# Installing, Configuring, and Administering Microsoft® Windows® XP Professional

## Exam 70-270

# Installing, Configuring, and Administering Microsoft® Windows® XP Professional

# Exam 70-270

**First Edition**

**Kenneth C. Laudon, Series Designer**
**Kenneth Rosenblatt**
**Robin L. Pickering**

**The Azimuth Interactive MCSE/MCSA Team**
Carol G. Traver, Series Editor
Russell Polo
David Langley
Brian Hill, MCSE, MCSA
Kevin Jensen, MCSE
Mark Maxwell
Stacey McBrine, MCSE, MCSA
Barbara Ryan
Richard Watson, MCSE, MCSA

PEARSON
Prentice
Hall

Upper Saddle River, New Jersey, 07458

Senior Vice President/Publisher: Natalie Anderson
Acquisitions Editor: Steven Elliot
Marketing Manager: Steven Rutberg
Assistant Editor: Allison Marcus
Editorial Assistant: Jasmine Slowick
Editorial Assistant: Jodi Bolognese
Marketing Assistant: Barrie Reinhold
Media Project Manager: Joan Waxman
Production Manager: Gail Steier de Acevedo
Editorial Production Project Manager: Tim Tate
Associate Director, Manufacturing: Vincent Scelta
Manufacturing Buyer: Tim Tate
Art Director: Pat Smythe
Design Manager: Maria Lange
Interior Design: Kim Buckley
Cover Designer: Pat Smythe
Cover Photo: Joseph DeSciose/Aurora Photos
Associate Director, Multimedia: Karen Goldsmith
Manager, Multimedia: Christy Mahon
Full Service Composition: Azimuth Interactive, Inc.
Quality Assurance: Digital Content Factory Ltd.
Printer/Binder: Banta Book Group, Menasha
Cover Printer: Phoenix Color Corporation

10 9 8 7 6 5 4
0-13-144132-9

*To our families,*
*for their love, patience,*
*and inspiration.*

# Brief Contents

# Contents

## Welcome to the Laudon MCSE/MCSA Certification Series!

You are about to begin an exciting journey of learning and career skills building that will provide you with access to careers such as Network Administrator, Systems Engineer, Technical Support Engineer, Network Analyst, and Technical Consultant. What you learn in the Laudon MCSE/MCSA Certification Series will provide you with a strong set of networking skills and knowledge that you can use throughout your career as the Microsoft Windows operating system continues to evolve, as new information technology devices appear, and as business applications of computers continues to expand. The Laudon Certification Series aims to provide you with the skills and knowledge that will endure, prepare you for your future career, and make the process of learning fun and enjoyable.

## Microsoft Windows and the Networked World

We live in a computer networked world—more so than many of us realize. The Internet, the world's largest network, now has more than 500 million people who connect to it through an estimated 171 million Internet hosts. The number of local area networks associated with these 171 million Internet hosts is not known. Arguably, the population of local area networks is in the millions. About 60% of local area networks in the United States are using a Windows network operating system. The other networks use Novell or some version of UNIX Netware (Internet Software Consortium, 2003). About 95% of the one billion personal computers in the world use some form of Microsoft operating system, typically some version of Windows. A growing number of handheld personal digital assistants (PDAs) also use versions of the Microsoft operating system called Microsoft CE. Most businesses—large and small—use some kind of client/server local area network to connect their employees to one another, and to the Internet. In the United States, the vast majority of these business networks use a Microsoft network operating system—either an earlier version called Windows NT, or the current version called Windows 2000. Many will soon upgrade to Windows Server 2003.

The Laudon MCSE/MCSA Certification Series prepares you to participate in this computer-networked world and, specifically, for the world of Microsoft Windows 2000 and XP Professional client operating systems, as well as Windows 2000 Server and Server 2003 operating systems.

## Laudon MCSE/MCSA Certification Series Objectives

The first objective of the Laudon MCSE/MCSA Certification Series is to help you build a set of skills and a knowledge base that will prepare you for a career in the networking field. There is no doubt that in the next five years, Microsoft will issue several new versions of its network operating system, and new versions of Windows client operating system. In the next five years—and thereafter—there will be a steady stream of new digital devices that will require connecting to networks. Most of what you learn in the Laudon Series will provide a strong foundation for understanding future versions of the operating system.

The second objective of the Laudon MCSE/MCSA Certification Series is to prepare you to pass the MCSE/MCSA certification exams and to receive certification. Why get certified? As businesses increasingly rely on Microsoft networks to operate, employers want to make sure their networking staff has the skills needed to plan for, install, and operate these networks. While job experience is an important source of networking knowledge, employers increasingly rely on certification examinations to ensure their staff has the necessary skills. The MCSE/MCSA curriculum provides networking professionals with a well-balanced and comprehensive body of knowledge necessary to operate and administer Microsoft networks in a business setting.

There is clear evidence that having the MCSE/MCSA certification results in higher salaries and faster promotions for individual employees. Therefore, it is definitely in your interest to obtain certification, even if you have considerable job experience. If you are just starting out in the world of networking, certification can be very important for landing that first job.

The Laudon Series teaches you real-world, job-related skills. About 90% of the work performed by MCSE/MCSAs falls into the following categories, according to a survey researcher (McKillip, 1999):

- Analyzing the business requirements for a proposed system architecture.
- Designing system architecture solutions that meet business requirements.

- Deploying, installing, and configuring the components of the system architecture.
- Managing the components of the system architecture on an ongoing basis.
- Monitoring and optimizing the components of the system architecture.
- Diagnosing and troubleshooting problems regarding the components of the system architecture.

These are precisely the skills we had in mind when we wrote this Series. As you work through the hands-on instructions in the text, perform the instructions in the simulated Windows environment on the CD-ROM, and complete the problem solving cases in the book, you will notice our emphasis on analyzing, designing, diagnosing, and implementing the Windows software. By completing the Laudon MCSE/MCSA Certification Series, you will be laying the foundation for a long-term career based on your specialized knowledge of networks and general problem solving skills.

Preparing you for a career involves more than satisfying the official MCSE/MCSA objectives. As you can see from the list of activities performed by MCSE/MCSAs, you will also need a strong set of management skills. The Laudon MCSE/MCSA Certification Series emphasizes management skills along with networking skills. As you advance in your career, you will be expected to participate in and lead teams of networking professionals in their efforts to support the needs of your organization. You will be expected to describe, plan, administer, and maintain computer networks, and to write about networks and give presentations to other business professionals. We make a particular point in this Series of developing managerial skills such as analyzing business requirements, writing reports, and making presentations to other members of your business team.

## Who Is the Audience for This Book?

The student body for the Laudon MCSE/MCSA Certification Series is very diverse, and the Series is written with that in mind. For all students, regardless of background, the Series is designed to function as a *learning tool* first, and, second, as a compact reference book that can be readily accessed to refresh skills. Generally, there are two types of software books: books aimed at learning and understanding how a specific software tool works, and comprehensive reference books. This series emphasizes learning and explanation and is student-centered.

The Laudon MCSE/MCSA Certification Series is well suited to beginning students. Many students will just be starting out in the networking field, most in colleges and training institutes. The Series introduces these beginning students to the basic concepts of networking, operating systems, and network operating systems. We take special care in the introductory chapters of each book to provide the background skills and understanding necessary to proceed to more specific MCSE/MCSA skills. We cover many more learning objectives and skills in these introductory lessons than are specifically listed as MCSE/MCSA objectives. Throughout all Lessons, we take care to *explain why things are done*, rather than just list the steps necessary to do them. There is a vast difference between understanding how Windows works and why, versus rote memorization of procedures.

A second group of students will already have some experience working with networking systems and Windows operating systems. This group already has an understanding of the basics, but needs a more systematic and in-depth coverage of MCSE/MCSA skills they lack. The Laudon MCSE/MCSA Certification Series is organized so that these more experienced students can quickly discover what they do not know, and can skip over introductory Lessons quickly. Nevertheless, this group will appreciate the emphasis on explanation and clear illustration that we emphasize throughout.

A third group of students will have considerable experience with previous Microsoft operating systems such as Windows NT. These students may be seeking to upgrade their skills and prepare for the Windows 2000/XP/2003 MCSE/MCSA examinations. They may be learning outside of formal training programs as self-paced learners, or in distance learning programs sponsored by their employers. The Laudon MCSE/MCSA Certification Series is designed to help these students quickly identify the new features of new versions of Windows, and to rapidly update their existing skills.

## Laudon Series Skills and MCSE/MCSA Objectives

In designing and writing the Laudon Certification Series, we had a choice between organizing the book into lessons composed of MCSE/MCSA domains and objectives, or organizing the book into lessons composed of skills needed to pass the MCSE/MCSA certification examinations (a complete listing of the domains and objectives for the relevant exam will be found inside the front and back covers of the book). We chose to organize the book around skills, beginning with introductory basic skills, and building to more advanced skills. We believe this is a more orderly and effective way to teach students the MCSE/MCSA subject matter and the basic understanding of Windows network operating systems.

Yet we also wanted to make clear exactly how the skills related to the published MCSE/MCSA objectives. In the Laudon Series, skills are organized into Lessons. At the beginning of each Lesson, there is an introduction to the set of skills covered in the Lesson, followed by a table that shows how the skills taught in the Lesson support specific MCSE/MCSA objectives. All MCSE/MCSA objectives for each of the examinations are covered; at the beginning of each skill discussion, the exact MCSE/MCSA objective relating to that skill is identified.

We also recognize that as students approach the certification examinations, they will want learning and preparation materials that are specifically focused on the examinations. Therefore, we have designed the MCSE/MCSA Interactive Series (on CD ROM) to follow the MCSE/MCSA domains and objectives more directly. Students can use these tools to practice answering MCSE/MCSA examination questions, and practice implementing these objectives in a realistic simulated Windows environment.

## What's Different About the Laudon Series—Main Features and Components

The Laudon MCSE/MCSA Certification Series has three distinguishing features that make it the most effective MCSE/MCSA learning tool available today. These three features are a graphical illustrated 2-page spread approach, a skills-based systematic approach to learning MCSE/MCSA, and an interactive *multi-channel pedagogy*.

**Graphical illustrated approach**. First, the Laudon Series uses a graphical, illustrated approach in a convenient *two-page spread format* (see illustration below). This makes learning easy, effective and enjoyable.

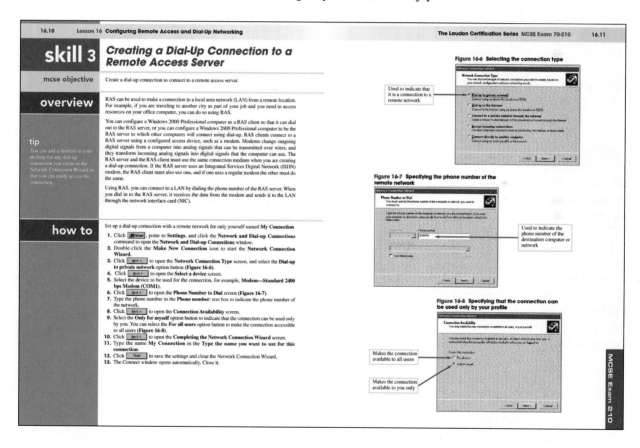

Each two-page spread is devoted to a single skill. On the left-hand side of the two-page spread, you will find a conceptual overview explaining what the skill is, why it is important, and how it is used. Immediately following the conceptual overview is a series of *How To Steps* showing how to execute the skill. On the right hand side of the two-page spread are screen shots that show you exactly how the screen should look as you execute the skills. The pedagogy is easy to follow and understand.

In addition to these main features, each two-page spread contains several *learning aids*:

- *More:* a brief section that explains more about how to use the skill, alternative ways to perform the skill, and common business applications of the skill.
- *Tips:* hints and suggestions to follow when performing the skill placed in the left margin.
- *Caution:* brief sections that tell you about the pitfalls and problems you may encounter when performing the skill placed in the left margin.

At the end of each Lesson, students can test and practice their skills using three end-of-Lesson features:

- *Test Yourself:* a multiple-choice examination that tests your comprehension and retention of the material in the Lesson.
- *Projects: On Your Own:* short projects that test your ability to perform tasks and skills in Windows without detailed step-by-step instructions.
- *Problem Solving Scenarios:* real-world business scenarios to help you analyze or diagnose a networking situation. The case generally requires you to write a report or prepare a presentation.

**Skills-based systematic approach**. A second distinguishing feature of the Laudon MCSE/MCSA Series is a *skills-based* systematic approach to MCSE/MCSA certification by using five integrated components:

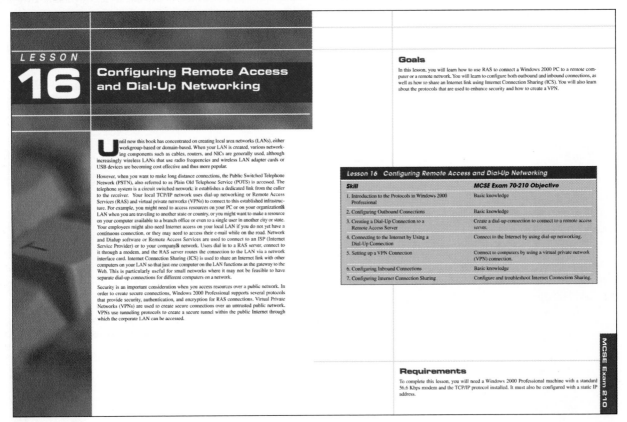

- Main Book—organized by skills.
- Student Project Book—for practicing skills in realistic settings.
- Examination Guide—organized by MCSE/MCSA domains and objectives to practice answering questions representative of questions you are likely to encounter in the actual MCSE/MCSA examination.
- Interactive multimedia CD ROM—organized by MCSE/MCSA domains and objectives—that allows students to practice performing MCSE/MCSA objectives in a simulated Windows environment.
- Powerful Website—provides additional questions, projects, and interactive training.

Within each component, the learning is organized by skills, beginning with the relatively simple skills and progressing rapidly through the more complex skills. Each skill is carefully explained in a series of steps and conceptual overviews describing why the skill is important.

The CD ROM is especially useful to students who do not have access to a Windows network on which they can practice skills. It also is useful to all students who want to practice MCSE/MCSA skills efficiently without disturbing an existing network. Together, these five components make the Laudon Certification Series an effective learning tool for students, increasing the speed of comprehension and the retention of knowledge.

**Interactive media multi-channel learning**. A third distinguishing feature of the Laudon MCSE/MCSA Certification Series is interactive media *multi-channel* learning. Multi-channel learning recognizes that students learn in different ways, and the more different channels used to teach students, the greater the comprehension and retention. Using the MCSE/MCSA Interactive Solutions CD ROM, students can see, hear, read, and actually perform the skills needed in a simulated Windows environment on the CD ROM. The CD ROM is based directly on materials in the books, and therefore shares the same high quality and reliability. The CD ROM and Website for the book provide high levels of real interactive learning—not just rote exam questions—and offer realistic opportunities to interact with the Windows operating system to practice skills in the software environment without having to install a new version of Windows or build a network.

## Supplements Available for This Series:

### 1.  Test Bank

The Test Bank is a Word document distributed with the Instructor's Manual (usually on a CD). It is distributed on the Internet to Instructors only. The purpose of the Test Bank is to provide instructors and students with a convenient way for testing comprehension of material presented in the book. The Test Bank contains forty multiple-choice questions and ten true/false questions per Lesson. The questions are based on material presented in the book and are not generic MCSE questions.

### 2.  Instructor's Manual

The Instructor's Manual (IM) is a Word document (distributed to Instructors only) that provides instructional tips, answers to the Test Yourself questions and the Problem Solving Scenarios. The IM also includes an introduction to each Lesson, teaching objectives, and teaching suggestions.

### 3.  PowerPoint Slides

The PowerPoint slides contain images of all the conceptual figures and screenshots in each book. The purpose of the slides is to provide the instructor with a convenient means of reviewing the content of the book in the classroom setting.

### 4.  Companion Website

The Companion Website is a Pearson learning tool that provides students and instructors with online support. On the Laudon MCSE/MCSA Certification Series Companion Website, you will find the Interactive Study Guide, a Web-based interactive quiz composed of fifteen or more questions per Lesson. Written by the authors, there are more than 255 free interactive questions on the Companion Website. The purpose of the Interactive Study Guide is to provide students with a convenient online mechanism for self-testing their comprehension of the book material.

**Exam 70-270 Installing, Configuring, and Administering Microsoft Windows XP Professional**

This book covers the subject matter of Microsoft's Exam 70-270. The focus in this book is on Windows XP Professional. You will learn about a variety of tools that are used to implement, configure, and administer the Windows XP operating system, such as the Microsoft Management Console, Task Scheduler, Control Panel, and the Registry. You will also learn about network protocols, especially TCP/IP (Transmission Control Protocol/Internet Protocol). You will be introduced to the Domain Name System (DNS), which is the hierarchical name service used on the Internet and by Microsoft's network operating system.

The following knowledge domains are discussed in this book:

- Installing Windows XP Professional.
- Implementing and Conducting Administration of Resources.
- Implementing, Managing, Monitoring, and Troubleshooting Hardware Devices and Drivers.
- Monitoring and Optimizing System Performance and Reliability.
- Configuring and Troubleshooting the Desktop Environment.
- Implementing, Managing, and Troubleshooting Network Protocols and Services.
- Configuring, Managing, and Troubleshooting Security.

### How This Book Is Organized

This book is organized into a series of Lessons. Each Lesson focuses on a set of skills you will need to learn in order to master the knowledge domains required by the MCSE/MCSA examinations. The skills are organized in a logical progression from basic knowledge skills to more specific skills. Some skills—usually at the beginning of Lessons—give you the background knowledge you will need in order to understand basic operating system and networking concepts. Most skills, however, give you hands-on experience working with Windows XP Professional and, in some cases, Windows 2000 Server. You will follow step-by-step instructions to perform tasks using the software.

At the beginning of each Lesson, you will find a table that links the skills covered to specific exam objectives. For each skill presented on a 2-page spread, the MCSE/MCSA objective is listed.

### The MCSE/MCSA Certification

The MCSE/MCSA certification is one of the most recognized certifications in the Information Technology world. By following a clear-cut strategy of preparation, you will be able to pass the certification exams. The first thing to remember is that there are no quick and easy routes to certification. No one can guarantee you will receive a certification—no matter what they promise. Real-world MCSE/MCSAs get certified by following a strategy involving self-study, on-the-job experience, and classroom learning, either in colleges or training institutes. Below are answers to frequently asked questions that should help you prepare for the certification exams.

### What Is the MCP Program?

The MCP program refers to the Microsoft Certified Professional program that certifies individuals who have passed Microsoft certification examinations. Certification is desirable for both individuals and organizations. For individuals, an MCP certification signifies to employers your expertise and skills in implementing Microsoft software in organizations. For employers, MCP certification makes it easy to identify potential employees with the requisite skills to develop and administer Microsoft tools. In a recent survey reported by Microsoft, 89% of hiring managers said they recommend a Microsoft MCP certification for candidates seeking IT positions.

### What Are the MCP Certifications?

Today there are seven different MCP certifications. Some certifications emphasize administrative as well as technical skills, while other certifications focus more on technical skills in developing software applications. Below is a listing of the MCP certifications. The Laudon MCSE/MCSA Certification Series focuses on the first two certifications.

- *MCSA:* Microsoft Certified Systems Administrators (MCSAs) administer network and systems environments based on the Microsoft Windows® platforms.
- *MCSE:* Microsoft Certified Systems Engineers (MCSEs) analyze business requirements to design and implement an infrastructure solution based on the Windows platform and Microsoft Server software.
- *MCDBA:* Microsoft Certified Database Administrators (MCDBAs) design, implement, and administer Microsoft SQL Server™ databases.
- *MCT:* Microsoft Certified Trainers (MCTs) are qualified instructors, certified by Microsoft, who deliver Microsoft training courses to IT professionals and developers.
- *MCAD:* Microsoft Certified Application Developers (MCADs) use Microsoft technologies to develop and maintain department-level applications, components, Web or desktop clients, or back-end data services.
- *MCSD:* Microsoft Certified Solution Developers (MCSDs) design and develop leading-edge enterprise-class applications with Microsoft development tools, technologies, platforms, and the Windows architecture.
- *Microsoft Office Specialist:* Microsoft Office Specialists (Office Specialists) are globally recognized for demonstrating advanced skills with Microsoft desktop software.
- *MCP:* Microsoft certified Professionals

### What Is the Difference Between MCSA and MCSE Certification?

There are two certifications that focus on the implementation and administration of the Microsoft operating systems and networking tools: MCSA and MCSE. The MCSA credential is designed to train IT professionals who are concerned with the management, support, and troubleshooting of existing systems and networks (see diagram below).

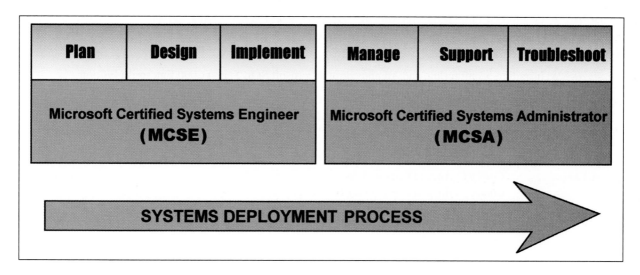

MCSA prepares you for jobs with titles such as Systems Administrator, Network Administrator, Information Systems Administrator, Network Operations Analyst, Network Technician, or Technical Support Specialist. Microsoft recommends that you have six to twelve months experience managing and supporting desktops, servers, and networks in an existing network infrastructure.

The MCSE certification is designed to train IT professionals who are concerned with the planning, designing, and implementation of new systems or major upgrades of existing systems. MCSE prepares you for jobs with titles such as Systems Engineer, Network Engineer, Systems Analyst, Network Analyst, or Technical Consultant. Microsoft recommends that you have at least one year of experience planning, designing, and implementing Microsoft products.

### *What Does the MCSA on Windows 2000 Require?*

MCSA candidates are required to pass a total of four exams: three core exams and one elective exam. The list below shows examinations that are included in the MCSA track.

### *Core Exams (3 Exams Required)*

(A) Client Operating System (1 Exam Required)

- *Exam 70-210:* Installing, Configuring, and Administering Microsoft Windows 2000 Professional
  **or**
- *Exam 70-270:* Installing, Configuring, and Administering Microsoft Windows XP Professional

(B) Networking System (2 Exams Required)

- *Exam 70-215:* Installing, Configuring, and Administering Microsoft Windows 2000 Server
  **and**
- *Exam 70-218:* Managing a Microsoft Windows 2000 Network Environment

### *Elective Exams (1 Exam Required)*

- *Exam 70-028:* Administering Microsoft SQL Server 7.0
- *Exam 70-081:* Implementing and Supporting Microsoft Exchange Server 5.5
- *Exam 70-086:* Implementing and Supporting Microsoft Systems Management Server 2.0
- *Exam 70-088:* Implementing and Supporting Microsoft Proxy Server 2.0
- *Exam 70-214:* Implementing and Administering Security in a Microsoft Windows 2000 Network
- *Exam 70-216:* Implementing and Administering a Microsoft Windows 2000 Network Infrastructure
- *Exam 70-224:* Installing, Configuring, and Administering Microsoft Exchange 2000 Server
- *Exam 70-227:* Installing, Configuring, and Administering Microsoft Internet Security and Acceleration (ISA) Server 2000, Enterprise Edition
- *Exam 70-228:* Installing, Configuring, and Administering Microsoft SQL Server 2000 Enterprise Edition
- *Exam 70-244:* Supporting and Maintaining a Microsoft Windows NT Server 4.0 Network

As an alternative to the electives listed above, you may substitute the following third-party certification combinations for an MCSA elective:

CompTIA Exams:  *CompTIA A+* and *CompTIA Network+*
 *CompTIA A+* and *CompServer+*

### *What Is the MCSE Curriculum for Windows 2000?*

MCSE candidates are required to pass a total of seven exams: five core exams and two elective exams. The list below shows the examinations that are included in the MCSA track.

### *Core Exams (5 Exams Required)*

(A) Client Operating System (1 exam required)

- *Exam 70-210:* Installing, Configuring, and Administering Microsoft Windows 2000 Professional
  **or**
- *Exam 70-270:* Installing, Configuring, and Administering Microsoft Windows XP Professional

(B) Networking System (3 Exams Required)

- *Exam 70-215:* Installing, Configuring, and Administering Microsoft Windows 2000 Server
- *Exam 70-216:* Implementing and Administering a Microsoft Windows 2000 Network Infrastructure
  **and**
- *Exam 70-217:* Implementing and Administering a Microsoft Windows 2000 Directory Services Infrastructure

(C) Design (1 Exam Required)

- *Exam 70-219:* Designing a Microsoft Windows 2000 Directory Services Infrastructure
- *Exam 70-220:* Designing Security for a Microsoft Windows 2000 Network
- *Exam 70-221:* Designing a Microsoft Windows 2000 Network Infrastructure
- *Exam 70-226:* Designing Highly Available Web Solutions with Microsoft Windows 2000 Server Technologies

## *Elective Exams (2 Exams Required)*

- *Exam 70-019:* Designing and Implementing Data Warehouses with Microsoft SQL Server™ 7.0
- *Exam 70-028:* Administering Microsoft SQL Server™ 7.0
- *Exam 70-029:* Designing and Implementing Databases with Microsoft SQL Server™ 7.0
- *Exam 70-056:* Implementing and Supporting Web Sites Using Microsoft Site Server 3.0
- *Exam 70-080:* Implementing and Supporting Microsoft Internet Explorer 5.0 by Using the Microsoft Internet Explorer Administration Kit
- *Exam 70-081:* Implementing and Supporting Microsoft Exchange Server 5.5
- *Exam 70-085:* Implementing and Supporting Microsoft SNA Server 4.0
- *Exam 70-086:* Implementing and Supporting Microsoft Systems Management Server 2.0
- *Exam 70-088:* Implementing and Supporting Microsoft Proxy Server 2.0
- *Exam 70-214:* Implementing and Administering Security in a Microsoft Windows 2000 Network
- *Exam 70-218:* Managing a Microsoft Windows 2000 Network Environment
- *Exam 70-219:* Designing a Microsoft Windows 2000 Directory Services Infrastructure
- *Exam 70-220:* Designing Security for a Microsoft Windows 2000 Network
- *Exam 70-221:* Designing a Microsoft Windows 2000 Network Infrastructure
- *Exam 70-222:* Migrating from Microsoft Windows NT 4.0 to Microsoft Windows 2000
- *Exam 70-223:* Installing, Configuring, and Administering Microsoft Clustering Services by Using Microsoft Windows 2000 Advanced Server
- *Exam 70-224:* Installing, Configuring, and Administering Microsoft Exchange 2000 Server
- *Exam 70-225:* Designing and Deploying a Messaging Infrastructure with Microsoft Exchange 2000 Server
- *Exam 70-226:* Designing Highly Available Web Solutions with Microsoft Windows 2000 Server Technologies
- *Exam 70-227:* Installing, Configuring, and Administering Microsoft Internet Security and Acceleration (ISA) Server 2000 Enterprise Edition
- *Exam 70-228:* Installing, Configuring, and Administering Microsoft SQL Server™ 2000 Enterprise Edition
- *Exam 70-229:* Designing and Implementing Databases with Microsoft SQL Server™ 2000 Enterprise Edition
- *Exam 70-230:* Designing and Implementing Solutions with Microsoft BizTalk® Server 2000 Enterprise Edition
- *Exam 70-232:* Implementing and Maintaining Highly Available Web Solutions with Microsoft Windows 2000 Server Technologies and Microsoft Application Center 2000
- *Exam 70-234:* Designing and Implementing Solutions with Microsoft Commerce Server 2000
- *Exam 70-244:* Supporting and Maintaining a Microsoft Windows NT Server 4.0 Network

## What About Windows Server 2003?

Windows Server 2003 is the latest release of Microsoft's family of network operating systems. In early 2003, Microsoft began releasing the full requirements for the MCSE and MCSA examinations on Microsoft Windows Server 2003. The MCP program will offer an upgrade path consisting of one or two exams that will enable current MCSEs and MCSAs on Windows 2000 to update their respective certification to the Windows Server 2003 track. You should check with the Microsoft Certification Program official Website at: **http://www.microsoft.com/traincert/mcp/default.asp** for the latest information. Microsoft recommends that until the software and examination requirements are released, individuals should continue to pursue training and certification in Windows 2000, because the skills acquired for Windows 2000 are highly relevant to, and provide a solid foundation for, Windows 2003 Server. To retain certification, MCSEs and MCSAs on Windows 2000 will *not* be required to pass Windows 2003 Server exams. If you are training on a Windows 2000 network for Windows 2000 certifications, you should continue to do so.

## Do You Need to Pursue Certification to Benefit from This Book?

No. The Laudon MCSE/MCSA Certification Series is designed to prepare you for the workplace by providing you with networking knowledge and skills regardless of certification programs. While it is desirable to obtain a certification, you can certainly benefit greatly by just reading these books, practicing your skills in the simulated Windows environment found on the MCSE/MCSA Interactive Series CD ROM, and using the online interactive study guide.

## What Kinds of Questions Are on the Exam?

The MCSE/MCSA exams typically involve a variety of question formats.

### (a) Select-and-Place Exam Items (Drag and Drop)

A select-and-place exam item asks candidates to understand a scenario and assemble a solution (graphically on screen) by picking up screen objects and moving them to their appropriate location to assemble the solution. For instance, you might be asked to place routers, clients, and servers on a network and illustrate how they would be connected to the Internet. This type of exam item can measure architectural, design, troubleshooting, and component recognition skills more accurately than traditional exam items can, because the solution—a graphical diagram—is presented in a form that is familiar to the computer professional.

### (b) Case Study-Based Multiple-Choice Exam Items

The candidate is presented with a scenario based on typical Windows installations, and then is asked to answer several multiple-choice questions. To make the questions more challenging, several correct answers may be presented, and you will be asked to choose all that are correct. The Laudon Certification Series Test Yourself questions at the end of each Lesson give you experience with these kinds of questions.

### (c) Simulations

Simulations test your ability to perform tasks in a simulated Windows environment. A simulation imitates the functionality and interface of Windows operating systems. The simulation usually involves a scenario in which you will be asked to perform several tasks in the simulated environment, including working with dialog boxes and entering information. The Laudon Certification Series Interactive Media CD-ROM gives you experience working in a simulated Windows environment.

### (d) Computer Adaptive Testing

A computer adaptive test (CAT) attempts to adapt the level of question difficulty to the knowledge of each individual examinee. An adaptive exam starts with several easy questions. If you get these right, more difficult questions are pitched. If you fail a question, the next questions will be easier. Eventually the test will discover how much you know and what you can accomplish in a Windows environment.

You can find out more about the exam questions and take sample exams at the Microsoft Website:
**http://www.microsoft.com/ traincert/mcp/default.asp**.

### How Long is the Exam?

Exams have fifty to seventy questions and last anywhere from 60 minutes to 240 minutes. The variation in exam length is due to variation in the requirements for specific exams (some exams have many more requirements than others), and because the adaptive exams take much less time than traditional exams. When you register for an exam, you will be told how much time you should expect to spend at the testing center. In some cases, the exams include timed sections that can help for apportioning your time.

### What Is the Testing Experience Like?

You are required to bring two forms of identification that include your signature and one photo ID (such as a driver's license or company security ID). You will be required to sign a non-disclosure agreement that obligates you not to share the contents of the exam questions with others, and you will be asked to complete a survey. The rules and procedures of the exam will be explained to you by Testing Center administrators. You will be introduced to the testing equipment and you will be offered an exam tutorial intended to familiarize you with the testing equipment. This is a good idea. You will not be allowed to communicate with other examinees or with outsiders during the exam. You should definitely turn off your cell phone when taking the exam.

### How Can You Best Prepare for the Exams?

Prepare for each exam by reading this book, and then practicing your skills in a simulated environment on the CD ROM that accompanies this series. If you do not have a real network to practice on (and if you do not build a small network), the next best thing is to work with the CD ROM. Alternatively, it is very helpful to build a small Windows 2000 network with a couple of unused computers. You will also require experience with a real-world Windows 2000 network. An MCSE/MCSA candidate should, at a minimum, have at least one year of experience implementing and administering a network operating system in environments with the following characteristics: a minimum of 200 users, five supported physical locations, typical network services and applications including file and print, database, messaging, proxy server or firewall, dial-in server, desktop management, and Web hosting, and connectivity needs, including connecting individual offices and users at remote locations to the corporate network and connecting corporate networks to the Internet.

In addition, an MCSE candidate should have at least one year of experience in the following areas: implementing and administering a desktop operating system, and designing a network infrastructure.

### Where Can You Take the Exams?

All MCP exams are administered by Pearson VUE and Prometric. There are 3 convenient ways to schedule your exams with Pearson VUE:

- Online: **www.pearsonvue.com/ms/**
- Toll Free in the US and Canada: call (800) TEST-REG (800-837-8734). Or, find a call center in your part of the world at: **http://www.pearsonvue.com/contact/ms/**
- In person: at your local test center. Pearson VUE has over 3,000 test centers in 130 countries. To find a test center near you, visit: **www.pearsonvue.com**

To take exams at a Prometric testing center, call Prometric at (800) 755-EXAM (755-3926). Outside the United States and Canada, contact your local Prometric Registration Center. To register online with Prometric, visit the Prometric web site, **www.prometric.com**.

### How Much Does It Cost to Take the Exams?

In the United States, exams cost $125 USD per exam as of January, 2002. Certification exam prices are subject to change. In some countries/regions, additional taxes may apply. Contact your test registration center for exact pricing.

### Are There Any Discounts Available to Students?

Yes. In the US and Canada, as well as other select regions around the globe, full-time students can take a subset of the MCP exams for a significantly reduced fee at Authorized Academic Testing Centers (AATCs). For details on which countries and exams are included in the program, or to schedule your discounted exam, visit **www.pearsonvue.com/aatc**.

*Can You Take the Exam More Than Once?*

Yes. You may retake an exam at any time if you do not pass on the first attempt. But if you do not pass the second time, you must wait fourteen days. A 14-day waiting period will be imposed for all subsequent exam retakes. If you have passed an exam, you cannot take it again.

*Where Can I Get More Information about the Exams?*

Microsoft Websites are a good place to start:

MCP Program (general): **http://www.microsoft.com/traincert/mcp/default.asp**

MCSE Certification: **http://www.microsoft.com/traincert/mcp/mcse/default.asp**

MCSA Certification: **http://www.microsoft.com/traincert/mcp/mcsa/default.asp**

There are literally thousands of other Websites with helpful information that you can identify using any Web search engine. Many commercial sites will promise instant success, and some even guarantee you will pass the exams. Be a discriminating consumer. If it was that easy to become an MCP professional, the certification would be meaningless.

# Acknowledgments

A great many people have contributed to the Laudon MCSE/MCSA Certification Series. We want to thank Steven Elliot, our editor at Prentice Hall, for his enthusiastic appreciation of the project, his personal support for the Azimuth team, and his deep commitment to the goal of creating a powerful, accurate, and enjoyable learning tool for students. We also want to thank David Alexander of Prentice Hall for his interim leadership and advice as the project developed at Prentice Hall, and Jerome Grant for supporting the development of high-quality certification training books and CDs for colleges and universities worldwide. Finally, we want to thank Susan Hartman Sullivan of Addison Wesley for believing in this project at an early stage and for encouraging us to fulfill our dreams.

The Azimuth Interactive MCSE/MCSA team is a dedicated group of technical experts, computer scientists, networking specialists, and writers with literally decades of experience in computer networking, information technology and systems, and computer technology. We want to thank the members of the team:

Kenneth C. Laudon is the Series Designer. He is Professor of Information Systems at New York University's Stern School of Business. He has written twelve books on information systems and technologies, e-commerce, and management information systems. He has designed, installed, and fixed computer networks since 1982.

Carol G. Traver is the Senior Series Editor. She is General Counsel and Vice President of Business Development at Azimuth Interactive, Inc. A graduate of Yale Law School, she has co-authored several best-selling books on information technology and e-commerce.

Kenneth Rosenblatt is a Senior Author for the Series. He is an experienced technical writer and editor who has co-authored or contributed to over two dozen books on computer and software instruction. In addition, Ken has over five years experience in designing, implementing, and managing Microsoft operating systems and networks.

Robin L. Pickering is a Senior Author for the Series. She is an experienced technical writer and editor who has co-authored or contributed to over a dozen books on computers and software instruction. Robin has extensive experience as a Network Administrator and consultant for a number of small to medium-sized firms.

Russell Polo is the Technical Advisor for the Series. He holds degrees in computer science and electrical engineering. He has designed, implemented, and managed Microsoft, UNIX, and Novell networks in a number of business firms since 1995. He currently is the Network Administrator at Azimuth Interactive.

David Langley is an Editor for the Series. David is an experienced technical writer and editor who has co-authored or contributed to over ten books on computers and software instruction. In addition, he has over fifteen years experience as a college professor, five of those in computer software training.

Kevin Jensen is a Technical Consultant and Editor for the Series. He is a Systems Consultant, Trainer, Administrator, and Independent Technical Editor. Kevin's industry certifications are MCSE on Windows 2000, Microsoft Certified Trainer (MCT), Certified Novell Engineer (CNE), Certified Netware Instructor (CNI), and Certified Technical Trainer (CTT). Kevin has specialized in enterprise network management, design, and interoperability between different network operating systems.

Mark Maxwell is a Technical Consultant and Editor for the Series. He has over fifteen years of industry experience in distributed network environments including TCP/IP, fault-tolerant NFS file service, Kerberos, Wide Area Networks, and Virtual Private Networks. In addition, Mark has published articles on network design, upgrades, and security.

## *Acknowledgments (cont'd)*

Stacey McBrine has spent more than 18 years configuring and supporting DOS and Windows based personal computers and local area networks, along with several other operating systems. He is certified as an MCSE for Windows NT 4.0, and was one of the first 2000 persons in the world to achieve MCSE certification for Windows 2000. He has brought his real world experience to the classroom for the last 5 years as a Microsoft Certified Trainer. He holds several other certifications for Cisco, Linux, Solaris, and Security.

Barbara Wilson Ryan has over 20 years of experience in technical education, teaching application software and network operating systems to students in the United States and Southeast Asia. Her recent focus has been on the Windows NT and Windows 2000 operating systems, both at the education and technical support levels. She has authored technical site-based courses, technical online courses, and computer operating system documentation.

Richard Watson has worked in the industry for 10 years, first as a Checkpoint Certified Security Engineer (CCSE), and then as a Lead Engineer for a local Microsoft Certified Solution Provider. Among his many other industry certifications are MCSE on Windows 2000 and NT4, Microsoft Certified Trainer (MCT), Cisco Certified Network Associate (CCNA), and IBM Professional Server Expert (PSE). Richard is currently the President of Client Server Technologies Inc., which provides network installation and support, website design, and training in Beaverton, Oregon.

## Quality Assurance

The Laudon MCSE/MCSA Certification Series contains literally thousands of software instructions for working with Windows products. We have taken special steps to ensure the accuracy of the statements in this series. The books and CDs are initially written by teams composed of Azimuth Interactive Inc. MCSE/MCSA professionals and writers working directly with the software as they write. Each team then collectively walks through the software instructions and screen shots to ensure accuracy. The resulting manuscripts are then thoroughly tested by an independent quality assurance team of MCSE/MCSA professionals who also perform the software instructions and check to ensure the screen shots and conceptual graphics are correct. The result is a very accurate and comprehensive learning environment for understanding Windows products.

We would like to thank the primary member of the Quality Assurance Team for his critical feedback and unstinting efforts to make sure we got it right. The primary technical editor for this book is Michael Aubert. Michael Aubert is a technical editor and technical author with over seven years of experience. He has also worked as an independent consultant and engineer on a variety of enterprise-level projects for clients in the United States. Michael's professional certifications include Microsoft Certified Systems Engineer (MCSE), Microsoft Certified Database Administrator (MCDBA), and Microsoft Certified Solution Developer (MCSD). His main areas of expertise include network engineering and security, directory services design, database administration, and solution architectures, including Microsoft .NET.

# LESSON 1

# Introducing Windows XP Professional

**W**elcome to Windows XP, Microsoft's multipurpose family of operating systems. Windows XP is used throughout the world by large and small corporations to build and administer corporate networks that can contain thousands of client user workstations. Windows and UNIX are the major corporate operating systems in use today.

Windows XP builds on Microsoft's earlier versions of the Windows operating system, combining many of the benefits of Windows 98, Me, and 2000, as well as Windows NT 4.0. The Windows 9.x operating systems concentrated on compatibility with older devices and the ability to perform well on systems without much memory. With Windows 2000, Microsoft decided to sacrifice these features in order to improve security and reliability. New features in Windows 2000 emphasized tighter security and strong central administrative controls for corporate networks, as well as improvements to the user interface. The most significant new feature was Active Directory. All of the information about how a server-based network is structured and organized is stored in Active Directory. Users access Active Directory in order to identify and locate resources on a network such as users and groups, as well as printers and computers. Active Directory serves as a central repository for network objects and as a central administrative site so that network administrators do not have to individually manage multiple servers.

Windows XP represents the next generation of reliability and performance in Microsoft operating systems. Windows XP features, such as a revamped Start menu and new graphical user interface, make the operating system more user-friendly. Updated dialog boxes, new Wizards, AutoComplete fields, and most recently used lists add to the convenience with which users can complete tasks. Windows XP also includes enhanced hardware support that improves power management and Plug and Play capabilities, and support for several new devices and buses. In terms of scalability, Windows XP supports small workgroups, as well as larger domain-based networks with thousands of clients. In this way, Windows XP can fulfill the networking needs of both small and large corporations.

The Windows XP family consists mainly of two products: Windows XP Professional and Windows XP Home. The Windows XP Home version is intended for home users who do not require their computer to be in a network or domain environment. It lacks several features that are useful in such environments, including file encryption, Internet Protocol Security, and Internet Information Server. This text will focus on Windows XP Professional. Windows XP functions with the Windows 2003 family to provide the same wide range of services that are provided by the Windows 2000 family of operating systems. Windows XP Professional can, of course, function just as well as a client computer in a Windows 2000 network environment.

## Goals

In this lesson, you will learn about the latest versions of the Windows operating system, as well as the key features of Windows XP Professional. You will also learn about both the workgroup and the domain networking models.

### Lesson 1  Introducing Windows XP Professional

| Skill | Exam 70-270 Objective |
|---|---|
| 1. Introducing the Windows XP Family of Operating Systems | Basic knowledge |
| 2. Introducing Windows XP Features and Enhancements | Basic knowledge |
| 3. Identifying the Range of Supported Hardware | Basic knowledge |
| 4. Introducing Windows XP Enhanced File Management Features | Basic knowledge |
| 5. Introducing Windows XP Security Features | Basic knowledge |
| 6. Introducing Workgroups and Domains | Basic knowledge |

## Requirements

There are no special requirements for this lesson.

# skill 1

# *Introducing the Windows XP Family of Operating Systems*

## exam objective

Basic knowledge

## overview

### tip
Microsoft recommends that workgroup networks contain fewer than 10 computers.

Windows XP is a multipurpose operating system that supports client/server networks (called domain-based networks), as well as peer-to-peer or workgroup networks. Windows XP is actually a family of closely integrated products that make up the Windows XP environment (**Figure 1-1**).

◆ **Windows XP Professional** is the primary Microsoft desktop operating system. It is used by businesses and organizations both large and small. Windows XP Professional combines the most useful and powerful features of its stand-alone and client workstation predecessors. It provides a user-friendly interface, a secure network-client environment, enhanced Plug and Play capabilities, improved power management features, and support for a broad range of hardware devices. Users can easily manage their system's hardware and software requirements and conserve power when they are not working. All of these features make Windows XP Professional a good fit for the corporate desktop. Using only Windows XP Professional, small businesses can create a workgroup or peer-to-peer network in which workstations can communicate with one another and share resources. Windows XP Professional can be used to its fullest potential when connecting to and interacting with a centralized domain-based Windows 2003 network. MCSE Exam 70-270 and this book focus on the Windows XP Professional operating system.

◆ **Windows Server 2003 Standard Edition** is a network operating system for client/server networks. It can be used for Web servers, as well as for file, print, and application servers. It has all of the features of Windows XP Professional along with a complete set of services based on Active Directory (AD). Active Directory services involve the management of users, groups, security services, and network resources. Windows Server 2003 Standard Edition provides a wide range of administrative features along with improved security and directory services. Centralized server-based networks that combine Windows XP Professional client computers and Windows 2003 servers allow network administrators to perform software updates and configure multiple workstations from a single location. Windows XP Professional users can take advantage of the automated network connectivity, desktop configuration, and software installation features of Windows Server 2003 that make it simple for users to set up their own workstations without any help from technical staff. Microsoft claims that total cost of ownership (TCO) for a network can be dramatically reduced when the centralized services available in Windows Server 2003 are used in conjunction with Windows XP Professional clients. Network administrators on a Windows 2003 network can more easily manage network resources such as file and print servers, and shared folders, files, and printers using Active Directory services. Its many security features provide for the protection of files and folders and the auditing of file, folder, and network access.

◆ **Windows Server 2003 Enterprise Edition** is a more powerful version of Windows Server 2003 that enables the use of up to eight processors in large sophisticated corporate networks. Windows Server 2003 Enterprise Edition has the improved scalability required for global corporations. With enhanced features for both Network Operating Systems (NOS) and the Internet, it can be used to host high-end network applications.

◆ **Windows Server 2003 Datacenter Edition** has even greater power and functionality than Windows Server 2003 Enterprise Edition. This product is ideal for data warehousing on a large scale. It is also used for econometric analysis and simulation-based applications in science and engineering. Datacenter Server can support up to 128 processors, with partitions up to 64 processors, and 512 GB of RAM in its 64-bit version.

◆ **Windows Server 2003 Web Edition** is a new product that is designed to be deployed specifically for Web serving and Web hosting.

**Figure 1-1  Products in the Window XP environment**

# skill 2

## Introducing Windows XP Features and Enhancements

**exam objective**

Basic knowledge

**overview**

The features and enhancements in the Windows XP family of products include **(Figure 1-2)**:

◆ **Reduced total cost of ownership:** Microsoft claims that Windows XP lowers the total cost of ownership (sometimes referred to as TCO) of corporate networks by using technologies that enable automatic installation and upgrading of the operating system and applications. Automation reduces the burden for technical support personnel. Windows XP's familiar interface, interactive help, and Wizards also enable users to successfully tackle many support tasks themselves, reducing the need for professional network technicians.

◆ **Security:** The Windows XP operating system incorporates a variety of enhanced security features, in particular, the Kerberos authentication protocol **(Figure 1-3)**. Files and folders can be encrypted using the Encrypting File System (EFS). The TCP/IP protocol, which is the core protocol for the Internet, allows for more secure communications using Internet Protocol Security (IPSec) and Layer 2 Tunneling Protocol (L2TP). Internet Connection Firewall adds another level to Internet security. There are many options for the stronger authentication of users before they can access resources or data from a computer or the network. Windows XP also has the ability to perform system audits and impose secure access to files, directories, printers, and other resources.

◆ **Multiprocessing, multitasking, and multithreading:** The Windows XP/2003 operating systems support multiprocessing, multitasking, and multithreading.

• *Symmetric multiprocessing (SMP)* enables a system to use any available processor. This contributes to the even distribution of system load and application needs across available processors. In SMP, each central processing unit (CPU) is equal, they share common memory and disk input/output resources, and process threads can be scheduled on any processor. This is in contrast to asymmetric multiprocessing in which processors are specialized, for example, for network processes, input/output processes, or graphics/video. In asymmetric multiprocessing, one CPU does the work for the system, while the other CPUs service user requests. Windows XP Professional can support up to two CPUs. When several CPUs are available, as could be the case, for example, with Windows 2003 Server, a number of different applications can run concurrently on different processors. Priority levels for each process can be set so that more important programs will be allocated more CPU capacity.

• Windows XP Professional also supports *preemptive multitasking* for system processes and programs. In preemptive multitasking, the computer runs multiple programs at the same time by allocating CPU time among the various applications. It can preempt or block an application that is currently running a process in order to run another process from a different application. The operating system essentially creates a timetable for how long one task in a multithreaded program, or a complete single-threaded program, will be allowed to access the CPU. Tasks can be preempted when they have taken up too much CPU time or when a more important application sends a request for attention. Preemptive multitasking is used by Windows 9.x, NT, and Windows 2000.

• *Multithreading*, in which a single application creates several execution threads that can carry on simultaneously, is also supported. For example, you can perform a spell check in Microsoft Word at the same time that the program executes a background process such as repagination. The term "threads" refers to units of code that the operating system can schedule to run. When multiple execution threads can run at the same time and the computer is also configured for SMP, threads can be executed simultaneously on different CPUs, greatly improving the speed of application processes and enabling both multiple foreground and multiple background tasks to run concurrently.

**Figure 1-2 Windows XP features and enhancements**

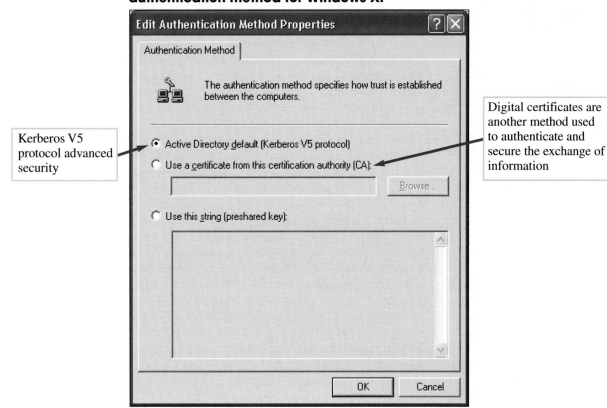

Security

Multitasking

Multiprocessing

Task Device Drivers

Microsoft® **Windows**ˣᵖ **Professional**

Networking and Communication services

Integration with the Internet

Hardware support

Customized administration tools

**Figure 1-3 The Kerberos V5 protocol, the default authentication method for Windows XP**

Kerberos V5 protocol advanced security

Digital certificates are another method used to authenticate and secure the exchange of information

**Edit Authentication Method Properties**

Authentication Method

The authentication method specifies how trust is established between the computers.

- Active Directory default (Kerberos V5 protocol)
- Use a certificate from this certification authority (CA):

  Browse...

- Use this string (preshared key):

OK    Cancel

# skill 2

## *Introducing Windows XP Features and Enhancements (cont'd)*

**exam objective**

Basic knowledge

**overview**

◆ **Connectivity:** Windows XP Professional supports a variety of network protocols such as TCP/IP (Transmission Control Protocol/Internet Protocol) and NWLink, as well as providing connectivity with UNIX systems **(Figure 1-4)**. Windows XP also supports dial-up networking.

◆ **Hardware support:** Windows XP Professional supports Plug and Play, a set of specifications developed by Intel that allows a computer to automatically detect and configure a hardware device and install the appropriate device drivers. Windows XP also supports the Universal Serial Bus (USB) standard, which allows a single port to support up to 127 peripheral devices and enables you to connect and disconnect devices without shutting down or restarting your computer **(Figure 1-5)**. While earlier versions of Windows, such as Windows 98, supported Plug and Play, the feature continues to be expanded. The IEEE 1394 high-performance serial bus, also known as FireWire, is also supported, allowing VCRs and camcorders to be connected to a Windows XP PC. DVDs, digital scanners, handheld devices, and cameras are supported as well. The Control Panel includes utilities for configuring such devices. Furthermore, additional monitors can be added to expand the desktop as long as either AGP (Accelerated Graphics Port) or PCI (Peripheral Component Interconnect) adapters are used.

◆ **Greater Ease of Use:** Windows XP features an enhanced user interface that makes the operating system easier to use and control. Ease of use features include:
  • A redesigned Start menu that enables you to display the most frequently accessed applications while hiding the less frequently used applications.
  • An improved taskbar that combines related open application windows into a single taskbar button.
  • More user-friendly dialog boxes, many of which automatically complete fields for you as you are entering data (Auto Complete).
  • New Wizards, notably the Files and Settings Transfer Wizard **(Figure 1-6)** and the Activate Windows Wizard.

◆ **Manageability:** Windows 2000 and 2003 networks offer many conveniences for network administrators, beginning with Active Directory. As noted, **Active Directory** is the central database for a network that stores information about users and groups, and manages logging on to the network. Active Directory provides a centralized method for managing workstation configuration, application installation, network resources, and network access. Other tools that add to a straightforward managerial environment include group policies, which are used to set up security rules and preferences for local workstations, network computers, or both. Group policies that are implemented at the network level are configured in the administrative tools in Active Directory. Windows XP computers also have the ability to automatically assign themselves IP addresses even if a network server is offline. For users who only need to interact with other computers on a LAN and do not need to access the Internet, this can be quite a useful feature. The Microsoft Management Console, or MMC also adds to the manageability of the operating system. MMC is simply a container object for "snap-ins," which are utilities that provide an interface and a set of administrative functions. Network administrators can add the snap-ins they use most often to an MMC to create a customized managerial tool. Finally, Windows Installer Package technology now helps network administrators with application deployment by providing an organized file format (.msi) that lists program functions so that they can manage user installation options. Windows Installer is an application installation technology that now augments the Add/Remove Programs Wizard. It also ensures the complete and safe removal of applications, including registry files, and is useful for its diagnostic capabilities for malfunctioning applications.

## Figure 1-4  Network protocols for connectivity

The NWLink protocol provides connectivity with Novell Netware computers

## Figure 1-5  USB controllers in the Device Manager

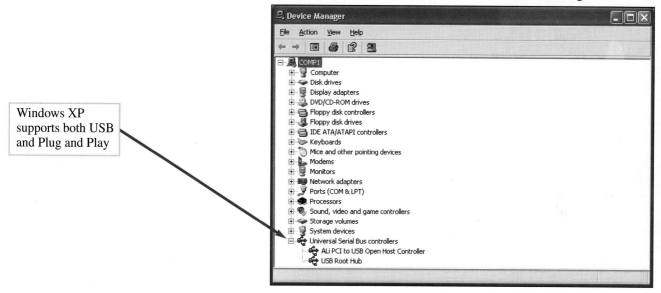

Windows XP supports both USB and Plug and Play

## Figure 1-6  The Files and Settings Transfer Wizard

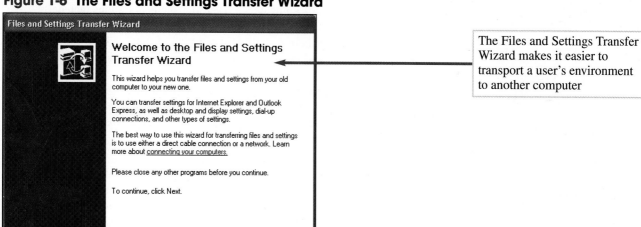

The Files and Settings Transfer Wizard makes it easier to transport a user's environment to another computer

# skill 3

## Identifying the Range of Supported Hardware

**exam objective**

Basic knowledge

**overview**

While Windows XP Professional supports thousands of hardware devices, including some of the latest technologies (such as infrared devices, digital cameras, and PDAs), users cannot assume that a device supported by earlier versions of Windows will necessarily work correctly. Every hardware device on a system should be systematically checked against the **Hardware Compatibility List (HCL)** to determine whether it will work with Windows XP Professional. You can find the HCL on the Windows XP CD-ROM, or for the most recent version go to the following Web address: **http://www.microsoft.com/hwdq/hcl/search.asp**.

Hardware support in Windows XP Professional includes the following features (**Figure 1-7**):

◆ **Add Hardware Wizard:** You use the **Add Hardware Wizard** to add, delete, upgrade, and troubleshoot computer peripherals (**Figure 1-8**). You can also stop the operation of devices or remove devices that are malfunctioning.

◆ **Win32 Driver Model (WDM):** WDM is a common model for device drivers supported across the Windows 98, Windows 2000, and Windows XP operating systems platforms. WDM supplies a cohesive architecture for device drivers that provides for cross-platform power management and supports Plug and Play capabilities. WDM was designed to function as a bridge between Windows 98 and Windows 2000 because drivers for certain components in Windows NT 4.0 and Windows 2000 are not compatible with Windows 98.

◆ **Plug and Play support:** Plug and Play gives Windows XP Professional the capability to configure newly connected hardware automatically and dynamically, to load the appropriate drivers, to register device notification events, and to use removable and changeable devices. Windows XP supports the latest in digital media and mobile technologies.

◆ **Power Options:** You can use the Power Options program in the Control Panel window to reduce the power consumption of the monitor and hard disks with additional settings for the entire system. You do this by choosing a power scheme, which is a collection of settings that manages the power usage of a computer. You can create your own power schemes or use the ones provided (**Figure 1-9**). Windows XP Professional supports two power management standards, the older standard, APM (Advanced Power Management), which is found on pre-1999 computers that were equipped with a power management system, and the newer standard, ACPI (Advanced Configuration and Power Interface), which allows users to control power management settings more precisely. Improved power management using the ACPI standard makes Windows XP Professional a practical operating system for notebook computers. Power Management options include:

  • **Hibernation:** You can use the **Hibernation** option to save the contents of your computer's memory before shutting down your system. When you restart your system, your files and documents will be open on your desktop just as you left them.

  • **Standby:** You can use the **Standby** option to shut off power to hardware components that are not in use, such as the monitor or hard drive, while maintaining power to the computer's memory so that your work is not lost.

**Figure 1-7  Windows XP hardware support features**

**Figure 1-8  Using the Add Hardware Wizard to troubleshoot a device**

**Figure 1-9  Creating a power scheme for a laptop computer**

# skill 4 *Introducing Windows XP Enhanced File Management Features*

**exam objective**    Basic knowledge

## overview

Windows XP Professional offers a number of facilities that make it easier to manage your files. File management features include (**Figure 1-10**):

◆ **The NTFS file system:** An advanced file system designed for use specifically within the Windows NT and Windows XP/2003 operating systems. It supports file system recovery, large storage media, long file names, file encryption, and disk quotas.

◆ **POSIX (Portable Operating System Interface for UNIX) subsystem:** POSIX is a standard set by the Institute of Electrical and Electronics Engineers (IEEE). This standard defines a set of operating-system services. Programs that adhere to the POSIX standard can easily be transported from one system to another.

◆ **The FAT32 file system:** A derivative of the File Allocation Table (FAT) file system. The **File Allocation Table** is a list maintained by the operating system that keeps track of the status of various segments of disk space used for file storage. FAT32 supports smaller cluster sizes than FAT, which results in more efficient space allocation on FAT32 drives. FAT32 is compatible with all Windows operating systems since the second version of Windows 95. To ensure compatibility with the first release of Windows 95 and DOS, Windows XP Professional also supports the FAT file system.

◆ **Disk Defragmenter utility:** A tool to help improve disk performance on systems (**Figure 1-11**). Defragmentation is the process of rewriting various parts of a file to contiguous sectors on a hard disk to increase the speed of file access and retrieval. The **Disk Defragmenter utility** optimizes stored data and unused space to help ensure that all related components of files and programs are placed in contiguous sectors of the hard disk. This means the processor does not have to spend excess time locating them during execution.

◆ **Backup utility:** Windows XP Professional provides a **Backup utility** to prevent the accidental loss of data due to hardware or software failure. You can use this utility to schedule automatic backups at regular intervals. The Backup utility can be used with a variety of storage media such as tape drives, logical drives, Zip disks, and CD-ROMs.

**Figure 1-10  Windows XP file management features**

**Figure 1-11  The Windows XP Disk Defragmenter utility**

| Volume | Session Status | File System | Capacity | Free Space | % Free Space |
|---|---|---|---|---|---|
| APTIVA (C:) | Defragmenting... | NTFS | 12.13 GB | 6.43 GB | 52 % |

Estimated disk usage before defragmentation:

Estimated disk usage after defragmentation:

| Analyze | Defragment | Pause | Stop | View Report |

■ Fragmented files   ■ Contiguous files   ■ Unmovable files   □ Free space

APTIVA (C:) Defragmenting... 3%  Moving File Craquelure.8BF

# skill 5

## *Introducing Windows XP Security Features*

**exam objective**

Basic knowledge

**overview**

The features of Windows XP Professional relating to system security include (**Figure 1-12**):

◆ **Kerberos V5:** This is an Internet standard authentication protocol for handling the authentication of user or system identity. With Kerberos V5, passwords that are sent across network lines are encrypted, not sent as plain text. Kerberos V5 is the primary authentication protocol for domains in the Windows XP operating system. This network authentication protocol uses powerful cryptography. Clients must prove their identity to a server, and vice versa, providing a more secure network connection.

◆ **Encrypting File System (EFS):** Using Windows XP Professional, users can encrypt files on a hard disk (**Figure 1-13**). Data is scrambled so that no one can access the file or folder unless they have a file encryption certificate and a private key. EFS encrypts data using a cryptographic key pair: a public key and a private key. Data is encrypted using a session key (file encryption key – FEK). The session key is then encrypted with the user's public key and later decrypted with the user's private key. Either the owner of the file or a user account that has been designated as a recovery agent for the file can simply log on with the correct user name and password in order to decrypt the file. The NTFS file system supports EFS.

◆ **Internet Protocol Security (IPSec):** IPSec is used to encrypt Transmission Control Protocol/Internet Protocol (TCP/IP) traffic to ensure that communications within an intranet or the Internet are more secure. Typically used to support VPNs (Virtual Private Networks), IPSec provides the highest level of Internet security currently possible. IPSec is a security addition to the IP protocol that, when enabled, protects communications so that no one except the receiver can read what is sent over the network.

◆ **Smart card support: Smart cards** are credit card sized devices that are used to store passwords, public and private keys, and other types of identifying data. You can attach a smart card reader to a Windows XP computer and use it to make certificate-based authentication possible. Users must have a personal identification number (PIN) for the smart card. Smart cards are often used to transfer identification and other confidential information between systems. With the help of smart cards, you can reduce the risks involved in transmitting sensitive information over the network.

**Figure 1-12  Windows XP security features**

**Figure 1-13  Using EFS to encrypt a folder on an NTFS disk**

Selecting this check box will encrypt a folder's contents using EFS

# skill 6

## *Introducing Workgroups and Domains*

### exam objective

Basic knowledge

### overview

The Windows XP operating system supports both workgroups and domains, the two basic network model types that enable users to share common resources.

A **workgroup (Figure 1-14)** is a logical group of computers that are interconnected, generally over a local area network (LAN). Workgroups allow users to easily share information and resources. A workgroup is also referred to as a **peer-to-peer network**. In a peer-to-peer network, all the computers in a workgroup share resources as equals, without a dedicated server. The main design features of workgroups are:

◆ The administration of user accounts and resource security in a Windows XP workgroup is decentralized. Each computer on the network maintains a **local security database**. This database lists user accounts and resource security information for the computer on which the database resides. All information about users and groups is stored in the local security database. Each computer user can share resources such as printers and folders with other users on the network. They can also control access to resources stored on their computer by setting access permissions for groups or individual users.

◆ In order for a user to gain access to any computer in the workgroup, he or she must have a user account on every computer. Furthermore, in order to maintain complete access to all computers on the network, if you make changes to a user account, you must update each computer in the workgroup with the changed information. If you forget to add a new user account on one of the computers in a workgroup, the new user will not be able to log on to that computer or access its shared resources over the network.

One key advantage to using Windows XP workgroups to share resources is that it does not require a computer running Windows 2000 or 2003 Server to store information.

Limitations: A workgroup model is practical only in smaller environments where the computers are located in close proximity **(Figure 1-15)**. Microsoft recommends less than 10 computers. If you require a more scalable network that includes machines located in different geographic locations, you should use domains. (***Note:** If all computers on a network are running Windows XP Professional, the only type of network option available is a workgroup. To implement a domain-based model, one of the Windows 2000 or Windows 2003 Server products is required to function as a domain controller.*)

A Windows **domain (Figure 1-16)** is a logical grouping of network computers that share a central **directory database**. The main features of a domain are as follows:

◆ The directory database, also referred to as **the Directory**, contains all user account and security information for the domain. This directory constitutes the database portion of the Windows directory service, known as **Active Directory**. One of the notable new components of Windows 2000, Active Directory stores information about network objects such as users and groups, printers, and computers. Users access Active Directory to locate the resources they need on the network. Active Directory now stores all network directory data, functionality migrated from the Registry in Windows NT. Since the entire network directory is stored on a single database rather than on multiple databases, the system is more structurally robust, offering extensibility that allows greater flexibility for modifications and additions.

**Figure 1-14  Windows XP workgroup**

A workgroup is the simplest form of a Windows network

**Figure 1-15  A Windows XP workgroup**

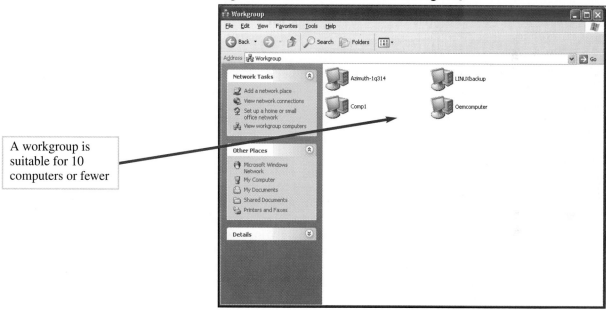

A workgroup is suitable for 10 computers or fewer

**Figure 1-16  Windows domain**

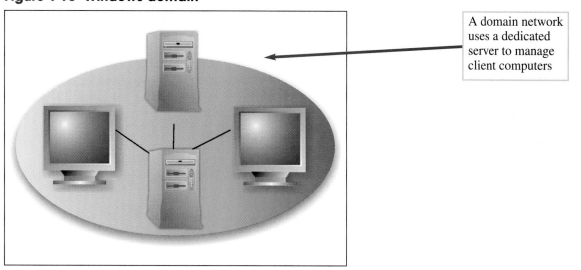

A domain network uses a dedicated server to manage client computers

# skill 6 *Introducing Workgroups and Domains (cont'd)*

**exam objective**    Basic knowledge

## overview

◆ All domains have a **domain controller**. A domain controller is a server on which the Directory resides. As noted above, this service must be run on one of the server versions of Windows 2000 or Windows 2003. This server manages security-related aspects of user/domain interactions. In a Windows domain, all domain controllers are equals, doing away with the concept of primary and backup domain controllers used in Windows NT.

◆ The computers in a domain can be in close physical proximity on a LAN, or can be located in different corners of the world using a WAN. These systems can use various media for communication such as dial-up lines, Integrated Services Digital Network (ISDN) lines, fiber optic lines, frame relay connections, satellite connections, or leased lines.

The two main advantages of a domain are as follows:

◆ Security and administration are centralized.

◆ It provides a single logon process for users to gain access to network resources, such as file, print, and application resources for which they have permissions.

## more

A Windows domain consists of three kinds of computers **(Figure 1-17)**:

◆ **Domain controllers running Windows 2000 Server or Windows Server 2003:** In a domain, when you create a user account, the Windows operating system records it in Active Directory, which resides on the domain controller. When a user logs on to a computer in a specific domain, a domain controller checks the directory for authentication of the user name and password, as well as any logon restrictions. This process helps prevent unauthorized access to computing resources. The domain controller performs this check by using the name specified by the user during the logon process. If a domain has multiple domain controllers, when you make changes to the Active Directory on one domain controller, they are automatically replicated to all other domain controllers in the domain.

◆ **Member servers running Windows 2000 Server or Windows Server 2003:** A computer that is not a domain controller for a Windows domain but that is running the Windows 2000 Server or Windows Server 2003 operating system is referred to as a member server. Member servers do not authenticate users, but are used to provide shared resources, such as printers and folders. These servers participate in a domain, but do not store a copy of the Active Directory database. Permissions are set locally for resources that reside on a member server, allowing users to connect to the server and use its resources.

◆ **Client computers running Windows XP Professional:** These are the computers that comprise the end user desktop environment. These computers allow users to access domain resources. (Note that Windows 2000 Professional client computers also function in this capacity.)

**Figure 1-17  Domain controller and Windows XP client computers in a Windows domain**

# Summary

- Windows XP is a multipurpose operating system that supports client/server (domain-based networks), as well as peer-to-peer networks (workgroups). Workgroup networks and domain networks are the two networking models that can be used to share common resources.

- Windows XP Professional and Windows XP Home are the two versions of Windows XP developed by Microsoft. Windows XP Professional works in conjunction with Windows 2000 Server or Windows Server 2003 to form the basis of a client/server network.

- General features and enhancements provided by Windows XP Professional include reduced total cost of ownership, enhanced security, support for symmetric multiprocessing, multitasking and multithreading, support for a variety of network protocols, Plug and Play hardware support, and greater ease of use.

- Windows XP supports thousands of different hardware devices. However, it is not necessarily the case that a device that works with Windows 95, Windows 98, or even Windows NT will be supported by Windows XP Professional. Every hardware device on a system should be systematically checked against the Hardware Compatibility List (HCL) to determine conclusively whether it will work with Windows XP Professional.

- File management features in Windows XP Professional include the NTFS file system, FAT 32 file system, disk defragmentation utility, and backup utility. The NTFS file system supports file system recovery, large storage media, long file names, file encryption, and disk quotas, which control disk usage by network users. (Disk quotas apply to local users also.)

- Kerberos V5, IPSec, EFS, and smart card support are some of the security features of Windows XP Professional. Kerberos V5 is the primary authentication protocol for domains in the Windows XP operating system. Internet Protocol Security (IPSec), which is typically used to support virtual private networks, is a security addition to the IP protocol that, when enabled, protects communications so that no one except the receiver can read what is sent over the network. EFS allows files and folders on NTFS disks to be encrypted. Smart cards are credit card sized devices that are used to store passwords, public and private keys, and other types of identifying information. A smart card reader can be attached to a Windows XP computer and used to make certificate-based authentication possible.

- The Windows XP operating system supports both the workgroup and domain network models. In a workgroup, the administration of user accounts and resource security is decentralized and each computer on the network maintains a local security database that stores information about users and groups on the local system.

- A Windows domain is a logical grouping of network computers that share a central directory database. The directory database, which contains user accounts and security information for the domain, constitutes the database portion of the directory service known as Active Directory. Active Directory, which was a new component in Windows 2000, stores information about network objects on a domain-based network. Users access Active Directory to locate the resources, such as users and groups, printers, and computers that they need on the network.

# Key Terms

| | | |
|---|---|---|
| Active Directory | File Allocation Table (FAT) | Plug and Play |
| Add/Remove Hardware Wizard | Hardware Compatibility List (HCL) | Smart card |
| Backup utility | Hibernation | Standby |
| Directory database | Internet Protocol Security (IPSec) | Win32 Driver Model (WDM) |
| Disk Defragmenter utility | Kerberos V5 | Windows 2000 Advanced Server |
| Domain | Local security database | Windows 2000 Datacenter Server |
| Domain controller | Member server | Windows 2000 Professional |
| Encrypting File System (EFS) | NTFS file system | Windows 2000 Server |
| FAT32 file system | Peer-to-peer network | Workgroup |

# Test Yourself

1. The Windows XP Professional operating system: (Choose all that apply)
   a. Can function with five processors.
   b. Supports automatic private IP addressing.
   c. Supports Plug and Play functionality.
   d. Supports asymmetric multiprocessing.

2. Which Windows XP operating systems feature allows a single port to support up to 127 peripheral devices, and enables you to connect and disconnect devices without shutting down or restarting your computer?
   a. The Universal Serial Bus (USB) standard
   b. Kerberos V5

c. Active Directory

d. Virtual private network support

**3.** What must you do to ensure that hardware devices are compatible with Windows XP Professional?

a. Nothing, all devices that work with Windows 95, Windows 98, or even Windows NT will work well with Windows XP Professional.

b. Check the Hardware Compatibility List (HCL) to determine conclusively whether they will work with Windows XP Professional.

c. You must have an IT professional install and configure any pre-1999 devices.

d. Make sure that they use the Win32 Driver Model.

**4.** Which of the following statements about the features in Windows XP Professional are true? (Choose all that apply.)

a. The Add/Remove Programs Wizard is used to add, remove, and repair peripheral devices.

b. Windows XP lowers the total cost of ownership by using technologies that enable automatic installation and upgrading of the operating system and applications.

c. Windows XP Professional supports only the Advanced Configuration and Power Interface (ACPI) for managing power consumption.

d. The Windows XP operating systems support symmetric multiprocessing (SMP), preemptive multitasking, and multithreading.

**5.** Which of the following hardware support options in Windows XP Professional has the capability to configure the installed hardware automatically and load the appropriate drivers?

a. Win32 Driver Model

b. Add/Remove Hardware Wizard

c. Plug and Play support

d. Install and drive support

**6.** Which of the following file-related options in Windows XP Professional ensures that all the related components of files and programs are placed in contiguous sectors of the hard disk?

a. NTFS file system

b. FAT32 file system

c. Disk Defragmenter utility

d. Backup utility

**7.** Which protocol uses encryption to support the secure exchange of data packets in the IP (Internet Protocol) layer?

a. Encrypting File System

b. Kerberos V5 Protocol

c. Internet Protocol Security (IPSec)

d. Smart card support

**8.** Which of the following are features of Windows XP workgroups? (Choose all that apply.)

a. Simple to design and implement.

b. Require a computer to run a Windows 2000 or 2003 Server to hold centralized security information.

c. A workgroup model is practical only in smaller environments where the computers are located in close proximity.

d. Support client/server relationships.

**9.** Which of the following statements about Windows domains are true? (Choose all that apply.)

a. They provide centralized administration and security.

b. They provide multiple logon processes.

c. A directory database contains user accounts and security information for the domain.

d. A domain controller is a client on which Active Directory resides.

## Problem Solving Scenarios

You are working for TechStaff, Inc., a small start-up company that provides job placement services for information technology specialists. TechStaff has ten employees with plans to expand to 15-20 within the next year. Currently, the office has eight PCs from various manufacturers running Windows 98 and a peer-to-peer network. The network supports two different printers and a scanner. All the employees use personal digital assistants. Colleen Williams, the founder of the company, is concerned that the Windows 98 network does not have the capacity to scale up as the organization grows, and that there is very poor file and communications security. She has asked you for recommendations and a report. Write a report for Colleen identifying the features of Windows XP that make it an appropriate solution and your recommendations for a new network.

# Installing Windows XP Professional

**W**indows XP Professional is an operating system that provides enhanced hardware compatibility, file management capabilities, and security as compared to earlier versions of Windows operating systems. Windows XP can be installed over a network, or by using a local CD-ROM.

For a smooth and successful installation, certain pre-installation tasks should be completed before you start. Computers on most networks have different configurations depending on their use. To specify variations in configuration at the time of installation, installation scripts are used. To create and modify scripts for a customized installation of the operating system, you can use the Windows XP Setup Manager Wizard. The Wizard enables you to input user settings during installation. It then creates an answer file that contains information about the settings that will be used in the installation process. This type of installation is called an unattended installation. The computer is set up with Windows XP Professional, and other applications if desired, with no user intervention.

Manual installation of Windows XP Professional on multiple computers in an organization with identical configurations can be a tedious and time-consuming task. Creating a disk image of the Windows XP Professional installation and copying this image to the other computers makes multiple installations simpler. A utility called Sysprep is used to prepare the system for duplication, also referred to as cloning. Sysprep does not perform the actual duplication. A third-party utility must be used to duplicate the master disk image onto the target computers. Sysprep makes sure that the security identifiers (SIDs) are unique on each of the target computers. It also initiates a Mini-Setup Wizard, which can be used on each of the targets to enter computer-specific information such as the user name, domain name, and time zone. Sysprep is included on the Windows XP Professional operating system CD in the **\Support\Tools\Deploy.cab** folder.

You can also perform remote installations of the operating system using the Remote Installation Service (RIS). In RIS installation a client computer is booted up, an image of the operating system is located, and the image is downloaded and installed. RIS helps you to simplify image management for client computers. It also supports recovery of the operating system in the event of system failures.

If you are currently using Windows 98, Me, 2000, XP Home, or NT 4.0 Workstation, you can upgrade the existing operating system on the computers in your network to Windows XP Professional. Microsoft periodically releases utilities and patches that contain error correction or improvements on widely used applications. These items are packaged together in the form of service packs. Using Windows XP Professional, you can install these service packs at the same time as you are installing the operating system, unlike previous versions of the operating system where service packs had to be installed separately.

## Goals

In this lesson, you will learn about the tasks that must be performed before you can install Windows XP Professional. You will use a CD-ROM to install Windows XP Professional and also install the operating system over a network. You will learn how to resolve setup problems, log on, and work with Setup Manager. You will also learn how to use the System Preparation tool and Windows XP Server Remote Installation Services to perform remote installations on client computers. Finally, you will learn how to configure Remote Installation Services, upgrade previous versions of Windows to Windows XP Professional and install service packs.

## Lesson 2   Installing Windows XP Professional

| Skill | Exam 70-270 Objective |
| --- | --- |
| 1. Identifying Pre-installation Tasks | Prepare a computer to meet upgrade requirements. |
| 2. Installing Windows XP Professional Using a CD-ROM | Perform and troubleshoot an attended installation of Windows XP Professional. |
| 3. Installing Windows XP Professional over a Network | Perform and troubleshoot an attended installation of Windows XP Professional. |
| 4. Resolving Problems Encountered During Setup | Troubleshoot failed installations. |
| 5. Logging On to Windows XP Professional | Basic knowledge |
| 6. Using the Windows XP Setup Manager | Perform and troubleshoot an unattended installation of Windows XP Professional. Create unattended answer files by using Setup Manager to automate the installation of Windows XP Professional. |
| 7. Using the System Preparation Tool | Perform and troubleshoot an unattended installation of Windows XP Professional. Install Windows XP Professional by using the System Preparation Tool. |
| 8. Performing Remote Installation on Client Computers | Perform and troubleshoot an unattended installation of Windows XP Professional. Install Windows XP Professional by using Remote Installation Services (RIS). |
| 9. Configuring Remote Installation Services | Perform and troubleshoot an unattended installation of Windows XP Professional. Install Windows XP Professional by using Remote Installation Services (RIS). |
| 10. Upgrading Previous Versions of Windows to Windows XP Professional | Upgrade from a previous version of Windows to Windows XP Professional. Perform post-installation updates and product activation. |
| 11. Updating Windows XP after Installation | Perform post-installation updates and product activation. |
| 12. Transferring Files and Settings | Migrate existing user environments to a new installation. |

## Requirements

To complete this lesson, you must have administrative rights, a distribution server, a domain, and a computer running Windows XP Professional that is connected to a network.

# skill 1

## *Identifying Pre-installation Tasks*

**exam objective**

Prepare a computer to meet upgrade requirements.

**overview**

Before you install Windows XP Professional, you should plan carefully and perform a number of checks to ensure that the installation proceeds without delays and bottlenecks. When you install, you can either upgrade an existing OS or do a clean installation of Windows XP Professional. You can upgrade from Windows 98, Me, 2000 or NT 4.0 Workstation. This will retain a number of settings including your desktop settings, user account and password information, and general computer and network configuration settings. Choose the upgrade option if you want to keep the Registry settings that allow you to run applications that are already installed.

You will choose a clean installation on computers with blank hard drives, when you want to overwrite an existing OS, or if you are going to create a dual-boot system in which the user will select the OS to use at startup. You can create a dual-boot system on machines that have Windows 98, 2000, and NT 4.0 Workstation installed. If you choose to overwrite an existing OS, you will have to reinstall all applications, reconfigure any customized settings, and recreate user account and password data. Following the guidelines outlined below will help ensure a successful installation:

◆ Check Microsoft's minimum hardware requirements list **(Table 2-1)** to make sure that the hardware on your computer is sufficient to install Windows XP Professional.

◆ If the computer meets the minimum hardware requirements, make sure all of your hardware devices are included on the **Hardware Compatibility List**. Only devices listed on the HCL are guaranteed to be compatible with Windows XP Professional. If you use a hardware device that isn't on the HCL, you might encounter problems during and after installation. A copy of the HCL is provided in the file called HCL.txt, which is in the Support folder on the Windows XP CD, or you can view or download the most current copy on the Internet at the URL **https://winqual.microsoft.com/download/default.asp** **(Figure 2-1)**. You can search the HCL at the following Internet address: **http://www.microsoft.com/whdc/hcl/search.mspx**.

◆ Check for software compatibility in the Windows Catalog on the Microsoft Web site at **http://www.microsoft.com/windowsxp/pro/howtobuy/upgrading/compat.asp**. You can search the Windows Catalog for specific hardware devices as well.

◆ Check to make sure the computer has the most recent BIOS (basic input/output system). The HAL (Hardware Abstraction Layer) that is installed is dependent upon the type and version of the BIOS.

◆ Run your virus scanning software, correct any problems, and then disable this software if it is BIOS-based. BIOS-based virus scanning software can impede an installation because it will react badly when the Setup program accesses the partition table on the hard disk.

◆ Find out how many partitions are on the hard disk of your computer and the file system with which they are formatted. (A **partition** is a part of your hard disk drive that has been formatted to act as a logically separate unit of storage.)

◆ Decide which file system you want to use for the installation partition.

◆ Select the domain or workgroup that your computer will join if it is to be a part of a network.

◆ A comprehensive method of checking that your system meets upgrade requirements is to use Microsoft's Upgrade Advisor, which you can access at the following URL: **http://www.microsoft.com/windowsxp/pro/howtobuy/upgrading/advisor.asp**.

**caution**

When you install the operating system on a partition that already contains data, all existing files will be overwritten.

**Table 2-1**  *Hardware requirements for installing Windows 2000 Professional*

| Component | Requirement |
| --- | --- |
| CPU | Intel Pentium/Celeron, AMD K6/Athlon/Duron or compatible processor; 233 MHz supported, 300 MHz recommended |
| Memory | 64 MB RAM supported, 128 MB recommended |
| Hard disk space | 1.5 GB available |
| Networking | Appropriate network adapter card |
| Display | Super VGA (800 x 600) resolution or higher Video Display Adapter (VDA) and monitor |
| Other devices | Recommended: CD-ROM or DVD drive 12 x or faster, unless you are installing Windows XP Professional over a network |
| Accessories | Keyboard and mouse or other pointing devices; 14.4 Kbps or higher modem for Internet access (33.6 or higher for voice and videoconferencing) |

**Figure 2-1  Search for compatible hardware devices**

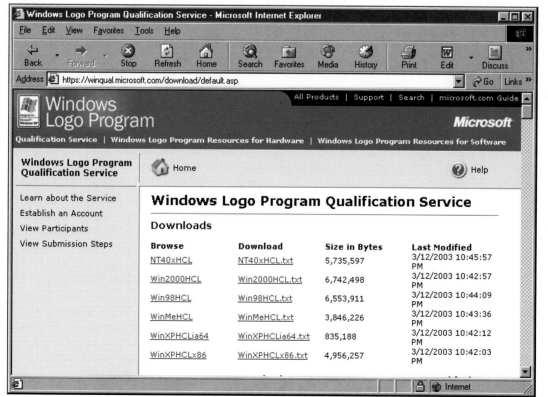

# skill 1

## *Identifying Pre-installation Tasks*
### *(cont'd)*

**exam objective**

Prepare a computer to meet upgrade requirements.

**overview**

During installation, you will select one of the following partition options according to the configuration of your computer's hard disk:

◆ **Unpartitioned hard disk:** Create a partition for the installation files and then choose the size you want for this partition.

◆ **Existing partition with enough free space:** You can install Windows XP Professional on an existing partition if it has enough free space, or you can create a new partition for the installation files if there is sufficient unpartitioned disk space. You can also delete an existing partition to create enough space, and then create a partition large enough for the installation files.

After installing Windows XP Professional on a partition, you must partition the remaining disk space to make it usable. Data cannot be stored until the disk is partitioned and formatted. The preferred method for formatting a disk is to use the Disk Management administrative tool after the installation process is complete rather than during setup, although this is possible.

According to the guidelines provided by Microsoft, the disk partition on which you install Windows XP should have 1.5 GB or more of free disk space. While this may be adequate in some situations, using a larger partition is highly recommended because the operating system alone consumes a substantial amount of disk space. This will allow for scalability, leaving room for updates and operating system tools or files that may be required later.

Next, you must select a file system for the Windows XP partition. Partitions can be formatted with any one of three file systems: NTFS, FAT, or FAT32 (**Figure 2-2**). A description of these file systems is provided below:

◆ **NTFS:** This is the file system recommended by Microsoft because it offers many benefits, including security at both the file and folder levels, compression for individual files and folders rather than just an entire drive, increased performance on large drives, and support for much larger disk and file sizes. NTFS 5, the new version of the file system (NTFS 4 was used for NT Workstation 4.0), also includes encryption, disk quotas, and support for mount points. Quotas are used to restrict the amount of disk space a user can consume on a particular partition or volume. Encrypted files provide additional security by preventing any user but the owner or the recovery agent (typically, the Administrator's account) from opening them. Mount points are used to create a path to a physical disk that points to a folder on a physical disk that acts as an entry to another partition. This means that you can add a second hard drive and, rather than labeling it the D: drive, you can assign it to a folder on the C: drive. Users will not have to access the D: drive to use the new storage space. Instead, what they will see is an extremely large new folder on a drive that is already familiar. NTFS also supports dynamic disks, which are divided into dynamic volumes. This storage method is superior to the partition-based storage on a basic disk because you can create an unlimited number of volumes on each disk. You use the Disk Management utility to create dynamic volumes.

◆ **FAT and FAT32:** Unlike NTFS, the FAT and FAT32 file systems do not allow you to control access to individual files. On FAT and FAT32 disks, you can only control access to shared folders. However, if you want to set up your computer for dual booting, in many cases you should format the system partitions as FAT or FAT32. When you configure a computer for dual booting, you can choose between one or more operating systems when you turn the computer on. The operating systems will be saved in different OS folders, which can be on the same partition or on different partitions. Generally, it is recommended that you install each operating system on a separate drive or on its own partition. This approach will prevent errors that can occur because each of the operating systems installs its own files into certain shared folders. Files installed by one OS may not work under the other OS; for example, files in the Common Files, Accessories, and Program

**tip**

The only operating systems you can use to access data from a hard disk that has been formatted with NTFS are Windows 2000, Windows NT, and Windows XP.

**Figure 2-2  Types of file systems supported by Windows XP**

# skill 1

## *Identifying Pre-installation Tasks*
### *(cont'd)*

**exam objective**

Prepare a computer to meet upgrade requirements.

**overview**

Files folders, as well as those in the Microsoft Internet Explorer and the Microsoft Outlook Express folders. You will want to format the disks with FAT or FAT32 because, generally, you will want to be able to read and write to other partitions, no matter which operating system you are presently using. As a Windows XP user, you likely will want to take advantage of such features as Encrypting File Systems (EFS) and disk quotas, which are available only on NTFS partitions. This creates a dilemma on many dual-boot systems. If you convert a partition to NTFS, only Windows 2000, Windows XP, and Windows NT 4.0 with the proper service pack (SP4) can read from and write to Windows XP NTFS volumes or partitions.

To create a dual-boot with either Windows 95 or Windows NT, the most important consideration is that you must install the earlier operating system first. You also can create a dual-boot configuration with Windows 98 and Windows 2000, or Windows 98 and Windows XP. In either case, you must install Windows 98 first. If you want to configure a multiple-boot situation in which you will have Windows 9x, Windows NT, Windows 2000, and Windows XP, first install Windows NT, then Windows 9x, then Windows 2000, and Windows XP last. In a dual-boot situation with Windows 95 OSR2 or Windows 98, the system partition must be formatted as either FAT or FAT32. FAT32 is recommended. For a dual-boot with earlier versions of Windows 95, the system partition must be FAT.

The Windows XP Setup program will automatically format the hard disk with FAT if the disk is smaller than 2 GB, and with FAT32 if it is larger than 2 GB. However, you can format another drive with NTFS.

You must also choose the type of network security model you will be using at the time of installation. Network security models can be either workgroups or domains. However, security in a workgroup must be implemented on an individual basis. A domain offers the advantage of global security. Other characteristics of these group types include:

◆ **Workgroup:** A workgroup is a logical grouping of networked computers that share resources without a dedicated server (**Figure 2-3**). Workgroups are used for small groups of approximately 10 computers. You must join either a workgroup or a domain during installation, although you can change a workgroup or domain membership later. To add a computer to an existing workgroup during installation, you must enter the name of the workgroup you want to join. You can also create a new workgroup during the installation.

◆ **Domain:** A domain consists of computers that are logically networked together for a similar purpose, regardless of their physical location. These logical groups share a central directory database. The directory database stores the user accounts and security information for the domain (**Figure 2-4**). During installation, you can join a domain, or you can add a computer to a domain after installation. (Whether you join a domain during or after installation, the domain must already exist before adding the computer.) In order to join a domain, your computer must have an account in the domain you want to join. You can create the account during installation if you have administrative privileges for the domain. You will have to enter the name and password for the administrative account. The Domain Administrator can also create a computer account for you before you begin the installation. In addition, you must ask your Domain Administrator to provide you with the DNS (Domain Name System) name for the domain you want to join. An example of a DNS domain name is techsoft.com. Techsoft is the organization's DNS identity. Finally, when you join a domain, there must be at least one domain controller and one DNS server online in the domain you want to join.

**caution**

If XP is joining an NT 4.0 domain, XP needs to use the NetBIOS name of the domain.

**Figure 2-3  Workgroup**

**Figure 2-4  Domain**

# skill 2

## *Installing Windows XP Professional Using a CD-ROM*

### exam objective

Perform and troubleshoot an attended installation of Windows XP Professional.

### overview

After you have completed the pre-installation tasks, you are ready to install Windows XP Professional on your computer. You can install the operating system from a CD-ROM or over a network. Booting a CD-ROM involves the following four stages:

1. **Running the Setup program:** This is the basic **setup** stage, in which a rudimentary version of the operating system is loaded into the memory of the computer. You accept the licensing agreement, create the installation partition and choose the file system for it, or select an existing partition as the installation partition.

2. **Running the Setup Wizard:** This is the graphical phase of installation, in which the Setup Wizard prompts you to provide information that is required to complete the installation. You will interact with the GUI interface in the Setup Wizard to perform the following tasks:
   - Selecting the regional settings
   - Entering your name and the organization's name
   - Entering the Product Key
   - Entering the computer name: The **computer name** (also known as the **NetBIOS name**) can contain no more than 15 characters and it must be unique. The same name cannot be given to another computer, workgroup, or domain. On a domain-based network, the NetBIOS name will appear in Active Directory as an object. It will be used in the UNC (Universal Naming Convention) path you will use to create connections to shared resources.
   - Entering the password of the Administrator's account
   - Selecting the modem dialing information
   - Selecting the date and time settings

3. **Installing Windows Networking Components:** Although the Setup Wizard is still running, this is considered the third stage of setup. The operating system attempts to detect the network card and copies a number of network software files to your computer. You enter the networking settings you want, either the typical setup, which includes installing Client for Microsoft Networks, File and Printer Sharing, and TCP/IP (Transmission Control Protocol/Internet Protocol), or a custom setup. These networking-related files, which you will learn more about in succeeding Lessons, will be used to send and receive files on the network. You will also join either a workgroup or a domain and the Setup program will install and configure the networking components.

4. **Completing the Installation:** In the final stage, the Setup program copies files onto the hard disk, registers the components, and configures the computer. The Installing Components screen shows the progress of the installation of various files, including the Fax Service, Indexing Service, games, and accessories. Next, the Performing Final Tasks screen displays the progress of installing the Start-menu items, registering the components, saving the configuration, and removing the temporary files. Finally, the computer is restarted and the installation is complete.

### how to

Install Windows XP Professional using a CD-ROM.

1. Insert the **Windows XP Professional CD-ROM** in the CD-ROM drive of your computer. The **Welcome to Windows XP** screen asks you what you want to do (**Figure 2-5**).

2. Click **Install Windows XP**. The **Welcome to Windows Setup** screen opens. Here you can specify whether you want to upgrade to Windows XP or install a new copy of Windows XP.

3. Click the **Installation Type** list box and choose **New Installation (Advanced)** (**Figure 2-6**). Then, click  Next >  to open the **License Agreement**.

**Figure 2-5  The Welcome to Microsoft Windows XP screen**

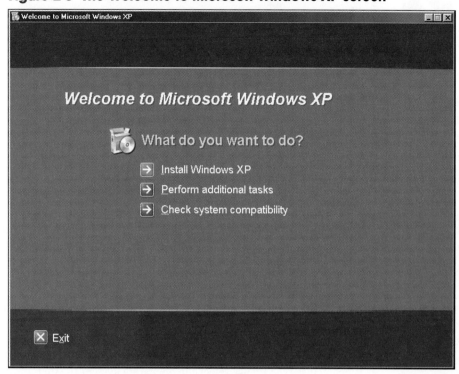

**Figure 2-6  The Welcome to Windows Setup screen**

# skill 2

## Installing Windows XP Professional Using a CD-ROM *(cont'd)*

**exam objective**

Perform and troubleshoot an attended installation of Windows XP Professional.

## how to

4. Click the **I accept this agreement** option button to accept the licensing terms and then click [ Next > ]. The **Your Product Key** screen opens **(Figure 2-7)**.
5. Enter the 25-character product key number for Windows XP Professional. The product key is provided with the Windows XP Professional CD.
6. Click [ Next > ]. The **Setup Options** screen opens. Here, you can customize the language, installation, and accessibility options for the setup. You do not need to modify the default settings. Click [ Next > ].
7. The **Get Updated Setup Files** screen opens. The **Yes** option button is selected by default. Accept the default selection and click [ Next > ]. While the system downloads the updated setup files, Setup describes some of the advantages and new features of Windows XP. This process may take several minutes.
8. Setup will load the information and determine the files that must be copied for the installation. After the information is loaded, Setup will copy the installation files to your computer and restart your computer. Restarting the computer enables Setup to inspect the hardware configuration and load the installation files to your computer. The Setup program prepares Microsoft Windows XP Professional to run on your computer.
9. When you see the **Please select the operating system to start** screen, press the **[Enter]** key to continue the installation. The **Welcome to Setup** screen displays three options:
   - To set up Windows XP now, press [Enter].
   - To repair a Windows XP installation, press R.
   - To quit Setup without installing Windows XP, press F3.

**tip**

If you only have a single partition, it will be automatically selected.

10. Press **[Enter]**. The next screen displays a list of the existing partitions and unpartitioned space on the computer and offers the following three choices **(Figure 2-8)**:
    - To set up Windows XP on the selected item, press [Enter].
    - To create a partition in the unpartitioned space, press C.
    - To delete the selected partition, press D.
11. Press **[Enter]** to select the default C: partition. If you are upgrading with a new install, you will receive a caution message. Press **C** to continue.
12. Setup states that it will install Windows XP on the C: partition. Leave **Convert the partition to NTFS** selected and press **[Enter]**. A caution message appears informing you that converting to NTFS will make the drive unusable by other operating systems. Press **C** to continue. A second caution message appears stating that a Windows folder already exists and will be overwritten. Press **L** to delete the existing folder and continue with the installation.
13. Setup will examine your disks, copy files to the installation folders, delete the existing Windows installation, and initialize your installation of Windows. When this portion of Setup is complete, the computer reboots.
14. When the computer restarts, Setup displays the file system type and checks the disk to verify its files and folders. Conversion of the file system from FAT32 to NTFS begins. When the file system conversion is complete, the computer restarts. Setup continues copying installation files, including those for devices such as the keyboard and mouse **(Figure 2-9)**. The screen may flicker during this process.
15. Next, the **Regional and Language Options** screen opens. Here, you can customize Windows XP for different regions and languages.
16. Accept the default settings and click [ Next > ]. The **Personalize Your Software** screen opens. Here you can personalize your software by providing information about yourself and your organization **(Figure 2-10)**.
17. After you have entered the required information, click [ Next > ]. The **Computer Name and Administrator Password** screen opens.

**Figure 2-7  The Your Product Key screen**

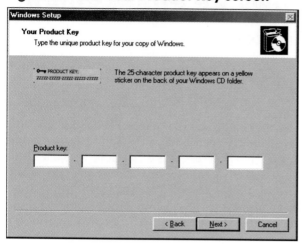

**Figure 2-8 Selecting a partition for Windows XP**

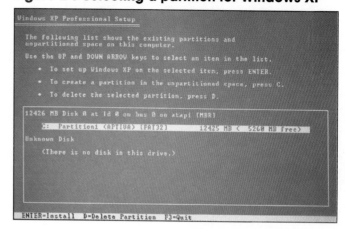

**Figure 2-9  Installing Windows XP components**

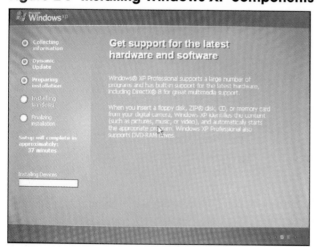

**Figure 2-10  The Personalize Your Software screen**

# skill 2

## Installing Windows XP Professional Using a CD-ROM (cont'd)

**exam objective**

Perform and troubleshoot an attended installation of Windows XP Professional.

**how to**

18. Type the computer name, for example, **comp1**, in the **Computer name** text box. The computer name will be entered in all capital letters. This is the NetBIOS name for the computer. It cannot contain more than 15 characters, and it cannot be the same as the name given to any other computer, workgroup, or domain. This computer name will appear as an object in Active Directory on a domain-based network.

19. Type a password, for example, **adminpass**, in the **Administrator password** and **Confirm password** text boxes. You will need to remember this password in order to have administrative rights on the computer.

20. Click [ Next > ] to advance to the Modem Dialing Information screen and enter the required information.

21. Click [ Next > ]. The **Date and Time Settings** dialog box opens. Make sure that the **Automatically adjust clock for daylight saving changes** check box is selected.

22. Set the correct date and time and click [ Next > ]. Setup now installs the network software that enables you to communicate with other computers, networks, and the Internet. The **Networking Settings** screen opens.

23. Here you can select typical or custom settings for configuring the networking settings. When you select the typical settings, you can create your network connections using **Client for Microsoft Networks, File and Printer Sharing for Microsoft Networks**, and the **TCP/IP** protocol with automatic addressing. If you choose custom settings, you can manually configure the networking components. Click the **Custom settings** option button and click [ Next > ]. The **Networking Components** dialog box opens. You must select the networking components so that your computer can connect to other computers.

24. Accept the default components and click [ Next > ]. The **Workgroup or Computer Domain** dialog box opens. Here you must specify whether your computer will join a workgroup or a domain.

25. If you are on a domain-based network, accept the default selection **Yes, make this computer a member of the following domain** and type the domain for your computer, for example, **Domain1**. If your computer is not on a network, or is on a network without a domain, select the workgroup option and enter a workgroup name.

26. Click [ Next > ]. The **Join Computer to DOMAIN1 domain** dialog box now opens **(Figure 2-11)**. Type a user name, for example, **user1**, in the User name text box.

27. After you have entered the required information, click [ OK ].

28. Setup continues copying files to complete the installation **(Figure 2-12)**. The final tasks include installing the **Start** menu items, registering the components, saving the settings, and removing any temporary files. When these tasks are completed, the computer restarts.

29. The **Welcome to Microsoft Windows** screen appears with the message **Let's spend a few minutes setting up your computer**. Click the **Next** icon [→] in the lower-right corner of the screen. The **Checking your Internet connectivity** screen appears.

30. Leave the default **Yes** option button selected and click [→].

31. On the **Ready to activate Windows?** screen, select **No, remind me every few days** and click **Next**. You will learn about activating Windows later in this lesson.

32. On the **Who will use this computer?** screen, enter the user names **user1** and **user2** in the first two text boxes and click [ Next > ].

33. A thank you message appears. Click **Finish** in the lower-right corner of the screen to complete the installation and configuration.

34. The Windows logon screen appears. Click **user1** on the right half of the screen to begin using Windows XP Professional. Windows applies user1's personal settings and the default desktop appears with the Start menu open.

**caution**

You may experience variances in some of these steps depending on whether you join your computer to a workgroup or a domain.

**Figure 2-11 Joining a Workgroup or Domain**

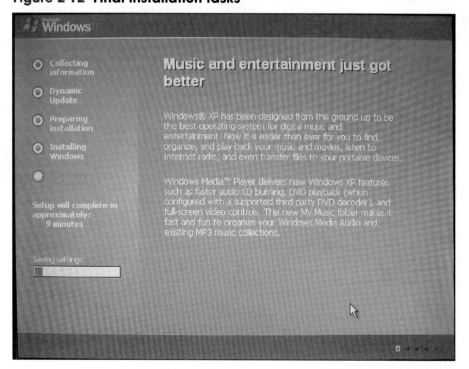

**Figure 2-12 Final installation tasks**

# skill 3

# Installing Windows XP Professional over a Network

## exam objective

Perform and troubleshoot an attended installation of Windows XP Professional.

## overview

To install Windows XP Professional over a network, you must first connect to a distribution server and then run the Setup program. The **distribution server** is a network file server that contains the Windows XP Professional installation files. In order to install Windows XP Professional over a network, you must adhere to the following pre-setup requirements (**Figure 2-13**):

◆ **Creating a distribution server:** A distribution server contains a set of distribution folders that store the installation files from the **i386** folder on the Windows XP Professional CD-ROM. It is a good idea to create more than one set of distribution folders if you have many computers on which to install the operating system, or if you must perform many installations at the same time. To create a distribution server, log on to the server as an administrator, create a distribution folder, and copy the contents of the i386 folder on the installation CD to the folder. If you have applications, drivers, or utilities that you want Setup to copy to the target computers, create a subfolder named **$OEM$** and place the executable files for these programs in the **$OEM$** subfolder. Setup will copy all files in this directory to a temporary directory during the setup process. Then, you must share the distribution folder so that it can be accessed on the network. To do this, right-click the distribution folder, select **Properties** to open the Properties dialog box for the folder, and open the **Sharing** tab of the dialog box. Select the **Share this folder** option button, and enter a name for the shared folder in the **Share name** list box. You can also install Windows XP Professional on systems with different hardware configurations by using one set of distribution folders. This set of folders is used with files that contain the inputs required for the Setup program. These files are referred to as the **answer files**. They contain information about how the computer should be configured during installation, as well as settings that will enable the computer to interact with the network.

◆ **Creating a partition on the target computer:** After creating a distribution server, you must make sure that a partition is available on the target computer that is large enough to accommodate the install. For installs from Windows 98, the partition can be formatted with FAT or FAT32; from Windows 2000, with FAT, FAT32, or NTFS.

◆ **Creating a client boot disk:** A network client is a software application that enables your computer to connect to the distribution server. If you are installing Windows XP Professional on a computer with no operating system, you must boot the computer from a system boot disk that includes a network client so that the target computer can connect to the distribution server.

## how to

Install Windows XP Professional over the network.

1. Boot the target computer.
2. Connect to the shared folder on the distribution server that contains the Windows 2000 Professional installation files.
3. If you are installing Windows XP Professional on a target computer running a Windows 3.x operating system or DOS, run the **Winnt.exe** file. If you are installing Windows XP Professional on a target computer running Windows 95, 98, Me, NT 4.0 (or NT 3.5), or 2000 operating system, run the **Winnt32.exe** file. You can locate the Winnt.exe and Winnt32.exe files in the shared folder on the distribution server. Running Winnt.exe from the shared folder results in the following:
   • Creation of the temporary folder $Win_nt$.~ on the target computer
   • Copying of the Windows XP installation files from the shared folder on the distribution server to the $Win_nt$.~ folder on the target computer

**Figure 2-13  Pre-setup requirements for installing Windows XP over a network**

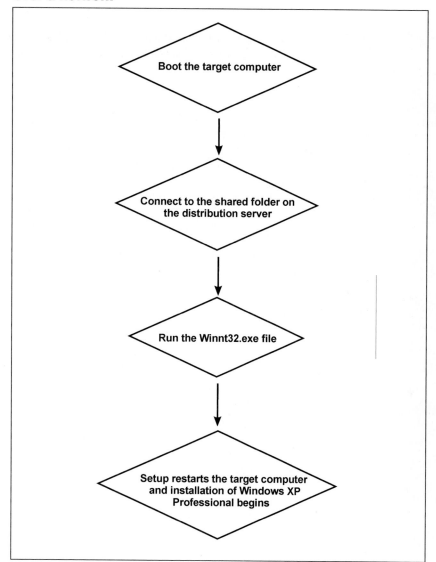

# skill 3

## *Installing Windows 2000 Professional over a Network (cont'd)*

### exam objective

Perform an attended installation of Windows 2000 Professional.

### how to

4. Setup restarts the computer and the installation of Windows XP Professional begins. The subsequent installation process is identical to that used in installation with a CD-ROM.

### more

Installing Windows XP Professional from a CD-ROM and installing it over the network differ only in the method of locating the installation files. To perform a network installation, you first locate and connect to the shared distribution folder, which contains the files from the i386 folder from the installation CD. After you locate and run either Winnt.exe or Winnt32.exe, the installation process is identical. You can modify a server-based installation by changing the way in which the Winnt32.exe and Winnt.exe files run the setup process. To do so, you can use the command line switches to customize the installation process.

**Table 2-2** provides a list of the switches that are used with the Winnt32.exe file. **Table 2-3** provides a list of the switches that are used with Winnt.exe.

### caution

Most of the command-line switches for Winnt32.exe and Winnt.exe have similar functionality with a different syntax. Thus, it is important to know the difference between them.

## Table 2-2   Switches used for Winnt32.exe

| Switch | Description |
| --- | --- |
| /checkupgradeonly | Used to verify whether the computer qualifies for an upgrade to Windows XP Professional. This switch also creates a report for upgrade installations. |
| /copydir:folder_name | Used to create an additional folder within the systemroot folder. Windows XP system files are copied to the systemroot folder. |
| /copysource:folder_name | Used to create an additional folder within the systemroot folder. Setup deletes the files created using this switch once the installation is complete. |
| /cmd:command_line | Used to allow the user to execute a command before the final phase of Setup. |
| /cmdcons | Used to install the Recovery Console. |
| /debug[level] [:file_name] | Enables you to create a debug log at the specified level. It creates the C:\Winnt32.log at level 2 (the warning level) by default. |
| /m:folder_name | Forces Setup to copy the replacement files from other locations. If the replacement files are on the computer, this switch asks Setup to use those files and not the files from the default location. |
| /makelocalsource | Used to copy all of the installation files to the local hard disk. You can use these files later if the CD-ROM drive is not available for installation. |
| /noreboot | Used to prevent Setup from restarting the computer when the file copy phase of Setup is over. Thus, the user is allowed to enter a command, if required, before completing setup. |
| /s:source_path | Used to determine where the Windows XP Professional installation files source is located. To copy files from multiple paths (up to 8) simultaneously, you use separate /s switches for all source paths. |
| /syspart:drive_letter | Used to copy the Setup startup files to the hard disk. The drive specified for installation is marked as the active drive. To install Windows XP Professional on another computer, you can install this drive on that computer and the Setup program will start from the next phase on that computer. Note that you cannot use the /syspart switch without the /tempdrive switch. |
| /tempdrive:drive_letter | Used to place temporary files on the specified drive. Windows XP Professional is installed on the same drive. |
| /unattend[number][:answerfile] | Used to perform an unattended installation. Used to give custom specifications to the Setup program. If an answer file is not specified, Setup takes the user settings from the previous installation. |
| /udf:id[,udf_filename] | Used to specify an identifier (ID) used by the Setup program. Setup uses this ID to find out how an answer file is changed by a Uniqueness Database File. |

## Table 2-3   Switches used with Winnt.exe

| Switch | Description |
| --- | --- |
| /a | Provides accessibility options. |
| /e[:command] | Used to specify a command to be executed on the completion of the GUI mode Setup program. |
| /r[:folder] | Used to specify an optional folder, which will be retained after installation. |
| /rx[:folder] | Used to specify an optional folder, which is copied to the hard disk. However, this folder is deleted by Setup after installation. |
| /s[:sourcepath] | Used to specify where the source files for Windows XP Professional are located. The syntax for this path is: **x:\[path] or \\server\share\ [path]** |
| /t[:tempdrive] | Used to specify the drive that will store temporary files. Windows XP Professional is installed on that drive. |
| /u[:answer file] | Used to perform an unattended setup using an answer file. |
| /udf [id],[UDB_filename] | Used to specify an identifier that Setup will use to modify the answer file. You can configure a Uniqueness Database File (udf) and tell Setup to use this file to override values in the answer file. The identifier tells Setup which values in the UDB file to use. If no UDB file is entered, you will be prompted to insert a disk containing the $Unique$.udb file. |

# skill 4
# *Resolving Problems Encountered During Setup*

**exam objective**

Troubleshoot failed installations.

**overview**

Despite following the hardware requirements, checking the HCL, and resolving all compatibility issues, you may still encounter installation problems. You can use several information files, called **log files**, which are generated during the GUI phase of the setup process, to help you to troubleshoot installation problems. These files contain information about the installation process. The files are located in the directory in which Windows XP Professional is installed. The four log files that are created are: **Setupact.log**, **Setuperr.log**, **Setupapi.log**, and **Setuplog.txt**. The action log (**Figure 2-14**) and the error log (**Figure 2-15**) are particularly valuable.

◆ **Action log:** The action log, which is stored in the **Setupact.log** file, contains information about the events that transpired during Setup, including the copying of files, the creation of registry entries, and any errors that might have occurred. Each event is recorded as it happened. Log files are created during the **GUI** phase of setup.

◆ **Error log:** The error log, which is stored in the **Setuperr.log** file, stores a description of the errors that have occurred and an entry indicating the magnitude of each error.

**more**

In addition to the action and error log files, the following device-specific or component-specific log files may also be created (**%windir%** is a system variable and represents the location of the main Windows directory.):

◆ **%Windir%\comsetup.log:** Registers the **Optional Component Manager** and **Com+** setup routines.

◆ **%Windir%\setupapi.log:** Registers an entry when a line from an **.INF** file is executed and error information if the execution was unsuccessful.

◆ **%Windir%\debug\netSetup.log:** Registers information about joining a domain or a workgroup, including the network computer name, workgroup, and domain validation.

Other problems you may encounter include media errors and CD-ROM drives that are not supported by Windows XP. These problems can usually be solved by replacing the CD-ROM you are using with a new one or replacing the CD-ROM drive. If you do not want to replace an unsupported CD-ROM drive, you can also simply use the network installation method and later add the adapter card driver for the CD-ROM drive, if available. If you find that you have insufficient disk space, simply create a new partition using the free space available on the hard disk or reformat one of the available partitions to create more space. If a dependency error occurs (such as that caused by a service that doesn't start or a driver that fails), make sure that you have installed the correct protocol and network adapter in the **Network Settings** dialog box in the Setup Wizard, that the network adapter has been configured correctly, and that the computer has a unique name on your network. If you cannot connect to a domain controller, check to see if the DNS server and the domain controller are online and running, and make sure that you have entered the correct domain name. If you cannot locate a domain controller, you must create and join a workgroup and join the domain after installation. Finally, if the operating system will not install or start, check to see if all hardware has been detected and confirm that it is all on the Hardware Compatibility List.

**Figure 2-14  Action log**

**Figure 2-15  Error log**

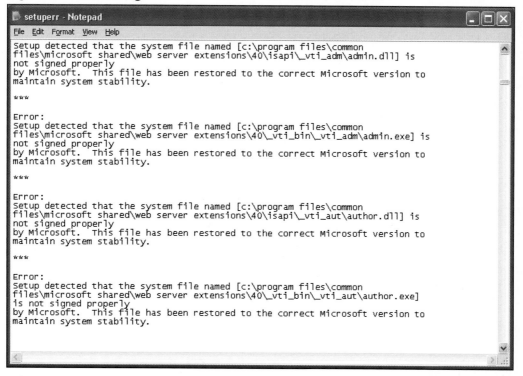

# skill 5

# *Logging On to Windows XP Professional*

**exam objective**

Basic knowledge

## overview

After you have installed Windows XP Professional, you must log on to the computer to access the data and resources on the system. The default settings for logging on to Windows XP allow a user to access the operating system quite easily: the user simply has to click his or her user name on the Welcome screen. In a business setting, however, you may want this procedure to be more secure. One level of security you can add is to require users to specify a user name rather than selecting one from the Welcome screen. To make the logon procedure even more secure, you can require users to supply a user name and a password. Windows XP uses logon authentication for network security purposes so that each user can have his or her own system preferences and private documents saved in a separate location. Logon authentication simply involves entering a user name and password in the **Log On to Windows** dialog box. Windows XP Professional uses the user name and password to verify the authenticity of a user, so that only a valid user can access the resources and data on a computer or network.

### tip

The Welcome screen that allows you to select a user is disabled if the computer is a member of a domain.

## how to

Set a password for a user and log on to Windows XP Professional using the password you set.

1. Click **start** and click **Control Panel** to open the Control Panel window.
2. Click **User Accounts** under the **Pick a category** heading to open the User Accounts window (**Figure 2-16**). Click the user name for whom you want to set a password in the **or pick an account to change** section of the User Accounts window.
3. On the **What do you want to change about <user_name>'s account** screen, click **Create a password**. The **Create a password for <user_name>'s account** screen opens (**Figure 2-17**).
4. Type a password, confirm the password, and type a password hint, as instructed.
5. Click **Create Password** to create the password.
6. Close the User Accounts window and the Control Panel window.
7. Click **start** and click **Log Off** to open the **Log Off** dialog box. Click **Log Off** to log off Windows.
8. On the logon screen, click the name of the user to whom you assigned a password. This user account is now password-protected. A text box appears so that you can enter the password (**Figure 2-18**). Type the password and press **[Enter]** on the keyboard. Windows XP Professional sends this information to the security subsystem of the computer. It then compares the logon information to the user information in the local security database to validate the authenticity of the user (ID). The user's identification for the local computer are contained in an **access token**, which stores the user's security identifiers (SIDs) and allows the user to gain access to system resources and to perform specific system tasks. If the user account is valid and the information matches the information stored in the local security database, Windows XP Professional creates an access token for the user and the user is able to log on.

### tip

To simply change the way in which users log on, click Change the way users log on or off in the Pick a task section of the User Accounts window. You can then deactivate the option of allowing users to log on using the Welcome screen. Instead, users will have to provide a user name in the Log On to Windows dialog box in order to log on to the operating system.

## more

There are actually two separate logon processes on a Windows XP workgroup. There is the process by which you access the local computer at which you are physically located, and the process by which you access network resources. If you log on locally but need to access a resource on another network computer, you will have to establish a network connection with that server. When you attempt to establish this connection, the user name and password that you used to log on locally are submitted. Another authorization process must take place to make sure that the Access Control List (ACL) for the resource you are attempting to use gives you permission to access it. As long as this authorization is granted, you will not be aware that this second authentication process is occurring. However, if the account name you used to log on locally does not have permission for this resource, you will be prompted to enter the user name and password for an account which does have permission for this resource.

**Figure 2-16  User Accounts window**

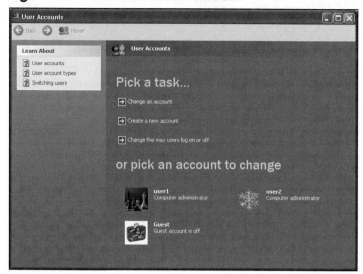

**Figure 2-17  Creating a password for a user**

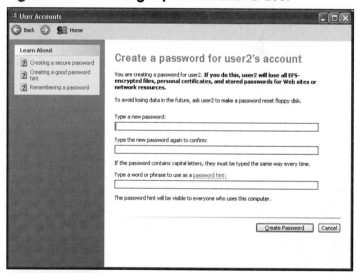

**Figure 2-18  Logging on to Windows with a password**

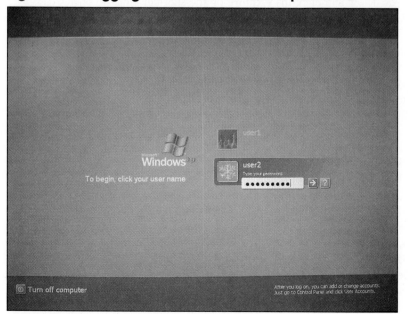

# skill 6

# Using the Windows XP Setup Manager

## exam objective

Perform and troubleshoot an unattended installation of Windows XP Professional. Create unattended answer files by using the Setup Manager to automate the installation of Windows XP Professional.

## overview

Before you perform an unattended installation of Windows XP Professional, you must set up the automatic install environment and create customized **installation scripts** using the Windows XP Setup Manager. Installation scripts specify variations in the software configurations of the computers depending upon their role and use.

You can also create and modify answer files using the Windows XP Setup Manager. Setup Manager asks you a series of questions and, as a result, a script is created for a customized installation of Windows XP. The answer files provide the responses to the questions that the Setup program asks.

In order to create customized installation scripts and answer files, you must copy the Windows XP Setup Manager Wizard to your hard disk. First, you must open the **Deploy.cab** (or **Deploy**) file on the Windows XP Professional CD. It is stored in the **Tools** sub-folder in the **Support** folder. Next, double-click the **Deploy** file to open the Deploy window. Select all of the files, right-click them, and select the **Extract** command on the shortcut menu (**Figure 2-19**).

After the files are extracted, you can use the Setup Manager to either create a new answer file, create an answer file that duplicates the configuration of the computer you are using, or to modify an existing answer file. When you create a new answer file, you must select from among three types of answer files, depending on the type of installation. You can either use the Sysprep utility along with an image replication tool to create a duplicate of the computer configuration that will be copied to other systems on the network, the Remote Installation Services (RIS) to install Windows XP Professional on computers with no operating systems, or you can perform an unattended installation. If you create an answer file that duplicates the configuration of the computer you are using, you can customize the level of user interaction with the Setup program.

Setup Manager has an easy-to-use graphical interface that will help you to create and modify answer files and UDFs (Uniqueness database files) that will contain all of the necessary computer-specific and user-specific data. Using Setup Manager, application setup scripting is straightforward and a distribution folder for the installation files is automatically created.

### tip

Create the destination folder before you begin.

## how to

Create unattended answer files by using Setup Manager.

1. Log on to Windows and insert the **Windows XP Professional CD** in the **CD-ROM** drive. Close the **Welcome to Microsoft Windows XP** window by clicking **Exit** or [X].
2. Right-click ❙❙ start ❙❙ and click the **Explore** on the shortcut menu to open **Windows Explorer**.
3. Click the **C:** drive.
4. Click **File** on the **Menu** bar, point to **New**, and select the **Folder** command to create a new folder on the C: drive.
5. Type **Deploy** to replace the default name for the folder. You will use this folder to store the files that you will extract from the **Deploy.cab** file on the Windows XP Professional CD. Click the **CD-ROM drive** icon in the left pane of the Windows Explorer window to display the contents of the CD-ROM in the right pane.
6. Double-click the **Support** folder to open the **Support** window.
7. Double-click the **Tools** folder to open the **Tools** window.
8. Double-click the **Deploy** file to open the **Deploy** window (**Figure 2-20**).
9. Open the **Edit** menu and click the **Select All** command to select all of the files in the window.
10. Right-click any file and click the **Extract** command on the shortcut menu. The **Select a Destination** dialog box opens.
11. Click My Computer to display the drives on folders available on your computer. Click the **C:** drive to display the folders stored on that drive.
12. Click the **Deploy** folder and then click [ Extract ]. Windows XP Professional copies the selected files to the Deploy folder.

### tip

To select all of the files in the Deploy.cab file, hold down the **[Ctrl]** key and select each of the files listed. If the file icons are listed within one column, you can also select the files by clicking the first file in the list, holding down the **[Shift]** key and then clicking the last file in the list.

**Figure 2-19  The files extracted from deploy.cab**

**Figure 2-20  The Deploy files in the Tools folder**

# skill 6

## *Using the Windows XP Setup Manager (cont'd)*

**exam objective**

Perform and troubleshoot an unattended installation of Windows XP Professional. Create unattended answer files by using the Setup Manager to automate the installation of Windows XP Professional.

## how to

**caution**

Different versions of Setup Manager will differ slightly in the names they give to some dialog boxes, check boxes, and/or option buttons. These steps were completed using Setup Manager version 5.1.2600.1106.

13. After Windows XP Professional has finished copying the files to the Deploy folder on your system's **C:** drive, open the Deploy folder to view the copied files.
14. Double-click the **readme** file to read its contents.
15. Close the readme file.
16. Double-click **setupmgr** in the Deploy folder to start the **Setup Manager Wizard**.
17. Click [ Next > ]. The **New or Existing Answer File** dialog box opens.
18. Make sure that the **Create new** option button is selected, as shown in **Figure 2-21**.
19. Click [ Next > ]. The **Type of Setup** dialog box opens.
20. Make sure that the **Unattended Setup** option button is selected. Click [ Next > ]. The **Product** dialog box opens.
21. Make sure that the **Windows XP Professional** option button is selected. Click [ Next > ]. The **User Interaction** dialog box opens.
22. Select the **Fully automated** option button, as shown in **Figure 2-22**.
23. Click [ Next > ]. The **Distribution Share** dialog box opens.
24. Leave the **Create a new distribution share** option button selected and then click [ Next > ]. The **Location of Setup Files** dialog box opens.
25. Leave the default option, **On the CD,** selected and click [ Next > ]. The **Distribution Share Location** dialog box opens.
26. Click [ Next > ] to accept the default settings. The **License Agreement** opens.
27. Click the **I accept the terms of the License Agreement** check box and click [ Next > ] to accept the agreement. The **Name and Organization** dialog box opens.
28. Enter your name in the **Name** text box and your organization name in the **Organization** text box. Click [ Next > ]. The **Display Settings** dialog box opens.
29. The list boxes for Colors, Screen area, and Refresh frequency are set to **Windows default**. Click [ Next > ] to accept the default display settings. The **Time Zone** dialog box opens.
30. Select the appropriate time zone setting and click [ Next > ]. The **Product Key** dialog box opens.
31. Enter the appropriate 25-character product key and click [ Next > ]. The **Computer Names** dialog box opens.
32. Type the computer name, **XPPRO2**, in the **Computer name** text box and click [ Add... ].
33. Repeat this step to add **XPPRO3** and **XPPRO4** to the list of computer names. These names appear in the **Computers to be installed** list box, as shown in **Figure 2-23**.
34. Click [ Next > ]. The **Administrator Password** dialog box opens.
35. Make sure that the **Use the following Administrator password (127 characters maximum; case-sensitive)** option button is selected and type the password, **password 2**, in the **Password** and **Confirm Password** text boxes.
36. Click [ Next > ]. The **Networking Components** dialog box opens.
37. Click [ Next > ] to accept the default option, **Typical settings**. The **Workgroup Or Domain** dialog box opens.
38. Click [ Next > ] to accept the default settings. The **Telephony** dialog box opens.
39. Provide the appropriate information for the **Country or region, Area code or city code, Number to dial for access to an outside line**, and **The phone system at this location uses** fields.
40. Click [ Next > ]. The **Regional Settings** dialog box opens.
41. Click [ Next > ] to accept the default settings. The **Languages** dialog box opens.

**Figure 2-21  New or Existing Answer File dialog box**

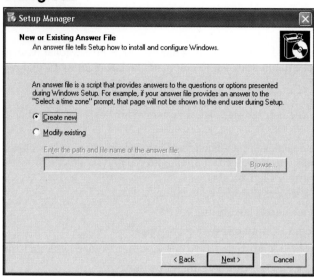

**Figure 2-22  The Fully automated option in the User Interaction dialog box**

**Figure 2-23  Computer Names dialog box**

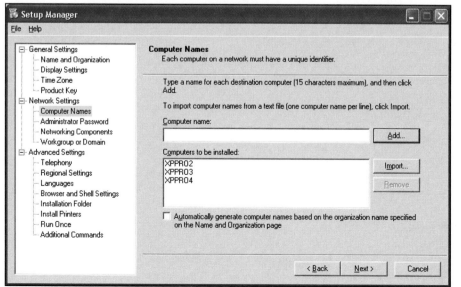

# skill 6

## *Using the Windows XP Setup Manager (cont'd)*

**exam objective**

Perform and troubleshoot an unattended installation of Windows 2000 Professional. Create unattended answer files by using the Setup Manager to automate the installation of Windows 2000 Professional.

**how to**

42. Click [ Next > ] to accept the default settings. The **Browser And Shell Settings** dialog box opens.
43. Click [ Next > ] to accept the default settings. The **Installation Folder** dialog box opens.
44. Select the **A folder with a name that I specify** option button and type **WXPPro** in the **Folder name** text box, as shown in **Figure 2-24**.
45. Click [ Next > ]. The **Install Printers** dialog box opens.
46. Click [ Next > ]. The **Run Once** dialog box opens.
47. Click [ Next > ]. The **Additional Commands** dialog box opens.
48. Click [ Finish ]. The **Setup Manager** dialog box opens with a default path and file name for the answer file selected in the **Path and file name** text box.
49. Type a new path for the answer file, **C:\Deploy\unattend.txt (Figure 2-25)**, and click [ OK ].
50. The **Setup Manager** copies distribution files to your computer's hard disk **(Figure 2-26)**.
51. After the files are copied, the **Completing Setup Manager** screen opens, stating that you have created 3 files: **unattend.txt**, **unattend.udb**, and **unattend.bat (Figure 2-27)**.
52. Close the Setup Manager Wizard window. The three files you created now appear in the Deploy window on your hard disk **(Figure 2-28)**. The Setup Manager has also created a folder called **windist** on the hard disk of your computer.
53. Open Unattend.txt and review its contents **(Figure 2-29)**. Open Unattend.udf using either Word or Notepad and review its contents. When you have finished, close all open windows.

### Figure 2-24  Installation Folder dialog box

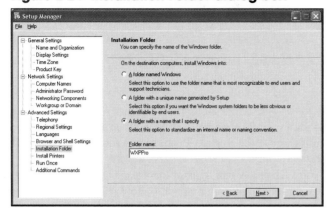

### Figure 2-25  Answer file name and path

### Figure 2-26  Copying distribution files

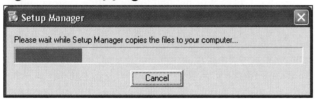

### Figure 2-27  New files in the Deploy window

### Figure 2-28  New files in the Deploy folder

### Figure 2-29  Unattend.txt

# skill 7

# *Using the System Preparation Tool*

## exam objective

Perform and troubleshoot an unattended installation of Windows XP Professional. Install Windows XP Professional by using the System Preparation Tool.

## overview

As a Network Administrator, you may work with a group of computers with identical hardware configurations. Installing Windows XP Professional individually on each of these computers would be a tedious task. You can use the **System Preparation tool (sysprep.exe)** in Windows XP Professional to prepare a hard disk so you can create a disk image of the Windows XP Professional installation. Then you can transfer that image to multiple computers with the same hardware configuration. The System Preparation tool works in conjunction with a third-party disk-imaging application such as Symantec Ghost or PowerQuest DriveImage. The tool removes computer-specific information, such as the computer name and security identifier (SID), so that you can safely transfer the image created with the disk-imaging software to other computers. This tool helps you create as many "carbon copies" of the distribution model as you require. Each hard drive will include the operating system and all applications that those workstations will need.

Before you use the System Preparation tool, you must prepare a distribution model computer. The distribution model machine cannot be a member of a domain. It must be a member of a workgroup, and you must leave the administrator password blank. First, perform a clean installation of Windows XP Professional and configure it as desired. Then copy the necessary files from the Deploy.cab file as outlined in the previous skill. Next, log on as the Administrator, and install all of the applications you will use on the network and all necessary update packs. This is the installation you will use to create what is called the **master disk image**. The master disk image will be transferred to the hard disks of the target computers to create clones of the distribution model.  ·

Next, run sysprep.exe (**Figure 2-30**). The Windows XP Professional System Preparation Tool dialog box will advise you that security parameters are going to be changed and will prompt you to shut down the computer. The **Sysprep.exe** file is the main Sysprep executable file. The syntax to run Sysprep.exe is as follows:

**Sysprep.exe [/quiet] [/nosidgen] [/pnp] [/reboot]**

**Table 2-4** explains the meaning of the various switches.

The primary function of the System Preparation tool is to remove the SID (security identifier) from the distribution model computer. If this were copied to the clone computers and you had the same SID on a group of computers on the network, it would cause major network security problems. SysPrep ensures that a unique SID will be created the first time one of the clone computers is booted up. It also installs a Mini-Setup Wizard on the distribution model computer so that, when a clone computer is booted up for the first time, the user will be prompted to accept the licensing contract and enter the Product ID, regional settings, user name, company name, network configuration, workgroup or domain, and time zone. The Mini-Setup program includes Plug and Play detection capability. This capability is necessary if the clones do not have the same hardware as the distribution model computer. The distribution model computer and the clone computers must have the same hardware abstraction layer (HAL), hard disk controller, boot device, and Ntoskrnl.exe. Ntoskrnl.exe, the microkernel file, creates a Registry key that contains information about the hardware components on a computer during the boot process. HAL is the layer that sorts out the differences between hardware components, presenting to the operating system a standard-looking set of computer hardware. The hard disk controller is an interface between the hard disk and the operating system. The mass-storage controllers (either IDE or SCSI) must also be identical.

Due to Windows XP's Plug and Play functionality, other hardware devices such as network adapters, sound cards, modems, and video cards do not have to be the same. However, if any device drivers for hardware devices on the clone computers are not included in Drivers.cab,

## caution

Disk duplication will only be successful if the master disk image computer and the clone computers have the same basic hardware (hardware abstraction layer or HAL), hard disk controller, power management, and number of processors.

**Figure 2-30  System Preparation tool**

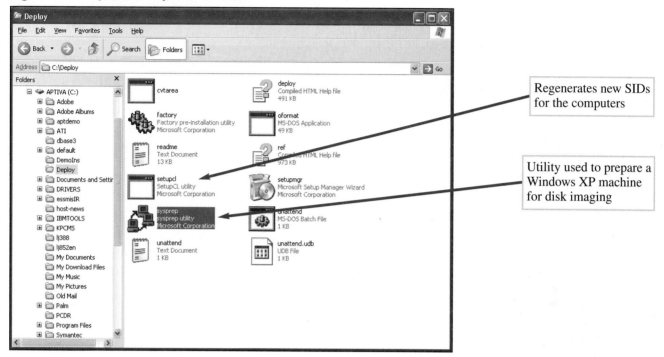

| **Table 2-4   Switches used by System Preparation Manager** | |
|---|---|
| **Switches** | **Description used by System Preparation Manager** |
| /quiet | Runs Sysprep in quiet mode. This switch stops the confirmation dialog boxes from displaying while Sysprep runs on the distribution model computer. It is used when you want to automate Sysprep by adding it to the GuiRunOnce key in the Unattend.txt file. |
| /pnp | Forces a full device detection on the target computer. This switch is optional. Use it when non-Plug and Play devices that cannot be dynamically detected exist on the target systems. |
| /reboot | Enables a reboot of the master computer after the image has been created instead of shutting down and then starting the Mini-Setup Wizard. Use this switch for auditing the system and verifying that Mini-Setup is operating correctly. |
| /nosidgen | Runs Sysprep without generating any security ID. This switch is useful for the Administrator who doesn't intend to clone the computer on which Sysprep is running. |

# skill 7

## *Using the System Preparation Tool*
### *(cont'd)*

**exam objective**

Perform and troubleshoot an unattended installation of Windows XP Professional. Install Windows XP Professional by using the System Preparation Tool.

**overview**

you must either install them on the distribution model computer before you run Sysprep, or you must ensure that the uninstalled drivers are available on the clone computers when you first boot them so that they can be detected and installed.

The master disk image can be saved on a shared network drive or on a CD-ROM. After you have transferred the master disk image to the clone computers, you can turn them on to initiate the Mini-Setup Wizard. You also can create a Sysprep.inf file so that the Mini-Setup Wizard can run without any user intervention. It will include the answers to all questions posed by the Wizard. Before you run Sysprep, use the Setup Manager Wizard (**Setupmgr.exe** from the **Deploy.cab** file) to create a Sysprep.inf answer file (**Figure 2-31**) that you can use to provide unique information for the target computers, including network and regional settings. When the Mini-Setup Wizard runs, it looks for the **Sysprep.inf** answer file (**Figure 2-32**) in the Sysprep folder on the distribution model's root drive and runs it if located. You also can save the Sysprep.inf answer file on a floppy and insert it in the clone computer right after the boot loader appears. If you use a Sysprep.inf answer file, three files: **Sysprep.exe**, **Setupcl.exe, and Sysprep.inf**, must all be saved in the same subfolder. Setupcl.exe is the utility that regenerates new SIDs for the computers.

**how to**

Use the **System Preparation** tool.

1. If you actually were going to mass deploy Windows XP Professional, and you wanted to prepare a hard disk so that you could create a disk image, you first would perform a clean installation of the operating system on a computer that was not a member of a domain, leaving the administrator password blank.
2. Next, log on as an **Administrator** and install and customize applications such as Microsoft Office or other business-specific programs that your target computers will need. You also can install any device drivers the clones may need that are not included in **Drivers.cab** (or not installed by the answer file if you have created one).
3. It is often recommended that you now use a third-party auditing tool to audit the system and verify that the image configuration is correct. Do not overwrite any system files when you audit. Sysprep cannot detect or restore system files that the auditing utility may have changed. It is all right to reboot as many times as needed during the auditing process.
4. When your audit is complete, delete any files or folders that the auditing utility added to the hard drive.
5. Open Windows Explorer. Create a new folder on your **%systemroot%** (usually **C:**) named **Sysprep**. Open the **Deploy** folder (extracted files from Deploy.cab) and move the **Sysprep.exe** and **Setupcl.exe** files to the Sysprep folder. If you used the Setup Manager Wizard to create a Sysprep.inf file, it must also be moved to this folder. You can create the Sysprep folder and store Sysprep.inf in it when you run the **Setup Manager Wizard** (**Figure 2-33**).

**Figure 2-31  Using the Setup Manager to create a Sysprep answer file**

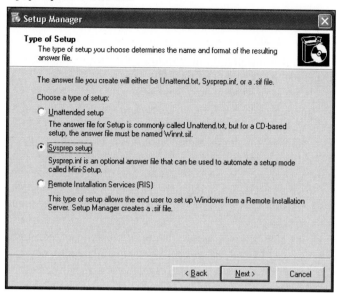

**Figure 2-32  The Sysprep folder after running the Setup Manager**

**Figure 2-33  Creating the Sysprep folder and Sysprep.inf with the Setup Manager**

# skill 7

## Using the System Preparation Tool
### (cont'd)

**exam objective**

Perform and troubleshoot an unattended installation of Windows XP Professional. Install Windows XP Professional by using the System Preparation Tool.

**how to**

6. Run Sysprep.exe. The Windows XP System Preparation Tool message box **(Figure 2-34)** warns you that running Sysprep may modify some of the security parameters on the computer. ACPI computers will automatically shut down. Otherwise, a dialog box will open to let you know that it is safe to shut down the computer.

7. The hard disk of the computer is now programmed to run Plug and Play detection, create new security identifiers (SIDs) (because Setupcl.exe has been copied to %systemroot%\SYSTEM32 and will run at the next boot), and run the Mini-Setup Wizard the next time the system is started.

8. Now you are ready to use an imaging utility to create the master disk image. Copy the image to a shared folder or onto a CD-ROM. The next time you boot up this computer, or any of the clones that were created from the master disk image, the system will detect and re-catalog the Plug and Play devices.

9. When the clone computers are booted up, first Plug and Play detection will take place. Then, the Mini Setup Wizard will run. Users will be prompted to accept the EULA (End-User License Agreement), enter their name and organization, join a workgroup or a domain, enter regional settings, enter TAPI (Telephony Application Program Interface) information, and choose the networking protocols and service to install. If you used a Sysprep.inf file **(Figure 2-35)**, only dialog boxes containing information that was not included in the .inf file will appear.

10. Finally, the local Sysprep folder containing Sysprep.exe, Sysprep.inf, and Setupcl.exe will be deleted, the computer will restart, and the logon dialog box will display.

**Figure 2-34  Windows 2000 System Preparation Tool 2.0 message box**

**Figure 2-35  Example of a Sysprep.inf answer file**

# skill 8

# Performing Remote Installation on Client Computers

## exam objective

Perform and troubleshoot an unattended installation of Windows XP Professional. Install Windows XP Professional by using Remote Installation Services (RIS).

## overview

RIS can eliminate much time and effort on the part of administrators by enabling them to create an image of the operating system that can be downloaded and installed automatically by client computers on a network. In a **remote installation**, the administrator connects to a Windows 2000 or Windows 2003 server called the **Remote Installation Server** (or **RIS server**), which stores the RIS image. RIS images, usually referred to as simply as images, are copies of the Windows XP installation files. An installation of Windows XP Professional, free of user interaction, can then be performed from a central location. This skill will utilize Windows 2000 Server to demonstrate RIS.

RIS is not included with Windows XP Professional. It comes with Windows 2000 Server, Advanced Server, and Datacenter Server. The RIS server can be either a member server or a domain controller. The RIS clients must have either a PXE (Pre-Boot Execution Environment) capable BIOS, a network card with remote boot functionality (PXE version .99c or higher), or a regular PCI (Peripheral Component Interconnect) bus network card that is supported by the RBFG.EXE (Remote Boot Disk Generator) program, which you can use to create an RIS boot disk.

Specific network services must also be available on the network, although they do not have to be on the RIS server. For example, there must be a DNS (Domain Name System) server because RIS needs the DNS service in order to locate the Active Directory. A DHCP (Dynamic Host Configuration Protocol) server is also necessary so that client computers that boot from a network card can get an IP (Internet Protocol) address. An IP address is needed in order for client computers to communicate with the RIS server on the network. If you have routers that do not support DHCP/BOOTP message relaying, you will need either a DHCP server or a DHCP relay agent on the same subnet as the RIS clients. It can be either a Windows 2000 or Windows 2003 server. Active Directory Services must also be running so that the RIS servers can be located. Active Directory will also handle RIS configuration settings and client installation options.

RIS must be installed on a separate partition from the system partition (the one on which Windows 2000 Server is installed). This partition must have enough space to store the RIS software and images and must be formatted with NTFS. This NTFS volume must then be shared.

## caution

In order to perform a remote installation, you must have a Windows 2000 Server computer and Active Directory; as well, the computers on the network must support remote boot.

## tip

Besides a Windows 2000 or Windows 2003 server, an NT 4.0 DHCP server will also work. However, it must be authorized in Active Directory. (Windows 2000/2003 DHCP Servers also must be authorized.)

## how to

Install **RIS** on a computer running Windows 2000 Server.
1. Log on as an **Administrator** and insert the **Windows 2000 Server CD** in the **CD-ROM** drive.
2. Open the **Control Panel** window and double-click the **Add/Remove Programs** icon to open the **Add/Remove Programs window (Figure 2-36)**.
3. Click **Add/Remove Windows Components** to initiate the **Windows Components Wizard**.
4. Select the **Remote Installation Services** check box in the **Components** list box **(Figure 2-37)**.

**Figure 2-36  Add/Remove Programs window**

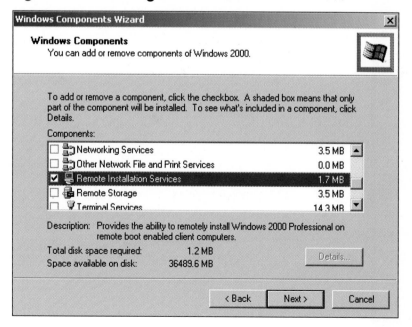

**Figure 2-37  Installing Remote Installation Services**

## skill 8

# *Performing Remote Installation on Client Computers (cont'd)*

**exam objective**

Perform and troubleshoot an unattended installation of Windows XP Professional. Install Windows XP Professional by using Remote Installation Services (RIS).

**how to**

5. Click [ Next > ]. This starts the installation of **Remote Installation Services**, as shown in **Figure 2-38**.
6. When the installation is complete, the **Completing the Windows Components Wizard** screen opens (**Figure 2-39**).
7. Click [ Finish ]. The **System Settings Change** dialog box informs you that you must reboot your system before the new settings will take effect.
8. Remove the Windows 2000 Server CD and click [ Yes ].

**more**

The RIS server stores the installation images that are used by client computers to download and install Windows 2000 Professional. These images are of two types:

- CD-based
- RIPrep

CD-based images are created from the Windows XP Professional installation CD and stored on the RIS server. You can use answer files to customize these images.

RIPrep images are created by taking a snapshot of a preconfigured computer and storing it on the RIS server. These images can also include application installations. An RIPrep image is created by two systems: the source computer (the computer that contains the basic operating system and applications) and the RIS server.

**tip**

The Remote Installation Preparation Wizard runs when the source computer is ready. Type \\RIS Server Name\reminst\admin\i386\Riprep.exe to run this Wizard.

**Figure 2-38  The Windows Components Wizard**

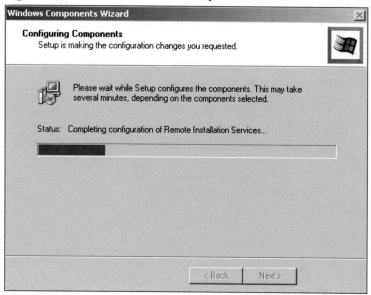

**Figure 2-39  Completing the Windows Components Wizard**

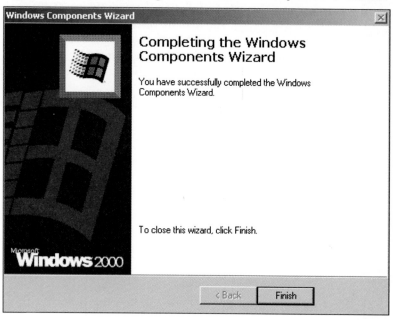

# skill 9

# *Configuring Remote Installation Services*

## exam objective

Perform and troubleshoot an unattended installation of Windows XP Professional. Install Windows XP Professional by using Remote Installation Services (RIS).

## overview

After you have installed Remote Installation Services, you must configure them to meet your requirements. First, the path to the remote installation folder location must be entered. This folder will not already exist. You will enter the drive letter where you installed RIS (remember, this drive must be formatted with NTFS), and the name for a new folder, which will be created as part of the configuration process. Next, the RIS server must be configured to support the RIS client computers. Finally, you must enter the path to the installation source files. The RIS server can be a:

- Domain controller
- Member server

## how to

Configure Remote Installation Services on a Windows 2000 Server computer.

1. After installing **RIS**, log on as an **Administrator**. The **Microsoft Windows 2000 Configure Your Server** window opens. If the Configure Your Server window does not open, open the **Control Panel**, double-click **Add/Remove Programs** and select **Add/Remove Windows Components**. Under **Setup Services**, select **Configure Remote Installation Services**. Then click the **Configure** button. Skip the second and third steps and go on to the fourth step.

2. Click **Finish Setup**. The **Add/Remove Programs** window opens, prompting you to **Configure Remote Installation Services (Figure 2-40)**.

3. Click [ Configure ]. The **Remote Installation Services Setup Wizard** opens.

4. Insert the **Windows 2000 Professional CD** in the **CD-ROM** drive of the server. The **Microsoft Windows 2000 CD** dialog box opens.

5. Click **Exit**. The **Welcome** screen for the **Remote Installation Services Setup Wizard** opens **(Figure 2-41)**.

6. Read the Welcome screen and click [ Next > ]. The **Remote Installation Folder Location** dialog box opens.

**Figure 2-40  Configure Remote Installation Services in the Add/Remove Programs window**

**Figure 2-41  The Remote Installation Services Setup Wizard**

# skill 9

## Configuring Remote Installation Services (cont'd)

### exam objective

Perform and troubleshoot an unattended installation of Windows XP Professional. Install Windows XP Professional by using Remote Installation Services (RIS).

### how to

7. In the path text box, type **D:\RemoteInstall (Figure 2-42)**. Note that you must enter a drive letter that is appropriate for your system. It must be a pre-existing NTFS drive with at least 300 MB of free space on the computer on which you installed RIS. The folder does not have to be pre-existing; it will be created as part of the configuration process.
8. Click ⌞Next >⌟. The **Initial Settings** page opens.
9. Select the **Respond to client computers requesting service** check box and click ⌞Next >⌟. The **Installation Source Files Location** dialog box opens.
10. Type the path to the installation source files, **x:\i386**, in the given text box, where **x** represents the drive letter for your CD-ROM drive.
11. Click ⌞Next >⌟. The **Windows Installation Image Folder Name** page opens.
12. Type the folder name **WINXP.PRO** and click ⌞Next >⌟. The **Friendly Description And Help Text** page opens.
13. Click ⌞Next >⌟ to accept the default friendly description and help text. The **Review Settings** page opens.
14. Review the information and click ⌞Finish⌟. The RIS setup program creates the remote installation folder, copies the RIS files and the Windows installation files, updates the Client Installation Wizard screen files, creates a new unattended Setup answer file, creates the Remote Installation Services (RIS), updates the Registry, and starts the necessary Remote Installation Services.
15. Click **Done** when the tasks are completed.
16. Close all open windows and dialog boxes.

### tip

You must authorize each RIS server in Active Directory for the server to respond to client requests. You can use the DHCP Management snap-in to authorize RIS servers.

### more

The most important thing to understand about RIS is that it comes with only the Windows 2000/2003 Server editions; also, networks that do not have at least one Windows 2000 Server cannot use it. Also remember that DNS must be running on a network server in order for RIS to locate Active Directory and the client computer accounts, and DHCP must be running so that computers with bootable network cards can be assigned an IP address. Client computers must have a BIOS version that supports PXE (Pre-Boot Execution Environment), a PXE network interface card, or a regular PCI (Peripheral Component Interconnect) network interface card that is supported by the Remote Boot Disk (Floppy) Generator (RBFG) program. PXE enables a workstation to boot from a server on a network before it boots the operating system on its hard drive. If the BIOS of the client computer or its network adapters don't support PXE, you can create and use an RIS boot disk to start the RIS client computers. Run the Windows 2000 Remote Boot Disk Generator (RBFG.EXE), which is stored on the RIS server to create the RIS boot disk.

If neither the BIOS nor the network interface card in the client computer supports PXE, you can use the Windows 2000 Remote Boot Disk Generator (RBFG.EXE) to create a boot disk or boot floppy that will mimic the PXE boot process. To create a boot floppy for a remote client, you use the following command at the command prompt on the RIS Server:
- The path to create a boot disk is: **\RemoteInstall\Admin\i386\Rbfg.exe.**
- Alternatively, you can double-click **Rbfg.exe** in the **\RemoteInstall\Admin\i386** folder to create the boot floppy.

**Figure 2-42  Remote Installation Folder Location screen**

# skill 10

## *Upgrading Previous Versions of Windows to Windows XP Professional*

**exam objective**

Upgrade from a previous version of Windows to Windows XP Professional. Perform post-installation updates and product activation.

## overview

When you upgrade from a previous version of Windows, you should first generate a report that identifies the system components that are compatible with Windows XP Professional. You can do this by running the **Windows 2000 Readiness Analyzer**. This utility runs by design during system upgrades; however, it is a good practice to discover hardware-related problems before the upgrade so that you can preempt any potential problems. To generate a hardware compatibility report, you can use the **Windows XP Compatibility tool** found on the Windows XP Professional CD-ROM. When you use the Windows XP Compatibility tool, you start the Setup program and check for compatible hardware and software, but Setup stops and produces the report. To run the Windows XP Compatibility tool, insert the Windows XP Professional CD-ROM into the CD-ROM drive and open a command prompt. Type **d:\i386\winnt32 /checkupgradeonly** (**d:** represents the drive letter of your CD-ROM drive) at the command prompt and press **[Enter]**. You can perform an automatic compatibility check by clicking Check system compatibility on the Windows XP Professional CD-ROM Welcome to Microsoft Windows XP screen.

The compatibility report is generated as a text document, which you can view in the %systemroot% folder. This folder is usually in the WINDOWS folder for Windows 9x upgrades. When you upgrade NT 3.51 or 4.0 or Windows 2000, the report is saved in the Winnt32.log in the %systemroot% folder.

**caution**

Third-party network protocols and client software that do not have an updated version in the i386 Winntupg folder on the Windows XP CD-ROM should also be removed.

In addition to identifying the compatibility of the hardware and software, the compatibility report lets you know if you need to upgrade your software, and it identifies any additional changes you might need to make so that the system functions without problems after Windows XP Professional is installed.

You should not encounter any problems with applications that you have installed on Windows NT 3.51 and 4, but there are certain applications that should be removed before you upgrade. Among those are antivirus applications and disk quota software, because the upgrade from NTFS 4 to NTFS 5 has instituted changes that may cause you problems. Any custom power management software and tools should also be removed because they are now irrelevant. Windows XP Professional includes the Advanced Configuration and Power Interface (ACPI) and Advanced Power Management (APM) to perform these functions.

## how to

Upgrade from a previous version of Windows to Windows XP Professional.
1. Insert the **Windows XP Professional CD-ROM** into the CD-ROM drive of your computer. The **Welcome to Microsoft Windows XP** screen asks you what you want to do **(Figure 2-43)**.
2. Click **Install Windows XP**. The **Welcome to Windows Setup** screen opens. Here you can specify whether you want to upgrade to Windows XP or install a new copy of Windows XP .
3. Make sure that the **Upgrade (Recommended)** is selected in the **Installation Type** list box **(Figure 2-44)** and click [ Next > ] to open the **License Agreement**.
4. Click the **I accept this agreement** option button to accept the licensing terms and click [ Next > ]. The **Your Product Key** screen opens **(Figure 2-45)**.
5. Enter the 25-character product key number for Windows XP Professional. The product key is provided with the Windows XP Professional CD.
6. Click [ Next > ]. Setup begins copying installation files and then restarts the computer. Upon restart, Setup continues preparing the installation, a process that can take several minutes.

**Figure 2-43  Welcome to Microsoft Windows XP screen**

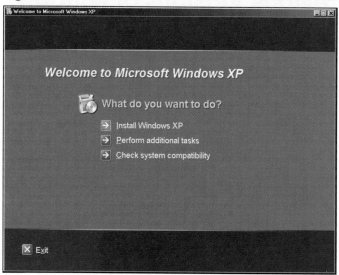

**Figure 2-44  Windows 2000 Setup Welcome screen**

**Figure 2-45  The Your Product Key dialog box**

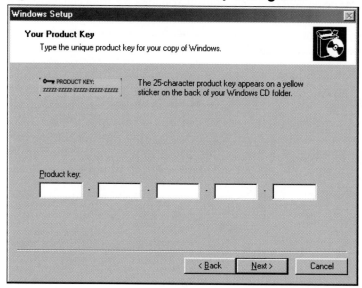

# skill 10

# *Upgrading Previous Versions of Windows to Windows XP Professional (cont'd)*

## exam objective

Upgrade from a previous version of Windows to Windows XP Professional. Perform post-installation updates and product activation.

## how to

7. When the preparation phase completes, the computer restarts again and the Installing Windows phase of the installation begins. Again, this phase will take some time (you can see how much time on the left side of the screen). Items such as devices and networking components are installed during this phase. Your screen may flicker occasionally.

8. When the Installing Windows phase completes, the computer restarts. The **Welcome to Microsoft Windows** screen appears with the message **Let's spend a few minutes setting up your computer**. Click the **Next** icon ➡️ in the lower-right corner of the screen.

9. On the **Ready to activate Windows?** screen, select **No, remind me every few days** and click ➡️. You will learn about activating Windows later in this lesson.

10. On the **Let's get on the Internet** screen, select **Do not set up an Internet connection at this time** and click ➡️.

11. A thank you message appears. Click **Finish** in the lower-right corner of the screen to complete the installation and configuration.

12. The Windows welcome screen opens. Windows applies the default user's personal settings and the default desktop appears with the Start menu open (**Figure 2-46**).

## more

You can upgrade systems running Windows 98, Windows Me, Windows NT Workstation 4, and Windows 2000 Professional directly to Windows XP Professional. Windows 95 computers must be upgraded to Windows 98 before Windows XP can be installed. Windows NT 3.1, 3.5, and 3.51 must likewise be upgraded to Windows NT 4 before they can be upgraded to Windows XP.

Product activation is a relatively new anti-piracy defense that Microsoft introduced in the Microsoft Office XP suite. With CD burners, high-capacity hard disks, and high-speed Internet connections now commonplace, it has become increasingly easier for computer users to spread, or even sell, software illegally. Product activation through the **Activate Windows Wizard** helps Microsoft guarantee that users adhere to the License Agreement. Activation differs from standard product registration in that it is required; you must activate Windows XP within 30 days of installing it or the operating system will cease to function, except for the Activate Windows Wizard. When you activate, you register your copy of Windows XP in a Microsoft database that includes the product key and a profile of the hardware used in your computer. The hardware profile prevents the same copy of Windows XP from being installed on more than one computer. The disadvantage to this is that if you significantly change the hardware components in your computer, Windows may not function. You will need to call Microsoft in order to activate the product again.

If you do not activate Windows XP during the install process, you can activate anytime within 30 days. During this time, an **Activate Windows** command will appear at the top of the **All Programs** menu (**Figure 2-47**). You can also run the Activate Windows Wizard from the **System Tools** menu. Once started, the Wizard presents you with three choices (**Figure 2-48**). The quickest and most convenient choice is **Yes, let's activate Windows over the Internet now**. You can also choose to activate Windows over the phone, or wait until another time to complete the activation. Activating over the Internet is accomplished with just a few simple clicks.

**Figure 2-46  Windows XP default desktop and Start menu**

**Figure 2-47  Activate Windows command on the All Programs menu**

**Figure 2-48  Joining a workgroup or domain**

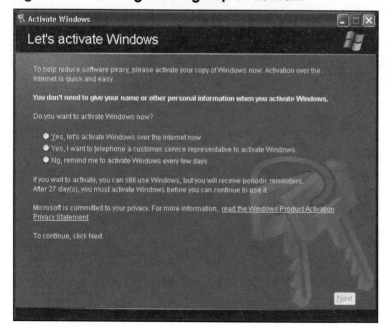

# skill 11

# Updating Windows XP after Installation

**exam objective**

Perform post-installation updates and product activation.

**overview**

Sometimes Microsoft releases update patches for various applications that are widely in use, or for the operating system itself. For example, there may be SMTP updates for Outlook Express or security updates for Internet Explorer. Updates can include new code, error corrections, or service-specific configuration settings from Microsoft. The purpose of updates is to correct or neutralize the deficiencies or vulnerabilities of the original product.

Some previous versions of the Windows operating system required a separate installation for service packs. In fact, if you reconfigured the operating system by adding a particular service, you would have to reinstall the existing service packs. Windows XP handles service packs through **Automatic Updates**.

**how to**

Configure your computer to receive Automatic Updates.
1. Click ⊞ start and click **Control Panel** to open the Control Panel window.
2. On the left side of the window, click **Switch to Classic View** to display all of the Control Panel icons (**Figure 2-49**).
3. Double-click the **System** icon to open the **System Properties** dialog box.
4. Click the **Automatic Updates** tab to view its options (**Figure 2-50**).
5. Make sure that the check box near the top of the tab, labeled **Keep my computer up to date, etc.**, is checked.
6. Make sure the option button labeled **Download the updates automatically and notify me when they are ready to be installed** in the middle of the tab is selected.
7. Click ⬚ OK ⬚ to close the System Properties dialog box and save the Automatic Update settings. You will be notified of updates that are ready to be installed by pop-up messages appearing from the notification area on the right end of the taskbar.
8. Close the Control Panel window.

**more**

Upgrade packs that include one or more .dll files to improve an application's compatibility with Windows XP are also released from third-party vendors. These types of files are most often used when you upgrade an older version of Windows to Windows XP so that you can update existing applications rather than having to reinstall them. Microsoft's Software Development Kit (SDK) provides information to vendors on how to design upgrade packs. In the graphical phase of installation, software upgrade packs can be integrated into the setup process. Open the **WIN9XUPG** subfolder in the **i386** directory to see the upgrade packs on the Windows XP CD.

**Figure 2-49  The Control Panel window in Classic View**

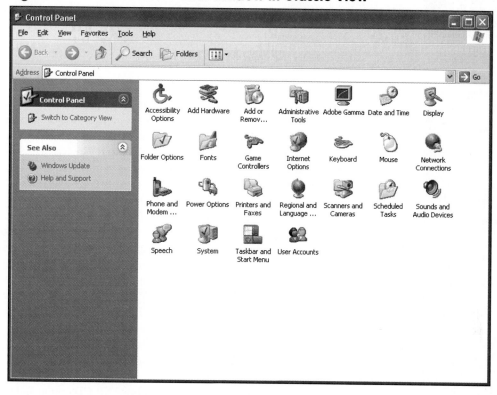

**Figure 2-50  Automatic Updates tab**

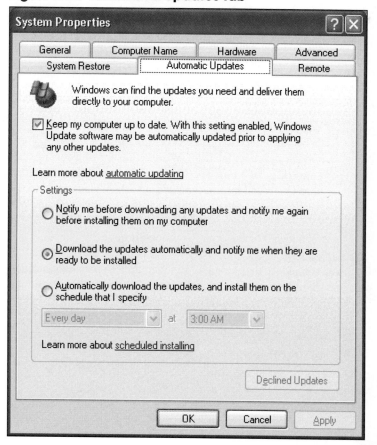

# skill 12   *Transferring Files and Settings*

## exam objective

Migrate existing user environments to a new installation.

## overview

Upgrading your operating system is a convenient way to improve your computing experience while maintaining your old files and preferred system settings. However, even if you upgrade to a new computer that uses Windows XP, you can still transfer your files and settings from your old computer using the **Files and Settings Transfer Wizard**. The Files and Settings Transfer Wizard is effective for salvaging your files and settings from any computer running Windows 95, 98, 98 SE, Me, NT 4, 2000, or XP. To utilize the Wizard, the two computers must be connected by means of a direct cable or a network connection such as that provided by a LAN. You can run the Files and Settings Transfer Wizard from the Windows XP Professional CD-ROM, or by clicking **Start**, pointing to **All Programs**, pointing to **Accessories**, pointing to **System Tools**, and clicking **Files and Settings Transfer Wizard**.

## how to

Transfer the files and settings from an older computer to a Windows XP computer.

1. On the Windows XP computer, click **start**, point to **All Programs**, point to **Accessories**, point to **System Tools**, and click **Files and Settings Transfer Wizard**.
2. Click **Next >** to open the **Which computer is this?** screen of the Wizard, as show in **Figure 2-51**. Leave the New computer option button selected.
3. Click **Next >**. The Wizard takes a moment to prepare for the next step and then opens the **Do you have a Windows XP CD?** screen.
4. Click the **I will use the wizard from the Windows XP CD** option and click **Next >**.
5. The **Now go to your old computer** screen opens with instructions for how to proceed. Follow the instructions by going to your old computer and inserting the Windows XP CD-ROM. When the Welcome to Microsoft Windows XP screen appears, click **Perform additional tasks**. Then click **Transfer files and settings**. The Files and Settings Transfer Wizard opens on the old computer. Follow the steps of the Wizard, choosing a transfer method and what you want to transfer. You may receive a message stating that you will have to install certain programs on the new computer so that transferred files that require those programs can be used. The Wizard will then collect the files and settings you have chosen (**Figure 2-52**). This process can take a significant amount of time.
6. During the collection, you will be asked to enter a password that is displayed on the new computer. Retrieve the password, enter it, and click **OK** (**Figure 2-53**).
7. When the collection phase is complete, click **Finish** on the old computer.
8. On the new computer, the Wizard finishes transferring and applying your files and settings (**Figure 2-54**). The **Completing the Files and Settings Transfer Wizard** screen then opens and informs you of any tasks it was unable to complete (**Figure 2-55**).
9. Click **Finish** to close the Files and Settings Transfer Wizard.
10. A message box opens to inform you that the changes will not take effect until you log off Windows. Click **Yes** to log off now.

## tip

If you do not have a Windows XP CD, select the option to create a Wizard disk on a floppy disk.

## more

You can reduce the amount of time required to transfer your files and settings by customizing the list of folders, settings, and file types that the Wizard will transfer. Look for the check box in the **What do you want to transfer?** dialog box that allows you to do this.

**Figure 2-51  Which computer is this? screen**

**Figure 2-52  Collection of files and settings**

**Figure 2-53  Entering a password**

**Figure 2-54  Transferring and applying settings**

**Figure 2-55  Completing the Files and Settings Transfer Wizard screen**

# Summary

◆ Windows XP is an operating system that provides enhanced compatibility, file management capabilities, and security compared to earlier versions of Windows.

◆ Performing certain pre-installation tasks enables you to avoid problems you may encounter while installing Windows XP Professional.

◆ Pre-installation tasks include determining the hardware requirements, cross-checking the hardware compatibility list, creating disk partitions, and determining the file system you will use.

◆ Windows XP Professional can be installed from a CD or over a network.

◆ When installing Windows XP Professional on a large number of computers, it is preferable to use the over-the-network installation method.

◆ Prerequisites for installing Windows XP Professional over a network are as follows:

  • Creating a distribution server.
  • Creating a partition on the target computer.
  • Installing a network client.

◆ Computers on most networks do not have identical configurations. To specify variations in software configurations, you must use installation scripts. Using the Windows XP Setup Manager Wizard, you can create a script for a customized installation of Windows XP Professional.

◆ You use disk duplication to create a master disk image of the Windows XP Professional installation that is copied to multiple computers with the same hardware configuration on the network.

◆ You use the System Preparation tool, Sysprep.exe, to prepare a computer's hard disk for disk imaging. The System Preparation (Sysprep) tool works in conjunction with a third-party, disk-imaging application. It removes computer-specific information, such as the computer name and security identifier (SID), so that the image that is created can be transferred to the other computers.

◆ Remote Installation can be used to install Windows XP Professional on client computers by connecting to a server running installation services, known as Remote Installation Services (RIS).

◆ If you are currently using Windows 98, Me, 2000, or NT 4.0 Workstation, you can upgrade directly to Windows XP Professional.

◆ Using Windows XP Professional, you can update setup files at the same time as you install the operating system, and then continue to update the operating system automatically as necessary.

# Key Terms

Access token
Action log
Answer file
Automatic Updates
checkupgradeonly switch
Computer name (NetBIOS name)
Distribution server
Error log
Hardware Compatibility List
Installation script

Log files
Master disk image
Mini-Setup Wizard
Partition
Remote installation
Remote Installation Server (RIS server)
Settings and Files Transfer Wizard
Setup
Setup Wizard

System Preparation tool
System service
Windir
Winnt.exe
Winnt32.exe

# Test Yourself

1. You are a systems administrator at Software Perfects Inc. Three employees have joined the Applications department. You need to install Windows XP Professional on their systems. They are Senior Software Developers and in order to develop a certain project they require different hardware from the rest of the employees in their organization. Which of the following options would you use to specify the software variations at the time of Windows XP Professional installation?
   a. Answer file
   b. Installation scripts
   c. Action log
   d. Distribution server

2. To prepare for disk imaging, which of the following would you need to use?
   a. Deploy folder
   b. Sysdiff.exe file
   c. System Preparation tool
   d. Winnt32.exe

3. At the time of master disk generation, if you need to install Windows XP without any user intervention, you use the:
   a. Sysprep.inf file.
   b. Sysdiff.exe file.
   c. Mini-Setup Wizard.
   d. Winnt.exe file.

**4.** As an administrator of a software company, GenX Inc., you are required to install Windows XP Professional on three computers with blank hard drives. Which of the following options will you use to install Windows XP Professional from a central location?
   a. HAL
   b. SID
   c. RIS
   d. i386

**5.** To locate the Active Directory on a network, RIS relies on a service called:
   a. DNS.
   b. DHCP.
   c. Active Directory.
   d. RIPrep.

**6.** To configure RIS, you need:
   a. A remote installation folder.
   b. Installation scripts.
   c. Sysprep.exe.
   d. RBFG.EXE.

**7.** To replicate the PXE process, you need to use the:
   a. Boot floppy.
   b. Remote Boot Disk Generator.
   c. Noreboot command.
   d. Convert command.

**8.** You can configure Automatic Updates on your Windows XP computer through the:
   a. Add Hardware Control Panel.
   b. Files and Settings Transfer Wizard.
   c. Activate Windows Wizard.
   d. System Control Panel.

**9.** Which of the following pre-installation tasks do you need to complete before installing Windows XP Professional? (Choose all that apply.)
   a. Selecting a file system
   b. Accepting the license

   c. Selecting the domain or work group that you want to join
   d. Ensuring that the hardware of your computer is included on the HCL
   e. Selecting the modem dialing information

**10.** Installing Windows XP Professional from a CD-ROM consists of four stages. One of these stages is:
   a. Identifying the hardware requirements.
   b. Determining the way in which you want to partition the hard disk of the computer on which you need to install Windows XP Professional.
   c. Identifying a file system that will be used by the installation partition.
   d. Running the Setup Wizard after the installation files are copied.

**11.** To install Windows XP Professional over the network, you need to connect to: (Choose all that apply.)
   a. RIS server.
   b. DNS server.
   c. Distribution server.
   d. Answer files.

**12.** Which of the following operating systems requires an additional step to be performed in order to be upgraded to Windows XP Professional?
   a. Windows 95
   b. Windows Me
   c. Windows NT Workstation 4
   d. Windows 98

**13.** Which of the following would you use to copy the important contents of a Windows 98 computer to a new Windows XP computer?
   a. Activate Windows Wizard
   b. Files and Settings Transfer Wizard
   c. Internet Connection Wizard
   d. Distribution folder

# Projects: On Your Own

**1.** Install the Windows XP Setup Manager.
   a. Insert the **Windows XP Professional CD** in the CD-ROM drive.
   b. Open the **Windows Explorer** window and create a folder named **Deploy** in the **C:** drive of your system.
   c. Access the **CD-ROM** drive.
   d. Open the **Support** window.
   e. Open the **Tools** window.
   f. Open the **Deploy** window.
   g. Select **all files** in this window.
   h. Extract these files into the **Deploy** folder on your hard disk partition.

   i. Access the **Deploy** folder on your hard disk partition and view the extracted files.
   j. Close all the windows that you have accessed.

**2.** Create a master disk image using the System Preparation tool.
   a. Open the **Windows Explorer** window.
   b. Access the **Windows XP System Preparation Tool** message box.
   c. Perform the steps to continue working as guided by the **System Preparation Tool Wizard**.
   d. Shut down your computer.

**3.** Configure Remote Installation Services.
   a. Log on to the Windows 2000 Server as an **Administrator**.
   b. Access the **Add/Remove Programs** window.
   c. Access the **Remote Installation Services Setup Wizard**.
   d. Insert the **Windows 2000 Professional CD** in the **CD-ROM** drive of the server.
   e. Start the **Remote Installation Services Setup Wizard**.
   f. Read the information on the **Welcome** screen and then access the **Remote Installation Folder Location** page.
   g. Specify the path as **D:\RemoteInst**.
   h. Access the **Initial Settings** page.
   i. Select the **Respond to client computer** check box.
   j. Access the **Installation Source Files Location** page.
   k. Specify the path to the installation source files.
   l. Access the **Windows Installation Image Folder Name** page.
   m. Accept the default name of **Win2000.pro**.
   n. Accept the default **friendly description and help** text.
   o. Review the information and then click the **Finish** button. Your system will perform certain tasks.
   p. Click the **Done** button when the tasks are completed.
   q. Close any open windows.

## Problem Solving Scenarios

You work as the Assistant Network Administrator for Northern Casualty Insurance, a regional commercial insurance agency. The agency has several departments, each with a different set of computers and networks. Some departments use Windows 95 without any network, while other departments use Windows 98 in small workgroups. Each of the Windows 98 departments has proprietary software that the insurance agents do not want to give up. Your job is to work with the Network Administrator to devise a plan for upgrading the company's 300 workstations into a single, coherent company network.

Specifically, the Network Administrator has asked you to prepare a PowerPoint presentation describing in general terms the steps required for a remote, unattended installation of a Windows XP domain network. This network must be able to run existing proprietary software used in some offices that operates only with Windows 98. You also will need to decide whether to do an upgrade or perform a clean install, and to justify the reasons for doing so. **Note**: The CEO has told the Network Administrator to minimize disruption to the business while making this transition.

# 3 Managing Hardware Devices

**D**uring the course of your work, you may need to add or change the hardware and peripheral devices connected to your computer. Some of the most common hardware devices that you work with on a daily basis are the mouse, keyboard, CD-ROM drive, modem, and printer. These devices can be categorized as either input devices such as the mouse and keyboard, or output devices such as the monitor and printer.

While these hardware devices enable you to work with data, removable media allow you to store data or to backup and archive data on alternatives to the hard drive such as CD-ROMs, DVDs, floppy disks, and tapes. Using removable media to store infrequently used data helps you to save hard disk space.

You may also need to exchange data with computers that are not on your network. Modems are used to exchange data between computers on the Internet using telephone lines. Modems are also used to connect computers to devices such as fax machines. Infrared light is used to connect a digital camera to a computer, whereas external communication lines are used to connect a Web camera to a computer.

These devices must interact with the operating system in order to process data. Windows XP Professional uses programs called device drivers to enable interaction with hardware devices. Device drivers serve as the translators for the operating system, converting commands from Windows into commands that the device can understand and process. A database of device drivers is installed along with the Windows XP Professional operating system. However, you may need to upgrade these drivers periodically when the manufacturers distribute newer versions or if the device is not functioning properly.

Windows XP Professional includes Plug and Play functionality. Any new Plug and Play devices you add to your system will be detected and the settings will be configured automatically after the device driver is located and installed. However, if the system cannot locate the required driver in the driver database because it was not included with the operating system, you will be prompted to install the driver. After the driver is installed, the hardware device will be configured automatically.

As you take on different kinds of tasks, you may also need to install new software on your system. Windows XP Professional uses digitally signed system files and Windows File Protection to ensure that any new software you install does not overwrite the existing system files. This protects your system against data corruption and general system failures.

## Goals

In this lesson, you will learn how to install, configure, and manage devices on your computer such as fax machines, removable devices, I/O devices, multimedia hardware, modems, IrDA, wireless devices, USB devices, hand held devices, network adapters and video adapters. You will also learn how to update device drivers on your system.

### Lesson 3  Managing Hardware Devices

| Skill | Exam 70-270 Objective |
| --- | --- |
| 1. Configuring I/O Devices | Implement, manage, and troubleshoot input and output (I/O) devices. Monitor, configure, and troubleshoot I/O devices, such as printers, scanners, multimedia devices, mouse, keyboard, and smart card reader. |
| 2. Configuring and Monitoring Removable Media Devices | Implement, manage, and troubleshoot disk devices. Install, configure, and manage DVD and CD-ROM devices. Monitor and configure removable media, such as tape devices. |
| 3. Adding a Modem | Install, configure, and manage modems. |
| 4. Configuring Fax Devices | Implement, manage, and troubleshoot input and output (I/O) devices. |
| 5. Updating Device Drivers | Manage and troubleshoot drivers and driver signing. |
| 6. Managing Driver Signing | Manage and troubleshoot drivers and driver signing. |
| 7. Managing Universal Serial Bus and Multimedia Devices | Install, configure, and manage USB devices. Monitor, configure, and troubleshoot multimedia hardware, such as cameras. Install, configure, and manage hand held devices. |
| 8. Installing Network Adapters | Install, configure, and manage network adapters. |
| 9. Installing Video Adapters | Install, configure, and troubleshoot a video adapter. |
| 10. Installing Infrared Data Association (IrDA) Devices | Install, configure, and manage Infrared Data Association (IrDA) devices. Install, configure, and manage wireless devices. |
| 11. Configuring Multiprocessor Computers | Monitor and configure multiprocessor computers. |

## Requirements

To complete this lesson, you will need a computer with Windows XP Professional installed on it. You will also need a modem, a scanner, a Web camera, a fax modem, and a CD-ROM. A second processor is optional for Skill 11.

# skill 1 *Configuring I/O Devices*

## exam objective

Implement, manage, and troubleshoot input and output (I/O) devices. Monitor, configure, and troubleshoot I/O devices, such as printers, scanners, multimedia devices, mouse, keyboard, and smart card reader.

## overview

Devices such as the mouse and keyboard that are attached to a computer externally are known as peripheral devices. Peripheral devices can be divided into input or output (I/O) devices. Input devices such as the mouse, keyboards, joystick, and scanners are used to provide input data to a computer. Processed data is redirected to the output devices, such as the monitor and printer. Most I/O devices are Plug and Play devices. This means that whenever you attach an I/O device to your computer, Windows XP Professional automatically detects the device. Then, the operating system installs the drivers for the device from the driver database on the system and installs the device. Many vendors choose to certify their drivers with Microsoft and have their drivers included in the driver database.

Often, when you attach an I/O device to a computer, an icon for that device will be placed in the Control Panel window. However, this is not always the case. For example, if you attach a FireWire device (used to connect VCRs and camcorders to a PC) or a USB hard drive, no additional icon for these devices will be added to the Control Panel. Some icons, such as those for the mouse, keyboard, and modems, are shown in the Control Panel window by default. Double-click an icon to install, configure, or troubleshoot the respective device.

In this skill, we will focus on configuring the mouse. You can install or configure a mouse in the **Mouse Properties** dialog box. The Mouse Properties dialog box generally contains five tabs: **Buttons**, **Pointers**, **Pointer Options**, and **Hardware**, although this can vary with the make and model. **Table 3-1** describes the tabs and the settings you can configure on each tab.

### caution

Make sure that the I/O devices that you use are included on the Hardware Compatibility List (HCL).

## how to

Configure your mouse pointer to snap to the default button in dialog boxes and change the acceleration speed of the pointer.

1. Click [ *start* ] and click **Control Panel** to open the **Control Panel** window. If necessary, click **Switch to Classic View** to display all of the Control Panel icons.
2. Double-click the **Mouse** icon to open the **Mouse Properties** dialog box.
3. Click the **Pointer Options** tab. In the section of the tab titled **Snap To**, click the **Automatically move pointer to the default button in a dialog box** check box **(Figure 3-1)**.
4. In the **Motion** section of the tab, drag the **Select a pointer speed** slider bar toward the **Fast** end **(Figure 3-2)**.
5. Click [ OK ] to apply the changes and close the Mouse Properties dialog box. You have configured the mouse to jump to the default button in a dialog box and increased the speed of the pointer. You can return to the default settings if you are uncomfortable with the new settings.
6. Close the **Control Panel**.

## more

The I/O devices attached to your system may malfunction occasionally due to various setting problems. If you have a wheel on your mouse and it is not functioning properly, open the **Hardware** tab in the Mouse Properties dialog box. In the **Devices** section, select the mouse you are using and click **Properties**. On the **Advanced Settings** tab, change the **Wheel Detection** setting to **Assume Wheel is Present**.

**Table 3-1   Tabs in the Mouse Properties dialog box**

| Properties Tab | Description |
| --- | --- |
| Buttons | You can configure your mouse for left-handed or right-handed use, set the double-click speed, and turn on ClickLock. In the Double-click speed section, you can test the double-click speed for your mouse. |
| Pointers | You can specify the look and feel for the mouse pointer. The shape of the pointer acts as a visual cue to indicate the process taking place. For example, the hourglass icon indicates that the computer is processing an event such as opening an application or a file. |
| Pointer Options | You can set the speed and visibility behaviors with which the mouse pointer moves on your screen. You can also set Snap To to program the mouse pointer to move automatically to the default button in dialog boxes. |
| Hardware | You can troubleshoot and access the port configuration, advanced settings, driver details, resource settings, and power management settings for the mouse. |

**Figure 3-1   Activating Snap To**

**Figure 3-2   Changing the speed of the mouse pointer**

# skill 2

# Configuring and Monitoring Removable Media Devices

## exam objective

Implement, manage, and troubleshoot disk devices. Install, configure, and manage DVD and CD-ROM devices. Monitor and configure removable media, such as tape devices.

## overview

You can also connect **removable media** devices to a computer. Common removable multimedia devices include CD-ROMs, DVDs, MIDI (Musical Instrument Digital Interface), scanning hardware, and tape devices. CD-ROMs and DVDs are used to store and view large amounts of data and multimedia. Tape devices are commonly used media for data backups, although today many large organizations are replacing tape systems with DVD-RWs for data archiving. The most commonly used tape devices are DAT (Digital Audio Tape), 8mm cassettes, quarter-inch cartridges, and DLTs (Digital Linear Tape).

CD-ROMs and Digital Video Discs (DVD) are used for audio/video data storage, are user-friendly, and are supported by all Windows platforms. Windows XP Professional uses the **Compact Disk File System (CDFS)** to read and write to CD-ROMs and the **Universal Disk Format** file system **(UDF)** to access DVD drives.

You can configure and manage removable media devices in the **Properties** dialog box for the device. To open the Properties dialog box for a media device, open the **My Computer** window, click **View system information**, and open the **Hardware** tab in the **System Properties** dialog box **(Figure 3-3)**. Click the **Device Manager** button to open the Device Manager window. Hard drives are listed under the **Disk drives** node. (Note that DVD/CD-ROM drives appear under the DVD/CD-ROM drives node, while floppy and tape drives appear under their own node as well.) Double-click the media device name to open the **Properties** dialog box for the device. The Properties dialog box for the device contains the following tabs:

**General:** Lists the type of the device, the name of the manufacturer, and the location of the device. It also shows the status of the device, indicating whether the device is working properly. You can also configure the device usage for a particular hardware profile. You can click <kbd>Troubleshoot...</kbd> to troubleshoot any problems with the device **(Figure 3-4)**. The Troubleshooter presents a series of questions for you to answer about the malfunctioning device. The answers you give will direct you to the information that is relevant to the problem. One main task you will often be asked to perform is to check the HCL (Hardware Compatibility List) to make sure that the device is supported by Windows XP. You will often be prompted to make sure that the appropriate drivers are installed and functioning properly. You may also be prompted to perform such actions as checking general or SCSI (small computer system interface) connections, cables and ID conflicts.

**Policies:** This tab is specific to hard drives and contains options for write caching, which affects disk performance and the procedure by which you can remove a device from the computer safely.

**Volumes:** Summarizes the volumes on a disk, including the type, status, partition style, capacity, and unallocated space.

**Driver:** Contains information about the device driver that is currently loaded on your system. On the Driver tab you can uninstall or update a driver, or roll back to the previously installed driver if the updated one does not function properly. When you click the **Update Driver** button, the **Hardware Update Wizard** will guide you through the process of updating the drivers.

**Figure 3-3  The System Properties dialog box**

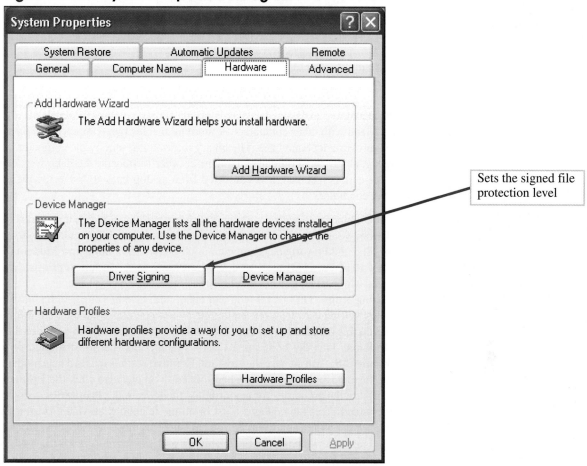

Sets the signed file protection level

**Figure 3-4  Modifying the properties for a removable media device**

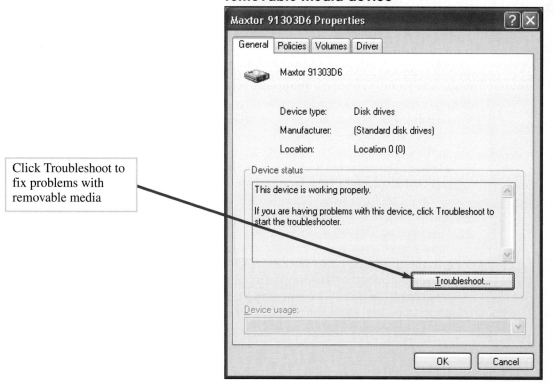

Click Troubleshoot to fix problems with removable media

# skill 3

# *Adding a Modem*

## exam objective

Install, configure, and manage modems.

## overview

A computer stores and processes data in digital format and uses binary digits to communicate internally and with other computers. A **modem** enables two computers to communicate with each other over telephone lines. The binary information sent by the computer is converted to analog signals by that computer's modem in order to transfer the data over telephone lines. When the data is received, it is converted from analog back to binary by the modem of the receiving computer.

If you add a modem to your computer that supports Plug and Play, it should be automatically identified by your system and the correct drivers should install. To add a modem that does not support Plug and Play to your computer, double-click the **Phone and Modems Options** icon in the **Control Panel** window to open the **Phone and Modem Options** dialog box. The Phone and Modems Options dialog box contains the following tabs:

- **Dialing Rules:** On this tab you can enter, add, or edit your geographical location, area codes, calling card features, and more. When you dial a number, the information specified on this tab assists Windows XP Professional in establishing links to the number.
- **Modems:** This tab contains a list of all modems that are installed on your system (**Figure 3-5**). You can use the **Add** and **Remove** buttons to add a new modem to your system or remove an already installed modem. You can also click the **Properties** button to configure the properties for any installed modems in the **Properties** dialog box.
- **Advanced:** This tab contains a list of all the telephony service providers that are available for telephony applications. You can add or remove service providers from the list or configure the properties for the telephony service providers using the **Add**, **Remove**, and **Configure** buttons.

When you click the **Add** button on the **Modems** tab, the **Add Hardware Wizard** will guide you through the installation process. You can either choose the modem to be installed, or have the system automatically detect the modem. If the modem is not automatically detected, or you want to choose the modem, select the **Don't detect my modem; I will select it from a list** check box on the **Install New Modem** screen. Then, follow the instructions in the Wizard to complete the installation.

You can configure any installed modem in the Properties dialog box for that modem. On the **Modems** tab, select the modem whose properties you want to access, and click the **Properties** button to open the **Properties** dialog box. The Properties dialog box for each modem contains the following basic tabs (**Figure 3-6**):

- **General:** This tab lists the type of the device, the name of the manufacturer, and the location of the device. It also shows the status of the device, indicating whether the device is working properly.
- **Modem:** This tab consists of three sections: **Speaker Volume**, **Maximum Port Speed**, and **Dial Control**. In these sections, you can set the speaker volume and the speed at which programs transmit data to the modem, and configure the modem to wait for the dial tone before dialing a given number.
- **Diagnostics:** This tab is used to troubleshoot the modem. You can view information about the performance of the modem and modify the modem settings.
- **Advanced:** Using this tab, you can configure any additional settings for initializing your modem. Additional settings for your modem can be found in the modem manual. You can also change the default modem settings, which may include call and data connection preferences, hardware settings, and terminal preferences.

## tip

The tabs you see in the Properties dialog box can change depending on what type of modem is installed.

**Figure 3-5  Selected modem is installed**

**Figure 3-6  Phone and Modem Options icon in Control Panel**

# skill 3

## *Adding a Modem (cont'd)*

**exam objective**

Install, configure, and manage modems.

**overview**

◆ **Driver:** Contains information about the device driver that is currently loaded on your system for the modem. On the Driver tab you can uninstall or update a driver, or roll back to the previously installed driver if the updated one does not function properly. When you click the **Update Driver** button, the **Hardware Update Wizard** will guide you through the process of updating the drivers.

◆ **Resources:** This tab displays the device resources currently assigned to the modem. These are settings that should not be changed unless you are an expert user. The tab also displays any device conflicts involving the device. You can resolve such conflicts by clicking the Troubleshoot button on the General tab.

**how to**

Configure a modem already installed on your system to wait for the dial tone before it starts dialing, and set the port speed to 57600.

1. Open the **Control Panel** window and switch to **Classic View** if necessary.
2. Double-click the **Phone and Modem Options (Figure 3-7)** icon to open the **Phone and Modem Options** dialog box.
3. Click the **Modems** tab to display the list of modems installed on your computer.
4. Select a modem and click ⎡ Properties ⎤ to open the **Properties** dialog box for the modem. The **General** tab opens by default.
5. Click the **Modem** tab.
6. In the **Maximum Port Speed** section, click the list arrow and select **57600** as the port speed for transmitting data **(Figure 3-8)**.
7. In the **Dial Control** section, the **Wait for dial tone before dialing** check box is selected by default. This will program the modem to detect the dial tone before it begins dialing out.
8. Click ⎡ OK ⎤ to apply the changes and to close the Properties dialog box, then click again to close the Phone and Modem Options dialog box. Close the Control Panel.

**more**

If you are unable to install a modem or encounter any other problems, check the following:

◆ Check that the modem or cables are not faulty or that the connections are not loose.
◆ Check the Hardware Compatibility List (HCL) on the Microsoft Web site to see if the modem you are trying to install is compatible with your system.
◆ Check that the COM port that the modem is using is recognized by Windows 2000. Double-click the **Ports** icon in the Device Manager to list all ports currently in use. If your COM port is on the list, Windows 2000 is recognizing it. If your COM port appears in the list with an exclamation point (!) in a yellow circle, or a red X, there may be a hardware conflict or a disabled modem device.

**Figure 3-7  The Control Panel window**

**Figure 3-8  Modem properties dialog box**

# skill 4

# *Configuring Fax Devices*

## exam objective

Implement, manage, and troubleshoot input and output (I/O) devices.

## overview

One of the most commonly used hardware devices today is a fax modem. Most fax modems are Plug and Play devices, so when you attach a fax modem, Windows XP Professional should detect it at startup and install it automatically. The operating system will also install the Windows fax driver and the Fax Service. If Windows XP Professional does not detect the device at startup, you can run the Add Hardware Wizard. The Wizard will search for and install the device and its drivers. You can access this Wizard in the Control Panel. After the Fax Service has been installed, you must start it. You start the Fax Service through the Services node in the Computer Management console. Right-click **My Computer** on the desktop and click **Manage** to open the **Computer Management console**. Expand the **Services and Applications** node, and click **Services** to display a list of the services on the computer in the Details pane. Then, either right-click **Fax Service** and click **Start**, or double-click **Fax Service** to open the **Fax Service Properties (Local Computer)** dialog box. In the **Service Status** section, click the **Start** button. Documents that you want to fax will be sent to the fax driver in the Printers folder. Faxes are received as TIFF (tagged image file format) images. They can be opened and read in **Microsoft Office Document Imaging** or in any other utility that can view TIFF files. The default behavior is for the TIFF file to be sent to the **Received Faxes** folder, but you can also save a received fax in a different folder, send it directly to a print device, or send it as an e-mail.

If you have already installed a fax modem and you want to set it up for faxing, open the **Control Panel** window and double-click the **Printers and Faxes** icon to open the **Printers and Faxes** window. Click **Set up faxing** on the left side of the window. The **Insert Disk** dialog box asks you to insert your Windows XP Professional CD. After you insert the CD, Windows configures your fax modem and adds a Fax icon to the Printers and Faxes window **(Figure 3-9)**. Double-click the Fax icon to configure your computer to send and receive faxes using the **Fax Configuration Wizard**. The Wizard prompts you to enter sender information for cover pages, select a device for sending or receiving faxes, choose routing information (such as to a printer or a folder), and enter transmitting subscriber and called subscriber identifiers. When you complete the Wizard, the Fax Console opens **(Figure 3-10)**. You will find that the Fax Console acts much like an e-mail client in that it enables you to send and receive faxes, and store received faxes in an inbox and sent faxes in an outbox. The Fax Console is always accessible by clicking **Start**, pointing to **All Programs**, pointing to **Accessories**, pointing to **Communications**, pointing to **Fax**, and clicking **Fax Console**.

Once you have configured a fax device, you can adjust its properties by right-clicking the Fax icon in the Printers and Faxes window and clicking **Properties**. In the **Fax Properties** dialog box, click the **Devices** tab, select the fax device, and click the **Properties** button. The properties dialog box for the particular fax device includes the following tabs:

◆ **Send:** This tab contains options for enabling/disabling the device to send faxes, including a banner on faxes, and increasing or decreasing the number of retries and minutes after a failed attempt will retry.

◆ **Receive:** This tab includes options for enabling/disabling the devices to receive faxes, setting the answer mode to manual or automatic, and routing faxes to a print device or folder.

◆ **Cleanup:** This tab enables you to delete failed faxes automatically after a certain number of days.

**Figure 3-9  The Printers and Faxes window**

**Figure 3-10  The Fax Console**

# skill 4

## *Configuring Fax Devices (cont'd)*

**exam objective**

Implement, manage, and troubleshoot input and output (I/O) devices.

**how to**

Start and configure the Fax Service on the local computer and configure a fax device.

1. Click [ *start* ] and click **Printers and Faxes**. Click **Set up faxing** on the left side of the window.
2. The **Insert Disk** dialog box asks you to insert your Windows XP Professional CD. After you insert the CD, Windows configures your fax modem and adds a Fax icon to the Printers and Faxes window.
3. Click [ *start* ] and click **Control Panel**. Double-click **Administrative Tools** and double-click **Computer Management** to open the Computer Management window.
4. Double-click **Services and Applications** to expand the node. Click **Services**.
5. Locate and right-click **Fax** in the list of services in the Details pane. Click **Start** on the context menu to start the fax service. You may receive a message saying that the service started and then stopped because it has no work to do. Click [ OK ] and close the Computer Management window.
6. Double-click the Fax icon in the Printers and Faxes window to open the **Fax Configuration Wizard**. Complete the steps of the Wizard as instructed on its screens. When you complete the final step, the **Fax Console** opens. Close the Fax Console.
7. Right-click the **Fax** icon in the Printers and Faxes window and click **Properties** to open the **Fax Properties** dialog box. By default, the **General** tab opens.
8. Click the **Devices** tab. Select the device whose properties you want to configure and click [ Properties... ] to open the Properties dialog box for that device.
9. On the **Send** tab **(Figure 3-11)**, make sure that the **Enable device to send** check box is selected and type **4** in the **Number of retries** text box.
10. In the **Retry after** text box, type **5**.
11. Click the **Receive** tab. Make sure that the **Enable device to receive** check box is selected.
12. In the **Answer mode** section of the tab, click the **Automatic after** option button, if necessary, and type **1** in the **rings** text box **(Figure 3-12)**.
13. Click [ OK ] to apply the changes and close the dialog box.
14. Close the **Fax Properties** dialog box, the **Printers and Faxes** window, and the **Control Panel**.

**more**

You can send a fax from either the Fax Console or the Printers and Faxes window. In the Fax Console, click **File** and click **Send a Fax**. In the Printers and Faxes window, click **Send a fax** in the **Printer Tasks** section on the left side of the window. Both techniques open the **Send a Fax Wizard**, which guides you through the steps of addressing the fax, selecting a cover page and subject line, composing the fax text, scheduling the transmission, setting the priority level, and previewing the fax. Using the Fax Console is a good way to track the success or failure of the transmission.

**Figure 3-11  Setting Send properties**

The number of times to attempt to resend a fax after the first attempt has failed

The minimum number of minutes between each attempt

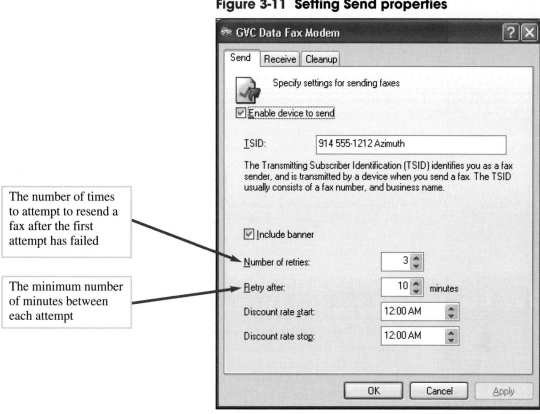

**Figure 3-12  Setting Receive properties**

Select number of rings before fax device starts receiving fax

# skill 5

## *Updating Device Drivers*

**exam objective**

Manage and troubleshoot drivers and driver signing.

**overview**

A **device driver** is software that enables a specific device such as a printer, modem, or network card to communicate with the computer. For example, to establish network connections using a modem, you need serial port drivers. Windows XP Professional includes the built-in drivers required for installing and configuring many commonly used devices. If you are installing a newer version of a device, adding new functionality to a device, or fixing device errors, you must update the drivers on your system.

You will also need to update a driver if the manufacturer of the hardware device has released a newer version. Moreover, some devices may contain additional features that can be enabled only if you update the driver. You can also upgrade drivers if the device is not functioning properly. You update device drivers in the **Device Manager**.

**how to**

Update the drivers for the modem attached to your system.

1. Click [ *start* ] and click **Control Panel**. Double-click **Administrative Tools** and double-click **Computer Management** to open the Computer Management window.
2. Click the **Device Manager** node to display all of the devices that are currently installed on the system. Alternatively, you can click **Start**, point to **Settings**, click **Control Panel**, and double-click **System** to open the **System Properties** dialog box. On the **Hardware** tab, click the **Device Manager** button to open the Device Manager.
3. Double-click **Modems** to display the modems installed on the computer.
4. Right-click the modem name, for example, **GVC Data Fax Modem**, and click the **Properties** command to open the **Properties** dialog box for the modem.
5. Click the **Driver** tab.
6. Click [ Update Driver... ] to open the **Hardware Update Wizard (Figure 3-13)**.
7. Click the **Install from a list or specific location (Advanced)** option button.
8. Click [ Next > ] to open the **Please choose your installation options** screen.
9. Click the **Don't search. I will choose the driver to install** option button.
10. Click [ Next > ] to open the **Install New Modem** screen.
11. Select the modem whose driver you want to update in the the **Models** list **(Figure 3-14)**. If you need to upgrade the drivers from a disk, you can click [ Have Disk... ]. This will allow you to select the path to the manufacturer's files so that they can be copied to the hard drive.
12. Click [ Next > ]. The Hardware Update Wizard installs the software for the device.

**Figure 3-13  The Hardware Update Wizard**

**Figure 3-14  The Install New Modem screen**

# skill 5

## *Updating Device Drivers (cont'd)*

### exam objective

Manage and troubleshoot drivers and driver signing.

### how to

13. The Completing the Update Hardware Wizard screen opens. Click [ Finish ] to complete the update procedure.
14. Close the modem **Properties** dialog box. The **System Settings Change** dialog box may prompt you to restart the system so that the changes can take effect.
15. If needed, click [ Yes ] to restart the system and apply the settings.

### more

You can also use **Windows Update** on the **All Programs** menu to connect to the **Microsoft Windows Update** page at **http://windowsupdate.microsoft.com**. When you connect to the site for the first time, a **Security Warning** will ask you if you want to install and run the **Windows Update V4 Control**. When you click **Yes**, ActiveX controls will be downloaded to your computer. Next, click **Scan for updates** to perform a scan of the software environment on your PC (**Figure 3-15**). Finally, click **Review and install updates**. Windows Update will create a catalogue of the latest updates available for your computer's operating system, software, and hardware (**Figure 3-16**). The list will be ranked to let you know if the update is critical or just recommended and may also include security updates and Internet and multimedia updates. This Web site is primarily intended for operating system service packs, but you can also update some drivers using this method. If an updated driver is available, you can follow a set of prompts to install it. You must use Internet Explorer to perform this operation because the system scan will not work with non ActiveX browsers such as Netscape.

Windows Update is a convenience for individual users, allowing them to keep their PCs up to date with the latest patches and fixes. However, network administrators may want to control what updates are downloaded on network computers to maintain system conformity for network technicians and troubleshooters. You can disable Windows Update by setting a Group Policy (See Lesson 12).

**Figure 3-15  Using Windows Update to scan for updates**

**Figure 3-16  Reviewing and installing updates**

# skill 6

# *Managing Driver Signing*

## exam objective

Manage and troubleshoot drivers and driver signing.

## overview

Microsoft uses digital signatures to assure users that the drivers they are using have been tested for quality and are safe for installation. A digital signature on a file certifies that the file is from the correct source, typically the hardware manufacturer or Microsoft. Windows XP Professional provides several ways of protecting digitally signed files.

◆ The **Windows File Protection** utility in Windows XP Professional works in the background to prevent the replacement of protected system files such as those files ending in **.sys**, **.dll**, **.ocx**, **.ttf**, **.fon**, and **.exe**. It detects any attempt by other programs to replace or move a protected system file. The Windows File Protection utility checks the digital signature on the file to determine if the correct Microsoft version is being installed. If an attempt is made to replace a digitally signed file, Windows XP Professional writes an event to the event log to record the file replacement attempt.

◆ The **System File Checker** utility scans and verifies the versions of all protected system files. If a protected file has been overwritten, the correct version of the file is retrieved from the **%systemroot%\system32\dllcache** folder. The **sfc** command can be run from the **Command Prompt**. To open the Command Prompt, click **Start**, point to **Programs**, point to **Accessories**, and click the **Command Prompt** command. The syntax for the System File Checker is:

**sfc [/scannow] [/scanonce] [/scanboot] [/revert] [/purgecache] [/cachesize=x]**

The parameters for the syntax are described in **Table 3-2**.

The **Windows File Signature Verification** utility is used to identify unsigned files on your computer and display the related information such as the file's name, location, last modification date, file type, and the file's version number. To launch this utility, click **Start**, click **Run**, type **sigverif**, and press **[Enter]**.

## how to

Set driver signing options to block the installation of unsigned files.

1. Open the **Control Panel** window in Classic View.
2. Double-click the **System** icon to open the **System Properties** dialog box.
3. Click the **Hardware** tab to display the hardware setting options (**Figure 3-17**).
4. Click [ Driver Signing ] to open the **Driver Signing Options** dialog box.
5. Click the **Block – Never install unsigned driver software** option button in the **What action do you want Windows to take?** section to prevent the installation of unsigned drivers (**Figure 3-18**).
6. Make sure that the **Apply setting as the system default** check box is selected in the **Administrator option** section to apply the default setting for all users who log on to the computer.
7. Click [ OK ] to apply the changes and close the **Driver Signing Options** dialog box.
8. Click [ OK ] to close the **System Properties** dialog box. Close the Control Panel.

## Table 3-2   Syntax for System File Checker

| Parameter | Description |
|-----------|-------------|
| /scannow | Scans all protected system files immediately. |
| /scanonce | Scans all protected system files once at the next restart. |
| /scanboot | Scans all protected system files every time the computer restarts. |
| /revert | Returns scan to its default operation. |
| /purgecache | Purges the Windows File Protection file cache and scans all protected system files immediately. |
| /cachesize=x | Sets Windows File Protection file cache size. |

**Figure 3-17  Selecting the driver signing option**

Configures properties for any device

**Figure 3-18  Setting driver signing options**

Allow all files to be installed regardless of whether they are digitally signed

Display a warning when an attempt is made to install any device driver without a digital signature

Prevents the installation of unsigned driver files

# skill 7

# Managing Universal Serial Bus and Multimedia Devices

## exam objective

Install, configure, and manage USB devices. Monitor, configure, and troubleshoot multimedia hardware, such as cameras. Install, configure, and manage hand held devices.

## overview

**Universal Serial Bus (USB)** is an external communication bus that is used to transfer data among the components in a computer system. USB lets you install devices such as keyboards, joysticks, tape drives, and hand held devices such as personal digital assistants (PDAs). It provides a faster and more manageable alternative to serial and parallel ports for devices such as keyboards and mice, and is expected to completely replace them in the future. USB is a better alternative to older I/O standards because all USB devices use the same kind of I/O connector so that you will no longer need different types of cables and connectors. USB technology also allows you to install multimedia devices such as scanners, audio players, CD-ROM drives, Web cameras, and speakers. It is supported by the WDM (Windows Driver Model) in Windows XP. Using one USB controller, you can attach a maximum of 127 USB devices simultaneously (with one or more USB hubs) to a single computer.

USB is a Plug and Play bus that supports **hot swapping** (also called **hot plugging**), which means that you can add and remove devices while the computer is running and have the operating system automatically recognize the change. USB moves the Plug and Play functionality for these peripheral devices outside the computer so that internal cards do not have to be added to the motherboard and the system does not have to be reconfigured. If USB is supported by the BIOS, you will find the **Universal Serial Bus controllers** in the Device Manager. You can configure and manage a USB device in the **Properties** dialog box for the device. You open the **Properties** dialog box by double-clicking any of several USB device names in the **Universal Serial Bus controller** node. (Be aware that a USB mouse will appear under **Mice and other pointing devices**. Typically, digital scanners and cameras will appear under **Imaging devices**.) The **Properties** dialog box for each USB controller often contains the following tabs:

- **General:** This tab lists the device type and device status. On this tab you can troubleshoot the device if it is not working properly and disable the USB device.
- **Advanced:** Each USB controller has a fixed amount of bandwidth, which the attached devices share. On this tab, you can view the distribution of bandwidth among the devices connected to the USB controller.
- **Driver:** On this tab you can view the driver properties and remove, update, or roll back the drivers for the USB device.
- **Resources:** On this tab, you can view the device resources that are currently assigned to the USB controller and the settings for each resource. The four types of device resources are: the **input/output (I/O) port**, the **direct memory access (DMA) channel**, the **interrupt request (IRQ) line**, and the **memory range**.

## how to

Install and configure a digital camera.

1. Plug the camera into the USB port and turn on the camera.
2. The **Found New Hardware Wizard** opens. Leave the **Install the software automatically (Recommended)** option button selected. If you have a disk containing the device drivers, insert the disk.
3. Click [ Next > ]. The Wizard searches for the proper device driver. When the driver is located, the Wizard installs the necessary software.
4. The **Completing the Found New Hardware Wizard** screen opens (**Figure 3-19**).
5. Click [ Finish ] to complete the installation of the camera.
6. Open the **Control Panel**, double-click the **System** icon, and click the **Hardware** tab.
7. Click [ Device Manager ] to open the Device Manager window.
8. Double-click the **Universal Serial Bus controllers** node. The camera you just installed is now listed (**Figure 3-20**). You can configure the properties of the camera by double-clicking it.
9. Close the Device Manager, the System Properties dialog box, and the Control Panel.

**Figure 3-19  Installing hardware device drivers**

**Figure 3-20  Installed camera in the Device Manager window**

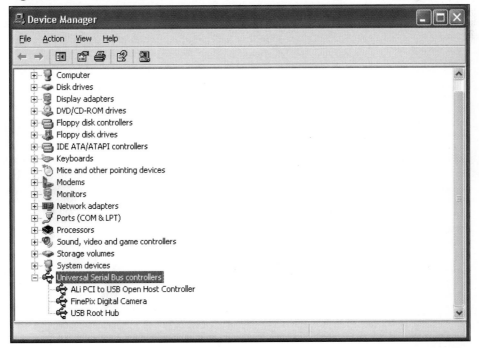

# skill 8 *Installing Network Adapters*

**exam objective**

Install, configure, and manage network adapters.

**overview**

Many network adapter models and the protocols and services that use adapter hardware are supported by Windows XP Professional. Although **network interface cards (NICs)** are crucial communications tools that are needed to connect computers to a network, they are just as simple to install as any other hardware device. First, you must install the NIC into a bus slot in the motherboard and attach the network cable to it. If the NIC is Plug and Play compatible and the driver is included in the driver.cab file from the Windows XP Professional installation CD, the device will be automatically detected and installed. If the device driver is not in the driver database, you may be prompted to insert the installation CD-ROM or third-party diskette. If the NIC is not Plug and Play compatible, you will have to run the Add Hardware Wizard from the Control Panel and follow the prompts to select the make and model.

You configure NICs in either the network connection **Properties** dialog box or in the **Device Manager**. To open the network connection Properties dialog box, first open the **Control Panel** and double-click the **Network Connections** icon to open the Network Connections window. Then, right-click the icon for the connection you want to configure (usually the **Local Area Connection** icon) and click the **Properties** command. Click [ Configure... ] to open the **Properties** dialog box for the network card **(Figure 3-21)**. The network card Properties dialog box contains the following tabs:

◆ **General:** On this tab you can view the manufacturer details for the network card. You can also enable or disable the device and troubleshoot problems you may be having with it.

◆ **Advanced:** The contents of this tab are specific to the adapter that you are configuring. In the **Property** list, choose the property you want to modify and change the entry in the **Value** list box to the appropriate setting **(Figure 3-22)**. You may find settings to select a regular Ethernet plug or a Fast Ethernet Plug, to select full or half-duplex communications, or to transfer error-checking calculations to the NIC. This is recommended because it will transfer error-checking from the main CPU to the NIC, freeing system resources.

◆ **Driver:** On this tab, you can view information about the drivers being used by the network adapter, including the manufacturer, date of manufacture, and digital signer. You can also use the Hardware Update Wizard to upgrade the driver.

◆ **Resources:** On this tab, you can view the device resources and settings currently assigned to the selected device. Improper settings can disable the hardware and cause the computer to malfunction.

To configure a NIC from the Device Manager, open the **Control Panel** and double-click the **System** icon to open the **System Properties** dialog box. Next, open the **Hardware** tab and click the **Device Manager** button to open the Device Manager window. Expand the **Network adapters** node to view the NICs installed on the computer. Right-click the NIC you want to configure and click **Properties** to open the Properties dialog box for the NIC.

**caution**

Only users who have expert knowledge of computer hardware and device resources should change resource settings.

**Figure 3-21  The Local Area Connection Properties dialog box**

**Figure 3-22  Configuring NIC properties**

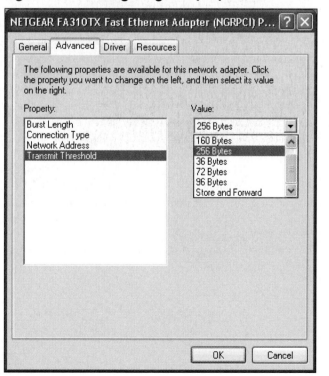

# skill 9 *Installing Video Adapters*

**exam objective**

Install, configure, and troubleshoot a video adapter.

## overview

A **video adapter** is an expansion board that plugs into a computer to give it display capabilities such as color and a choice of different resolutions. Modern video adapters contain memory so that system RAM is not used for storing displays. Video adapters are also called video cards, video boards, video display boards, graphics cards, and graphics adapters. Most computers manufactured today have built-in video adapters. If a computer does not have a built-in video adapter, you can attach one to the motherboard. The video adapter can then be installed using the Plug and Play method or the Add Hardware Wizard.

You can configure and manage video adapters on the **Settings** tab in the **Display Properties** dialog box. Right-click any free space on the desktop and click **Properties** to open the Display Properties dialog box. On the Settings tab, you can modify the color quality and screen resolution settings. You can also solve any problems related to the screen display by clicking [ Troubleshoot... ]. On the **Advanced** tab, you can change the font size, select the color profile for your monitor, and extend the desktop to span multiple monitors.

## how to

Change the color quality of your monitor to Highest (32-bit) and the screen resolution to 1024 by 768.

1. Right-click any free space on the desktop and click **Properties** to open the **Display Properties** dialog box.
2. Click the **Settings** tab to view the options for changing the monitor display.
3. Click the list arrow on the **Color quality** list box and select the **Highest (32-bit)** option. (If your video adapter does not support 32-bit color, choose the highest setting available.)
4. In the **Screen resolution** section, move the slider to change the screen area to **1024 by 768** pixels (**Figure 3-23**).
5. Click [ Apply ] to apply the changes. Your screen may flicker and a message box states that the desktop has been reconfigured and asks you if you want to keep the new settings.
6. Choose Yes or No and close the Display Properties dialog box.

## more

If you encounter problems when you install a video adapter on your system, refer to **Table 3-3**, which lists some common problems and their solutions. If the screen of your computer stays blank when you start up Windows XP Professional after configuring the video adapter, you should reboot the system. When the system displays the **Starting Up** progress bar or the message **Please select the operating system to start**, press the **[F8]** key on your keyboard. The **Windows Advanced Options Menu** will open. Select the **Last Known Good Configuration** option to boot the machine. You can also try restarting the computer in either safe mode or VGA mode (Enable VGA Mode command on the Windows Advanced Options Menu). When Windows XP boots into either Safe or VGA (video graphics array) mode, it uses a basic set of drivers, including a VGA adapter with low resolution and a limited number of colors. In Safe mode, you will generally be able to view the screen so that you can open the Display Properties dialog box and fix the settings to make the monitor work again. VGA mode is specifically designed for instances of corruption or incompatibility with the currently installed video driver.

**Figure 3-23  Changing the Display Properties**

---

**Table 3-3   Common problems encountered while installing video adapters**

| Problem | Solution |
|---|---|
| The video adapter is not supported by Windows XP Professional. | Check the Hardware Compatibility List or the manufacturer of the video adapter. |
| Video Mode is not supported by the Video driver. | Select the 640 by 480 or 800 by 600 screen resolution and 16-bit color from the Display Properties dialog box. |
| You have the wrong driver for the adapter. | To locate the correct video driver, check the documentation for the video adapter. |

# skill 10 *Installing Infrared Data Association (IrDA) Devices*

**exam objective**

Install, configure, and manage Infrared Data Association (IrDA) devices. Install, configure, and manage wireless devices.

**overview**

**Infrared Data Association (IrDA)** devices communicate with computers using infrared light instead of cables. Computers with built-in IrDA hardware such as Infrared Ports automatically detect and install infrared devices. Users who do not have computers with built-in IrDA hardware can attach a serial IrDA transceiver to a serial COM Port to allow the synchronous transmission of data. The Add Hardware Wizard is used to install infrared devices if a computer does not have an internal IrDA device or if the device is not automatically detected and installed.

After you install an IrDA device, Windows XP Professional adds the **Wireless Link** icon to the **Control Panel** window. The Wireless Link icon appears on the desktop and on the taskbar when another IrDA transceiver comes into range. This enables the transfer of data over the infrared connection.

You configure and manage wireless devices in the **Wireless Link** dialog box. To open the Wireless Link dialog box, double-click the **Wireless Link** icon in the **Control Panel** window. The Wireless Link Properties dialog box contains the following tabs (**Figure 3-24**):

◆ **File Transfer**: This tab allows you to decide if you want a wireless link icon to display on the taskbar when another wireless device comes into range. It also allows you to specify whether other computers can send files to your computer over the wireless link connection. If you allow other computers to send files to your computer, you can display the transfer status when your computer is receiving files. You can also set a default location where the received files can be stored.

◆ **Image Transfer**: This tab allows you to designate if the wireless link will be allowed to transfer images from a camera to your computer. If you allow the transfer of images, you can choose the location of the folder where the files are to be saved. You can also specify that Windows Explorer automatically open the folder after the images have been copied.

◆ **Hardware**: This tab displays a list of the wireless devices installed, the names of the manufacturers, and the physical location of the file. Using the options on this tab, you can troubleshoot problems associated with a wireless device and change the properties for the device. Click [ Properties ] to open the **Properties** dialog box for a wireless device (**Figure 3-25**). The functions of the tabs on the Properties dialog box for an infrared device are described in **Table 3-4**.

**more**

If you are unable to set up communication between two infrared devices, for example a computer and a digital camera, you must:

◆ Make sure that you have installed the infrared device properly by checking the properties for the device in the **Properties** dialog box.

◆ Check the placement of the two devices. They should be facing each other and not more than three feet apart. If the devices are properly placed, an icon for an infrared device will display on the taskbar.

◆ Check that the device is compatible with Windows XP Professional by referring to the Hardware Compatibility List.

**Table 3-4  Functions of various tabs on the Properties dialog box of an infrared device**

| | |
|---|---|
| General | The General tab displays the information about the device that you have selected and the status of the device. You can click the Troubleshooter button to receive help in solving problems with the device. You can also set the device usage (either enabled or disabled) for the device. |
| IrDA Settings | This tab displays the current setting for the maximum speed at which the infrared device can transfer data. The speed can be changed according to the specifications for the device. |
| Driver | This tab displays the details, such as the manufacturer's name, for the driver for the infrared device. You can also uninstall or upgrade drivers here. |
| Resources | This tab displays the device resources that are currently assigned to the selected device and the settings for each resource. Improper resource settings can cause your computer to malfunction. Therefore, only users who have expert knowledge of computer hardware and device resources should change these settings. |

**Figure 3-24  Configuring the properties for a wireless link**

**Figure 3-25  The Properties dialog box for an infrared device**

# skill11 *Configuring Multiprocessor Computers*

## exam objective

Monitor and configure multiprocessor computers.

## overview

**Multiprocessing** occurs when two or more CPUs carry out one or more processes simultaneously. Each processing unit works on a different set of instructions or on different parts of the same process. You can use a multiprocessor system to provide scalability and increased speed of access to network resources and services. Generally, a multiprocessor system will only be configured on a server, but some graphics-intensive applications, scientific analysis programs, or engineering design software may require added CPU power on a client system. You can improve the performance of a system for use by applications such as these by distributing the workload between the two processors.

You can upgrade your system from a uniprocessor to a multiprocessor system if there is an expansion slot available. Then, you can either reinstall Windows XP Professional over itself or you can upgrade the drivers to convert the configuration of your system from single processor to multiple processors. You use the Device Manager to upgrade the HAL for SMP (symmetric multiprocessing). You will probably have more luck performing a fresh installation of Windows XP. However, you can follow the steps in the **How to** section to update the drivers. (***Note:*** *This exercise is optional and should not be performed unless you have installed a second CPU. Your system may be severely compromised if you upgrade to a HAL that supports two processors when only one is installed.*)

If this method does not work, perform a fresh installation of Windows XP Professional. If you install Windows XP Professional on a computer that already has two processors, Setup should automatically detect both processors and install the correct HAL. When you add a second processor on the other hand, a different HAL is used for SMP, resulting in a completely different method of handling the hardware attached to your system.

When a second processor is installed on your system, you can use the Performance console to monitor the system, which is now a Symmetric Multiprocessing System (SMP). To open the Performance console, double-click **Performance** in the **Administrative Tools** window.

### tip

The Hardware Abstraction Layer (HAL), a hardware-specific operating system component, provides support for multiprocessors.

### caution

Windows XP does not support Asymmetric Multiprocessing (ASMP), a process in which each processor can operate on an independent task.

## how to

Update the driver for the computer for multiprocessor support.
1. Open the **Device Manager** window.
2. Double-click **Computer**.
3. Double-click the model name of your computer, for example, **Advanced Configuration and Power Interface (ACPI) PC** to open the **Properties** dialog box for the computer.
4. On the **Driver** tab, click the **Update Driver** option button to open the **Hardware Update Wizard**.
5. Click the **Install from a list or specific location (Advanced)** option button and click [ Next > ] to open the **Please choose your search and installation options** screen.
6. Leave the **Search for the best driver in these locations** option button selected (**Figure 3-26**) and click [ Next > ].
7. The Wizard searches for an updated driver. If one is found, you may install it. If the Wizard cannot find a better driver, the Wizard asks you to search in another location or keep the current driver (**Figure 3-27**).
8. Click [ Finish ] to exit the Hardware Update Wizard. Close the Device Manager window.

**Figure 3-26  Searching for drivers**

**Figure 3-27  Finishing the Hardware Update Wizard**

# Summary

♦ Plug and Play devices are installed automatically by Windows XP Professional.

♦ Devices installed on your system can be managed using the Device Manager.

♦ Input devices such as the mouse, keyboard, joystick, and scanners are used to provide input data to a computer. Processed data is redirected to the output devices such as the monitor and the printer.

♦ Before installing a mouse on your system, make sure that the drivers for the mouse are compatible with Windows XP Professional.

♦ When you plug in a mouse, Windows XP Professional automatically detects this new hardware and installs the drivers.

♦ Removable media are devices such as the CD-ROM, DVD, and tape devices that can be removed from your system without having to shut down the system.

♦ Removable media are used to store data in alternative storage devices other than the hard drive.

♦ A DVD is a removable device that is commonly used to store large amounts of multimedia data.

♦ A modem converts analog signals to digital signals and vice versa, making it possible for data to be transferred over telephone lines.

♦ You can configure the modems installed on your system in the Properties dialog box for that modem.

♦ You must be careful when selecting your modem speed. If you select a high speed for your modem and the speed of the Internet service provider is slow, you may have problems with your connections to the Internet.

♦ You must install the Fax service and a fax device in order to send faxes through Windows XP.

♦ Device drivers are software that enables a specific device, such as a printer, modem, or network card, to communicate with Windows XP Professional computers.

♦ Windows XP Professional has built-in drivers for installing and configuring commonly used devices.

♦ The Windows File Protection feature checks the digital signature of the file to determine if the correct Microsoft version is being installed.

♦ The System File Checker utility scans and verifies the versions of all protected system files.

♦ Universal Serial Bus (USB) is an external communication bus that is used to transfer data among the components of a computer system.

♦ USB allows you to install multimedia devices such as scanners, audio players, CD-ROM drives, Web cameras, and speakers.

♦ Network interface cards (NICs) enable you to be connected to a network.

♦ A video adapter is an expansion board that plugs into a computer and provides display capabilities such as color and a choice of different resolutions.

♦ IrDA devices communicate with computers using infrared light.

♦ After an IrDA device is installed on a computer, Windows XP Professional adds the Wireless Link icon to the Control Panel window.

# Key Terms

Compact Disk File System (CDFS)
Device driver
Device Manager
Hot swapping (hot plugging)

IrDA protocols
Modem
Multiprocessing
Network Interface Card (NIC)
Protocol binding

Removable media
Universal Disk Format (UDF)
Universal Serial Bus (USB)
Video adapter

# Test Yourself

1. Which of the following devices is used to store data offline?
   a. UDF
   b. NIC
   c. Modem
   d. DVD

2. A NIC is used to:
   a. Connect to the network.
   b. Configure dial-up options.
   c. Store data on removable media.
   d. Upgrade drivers.

3. You are working as an administrator of a Windows XP Professional network environment. One of your team members is facing problems in starting the fax service on his system. He reports that the Control Panel does not display the fax icon. Which of the following may be the cause of this problem?

   a. No fax device is physically attached to the computer.
   b. Supporting fax software is not present.
   c. Windows XP Professional registry files are corrupt.

4. Which of the following options is used to set the number of times a fax device will attempt to send a fax after the initial attempt has failed?
   a. Local dial-up settings
   b. Number of rings before the fax is answered
   c. Number of retries
   d. Retry after

5. Which of the following options in the Computer Management console will you use to upgrade drivers?
   a. Hardware Resources
   b. Disk Management
   c. Device Manager
   d. System Information

6. Which of the following is used to install devices such as keyboards, joysticks, and tape drives, and provides a faster and more manageable alternative to serial and parallel ports for devices such as keyboards and mice?
   a. Parallel port
   b. COM port
   c. Serial port
   d. Universal Serial Bus

7. If you cannot use the your mouse wheel, which of the following tabs in the Mouse Properties dialog box, enables you to modify the wheel settings?
   a. Buttons
   b. Motion
   c. Advanced Settings
   d. Hardware

8. You need to configure a video adapter on a Windows XP Professional computer. Which of the following tabs is used to change the screen resolution of the display?
   a. Settings tab
   b. Hardware tab
   c. Appearance tab
   d. Drivers tab

9. Which of the following is used to install an IrDA device on a computer running Windows XP Professional?
   a. Device Manager
   b. Wireless Link icon in the Control Panel

   c. Add or Remove Programs icon in the Control Panel
   d. Add Hardware icon in the Control Panel

10. If you upgrade the drivers for a single processor computer to multiple processors, which of the following is likely to happen?
    a. There will be no change in the functioning of the computer.
    b. The computer will stop functioning.
    c. The computer will be upgraded to a multiple processor computer.
    d. The first processor will be disabled and the second processor will be enabled.

11. The SFC [/scannow] syntax of the System File Checker is used to:
    a. Scan all files for digital signatures each time the system is rebooted.
    b. Cancel all pending scans of protected system files.
    c. Scans all protected system files immediately.
    d. Return Windows File Protection to default operation.

12. In the Mouse Properties dialog box, which of the following tabs can be used to set the pointer speed for the mouse?
    a. Pointer Options tab
    b. Buttons tab
    c. Pointers tab
    d. Hardware tab

13. In the Properties dialog box for a modem, which of the following tabs can be used to set the speed at which programs transmit data to the modem?
    a. General
    b. Modem
    c. Advanced
    d. Diagnostics

14. Universal Serial Bus controllers are displayed in the Device Manager.
    a. True
    b. False

## Projects: On Your Own

1. Configure a fax device to retry after 10 minutes and disable the device from receiving faxes.
   a. Open the **Printers and faxes** window.
   b. Open the **Fax Properties** dialog box.
   c. Open the **Devices** tab.
   d. Open **Properties** dialog box for the fax device you want to configure.
   e. Set the **Retry after** value to 10.
   f. Open the **Receive** tab.
   g. Clear the **Enable device to receive** check box.

2. Configure your mouse to use a faster double-click speed.
   a. Open the **Control Panel** window.
   b. Open the **Mouse Properties** dialog box.
   c. Set the double-click speed to a fast setting.

3. Configure a modem installed on your system to wait for the dial tone before it starts dialing and set the port speed to 115200.
   a. Open the **Control Panel** window.
   b. Open the **Phone and Modem Options** dialog box.
   c. Select a modem on the **Modems** tab.

d. Open the Properties dialog box for the selected modem.

e. Open the **Modem** tab.

f. Click the list arrow and select **115200** as the port speed in the **Maximum Port Speed** section.

g. Select the **Wait for dial tone before dialing** check box in the **Dial Control** section.

## Problem Solving Scenarios

1. You are working as the Network Administrator at Nationwide Trucking, a transportation company that specializes in long distance moving of heavy construction equipment. Nationwide is located in Moline, Illinois, but has regional offices in Sacramento, Austin, Minneapolis, and Albany. The marketing manager would like to be able to hold virtual meetings with his marketing staff located in the regional offices. Currently the marketing manager uses telephone conference calling, but he would like to switch to Microsoft's NetMeeting software using a Web camera. He has asked you to configure a Web camera on his Windows XP desktop computer using his USB port to enable video conferencing. Once you have accomplished this, he has asked that you write down the steps you have taken to install the Web camera so that other regional offices can also install them. Create a series of PowerPoint slides that provide instructions for employees in the regional offices (if you wish, you can include screenshots in your answer).

2. Beryl Williams, an advertising representative at Pique Fashion Design, Inc. in New York City, uses a modem to connect to the Internet. A few weeks after she purchased a new modem, the manufacturer sent her an e-mail notice that a new set of modem device drivers had just been released and that, in order to ensure proper operation of her modem, she should install the new drivers on her system. She has asked you to install the new drivers and to write a memo indicating the steps you followed to do so.

# Working with the Control Panel

In Windows XP Professional, the Control Panel is used to customize many different system settings to suit users' tastes and needs. For example, you may want to change the screen resolution, screen colors, language support, or keyboard and mouse functionalities. In the Control Panel, you can configure many different options to control the basic functionality and administration of your system.

The Control Panel includes the following utilities. The System and Display utilities are most commonly used.

◆ System: You can use the System properites to manage hardware profiles, configure system devices, optimize system performance, configure automatic updates, activate remote assistance, and configure the system for restoration.

◆ Regional and Language Options: You can configure multiple-language support on your computer and designate location-specific settings, such as the currency that will be used in monetary calculations, and the date and time.

◆ Accessibility Options: This applet is used to configure a system for users with visual, auditory, or physical impairments. For example, you can configure the system to display visual effects or captions when the computer makes a sound, or you can use the MouseKeys setting to allow users to control the pointer using the number pad instead of the mouse.

◆ Display: You can use the Display properties to define and modify the screen resolution, color scheme, color quality, and other properties that affect the appearance of the desktop and application interfaces. You can also set up multiple displays to expand the size of your desktop across more than one monitor.

In the Control Panel, you will also find the Power Options utility, which is used to configure the power management functions in the Windows XP environment. The contents of this dialog box will vary depending on the particular power-saving features of the computer. Typically, however, it allows you to implement or create power schemes that will dictate when to turn off the monitor and hard disk, when to put the computer into Standby mode, and when to put it into Hibernate mode (if you so choose). Power-saving capabilities are particularly important when you are using a laptop or notebook computer because they help you to extend the life of the computer's battery. The PCMCIA (Personal Computer Memory Card International Association) or PC card is another important mobile computer hardware device. These card devices are used to change laptop configurations by adding memory, a NIC, modem, or portable hard drive. Card services do not have a utility in the Control Panel. The operating system automatically carries out most of the functions that are needed to administer PC card support. The main thing you will need to know about configuring card services is that you should make sure that the system stops using the PC card before you remove it.

# Goals

In this lesson, you will learn to configure hardware profiles, optimize system performance, and set parameters for system startup and recovery, language and locale support, and display properties. You will also learn to customize the accessibility options, manage power consumption, and configure PC card services.

## Lesson 4: Working with the Control Panel

| Skill | Exam 70-270 Objective |
|---|---|
| 1. Configuring Hardware Profiles for Mobile Users | Manage, monitor, and optimize system performance for mobile users. |
| 2. Tuning System Performance | Monitor, optimize, and troubleshoot performance of the Windows XP Professional desktop. Optimize and troubleshoot application performance. Optimize and troubleshoot memory performance. |
| 3. Specifying System Startup and Recovery Settings | Monitor, optimize and troubleshoot performance of the Windows XP Professional desktop. |
| 4. Customizing Language and Locale Support | Configure support for multiple languages or multiple locations. Enable multiple-language support. Configure multiple-language support for users. Configure local settings. Configure Windows XP Professional for multiple locations. |
| 5. Customizing the Accessibility Options | Basic knowledge |
| 6. Setting Display Properties | Implement, manage, and troubleshoot display devices. Configure and manage user profiles and desktop settings. |
| 7. Configuring Multiple Displays | Implement, manage, and troubleshoot display devices. Configure multiple-display support. |
| 8. Configuring Power Options | Manage, monitor, and optimize system performance for mobile users. Configure Advanced Configuration Power Interface (ACPI). |
| 9. Configuring Card Services | Manage, monitor, and optimize system performance for mobile users. |

# Requirements

To complete this lesson, you will need a computer running Windows XP Professional. The computer should be connected to a network. You will also need a laptop and, to complete Skill 7, you will need multiple monitors, as well as PCI or AGP video adapters.

# skill 1

## Configuring Hardware Profiles for Mobile Users

### exam objective

Manage, monitor, and optimize system performance for mobile users.

### overview

The typical hardware requirements for a computer include a CPU, RAM, hard disk, sound card, and probably a network card. In addition to this standard equipment, you may need other hardware, such as a multimedia card and speakers. You can easily install these devices on your system; however, when you install additional hardware devices, each time you boot your computer the system tries to establish a connection with each device, even when you do not need to use them. This can adversely affect system performance. Using Windows XP, you can prevent this by creating hardware profiles.

**Hardware profiles** enable you to set up and store different hardware configurations for your computer. A hardware profile contains configuration information about computer hardware or devices. It notifies the computer at startup about the devices to be used and the type of settings for each device. Usually, client desktops will not change hardware configurations; however, mobile computers may do so frequently. Although you could depend on Plug and Play to detect hardware changes at startup, this can increase the amount of time it takes the computer to boot, and not all of your hardware devices may be Plug and Play compatible. If the operating system tries to detect devices that are not present, startup will be considerably delayed while Windows waits a set time period for those devices to respond before deciding that they are not attached.

Multiple hardware profiles are most commonly required for mobile computers. While working with a mobile computer at home, the office, or other sites, you often need to enable or disable network support, docking stations, modems, and monitors.

To create different types of hardware profiles, you use the System Properties dialog box. Each system has a default hardware profile named **Profile 1**. To create a new hardware profile, you must first make a copy of Profile 1 for backup reasons and then modify it according to your requirements. Although, by default, new hardware profiles are named **Profile 2** or **Profile 3**, depending on the number of existing profiles, you can easily rename them.

### how to

Create a new hardware profile for a laptop.

1. Click **⊞ start** and click **Control Panel** to open the **Control Panel** window.
2. Double-click the **System** icon to open the **System Properties** dialog box.
3. Click the **Hardware** tab (**Figure 4-1**).
4. Click [ Hardware Profiles ] to open the **Hardware Profiles** dialog box (**Figure 4-2**).
5. Click **Profile 1 (Current)** and then click [ Copy ] to make a copy of the default profile. The **Copy Profile** dialog box opens with the default name **Profile 2** shown for the new profile.
6. Click [ OK ]. The new hardware profile is listed in the **Available hardware profiles** list box.
7. Click [ Properties ] to open the **Profile 2 Properties** dialog box.
8. Select the **This is a portable computer** check box to specify that you are using a portable computer, a laptop (**Figure 4-3**).
9. Click [ OK ] to save the settings and again to close the Hardware Profiles dialog box.

### more

If there are two or more hardware profiles on your computer, Windows XP Professional will prompt you to select one at startup. You can specify a default profile that Windows XP Professional will automatically initiate after the specified number of seconds during startup. If you do not want to select a profile, Windows XP can, by default, select the first profile as the default profile. To do this, select the **Select the first profile listed if I don't select a profile in** option button in the Hardware Profiles dialog box. Then, in the **Seconds** spin box, enter the number of seconds your computer should wait before selecting the default profile.

**Figure 4-1  Hardware tab in System Properties dialog box**

**Figure 4-2 Hardware Profiles dialog box**

**Figure 4-3 Properties of the new profile**

# skill 2

# *Tuning System Performance*

## exam objective

Monitor, optimize, and troubleshoot performance of the Windows XP Professional desktop. Optimize and troubleshoot application performance. Optimize and troubleshoot memory performance.

## overview

You can optimize your system's performance by configuring the application response and the virtual memory settings in the **Performance Options** dialog box to meet the requirements of your individual system. The Performance Options dialog box contains two tabs: Visual Effects and Advanced. On the **Visual Effects** tab, you can adjust your system's performance so that it is geared for best appearance or best performance. You can also customize the performance by setting options for how different screen elements appear and animate.

On the **Advanced** tab, the **Processor scheduling** setting is used by Windows XP Professional to distribute microprocessor resources between programs that are being executed simultaneously on the system at any given point in time. Scheduling is categorized as either active foreground programs or background services. If you select the **Programs** option button, more processor resources will be allocated to foreground programs than to background services. This option is generally used for client workstations where more resources are required for the program running in the foreground. If your system is often used as a file, print, or e-mail server, you should change the application response option to background services. Likewise, the **Memory usage** setting should only be set to **System cache** on computers that are acting as servers. Otherwise, leave Memory usage set to **Programs** so that a greater share of your system's memory is devoted to running the programs on your workstation.

**Virtual memory** is defined as temporary storage, composed of a paging file, pagefile.sys, used by a computer to run programs that need more memory than is available at a given time. For example, programs could have access to 4 GB of virtual memory on a hard drive, even if the computer has only 32 megabytes of RAM. The program data that does not fit in the computer's memory is saved in the paging file. Virtual memory enables you to run larger and/or more applications than is normally possible with physical memory. Windows XP Professional uses the **Virtual Memory Manager (VMM)** to coordinate the use of physical memory and virtual memory. You can improve virtual memory somewhat by moving the paging file to a faster drive or by making the initial size and the maximum size of the paging file the same. This will make access to virtual memory faster by reducing fragmentation of the swap file; however, system performance will not be significantly increased because memory performance will only be slightly improved. Since physical memory is up to 1000 times faster than virtual memory, installing more physical memory (RAM) is a more productive way to improve memory performance. Making the paging file's initial size and maximum size the same is typically done for machines using heavy applications, for example, a database server.

### caution

Selecting Background services may slow down system performance for foreground applications.

## how to

Set both the initial size and the maximum size of the paging file to equal values to reduce fragmentation in the swap file and improve memory performance.

1. Open the **System Properties** dialog box, if necessary, and click the **Advanced** tab.
2. In the **Performance** section, click [ Settings ] to open the **Performance Options** dialog box (**Figure 4-4**).
4. Click the **Advanced** tab, and then click [ Change ] in the **Virtual memory** section to open the **Virtual Memory** dialog box.
5. Select the **Custom size** option button, if necessary, and change the **Initial size (MB)** value so that it matches the **Maximum size (MB)** value (**Figure 4-5**).
6. Click [ Set ] to set the initial and maximum sizes of the paging file.
7. Click [ OK ] to close the **Virtual Memory** dialog box.
8. Click [ OK ] to close the **Performance Options** dialog box.

**Figure 4-4  Performance Options dialog box**

**Figure 4-5  Virtual Memory dialog box**

# skill 3

## *Specifying System Startup and Recovery Settings*

**exam objective**

Monitor, optimize, and troubleshoot performance of the Windows XP Professional desktop.

## overview

When you have installed multiple operating systems on your computer, you may want to specify a particular operating system as the default so that it will be initialized automatically each time you start your computer. Alternatively, you might want to be able to choose one of the installed operating systems at startup. In the **Startup and Recovery** dialog box you can set or change the default operating system options. You can also select the course of action to be followed in case the system stops unexpectedly. To change these settings, you must be logged on as a member of the **Administrators** group.The Startup and Recovery dialog box is divided into two sections:

◆ **System Startup:** In this section you can specify which operating system you want as the default at startup, the number of seconds the system should wait for you to select an operating system during startup before the default operating system initializes, and the number of seconds to display recovery options when the situation calls for them.

◆ **System Failure:** In this section you can control the actions Windows XP Professional will take when a system failure occurs. You can configure Windows XP Professional to perform any of the following actions in the event of a system failure:
  • Write an event to the system log.
  • Send an administrative alert.
  • Automatically reboot the system.
  • Write debugging information.

You can specify the kind of debugging information Windows XP Professional will write to the specified dump file, MEMORY.DMP. **Table 4-1** describes the four options for writing debugging information.

## how to

Limit the duration of display for the list of operating systems to zero seconds so that the default operating system will be started without any boot delay. Set the system properties so that, if a system failure occurs, an alert will be sent to the administrator and an entry will be made in the system log giving a brief description of the problem.

1. Open the **System Properties** dialog box, if necessary.
2. Click the **Advanced** tab (**Figure 4-6**).
3. Click [ Settings ] in the **Startup and Recovery** section to open the **Startup and Recovery** dialog box.
4. In the **Time to display list of operating systems** spin box, type **0** (**Figure 4-7**). The default setting is 30 seconds.
5. In the **System failure** section, make sure that the **Write an event to the system log** check box is selected. If a system failure occurs, this will create an entry in the system log.
6. Make sure that the **Send an administrative alert** check box is selected. This will send an alert message to the system administrator informing him or her of the system failure.
7. Make sure that the **Automatically restart** check box is selected. This will restart the system in case of a system failure.
8. In the **Write debugging information** list box, select the **Small memory dump (64 KB)** option. This will record the minimum information about the system problem on the system log.
9. Click [ OK ] to apply the changes and close the dialog box.
10. Click [ OK ] to close the **System Properties** dialog box. Close the **Control Panel**.

**Table 4-1   Options for writing debugging information in the dump file**

| Write Debugging Information Option | Function |
|---|---|
| None | No information is written to the dump file. |
| Small Memory Dump | A minimum amount of useful information is written to the dump file. This option requires a 2 megabyte (MB) paging file on the boot volume and Windows XP Professional must create a new file each time there is a system failure. A history of these files is maintained in the small dump directory named %SystemRoot%\minidump. |
| Kernel Memory Dump | Kernel memory is written to the dump file. Kernel memory is protected memory used by the operating system and is typically a smaller portion of the total memory in use by the system. This enables faster recording of information in a log when the system stops unexpectedly. You must have 50 MB to 800 MB available in the paging file on the boot volume, depending on the amount of RAM on your computer. The more RAM you have, the less space you will need for the paging file. |
| Complete Memory Dump | The entire contents of the system memory are written to the dump file when a system failure occurs. The system must have a paging file on the boot partition that is large enough to store the physical RAM plus 1 MB. |

**Figure 4-6  Advanced tab in System Properties dialog box**

**Figure 4-7  Startup and Recovery dialog box**

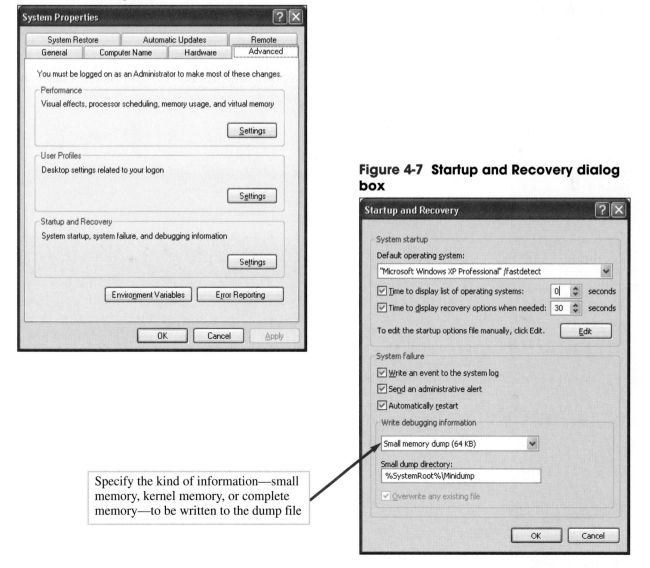

Specify the kind of information—small memory, kernel memory, or complete memory—to be written to the dump file

# skill 3

## *Specifying System Startup and Recovery Settings (cont'd)*

**exam objective**

Monitor, optimize, and troubleshoot performance of the Windows XP Professional desktop.

## more

In the **System Properties** dialog box, you can also specify the environment variables. Environment variables provide system and user environment information, such as drives, paths, or file names. All of the various initialization parameters and paths for globally used variable parameters are also stored as environment variables. Since applications use some common variables across the platform to interpret behavior or data in an operating system, these variables must be stored in a common place where they are accessible to all. To display the **Environment Variables** dialog box, click [ Environment Variables ] on the **Advanced** tab in the System Properties dialog box. There are two types of environment variables (**Figure 4-8**):

## caution

System environment variables can only be added, changed, or deleted by an Administrator.

◆ **User variables for <username>:** User environment variables are personalized settings for different users using the same system. For example, users may have defined personal settings such as a particular desktop pattern or display colors or menu options in a specific application. The paths to the locations of application files are also stored as environment variables. Thus, user environment variables differ for each user and are loaded according to the user who logs on to the system. Users can add, delete, or edit their user environment variables to suit their specific requirements.

◆ **System variables:** The Setup program in Windows XP Professional configures the system environment variables during installation. These variables contain information such as the path used by the Windows XP Professional registry files. For example, the **TEMP** environment variable indicates where the operating system stores temporary files, while the **ComSpec** environmental variable indicates the path for the **Command Prompt** executable file.

**Figure 4-8  Environment Variables dialog box**

Used to set a variable name and variable value for a particular user

# skill 4

## *Customizing Language and Locale Support*

### exam objective

Configure support for multiple languages or multiple locations. Enable multiple-language support. Configure multiple-language support for users. Configure local settings. Configure Windows XP Professional for multiple locations.

### overview

When you use Windows XP Professional, you can customize your desktop for multiple languages and locations. In the English version, users can view, edit, and print information in several languages. In the Translated version, users can access menus, help files, dialog boxes, and file system components in multiple languages. The MultiLanguage version allows bilingual users to switch back and forth between several language interfaces, which is particularly useful for employees of multinational companies that have offices and customers in numerous countries. The MultiLanguage version of the operating system uses a single worldwide executable file that supports Arabic, Hebrew, and most European and East Asian languages. Rather than having to use a different translated version of Windows for each language, you can install Windows XP with the MultiLanguage Pack to support multilingual document editing and the deployment of multiple language interfaces. The MultiLanguage Pack is available to customers who participate in the Microsoft Open License Program and to Select and Enterprise agreement customers.

On the English language version, you can configure your system to display and sort numbers, currency, and the date and time according to the location you select. To specify the language you want to use, you must add the required input language. When you add an input language, a keyboard layout or Input Method Editor (IME) for that language is also added. Keyboard layouts or IMEs are designed to accommodate the special characters and symbols used in different languages.

To customize the language and local support for your desktop, you use the **Regional and Language Options** dialog box (**Figure 4-9**). This dialog box contains several tabs where you can specify and configure the languages you need your computer to support, the current locale, and any additional locales you need supported. You can also modify input locales to alter keyboard layouts. A brief description of each tab is given in **Table 4-2**.

### how to

Configure your desktop to support both English and Spanish.

1. Click ⊞ start and click **Control Panel** to open the Control Panel window.
2. Double-click the **Regional and Language Options** icon to open the **Regional and Language Options** dialog box (**Figure 4-9**).
3. Click the **Languages** tab. In the **Text services and input languages** section, click Details... to open the **Text Services and Input Languages** dialog box. **English (United States) - US** is listed as the default input language in the **Default input language** list box. In order to support another language on your system, you must add another language.
4. Click Add... in the **Installed services** section of the tab to open the **Add Input Language** dialog box.
5. Click the **Input language** list arrow to view a list of available input locales. Select the **Spanish (Internations Sort)** option (**Figure 4-10**).

**Table 4-2  Tabs in the Regional and Language Options dialog box**

| Tab | Offers options that enable you to: |
|---|---|
| Regional Options | Set standards and formats for items such as numbers, currency, time, and dates. Select your location for customized information from services such as news and weather. |
| Languages | Add additional input languages and install languages not installed by default. |
| Advanced | Select a language for non-Unicode programs so that features such as menus and dialog boxes that were originally in the selected language will display properly. Install and uninstall code page conversion tables to convert to, and from Unicode. |

**Figure 4-9  The Regional and Language Options dialog box**

You can select the code page conversion tables on the Advanced tab

**Figure 4-10  Adding a new input language**

Select the language you want to add

# skill 4

## *Customizing Language and Locale Support (cont'd)*

**exam objective**

Configure support for multiple languages or multiple locations. Enable multiple-language support. Configure multiple-language support for users. Configure local settings. Configure Windows XP Professional for multiple locations.

## how to

6. Click [ OK ] to close the dialog box. The selected language, **Spanish (International Sort)** is displayed in the **Input language** list box, along with the default language **English (United States) (Figure 4-11)**.

7. Click [ OK ] to apply the new settings. A language indicator, **EN**, is shown on the taskbar **(Figure 4-12)**.

8. Click [ OK ] to close the Regional and Language Options dialog box.

9. To switch to the Spanish language, click EN on the Taskbar. A menu listing the languages you have configured appears **(Figure 4-13)**. Click **Spanish (International Sort)** to switch to the **Spanish** language.

## more

After changing to some languages, you will find that certain characters have a different appearance when you type them. For example, if you press the [;] key when using the Spanish language, a Spanish character [ñ] is displayed on the screen. This indicates that the internal layout of the keyboard has changed to suit the Spanish language.

Each language has a default keyboard layout, but many languages support alternative keyboard layouts. Even if you work mainly with one language, you can try other layouts.

You can use a different input language for each program you use. For example, you can use one input language to create documents using **WordPad** and another input locale at the **Command Prompt**. To do this, open the program and select the input language to be used for that program by using the language indicator on the taskbar.

**Figure 4-11  The Text Services and Input Languages dialog box**

New language added

Specify key sequence to switch between locales

**Figure 4-12  Indicator representing the current input language**

Current input language on the taskbar

**Figure 4-13  Switching the language**

All added languages will be visible

# skill 5 *Customizing the Accessibility Options*

## exam objective

Basic knowledge

## overview

You can customize your computer to meet your special visual, auditory, or mobility needs in the **Accessibility Options** dialog box. This dialog box has five tabs: Keyboard, Sound, Display, Mouse, and General (**Figure 4-14**). A brief description of the functions you can configure on each of these tabs is given below.

On the **Keyboard** tab you can configure the following support:

◆ **StickyKeys:** To use a multiple-key combination, such as **[Ctrl]+[Alt]+[Delete]**, normally you must press the required keys simultaneously. For people who find it difficult to press more than one key at a time, such as those with arthritis, you can set the StickyKeys function so that they can perform the same action by pressing one key at a time.

◆ **FilterKeys:** This function adjusts the response of your keyboard to your actions. For example, normally if you press a key on the keyboard and hold it down, multiple instances of the character are inserted until you release the key. With the FilterKeys function activated, the character will appear only once regardless of how long you hold down the key. You can also adjust the length of time a key must be pressed before the keystroke is accepted. The FilterKeys function should be used carefully, however, because a key press can be ignored after a letter has been entered once, even when the character is intended to be displayed twice in succession such as in the word "succeed".

◆ **ToggleKeys:** Activating the ToggleKeys function configures your computer to emit sounds when certain locking keys are pressed. For example, the computer will make a high-pitched sound each time the **[Caps Lock]**, **[Num Lock]**, or **[Scroll Lock]** keys are toggled on. Similarly, each time these keys are toggled-off, the computer will make a low-pitched sound.

The **SoundSentry** function on the **Sound** tab can be extremely helpful for the hearing impaired. It programs Windows XP Professional to generate visual warnings when the system's built-in speaker plays a sound. The visual warning is in the form of a flash on a part of the screen when the user performs an action that causes a sound to be generated. You can specify the part of the screen where you want the warning to appear, either in the caption bar, the active window, or the entire desktop. You can also set the **ShowSounds** function to display captions to replace the speech and sounds generated by programs.

On the **Display** tab, you can set the display to use high contrast color schemes that are specially designed to improve the legibility of text. For example, you can make the color scheme black on white, white on black, or any other color scheme you prefer. You can also set cursor options to improve the visibility of the cursor by changing its blink rate and width.

On the **Mouse** tab, you can set the **MouseKeys** function so that users can perform mouse functions using the numeric keypad. The arrow keys on the numeric keypad located at the extreme right of your keyboard can be used to control the pointer movement and actions on the screen. Before you set the MouseKeys function, you must deactivate the **NumLock** key. If you encounter problems implementing this function, verify that NumLock has been deactivated and try again.

On the **General** tab, you can configure settings related to automatic resetting, notification, SerialKey devices, and administrative options (**Figure 4-15**). **Table 4-3** contains a description of each of these functions.

**Figure 4-14  Accessibility Options dialog box**

Multiple-key combinations can be executed while pressing one key at a time

Adjusts the response of your keyboard

Emits sounds when certain locking keys are pressed

**Figure 4-15  The General tab in the Accessibility Options dialog box**

You can select the port where you will connect an alternative input device

## Table 4-3  Options on the General tab

| Options | Description |
|---|---|
| Automatic reset | Deactivates all of the accessibility functions, except the SerialKeys device, after the computer has been idle for a specified time. The SerialKeys device is designed for people who are unable to use the computer's standard keyboard and mouse. |
| SerialKey devices | Allows alternative access to keyboard and mouse functions. SerialKey devices are designed for people who are unable to use the computer's standard keyboard and mouse. Selecting the Support SerialKey devices check box activates SerialKey support, and you can attach an alternative input device to your computer's serial port. These devices are also referred to as augmentative communicative devices. |
| Administrative options | Program the system to apply the newly configured accessibility options as the default settings for a particular user and/or for all new users. |

# skill 5

## Customizing the Accessibility Options *(cont'd)*

### exam objective

Configure and troubleshoot accessibility services.

### how to

Configure accessibility options so that the numeric keypad can be used instead of a mouse, and change the display settings to provide a high contrast of black text on a white background.

1. In the **Control Panel** window, double-click the **Accessibility Options** icon to open the **Accessibility Options** dialog box.
2. Click the **Mouse** tab to display the options on the tab.
3. Select the **Use MouseKeys** check box to activate the numeric pad on your keyboard to control the mouse pointer on the screen (**Figure 4-16**), and click the [ Apply ] button. The MouseKeys indicator is displayed at the bottom right of the screen (**Figure 4-17**).
4. To confirm that the MouseKeys function has been activated, press the up arrow key on the numeric keypad. The cursor on the screen moves up in the same way it would if you were using a mouse. Hold down the up arrow key. The cursor moves up more quickly the longer you hold down the key.
5. Click the **Display** tab.
6. Select the **Use High Contrast** check box.
7. Click [ Settings ] to open the **Settings for High Contrast** dialog box.
8. Select the **High Contrast White (large)** option in the **Your current high contrast scheme is** list box (**Figure 4-18**), and then click [ OK ] to confirm the selection.
9. Click [ OK ] in the **Accessibility Options** dialog box to apply the changes. **Figure 4-19** displays the **High Contrast White (large)** high contrast color scheme.
10. Reopen the **Accessibility Options** dialog box and remove any settings you do not want to retain. Close the dialog box.

### more

In addition to the accessibility functions, there are many other desktop settings in Windows XP Professional that are configured through the **Control Panel** such as **Folder Options**, **Sounds and Audio**, and **Internet Options**. You can configure these settings by double-clicking the relevant icon in the Control Panel, opening the relevant tab, and configuring the required settings.

A few accessibility related problems that you may encounter, along with their solutions, are listed below:

1. If the accessibility options you have set are not working, make sure that the **Turn off accessibility features after idle for** check box on the **General** tab in the **Accessibility Options** dialog box is not selected.
2. If accessibility options are active for users who do not require them, make sure that the **Apply all settings to defaults for new users** check box is not selected in the **Administrative options** section of the General tab.
3. If the numeric keypad is not producing the typed characters you are pressing, make sure that **Num Lock** is enabled on the keyboard.

**Figure 4-16  The Mouse tab in the Accessibility Options dialog box**

**Figure 4-17  The System Tray displaying the MouseKeys indicator**

Click to set the pointer speed

MouseKeys indicator in the notification area

**Figure 4-18  Changing the High Contrast setting**

**Figure 4-19  The High Contrast White (large) high contrast scheme**

# skill 6

# Setting Display Properties

## exam objective

Implement, manage, and troubleshoot display devices. Configure and manage user profiles and desktop settings.

## overview

You can also modify the display properties for your computer such as the screen resolution, color depth, and background colors. To configure the display properties, you use the **Settings** tab on the **Display Properties** dialog box. The Settings tab contains the following options:

- ◆ **Colors:** Provides a list of color depths available for the display adapter.
- ◆ **Screen Area:** Enables you to set the screen resolution.
- ◆ **Troubleshoot:** Enables you to diagnose display problems.
- ◆ **Advanced:** Enables you to configure the properties for the display adapter to support the multiple display feature. The options on the Advanced tab are explained in **Table 4-4**. (Note: not all systems will include all of the tabs shown in the table.)

## how to

Change the screen area for your computer to **1024 by 768** pixels.

1. Double-click the **Display** icon in the **Control Panel** window to open the **Display Properties** dialog box.
2. Click the **Settings** tab.
3. In the **Screen resolution** section, drag the slider in the appropriate direction to change the screen area to **1024 by 768 pixels (Figure 4-20)**.
4. Click [ Apply ] to apply the changes. Your screen may flicker. The **Monitor Settings** box then informs you that the desktop has been reconfigured and asks you if you want to keep the new settings. If you do not respond within 15 seconds, the display will revert to its previous setting.
5. Click [ Yes ].
6. Click [ OK ] to close the Disiplay Properties dialog box.

## more

Troubleshooting Display Settings:

- ◆ Changing the screen resolution: There may be times when you are not able to view graphics on the monitor properly. Some of the graphics may be only partly visible because they extend beyond the screen area. You can change the resolution of the screen to view a graphic in its entirety. A higher screen resolution reduces the size of objects on your screen and increases the size of your desktop. Your monitor and the drivers for the video adapter determine whether you can change your screen resolution.
- ◆ Changing the refresh frequency of your monitor: If your screen seems to flicker, causing distortion and disturbance, increase the refresh setting for your screen to a higher rate. The default refresh frequency setting is 60 Hertz, but your monitor may support a higher setting. Check your manufacturer's documentation for information regarding the settings your monitor supports. A higher refresh frequency will reduce the flickering, but choosing a setting that is too high for your monitor can make your display unusable and cause damage to your hardware.

## Table 4-4 Options in the Graphics Controller Properties dialog box

| Tab | Option group | Description |
|---|---|---|
| General | Display | Displays the DPI setting for the current monitor. You can set the DPI to a predefined small or large size, or you can set a custom DPI value. |
| | Compatibility | Specifies the action to be taken after you have changed the display settings. You can select any of the three options:<br>• Restart the computer before applying the new display settings<br>• Apply the new display settings without restarting<br>• Ask me before applying the new display settings |
| Adapter | Adapter Type | Provides information about the type of video adapter used on your system. This includes information about the manufacturer and model number and about the device status, resource settings, and whether there are any conflicting devices. |
| | Adapter Information | Provides information about the video adapter. This includes information such as the video chip type, DAC type, memory size, and BIOS. |
| | List All Modes | Lists all of the compatible modes for your video adapter. You can select the resolution, color depth, and refresh frequency in a single step. |
| Monitor | Monitor Type | Provides information about the monitor your system is using. You can also troubleshoot the display by clicking Properites to diagnose display problems. The Windows Help and Support Center guides you through a series of questions to help you solve display problems. |
| | Monitor Settings | You can set the refresh rate frequency. |
| Troubleshoot | Hardware Acceleration | You can gradually decrease the display hardware's acceleration so that you can segregate and fix display problems. |
| Color Management | | You can select the color profile for your monitor. |

### Figure 4-20 Changing the resolution

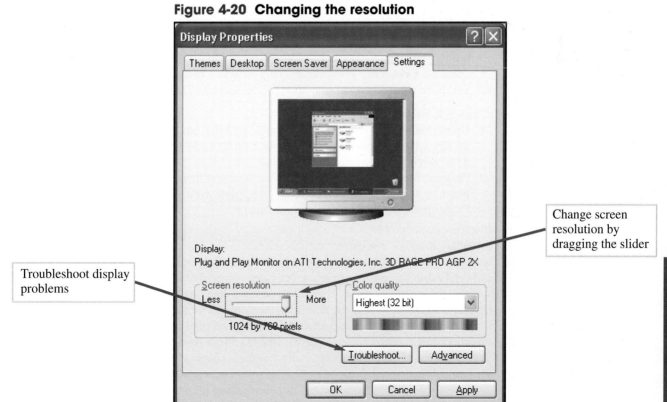

Change screen resolution by dragging the slider

Troubleshoot display problems

# skill 7

# *Configuring Multiple Displays*

## exam objective

Implement, manage, and troubleshoot display devices. Configure multiple-display support.

## overview

You can configure your computer for **multiple displays** to expand the size of your desktop to more than one monitor (**Figure 4-21**). A maximum of ten monitors can be connected to create a desktop large enough to hold multiple displays. For example, if you want to view the contents of a Microsoft Excel spreadsheet without having to scroll, you can set up a multiple display to stretch the spreadsheet across three or four monitors.

## how to

**Install additional monitors. (Activity 1)**

Requirements:

◆ A Windows XP Professional computer equipped with a peripheral Component Interconnect (PCI) or Accelerated Graphics Port (AGP) video adapter for each monitor.

◆ A multiple-display compatible onboard adapter set as VGA. The motherboard adapter becomes the secondary display adapter when you add a display adapter, unless the BIOS gives you the option of selecting the primary display adapter.

◆ Windows XP Professional completely set up before installing another adapter. (Windows XP Professional Setup will use the default display adapter and disable other display adapters if they are detected.)

1. Shut down the computer.
2. Insert an additional **Peripheral Component Interconnect (PCI)** or **Accelerated Graphics Port (AGP)** video adapter into an available slot.
3. Plug your additional monitor cable into the display adapter.
4. Restart the computer. Windows XP will detect the new video adapter and install the appropriate drivers.
5. Click **start** and click **Control Panel** to open the Control Panel window.
6. Double-click the **Display** icon to open the Display Properties dialog box.
7. Click the **Settings** tab.
8. Click the **Monitor** icon that represents the monitor you want to use in addition to your primary monitor.
9. Click the **Extend my Windows desktop onto this monitor** check box (**Figure 4-22**).
10. Select the color depth and resolution for the secondary display.

**Arrange multiple monitors. (Activity 2)**

1. On the Settings tab in the Display Properties dialog box, click **Identify** (**Figure 4-23**) to display a large number on each of your monitors, showing which monitor corresponds with each icon.
2. Drag the Monitor icons to positions that represent how you want to move objects from one monitor to another, and click **OK** to view the changes. Close the Display Properties dialog box and the Control Panel.

If you encounter problems with a multiple-display configuration, such as output failure on the secondary displays, you can try various solutions. For example, if you are unable to see the output on the secondary displays, open the **Display Properties** dialog box, select the device, and verify that you are using the correct video driver. Then, restart your computer to make sure that the secondary display starts. If it does not start, open the Device Manager and check the status of the device. If the device is operating correctly, try switching the order of the adapters in the slots on the motherboard. If the **Extend my Windows desktop onto this monitor** check box is not presented, open the **Display Properties** dialog box, select the secondary display instead of the primary one, verify that the secondary display adapter is supported, and verify that Windows XP Professional can detect the secondary display. If a particular application will not display on the secondary display, first run the application on the primary display, then use full-screen mode to run the application (i.e., maximized). Finally, to find out if the problem is chiefly related to multiple-display support, disable the secondary display.

## tip

You can resize a window to stretch it across more than one monitor.

## tip

If you are using two monitors and you want to move objects from one monitor to the other by dragging left and right, place the respective monitor icons side by side. To move objects between monitors by dragging up and down, place the icons one above the other.

**Figure 4-21  Multiple displays**

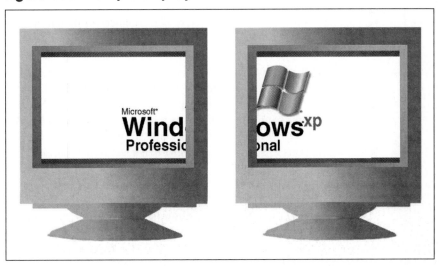

**Figure 4-22  Extending the desktop**

Select this check box
to extend the display
to the second monitor

**Figure 4-23  Identifying the monitors**

Click to see which
monitor corresponds
to the selected icon

# skill 8 | *Configuring Power Options*

**exam objective**

Manage, monitor, and optimize system performance for mobile users. Configure Advanced Configuration Power Interface (ACPI).

## overview

Windows XP Professional supports two power management standards: **Advanced Power Management** (APM) and **Advanced Configuration and Power Interface (ACPI)**. These standards are used to control and manage power consumption. APM is the older standard and it may be all that the hardware in older computers supports. You use the **Power Options** utility in the **Control Panel** to configure the APM or ACPI power settings. If the APM tab is there, your computer supports this standard. If APM is not yet turned on, select the **Enable Advanced Power Management** check box. ACPI is the newer standard. It improves power management capabilities considerably. To find out if your computer's hardware supports this standard, open the **Control Panel**, double-click the **System** icon, open the **Hardware** tab and click the **Device Manager** button. Then, expand the **Computer** icon and read the label. If it says Advanced Configuration and Power Interface (ACPI), ACPI Uniprocessor PC, or ACPI Multiprocessor PC, your computer supports the standard. If it says Standard PC, MPS Uniprocessor, or MPS Multiprocessor, it does not.

The Power management features in Windows XP are primarily designed for laptop computers so that you can optimize the life span of the battery, although they can also be used to reduce the amount of energy consumed by a desktop computer. You configure either the APM or ACPI power management settings in the Power Options applet, which has the following tabs:

◆ **Power Schemes:** The Power Schemes tab provides you with options to switch off the monitor and hard disk temporarily when you are not using your system (**Figure 4-24**). This conserves energy when the system is not in use. You can use the **Power Options Properties** dialog box to configure power schemes. First, however, you must make sure that your system supports automatically switching off the monitor and hard disk.

◆ **Advanced:** The Advanced tab is used to designate if a power management icon will display in your system tray. When you select the **Always show icon on the taskbar** check box (**Figure 4-25**), an icon will appear in the system tray. If you select a standby option on the Power Schemes tab, you can configure your computer to ask for a password when it is taken out of standby.

◆ **Hibernate:** Hibernate mode can also be used to conserve energy while you are not working on your system. When you configure your system to Hibernate, it saves your current system state to your hard disk and then shuts down the system when you are not working. The contents of memory are saved to a disk file. When you restart your system, the operating system gets this information from the disk file and returns the computer to its previous state. Any program that was running before the hibernation will automatically restart and any network connections will be restored. To configure the Hibernate mode, click the **Hibernate** tab in the Power Options Properties dialog box and select the **Enable hibernation** check box (**Figure 4-26**).

◆ **UPS:** The **UPS (Uninterruptible Power Supply)** tab is used to configure backup battery power for the system. This protects the system from a sudden loss of electrical power. The battery power gives you enough time to shut down your system safely and save all of your current work. The UPS is physically connected to a system's serial port, allowing the asynchronous transmission of data. The information on whether your system is running on UPS or on power supply appears on the UPS tab in the Power Options dialog box. The UPS tab is used to configure the behavior of your system in the event of a power failure.

**Figure 4-24  Power Schemes tab**

**Figure 4-25  Advanced tab**

**Figure 4-26  Showing the Power Options icon on the taskbar**

# skill 8

## *Configuring Power Options (cont'd)*

**exam objective**

Manage, monitor, and optimize system performance for mobile users. Configure Advanced Configuration Power Interface (ACPI).

**overview**

The Power Options dialog box can also contain other tabs with additional capabilities, depending on the computer. Additionally, the Power Options utility provides a feature to warn the user when the power of the battery is below the critical level. You can easily change the battery level at which the alarm or message is to be activated. This ensures that you can save your data on time and shut down the system.

**how to**

Configure the Power options on a laptop.

1. Click ***start*** and click **Control Panel** to open the **Control Panel** window.
2. Double-click the **Power Options** icon to open the **Power Options Properties** dialog box.
3. Select the **Portable/Laptop** option in the **Power schemes** list box, as shown in **Figure 4-27**.
4. In the **Settings for Portable/Laptop power scheme** section, click the **After 10 mins** option in the **Turn off monitor** list box. This programs the monitor to automatically switch off after 10 minutes when it is not in use.
5. Click the **After 20 mins** option in the **Turn off hard disks** list box. This programs the hard disk to automatically switch off after 20 minutes when it is not in use.
6. Select **After 30 mins** in the **System standby** list box. Then click [ Save As... ] to save the scheme. This opens the **Save Scheme** dialog box.
7. Type **Laptop Settings** as the name of the power scheme in the **Save this power scheme as** text box.
8. Click [ OK ] to close the **Save Scheme** dialog box.
9. Click [ Apply ] to apply the saved scheme to the system.
10. Open the list box in the **Power schemes** section to make sure that your newly created power scheme is on the list (**Figure 4-28**).
11. Close the list and click the **Hibernate** tab.
12. Make sure that the **Enable hibernation** check box is selected and click [ Apply ].
13. Click [ OK ] to close the **Power Options Properties** dialog box. You have now successfully configured Power options.
14. Close the **Control Panel**.

**Figure 4-27  Setting power schemes**

Power Schemes tab provides different power settings for a system

Switches off the monitor after a specified time

Switches off the hard disk after a specified time

**Figure 4-28  Saved power scheme**

Your power scheme added to the list of preset schemes

# skill 9

## *Configuring Card Services*

**exam objective**

Manage, monitor, and optimize system performance for mobile users.

## overview

**PCMCIA (Personal Computer Memory Card International Association) card** devices or PC cards are mainly found on laptop computers, although you might occasionally find a desktop computer with one. They are used to add a network interface card (NIC), a modem, or occasionally, memory to a laptop, or to connect to a portable hard drive, among other things. They are credit-card-sized devices that are inserted into an expansion slot or a port and are immediately recognized by the operating system without you having to shut down and restart the system. When you disconnect PC cards, you simply need to notify the operating system that you are unplugging or ejecting them, and you do not need to reboot for the new configuration to be operational. This ability to insert and remove PC cards while the computer is running is referred to as hot swapping and it makes it very convenient for users to quickly change the configuration of a laptop. The two keys to this technology are Plug and Play support and the ACPI power management standard. Plug and Play was designed to allow computer users to disconnect and reconnect devices without the need to install and uninstall the corresponding device drivers, reallocate resources, or reboot the computer. It works best with the ACPI power management standard because ACPI computers can dynamically reconfigure PC cards. However, some APM machines do have the same functionality. Dynamic reconfiguration is a term closely related to hot swapping that refers to the ability of the operating system to automatically detect and configure devices when they are plugged in with no need to reboot. When you remove a PC card device, the best practice is simply to double-click the **Safely Remove Hardware** icon in the notification area of the taskbar **(Figure 4-29)** to open the corresponding dialog box where you can use the Stop button to stop the device driver for the device **(Figure 4-30)**. This dialog box is also used to stop the device drivers for all removable devices, preventing system errors or possible data loss that could occur when you do not allow the system to complete any processes in progress, clear the related buffers, and disable the drivers and any dependent services.

The operating system software that is used to manage PC cards is referred to as card services and it is automatically installed when you install Windows XP Professional on a desktop computer that has a PCMCIA expansion slot, or on a HAL supported notebook or laptop computer. Three types of PCMCIA card standards are currently available. Type I cards are generally used to add memory to a laptop. Type II cards are used to add modems or NICs. Type III cards are generally used to connect a portable hard drive. These cards also differ in their thickness, ranging from a width of up to 3.3 mm for a Type I card, up to 5.5 mm for Type II, and up to 10.5 mm for a Type III card. When the card services software is installed on a computer, the operating system carries out most of the functions that are needed to administer PC card support, without the need for any user intervention. The Unplug or Eject Hardware dialog box is all you will need to use to make sure that the system stops using the PC card before you remove it.

**Figure 4-29** **The Safely Remove Hardware icon in the notification area**

Safely Remove Hardware icon

**Figure 4-30** **The Safely Remove Hardware dialog box**

# Summary

- In the Control Panel, you can configure a system according to your requirements. It contains basic applets including the System, Regional and Language Options, Accessibility Options, and Display utilities.
- The System program is used to optimize your system performance by:
  - Creating and managing different hardware profiles for your computer.
  - Configuring the application response settings to distribute microprocessor resources between foreground and background programs.
  - Configuring the virtual memory settings by adjusting the size of the paging file.
  - Setting the system startup settings.
  - Designating the actions the system should perform in the event of a system failure.
  - Configuring the user and system environment variables.
- The Regional and Language Options program is used to customize your system to support multiple languages and locations. You can configure the system to display and sort numbers, currency, and date and time according to the location you select.
- The Accessibility Options program is used to customize your computer to meet special visual, auditory, or mobility needs. You can configure the keyboard, sound, display, and mouse settings according to your requirements.
- The Display program helps you to define, modify, and troubleshoot the display properties for your computer such as the screen resolution, color quality, background colors, and other display features.
- The multiple display feature allows you to expand the size of your desktop across more than one monitor.
- Windows XP Professional supports two power management standards: Advanced Power Management (APM) and Advanced Configuration and Power Interface (ACPI). These standards are used to control and manage power consumption.
- You use the Power Options dialog box to configure power scheme options and to manage the power consumption of a system.
- PCMCIA (Personal Computer Memory Card International Association) card devices or PC cards are credit-card-sized devices that are inserted into an expansion slot or a port, mainly on laptop computers, although some desktop computers now have them. They are used to add memory, a network interface card (NIC), or a modem to a laptop, or to connect to a portable hard drive. They are immediately recognized by the operating system without you having to shut down and restart the system. When you disconnect the cards, you simply need to notify the operating system that you are unplugging or ejecting them and you do not need to reboot for the new configuration to be operational.
- This ability to insert and remove PC cards while the computer is running is referred to as hot swapping.
- Dynamic reconfiguration is a term closely related to hot swapping that refers to the ability of the operating system to automatically detect and configure devices when they are plugged in, with no need to reboot.

# Key Terms

ACPI (Advanced Configuration and Power Interface)
APM (Advanced Power Management)
Application response setting
FilterKeys
Hardware profiles
MouseKeys

Multiple displays
PCMCIA (Personal Computer Memory Card International Association) card
Power options
Power schemes
ShowSounds

SoundSentry
StickyKeys
ToggleKeys
UPS
Virtual memory
Virtual Memory Manager (VMM)

# Test Yourself

1. Which of the following utilities will you use to specify the devices, and their configuration settings, that should be loaded during system startup?
   a. Device Manager
   b. Hardware Profiles dialog box
   c. Hardware Wizard
   d. Computer Management snap-in

2. Which of the following dialog boxes or tabs would you use to specify the default operating system in case you have multiple operating systems installed on your system?
   a. Startup and Recovery
   b. Virtual Memory
   c. Hardware Profiles
   d. User Profiles

3. Which of the following settings do you specify in the Startup and Recovery dialog box? (Choose all that apply.)
   a. System environment variables
   b. Wait time before the default operating system is loaded
   c. Method for writing the debugging information to the dump file
   d. Application response time
   e. Paging file size

4. Which of the following program options in the Control Panel enables you to customize your desktop settings for multiple languages and locations?
   a. Accessibility Options
   b. Regional and Language Options
   c. Power Options
   d. Display Options

5. Which of the following functions can you use to perform the same action by pressing one key after the other, instead of holding down multiple keys simultaneously?
   a. FilterKeys
   b. StickyKeys
   c. ToggleKeys
   d. SoundSentry

6. Which of the following command sequences will you use to specify the option to start the MouseKeys utility automatically at login?
   a. Start → Control Panel → Accessibilty Options → Mouse → General
   b. Start → Programs → Accessories → System Tools → Accessibility Options
   c. Start → Control Panel → Accessibilty Options → Advanced
   d. Start → Control Panel → Power Options → UPS → General

7. Which of the following statements about a hardware profile are true? (Choose all that apply.)
   a. Notifies the system about the type of settings to be used for the devices.
   b. Notifies the system about the desktop environment settings to be loaded in the system.
   c. Optimizes a system's performance.
   d. Specifies the actions that the system should perform in the event of a system failure.

8. Which of the following is used to distribute microprocessor resources between programs that are being executed simultaneously on a system at a given point in time?
   a. Registry
   b. Virtual memory
   c. Processor scheduling
   d. System environment variables

9. Which of the following options, available for writing the debugging information, requires the system to have a paging file on the boot partition that is large enough to store the physical RAM plus 1 MB?
   a. Small Memory Dump
   b. Kernel Memory Dump
   c. Complete Memory Dump
   d. None of the above

10. You have configured your system to enable you to perform mouse functions using the numeric keypad; however, you are facing a problem implementing this function. To resolve the problem, you should ensure that the: (Choose all that apply.)
    a. ToggleKeys function is enabled.
    b. MouseKeys function is activated.
    c. Numlock key is deactivated.
    d. StickyKeys function is activated.

11. You are the Administrator of Excel Inc. and you want to configure the power options on your laptop to shut off the monitor after the machine has been idle for a specific time period. To do this, you open the Power Options applet in the Control Panel. Once there, you decide to configure your battery backup power options as well. Which Power Options tabs will you use to complete these tasks?
    a. Power Schemes and APM
    b. Advanced and UPS
    c. Power Schemes and Advanced
    d. Power Schemes and UPS

12. Which of the following writes all of the contents of memory to a file on the hard disk and then turns the power to the computer off?
    a. APM
    b. Power Schemes
    c. Hibernate
    d. Caching

## Projects: On Your Own

1. Create a new hardware profile on your system with the name **hardware_nu** and configure your system to wait for you to select a hardware profile during startup.
   a. Open the **Hardware Profiles** dialog box through the **System** applet in the **Control Panel**.
   b. Create a copy of the default profile and name it **hardware_nu**.

   c. In the **Hardware profiles selection** section, click the **Wait until I select a hardware profile** option button.
2. Configure your system so that every time there is a system failure, your network administrator receives an alert.
   a. Access the **System Properties** dialog box through the **Control Panel** and click the **Advanced** tab.
   b. Open the **Startup and Recovery** dialog box.

c. In the **System Failure** section, ensure that the **Send an administrative alert** check box is selected.

3. Configure your system in such a way that a flash is visible in the active window each time the system generates a sound.

   a. Display the **Sound** tab in the **Accessibility Options** dialog box through the **Control Panel**.

b. In the **SoundSentry** section, click the **Use SoundSentry** option button.

c. In the **Choose the visual warning** list box, select the visual warning option **Flash active window**.

# Problem Solving Scenarios

1. The number of complaints about slow computers, poor network response times, and frequent network crashes at Delphi Engineering—a small highway engineering firm in Minden, Nevada—is reaching unusual levels. Delphi's Systems Administrator has asked you to figure out what's wrong and fix the problem. You suspect one issue is that many of the workstations may not be optimized for the kind of intensive desktop programs being used. You believe it may be helpful to increase the size of virtual memory being used because several of the older machines have limited RAM. You are not sure about the network crashing frequency, duration, or time to recover. Outline in a memo or PowerPoint slides the steps you will take to optimize the performance of Delphi's desktop workstations and improve the reporting of system failures.

2. DigitalForge Media, Inc., specializes in creating corporate presentations, as well as Web-related graphic and multimedia material. The firm's chief graphic designer, Harry Bridges, recently injured his left hand in a skiing accident. Unfortunately, Harry was working on a very important project for the firm. Harry is left-handed and has a cast on his left hand, but he can still use his fingers freely to hold a pencil and draw. He requests that you install a tablet on his system so he can work without having to use the mouse. He also wants you to change the keyboard functionality so he does not have to hold down the ALT key simultaneously with other keys to use various functions in his graphics software. To practice, log on to your Windows XP client and use the Accessibility Options dialog box through the Control Panel to activate the Support SerialKey devices feature so Harry can use a tablet and stylus as input devices instead of a mouse. Change the keyboard to use StickyKeys. Write a memo describing the steps you have taken.

# Managing Data Storage

In order to save and share your work, you must learn how to properly store your data. In Windows XP Professional there are two data storage types: basic and dynamic. In basic storage, the hard disk is divided into primary partitions, extended partitions, and logical drives. In dynamic storage, the entire physical hard disk is viewed as a single entity, which can be divided into volumes. These volumes consist of portions of one or more physical disks. You can change the storage type of the disk from basic storage to dynamic storage.

Effective data storage involves more than storing data in volumes. You must compress data, assign disk quotas, and perform disk maintenance, such as deleting files that are no longer needed, and organizing your hard disk for effective data storage. NTFS compression allows you to store large amounts of data on a hard disk by compressing entire volumes, folders, sub-folders, and files. Using Windows XP Professional, you can also limit the disk space assigned to specific users or groups by assigning disk quotas so that users will not be able to consume excess disk space.

You can also improve file access speed by using the Disk Defragmenter utility to organize the files on the hard disk into continuous clusters, rather than having them scattered over the hard disk. NTFS compression produces a self-defragmenting file system, but you will still need to run the Disk Defragmenter occasionally to optimize the speed with which the system locates and retrieves files.

## Goals

In this lesson, you will learn how to create a simple volume, upgrade a basic disk to a dynamic disk, assign disk quotas, compress and manage files and folders, and use the Disk Defragmenter to organize a hard disk.

### Lesson 5  Managing Data Storage

| Skill | Exam 70-270 Objective |
|---|---|
| 1. Introducing Storage Types | Configure and manage file systems. Configure NTFS, FAT32, or FAT file systems. Monitor, configure, and troubleshoot volumes. |
| 2. Upgrading a Basic Disk to a Dynamic Disk | Monitor and configure disks. |
| 3. Creating Volumes | Monitor, configure, and troubleshoot volumes. |
| 4. Identifying the Properties of a Disk | Basic knowledge |
| 5. Converting File Systems | Convert from one file system to another file system. |
| 6. Introducing Disk Quotas | Monitor and configure disks. |
| 7. Introducing NTFS Compression | Configure, manage, and troubleshoot file compression. |
| 8. Copying and Moving Compressed Files and Folders | Configure, manage, and troubleshoot file compression. |
| 9. Optimizing Hard Disk Performance | Optimize and troubleshoot disk performance. |

## Requirements

To complete the skills in this lesson, you will need a computer with Windows XP Professional installed, as well as a disk with free disk space to create volumes and partitions.

# skill 1

# Introducing Storage Types

## exam objective

Configure and manage file systems. Configure NTFS, FAT32, or FAT file systems. Monitor, configure, and troubleshoot volumes.

## overview

A storage type is a pattern or format in which data is stored on a hard disk. In order to store any kind of data on a hard disk, you must partition and format the hard disk. The tasks involved in setting up a hard disk for data storage are as follows:

◆ Initialize the disk with a storage type.
◆ Create partitions on a basic disk or volumes on a dynamic disk.
◆ Format the disk with a specific file system such as FAT, FAT32, or NTFS.

Windows XP Professional supports the basic and dynamic storage types.

◆ **Basic storage** is the method of dividing a hard drive into partitions, which function as logically separate units of storage **(Figure 5-1)**. Partitions are used to store different types of information separately (such as user data and applications). All versions of Microsoft Windows, MS-DOS, and Windows NT support basic storage. A disk initialized for basic storage is referred to as a basic disk and it can contain two types of partitions:

  • **Primary partition:** This type of partition can be created using the unallocated space on a basic disk. Windows XP Professional uses a primary partition, called an **active partition**, to boot the machine. Only one partition on a single hard disk drive can be designated as an active partition. Primary partitions are created only on basic disks and cannot be partitioned further. You can isolate different types of data by using multiple partitions.

  • **Extended partition:** This type of partition can be created from any free space that is left after the primary partitions have been set up. You can create only one extended partition on a basic disk. Extended partitions are divided into segments in which each segment forms a logical drive. On a basic disk, you can create up to four primary partitions, or three primary partitions and an extended partition.

◆ **Dynamic storage**, which was first supported by Windows 2000 Professional and Server, uses volumes instead of partitions. A disk that you initialize for dynamic storage is referred to as a **dynamic disk**. There is no limit on the number of volumes a dynamic disk can contain. A volume can consist of parts of one or more physical disks **(Figure 5-2)**. When you create a dynamic disk by upgrading a basic disk, the partitions are changed to volumes. Additional volumes can then be created from any leftover free space. Dynamic storage is free from the constraints that apply to basic storage. For example, unlike in basic storage, the volumes on a dynamic disk, except the boot volume and system volume, can be sized and resized without restarting Windows XP Professional. The disk configuration data is stored on the drive rather than in the operating system, which is beneficial because it supports drive recovery if the operating system becomes corrupt. On a dynamic disk, you can create the following volumes:

  • **Simple volume:** This kind of a volume contains disk space from a single disk. You can extend a simple volume to include unallocated space on the same disk. However, you cannot extend either the boot volume or the system volume. A simple volume is not fault tolerant. **Fault tolerance** is the ability of a computer or operating system to respond to a crisis without losing data.

## tip

A physical disk must be either basic or dynamic. Both storage types cannot be used on one disk. However, you can use both types of disk storage in a multi-disk system.

## caution

Before creating a partition, make sure that the drive has only three primary partitions, or two primary partitions and an extended partition.

**Figure 5-1  Basic storage**

**Figure 5-2  Dynamic storage**

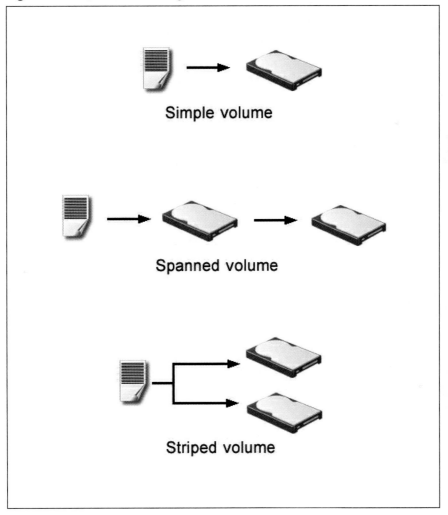

# skill 1

## *Introducing Storage Types (cont'd)*

### exam objective

Configure and manage file systems. Configure NTFS, FAT32, or FAT file systems. Monitor, configure, and troubleshoot volumes.

### overview

### tip

If you want to dual boot Windows XP Professional with Microsoft Windows 95 or MS-DOS, the active partition must be formatted as FAT because Windows 95 cannot read a partition formatted with FAT32 or NTFS.

- **Spanned volume:** This volume can include disk space from up to 32 disks. Starting from a spanned volume on the first disk, Windows XP Professional writes data, disk by disk, on each disk included in the spanned volume. A spanned volume is also not fault tolerant. Therefore, data in the entire volume is lost if any disk in the spanned volume fails.
- **Striped volume:** This volume combines areas of free space from multiple hard disks. The maximum number of hard disks that can be included in a logical striped volume is also 32. In a striped volume, data is written evenly across all of the disks so that it is added to each disk at the same rate. All hard disks in a striped volume perform the same functions as a single hard disk. Thus, Windows XP Professional can issue and process I/O commands simultaneously on all hard disks. This increases the speed of the system. Like simple and spanned volumes, striped volumes do not provide fault tolerance. Thus, if one disk in a striped volume fails, the data in the entire volume will be lost.

After you have decided on the storage type and created the necessary partitions or volumes, you must format the disk using one of the file systems supported by Windows XP Professional, **NTFS, FAT,** or **FAT32.** You should use the NTFS file system if you need partitions that feature file-level and folder-level security, disk compression, disk quotas, or encryption. NTFS is the most commonly used file system because it supports these features.

### more

When a new basic disk is added to the computer, the space on the new disk can be divided into partitions. Open the **Start** menu, right-click **My Computer**, and click **Manage** to open the **Computer Management** window. Click the **Disk Management** node. In the **Disk Management** snap-in, right-click the unallocated space where you want to create the partition and click **New Partition (Figure 5-3)**. In the **New Partition Wizard,** click [ Next > ] . In the **Select Partition Type** window, click the **Primary partition** or **Extended partition** option button to select the partition type (**Figure 5-4**). Follow the subsequent instructions in the Wizard to complete the process of creating a partition. You can also manage disks on a remote computer on the network. For example, you can create partitions as long as the remote computer is running Windows XP Professional or Windows 2000. To manage disks in a domain or on a remote computer, you must be a member of either the **Administrators** or **Server Operators** group on the remote computer.

**Figure 5-3  Creating a new partition**

**Figure 5-4  Selecting a partition type**

# skill 2

# *Upgrading a Basic Disk to a Dynamic Disk*

## exam objective

Monitor and configure disks.

## overview

Windows XP Professional uses basic storage to initialize a hard disk by default. However, you may want to convert a basic disk to a dynamic disk in order to take advantage of the additional features offered by dynamic disks. For example, if you are working on an important project and the basic disk you are working on becomes corrupt, you may end up losing data. Using a dynamic disk, you can duplicate the hard disk on one or more hard disks. This process is referred to as **disk mirroring** and it will ensure that you do not lose data.

Other important features of dynamic disks are as follows:
◆   Fault tolerance
◆   Disk striping
◆   Extending volumes without restarting the computer

You can upgrade a basic disk to a dynamic disk using the **Disk Management** snap-in. Before upgrading, you need to make sure that:
◆   All programs running on the hard disk are closed.
◆   There is at least 1 MB of unallocated space on the hard disk.
◆   The disk to be upgraded has been backed up.

When you convert a basic disk to a dynamic disk, the existing partitions on the basic disk are converted to simple volumes. A dynamic disk can be changed to a basic disk, but if you do so, you will lose all of the data stored on that disk.

## caution

Dynamic disks are unique to Windows 2000 and XP Professional and are not recognized by other operating systems.

## how to

Convert a basic disk to a dynamic disk.
1. Click **start**, right-click **My Computer** and click **Manage** to open the **Computer Management** console.
2. Click the **Disk Management** node under **Storage**.
3. In the lower-right pane of the **Computer Management** window, right-click the disk that you want to upgrade, for example, **Disk 1 (Figure 5-5)**.
4. Click the **Convert to Dynamic Disk** command to open the **Convert to Dynamic Disk** dialog box (**Figure 5-6**).
5. Click ☐ OK ☐ to open the **Disks to Convert** dialog box (**Figure 5-7**).
6. Click ☐ Convert ☐. The **Disk Management** message box opens, warning you that once you upgrade to a dynamic disk, you will not be able to boot other installed operating systems from any volume on this disk (**Figure 5-8**).
7. Click ☐ Yes ☐ to confirm the conversion of the disk. The **Convert Disk to Dynamic** message box informs you that file systems on any of the disks to be converted will be dismounted.
8. Click ☐ Yes ☐. Windows converts the disk from basic to dynamic.
9. Close the Computer Management console.

## more

Besides changing the storage type that your system uses, you can also add new disks to a computer running Windows XP Professional. You can install a new disk by attaching the disk to your computer and clicking the **Rescan Disks** command on the **Action** menu in the Computer Management console.

### Figure 5-5  Converting a disk

### Figure 5-6  The Convert to Dynamic Disk dialog box

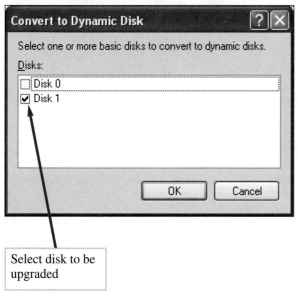

Select disk to be upgraded

### Figure 5-7  Checking the details of disks that can be upgraded

Click to convert basic disk to dynamic

### Figure 5-8  Disk Management message box

# skill 3 *Creating Volumes*

**exam objective**

Monitor, configure, and troubleshoot volumes.

**overview**

Before deciding on the type of file system that you want, you should consider which volume type best suits your needs for efficient utilization of disk space and performance. A simple volume consists of disk space from a single disk. However, it can be extended to include any available free space on the disk. To create a simple volume, you can format the hard disk with FAT, FAT32, or NTFS; however, you can extend a volume only if the hard disk is formatted with NTFS.

**how to**

Create a simple volume.

1. Click **start** and click **Control Panel** to open the Control Panel window.
2. Double-click the **Administrative Tools** icon to open the Administrative Tools window.
3. Double-click the **Computer Management** icon to open the Computer Management console.
4. Click **Disk Management** under **Storage** on the left side of the **Computer Management** console.
5. In the lower-right pane of the **Computer Management** console, right-click the unallocated space on the dynamic disk where you would like to create the volume and select the **New Volume** command (**Figure 5-9**).
6. The **New Volume Wizard** is initialized and the first screen **Welcome to the New Volume Wizard** opens.
7. Click **Next >** to display the **Select Volume Type** screen.
8. The **Simple** option button is selected by default (**Figure 5-10**). Click **Next >** to display the **Select Disks** screen.
9. In the **Select the amount of space in MB** spin box, type **200** to specify the disk size (**Figure 5-11**).
10. Click **Next >** to display the **Assign Drive Letter or Path** screen.
11. The **Assign the following drive letter** option button is selected by default. Select **F** in the list box if necessary.
12. Click **Next >** to display the **Format Volume** screen. The **Format this volume with the following settings** option button is selected by default.
13. Select a file system in the **File system** list box.
14. Make sure that **Default** is selected in the **Allocation unit size** list box.
15. Type **SimpleVol** in the **Volume label** text box to enter a label for the volume (**Figure 5-12**).
16. Select the **Perform a Quick Format** check box.
17. Click **Next >** to display the final screen, **Completing the New Volume Wizard**. This screen displays the settings that you have selected.
18. Click **Finish** to complete the process of creating a simple volume.

**more**

The process of creating a spanned volume or a striped volume is similar to the process of creating a simple volume. In the **Disk Management** snap-in, right click the **Dynamic** disk where you want to create the striped or spanned volume and then click the **New Volume** command. In the **New Volume Wizard**, click **Next >**, click either the **Striped Volume** or the **Spanned Volume** option button, and follow the remaining instructions in the Wizard.

**Figure 5-9  Selecting unallocated space on the dynamic disk to create a volume**

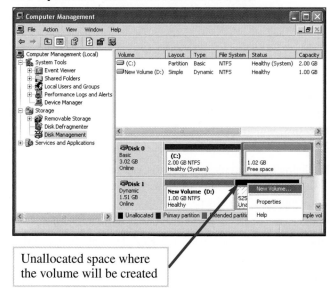

Unallocated space where the volume will be created

**Figure 5-10  Selecting the volume type**

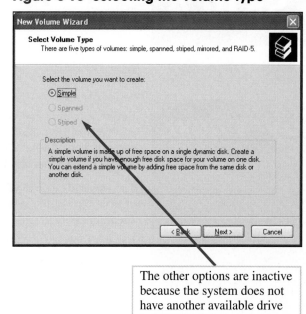

The other options are inactive because the system does not have another available drive

**Figure 5-11  Selecting the disk where the volume will be created**

Set volume size

Remove all selected disks

Remove the selected dynamic disk

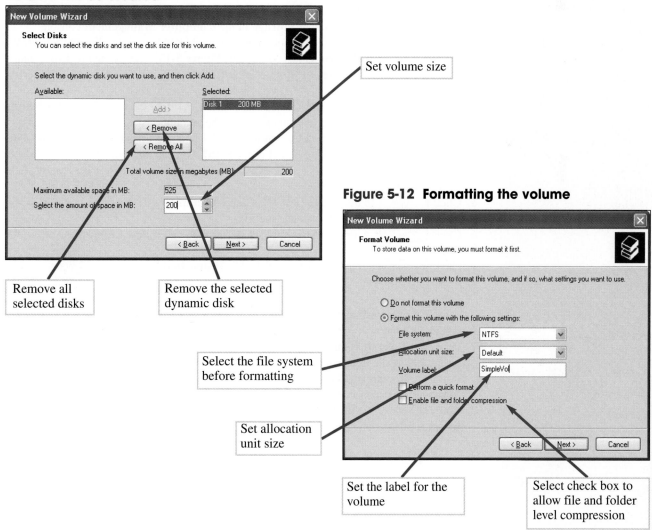

**Figure 5-12  Formatting the volume**

Select the file system before formatting

Set allocation unit size

Set the label for the volume

Select check box to allow file and folder level compression

# skill 4 — *Identifying the Properties of a Disk*

**exam objective**

Basic knowledge

## overview

Before installing new software on your system, you should determine the amount of free space available on the disk so that you can make sure that there is enough disk space to install and run the software. **Disk properties**, which are the attributes of your hard disk, can be found in the **Properties** dialog box.

The **General** tab in the Properties dialog box provides information on the volume label, type of disk, type of file system, and the disk usage. In this window, you can also run the **Disk Cleanup** utility to remove deleted, temporary, and downloaded files.

Use the **Tools** tab to perform volume error checking, backup, and disk defragmentation.

Use the **Hardware** tab to check the properties of the physical disks and troubleshoot physical disk problems.

The **Sharing** tab allows you to set the network shared volume parameters and permissions.

The **Security** tab provides NTFS access permissions.

Use the **Quota** tab to set user quotas for NTFS volumes.

## how to

Use the **Disk Cleanup** utility in the **Properties** dialog box.

1. Click **Disk Management** under **Storage** in the **Computer Management** console.
2. In the lower-right pane of the Computer Management window, right-click the **SimpleVol (F:)** drive and click the **Properties** command **(Figure 5-13)** to open the Properties dialog box. Review the properties of SimpleVol (F:) **(Figure 5-14)** and close the Properties dialog box.
3. Right-click the **(C:)** drive and select **Properties**. Click [ Disk Cleanup ]. The **Disk Cleanup** message box opens, and the system calculates the amount of space that can be freed.
4. Select the check boxes of the files you want to delete in the **Files to delete** list box in the **Disk Cleanup for (C:)** dialog box **(Figure 5-15)**. You can also choose to compress old files. You can view the details for the files selected in the **Files to delete** list box by clicking the [ View Files ] button.
5. Click [ OK ] to delete the files. The **Disk Cleanup for (C:)** message box asks you if you are sure that you want to delete the files.
6. Click [ Yes ]. A progress bar appears so that you can follow the progress of the file deletion.
7. Click [ OK ] to close the **Local Disk (C:) Properties** dialog box.
8. Close the Computer Management console.

### caution

When you run the Disk Cleanup utility, the scanning process can take several minutes. It is best to run this utility when the machine is not in use.

## more

You can use the **Refresh** and **Rescan Disks** commands on the **Action** menu in the **Computer Management** window to update the information in the **Disk Management** snap-in.

◆ Using the **Refresh** command, you can update the drive letter, file system, volume, and removable media information.

◆ Using the **Rescan Disks** command, you can update the hardware information in the **Disk Management** snap-in and scan the attached disks for any disk configuration changes. You can also use this command to update information on removable media, basic volumes, file systems, and drive letters.

### caution

Rescanning disks may take several minutes, depending on the number of hardware devices installed.

**Figure 5-13  Viewing the Properties for SimpleVol (F:)**

**Figure 5-14  Properties dialog box for a disk**

Click the Disk Cleanup button to start disk cleanup

**Figure 5-15  Listing the files that can be deleted**

Select check box for files to be deleted

# skill 5

# *Converting File Systems*

## exam objective

Convert from one file system to another file system.

## overview

### caution

FAT and FAT32 can be upgraded to the NTFS format without data loss. However, to convert from NTFS to FAT, you will have to back-up the data on the volume, delete the volume, recreate it, format it, and then restore the data from the backup.

Windows XP Professional supports the FAT, FAT32, and NTFS file systems. The FAT (File Allocation Table) formatting structure provides backward compatibility with other operating systems, such as DOS, Windows 3.1x and Windows for Workgroups, thus allowing upgrades from other operating systems to Windows XP. Under Windows XP, FAT supports volumes up to 4 GB in size, while the updated version, FAT32, supports volumes up to 2 TB in size (although, if you create the FAT32 partition on a Windows 2000 or Windows XP system, this size is limited to 32 GB). The FAT file system is most efficient for volumes smaller than 256 MB, and can contain 512 entries in the root directory. However, FAT does not support file-level compression and has no file security capabilities. FAT32 can provide adequate functionality for a desktop station, but it is not usually used with servers.

NTFS supports large volumes, is most efficient for volumes larger than 512 MB, and can contain unlimited entries in the root directory. It also has capabilities for file-level compression and security, and you can set disk quotas to restrict users to a specific amount of space on a drive.

## how to

### caution

You cannot convert the active drive. If you only have a C: drive, the Convert utility will warn you that it cannot gain exclusive access to the drive and will ask you if you want to schedule the conversion for the next time the system starts.

Convert a **FAT** partition to **NTFS**.

1. Click **start**, point to **All Programs**, point to **Accessories**, and click **Command Prompt** to open the **Command Prompt** window.
2. Type **convert *x*: /fs:ntfs /v** and press **[Enter]**. The *x* represents the drive letter of whichever volume you are converting and the **/v** indicates that the command should be run in **verbose mode**. In verbose mode, all of the messages generated during the conversion are displayed **(Figure 5-16)**. Note that if you have a dual-boot system, only Windows 2000, XP, and NT 4.0 with Service Pack 4 or later applied can read from and write to NTFS 5.0 volumes or partitions.
3. Enter **SimpleVol** as the current volume label and press **[Enter]** to perform the conversion.
4. Type **Exit** and press **[Enter]** to exit the command prompt window and return to the Windows XP desktop.

## more

Both FAT16 and FAT32 are referred to as FAT unless it is important to differentiate between the two. The FAT file system, and in most cases, the FAT32 file system, can also be used if you want to be able to dual boot the system with Windows XP and another operating system. However, NTFS is the preferred file system because it supports larger volumes, file level compression and security, and many other useful features. The Convert utility used in the exercise converts your disk while maintaining all of the files on the disk. However, it is still recommended that you back up the drive before the conversion. You can also reformat a volume or partition in the Disk Management snap-in by right-clicking the volume and selecting **Format** on the context menu **(Figure 5-17)**. The **Format (drive letter)** dialog box will open **(Figure 5-18)**. In the **File system** list box, select the format you want and click **OK**. A warning dialog box will caution you that formatting will erase all data on the volume **(Figure 5-19)**.

**Figure 5-16  Convert command in the Command Prompt window**

Convert command
for converting
from FAT to NTFS

**Figure 5-17  Formatting a drive in the Disk Management snap-in**

**Figure 5-18  Formatting a volume**

**Figure 5-19  The Format F: warning message**

# skill 6  *Introducing Disk Quotas*

## exam objective

Monitor and configure disks.

## overview

When users are asked to back up their important data on a central machine, they will often dump their entire data load onto that machine. This can drastically decrease the available space on the disk. Disk quotas enable you to track and control disk usage on a per-user, per-volume basis. The number of files and folders owned by a user determines their disk space allotment.

Windows XP Professional collects information about disk usage for all users who have files and folders on a volume.

### caution

Disk quotas can be applied only to Windows 2000 and XP NTFS volumes.

You set disk quotas on the **Quota** tab in the **Properties** dialog box for an NTFS volume or partition. You can set two values: the **disk limit** and the **warning level**. The disk limit designates the amount of space a user is allowed to use and the warning level sets the storage level at which a warning will be issued to the user. For example, if a user's disk space requirement generally does not exceed 60 MB, you can set the disk limit for a particular volume to 60 MB and the warning level to 55 MB. When the user's storage capacity exceeds 55 MB, a warning will be issued. The user can then either delete some files to free space or ask the Administrator to increase the quota limit.

By default, Windows XP Professional allows only members of the **Administrator** group to view and modify quota settings. The disk quotas you assign are based on the sizes of uncompressed files, so take this into account when determining the appropriate storage requirement for a user.

## how to

Limit the disk space of a drive to **20 MB** and set the warning level to **16 MB** for the **Guest** account.

1. Click ⟨*start*⟩, point to **All Programs**, point to **Accessories**, and click **Windows Explorer** to open the Explorer window.
2. Click the **My Computer** icon, right-click the **F:** drive in the left panel, and click the **Properties** command to open the Properties dialog box on the **General** tab.
3. Click the **Quota** tab to display the options for setting disk quotas. By default, disk quotas are disabled.
4. Select the **Enable quota management** check box.
5. Select the **Deny disk space to users exceeding quota limit** check box. This will send an "out of disk space" message when users exceed the limit. To track and generate hard disk usage information without preventing users from saving data, you can clear the **Deny disk space to users exceeding quota limit** check box.
6. Select the **Limit disk space to** option button and type **20** in the **Limit disk space to** text box.
7. Type **16** in the **Set warning level to** text box.
8. Specify the unit size by opening the list boxes next to the **Limit disk space to** and **Set warning level to** text boxes and selecting the MB option for both values (**Figure 5-20**).
9. Click ⟨Apply⟩. The **Disk Quota** message box opens (**Figure 5-21**) to warn you that if you enable disk quotas, the volume will be rescanned to update disk usage statistics.
10. Click ⟨OK⟩ to enable disk quotas.
11. Click ⟨Quota Entries...⟩ on the **Quota** tab to open the **Quota Entries for SimpleVol (F:)** window.
12. Click **Quota** on the Menu bar and click the **New Quota Entry** command (**Figure 5-22**) to open the **Select Users** dialog box.
13. Make sure the object type is set to Users and the location is set to the local computer name. Type **Guest** in the **Enter the object names to select** text box.

### tip

Right clicking Start and selecting Explorer will also open the Windows Explorer window.

### Figure 5-20  Setting Disk Quotas

Check box selected to deny extra disk space

Size of the quota

Select to log an event when the quota limit has been exceeded

Select to log an event when the quota warning level is reached

### Figure 5-21  Disk Quota message box

### Figure 5-22  Quota Entries for SimpleVol (F:) window

# skill 6

## Introducing Disk Quotas (cont'd)

### exam objective

Monitor and configure disks.

### how to

14. Click [ OK ] to open the **Add New Quota Entry** dialog box (**Figure 5-23**).
15. Type **10** in the **Limit disk space to** text box.
16. Type **8** in the **Set warning level to** text box.
17. Select the MB unit size in the **Limit disk space to** and **Set warning level to** list boxes.
18. Click [ OK ] to return to the **Quota Entries** window (**Figure 5-24**). The quota entry you created for the Guest account now appears in the window.
19. Close the **Quota Entries** window.
20. Click [ OK ] to close the **Properties** dialog box.
21. Close Windows Explorer.

### more

The guidelines for assigning disk quotas are listed below:

◆ Log on as the Administrator when you need to install additional Windows XP Professional components and applications so that the disk space that you use is not deducted from the disk quota limit for your user account.

◆ Set restrictive limits for all user accounts; however, you can modify these limits according to the requirements of the users. For example, you can increase the limit for users who need to store large files.

◆ If a user currently has files stored on the volume, you must either delete those files, move them elsewhere, or have another user such as the Administrator take ownership of the files before you can delete the quota entry for the user account.

◆ You do not have to deny disk space to users as you did in the exercise. Instead, you can set disk quotas simply to keep an eye on how much space users are consuming. Then, you can periodically check the Quota Entries window. If a user has exceeded the warning level, a yellow warning symbol will appear in the Status column. If a user has exceeded the quota, a red circle with an exclamation point will immediately inform you that the user is above the limit (**Figure 5-25**). You can either increase the disk space allotment for the user, set the deny disk space to users exceeding limit option, or inform the user that he or she must delete some files or store new documents elsewhere.

**Figure 5-23  Setting a quota entry for a user**

Quota limit for
selected user(s)

**Figure 5-24  Quota entry set for the Guest account**

**Figure 5-25  Quota entry status**

Status of quota limit—
whether it is OK, has
exceeded the warning
level, or exceeded the
quota level

# skill 7

# *Introducing NTFS Compression*

## exam objective

Configure, manage, and troubleshoot file compression.

## overview

You can use **NTFS compression** to compress files and folders such as Word or other Office documents and bitmaps to conserve disk space. All NTFS files and folders have a compression state, either compressed or uncompressed. Compressed files and folders exhibit the following features:

◆ **Display color:** Compressed files and folders can be displayed in a different color to distinguish them from uncompressed files and folders.

◆ **Space allocation:** When using disk quotas on an NTFS volume, usage is based on the uncompressed file size. For example, if there is enough space in the NTFS volume for you to store a compressed file, but there is not enough space to store that file in the uncompressed format, when you try to copy the file to the disk, you will receive an error message stating that there is not enough disk space available for the file.

◆ **Access to compressed files and folders by applications:** Compressed NTFS files are automatically uncompressed when accessed by Microsoft Windows-based or MS-DOS-based applications. For example, when an application, such as **Microsoft Excel**, opens a compressed file, the file is automatically uncompressed by the NTFS file system. When the file is closed or saved, it is again compressed.

### tip

Windows XP includes built-in support for writing data to CD-R and CD-RW, provided your computer is equipped with a CD-R or CD-RW drive. Burning CDs is an effective way to save hard disk space while maintaining data archives.

## how to

Compress a folder in an **NTFS** volume and change the display color of the compressed folder.

1. Create a folder called **Compfolder** on the C: drive.
2. Right-click the **Compfolder** folder and click **Properties** to open the **Compfolder Properties** dialog box.
3. Click [ Advanced... ] to open the **Advanced Attributes** dialog box.
4. Select the **Compress contents to save disk space** check box in the **Compress or Encrypt attributes** section (**Figure 5-26**).
5. Click [ OK ] to close **Advanced Attributes** dialog box and display the **Properties** dialog box for the folder.
6. Click [ OK ] to close the **Properties** dialog box for the folder.
7. Next, you need to change the display color for the compressed folder. Right-click [ *ij start* ] and click the **Explore** command.
8. Open the **Tools** menu and click the **Folder Options** command to open the **Folder Options** dialog box.
9. Click the **View** tab.
10. In the **Advanced Settings** list box, select the **Display encrypted or compressed files in color** check box (**Figure 5-27**).
11. Click [ OK ] to apply the changes. The names of the compressed files and folders are displayed in blue in the **Windows Explorer** window.

### tip

Steps 7–11 will only be necessary if the default setting, Display encrypted or compressed files in color, has been turned off previously.

## more

To troubleshoot file compression, you may have to recompress or remove file compression from the file, or restore the backup of a file that was damaged due to compression.

Windows XP Professional offers a new method of file compression in the form of **compressed folders**, which are standard ZIP files but appear as normal folders. Files that you move into a compressed folder are compressed automatically. If you move a file out of the compressed folder, the file will no longer be compressed. However, you can open and work with files that are in a compressed folder just like you can open and work with uncompressed files. When you close a file that is in a compressed folder, the file is compressed automatically again. Some programs will even run from a compressed folder. Using compressed folders will enable you to save space and store more files on a particular disk just like .zip archives do. To create a compressed folder, open **Windows Explorer**, click **File**, point to **New**, and click **Compressed (zipped) Folder**. The compressed folder, with a zipper icon to identify it as such, will appear in the current folder (**Figure 5-28**).

**Figure 5-26  Setting the Compress attribute**

Select check box to compress data

**Figure 5-27  Displaying compressed NTFS files and folders in color**

Select check box to change color of compressed folders

**Figure 5-28  Creating a compressed folder in Windows Explorer**

Compressed folders can be created on both NTFS and FAT volumes and are compatible with other popular zip programs

# skill 8

## Copying and Moving Compressed Files and Folders

**exam objective**

Configure, manage, and troubleshoot file compression.

**overview**

While working with a compressed file, you might need to copy it onto another machine or move it from its original location. When you copy or move a file, the compression state of the file depends on whether you are copying or moving the file from a different location within the same NTFS volume, between two NTFS volumes, or between NTFS and FAT volumes.

Changes in the compression state of a file or folder are different depending on the situation (**Figure 5-29**):

◆ When a file is copied from one location to another within an NTFS volume or between two NTFS volumes, it inherits the compression state of the target folder.

◆ Moving a file or folder within an NTFS volume does not change the compression state of the file or folder. The file or folder retains its original compression state. For example, if you move a file or folder within the same volume, it retains its original compression state, either compressed or uncompressed. However, if you move it to another volume, it will inherit the attribute of the destination folder.

◆ You can compress only NTFS files using the Advanced Attributes dialog box. Thus, when you move or copy a compressed file or folder from an NTFS volume to a FAT volume, or to a floppy disk, Windows XP uncompresses the file or folder automatically. To compress files and folders on a FAT volume, create a compressed folder in Windows Explorer by clicking File, pointing to New, and clicking Compressed (zipped) Folder.

**more**

When compressing files and folders, choose appropriate file types because some file types can be compressed to a larger extent than others. For example, .zip, .cab, .gif, and .jpg files are already compressed, while **bitmap** files can be compressed to less than 50 percent of their original size, and application files can often be compressed to less than 75 percent of their original size.

Compress static data and not files that are frequently changed because compressing and uncompressing files is a waste of system time. Copying a compressed file may affect the performance of the system because Windows XP Professional must first uncompress the file, copy it, and then compress it again, using valuable system resources.

**Figure 5-29 Copying compressed files and folders**

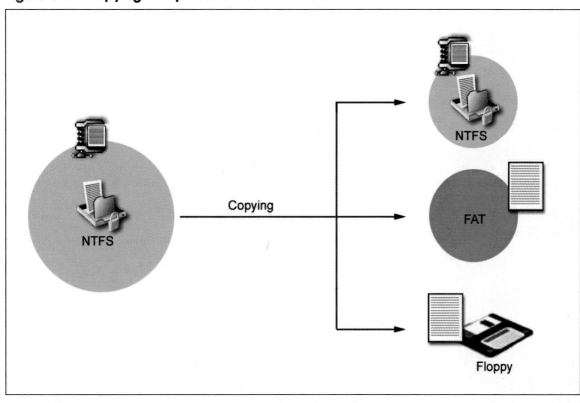

# skill 9 *Optimizing Hard Disk Performance*

## exam objective

Optimize and troubleshoot disk performance.

## overview

When you save files and folders in Windows XP Professional under the FAT or FAT32 file system, they are saved in the first available space on the hard disk (NTFS will attempt to find a segment on the hard disk that is large enough for the entire file, regardless of whether it is the first available space). This causes file and folder fragmentation, as pieces or fragments of large files are stored on different parts of the hard disk. As data becomes increasingly scattered over different parts of the hard disk, the computer takes longer to access files, leading to a general deterioration in system performance. The computer takes longer to create new files and folders because free space is also scattered on the hard disk. You can use the **Disk defragmenter** utility to reorganize the files on the hard disk. The Disk Defragmenter rearranges files and unused space moving the segments of each file and folder to one location so that they occupy a single, contiguous space on the hard disk. This process of finding and consolidating files and folders, called **defragmentation,** enables the system to access files quickly and makes programs run faster.

### tip
You can defragment FAT and FAT32, as well as NTFS volumes.

The **Disk Defragmenter** window is divided into three parts:

◆ **Partitions to analyze and defragment:** Lists the volumes that you can view and defragment. It also provides details such as the type of **File System,** amount of **Free Space,** and drive **Capacity.**

◆ **Analysis display:** Provides a graphical depiction of how the selected volume is fragmented.

◆ **Defragmentation display:** Provides a constantly-updating representation of the volume during defragmentation.

## how to

Analyze a volume to determine its fragmentation level and defragment the volume using the **Disk Defragmenter**.

1. Right-click ⟨ *start* ⟩ and click **Explore** to open the **Windows Explorer** window.
2. Right-click the **C:** drive and click **Properties** to open the **Properties** dialog box for the **C:** drive.
3. Click the **Tools** tab **(Figure 5-30)**.
4. Click ⟨ Defragment Now... ⟩ to open the **Disk Defragmenter** window **(Figure 5-31)**.
5. Click ⟨ Analyze ⟩. The system analyzes the fragmentation state of the disk. When the analysis is complete, the **Analysis Complete** dialog box opens.
6. It will be recommended either that you defragment or that the volume does not need defragmenting **(Figure 5-32)**.
7. Click ⟨ View Report ⟩ to open the **Analysis Report** dialog box **(Figure 5-33)**, which displays information about the fragmented files.
8. Click ⟨ Defragment ⟩ to start the defragmenting process **(Figure 5-34)**.
9. After the disk is defragmented, the **Disk Defragmenter** message box will display.
10. Click ⟨ Close ⟩ to close the message box.
11. Close the Disk Defragment window and the Properties dialog box. Close Windows Explorer.

## more

Run the **Disk Defragmenter** only when your computer is not being used extensively. Defragmentation can adversely affect the time it takes to access other disk-based resources. It is a good practice to defragment your local hard disk at least once a month to prevent the accumulation of fragmented files, and also before installing large applications. Analyze the volume and defragment it, if necessary, to ensure faster installation and to speed up access to resources.

**Figure 5-30  The Tools tab in the Properties dialog box**

Click the Defragment Now button to start the defragmenting process

**Figure 5-31  The Disk Defragmenter**

**Figure 5-32  Analyzing the fragmentation of the disk**

**Figure 5-33  The Analysis Report dialog box**

**Figure 5-34  Defragmenting the disk**

# Summary

- There are two storage types: basic and dynamic.
- Basic storage or a basic disk can have primary partitions, extended partitions, and logical drives.
- Dynamic storage or a dynamic disk can be divided into simple, spanned, or striped volumes.
- Disk Cleanup is used to free space on hard drives.
- Before upgrading a basic disk to a dynamic disk, make sure that 1 MB of free disk space is available and that all running programs are closed.
- FAT provides backward compatibility with other operating systems, thus allowing upgrades from other operating systems to Windows XP.
- NTFS is preferred over FAT because it supports file-level compression and security, larger volumes, and other useful features.
- Reverting from a dynamic disk to a basic disk will result in the loss of data.
- Disk quotas can be assigned only in Windows 2000 or XP Professional on an NTFS volume or partition.

- NTFS compression can reduce some types of files to less than half of their original sizes.
- NTFS automatically uncompresses files when they are accessed by Microsoft Windows-based or MS DOS-based applications.
- Windows XP Professional automatically uncompresses an NTFS file or folder copied or moved to a FAT folder.
- Compressed files and folders can be displayed in a different color to distinguish them from uncompressed files and folders.
- Preferably, static data should be compressed to avoid performance degradation.
- The Disk Defragmenter utility rearranges the files on the hard disk in order to increase the speed of access and retrieval.
- A hard disk should be defragmented once a month, and also before installing large applications.

# Key Terms

Active partition
Basic storage
Compressed folders
Defragmentation
Disk cleanup
Disk defragmenter
Disk limit
Disk mirroring

Disk properties
Disk quotas
Disk striping
Dynamic disk
Dynamic storage
Extended partition
Fault tolerance

Logical drives
NTFS compression
Primary partition
Simple volume
Spanned volume
Striped volume
Verbose mode

# Test Yourself

1. You have 3 hard disks of 2 GB each on your Windows XP Professional computers. You want to save data sequentially on your hard disk, that is, the first hard disk should be filled before the system starts writing on the second disk, and so on. What kind of a volume will you format the hard disk with?
   a. Simple
   b. Spanned
   c. Striped
   d. Mirrored

2. The compression state of a file or folder does not change when you:
   a. Move a file or folder within an NTFS volume.
   b. Copy a file or folder between NTFS volumes.

   c. Copy or move a file or folder to a FAT volume.
   d. Copy or move a file or folder to a floppy.

3. Your computer is being used as the backup computer for your team. You want to limit the amount of data that can be stored on your computer by the team. However, the Properties dialog box does not show the Quota tab. The reason could be that: (Choose all that apply.)
   a. It is not an NTFS volume.
   b. You are not logged on as an Administrator.
   c. You are not viewing the properties for a volume or partition.
   d. The operating system is not configured properly.

**4.** As the System Administrator of a company, you need to set up and configure new training software on the computers in the training room. At present, the computers in the training room are running Windows 98. However, the prerequisite for installing new software is that the computer should be running Windows XP. The users want to use both Windows 98 and Windows XP and be able to access all of the files on their computers while using either operating system. You also want to provide them with optimum performance of the system. What should you do?

   a.  Create and format a FAT32 Partition.

   b.  Create and format an NTFS volume.

   c.  Create and format a FAT16 Partition.

   d.  Configure Windows XP Professional to enable disk compression.

   e.  Configure Windows XP Professional to implement dynamic volumes.

**5.** Which of the following volumes does Windows XP Professional support? (Choose all that apply.)

   a.  Striped volumes

   b.  Mirrored volumes

   c.  Spanned volumes

   d.  Striped volumes with parity

**6.** Which of the following disks can be upgraded to dynamic disks?

   a.  Disks on laptops

   b.  Disks that have less than 1 MB free disk space

   c.  Disks that are part of a striped set

   d.  Disks that are part of a volume set

**7.** Which of the following statements are true for disk quotas?

   a.  Quotas are set for individuals and not groups.

   b.  You can implement quotas on FAT volumes.

   c.  By default, quotas are enabled for all volumes.

   d.  The Administrator group is exempt from quota limit.

   e.  You cannot configure guest accounts for disk quotas.

## Projects: On Your Own

**1.** Create a volume.

   a.  Log on as **Administrator**.

   b.  Access the **Disk Management** option.

   c.  Right-click the unallocated disk space on the lower right pane.

   d.  Initialize the **New Volume Wizard**.

   e.  Create a **Simple** volume.

**2.** Defragment a disk.

   a.  Open **Windows Explorer**.

   b.  Access the **Properties** dialog box.

   c.  Access the **Tools** tab.

   d.  Access the **Defragment** tab.

   e.  **Defragment** drive **C:**.

**3.** Use the Disk Cleanup utility.

   a.  Open **Windows Explorer**.

   b.  Access the **Properties** dialog box.

   c.  Click the **Disk Cleanup** Tab.

   d.  Run the utility on drive **C:**.

## Problem Solving Scenarios

The Financial Manager at Market Forecasts, Inc., a market forecasting firm, complains that his employees are experiencing long delays in accessing and saving files on the server. Employees create detailed financial spreadsheets and Microsoft Word documents for the companies they analyze, and these files are frequently updated. The employees also store a large library of financial research documents on the file server. Each of these documents is accessed infrequently, and they are all read-only. The Financial Manager has asked you to find out what is wrong. After interviewing the employees, you discover that they frequently save updated spreadsheets as new files with the current date, keeping copies of each day's work as a new file. Old files are supposed to be deleted after two weeks, but often are not. Disk space on the file server is being consumed at an alarming rate. Moreover, the frequent writing to and deleting from the disk is causing files to be saved on different sectors of the disk. Outline the steps you would take to improve the efficiency of data storage on the server.

# 6

# Installing and Configuring Network Protocols

**A** protocol is a set of rules and conventions for sending information over a network. These rules manage the content, format, timing, sequencing, and error control for messages exchanged among network devices. The protocol explains how the clients and servers on a network must arrange data in order to deliver it to other computers on the network and how they can interpret data that is delivered to them. In addition, computers on a network must "speak the same language" in order for data transfers to be possible. Windows XP Professional supports several protocols that networks follow when transferring data. The main protocol is TCP/IP (Transmission Control Protocol/Internet Protocol), which is the core protocol for the Internet. TCP/IP is a scalable and routable protocol. It is scalable because it can be used for both large and small networks, and data can be transferred across networks and between computers using different operating systems with widely varying structural designs. TCP/IP is a routable protocol because it ensures that data can cross a router, which is a special computer used to transfer data between networks. Networking protocols today are put into practice as a suite of protocols. A protocol suite is a combination of several different networking applications and services that function jointly to make network communications possible. The protocol suite outlines the stages involved in packaging data so that it can be sent and received on the network. Each packet of data must be correctly formatted, ordered, compressed, and checked for errors. Therefore, each computer on a network must be configured with the same protocol suite if intercommunication between them is required.

If your network uses computers running Microsoft operating systems and you must access the resources on servers running a version of Netware that predates 4.0, you must use the NWLink protocol. Netware 4.0 servers and above support TCP/IP. NWLink can also be used in an exclusively Microsoft environment; however, you will not be able to use Active Directory because it is only compatible with TCP/IP. If a Microsoft client needs to access file and print resources on a NetWare server, Client Service for NetWare (CSNW), the redirector that is compatible with NetWare, must also be installed. Alternatively, you can install Novell's redirector, Novell Client for Windows NT/2000/XP.

Network bindings are used to set the order in which the protocols that are configured on a system will be used. When a network connection is initiated, the bindings set the order in which the system will attempt to use protocols to establish links.

On computers running Windows XP Professional, you can use Network Bridge to connect segments of a LAN without implementing routers. Network Bridge greatly simplifies the process of combining multiple media types that use multiple protocols in one network.

## Goals

In this lesson, you will learn how to configure TCP/IP to use a static IP address, troubleshoot TCP/IP problems, and install the NWLink protocol. You will also learn about other protocols supported by Windows XP Professional, and how to configure network bindings and Network Bridge.

### Lesson 6  Installing and Configuring Network Protocols

| Skill | Exam 70-270 Objective |
|---|---|
| 1. Introducing the TCP/IP Protocol | Basic knowledge |
| 2. Configuring TCP/IP to Use a Static IP Address | Configure and troubleshoot the TCP/IP protocol. |
| 3. Introducing WINS and DNS | Basic knowledge |
| 4. Troubleshooting TCP/IP Problems | Configure and troubleshoot the TCP/IP protocol. |
| 5. Installing NWLink on a System | Basic knowledge |
| 6. Introducing Other Protocols Supported by Windows XP Professional | Basic knowledge |
| 7. Configuring Network Bindings | Configure and troubleshoot the TCP/IP protocol. |
| 8. Configuring Network Bridge | Basic knowledge |
| 9. Optimizing and Troubleshooting Network Performance | Basic knowledge |

## Requirements

A system with Windows XP Professional installed on it.

# skill 1 — *Introducing the TCP/IP Protocol*

**exam objective**

Basic knowledge

**overview**

**TCP/IP (Transmission Control Protocol/Internet Protocol)** is a set of protocols that enables you to route messages between networks. A message is broken down into packets before it is transmitted. Although the packets can follow different routes, they generally follow one common path. When the packets reach their destination, TCP/IP uses a sequencing function to ensure that they are reassembled in the correct order to recreate the original message. It also includes procedures for acknowledging the delivery of the correct packets and for requesting that lost or damaged packets be resent.

TCP/IP defines the rules for connecting networks to each other and for communication between computers on a network. These rules are used to correct errors, manage the routing and delivery of data, and to control all aspects of data transmission. Protocols within the TCP/IP protocol suite also provide logon, file, and print services, as well as other services such as FTP (File Transfer Protocol), Telnet, and DNS (Domain Name Service).

TCP/IP is suitable for most large networks because it is supported by most operating systems and multiple hardware configurations. It provides an infrastructure that is cross-platform, client/server based, scalable, dependable, and time-tested. IP is a routable protocol, meaning that it can be used to send packets across a router so that messages can leave physical and logical networks. Since a domain-based Windows network uses the TCP/IP protocol suite, understanding how a TCP/IP network operates is the equivalent of understanding how an Active Directory-based network functions.

From a conceptual standpoint, the TCP/IP suite can be viewed as consisting of four layers **(Figure 6-1)**:

- ◆ Application
- ◆ Transport
- ◆ Internet
- ◆ Network Interface

**Application layer:** This layer is used by applications to gain access to the network. The application layer is at the top of the conceptual model. It includes many standard TCP/IP utilities and services such as FTP, Telnet, and DNS.

**Transport layer:** This layer sets up communication sessions between computers and makes sure that messages are reassembled in the correct sequence without errors, and with no data duplication or data loss. The transport protocol used depends upon the method chosen to deliver the data. It is a function of the standards associated with the type of data transmission. There are two types of transport layer protocols:

- ◆ **Transmission Control Protocol (TCP):** TCP is used to establish a connection between two hosts so that they can exchange streams of data. Whereas IP handles packets, TCP handles streams of data. TCP establishes the connections between sending and receiving computers and provides connection-oriented communications. Connection-oriented communications require the sender and the receiver to establish a channel. The term "channel" refers to any communication path between two computers or devices. It can refer to the physical medium such as the wires or network cables, or to the virtual circuits that act as a direct connection. Virtual circuits are connections between two hosts, usually on a packet-switching network, through which they can communicate as though they have a dedicated connection, when in fact the packets may be following a very different

**Figure 6-1  The four layers in the TCP/IP suite**

| | | |
|---|---|---|
| **NetBIOS applications** | **Windows Sockets applications** | **Application** |
| **NetBT** | **Windows Sockets** | |
| **UDP** | **TCP** | **Transport** |
| ARP   IP   ICMP  IGMP | | **Internet** |
| **LAN technologies: Ethernet, Token Ring, FDDI** | **WAN technologies: Serial Lines, Frame Relay, ATM** | **Network Interface** |

# skill 1

## *Introducing the TCP/IP Protocol*
### *(cont'd)*

**exam objective**

Basic knowledge

**overview**

route. TCP ensures that data is reassembled in the correct sequence, with no data loss or duplication, and it reports the receipt of data. The receiver reports back to the sender whether it received all of the consecutively numbered packets, or if some need to be resent. If the sender does not receive this notification, either the acknowledgement has been lost, or the connection has been broken. The sender will then keep retransmitting the data at increasingly longer intervals, until finally, if it still receives no acknowledgement, it breaks the connection. Not all applications use TCP. However, many use UDP.

◆ **User Datagram Protocol (UDP):** UDP is used by applications to transfer small amounts of data at one time. It provides **connectionless communication**, wherein the host can send a message to the recipient without establishing a channel. This is in contrast to connection-oriented protocols, which require a channel to be established between the sender and receiver before any messages are transmitted. Like TCP, UDP runs on top of IP networks, but it provides very few recovery services. Instead, it provides a direct way to send and receive datagrams on an IP network and is often used for broadcasting messages. A datagram is a unit of data similar to a packet. A connectionless protocol, such as UDP, is used by a host to send a message to the network with the destination address, but there is no guarantee that it will reach its destination. There is no acknowledgement that the data packets have been received and, therefore, no data retransmissions. This is why it is considered to be a less reliable protocol (**Table 6-1**).

**Internet layer:** This layer determines what route data will take when the data packets are transferred from the source computer to the destination computer. The Internet layer ultimately forms packets by encapsulating segments or datagrams. The term packet refers to a piece of a message transmitted over a packet-switching network. Packets contain the source computer address and the destination address in addition to the data. In IP networks, packets are often called datagrams. **Routers** are computers that interconnect the multiple computers on a network or the Internet. They use headers, as well as a routing table, to determine where packets go. They also use ICMP (Internet Control Message Protocol), an extension of IP, to communicate with each other and configure the best route between any two hosts. Routing algorithms are also sometimes used at this level to determine the best available path for the data packets, although often the paths are statically defined in the routing table.

The Internet layer consists of the following protocols:

◆ **Internet Protocol (IP):** This protocol in the TCP/IP protocol suite is responsible for addressing and routing. It provides the addressing scheme for the network and for the Internet. Packets sent between two hosts may take different routes, but IP does not ensure either the arrival of the packets or their correct sequencing. It relies on other protocols to perform these functions. Routing protocols also include several key IP protocols such as Routing Internet Protocol (RIP), Open Shortest Path First (OSPF) protocol, and Border Gateway Protocol (BGP).

◆ **Address Resolution Protocol (ARP):** This protocol is used to map an IP address to the **Media Access Control (MAC)** address. A MAC address is a unique 48-bit or 6-byte number, usually represented as 12 hexadecimal digits. It is also referred to as a hardware address, physical address, or Ethernet address. There are two types of ARP resolution:

**Table 6-1 Internet Applications and Underlying Internet Protocols**

| Application | Application-layer protocol | Underlying transport protocol |
|---|---|---|
| Electronic mail | SMTP | TCP |
| Remote terminal access | Telnet | TCP |
| World Wide Web (www) | HTTP | TCP |
| File transfer | FTP | TCP |
| Remote terminal access | NFS | typically UDP |
| Streaming multimedia | proprietary | typically UDP |
| Internet telephony | proprietary | typically UDP |
| Network management | SNMP | typically UDP |
| Name translation | DNS | typically UDP |

The Internet uses two transport protocols: TCP and UDP. TCP is used where reliability is more important than speed. UDP is used where speed is more important than reliability.

TCP requires the establishment of a connection between sender and receiver, and maintains a connection state that includes buffers, congestion control, sequencing of packets, and acknowledgment numbers. This makes TCP extremely reliable and manageable. UDP, in contrast, has no regulation on its send rate; it is "connectionless" in the sense that it sends data without verifying a connection—it simply blasts out data. UDP is very fast, in part because it does not have all the overhead of TCP. UDP has only 8 bytes of overhead for a data segment compared to 20 bytes for a TCP segment. For Internet phone, multimedia, and real-time Internet conferencing, UDP is preferred. Internet network managers and other users, however, do not appreciate UDP's ability to congest networks. A part of the "World Wide Wait" is due to UDP's unmanageable behavior.

# *Introducing the TCP/IP Protocol*
## *(cont'd)*

**exam objective**

Basic knowledge

**overview**

local and remote. In either case, first the ARP request is initiated, and it is determined whether the IP address is local or remote. If it is local, the ARP cache is checked. Address mappings are stored in the ARP cache for future reference. In local ARP resolution, if no mapping is found in the ARP cache, an ARP request is broadcast to all hosts. When the target host validates the IP address in the request, it generates an ARP reply. The sender then updates its ARP cache. If the IP address is identified as remote, the IP address of the default gateway must be determined. The ARP cache is checked for the MAC address of the default gateway. If it is not found, an ARP request for the default gateway's hardware address is generated. After the response is received from the default gateway, the data packet is sent to the default gateway. Then the default gateway must determine if the address is local or remote. If it is local, it broadcasts an ARP request and obtains the MAC address. If it is remote, the hardware address for the next default gateway must be determined, and the process is repeated.

◆ **Internet Control Message Protocol (ICMP):** This protocol enables hosts to exchange status and error information. ICMP supports packets containing error, control, and informational messages. This information, also called an ICMP packet, is used by higher-level protocols to solve transmission problems and by network administrators to discover where network problems are located. ICMP packets are also used by the ping utility to find out if an IP device on the network is working.

◆ **Internet Group Management Protocol (IGMP):** This protocol is used so that multicast routers on a network can communicate with all member devices in a multicast group. On a network, broadcasting refers to sending data to everyone on the network, while multicasting refers to a transmission method for sending identical data to a select group of recipients. The server can transmit a single stream, regardless of how many clients have requested it. When the data stream crosses a multicast-enabled switch or router, it is copied to the paths where the clients that requested the stream are located. IGMP is used to establish memberships in certain groups on a network and to communicate group membership information to the multicast routers. It is used by a host computer to tell its local routers to send messages to it that are addressed to a particular multicast group.

**Network Interface layer:** This layer is at the base of the TCP/IP conceptual model. It consists of the physical media, network adapter card, and driver information. When sending data, the network interface layer encapsulates packets into frames that will be sent across the network as a series of bits. It is responsible for placing TCP/IP packets on the network medium and receiving TCP/IP packets off the network medium (**Figure 6-2**). The Network Interface layer interacts directly with the physical medium on which the TCP/IP packets will be traveling. The Network Interface layer can connect to a wide variety of older media (like Ethernet and X.25), as well as to new optical media like FDDI and Sonet (not shown). This layer makes TCP/IP communication independent of whatever physical media evolve in the future, and provides organizations tremendous flexibility in the choice of physical media.

**Figure 6-2  Network Interface layer**

# skill 2

# Configuring TCP/IP to Use a Static IP Address

## exam objective

Configure and troubleshoot the TCP/IP protocol.

## overview

TCP/IP works in conjunction with the **Dynamic Host Configuration Protocol (DHCP)** service. DHCP provides TCP/IP configuration information to client computers running Windows XP Professional, Windows 2000 Professional, Windows 95, Windows 98, and many other types of client operating systems. The default setup in Windows XP Professional is that the operating system will retrieve an IP address from another computer on the network called a DHCP server. The DHCP server's job is to dynamically assign or "lease" IP addresses from a range of IP addresses to computers as they boot. This simplifies the administration of TCP/IP configuration because it automates the process of assigning IP addresses to clients. However, certain computers on the network must be assigned a static IP address. For example, a data application server may have to have an IP address that remains constant so that your customers or employees can access it. The DHCP server itself must have a constant IP address. Print servers will also have a static IP address and you may decide to assign a static IP address to each server running either the WINS or DNS service, which are discussed in the next skill. In these cases, you can assign IP addresses manually or you can use client reservations. A client reservation refers to a specific IP address within a range of permanently reserved addresses that is only leased to a specific DHCP client. In this way you can ensure that a host will always receive the same IP address.

IP addresses consist of four octets separated by periods. Within these four octets, there are two identifiers: one for the network (the network ID) and one for the computer or host (the host ID). Another number, called the **subnet mask**, which is also made up of four octets, is used by TCP/IP to divide the network ID from the host ID. For example, the subnet mask is used to determine if an IP address is on the local network or on a remote network. A subnet, therefore, is a part of a network that has a portion of the address in common. On TCP/IP networks, subnets have the same IP address prefix and the subnet mask helps to identify the subnet to which an IP address belongs.

A **default gateway** must also be set up in order to connect your network to other networks, unless your computer is using its local routing table. **Routing tables** are used to provide routers with the directions they will use to forward data packets to locations on other networks. Routing table data will determine how to send a data packet and where to send it. A router uses the destination address and the information in the table, which outlines potential routes. The routes are delineated into the steps it will take to forward the data packets from the origin and through the succeeding routers to reach the destination. You can keep a routing table that contains an entry for every computer or network with which you need to communicate. However, continually updating static routes is not practical and generally a default gateway is used instead. A default gateway is simply a router that links networks. The typical setup is that the DHCP server will dynamically assign IP addresses, subnet masks, and default gateways when a computer establishes its connection to the network during startup. It can also automatically assign a DNS server address.

**Table 6-2** explains the elements involved in configuring a static TCP/IP address.

## how to

Configure TCP/IP to use a static IP address.
1. Click ⟦ *start* ⟧, click **Control Panel** on the Start menu, and double-click the **Network Connections** icon to open the **Network Connections** window (**Figure 6-3**).
2. Right-click the **Local Area Connection** icon and select **Properties** to open the **Local Area Connection Properties** dialog box.

## Table 6-2 Configuring a static TCP/IP address

| Option | Description |
| --- | --- |
| IP address | Used to identify a TCP/IP host as a logical 32-bit address divided into four octets. Computers connected to a TCP/IP network are referred to as TCP/IP hosts. For identification purposes, you must have a unique IP address for each network adapter card in a computer running TCP/IP. An IP address consists of a network ID and a host ID. The network ID identifies all hosts on the network, while the host ID represents a specific computer. For example, in the IP address **198.154.1.207**, 198.154.1 is the network ID and 207 is the host ID. |
| Subnet mask | Another 32-bit number, divided into four octets, that is used to break up the IP address into the two parts: the network ID and the host ID. The subnet mask blocks or "masks" a part of the IP address in order to differentiate between the two. Companies generally either use the same subnet mask throughout their network or a VLSM (variable length subnet mask) subnetting scheme. Variable length subnetting is a method of allocating subnetted network IDs that use subnet masks of different sizes. |
| Default gateway | Gateways or routers are used to connect different networks. A default gateway acts as an intermediate device between hosts on different network segments. TCP/IP sends packets to the IP address for the router, which acts as a gateway to remote networks. The default gateway dispatches the data packets to the destination network.<br><br>You must configure an IP address with a default gateway in order to make remote communications possible. You do not need to configure a default gateway unless you are connecting to an external network. |

### Figure 6-3 Network Connections window

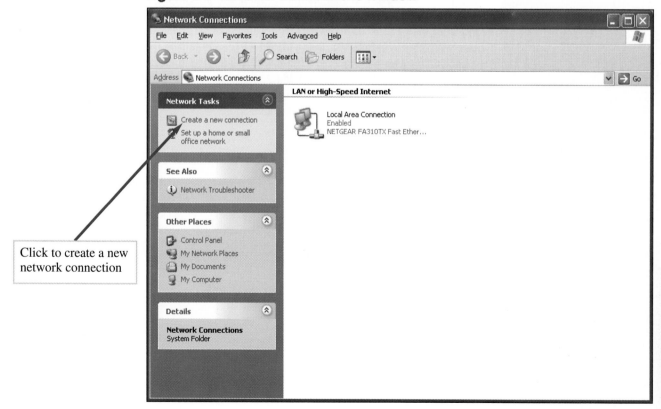

Click to create a new network connection

# skill 2

## Configuring TCP/IP to Use a Static IP Address *(cont'd)*

**exam objective**

Configure and troubleshoot the TCP/IP protocol.

## how to

3. Select **Internet Protocol (TCP/IP) (Figure 6-4)**.
4. Click [ Properties ] to open the **Internet Protocol (TCP/IP) Properties** dialog box.
5. Click the **Use the following IP address** option button.
6. Click in the **IP address** text box and type **198.164.1.204 (Figure 6-5)**.
7. Click in the **Subnet mask** text box. Windows XP Professional automatically assigns an appropriate subnet mask according to the given IP address.
8. Click [ OK ] to confirm the settings.
9. Click [ OK ] to close the Local Area Connection Properties dialog box.
10. Close the Network Connections window.

## more

When TCP/IP is installed on a Windows XP Professional computer, it is automatically set up to be a DHCP client; a Windows XP Professional computer cannot be a DHCP server. The DHCP service is only included in the Windows 2000 Server and Windows Server 2003 products. However, a DHCP client does not necessarily need a DHCP server in order to use a dynamic IP address. If a DHCP client cannot locate a DHCP server, it will use a service called automatic private IP addressing (APIPA) to randomly choose an IP address from a private APIPA address series, which is not in use on the Internet. In this way, computers on a LAN, where there is no DHCP server, or on a network, where the DHCP server is down, can still be assigned an IP address and communicate with other computers on the same subnet. APIPA generates an address and broadcasts that address across the network. If no other computer responds to this address, the computer knows that it can assign the address to itself. The IP address will always be in the format 169.254.x.x and the subnet mask will always be 255.255.0.0. However, APIPA cannot assign a default gateway, so remote access, such as communication on the Internet or with outside networks, will not be possible. Windows XP computers that have used APIPA to assign themselves an IP address can usually only communicate with other Windows (98, 2000, ME or XP) computers on the same subnet that have also assigned themselves an IP address using APIPA. The IP addresses generated by APIPA are in the range from 169.254.0.0 to 169.254.255.255 because the Internet Assigned Numbers Authority (IANA) has set aside this series of addresses for this purpose. This ensures that the IP address does not conflict with any routable addresses.

### tip

On a subnet where there is no DHCP server, Windows XP Professional computers can still use DHCP rather than APIPA if there is a router on the subnet that supports DHCP/BOOTP forwarding, or if there is a Windows 2000, 2003, or NT4 Server that is running the DHCP Relay Agent service. The DHCP Relay Agent has the IP address for the remote DHCP Server and can transfer messages between subnets.

**Figure 6-4  Local Area Connection Properties dialog box**

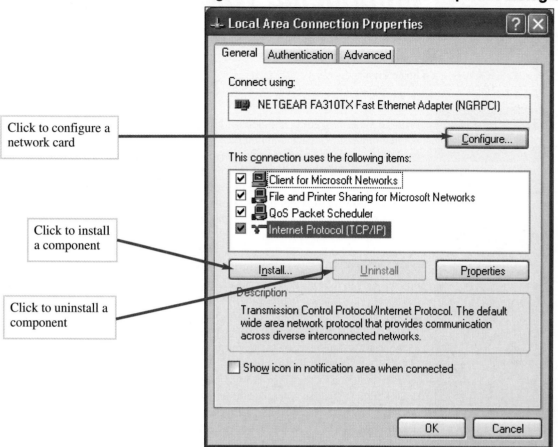

**Figure 6-5  Configuring a static IP address**

# skill 3   *Introducing WINS and DNS*

**exam objective**

Basic knowledge

**overview**

Prior to Windows 2000, the default computer naming convention was NetBIOS. As you learned in Lesson 2, each computer has a computer or NetBIOS name. The NetBIOS name is used to identify the computer on a Microsoft network. When network users want to find your computer on a TCP/IP network using the NetBIOS name, there must be a method for assigning or mapping an IP address to the computer name. This method is the **WINS (Windows Internet Naming Service)** database on a WINS server, which functions as the lookup directory. The WINS database is dynamically updated so that as client computers are assigned different IP addresses by the DHCP server, the database stays current. Since NetBIOS was used by default in Windows NT 4, setting up a WINS server is necessary if some of the client computers on your network are running that operating system or Windows 9.x or NT 3.5. If you do not set up WINS and there are no LMHOSTS files configured (see below), users can still browse on their subnet using NetBIOS names, but they cannot make connections to computers on other subnets using NetBIOS names. Furthermore, in the absence of WINS or an LMHOSTS file, NetBIOS packets must be broadcast to all computers on the network in order to request and announce network resources. To configure WINS, open the Internet Protocol (TCP/IP) Properties dialog box and click the **Advanced** button to open the **Advanced TCP/IP Settings** dialog box. On the **WINS** tab, select the **Enable NetBIOS over TCP/IP** option button. You can enter a static IP address in the **WINS addresses, in order of use** text box, or you can have the DHCP server assign the address for the WINS server by leaving the default **Use NetBIOS setting from the DHCP server** option button selected (**Figure 6-6**).

In the Advanced TCP/IP Settings dialog box, you will also see the **Enable LMHOSTS lookup** check box selected by default. HOSTS and LMHOSTS are text files, stored on the local computer, that also contain name-to-IP address correlations. The LMHOSTS file correlates NetBIOS names to IP addresses. The HOSTS file correlates host names or fully qualified domain names (FQDNs) to IP addresses. These files must be updated manually by an Administrator. Since this would be extremely difficult on a network in which IP addresses are being dynamically generated, these files are now all but obsolete as a method for mapping IP addresses to computer or domain names. However, you should know of their existence as the precursor to WINS and DNS. DNS, like the HOSTS file, correlates FQDNs to IP addresses. Name resolution, which will be discussed in detail in Lesson 17, simply means the process we have been discussing of translating names into corresponding IP addresses.

**DNS (Domain Name Service)**, which will also be discussed in detail in Lesson 17, is the main name resolution service for Windows XP. It is a method of accessing computers on a TCP/IP network using the FQDN or host name. Fully qualified domain names consist of a host and a domain name, including a top-level domain, which is the attached Internet suffix, com, edu, gov, org, mil, net, or a country code such as ca for Canada. They look like the URLs you use to access a Web page on the Internet, for example, **www.ebay.com**. Although it is not required that TCP/IP networks use domain names, you cannot have an Active Directory domain-based network without a DNS server. The DNS service only runs on Windows 2000 or 2003 Server, but you will need to know how to configure a Windows XP Professional client computer to use the DNS server for the name resolution process. Usually, you will leave the **Obtain DNS server address automatically** option button selected in the **Internet Protocol (TCP/IP) Properties** dialog box (**Figure 6-7**). This will result in the IP address for the DNS server being automatically retrieved from the DHCP server. The other method is to manually enter a static IP address for the DNS server. First, you must select the **Use the following DNS server addresses** option button, and then you can type in the IP addresses for a preferred and an alternate DNS server (if applicable) in the corresponding text boxes.

**Figure 6-6  WINS tab in the Advanced TCP/IP
Settings dialog box**

**Figure 6-6  WINS tab in the Advanced TCP/IP
Settings dialog box**

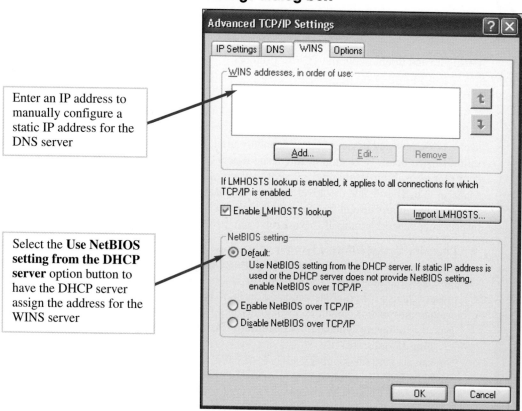

Enter an IP address to manually configure a static IP address for the DNS server

Select the **Use NetBIOS setting from the DHCP server** option button to have the DHCP server assign the address for the WINS server

**Figure 6-7  Configuring a Windows XP Professional
computer to be a DNS client**

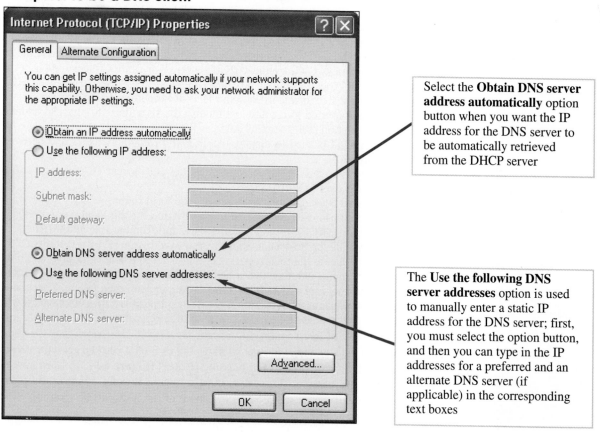

Select the **Obtain DNS server address automatically** option button when you want the IP address for the DNS server to be automatically retrieved from the DHCP server

The **Use the following DNS server addresses** option is used to manually enter a static IP address for the DNS server; first, you must select the option button, and then you can type in the IP addresses for a preferred and an alternate DNS server (if applicable) in the corresponding text boxes

# skill 4 | Troubleshooting TCP/IP Problems

**exam objective**

Configure and troubleshoot the TCP/IP protocol.

**overview**

Network Administrators will find that they must frequently troubleshoot TCP/IP problems. Client configuration problems are frequent. More frequent, however, are everyday calamities such as disconnected devices and accidentally unplugged cables. Before you use any of the utilities listed below, you should troubleshoot network communication problems by making sure that everything is plugged in, switched on, and connected. Next, check the Device Manager to make sure that the driver for the network adapter is set up and functioning properly. Finally, you can use several troubleshooting utilities included in Windows XP Professional to inspect your network protocols. All are run from the Command Prompt window.

◆ **Ping:** The **Packet Internet Groper** utility is used to test TCP/IP configurations and identify connection failures. A packet of information is sent to check the connection between the client and the server. The Ping utility also reports the interval required for the complete exchange (original message and reply) to take place. You can use the ping utility to provide information about the availability and functionality of a particular TCP/IP host. Type the following syntax at the **Command Prompt:**

   **ping IP_address**

You can also use the loopback address, 127.0.0.1 (or simply enter ping loopback) to confirm that TCP/IP is bound to your network adapter. The Reply From message will be repeated four times if the protocol is bound to the network adapter when you use the loopback address, and whenever you have successfully communicated with an IP address.

◆ **Ipconfig:** This utility is used to confirm that the TCP/IP protocol is running. You can run it without any switches to get the IP address, subnet mask, and default gateway to confirm that the configuration has been initialized. You can also use the ipconfig command with the **/all** switch to include information about any DNS or WINS servers, to find out if the IP address is static or dynamic and discover the name of the host, and to make sure that there is no duplicate IP address. If there is a duplicate address, the IP address and subnet mask will be 0.0.0.0. You use the **/release** switch with ipconfig to release the IP address that has been assigned by the DHCP server. You cannot release a leased IP address in the TCP/IP Properties dialog box. The **/renew** switch is used to renew a DHCP address, which you are also unable to do in the TCP/IP Properties dialog box.

◆ **ARP:** This command is used to display and modify the IP address to physical address (MAC address) translation tables used by Address Resolution Protocol.

◆ **Netstat:** This command is used to display the TCP/IP protocol statistics and network connections (**Figure 6-8**).

◆ **Nbtstat:** This utility is used to display protocol statistics and current TCP/IP connections using **NBT** (NetBIOS over TCP/IP).

◆ **Route:** This command is used to display or modify the local routing table.

◆ **Hostname:** This utility is used to validate the host name for the local computer. The Remote Copy Protocol (RCP), remote shell (RSH), and Remote Execution (REXEC) utilities will authenticate the host name after it is retrieved by the Hostname utility.

◆ **Tracert:** This utility checks the route a packet is following to reach its destination point. Tracert shows every router interface that a TCP/IP packet passes through on the path to the destination. It can be used to determine where a data transmission failure is occurring and/or where a slow transmission is taking place. If data transmission is complete, it will trace the route the packets have taken to get from sender to receiver.

To find out how to use any of these commands, except Tracert and Hostname, type the command followed by **/?** in the Command Prompt window. For example, you can get information on the ARP command by typing **ARP/?** and pressing **[Enter] (Figure 6-9)**. To learn how to use the Tracert utility, simply type **Tracert** in the Command Prompt window and press **[Enter]**. If you enter **hostname** at the prompt, the name of the host will be returned. This command has no other switches or parameters.

**Figure 6-8  Using the Netstat utility**

**Figure 6-9  Using the ARP utility**

# skill 4

## *Troubleshooting TCP/IP Problems*
### *(cont'd)*

**exam objective**

Configure and troubleshoot the TCP/IP protocol.

**how to**

Test the TCP/IP configuration of your computer by using the **ipconfig** and **ping** commands.
1. Open the **Command Prompt** window.
2. At the Command Prompt, type **ipconfig/all** and press **[Enter]**. This displays the details of the **Ethernet adapter Local Area Connection (Figure 6-10)**. (If you want to stop the ipconfig results from scrolling off the screen, type ipconfig/all|**more**. Now you can press the **[Spacebar]** to scroll down and view further results.)
3. At the Command Prompt, type the default value, **ping 127.0.0.1** and press **[Enter]**. This IP address is called the **local loopback** address and it is used to confirm that TCP/IP is bound to your network adapter. If a "Reply from" message is repeated four times **(Figure 6-11)**, your network adapter is properly configured.

**more**

In addition to the troubleshooting utilities, and those used to test TCP/IP connectivity, Windows XP Professional includes other useful utilities and protocols. For example, **File Transfer Protocol (FTP)** is used to transfer files between a computer running Windows XP Professional and a TCP/IP host running both server software and FTP. It also provides directory and file handling services such as listing directory contents, deleting files, and selecting file formats. **Trivial File Transfer Protocol (TFTP)**, a simpler form of FTP, is used to transfer files between a computer running Windows XP Professional and a TCP/IP host running both server software and TFTP. TFTP uses the User Datagram Protocol (UDP), and thus includes no security features, acknowledgements, or data retransmissions. Servers often use it to boot diskless workstations or routers. **Remote Copy Protocol (RCP)** is used to copy files between computers running Windows XP Professional and hosts that support the RCP service (frequently a UNIX host). **Remote shell (RSH)** is used to execute commands on a UNIX host.

**Telnet** is a terminal emulation protocol that runs over TCP/IP. When you run Telnet from a client machine and connect to a server on the network, you can enter commands which will be carried out as if you were performing them directly on the server terminal. Telnet is often used to manage a remote Web server. It is used to control the server and to communicate with other servers on the network. You can also connect to a computer on the Internet that supports Telnet to run programs from that computer. Telnet was the first way in which remote access was accomplished. **Finger** is a utility, supported by UNIX computers, that is used to retrieve information about users, including their user name and how long they have been logged on. You can find out who is logged on to a remote network by first connecting to a Telnet server and then typing **finger** at the prompt. Most Internet host computers no longer support finger due to security concerns.

**Figure 6-10  Using the ipconfig/all command**

```
C:\  Command Prompt                                                    _ □ ×

Microsoft Windows XP [Version 5.1.2600]
(C) Copyright 1985-2001 Microsoft Corp.

C:\Documents and Settings\user1>ipconfig/all

Windows IP Configuration

        Host Name . . . . . . . . . . . . : comp1
        Primary Dns Suffix  . . . . . . . :
        Node Type . . . . . . . . . . . . : Unknown
        IP Routing Enabled. . . . . . . . : No
        WINS Proxy Enabled. . . . . . . . : No

Ethernet adapter Local Area Connection:

        Connection-specific DNS Suffix  . :
        Description . . . . . . . . . . . : NETGEAR FA310TX Fast Ethernet Adapte
r (NGRPCI)
        Physical Address. . . . . . . . . : 00-02-E3-07-BD-7C
        Dhcp Enabled. . . . . . . . . . . : Yes
        Autoconfiguration Enabled . . . . : Yes
        IP Address. . . . . . . . . . . . : 192.168.0.59
        Subnet Mask . . . . . . . . . . . : 255.255.255.0
        Default Gateway . . . . . . . . . : 192.168.0.1
        DHCP Server . . . . . . . . . . . : 192.168.0.1
```

**Figure 6-11  Using the ping 127.0.0.1 command**

```
C:\  Command Prompt                                                    _ □ ×

C:\Documents and Settings\user1>ping 127.0.0.1

Pinging 127.0.0.1 with 32 bytes of data:

Reply from 127.0.0.1: bytes=32 time<1ms TTL=128
Reply from 127.0.0.1: bytes=32 time<1ms TTL=128
Reply from 127.0.0.1: bytes=32 time<1ms TTL=128
Reply from 127.0.0.1: bytes=32 time<1ms TTL=128

Ping statistics for 127.0.0.1:
    Packets: Sent = 4, Received = 4, Lost = 0 (0% loss),
Approximate round trip times in milli-seconds:
    Minimum = 0ms, Maximum = 0ms, Average = 0ms

C:\Documents and Settings\user1>_
```

# skill 5

## *Installing NWLink on a System*

**exam objective**

Basic knowledge

## overview

The IPX/SPX (Internet Package eXchange/Sequenced Packet eXchange)/NetBIOS compatible protocol, also known more simply as **NWLink**, is used on Microsoft networks so that they can communicate with Novell Netware networks. It can also be used in exclusively Microsoft environments, but the advantages of Active Directory will be foregone because Active Directory needs TCP/IP in order to function. Therefore, NWLink is mainly used to access resources on NetWare servers. Simply configuring the NWLink protocol, however, is not always sufficient. NWLink is all you will need to connect to client/server applications (for example, a NetWare file server) that are running on a NetWare server. However, in order to access file and print resources on a Netware server, a software component called a redirector is needed to determine if a request for a resource should be handled locally by one of the disk drivers or by the network server. The redirector for Windows networks is called Client for Microsoft Networks, or the Workstation service, while the redirector for a Novell NetWare server is called Client Service for Netware (CSNW). Either a CSNW redirector or the Novell client must be installed in order for a Microsoft client to access file or print resources on a NetWare server. NWLink runs programs that use Winsock or NetBIOS-over-IPX interfaces. Configuring NWLink entails setting up three different components: the frame type, the network number, and the internal network number.

NWLink supports the following types of networking APIs that provide interprocess communication (IPC) services:

◆ **Winsock:** Winsock supports existing NetWare applications that are compatible with the IPX/ SPX socket interface in NetWare applications.
◆ **NetBIOS over IPX:** Communication with a computer running Windows XP Professional and NWLink NetBIOS is made possible using the **NetBIOS** protocol.

Resources on a Windows 2000 server, such as Microsoft SQL Server or Microsoft SNA Server, can also be accessed with NWLink. You can install **File and Print Service for Netware (FPNW)** to enable a Netware or Macintosh client to use file and print resources on a computer running Windows 2000 Server. However, FPNW is not included with Windows 2000 by default. In addition, to run FPNW, you cannot use the generic internal network number provided by Windows 2000 by default when installing NWLink. You must specify an internal network number manually.

## how to

Install NWLink and Client Service for Netware (CSNW) on your computer.

1. Click ⟨start⟩, click **Control Panel**, and double-click the **Network Connections** icon in the Control Panel window to open the **Network Connections** window.
2. Right-click the **Local Area Connection** icon and click **Properties** on the shortcut menu to open the **Local Area Connection Properties** dialog box (**Figure 6-12**).
3. Click [ Install... ] to open the **Select Network Component Type** dialog box.
4. Select the **Protocol** option in the **Click the type of network component you want to install** box (**Figure 6-13**).
5. Click [ Add... ]. The **Select Network Protocol** dialog box opens.

## tip

If you have not already installed NWLink, it will be automatically co-installed as part of installing CSNW.

**Figure 6-12  The Local Area Connection Properties dialog box**

**Figure 6-13  Select Network Component Type dialog box**

# skill 5

# Installing NWLink on a System *(cont'd)*

## exam objective

Basic knowledge

## how to

6. Select the **NWLink IPX/SPX/NetBIOS Compatible Transport Protocol** option in the **Network Protocol** section (**Figure 6-14**).

7. Click [ OK ] to apply the changes. In addition to the NWLink IPX/SPX/NetBIOS Compatible Transport Protocol, the NWLink NetBIOS protocol has been added (**Figure 6-15**). This is to ensure backward compatibility with earlier Microsoft networks. The additional protocol is needed to make IPX/SPX NetBIOS compatible.

8. Click [ Install... ] to open the **Select Network Component Type** dialog box again.

9. Select **Client** in the **Click the type of network component you want to install** box.

10. Click [ Add... ] to open The **Select Network Client** dialog box.

11. Select **Client Service for Netware** in the **Network Client** box. (This will be the only client available if the default Windows XP Professional installation was performed.) Click [ OK ]. The **Local Network** dialog box informs you that you must restart the computer. Click **Yes** to restart the computer.

12. When the computer has rebooted, the **Select NetWare Logon** dialog box opens. You must have ready the name of the NDS (Novell Directory Services) **tree**, and the location of the server object (**context**) to which the client computer will be connecting. If you have access to a Netware Server and this information, enter it in the **Tree** and **Context** text boxes. If not, simply click **Cancel** and then **Yes** in the **NetWare Network** dialog box to continue without setting a preferred server.

13. Open the Control Panel window. A **CSNW** icon has been added to the Control Panel. You can enter or change the default **NDS** tree and context settings, and other **CSNW** settings by double-clicking this icon to open the Client Service for Netware dialog box (**Figure 6-16**).

## more

The NWLink protocol is configured in the Properties dialog box for the protocol. You open this dialog box by opening the Properties dialog box for the connection (for example, Local Area Connection Properties), selecting the **NWLink IPX/SPX/NetBIOS Compatible Transport Protocol** in the **Components checked are used by this connection** box on the **General** tab, and clicking the **Properties** button. It is configured by setting the following three components:

◆ Frame type
◆ Network number
◆ Internal network number

**Frame type:** The frame type determines how the network card will format data. The frame type of the Windows XP computer and the NetWare server must match or data will not be formatted in the same way and you will not be able to connect to the server. The default setting is AutoDetect, which means that the operating system will attempt to figure out the right frame type when you install NWLink. If it cannot do so, the default 802.2 will be used. This is the default frame type for newer versions of NetWare. You can manually set the frame type so that you do not have to rely on AutoDetect.

**Network Number:** The network number is a unique number for each NWLink network segment that must be specified for each frame type on a network adapter card. All computers on an NWLink network segment must have the same network number in order to be able to see each other. In this case, you can rely on Windows XP Professional to automatically find the network number and, for the most part, you will not need to change this setting. In fact, if there is a technical problem and you must manually assign a network number to the NWLink protocol, you must use the **Registry Editor**. This involves providing two corresponding entries:

**Figure 6-14  Select Network Protocol dialog box**

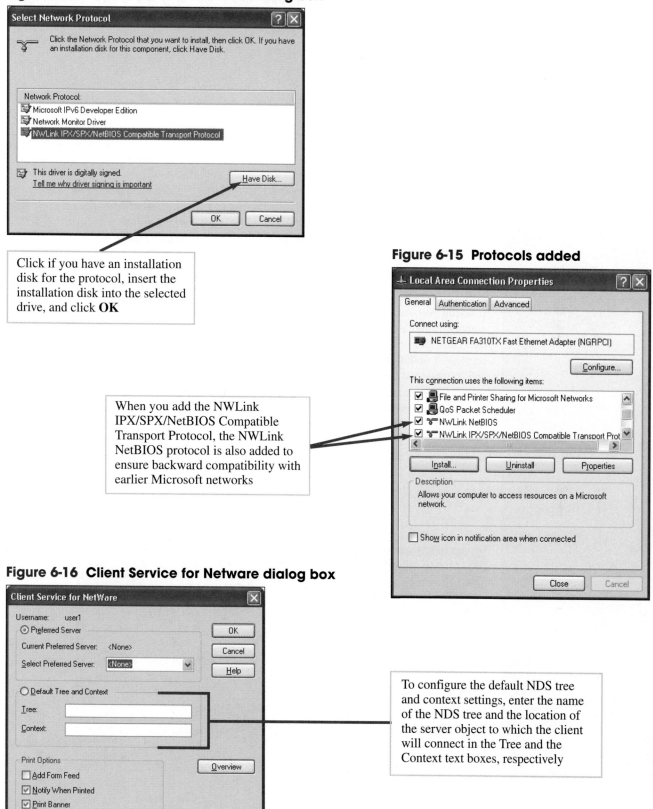

Click if you have an installation disk for the protocol, insert the installation disk into the selected drive, and click **OK**

**Figure 6-15  Protocols added**

When you add the NWLink IPX/SPX/NetBIOS Compatible Transport Protocol, the NWLink NetBIOS protocol is also added to ensure backward compatibility with earlier Microsoft networks

**Figure 6-16  Client Service for Netware dialog box**

To configure the default NDS tree and context settings, enter the name of the NDS tree and the location of the server object to which the client will connect in the Tree and the Context text boxes, respectively

# skill 5

## Installing NWLink on a System (cont'd)

**exam objective**

Basic knowledge

### more

**tip**

If the NetWare server is functioning as a router, there can be two different frame types, but this is not the optimum setup, and inefficient connections may result.

◆ **NetworkNumber:** A four-byte-long hexadecimal number used to specify the network number for the adapter. To view the network number, frame type, and device in use on a computer running Windows XP Professional, type **ipxroute config** as the NetworkNumber entry at the Command Prompt (**Figure 6-17**).
The NetworkNumber entry uses the **REG_MULTI_SZ** data type. If you specify the value for this entry as **zero**, NWLink takes the network number from the network. The default frame type for **NetWare 2.2** and **NetWare 3.11** on Ethernet networks is **802.3**. The default frame type for **NetWare 3.12** and later is **802.2** (**Figure 6-18**).

◆ **PktType:** The packet form (for example, Ethernet_II, SNAP, or ArcNet) is identified in the PktType.entry, and it uses the REG_MULTI_SZ data type. **Table 6-3** lists the PktType entry and packet forms supported by NWLink.

**Internal Network Number:** The internal network number, also called a virtual network number, is another unique number that is used for internal routing purposes to identify a specific computer on the network. It is an eight-digit hexadecimal number that by default is given a value of **00000000**. You must change this when FPNW is installed on a Windows 2000 server, when NWLink is configured on multiple adapters in the computer, when there are several different frame types on one adapter, or if an application is using the **NetWare Service Advertising Protocol (SAP)** such as **SQL Server** and **SNA Server**.

### Table 6-3 NWLink supports the following Pkt Type entries and packet forms

| Value | Packet form |
| --- | --- |
| 0 | Ethernet_II |
| 1 | Ethernet_802.3 |
| 2 | Ethernet_802.2 |
| 3 | SNAP |
| 4 | ArcNet |
| FF (default) | Auto-detect |

**Figure 6-17  Using the ipxroute config command**

**Figure 6-18  NWLink/SPX/NetBIOS Compatible Transport Protocol Properties dialog box**

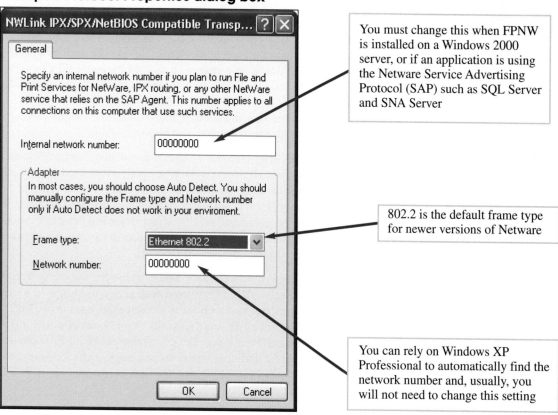

<table>
<tr><td>**skill 6**</td><td>*Introducing Other Protocols Supported by Windows XP Professional*</td></tr>
</table>

**exam objective**    Basic knowledge

## overview

Windows XP Professional supports several other protocols that increase authentication, encryption, and multilinking options, as shown in **(Figure 6-19)**. These protocols are as follows:

- Extensible Authentication Protocol (EAP)
- Remote Authentication Dial-In User Service (RADIUS)
- Internet Protocol Security (IPSec)
- Layer Two Tunneling Protocol (L2TP)
- Bandwidth Allocation Protocol (BAP)

**Extensible Authentication Protocol (EAP):** EAP performs arbitrary authentication of a dial-in connection and is an extension of the Point-to-Point Protocol (PPP). PPP works with Dial-Up, PPTP (Point-to-Point Tunneling Protocol), and L2TP clients. EAP uses the following to extend logon security services so that smart cards or other types of certificates can be used as part of the authentication process:

- **Generic token cards:** These are physical cards that provide passwords. They can handle several authentication methods, such as codes that change with each use.
- **MD5-CHAP (Message Digest 5 Challenge Handshake Authentication Protocol):** User names and passwords are encrypted with an MD5 algorithm using this protocol.
- **Transport Layer Security (TLS):** This protocol is used to support smart card authentication systems.

**Remote Authentication Dial-In User Service (RADIUS):** RADIUS is an authentication and accounting system used to facilitate the management of remote access services. It provides a suite of services designed to check user logon information to make sure it is correct in order to authorize access to a system. It is used by many ISPs to authenticate users as they dial in to the ISP. Logon data is forwarded to a RADIUS server, which verifies the data and authorizes access to the ISP system. The suite of services provided by RADIUS is referred to as **AAA** for authentication, authorization, and usage accounting. The protocol design is vendor-independent, reliable, and highly scalable.

**Internet Protocol Security (IPSec):** To ensure secure communication over IP networks, the Internet Protocol Security (IPSec) is used. IPSec policies are used to configure IPSec security services, which provide a variable level of protection for most types of traffic in existing networks. Configuring IPSec policies can fulfill the security requirements for a user, group, application, domain, or global enterprise. You can create and manage IPSec policies using the **IP Security Policy Management** snap-in. This snap-in can be added to any custom console created with the **Microsoft Management Console**.

**Layer Two Tunneling Protocol (L2TP):** This is an Internet tunneling protocol used to create a channel through a network. L2TP is used with IPSec to provide a secure tunnel for the transfer of data. The encryption functions of IPSec can be used in conjunction with L2TP to create a secure VPN (Virtual Private Network). A VPN can also use only PPTP (Point-to-Point Tunneling Protocol), which provides encryption via PPP. PPP (Point-to-Point Protocol) is the default selection for dial-up connections because it is efficient, supports error-checking, and can be used on NetBEUI, TCP/IP, and IPX/SPX networks.

**Bandwidth Allocation Protocol (BAP):** This protocol is used when you use multilinking to combine phone lines and modems to optimize bandwidth. BAP and BACP (Bandwidth Allocation Control Protocol) are sometimes used interchangeably. They provide bandwidth-on-demand functionality and are PPP control protocols.

## tip

Microsoft has scaled back its support of some older protocols whose functions are generally replaced by newer protocols. You can no longer install Microsoft Data Link Control (DLC) and NetBIOS Enhanced User Interface (NetBEUI) from the Local Area Connection dialog box. Network Monitor Driver, which reports statistics about activity detected by the network card to a Windows server, is still available.

**Figure 6-19  Other protocols supported by Windows XP Professional**

# skill 7 *Configuring Network Bindings*

**exam objective**

Configure and troubleshoot the TCP/IP protocol.

**overview**

On a client computer that is using multiple protocols, you must set the **binding order** for the protocols. The binding order establishes which protocol should be used first when a network connection is initiated. Binding refers to an operational link between network layers, and it is the *client* computer that determines which protocol will be used to establish the connection. For example, if you most frequently use your computer to access a Microsoft network and the Internet, and only occasionally need to locate files on a NetWare server (either 4.0 or versions that predate it), you will have both TCP/IP and NWLInk configured on your network adapter. Since your most frequent tasks involve the use of TCP/IP, you will position the protocols so that TCP/IP is the protocol of choice for the Client for Microsoft Networks (Workstation) service.

**how to**

Configure the network bindings on your computer.

1. Open the Control Panel and double-click the Network Connections icon to open the **Network Connections** window.
2. Open the **Advanced** menu and select the **Advanced Settings** command to open the **Advanced Settings** dialog box **(Figure 6-20)**.
3. Select **Local Area Connection** in the **Connections** section of the **Adpaters and Bindings** tab.
4. In the **Bindings for Local Area Connection** scrolling list box, under **File and Printer Sharing for Microsoft Networks**, select the **Internet Protocol (TCP/IP)**.
5. Click 🔼 once to move the selected protocol above **NWLink IPX/SPX/NetBIOS Compatible Transport Protocol**.
6. Under **Client for Microsoft Networks**, select **Internet Protocol (TCP/IP)**. Click 🔼 again to position Internet Protocol (TCP/IP) above NWLink here, as well **(Figure 6-21)**.
7. Click 🔲 OK 🔲 to apply the changes.
8. Close the Network Connections window.

**more**

You should disable any adapter bindings that you do not use to increase the speed of your connections, and the security of your system. Simply clear the check boxes for bindings you do not need. Use the up and down arrow keys to correctly position the bindings in the protocol priority order you want used. This will also increase system efficiency because the operating system will not attempt to create unsuitable connections.

**Figure 6-20  Advanced Settings dialog box**

**Figure 6-21  Protocol binding order changed**

Click buttons to move a selected protocol up or down in the binding order

# skill 8

# *Configuring Network Bridge*

## exam objective

Basic knowledge

## overview

With Windows XP Professional, Microsoft has introduced a new networking feature to the Windows operating system. **Network Bridge** simplifies the process of connecting different segments of networked computers on the same LAN that use different types of network media. In the past, such connections required physical routers and bridges, as each media type would be located in a different subnet on the network. Since different media types also use different protocols to communicate, some method of transmitting packets was necessary. Network Bridge enables you to create a virtual hub through which the different media types can communicate automatically.

## how to

Configure Network Bridge on a Windows XP Professional computer.

1. Click ![start], click **Control Panel**, and double-click the **Network Connections** icon to open the **Network Connections** window.
2. Select the network connections you wish to bridge in the Network Connections window under **LAN or High-Speed Internet** (**Figure 6-22**).
3. Right-click any of the selected network connections and click **Bridge Connections** on the shortcut menu.
4. Windows takes a few moments to create the bridge. A bridge icon then appears in the Network Connections window (**Figure 6-23**).
5. Close the Network Connections window.

## more

To remove a network connection from a bridge, simply right-click the individual connection and click **Remove from Bridge** on the shortcut menu. You can configure the properties of a Network Bridge and the connections it bridges by right-clicking the Network Bridge icon and selecting Properties from the shortcut menu. You can join multiple connections in a Network Bridge, but you may only create one bridge per computer. A Network Bridge can only consist of Ethernet or Ethernet-compatible adapters or IEEE-1394 adapters. However, if these adapters are running under Internet Connections Sharing (ICS) or Internet Connection Firewall (ICF), they cannot be part of a Network Bridge.

**Figure 6-22  Network connections selected for Network Bridge**

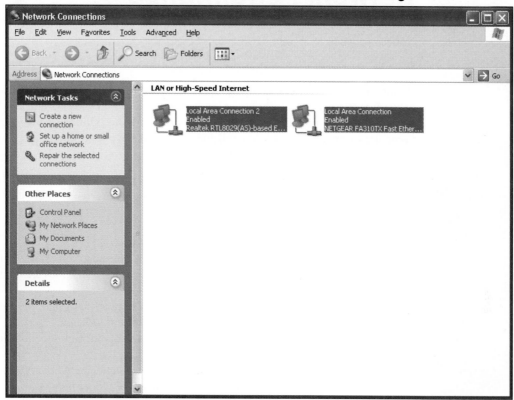

**Figure 6-23  Network Bridge created**

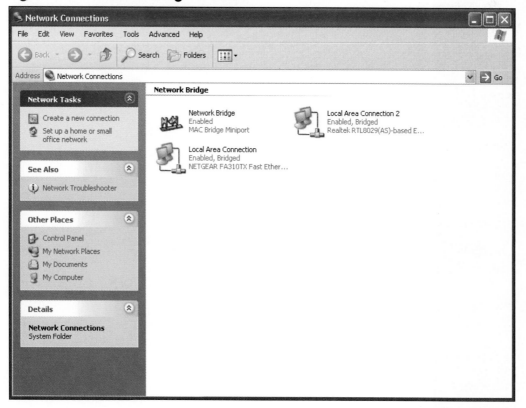

# skill 9 *Optimizing and Troubleshooting Network Performance*

**exam objective**

Basic knowledge

**overview**

Communications between computers in a network generate network traffic. Increases in network traffic may adversely affect the performance of a network **(Figure 6-24)**. Network Administrators must follow certain guidelines in order to optimize network performance. Some useful guidelines for accomplishing this, and for troubleshooting common network problems, are given below:

◆  If the computers on a network are communicating over Token Ring, FDDI, or switched Ethernet networks, you can balance network traffic by distributing client connections across multiple network adapters.

◆  Use adapters with the highest bandwidth available.

◆  Use adapters that support task-offloading capabilities.

◆  If your network uses multiple protocols, bind each protocol on a different adapter and make sure that the most efficient protocols are used, preferably ones that minimize broadcasts.

◆  To reduce congestion on the server, divide your network into multiple subnets or segments. Attach the server to each segment with a separate adapter.

◆  Do not reorder the server bindings. The server accepts incoming connections based on the protocol used by the client computer.

◆  Promote the use of offline files and folders for working on network applications. Offline folders make use of client-side caching, and therefore reduce network traffic.

**Figure 6-24** **Increases in network traffic may adversely affect the performance of a network**

# Summary

- TCP/IP is a set of protocols that enable you to route messages over a network.
- TCP/IP defines the rules for connecting networks to each other and for communication between computers on a network.
- TCP/IP consists of four layers: Network Interface, Internet, Transport, and Application.
- DHCP (Dynamic Host Configuration Protocol) provides configuration information to any standard TCP/IP DHCP-compatible client including Windows, Linux, and every other mainstream operating system on the market. The DHCP server's job is to dynamically allocate IP addresses. This simplifies the administration of the TCP/IP configuration because it automates the process of assigning IP addresses to clients.
- If a DHCP client cannot locate a DHCP server, automatic private IP addressing (APIPA) is used to randomly choose an IP address from a private APIPA address series that is not in use on the Internet. In this way, computers on a LAN where there is no DHCP server, or on a network where the DHCP server is down, can still be assigned an IP address and communicate with other computers.
- You may need to add a static IP address to selected computers on a network such as application servers and the DHCP server.
- The IANA reserves all IP addresses that fall in the range of 169.254.0.0 to 169.254.255.255.
- The Ping utility is used to test the TCP/IP configuration on your system.
- The ipconfig utility is used to confirm the TCP/IP parameters on a host computer.
- ARP is responsible for finding the MAC address associated with a known IP address.
- A MAC address is a unique 48-bit or 6-byte number, usually represented as 12 hexadecimal digits. It is also referred to as a hardware address, physical address, or Ethernet address.
- When communication is initiated between a system and a host for which the system does not have a MAC address, the system sends an ARP broadcast packet asking for a MAC address that corresponds to a local IP address, or for the MAC address of the default gateway if it is a remote host.
- Netstat displays the TCP/IP protocol statistics and the network connections related to it.
- Route displays and modifies the local routing table.
- Hostname returns the host name of a local computer for authentication by the RCP, RSH, and REXEC utilities.
- File Transfer Protocol (FTP) is used to transfer files between a computer running Windows XP Professional and a TCP/IP host running both server software and FTP. It also provides directory and file handling services such as listing directory contents, deleting files, and selecting file formats.
- Trivial File Transfer Protocol (TFTP), a simpler form of FTP, is used to transfer files between a computer running Windows XP Professional and a TCP/IP host running both server software and TFTP. TFTP uses the User Datagram Protocol (UDP), and thus includes no security features, acknowledgements, or data retransmissions. It is often used by servers to boot diskless workstations or routers.
- Telnet is a terminal emulation protocol that runs over TCP/IP. When you run Telnet from a client machine and connect to a server on the network, you can enter commands, which will be carried out as if you were performing them directly on the server terminal.
- Telnet is often used to manage a remote Web server. It is used to control the server and to communicate with other servers on the network. You can also connect to a computer on the Internet that supports Telnet to run programs from that computer. Telnet was the first way in which remote access was accomplished.
- RCP copies files between a computer running Windows XP Professional and a host supporting RCP.
- RSH runs commands on a Unix host.
- Finger is a utility, supported by UNIX computers, that is used to retrieve information about users, including their user name and how long they have been logged on.
- NWLink is used by Microsoft computers to access resources on NetWare 4.0 servers and on servers running NetWare versions that predate 4.0.
- NWLink also helps computers to communicate with network devices that use IPX/SPX socket interfaces.
- NWLink supports Winsock and NetBIOS over IPX networking APIs.
- You must install either the CSNW redirector or Novell Client for Windows NT/2000/XP on a Windows XP Professional machine in order to access file and print resources on a NetWare server.
- You must install FPNW to enable NetWare clients to use file and print resources on a computer running Windows 2000 Server or Windows Server 2003.
- You configure three components when you install the NWLink transport protocol: Frame type, Network number, and Internal Network number.
- To increase authentication, encryption, and multilinking, Windows XP Professional uses protocols such as EAP, RADIUS, IPSec, L2TP, and BAP.
- Network binding links network adapter card drivers, protocols, and services by establishing an initial connection between them, allowing communication to occur at different levels.
- You can specify a binding order for the various protocols to optimize network performance.
- Network Bridge enables you to connect existing LAN segments without using a physical router or bridge.

# Key Terms

Application layer
Address Resolution Protocol (ARP)
Binding order
Connectionless Communication
Default gateways
DNS (Domain Name System)
Dynamic Host Configuration Protocol (DHCP) service
Extensible Authentication Protocol (EAP)
File Transfer Protocol (FTP)
File and Print Services for NetWare (FPNW)
Finger
Frame type
Host ID
Host Name
Hostname
Internet Control Message Protocol (ICMP)
Internet Group Management Protocol (IGMP)
Internet layer

Internal network number
Internet Protocol (IP)
Internet Protocol Security (IPSec)
IP address
Ipconfig
Layer Two Tunneling Protocol (L2TP)
Media Access Control (MAC) address
Multicasting
Nbtstat
Netstat
NetBIOS over IPX
Network Bridge
Network ID
Network Interface layer
Network Monitor Driver 2
Network number
NWLink
Ping
PktType
Remote Authentication Dial-In User Service (RADIUS)
Remote Copy Protocol (RCP)
Remote shell (RSH)

Route
Router
Routing table
Subnet mask
TCP/IP host
Telnet
Tracert
Transmission Control Protocol (TCP)
Transmission Control Protocol/ Internet Protocol (TCP/IP)
Transport layer
Trivial File Transfer Protocol (TFTP)
User Datagram Protocol (UDP)
WINS (Windows Internet Naming Service)
Winsock

# Test Yourself

1. Which of the following protocols is responsible for providing the addressing scheme for networks and for the Internet?
   a. TCP
   b. IP
   c. UDP
   d. DHCP

2. Which of the following is a function of the Internet layer in the TCP/IP conceptual model?
   a. Responsible for placing TCP/IP packets on the network medium and receiving TCP/IP packets off the network medium.
   b. Determines the route the data packets will take.
   c. Enables applications to gain access to the network.
   d. Makes sure that messages are delivered in the correct sequence without errors, and with no data duplication or data loss.

3. Which of the following protocols enables hosts to exchange status and error information over the network?
   a. UDP
   b. ICMP
   c. IGMP
   d. ARP

4. The Internet Group Management Protocol provides:
   a. Multicasting.
   b. Automatic IP address assignment.
   c. Connectionless packet delivery.
   d. Passwords for accounts.

5. Which protocol ensures the delivery of data packets in the correct sequence to the destination computer?
   a. Transmission Control Protocol
   b. User Datagram Protocol
   c. Address Resolution Protocol
   d. Internet Control Message Protocol

6. Which of the following utilities enables you to check the route a packet is following to reach its destination point?
   a. Netstat
   b. Route
   c. Tracert
   d. ARP

7. Which of the following protocols will you use to enable clients running Microsoft operating systems to access resources on NetWare 4.0 or earlier servers?
   a. AppleTalk
   b. DLC
   c. NWLink
   d. NetBEUI

8. The Ping utility is used primarily to:
   a. Test TCP/IP configurations and identify connection failures.
   b. Validate the host name for the local computer.
   c. Display protocol statistics and current TCP/IP connections using NBT.
   d. Check the route a packet is following to reach its destination point.

9. Transport Layer Security is used by EAP to:
   a. Be the authentication standard when a smart card is in use.
   b. Provide passwords for accounts.
   c. Encrypt user names and passwords.
   d. Create an encrypted tunnel through a network.

10. Which of the following is used to divide the network ID from the host ID?
    a. IP address
    b. Subnet mask
    c. Default gateway
    d. BAP

11. Which of the following is used to optimize network performance?
    a. Frame type
    b. Binding order
    c. Network Monitor Driver 2
    d. Subnet mask

## Projects: On Your Own

1. Verify the configuration of a computer.
   a. Open the **Command Prompt**.
   b. Type **ipconfig/all | more** at the Command Prompt.
   c. Press **[Enter]**.

2. Install NWLink on your computer.
   a. Access the **Network Connections** window.
   b. Access the **Local Area Connection Properties** dialog box.
   c. Display the **Select Network Component Type** dialog box.
   d. Select the **Protocol** option from the dialog box and access the **Select Network Protocol** dialog box.
   e. Select the **NWLink IPX/SPX/NetBIOS Compatible Transport Protocol** option from the Network Protocol section.
   f. Apply the changes.

   g. Close the Local Area Connections Properties dialog box.
   h. Close the Network Connections window.

3. Configure the network bindings in your computer.
   a. Access the **Network and Dial-up Connections** window.
   b. Access the **Advanced Settings** dialog box.
   c. Select the **Internet Protocol (TCP/IP)** check box from the Advanced Settings dialog box.
   d. Apply changes.
   e. Close all the windows.

## Problem Solving Scenarios

1. Your company, Bay View Architects, has just landed a large project from a client in Philadelphia. To service this client, Bay View has purchased a new print server. Outline, in a memo, the specific steps you would take to assign a static IP address to this print server.

**W**indows XP Professional includes various administrative tools that you can use in order to centralize administrative tasks and perform them efficiently. The Microsoft Management Console (MMC) is used to create a set of tools for performing administrative tasks. MMC acts as a container for other administrative tools and displays them as consoles. Consoles consist of one or more applications called snap-ins that are designed to perform specific administrative functions. Windows XP Professional provides certain predefined consoles, and you can also create custom consoles by combining multiple preconfigured snap-ins into one console. You can also add extensions to custom snap-ins in order to provide additional administrative functionality.

The Task Scheduler is another administrative tool. The Task Scheduler can be programmed to carry out certain routine tasks, such as performing a backup every Friday or a virus check on all systems at the start of each day. You can use the Task Scheduler to schedule system tasks and programs, such as the Disk Cleanup utility, to run at specific time intervals.

## Goals

In this lesson, you will learn about the MMC console and snap-ins. You will also learn to create a custom console, add an extension snap-in to a console, and schedule administrative tasks.

## Requirements

To complete the skills in this lesson, you will need a computer with Windows XP Professional installed on it.

# skill 1 | *Introducing the Microsoft Management Console*

**exam objective**

Basic knowledge

**overview**

The primary administrative tool in Windows XP Professional is the **Microsoft Management Console (MMC)**, which is the foundation for all of the management tools in the operating system. The MMC, which provides a simple, uniform, user-friendly interface, is used to manage hardware, software, and network components. It provides a framework for creating, saving, and opening a collection of tools called **consoles**. A console consists of management applications called **snap-ins** that integrate applications, information, and views of your network and enable you to perform administrative tasks. For example, the Computer Management console combines various administration utilities into a single console tree. Using this console, you can manage a local or remote computer and view the list of users connected to the computer. You can also start and stop system services, such as the Task Scheduler, and view device configurations.

The MMC management interface is used to create consoles with which you can easily perform administration tasks. The benefits of the MMC are listed below:

◆ It provides a single interface from which to administer tasks and troubleshoot problems. For example, the **Disk Management** snap-in is used to create, delete, and format partitions on a basic disk and lets you create simple, spanned, or striped volumes on dynamic disks.

◆ You can use consoles to perform administrative tasks on all of the computers in a network through a central machine as long as you have administrative access to each of the target computers.

◆ Snap-ins can administer tasks and troubleshoot problems on remote computers. Most, but not all snap-ins, such as the **Disk Defragmenter** snap-in, are designed for remote administration.

◆ You can create custom consoles to perform the tasks you most often undertake. Your custom consoles are saved as .msc files, which can be reused on the computer on which you created them, or transferred to other computers.

The MMC has two types of console modes: **Author mode** and **User mode**. You choose between these two modes to designate the operating mode and functionality for each console.

**Author mode:** In this mode, you have complete access to the MMC functionality of the saved console. You can save the console, view all portions of the console tree, add or remove snap-ins, and create new windows. Author mode is the default mode for new consoles that you save.

**User mode:** When you save a console in User mode, you can distribute it to other Administrators. There are three User mode types: full access; limited access, multiple window; and limited access, single window. **Table 7-1** provides a description of the three user mode types.

To set the console mode, open the **File** menu and click the **Options** command to open the **Options** dialog box. On the **Console** tab, select the console mode in the **Console mode** list box. Even if you save a console in one of the User modes, you can right click it and select **Author** on the context menu at any time to open it in Author mode.

### Table 7-1   User Mode Types

| | |
|---|---|
| Full access | Allows users to:<br>• View the entire console tree.<br>• Add and delete new windows.<br><br>Prevents users from:<br>• Adding/removing snap-ins.<br>• Changing console properties. |
| Limited access, multiple windows | Allows users to:<br>• Create new windows.<br>• Add and delete new windows.<br>• Access only those areas that were visible when the console was saved.<br><br>Prevents users from:<br>• Closing existing windows.<br>• Changing console properties. |
| Limited access, single window | Allows users to:<br>• Access only one window.<br><br>Prevents users from:<br>• Opening new windows.<br>• Gaining access to other portions of a console tree. |

# skill 2 | *Creating Custom Consoles*

## exam objective

Basic knowledge

## overview

Consoles contain snap-ins that facilitate management of system services, processes, and applications. Each console is saved with a **.msc** extension. Note that some important snap-ins, including the Group Policy, Security Templates, and Security Configuration and Analysis snap-ins, are not supplied in any of the preconfigured consoles. You will have to build a custom console in order to use them.

Each console window is divided into a **console tree** and a **details pane**. The console tree organizes the snap-ins that are available in the console in hierarchical order. The details pane displays the contents of the snap-in that is selected in the console tree.

Windows XP Professional supports two types of consoles: preconfigured and custom. The predefined consoles are installed on your system during the installation of Windows XP Professional. Preconfigured consoles contain commonly used snap-ins, such as the Computer Management, Event Viewer, and Local Security snap-ins, which are used to perform administrative tasks. You cannot modify a preconfigured console or add any new snap-ins to it.

You can also create your own **custom consoles** by combining multiple preconfigured snap-ins into one console. For example, you can create the **Administering Events** custom console by combining the **Computer Management** and **Component Services** snap-ins. You can then view and manage all of the services running on a particular system rather than searching for specific services.

After you create custom consoles, you can:

◆ Save them and use them in the future.
◆ Distribute them to other Administrators to meet their administrative needs.
◆ Use them to carry out remote administration. This centralizes and unifies administrative tasks.

### tip

When you add items to the console tree, they are displayed under the console root.

## how to

Create a custom console named **Administering Events** and add the **Computer Management** snap-in to it to manage your computer.

1. Click ⊞ start and then click the **Run** command to open the **Run** dialog box.
2. Type **MMC** in the **Open** list box (**Figure 7-1**).
3. Click OK . MMC is initialized and displays the default empty console.
4. Open the **File** menu and click the **Add/Remove Snap-in** command to open the **Add/Remove Snap-in** dialog box with the **Standalone** tab active by default. The **Console Root** option is selected by default in the **Snap-ins added to** list box.
5. Click Add... to open the **Add Standalone Snap-in** dialog box. This dialog box lists all available snap-ins.
6. Click the **Computer Management** snap-in to select it to be added to the custom console (**Figure 7-2**).
7. Click Add . The **Computer Management** dialog box prompts you to select the computer you want the snap-in to manage (**Figure 7-3**).
8. Most of the time you will select the local computer. Make sure that the **Local computer: (the computer this console is running on)** option button is selected.
9. Click Finish to close the **Computer Management** dialog box.
10. In the Add Standalone Snap-in dialog box, click the **Component Services** snap-in, and then click Add . This adds this snap-in to the Add/Remove Snap-in dialog box.

### tip

The Console1 window is the default MMC window. It does not contain any snap-ins.

**Figure 7-1  Opening a blank MMC**

Used to select the program
you want to run

**Figure 7-2  Windows XP standalone snap-ins**

Select the snap-in that you
want to add to the console

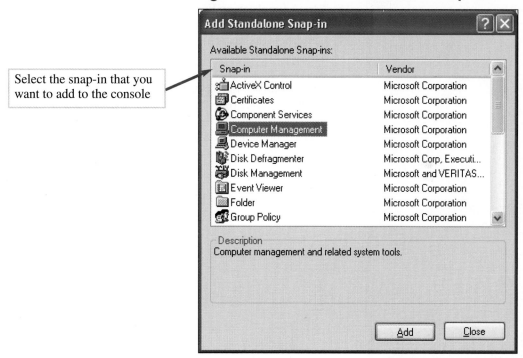

**Figure 7-3  Selecting the computer to manage**

Select this option to
manage a local computer

Select this option to
manage a remote computer

Used to locate the remote
computer that will be
managed by the snap-in

# skill 2

## Creating Custom Consoles *(cont'd)*

**exam objective**

Basic knowledge

**how to**

11. Click [ Close ] to close the **Add Standalone Snap-in** dialog box.
12. Click [ OK ] to close the **Add/Remove Snap-in** dialog box.
13. In order to use the console again, you must save it. Open the **Console** menu and click the **Save As** command to open the **Save As** dialog box.
14. To save the console on the desktop, select **Desktop** in the **Save in** list box.
15. Type **Administering Events** in the **File name** text box (**Figure 7-4**).
16. Click [ Save ]. The console name appears in the MMC title bar (**Figure 7-5**).
17. **Close** the **Administering Events** console. The Administering Events icon is added to the desktop (**Figure 7-6**).

**more**

Custom consoles are saved in the **Administrative Tools** folder of the currently logged on user by default. Therefore, only the user who saves a custom console will be able to see it displayed in the Administrative Tools folder. You can access the Administrative Tools folder through the Control Panel. Shortcuts to the preconfigured MMCs are stored in the **All Users** profile.

**Figure 7-4  Saving a console on the desktop**

**Figure 7-5  New Administering Events console**

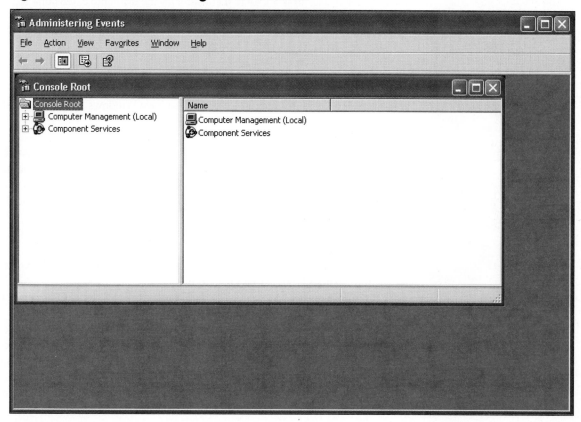

**Figure 7-6  Administering Events icon on the desktop**

# skill 3 | *Adding Extensions to Snap-Ins*

## exam objective

Basic knowledge

## overview

MMC provides an interface, as well as the architecture for adding snap-ins to a console. You can combine snap-ins from various vendors, such as Microsoft or ISVs, and those created by in-house developers, into a single console. MMC acts as a common link between the snap-ins provided by different vendors. Windows XP Professional supports two types of snap-ins:

◆ **Standalone snap-ins:** These snap-ins are used to perform administration tasks. They are simply referred to as snap-ins.

◆ **Extension snap-ins:** These are referred to as extensions. Extension snap-ins expand the administrative functionality of other snap-ins. For example, you can add the **Event Viewer Extension** snap-in to the **Computer Management** snap-in in order to view the task processing results on a system. Extension snap-ins are designed to work with one or more standalone snap-ins or other extension snap-ins, depending on the function of the parent snap-in. An extension provides functionality only when you are in the parent snap-in. When a snap-in is added to a console, all the available extensions of that snap-in are added to the console by default. However, you can remove an extension from a snap-in as needed. When you add an extension to a snap-in, Windows XP Professional displays only those extensions that are compatible with the standalone snap-in.

You can add the preconfigured consoles for Windows Server 2003 to Windows XP Professional by running the **Adminpak.msi** program. This application can be found on the Windows Server 2003 installation CD. You must have Windows XP Professional with Service Pack 1 or later.

## how to

Add the **Event Viewer Extension** snap-in to the **Administering Events** custom console.

1. Double-click the **Administering Events** icon on the desktop to open the **Administering Events** console.
2. Open the **File** menu and click the **Add/Remove Snap-in** command to open the **Add/Remove Snap-in** dialog box.
3. Click the **Extensions** tab to display the extension snap-ins available in the Administering Events console.
4. In the **Snap-ins that can be extended** list box, select **Computer Management**.
5. Clear the **Add all extensions** check box.
6. Clear all of the check boxes except the **Event Viewer Extension** option in the **Available extensions** list box (**Figure 7-7**).
7. Click [ OK ] to add the **Event Viewer Extension** snap-in to the console tree.
8. Expand the **Computer Management (Local)** node. Expand the **System Tools** node. The Event Viewer extension has been added to the Computer Management snap-in (**Figure 7-8**).
9. Close the **Administering Events** window, and save the changes you have made.

**Figure 7-7 Adding snap-in extensions**

Select the snap-in to which you are adding the extension

Select the extension to be added to the snap-in

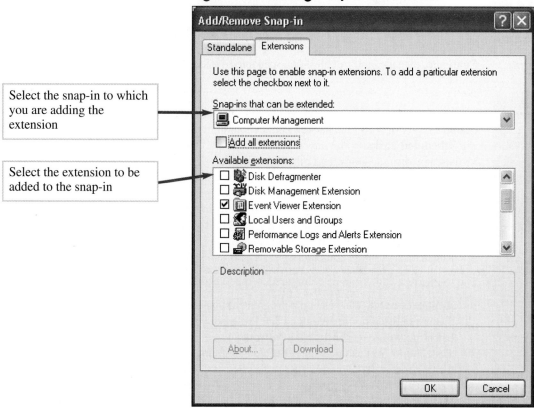

**Figure 7-8 Adding snap-in extensions**

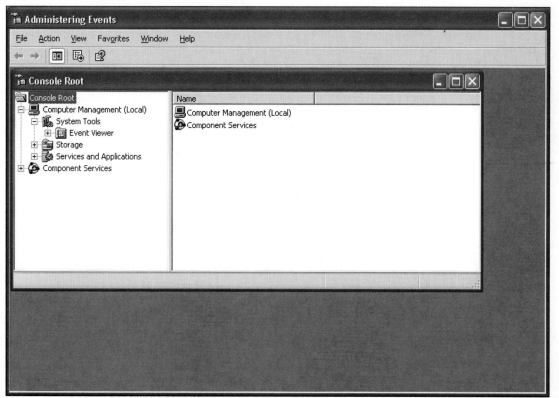

# skill 4

# *Working with Scheduled Tasks*

## exam objective

Configure, manage, and troubleshoot Scheduled Tasks.

## overview

As a Network Administrator, you will need to perform certain tasks at regular intervals. For example, you might run the backup application on the first Monday of every month. You can use **Scheduled Tasks** to run any application, script, or document at specified time intervals. Virus scans, disk cleanups, and other administrative utilities can be configured to run daily, weekly, monthly, at system startup, at logon, or when the system is idle. You can also use Scheduled Tasks to:

◆ Schedule maintenance utilities at specific time intervals.
◆ Customize the running of a task at a specified time.
◆ Stop a scheduled task from running.
◆ Run tasks on remote computers.

The following options can be configured in the Scheduled Task Wizard:

◆ **Application:** You can select the program you want to schedule from a list of applications that are registered with Windows XP Professional. You can also specify any program or batch file that is available on the network.
◆ **Task Name:** You can give the scheduled task a logical name. For example, you can name the task that starts the virus check utility, Virus Check.
◆ **Frequency:** You can specify the number of times the task should be performed by Windows XP Professional and whether the task should be performed daily, weekly, monthly, one time only, when the computer starts, or when you log on.
◆ **Time and Date:** You can specify the start time and start date for the task. Where appropriate, you can also specify the days on which the task should be repeated.
◆ **Name and Password:** You can enter a user name and password, and specify that a particular task be run under the security settings for that user.

The **Task Scheduler** also includes some advanced options that can be set in the **Properties** dialog box for the scheduled task (**Figure 7-9**). **Table 7-2** lists the tabs in the Properties dialog box and their descriptions.

## tip

Scheduled tasks are saved in the Scheduled Tasks folder in the Control Panel.

## how to

Configure your system to run the **Backup** application on the first **Monday** of every month at **9:00 AM**.

1. Click ⟦ *start* ⟧ and click the **Control Panel** command to open the Control Panel window.
2. Double-click the **Scheduled Tasks** icon to open the Scheduled Tasks window.
3. Double-click the **Add Scheduled Task** icon to open the **Scheduled Task Wizard**.
4. Click ⟦ Next > ⟧. A list appears showing the programs you can schedule.
5. Scroll down and select the **Backup** option to schedule the backup application (**Figure 7-10**).
6. Click ⟦ Next > ⟧ to name the task and select when it will run.
7. Type **Running Backup** in the **Type a name for this task** text box.
8. In the **Perform this task** section, click the **Monthly** option button (**Figure 7-11**) and then click ⟦ Next > ⟧.
9. Type **9:00 AM** in the **Start time** spin box. You can also use the spin arrows to set the time.

## Table 7-2   Advanced Properties of the Task Scheduler

| | |
|---|---|
| Task | The Task tab allows you to configure command-line programs that run tasks. You can also enter information or comments about the task, assign a different user and password to run the task, or disable the task by clearing the Enabled check box. |
| Schedule | Using the Schedule tab, you can set multiple schedules for a particular task or change when a task is scheduled to run. |
| Settings | On the Settings tab, you can change the options that affect the execution of a task. For example, you can specify that the task be run only when the computer is idle, or you can specify that the task be disabled if the computer is running on battery power. |

### Figure 7-9 **Running Backup dialog box**

### Figure 7-10 **Scheduling a task**

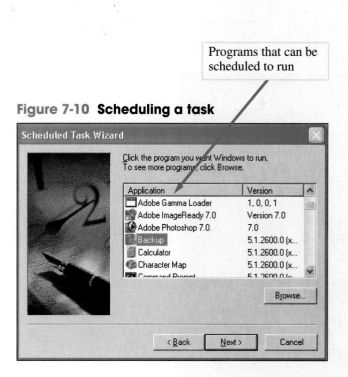

Programs that can be scheduled to run

### Figure 7-11 **Setting the name and frequency for the task**

Name under which the task will be saved

Frequency selected here determines the options to be displayed on the next screen

# skill 4

## *Working with Scheduled Tasks (cont'd)*

### exam objective

Configure, manage, and troubleshoot the Task Scheduler.

### how to

10. Click the **The** option button. By default, the Wizard displays **the first Monday** of each month option (**Figure 7-12**). Click [ Next > ].
11. The Wizard displays the name of the user who is currently logged on to the system. Enter the password for the user account in the **Enter the password** text box. Re-type the password in the **Confirm password** text box (**Figure 7-13**). You can specify a user account and password that is different from the administrative account that you used to log on, as long as that user is a member of either the **Backup Operators** or **Administrators** group. Only members of these groups have the right to perform backups.
12. Click [ Next > ]. A summary of the settings you have entered for the Backup application is displayed (**Figure 7-14**).
13. Click [ Finish ] to add the **Running Backup** task to the list of scheduled tasks. The task is saved with a **.job** file extension (if you have Windows set to display file extentions) and added to the **Scheduled Task** window.

### more

You cannot schedule, run, or modify a task if the Task Scheduler service is stopped. You can use the **Services** snap-in in the **Administrative Tools** window to check the status of the Task Scheduler service. The service can be stopped, started, paused, or resumed by the user. Alternatively, you can check which services are running in the Computer Management console. The Computer Management console is in the Administrative Tools folder in the Control Panel. You can also right-click **My Computer** on the desktop or on the Start menu and select the **Manage** command on the shortcut menu to open the **Computer Management** console. In the **details** pane, double-click the **Services and Applications** node to display its contents. Double-click the **Services** snap-in to view all of the services that are running on your machine and their status.

**Figure 7-12  Selecting the time and day for the task**

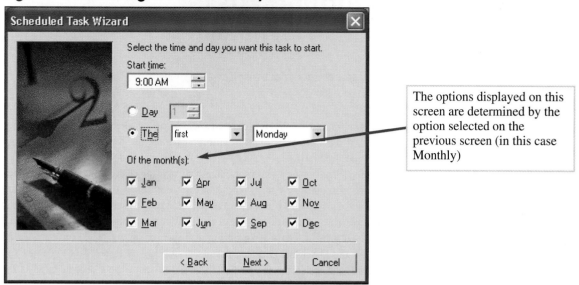

The options displayed on this screen are determined by the option selected on the previous screen (in this case Monthly)

**Figure 7-13  Specifying the user account details**

**Figure 7-14  Summary of the scheduled task**

Select this check box if you want to set advanced properties for the task

# Troubleshooting Tasks

**exam objective**

Configure, manage, and troubleshoot Scheduled Tasks.

## overview

If you find that the Task Scheduler service is not functioning properly and that scheduled tasks are not running as programmed, you can explore several possible reasons. Some troubleshooting measures are given below:

**tip**

The notification area is the bar on the right end of the taskbar that contains the system clock and various program icons.

◆ Incorrect time/date setting on the computer. The system checks the date and time on the local computer before starting a task. If the date or time settings on the computer are different from the actual date and time, the task will not run on schedule. You can check the system date and time in the notification area. When you double-click the clock (**Figure 7-15**), the **Date and Time Properties** dialog box opens. You can correct the time, if necessary, in the Date and Time Properties dialog box (**Figure 7-16**). (Note: You can also access the Date and Time Properties dialog box from the Control Panel if the system clock is not displayed in the notification area.)

◆ The path for the tool or program that is supposed to be launched is not correct. You can check the path for the task by right-clicking the task in the **Scheduled Tasks** window and clicking **Properties** on the shortcut menu to open the **Properties** dialog box for the task. Here, you can check to see if the displayed path is correct.

◆ The Task Scheduler service has been stopped or paused. You can check this by opening the **Advanced** menu in the Scheduled Tasks window. If the Task Scheduler service has been stopped, the Advanced menu will display the **Start Using Task Scheduler** command. Usually the Advanced menu displays the **Stop Using Task Scheduler** command because the service runs by default. If the Task Scheduler service has been paused, the Advanced menu will display the **Continue Task Scheduler** command. By default, the menu displays the **Pause Task Scheduler** command.

◆ If you create several scheduled tasks and all but one of them runs, you may have a user rights conflict. When you enter a user name and password in the Scheduled Task Wizard, you must be sure that this user has the right to perform the specific system task. Many tasks require administrative rights.

## how to

Troubleshoot the **Running Backup** task.
1. Double-click the **Scheduled Tasks** icon in the **Control Panel** window to open the Scheduled Tasks window.
2. Open the **Advanced** menu (**Figure 7-17**) and click the **Stop Using Task Scheduler** command to stop the Task Scheduler service.
3. Right-click the **Running Backup** task and click **Run** on the context menu.
4. A message box informs you that the service is currently stopped and that no services will run unless it is started. Click [ Yes ] to start the Task Scheduler service (**Figure 7-18**).
5. Close the Task Scheduler.

## more

The other commands on the **Advanced** menu in the Scheduled Tasks window are given below:

◆ **Notify Me of Missed Tasks:** This command is toggled off by default. When you activate this command, a check mark will indicate that the service has been turned on.

◆ **AT Service Account:** You use this command to specify the user account that will be used for all tasks that are created with the AT.exe command-line utility (discussed below).

**Figure 7-15 The notification area**

**Figure 7-16 Date and Time Properties dialog box**

**Figure 7-17 Stopping the Task Scheduler service**

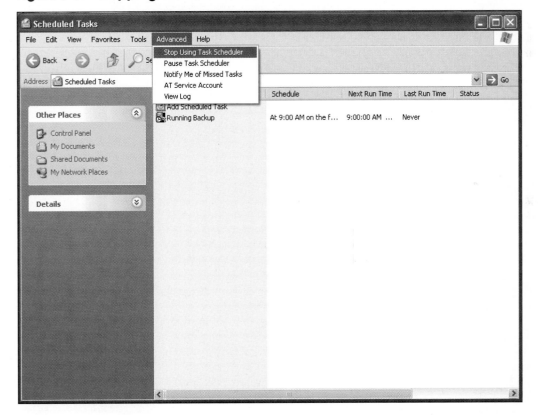

**Figure 7-18 Restarting the Task Scheduler service**

# skill 5

## Troubleshooting Tasks *(cont'd)*

**exam objective**

Configure, manage, and troubleshoot the Task Scheduler.

**more**

◆ **View Log:** This command is used to open **SchedLgU.Txt** in Notepad (**Figure 7-19**). This file contains the actions of the Scheduled Tasks utility and can be used to troubleshoot problems. Specific error messages will be recorded when a task fails to execute.

The command-line version of the Scheduled Tasks tool is **AT.exe**. When you create tasks using the command-line tool, those tasks must all run under the account that you specify in the AT Service Account Configuration dialog box (AT Service Account command on the Advanced menu). The graphical tool is more user-friendly and you can run different tasks under different user accounts. To learn about the syntax for the AT command, type: **at /?** at the command line (**Figure 7-20**).

**Figure 7-19 SchedLgU.Txt file in Notepad**

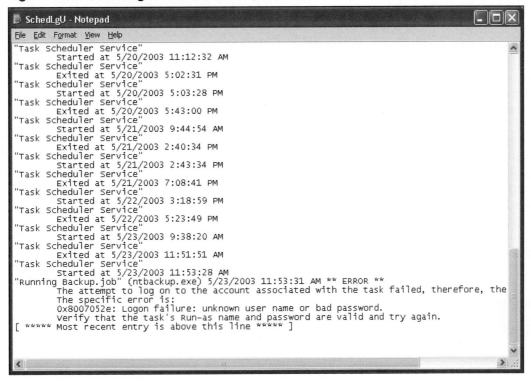

**Figure 7-20 Syntax of the AT command**

# Summary

- The Microsoft Management Console (MMC) is an administrative tool that you use to manage hardware, software, and network components using snap-ins. It provides a framework that you can use to create, save, and open a set of administrative tools called consoles.
- There are two types of consoles: predefined and custom.
- Predefined consoles are installed on a system during the installation of Windows XP Professional. You cannot modify a preconfigured console or add any new snap-ins to it.
- Custom consoles are created by combining multiple pre-configured snap-ins into one console. You can save and reuse custom consoles, distribute them to other administrators, and use them to carry out remote administration.
- A custom console can be saved in either of the two modes: Author or User.
- A console tree organizes the available snap-ins in hierarchical order.

- Snap-ins are management applications that are used to perform specific administrative tasks.
- There are two types of snap-ins: Standalone snap-ins and Extension snap-ins.
- Standalone snap-ins are used to perform administration tasks.
- Extension snap-ins provide additional administrative functionality to other snap-ins.
- The Scheduled Tasks tool can be used to schedule programs and batch files to run at specified intervals.
- You can troubleshoot tasks that are not running by checking the system date and time, checking the path for the task that has been scheduled, checking to see if the Task Scheduler service has been stopped or paused, and checking for a user rights conflict. You can also check the log file, SchedLgU.txt, to view the error messages for the Scheduled Task utility.

# Key Terms

Author mode
Console tree
Console
Custom console
Details pane

Disk Management snap-in
Extension snap-in
Microsoft Management Console (MMC)
Preconfigured console
Scheduled Tasks

Snap-in
Standalone snap-in
Task Scheduler
User mode

# Test Yourself

1. Which of the following statements about a console are correct?
   a. A standalone snap-in can be used to administer only a local computer.
   b. An extension snap-in provides functionality only when you invoke the parent snap-in.
   c. You can add the preconfigured consoles of Windows Server 2003 to Windows XP Professional.
   d. To use the predefined consoles, you need to install them on your system from the Windows XP Professional Installation CD.

2. Which of the following types of console modes allows users to create new windows, but does not grant access to close the existing windows?
   a. Full access
   b. Limited access, single window
   c. Limited access, multiple windows
   d. Author

3. Console snap-ins that are designed to work only in conjunction with one or more standalone snap-ins, and that can only provide functionality when added to a parent snap-in, are called:
   a. Extensions.
   b. Supplements.
   c. Add-on snap-ins.
   d. Supplements.

4. Microsoft Management Console:
   a. Is stored in an administrative template file.
   b. Is a framework to which management tools can be added.
   c. Contains a comprehensive list of applications for which a task can be scheduled.
   d. Is saved with a .job extension.

**5.** Which of the following statements about a console is correct?
   a. You can create a custom console by combining multiple preconfigured snap-ins in one console.
   b. When you add a snap-in to a console, you need to select the extensions that should be included in that snap-in.
   c. Standalone snap-ins provide additional administrative functionality to other snap-ins.
   d. You can add or remove an extension from a preconfigured console.

**6.** You are logged on to a Windows XP Professional machine as an Administrator and you create a scheduled task to run a backup of the C: drive after business hours. You enter the user name and password for the workstation user, who is a member of the Users group, in the Scheduled Task Wizard. The next day you discover that the backup did not run. What happened?
   a. You can only create a backup task when you are logged on as a member of the Backup Operators group.
   b. You must change the user name and password for the task to a member of the Backup Operators or Administrators groups, because only members of these groups have the right to perform backup jobs.
   c. You forgot to start the Task Scheduler service.
   d. You must use the AT.exe command to create a backup task.

## Projects: On Your Own

**1.** Create a custom console, add a Computer Management snap-in, and save it with the name Managing System.
   a. Access the **Run** dialog box.
   b. Type **MMC**.
   c. Access the **Add/Remove Snap-in** in the Console1 dialog box.
   d. Select the **Computer Management** option.
   e. Save the console.
**2.** Schedule a disk cleanup task to run once a week on Friday.
   a. Access the **Control Panel** window.
   b. Run the **Scheduled Task Wizard**.
   c. Select the **Disk Cleanup** utility.
   d. Set the task to run once a week.
   e. Set the start time for the task as **6:00 AM** on **every Friday**.
   f. Set the security context for the task. (Enter the user name and password for the task to run under.)
   g. Click **Finish**.

## Problem Solving Scenarios

1. You are the coordinator at Expert Trainers Center. You have 20 computers at the training center. The training at the center requires students to access the network frequently. Therefore, many temporary files are created on each workstation, unnecessarily using up disk space. You decide that every morning when the computers are switched on, the Disk Cleanup utility should run. Outline in a memo the steps you would take to run Disk Cleanup every morning, on each of the 20 client computers.

2. The Systems Administrator at CarbonTec Inc., a fabricator of carbon fiber parts for aircraft, would like help in administering the Windows network. Write a memo explaining how he can configure the Microsoft Management Consoles that will allow him to do so.

# 8

# Administering User Accounts and Groups

I n Windows XP Professional, user accounts are used to store relevant details about network users and to distinguish one user from another. There are three types of user accounts: local user accounts, domain user accounts, and built-in user accounts. With a local user account, the account can only be assigned permissions to resources on the computer on which the account was created. Conversely, with a domain user account, you can assign permissions for the user to access resources on any computer on the domain or trusting domains. Built-in user accounts are created when you install Windows XP Professional. The Administrator and Guest accounts are the two built-in user accounts.

In a peer-to-peer or workgroup network, where there is no dedicated server and no central logon authority, resources such as printers, disks, and folders are shared using local user accounts and group names. Microsoft recommends that workgroup networks contain no more than 10 computers. Windows XP Professional is all you will need to create a workgroup network. However, if you want to create a domain-based network, you will have to create at least one central server (domain controller) that stores Active Directory. Active Directory is the database that stores all of the information about users and groups, and manages logging on to the network. In order to create a domain controller you must have Windows 2000 Server or Windows Server 2003 installed. You primarily use only domain user accounts in a domain-based network.

Setting up user accounts in either type of network is the first line of defense against unauthorized access to network resources. You create local user accounts and groups to allow multiple users to access resources on a particular standalone or workgroup computer. Then, you assign permissions to the groups and to individual users so that they can access only certain resources and folders on the machine. A group is, therefore, a collection of user accounts that require similar permissions and rights. In order to create local user accounts, you use the Computer Management console, which is one of the Administrative Tools in the Windows XP Professional operating system. You can also modify existing user accounts by changing their properties.

## Goals

In this lesson, you will identify the user accounts and groups available in Windows XP Professional, plan and create user accounts, explore the user's Properties dialog box, and set properties for user accounts. You will also create local groups, add members to a group, and put built-in groups into operation.

## Lesson 8   Administering User Accounts and Groups

| Skill | Exam 70-270 Objective |
|---|---|
| 1. Introducing User Accounts | Configure, manage, and troubleshoot local user and group accounts. |
| 2. Planning User Accounts | Configure, manage, and troubleshoot local user and group accounts. |
| 3. Creating User Accounts | Configure, manage, and troubleshoot local user and group accounts. |
| 4. The User Accounts Utility | Configure, manage, and troubleshoot local user and group accounts. |
| 5. Identifying User Properties | Configure, manage, and troubleshoot local user and group accounts. Configure, manage, and troubleshoot account settings. Configure and manage user profiles and desktop settings. |
| 6. Setting User Account Properties | Configure, manage, and troubleshoot local user and group accounts. Configure, manage, and troubleshoot account settings. |
| 7. Creating Local Groups | Configure, manage, and troubleshoot local user and group accounts. |
| 8. Adding Members to a Group | Configure, manage, and troubleshoot local user and group accounts. |
| 9. Implementing Built-in Groups | Configure, manage, and troubleshoot user and group rights. |
| 10. Application Installation and Recovery | Manage applications by using Windows Installer packages. |

## Requirements

Administrative rights on a Windows XP Professional computer and on a Windows 2000 Server computer.

# skill 1

# *Introducing User Accounts*

## exam objective

Configure, manage, and troubleshoot local user and group accounts.

## overview

A **user account** is an account that contains all of the personal information related to a user. It also identifies a user on the network. The personal information includes the **user name** and **password**, which are required for logon.

The types of user accounts supported by Windows XP are listed below:

◆ Local
◆ Domain
◆ Built-in

A **local user account** is used to access resources on the computer where the account was created. You cannot replicate local user accounts to any other computer in a workgroup. For example, if you have created a local user account named **user1** on a computer named **comp1**, you can log on to this computer as user1 and access the local resources. If this computer is part of a workgroup that consists of three more computers, **comp2**, **comp3**, and **comp4**, and you want to use the local user account user1 on the other computers in the workgroup, you will have to create the account on each computer. Furthermore, if you want to change the password for the user1 account, you must change the password on each of the computers on which it was created, because each computer maintains its own **local security database**. Local user accounts are created in the local security database and all information pertaining to local user accounts and groups is stored there.

A **domain user account** is used to access the resources of a computer in a domain. A domain can be defined as a group of computers on a network that access a common directory database (**Active Directory**) for authentication purposes. Domains have common rules and procedures such as password policies and account policies. Domain user accounts are created in Active Directory in Windows 2000/2003. Domain user accounts do not need to be created on multiple computers on the network because Active Directory serves as the central storage area for all account information on the network. In order to gain access to resources on the network, a user must enter his or her user name, password, and the domain name during the logon process. Windows XP Professional verifies that the user is authorized to access the domain and creates an **access token**. The access token stores the user information and the security identifiers so that it can be used by the operating system to identify the user.

As you have learned, the authentication protocol used in a Windows 2000/2003 domain is the Kerberos protocol. Kerberos uses a Key Distribution Center (KDC) as an interface between the user at a client workstation and a resource such as a server. The logon process begins when the client sends a request for authentication to the KDC, which replies with a Ticket-Granting Ticket (TGT). The TGT includes the user's security identifiers (SIDs) in the authorization data. Windows XP Professional builds the access token based on this authorization data and any local groups of which the user is a member. Once in possession of the TGT, the user is admitted to the KDC and able to request a session ticket from the KDC for access to a resource in the domain, the server. The KDC then returns a session ticket to the client. The client sends this session ticket to the server in order to gain access to its resources. The server now extracts the authorization data and builds an access token based on the data and the user's local group affiiations, if any. If a user wants to access a resource in another domain, the user must go to the KDC in its domain and request a TGT for the KDC in the resources's domain.

On a workgroup network (**Figure 8-1**), users log on locally and access shared resources on other computers in the workgroup seamlessly, but only if they have an account with the same username and password on the computer they are accessing. When a user attempts to access another computer, the **Connect to** dialog box (**Figure 8-2**) will open and he or she will be required to enter a user name and password with permission to access that computer.

## tip

It is not a good practice to create local user accounts on computers running Windows XP Professional that are part of a domain, because a local user account's scope does not allow it to be used on the domain, and, therefore, it can't be assigned permissions to domain resources.

**Figure 8-1  A workgroup network**

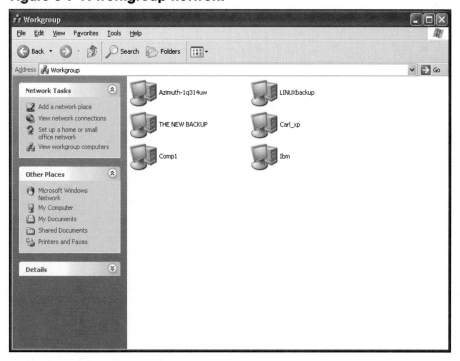

**Figure 8-2  The Connect to dialog box**

Requires you to enter a valid username and password to access another computer on the network

# skill 1

## *Introducing User Accounts (cont'd)*

**exam objective**

Configure, manage, and troubleshoot local user and group accounts.

**overview**

The logon process can be customized to include such features as not displaying the last user name on the logon screen, adding a logon security warning, enabling or disabling the Shutdown button, allowing automated logons, and automatically locking a user account from use after a specific number of invalid logon attempts. These changes to the logon process are accomplished locally through the use of local security policies (see Lesson 12), although they can also be accomplished in the Registry (see Lesson 15) in the HKEY_LOCAL_ MACHINE\SOFTWARE\Microsoft\Windows NT\CurrentVersion\Winlogon key. Setting security policies is the preferred method because it is far safer and easier than making manual changes to a Registry key. In a domain environment, these types of security settings are set using a Group Policy.

**Built-in user accounts** are the default accounts created by Windows XP. The two built-in user accounts are the **Administrator** and **Guest** accounts **(Figure 8-3)**. You can rename these accounts (and should do so for the Administrator account), but you cannot delete them.

The **Administrator account** is used to manage the overall functioning of a computer. You use it to manage and configure the local computer or a domain. The Administrator account should always be renamed, and you should not use it for any other work besides administrative tasks so that you do not run the risk of inadvertently harming your system. The Administrator account cannot be deleted, and it cannot be locked out due to invalid logon attempts. You also cannot remove it from the Administrators local group to which it automatically belongs. The administrative tasks you can perform include:

- ◆ Creating and modifying user accounts and groups
- ◆ Managing security policies
- ◆ Assigning rights and permissions to user accounts
- ◆ Installing printers
- ◆ Installing hardware devices and drivers
- ◆ Changing system date and other system settings

The **Guest account** can be used by people who only need to access computer resources infrequently or on a temporary basis. The Guest account has limited rights, which restrict users from changing the system date and other system settings. Guests cannot perform any administrative tasks and have only limited access to resources. For example, a student who sits for an online exam will likely be assigned the Guest account so that they can answer the questions on the exam, but cannot change any questions or tamper with any other resources on the computer. A new password should always be set for the Guest account, which is blank by default. The Guest account also cannot be deleted or locked out due to invalid logon attempts, but it can be disabled and, in fact, is disabled by default. You can rename the Guest account if you do not want it to be used.

**more**

The prerequisite for creating a domain user account is a domain. This means that at least one computer on the network must be running one of the Windows 2000 Server or Windows Server 2003 products, and be configured as a domain controller.

Administrator and Guest accounts are the two built-in local user accounts

**Figure 8-3  The built-in local user accounts**

# skill 2

## *Planning User Accounts*

**exam objective**

Configure, manage, and troubleshoot local user and group accounts.

## overview

**tip**

Using a naming convention might not seem imperative in a small network, but small networks often end up growing, sometimes rapidly. If you use a naming convention from the beginning, you will be prepared for network expansion and it will be easier to keep track of user names on your network.

**tip**

Typically, the best practice is to let users control their own passwords.

Before you start creating user accounts, you should determine the naming convention you will use, and plan how you will assign and structure the passwords on the network. The **naming convention** is a pattern that users will follow to identify themselves on the network. Following a specific naming convention will make it easier for network users to remember their logon names. For example, as an Administrator, you may create user accounts for the employees in your organization using the first name and last initial of each employee such as **JoeyM** for **Joey Mathews**. When planning your naming convention, there are specific guidelines you should follow. First, local user account names must be unique. There cannot be two accounts with the same name in a local security database; likewise, each domain user account name stored in Active Directory must be unique. Second, logon names can contain a maximum of **20** characters, which can be either upper or lower case. You can actually enter more than 20 characters in the user logon field, but the operating system only accepts the first 20. Third, some characters, including " / \ [ ] : ; | = , + * ? < > are not acceptable. You cannot use these characters in a user logon name. Fourth, although the operating system saves the case when you create a logon name, it is not case sensitive. In other words, Joey Mathews can enter either JoeyM or joeym in the user logon field. Alphanumeric and special characters can also be used to create unique logon names. Finally, if two users have the same name, you must determine a method for differentiating between the two users. You may decide to use the second letter in the last name for one user, or you can add a number to each user name. For example, if two users are named **Erin Williams**, the user names can be **ErinW** and **ErinWi**, or **ErinW1** and **ErinW2**.

Next, you must decide how you will assign and structure the passwords on your network. The password is used in conjunction with the user name to log on to the network. It is imperative that the Administrator account be renamed and assigned a password in order to prevent unauthorized access. Next, you must decide who will be responsible for controlling passwords— the Administrator or the users. If the Administrator controls the passwords, only he or she will be able to change them. Passwords should be difficult for hackers to guess. Employees should be warned against using birth dates, children's names, street names and numbers, college names, and other easily available identifying information in their passwords. Passwords can have a maximum length of **128** characters. It is a good practice to have at least **8** characters in every password. Valid password characters include all upper and lower case letters, numbers, and many non-alphanumeric characters. The same characters that are invalid for logon names are recommended for use in passwords (` ~ ! @ # $ % ^ & * ( ) _ + - = { } | [ ] \ : " ; ' < > ? , . / ). **Table 8-1** sets forth some useful guidelines to follow with respect to the creation of logon names and passwords.

## Table 8-1   Guidelines for Logon Names and Passwords

### Guidelines for Logon Names

1. **Must be Unique:** Local user logon names must be unique on the local computer on which they are created. Domain user logon names must be unique in the domain. No two user logon names in the same parent container can have the same RDN (relative distinguished name) or common name. (See Lesson 17.)

2. **Maximum of 20 characters:** You can enter more than 20, but Windows only recognizes the first 20.

3. **Cannot use invalid characters:** " / \ [ ] : ; | = , + * ? < >

4. **Not case sensitive:** Windows saves the case in which a user logon name was created, but the letters in the logon name can be entered in either upper or lower case when the user is logging on.

5. **Have a system for handling duplicate names:** Devise a consistent system for differentiating between users with the same name. This might involve using the second letter in the last name for one user or adding a number to each user name. You can also use department names in the user name in order to cut down on this type of conflict.

### Guidelines for Passwords

1. **Rename and assign a password to the Administrator account.**

2. **Create passwords that are difficult for hackers to guess.** Strong passwords contain characters from three groups: letters (both uppercase and lower case), numbers, and the non-alphanumeric characters: ` ~ ! @ # $ % ^ & * ( ) _ + - = { } | [ ] \ : " ; ' < > ? , . /

3. **Minimum length of 8 characters.**

4. **Use at least one symbol in the second through sixth spots.**

5. **Keep them different from previously used passwords.**

6. **Can have a maximum of 128 characters.**

7. **Do not use easily available identifying information:** Avoid using common words or names and do not use birth dates, children's names, street names and numbers, or college names.

8. **If your network includes Windows 95 or 98 computers, keep password length to no more than 14 characters.** These operating systems do not support passwords longer than this.

9. **Decide who will control passwords:** If the Administrator controls the passwords, only he or she will be able to change them.

# skill 3

## *Creating User Accounts*

### exam objective

Configure, manage, and troubleshoot local user and group accounts.

### overview

When you are setting up a workgroup network, you will want to create local user accounts for the primary user of each computer, as well as for anyone else who shares the computer. Local user accounts will not have the unrestricted access of the Administrator account, but will allow broader access than the Guest account. One way to create local user accounts on a workgroup workstation is in the **Local Users and Groups** snap-in in the **Computer Management** console **(Figure 8-4)**, using the **New User** dialog box **(Figure 8-5)**.

In the New User dialog box you enter the user information, including the user's logon name (which cannot be left blank), the user's full name (first and last, with a middle initial if desired), a description of the user (for example, their job title or department), and the user's password. The password text is entered as a series of asterisks. Although this is an optional field and it can be left blank when you are first creating an account, all users should be instructed to create a password for their account in order to ensure network security. The password must be re-entered in the **Confirm password** text box to make sure that it has been entered correctly. You can also set a temporary password when you create the account and specify that the user can change the password the first time they log on. This option is selected by default. If the Network Administrator is going to control the passwords, you can select the **User cannot change password** option to disallow users from changing their own passwords. If you want the password to remain unchanged (for example, passwords that a particular program will use), you will set the **Password never expires** option. If you are setting up an account that will not be put into use immediately, or you have an employee who is going on a long leave, you can select the **Account is disabled** option to prevent the account from being used until it is needed.

### how to

Create and test a local user account, **JForester**, on your machine.
1. Log on as the default local user or as an **Administrator**.
2. Click **｜ start｜** and click the **Control Panel** command to open the **Control Panel** window (switch to Classic View, if necessary) **(Figure 8-6)**.
3. Double-click the **Administrative Tools** icon to open the **Administrative Tools** window **(Figure 8-7)**.
4. Double-click the **Computer Management** icon to open the **Computer Management** console.
5. Double-click the **Local Users and Groups** node to open it. There are two folders in the node: **Users** and **Groups**.

**Figure 8-4  Computer Management snap-in**

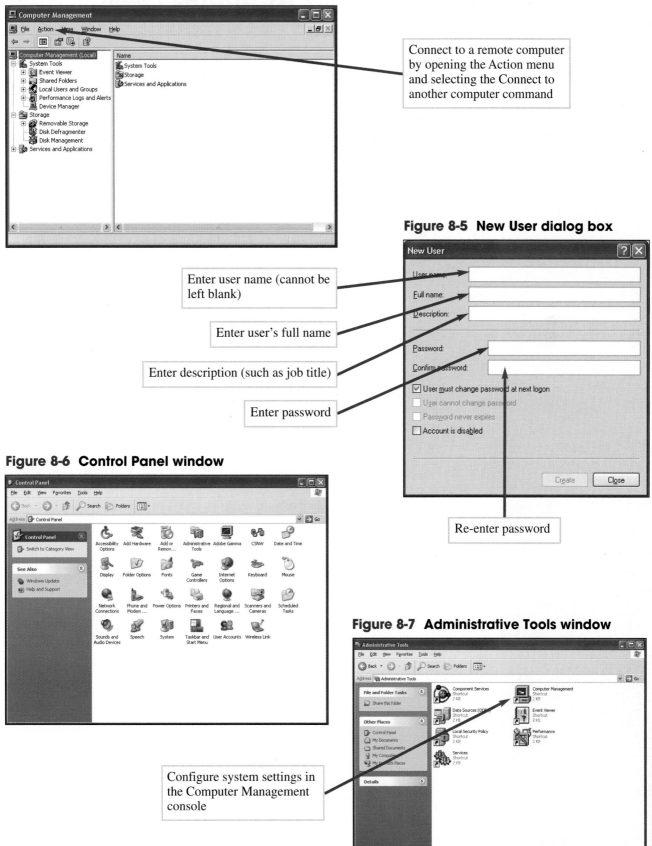

Connect to a remote computer by opening the Action menu and selecting the Connect to another computer command

**Figure 8-5  New User dialog box**

Enter user name (cannot be left blank)

Enter user's full name

Enter description (such as job title)

Enter password

Re-enter password

**Figure 8-6  Control Panel window**

**Figure 8-7  Administrative Tools window**

Configure system settings in the Computer Management console

# skill 3

## Creating User Accounts *(cont'd)*

**exam objective**

Configure, manage, and troubleshoot local user and group accounts.

## how to

**tip**

Always have new users change their passwords the first time they log on in order to ensure that their password is known only to them.

6. Right-click **Users** and click the **New User** command on the shortcut menu **(Figure 8-8)** to open the **New User** dialog box.

7. Type **JForester** in the **User name** text box.

8. Type **Joe Forester** in the **Full name** text box.

9. Type **daylight** in the **Password** text box. Notice that the password appears as a series of asterisks.

10. Re-type the password in the **Confirm password** text box.

11. The **User must change password at next logon** check box is selected by default. **Figure 8-9** illustrates steps **7** to **10**.

12. Click [ Create ]. A local user account is now created. The New User dialog box remains open so that you can create another user account, if necessary.

13. Close the New User dialog box.

14. Close the Computer Management snap-in and the Administrative Tools window.

15. To test the local user account, click [ start ] and click **Log Off**. Next, click **Switch User**. (Note: The Fast User Switching feature is not available on computers that are members of a domain. If your computer is a member of a domain, you will have to log off the current user account and log on to the JForester account using the **Log On to Windows** dialog box.)

16. When the list of user accounts appears, click **Joe Forester**. Type **daylight** in the password text box that opens and press **[Enter]**.

17. The Logon Message, **You are required to change your password at first logon** appears. Click [ OK ]. The **Change Password** window opens.

18. Type a new password, such as **night**, in both the **New Password** and **Confirm New Password** text boxes.

19. Click [ OK ]. The Change Password window displays the message, **"Your password has been changed."**

20. Click [ OK ]. You are now successfully logged on as Joe Forester.

**Figure 8-8  Computer Management snap-in**

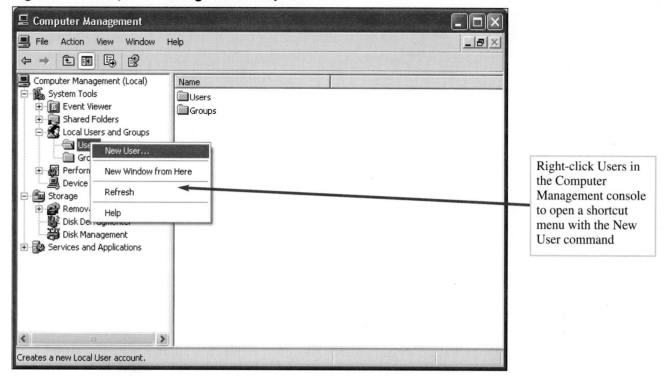

Right-click Users in the Computer Management console to open a shortcut menu with the New User command

**Figure 8-9  New User dialog box**

Optional

Password appears as a series of asterisks

Re-enter password

Check box is selected by default

# skill 4    *The User Accounts Utility*

## exam objective

Configure, manage, and troubleshoot local user and group accounts.

## overview

The other tool you can use to create and manage user accounts is the **User Accounts** utility in the Control Panel. You will only be able to open this utility if you log on with the Administrator account or another user account that is a member of the Administrators group. If you are not currently logged on as an Administrator when you attempt to open the applet, the **User Accounts** utility will offer limited options only: those geared toward modifying the account that is logged on currently. On the Administrator account, the User Accounts tool lists all local user accounts, the groups to which they belong, and if the accounts are password protected. You can add new accounts to the computer, change existing accounts, or change the way users log on or off. If you choose to modify an existing account, your options include changing the name of the account, changing the password, removing the password, changing the picture associated with the account, changing the account type, and deleting the account. However, if you want to change the group to which an account belongs, you will need to use the Local Users and Groups snap-in. Furthermore, you can only create groups in the Local Users and Groups snap-in. You can also use the Local Users and Groups snap-in to make a user a member of several groups.

## how to

Create a local user account using the User Accounts utility.

1. Log on as an **Administrator**.
2. Click  *start*  and click the **Control Panel** command to open the **Control Panel** window.
3. Double-click the **User Accounts** icon to open the User Accounts window dialog box (**Figure 8-10**).
4. Click **Create a new account** to open the **Name the new account** screen.
5. Type **JSimmons** in the text box provided.
6. Click  Next >  to open the **Pick an account type screen**.
7. Select the **Limited** option button (**Figure 8-11**). (Note: If this is the first time you have created an account with this Wizard, you will be required to make the first user a Computer administrator; the Limited account type will be unavailable.)
8. Click  Create Account . The JSimmons account now appears on the main screen of the User Accounts window with the other existing user accounts.
9. Click the JSimmons account in the **or pick an account to change** section of the window.
10. On the **What do you want to change about JSimmons's account?** screen, click **Create a password**.
11. The **Create a password for JSimmons's account** screen explains the ramifications of creating a password for the account. Since the account was just created, the likelihood of losing important data is minimal.
12. Type a password in the **Type a new password** text box and confirm the password in the next text box. Leave the password hint text box blank.
13. Click  Create Password . The JSimmons account is now password protected.
14. Close the User Accounts window and the Control Panel.

## tip

The steps in this exercise describe the process of creating a local user account on a computer that is a member of a workgroup. The process and the screens that you will see will be different if your computer is a domain member.

**Figure 8-10  User Accounts window**

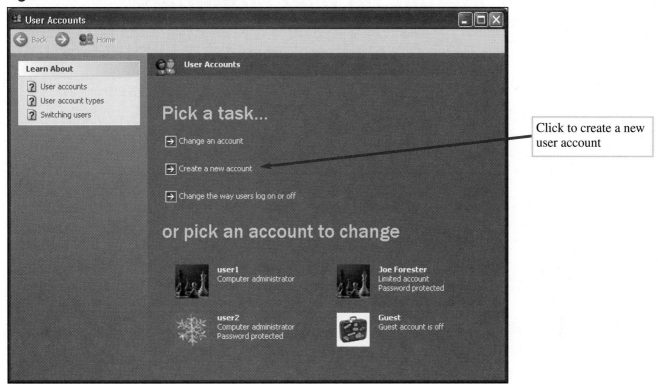

**Figure 8-11  Pick an account type screen**

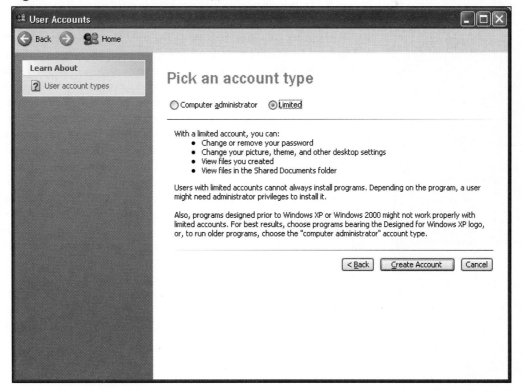

# skill 5

## *Identifying User Properties*

**exam objective**

Configure, manage, and troubleshoot local user and group accounts. Configure, manage, and troubleshoot account settings. Configure and manage user profiles and desktop settings.

**overview**

Every local user account you create has a set of default properties that can be modified in the **Properties** dialog box for that user. To access the Properties dialog box for a specific user account, first open the **Computer Management** console. Select the **Local Users and Groups** snap-in, and double-click the **Users** folder in the details pane to view all of the local user accounts. Double click the **user account name** to open the Properties dialog box. The Properties dialog box contains three tabs (**Figure 8-12**):

◆ General
◆ Member Of
◆ Profile

On the **General** tab, you can change the full name or the description of a user, configure the account so that the user must change his or her password at their next logon, set the password so that it cannot be changed by the user, set the password to never expire, disable the account, or, if the account has been locked out of the system, you can clear the **Account is locked out** check box. Account lockout happens when the user has surpassed a set number of invalid logon attempts. The check box will be activated if the user has been unable to log on within this specified number of attempts. This is a security feature that helps prevent unauthorized users from accessing the resources on the network. Only an Administrator can clear the check box to reactivate the account.

On the **Member Of tab**, you can add or remove user accounts from a group.

On the **Profile tab**, you can set the path for the user profile, logon script, and home folder (**Figure 8-13**). A **user profile** is created the first time a user logs on to a particular computer. It stores directories that contain user-specific data for applications, the user's cookies from their Web-surfing activities, the history list of URLs from Internet Explorer, all of their network and printer mappings, their Microsoft Office templates, and their desktop settings. This includes many settings that the user can specify such as the color scheme, resolution, and application settings, as well as the location of their My Documents folder and user-specific Registry data. Also included in the user profile are directories that store the user's history list of files recently accessed, as well as temporary files, their Start menu layout, and the links they have used with the Send To command. There are two main types of user profiles: either local or roaming. **Local user profiles** are stored locally and are accessed from the logon computer. When a user logs on to a computer, their individual desktop settings and connections are accessed. Different users can log on to the same computer and each can access their own individualized desktop environment, application settings, network connections, and history, as well as most recently used lists. When a user logs on to a computer running Windows XP Professional for the first time, a user profile for that user is created by default and is stored in a folder named after the user logon name under **C:\Documents and Settings**. A **My Documents** folder is created for each user profile and an icon for that folder is available for the desktop. This folder is the default location for the **Open** and **Save As** commands on the **File** menu. When the user modifies their desktop settings, the changes are saved in the user profile. For example, if a user adds a file to the My Documents folder and logs off, the file will be incorporated into the user profile and will be available the next time the user logs on.

**tip:**

If you have upgraded from a previous version of Windows to Windows XP, user profiles may be stored in an alternate location.

**Figure 8-12  JForester Properties dialog box**

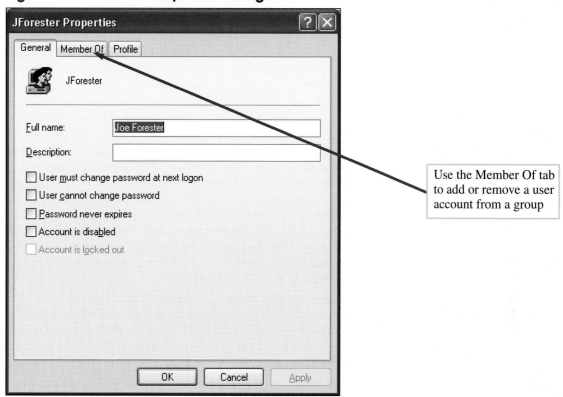

Use the Member Of tab to add or remove a user account from a group

**Figure 8-13  Profile tab of Usr1 Properties dialog box**

Enter the path to the user profile

Enter the path to the logon script you want a user to use; logon scripts run executable files (e.g., anti-virus applications) every time users log on, and for mapping drive letters, initiating programs, and executing command-line operations when the user logs on

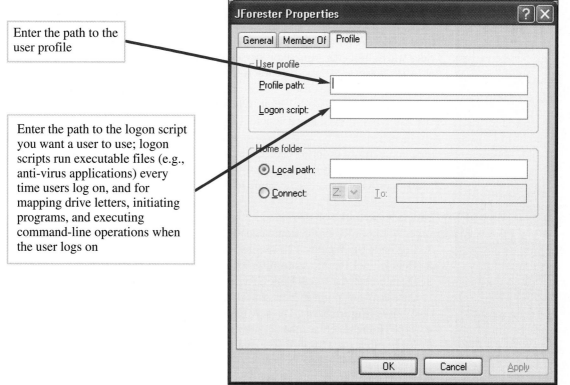

# skill 5

## *Identifying User Properties (cont'd)*

### exam objective

Configure, manage, and troubleshoot local user and group accounts. Configure, manage, and troubleshoot account settings. Configure and manage user profiles and desktop settings.

### overview

As an Administrator, you can delete, copy, or change the type of user profile. For instance, a user profile can be changed from a local user profile to a **roaming user profile**. A roaming user profile sets up the same desktop environment for a user, no matter which computer he or she is using to log on to the domain. Roaming user profiles are one of the distributed computing technologies that were grouped under the name **IntelliMirror** beginning with Windows 2000. The objective behind the IntelliMirror concept is to create an environment in which users can easily move between computers while still being able to access their own data, applications, and settings. A complete IntelliMirror system will include both server-side and client-side features on a domain-based system that includes using Active Directory and Group Policy to centrally manage users' desktops. When you create a roaming user profile, the user can log on to any computer in the domain, and a server will automatically download all of their customized user settings to the local computer.

There are also read-only user profiles called **mandatory user profiles**. Users of mandatory profiles cannot save any changes that are made to the desktop while they are logged on. Mandatory user profiles are generally used when many users share the same profile. Desktop settings can be changed during each session, but the changes will not be available when the user logs on for their next session.

**Logon Script: Logon scripts** are used to set the desktop and working environment for a user. The script is run each time the user logs on. Logon script files can also be useful for running particular executable files, such as anti-virus applications every time a user logs on. Windows 2000, 2003, and XP use logon scripts from group policy. However, logon scripts in the user's account properties are still used to create backwards compatibility with client computers on the network that run older versions of Windows such as NT 4.0 Workstation, Windows 98, and Windows 95.

**Home folder:** A **home folder** is a private network location in addition to the My Documents folder where users can store their personal files. The home folder can be located on a client computer; however, its true function is to serve as a storage area on the network that users can access from any workstation. Therefore, a home folder is more appropriately stored in a shared folder on a network server. When you create the home folder on a network server, users can access it from any computer on the network. Administrators can use this centralized storage area to easily backup important network files instead of going from client computer to client computer in order to make sure that all relevant files are backed up. Users of client computers running any of the Microsoft operating systems, such as MS-DOS, Windows 95, 98, 2000, or XP, can access the home folder.

### tip

It is a good practice to store home folders on an NTFS volume and to use NTFS permissions for security, because this is superior to the shared folder permissions available on a FAT volume.

### how to

Create a home folder on a Windows 2000 network file server and connect to the home folder from a Windows XP Professional client.

1. Log on to the Windows 2000 network file server as an **Administrator**.
2. Double-click the **My Computer** icon on the desktop to open the **My Computer** window.
3. Double-click the **Local Disk C:** icon to display the folders and files on the C: drive. Open the **File** menu, point to **New**, and click the **Folder** command to create a new folder on the C: drive (**Figure 8-14**). The new folder displays the default name **New Folder**.
4. Type **Home** to replace the default name.
5. Right-click the **Home** folder and click the **Properties** command to open the **Home Properties** dialog box.
6. Click the **Sharing** tab. Select the **Share this folder** option button. The Sharing tab is shown in **Figure 8-15**.

### caution

You may have to run the Network Setup Wizard from the Sharing tab before completing step 6 in order to enable remote access to your computer.

**Figure 8-14  Local Disk (C:) window**

New folder created by clicking
on File, pointing to New, and
clicking Folder command

**Figure 8-15  Home Properties dialog box**

# skill 5

## *Identifying User Properties (cont'd)*

**exam objective**

Configure, manage, and troubleshoot local user and group accounts. Configure, manage, and troubleshoot account settings. Configure and manage user profiles and desktop settings.

## how to

7. Click [Permissions] to open the **Permissions for Home** dialog box.
8. Select the **Everyone** group, if necessary **(Figure 8-16)**, and click [Remove].
9. Click [Add...] to open the **Select Users, Computers, or Groups** dialog box.
10. Click the **Users** group in the **Name** section **(Figure 8-17)**, and then click [Add]. The Users group is added to the bottom section of the Select Users, Computers, or Groups dialog box. Click [OK] to close the dialog box and add the Users group to the Permissions for Home dialog box. This way, only users with a valid domain user account will be able to access the folder.
11. Click the **Allow** check box to the right of **Full Control** in the **Permissions** section **(Figure 8-18)**. Then, click [OK].
12. Click [OK] to close the Home Properties dialog box. Close the C: drive window and the My Computer window.
13. On the Windows XP Professional client workstation, click [start] and click **Control Panel** to open the **Control Panel** window.
14. Double-click the **Administrative Tools** icon to open the **Administrative Tools** window.
15. Double-click the **Computer Management** icon to open the **Computer Management** window.
16. Double-click the **Local Users and Groups** snap-in to expand it.
17. In the right pane of the Computer Management window, double-click the **Users** folder to display a list of users on the network.
18. Select a user for whom you would like to create a home folder in the shared Home directory, in this case **JForester**.
19. Right-click **JForester** and click the **Properties** command to open the **JForester Properties** dialog box.
20. Click the **Profile** tab.
21. Select the **Connect** option button in the **Home folder** section of the tab.

**Figure 8-16 Permissions for Home dialog box**

**Figure 8-17 Select Users, Computers, or Groups dialog box**

Select the Everyone group and click Remove

Select Users in the Name section and click the Add button

**Figure 8-18 Permissions for Home folder**

Select proper check boxes to allow or deny permissions to the Users group selected in the Name pane

# skill 5

## *Identifying User Properties (cont'd)*

### exam objective

Configure, manage, and troubleshoot local user and group accounts. Configure, manage, and troubleshoot account settings. Configure and manage user profiles and desktop settings.

### how to

22. In the **To:** text box, specify the UNC (Universal Naming Convention) path for the home folder. The UNC path contains the name of the server (the NetBIOS name for the computer where it is stored), the share name, and, typically, the %username% variable or the user name such as **\\pubserver\home\JForester (Figure 8-19)**. When you use the username variable, each user's home folder is given the user logon name automatically.
23. Click [ OK ]. Close all open windows. You have now successfully created a Home folder on a network file server.

### more

Windows contains a hidden file, known as **Ntuser.dat**, for each user account. This file contains the system settings for an individual user account, along with the environment settings for the user. Log on as an **Administrator** and create a user account that you can use to create user profiles. Log off and log on again using the account you have just created. Configure the desktop environment that you want, for example, select wallpaper, a screen saver, and screen resolution. Log off and log on again using the **Administrator** account. Locate the Ntuser.dat file in **C:\Documents and Settings\user_logon_name (Figure 8-20)**. Make this file a mandatory roaming user profile by changing its name from Ntuser.dat to **Ntuser.man**. Now you can copy this file and apply the mandatory user profile to any user account.

Although this lesson deals mainly with local user accounts, at this point there are several concepts you must understand about domain accounts. They are created in the **Active Directory Users and Computers** console. This console will be created by default on a domain controller. However, you can install it on a Windows XP Professional computer with Service Pack 1 if you have a Windows Server 2003 installation CD. Simply insert the CD and double-click **Adminpak.msi** in the \I386 folder to install the **Windows Server 2003 Administration Tools Pack**. You configure domain user accounts by opening the Users node, right-clicking the user account icon in the details pane, and selecting Properties to open the Properties dialog box for the user. For a domain user account, you can also specify the location of a roaming user profile on a domain server (**Profile** tab), as previously discussed. On the **Account** tab, you can designate certain logon hours to restrict the times the user will be allowed to log on to the domain. On the **Sessions** tab, you can set the **Idle** session limit to log off a user after a set amount of time. As with local user accounts, you can use the **Member of** tab to change the group memberships for a user, and you can also use the **Dial-in** tab to designate if a user has permission to dial in to a Remote Access Server (RAS). Administrators can also disable accounts, change passwords, move domain user accounts to different OUs (organizational units), and delete and rename domain user accounts, just as the Local Administrator can do for local user accounts. On a domain-based network, it will often take some time for new domain user accounts to be replicated to the other domain controllers on the network. Therefore, if a new user cannot log on, simply waiting a bit may solve the problem. Another common reason users may report an inability to log on is that they have inadvertently selected an incorrect domain in the list box in the logon dialog box. Other logon problems include the setting needing to be adjusted on the Account tab or users attempting to log on during hours that have been placed off limits. If the user cannot connect to a remote server, check to make sure that permission has been granted on the Dial-in tab. In Lesson 12, you will learn about group policies. Domain group policies take precedence over local group policies. If a user is having trouble logging on, you may need to open the Active Directory Users and Computers console (in the Administrative Tools folder), right-click the domain to which the user belongs, and open the Properties dialog box for the domain on the **Group Policy** tab. Here, you can select a Group Policy object and click the **Edit** button to open the Group policy snap-in, where you can view the policy settings to determine if a policy setting for the domain is overriding a local computer policy and is affecting the ability of the user to log on.

### tip

To display hidden files, open the Tools menu and click Folder Options. On the View tab of the Folder Options dialog box, select the Show hidden files and folders option button.

### caution

If you have upgraded a Windows 2000 computer to Windows XP Professional, the Windows 2000 Adminpak.msi file is not compatible.

**Figure 8-19  JForester Properties dialog box**

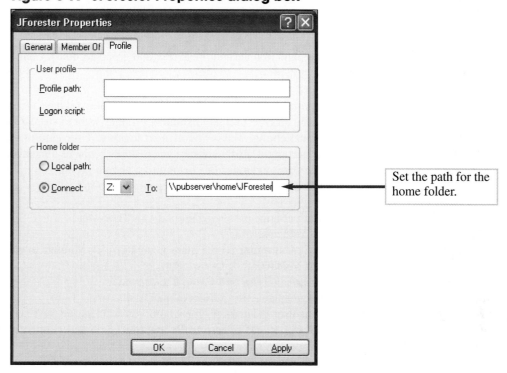

Set the path for the home folder.

**Figure 8-20  NTUSER.DAT file**

NTUSER.DAT file containing system settings for user2

# skill 6

## *Setting User Account Properties*

**exam objective**

Configure, manage, and troubleshoot local user and group accounts. Configure, manage, and troubleshoot account settings.

**overview**

If you need to modify the properties of a user account after you have created it, you use the **Properties** dialog box for the user. For example, you may want to change the password property from **User must change Password at next logon** to **User cannot change password.** Modifying a user account is also necessary when a user becomes a member of an additional group or when they no longer need to belong to a certain group. You access the Properties dialog box for a user in the **Computer Management** snap-in.

**how to**

Set the **User cannot change password** property for **JForester**.

1. Log on as an **Administrator**.
2. Right-click **My Computer** on the Start menu and click **Manage** to open the **Computer Management** window.
3. Double-click **Local Users and Groups** to expand it.
4. Click **Users** to display a list of users in the Details pane.
5. Right-click the user (**JForester**) for whom you want to set the **User Cannot Change Password** property, and select the **Properties** command (**Figure 8-21**) to open the **JForester Properties** dialog box.
6. Select the **User cannot change password** check box (**Figure 8-22**), and click ⌷ OK ⌷. Close the Computer Management window.
7. Click **Log Off** on the Start menu, click Switch User, and log on as **JForester**. (Note: The Fast User Switching feature is not available on computers that are members of a domain. If your computer is a member of a domain, you will have to log off the current user account and log on to the JForester account using the **Log On to Windows** dialog box.)
8. Open the Control Panel and double-click **User Accounts** (single click in Category View).
9. Click **Change my password** on the **Pick a task...** screen.
10. Type **night** as the password in the **Type your current password** text box, and then type **daybreak** in the **Type a new password** and **Type the new password again to confirm** text boxes.
11. Click ⌷ Change Password ⌷. The **User Accounts** message box informs you that Windows cannot change the password.
12. Click ⌷ OK ⌷ to close the User Accounts message box. Close the User Accounts window and the Control Panel.
13. Log Off the JForester account and log back on as an Administrator or as the defaul local user.

**caution**

You will find variations in these steps if your computer is a member of a domain.

**more**

If a user is having trouble with his or her account, open the Properties dialog box for that user and check the settings. For example, if the user wants to change the password but is unable to do so, open that user's **Properties** dialog box and make sure that the **User cannot change password** check box is not selected. Similarly, if a user is unable to access his or her account, make sure that the **Account is disabled** or **Account is locked out** check boxes are not selected.

**Figure 8-21 Computer Management window**

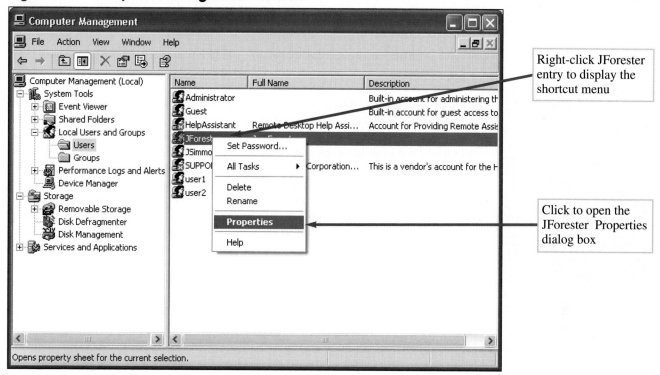

Right-click JForester entry to display the shortcut menu

Click to open the JForester Properties dialog box

**Figure 8-22 Setting the User cannot change password property**

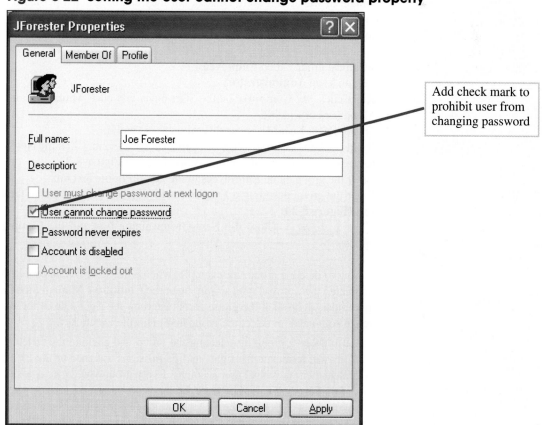

Add check mark to prohibit user from changing password

# skill 7 *Creating Local Groups*

**exam objective**

Configure, manage, and troubleshoot local user and group accounts.

**overview**

Groups are used to make it easy to assign permissions and rights to users with similar needs. It is much easier to assign permissions and rights to a group of users rather than having to assign permissions and rights on an individual basis. **Permissions** are used to assign the capabilities a user has when he or she gains access to a resource. For example, students in a class would likely be assigned permission to read the files in a professor's folder, but would not be able to modify them. First, to assign permissions to such a group, you create a Students group and give that group the Read-only permission. Then, you add the user accounts for these students to the Students group. **Rights** give users the ability to perform system tasks such as changing the time on the computer or shutting down the system. A member of a group receives all of the permissions and rights that are given to a group. Users can belong to multiple groups, and one group can belong to another group in a domain.

**Local Groups:** A **local group** resides in the local security database on a single computer and is a used to assign permissions and rights to local user accounts for the resources on that computer. Local groups are used in peer-to-peer or workgroup networks. For the most part, they should not be used on domain-based networks. Windows XP Professional can only create and manage local groups. A local group cannot be a member of any other group.

On a domain-based network, you can create **global groups** that can be added to a local group in order to access resources in the domain. If you use local groups in a domain-based network, they will not appear in Active Directory, so you will have to administer them individually.

On a domain-based network **domain local groups** are used to assign rights and permissions to resources in a particular domain for any user. Global groups can have members only from the domain in which they were created, but they can be granted permissions in any domain within a forest of domains (See Lesson 17). Domain local groups can only be assigned permissions in the domain in which it is created.

**how to**

Create a local group called **Employees**.

1. Log on as an **Administrator**.
2. Right-click **My Computer** on the Start menu and click **Manage** to open the **Computer Management** window.
3. Double-click **Local Users and Groups** to expand it.
4. Right-click the **Groups** folder to open a shortcut menu. Click the **New Group** command to open the **New Group** dialog box, as shown in **Figure 8-23**.
5. Enter the group name **Employees** in the **Group name** text box.
6. Enter the group description **Employees of Blossoms Creations** in the **Description** text box (**Figure 8-24**).
7. Click [ Create ]. Close the New Group dialog box and the Computer Management window.

**more**

If you want to delete a group, for example, when a group of freelancers in your organization has completed their project, you simply open the **Computer Management** window, open the **Groups** folder, right-click the group name listed on the right side of the window, and select the **Delete** command, or select the group and press the Delete key.

You can also delete a group by selecting the group and clicking the Delete ☒ button on the toolbar. This will terminate the rights and permissions assigned to the Freelancers group, but will not delete their individual user accounts. Every group you create is assigned a unique **SID** (security identifier) that is used by the operating system to recognize the group and its permissions. When a group is deleted, the SID will not be reused even if you create another group with the same name. In order to recreate the group, you must reassign the rights and permissions.

**Figure 8-23  New Group dialog box**

**Figure 8-24  New Group dialog box showing the Group name and Description**

# skill 8

# Adding Members to a Group

## exam objective

Configure, manage, and troubleshoot local user and group accounts.

## overview

As new employees join your organization, you will have to add their user accounts to various groups that are relevant to the projects they will be working on. This will help you to effectively manage the rights and permissions of employees working on different projects or in different departments. To add members to a group, you use the Select Users and Groups dialog box, which is accessed in the Computer Management console.

## how to

Add a user, **JForester**, to the **Power Users** group.

1. Open the **Computer Management** window and expand the **Local Users and Groups** node.
2. In the left pane of the Computer Management window, click **Groups** to display a list of all the available groups in the details pane.
3. Double-click **Power Users** to open the **Power Users Properties** dialog box (**Figure 8-25**).
4. Click [ Add... ]. **The Select Users or Groups** dialog box opens.
5. Make sure that **Users or Built-in security principals** appears in the **Select this object type** text box. If it does not, click [ Object Types... ] and select **Users**.
6. Make sure that the computer on which you are working appears in the **From this location** text box. If it does not, click [ Locations... ] and select the computer.
7. Type **JForester** in the **Enter the object names to select** text box (**Figure 8-26**).
8. Click [ OK ]. The Power Users Properties dialog box displays the selected user's name in the **Members** section, as shown in **Figure 8-27**.
9. Click [ OK ] to close the Power Users Properties dialog box. Close all other open windows.

### tip

You can add multiple user names at the same time by separating each name with a semicolon.

## more

When an employee is transferred or promoted to a different department, you may have to remove his or her user account from a particular group. To remove a member from a group, open the **Properties** dialog box for the group, select the member, and click [ Remove ]. The selected user or users will be removed from the group. Click [ OK ] to close the Properties dialog box.

### tip

You can use the **Member Of** tab in the **Properties** dialog box for the user to add a user account to multiple groups.

**Figure 8-25  Power Users Properties dialog box**

**Figure 8-26  Select Users or Group dialog box**

**Figure 8-27  Adding a user to a group**

Specified user's name appears in Members section

# skill 9 *Implementing Built-in Groups*

**exam objective**

Configure, manage, and troubleshoot user and group rights.

**overview**

Built-in groups are created automatically by Windows XP Professional during installation. There are two types of built-in groups: either local or system. **Built-in local groups** are found on all Windows XP Professional computers, as well as on Windows 2000/2003 servers that are not domain controllers. They have preset rights or privileges for the local computer such as modifying the desktop, installing a program, sharing a folder, or backing up the hard drive. You can view the rights that each built-in group has by opening the **Local Security Policy** console in the Administrative Tools folder. Expand the **Local Policies** node and double-click **User Rights Assignment (Figure 8-28)**. For example, only Administrators will have the right to **Increase quotas** and **Load and unload device drivers**. You can change the rights that built-in groups are granted by default by applying security templates (See Lesson 12). In Windows XP Professional, the built-in local groups can be found in the **Groups** folder in the **Computer Management** window **(Figure 8-29)**. You add users to these built-in local groups to give them the appropriate level of interaction with the operating system. A list of the built-in local groups and their capabilities is given below:

- ◆ **Users:** These users cannot share folders, install programs that other users will be able to run, create local printers, or modify system settings in the operating system, the Registry, or in applications. All local user accounts you create automatically become members of this group, which enables them to run all Windows XP applications but may not allow them to run some older Windows NT 4.0 applications. The compatible security template **(compatws.inf)** reduces some of the user rights restrictions on the Users group so that members can run older Windows NT 4.0 applications.
- ◆ **Administrators:** Users with unlimited access, rights, and permissions. The built-in local user account, Administrator, is automatically added to this group.
- ◆ **Guests:** Users with restricted access who cannot change the desktop environment. The built-in local user account, Guest, is automatically made a member of this group. These users will generally have to be given individual rights in order to perform even the most basic tasks.
- ◆ **Power Users:** These users can create local user accounts, install applications that do not involve operating system services or change operating system files, run and halt system services that did not start automatically, and remove users from the Guests, Users, and Power Users groups. They cannot, however, change or delete user accounts that they did not create, change the memberships in the Administrators or Backup Operators groups, or take ownership of files.
- ◆ **Backup Operators:** These users can back up and restore any file on the system. Members of the Users group can only do so if they have the proper file access permissions.
- ◆ **Network Configuration Operators:** This group is intended for users who might need to switch networks, but shouldn't have the wide range of rights afforded to power users.
- ◆ **Remote Desktop Users:** Members of this group are able to connect to the Windows XP Professional computer and use it as though they were a local user via the Remote Desktop feature, a form of Terminal Services.
- ◆ **HelpServicesGroup:** This group exists exclusively for the Microsoft support account that is created when you install Windows XP Professional. The support account is the singular default member of the group, which provides the necessary rights for a remote assistant to conduct support services.
- ◆ **Replicators:** These users can perform file replication in a domain.

**Figure 8-28  User rights assignments for built-in local groups**

**Figure 8-29  Groups node in the Local Users and Groups snap-in**

All local groups on the computer are included in the Groups folder; the groups shown are the built-in local groups and the Employees group created in Skill 7

# skill 9

## Implementing Built-in Groups *(cont'd)*

**exam objective**

Configure, manage, and troubleshoot user and group rights.

**overview**

**Built-in system groups** are found on all computers that run Windows XP Professional. Built-in system groups do not have any specific members. Therefore, you cannot add, modify, or remove users from this group. Members of a built-in system group are based upon how a user gains access to the computer or the network rather than on which user is accessing the computer. You may recognize the names of the built-in system groups if you have assigned permissions to resources on a network **(Figure 8-30)**. The commonly used system groups are given below:

◆ **Everyone:** All users who are accessing the computer, including the Guest account. This, however, no longer includes anonymous logins as in versions of Windows prior to Windows 2000. The inclusion of the Anonymous Logon group in the Everyone group posed significant security risks because users without valid user accounts could access a computer without having to log on, and receive all of the rights and permissions assigned to the Everyone group.

◆ **Authenticated Users:** All users who have been authenticated either on the local computer or in the domain (those with valid user accounts in the local security database or in the domain database in Active Directory). In contrast to the Everyone group, this excludes the Guest account.

◆ **Creator Owner:** Users who create or take ownership of a resource, for example, a folder.

◆ **Interactive:** Users who are accessing local resources on the computer with which they are physically interacting.

◆ **Network:** Users who are accessing a shared resource on a computer via a network connection.

◆ **Anonymous Logon:** Users with accounts that were not authenticated by Windows XP Professional.

◆ **Dialup:** Users who are accessing a shared resource on a computer via a dial-up connection or virtual private network (VPN).

**Figure 8-30  Assigning permissions to the Everyone group**

# skill 10

# *Application Installation and Recovery*

## exam objective

Manage applications by using Windows Installer packages.

## overview

Windows Installer is an application installation technology that augments the Add or Remove Programs Wizard. It is touted by Microsoft as one of the main features that reduces the TCO (Total Cost of Ownership) of a Windows network and, as previously mentioned, one of the IntelliMirror technologies that facilitates users moving from computer to computer. Microsoft's other applications, as well as many other application providers, now include this technology in order to manage user installation options and to ensure the complete and safe removal of applications. Windows Installer is also useful for its diagnostic capabilities for malfunctioning applications. It can find which key files have been deleted or are corrupt, and easily repair them in order to restore functionality. It also includes the ability to take a snapshot of the current system configuration so that the computer can return to its original state in the event of an aborted or failed application installation. Windows Installer packages are autonomous databases that contain a set of rules and instructions for application program interfaces (APIs), which software developers must follow in order for Windows Installer to process the commands they present for installation. The benefits of the Windows Installer service include improved management facilities such as advertising features without installing them, user customization, and installing software on demand.

In order for applications to use the Windows Installer service, the installation routines must be written in an MSI file. MSI stands for Microsoft Installer, which is the name given to the previous version of the service. Installing applications on a Windows XP Professional computer simply involves double-clicking an .msi file, or right-clicking it and selecting the Install command on the shortcut context menu. If you have a Windows-Installer-"aware" application on a CD-ROM (**Figure 8-31**), you can conserve disk space by installing only the minimum files required for the application. Then, you can subsequently install additional files as they become necessary. You can also use the Microsoft Installer Executive, MSIEXEC.EXE, at the command prompt or in the Run dialog box. To install an application, you would add the command line parameter /I. Some of the other command line parameters you can use with MSIEXEC.EXE are outlined in **Table 8-2**. Windows Installer is one of the services listed when you open the **Services** node in the **Administrative Tool**s window (click **Start**, click **Control Panel**, double-click **Administrative Tools**, double-click **Services**).

However, the true capabilities of Windows Installer can only be taken advantage of on a domain-based Active Directory system, where the .msi files can be copied to a network share, and a Group Policy can be created to manage the installation of applications. When MSI files are deployed via a GPO (Group Policy Object), they can be stored on a member server, or on any other server that is given the appropriate UNC path and permissions. This process is a bit more complex and involves deciding whether to publish an application for users or whether to assign it to users or computers. When you publish an application, it is made available to any user who wants it and will appear in the Add or Remove Programs control panel. Users will simply have to run the Add or Remove Programs Wizard to install the application. Applications are published only to specific users, not to computers. On the other hand, when you assign an application, you designate the users *or computers* to which it will be made available. If the application is assigned to a user, he or she will simply have to open the application from the Start menu, or attempt to open a file created using the application and it will be automatically installed. The application will always be included on the user's Start menu and cannot be deleted. If the program is removed, it will reappear on the Start menu. If it is assigned to a computer, it will install the next time the computer is started. Administrators generally choose to assign applications to computers when several users share a workstation, and they will all need the same program, or if an application is only needed on one or several computers.

**Figure 8-31  Windows Installer Package files on a CD-ROM**

## Table 8-2   Command Parameters for MSIEXEC.EXE

| Variable | Function |
|----------|----------|
| /I | Installs or configures a product. For example, to install an application from the D: drive, you would type: **msiexec /I D:\\<*filename*>.msi** |
| /F | Fix or repair: This is the command-line version of the Repair option. It is used with a number of other variables that designate exactly what to repair. For example, **p** is used to designate that you only want to reinstall if a file is missing, **o** is used to reinstall if a file is missing or if an older version is installed, **e** is used to reinstall if a file is missing or an equal or older version is installed, and **d** is used to reinstall if a file is missing or a different version is installed. |
| /L | Log: Windows Installer automatically logs noteworthy events in the Application event log by default. If you want to designate other events that you want recorded, you will use this variable in conjunction with other variables to specify the events you want the log file to include. For example, **i** is used to record Status messages, **w** is used to record nonfatal warnings, **e** is used to record all error messages, **a** is used to record the startup of actions, and **u** is used to record user requests. |
| /P | Patch: This variable modifies an existing administrative image on a server that client workstations will use to install the application. For example, if you want to apply a patch to an administrative installation package, type: **msiexec /p <*PatchPackage*> /a <*filename*>.msi** |
| /X | Extract or Uninstall: This is the command line version of the Remove option in the Add or Remove Programs Wizard. |
| /J | This variable is used to advertise an application. It is used with a number of other variables to designate how you want the application to be advertised. For example, **u** is used to advertise to the current user, and **m** is used to advertise to all users of the computer. For example, to advertise a package to all users of this computer you would type: **msiexec /jm <*filename*>.msi** |

# skill 10

## *Application Installation and Recovery (cont'd)*

**exam objective**

Manage applications by using Windows Installer packages.

**overview**

The benefits that are conveyed to the Add or Remove Programs Wizard (**Figure 8-32**) include the repair process, which can replace any necessary application or system files that may have been unintentionally deleted or lost in a system crash. This is where the IntelliMirror capability comes in. Users can reconfigure their computers with the same applications and settings they had previously. The Add or Remove Programs Wizard can also perform a more thorough un-installation than was previously possible. Registry entries, shortcuts, and other odds and ends files are now removed from the system. To uninstall an application, users simply have to open the Add or Remove Programs window, select the application in question, and click the **Change/Remove** button. You will then receive information or instructions on how to proceed with the removal of the program (**Figure 8-33**).

**Figure 8-32  Add or Remove Programs window**

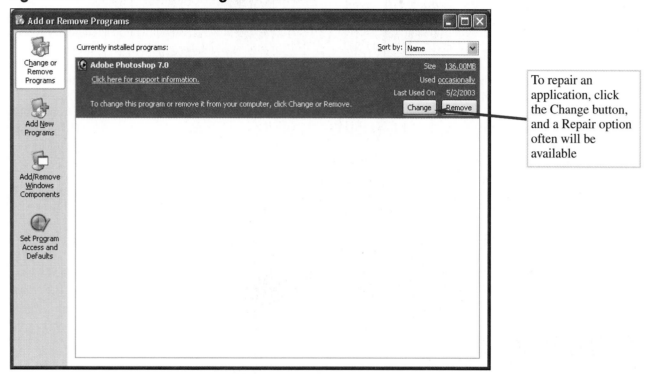

> To repair an application, click the Change button, and a Repair option often will be available

**Figure 8-33  Removing an application**

# Summary

- A user account stores the personal information of a user and is used to identify the user on the network.
- There are three types of user accounts in Windows XP Professional: local user accounts, domain user accounts, and built-in user accounts.
- You create user accounts in the Computer Management snap-in, which is found in the Administrative Tools window.
- Local user accounts are used to access the local resources on a computer.
- Local user accounts cannot be replicated automatically in a workgroup.
- Domain user accounts are used to logon to a domain and gain access to resources on computers on the network. A client requests authentication from a KDC, which sends the client a TGT. The client can then use the TGT to request a session ticket for a resource from the KDC.
- Built-in user accounts are default accounts created by Windows XP Professional.
- There are two built-in user accounts: Administrator and Guest.
- The Administrator account is used to manage the overall functioning of a computer.
- The Guest account is assigned to users who use the computer only occasionally or on a temporary basis, and thus the account has very limited rights.
- Windows Installer is an application installation technology that augments the Add or Remove Programs Wizard.
- The benefits of the Windows Installer service include improved management facilities such as advertising features without installing them, user customization, and installing software on demand.
- In order for applications to use the Windows Installer service, the installation routines must be written in an MSI file.
- You can also use the Microsoft Installer Executive, MSIEXEC.EXE, at the command prompt or in the Run dialog box.
- Windows Installer is one of the services listed when you open the Services node in the Administrative Tools window.

# Key Terms

Access token
Administrator account
Assigned application
Built-in local groups
Built-in system groups
Built-in user accounts
Domain local group
Domain user account
Global group
Group
Guest account

Home folder
IntelliMirror
Local group
Local user account
Local user profile
Logon script
Mandatory user profile
Member Of tab
My Documents
Naming convention
Ntuser.dat

Password
Permissions
Profile tab
Publishing an application
Rights
Roaming user profile
User account
User account properties
User profile
Windows Installer

# Test Yourself

1. Users who do not need to access the resources of a computer frequently, would typically be:
   a. Assigned a local user account.
   b. A member of a built-in system group.
   c. A member of a built-in local group.
   d. Using the Guest account.

2. Carole has transferred to a different department in your organization and you must remove her account from the Accounting group. Which of the following tabs will you use?
   a. General
   b. Member Of

   c. Profile
   d. Sharing

3. This type of user profile sets up the same desktop environment for a user no matter which computer he or she is using to log on to the domain.
   a. Mandatory user profile
   b. Local user profile
   c. Roaming user profile
   d. Home folder user profile

4. You set these to assign the capabilities a user will have after they gain access to a resource:

a. User profile
b. Passwords
c. Permissions
d. Logon script

5. Your company has recruited new Instructional Designers who are required to work on a project on Windows 2000 Server. To make their storyboards, they need to take screenshots and edit them using Adobe Photoshop. Your company has only one licensed copy of Adobe Photoshop, so it can be installed only on one computer. The Instructional Designers will have to work in shifts to use Photoshop. The computer on which you have installed Photoshop has critical files stored on it, so you cannot give Full Control to the Instructional Designers. You need to make a collection of their accounts on this computer, and then assign them permissions. Which of the following options best describe this collection?
   a. Local group
   b. Domain
   c. User profile
   d. Power user

6. A group that does not have any specific members is known as a:
   a. Built-in system group.
   b. Built-in local group.
   c. Local group.
   d. Domain local group.

7. A group that can create or modify a local user account is known as:
   a. A Replicator.
   b. Power Users.
   c. Authenticated Users.
   d. Creator Owner.

8. A roaming user profile enables you to:
   a. Create a group of computers on a network sharing a common directory database.
   b. Store user-specific settings on a computer on which the user has logged on.
   c. Set up the same desktop environment, application settings, network connections, and history and most recently used lists for a user in a domain no matter which computer they use to log on.

d. Store information for a user that defines him/her on the network.

9. In order to gain access to resources on a domain, a user must enter his or her user name, password, and the domain name during the logon process. The logon request is received by a Key Distribution Center. The KDC issues a/an _____ to the client, which stores the user information and security identifiers so that the client can go back to the KDC to request a session ticket for the resource that the client wants to access.
   a. Permission
   b. User profile
   c. Ticket-Granting Ticket
   d. Server license

10. Which of the following best describes a group of computers on a network that use a common directory database to authenticate users who attempt to log on?
   a. User accounts
   b. Domain
   c. Access tokens
   d. Security database

11. The account that is created in the local security database of a computer is the:
   a. Domain user account.
   b. Guest account.
   c. Local user account.
   d. Built-in system account.

12. You can have a maximum of 25 characters in user logon names.
   a. True
   b. False

13. The Password never expires option is useful if you have more than one user accessing the same account.
   a. True
   b. False

14. To add members to a group, you use the Select Users dialog box, which is accessed from the Computer Management window.
   a. True
   b. False

## Projects: On Your Own

1. Create a local user account.
   a. Log on as an **Administrator**.
   b. Click **Start** on the taskbar of your computer, then click **Control Panel**.
   c. Double-click the **Administrative Tools** icon.
   d. Double-click the **Computer Management** icon.
   e. Expand **Local Users and Groups** by double-clicking it.

   f. Right-click **Users** and click **New Users**.
   g. Type **VWilliams** in the **User Name** text box.
   h. Type **Victoria Williams** in the **Full Name** text box.
   i. Type any password, such as **daylight**, in the **Password** text box if you wish to assign a password to the user.
   j. Type the same password in the **Confirm Password** text box.

k.  Select the check box to specify whether the user can change the password or not.

l.  Click **Create**.

**2.** Set the User cannot change password property.

a.  Log on as an **Administrator**.

b.  Click **Start** on the taskbar and click **Control Panel**.

c.  Double-click the **Administrative Tools** icon.

d.  Double-click the **Computer Management** icon.

e.  Expand **Local Users and Groups** by double-clicking it.

f.  Click **Users** in the left pane.

g.  Right-click the user for whom you want to set the **User cannot change password** property.

h.  Click the **Properties** option.

i.  Check the **User cannot change password** option in the user's **Properties** dialog box and click **OK**.

## Problem Solving Scenarios

1. You have just been hired as an Assistant Network Administrator by Sureflow Baggage Inc., a company in Pewaukee, Wisconsin that manufactures computer-controlled baggage handling equipment for the airlines. There are 140 employees, all of whom will be given access to the shared resources stored on workstations on the company's Windows peer-to-peer network. You want to ensure that executives, managers, and regular employees are assigned permissions giving them access to only the information they require, as determined by senior management. You will need to establish three local groups and assign different rights and permissions to each group. Outline in a memo the steps you will take to create the three local groups. Include information on how you will structure users' logon names and passwords.

2. Senior management at Sureflow Baggage is very concerned about the security of data on the company's network. They want executives and managers to be required to enter a new password every time they logon, but they want regular employees to have just one password. Executives and managers will be issued a small password generator that generates a unique eight-character password each time it is activated. Outline the steps you will take to create this capability.

# Working with Shared Folders

**S**ince the main function of any network of computers is to share resources, providing accessibility to files and folders, as well as making sure that the correct levels of access are granted, is crucial to a functional and secure system. Shares are segments of a computer's resources that are made available to other users on a network. If you do not grant sufficient access, users may be hampered in performing their duties. On the other hand, if the access you grant is too liberal, you risk the inadvertent, or even intentional, loss or destruction of vital enterprise data. There are three levels of control in a Windows XP environment: local, network, and Internet. You must control access to shared resources on a local computer, as well as resources that are shared over the network, and you can also control network access to an intranet, or the Internet, using the Internet Information Service (IIS) snap-in. Network sharing is controlled by the File and Printer Sharing for Microsoft Networks service (also known more simply as the Server service), which is automatically configured on all Windows XP Professional computers, and starts as soon as the operating system is initiated. The Server service uses the Server Message Block (SMB) protocol to communicate with other Windows computers so that file and print resources can be shared between network users.

As you have learned, access to both a local PC and networked computers can be controlled by setting group policies. Beyond that, the type of local and network access that can be granted depends upon the type of disks in use. On FAT, FAT32, and NTFS partitions and volumes, you can use what are called **share permissions**, or shared folder permissions, to control access to network resources. On NTFS volumes, you can also use NTFS permissions to control access to both files and folders on the local computer. You can use share permissions in conjunction with NTFS permissions to control network access if a folder resides on an NTFS partition. Using share permissions, you can permit particular users to access only certain folders and, to some degree, you can control the level of access or the tasks they will be able to perform after they have opened the folder. In this lesson, we will concentrate on how to create share permissions.

After you assign permissions, you will also need to monitor user access to shared folders in order to maintain and secure the data. To do this, you can view a list of open files that are located in the shared folders, as well as the users who are currently using the files. Additionally, you can make the shared folders available offline by storing copies of the files in a reserved portion of disk space on the client machine called the cache. This enables you to work on the latest version of files even when you are not connected to the network.

## Goals

In this lesson, you will learn how to share folders, assign permissions to shared folders, and connect to a shared folder. You will also learn how to monitor access to shared folders and how to configure offline files and folders.

| Skill | Exam 70-270 Objective |
| --- | --- |
| 1. Introducing Shared Folders | Basic knowledge |
| 2. Sharing a Folder | Create and remove shared folders. |
| 3. Introducing Types of Permissions for Shared Folders | Control access to files and folders by using permissions. Control access to shared folders by using permissions. |
| 4. Accessing Shared Resources on a Windows Network | Basic knowledge |
| 5. Monitoring Access to Shared Folders | Manage and troubleshoot access to shared folders. Monitor, manage, and troubleshoot access to files and folders. |
| 6. Configuring and Managing Offline Files and Folders | Manage and troubleshoot access to and synchronization of offline files. Optimize access to files and folders. |

## Requirements

To complete this lesson, you will need a system with Windows XP Professional installed on it.

# skill 1 *Introducing Shared Folders*

**exam objective**

Basic knowledge

## overview

In Windows XP Professional, members of the Administrators or Power Users groups can create shared folders on FAT and FAT32 partitions, or on NTFS volumes using one of three methods: Windows Explorer, the Shared Folder utility, or the NET SHARE command. This type of access control is only for folders. Individual files within the folders cannot be given their own sets of permissions. To control who can access a particular file, you must grant the appropriate privileges to the folder in which it is stored. Unless a contradictory group policy has been set, shared folders can be made available on removable disks and CD-ROM drives. However, shared folder permissions are not applicable at the local computer level. It is very important that you understand this. They cannot be used to control what users can access locally. By default, all local resources can be accessed by any user, except on NTFS volumes where many system folders and files are protected from access by users. In contrast, shared folders are used for networks and share permissions must be set up or these folders cannot be accessed by anyone.

When you set up shared folder permissions, you grant different levels of access to individual users or groups. As you have learned, using groups is the best method, because it is much easier for Administrators to set permissions for groups of users. After you determine which folders will be shared and which groups or individuals will be able to access them, you set permissions to control what these users will be allowed to do, depending on the type of resource. For example, you can assign the Change permission for a folder in order to allow users to modify the data in the folder, as well as delete files in the folder. On the other hand, the Manage Printers permission allows users to have administrative control over a printer so that they can change the properties for the printer, pause and restart it, and share and remove sharing permissions from the printer.

You set share permissions in the ACL (Access Control List) for that resource. Most objects in Windows XP Professional have an ACL. The ACLs you will access to set share permissions are for folders, Registry keys, and printers. The default permission for a shared resource is Full Control for the Everyone group. Generally, you will remove this permission and set your own according to your organizational needs. You can also organize the shared folders according to their function in order to make it easy for users to locate them. You can store different types of content, such as applications or data, in a shared folder. Based on the contents, you can categorize shared folders in the following ways (**Figure 9-1**):

◆ **Shared Application folders:** A Shared Application folder contains the applications that users can access over the network. Storing applications in one place is an organizationally sound design because it creates a single location from which programs can be installed and upgraded. This way you will not have to install applications on each system separately. Shared Application folders are stored on a network server where they can be used by the client systems.

◆ **Shared Data folders:** A Shared Data folder is used to store either Working Data or Public Data. Working data folders contain centralized information that a select group of users needs to perform their duties. Public data folders contain more general centralized data that is used by a large group of users.

**tip**

In a domain, the **Administrators** and **Server Operators** groups can share folders on any computer in the domain. The local **Power Users** group can only share local resources.

## more

Windows XP Professional automatically shares certain folders, whose contents are available only to Administrators. These **administrative shares** are appended with a **dollar** sign (**$**) to

**Figure 9-1 Shared Application folders and Shared Data folders**

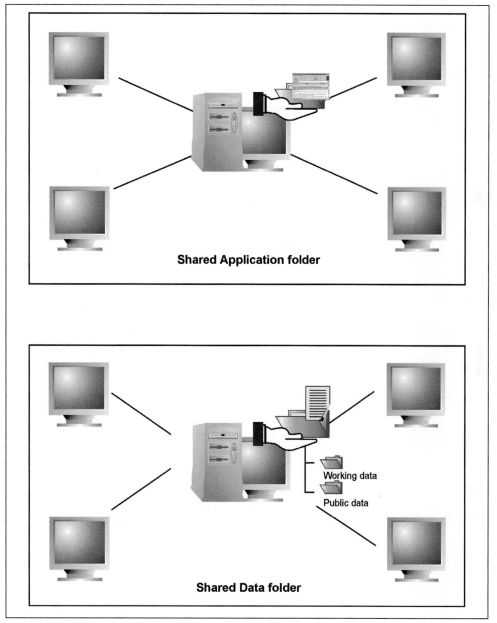

Shared Application folder

Working data

Public data

Shared Data folder

# skill 1

## *Introducing Shared Folders (cont'd)*

**exam objective**    Basic knowledge

**more**

hide them from other users on the network **(Figure 9-2)**. For example, the %systemroot% folder, the root of each volume, and the location of the printer drivers are hidden administrative shares.

Some of the administrative shared folders that Windows XP automatically creates are listed below:

◆ **Admin$:** Admin$ is the shared folder used by Administrators to administer Windows XP Professional. By default, **C:\Windows**, the system root folder, is shared as **Admin$ (Figure 9-3)**. Only members of the **Administrators** group have the **Full Control** permission to access this folder. Members of other groups such as Everyone, Power Users, and Server Operators have no rights to access these folders.

◆ **C$, D$, E$:** The drive letter administrative shares point to the roots of the corresponding logical drive. For example, D$ is the shared folder name for the shared D: drive. The Administrator accesses these shared folders to connect to the entire volume of a remote computer in order to perform administrative tasks.

◆ **Print$:** The Print$ administrative share is used by Administrators to monitor shared printers remotely by providing access to the printer driver files. Members of the **Administrators** and **Power Users** groups have the **Full Control** permission for this folder. The **Everyone** group is given only the **Read** permission.

◆ **IPC$ (Interprocess Communications):** The IPC$ administrative share is used to facilitate IPC communication between systems. Interprocess communications refers to the capacity supported by multiprocessing systems that allows one process, or executing program, to exchange information with another process that is either executing on the same computer or on another computer on a network. It allows client computers to submit requests for service to servers and enables servers to answer those requests.

Only members of the Administrators and Backup Operators local groups have the right to use the administrative shares on Windows XP Professional and Windows 2000 Server or Windows Server 2003 member servers. Users in the Administrators, Backup Operators, and Server Operators groups can access administrative shares on a domain controller.

Additionally, you can create shared hidden folders, or you can share folders and append a dollar sign to the end of the share name. This will enable only users who know the folder name and have appropriate permissions to gain access to the folder. You can use this to share applications with other Administrators so that other users will not be able to see these folders when they use My Network Places to access shared resources.

**Figure 9-2  Built-in administrative shares in the Shares node of the Shared folders snap-in**

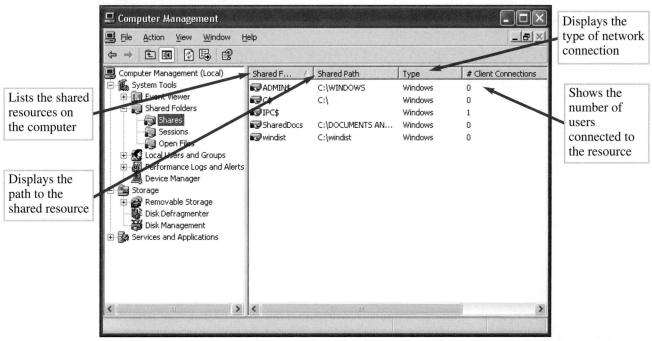

Displays the type of network connection

Shows the number of users connected to the resource

Lists the shared resources on the computer

Displays the path to the shared resource

**Figure 9-3  The WINDOWS Properties dialog box**

By default, %systemroot%, usually C:\Windows, is shared as Admin$

# skill 2

# *Sharing a Folder*

**exam objective**

Create and remove shared folders.

## overview

To create a shared folder, you use the **Sharing tab** in the Properties dialog box for that folder. By default, the name that is given to the shared folder will be the original folder name, but you can change this if you want. This way you can use one name for opening the folder locally and another name for accessing it over the network. On the Sharing tab, you can set various options for sharing the folder, as well as set the properties for the shared folder. Some of the options are listed below:

### caution

The options available on the Sharing tab will be different depending on whether the computer is a member of a workgroup or a domain.

◆ **Share this folder:** This option makes the contents of the folder available to network users.
◆ **Share name:** This is the name assigned to the folder that you want to share. Network users will use this name to access the shared folder.
◆ **Comment:** This is a description of the shared folder.
◆ **User limit:** This option is used to set the number of users who can simultaneously access a shared folder over a network. If you click the **Maximum allowed** option button, Windows XP Professional will allow ten users to connect to the shared folder, or you can specify a lower number. A maximum of ten simultaneous users is allowed because Windows XP Professional is designed for workgroup or peer-to-peer networks. Windows 2000 Server and Server 2003, on the other hand, allow a maximum number of users to simultaneously access a shared folder based on licensing terms.
◆ **Permissions:** This button is used to assign access permissions to ensure that only authorized users can connect to the shared folder.
◆ **Caching:** This button is used to designate how the contents of a shared folder can be accessed offline.

You can also disallow the sharing of a folder to make its contents unavailable over the network. To do this, click the **Do not share this folder** option button on the **Sharing** tab.
You can also create a shared folder using the **Create Shared Folder Wizard**. This Wizard guides you through the process of selecting the folder you want to share, making it available to network users, and assigning permissions to the various users who will be accessing it. You access the Create Shared Folder Wizard in the **Computer Management** window.

## how to

Share a folder named **General**.

1. Right-click **start**, and click the **Explore** command on the shortcut menu to open the **Windows Explorer** window.
2. Right-click the folder that you want to share, for example **General**. Then click the **Properties** command on the shortcut menu to open the **General Properties** dialog box.
3. Click the **Sharing** tab.
4. Click the **Share this folder** option button to make the contents of the folder accessible to other users on the network **(Figure 9-4)**. The name of the folder you have chosen to share, in this case **General**, appears by default in the **Share name** text box, and the **Maximum allowed** option button is selected by default.
5. Accept the defaults, and click **OK** to close the **General Properties** dialog box.

## more

In order to create shortcuts for your users to connect to a shared folder, you use one of the following methods:

◆ **My Network Places:** First, click the **Add a network place** link in the My Network Places window to open the **Add Network Place Wizard (Figure 9-5)**. Click **Next**, and then select **Choose another network location** on the **Where do you want to create this network place?** screen. Click **Next**, and then, on the **What is the address of this network place** screen, enter the **UNC (Universal Naming Convention) pathname** for the

**Figure 9-4  Sharing tab in General Properties dialog box**

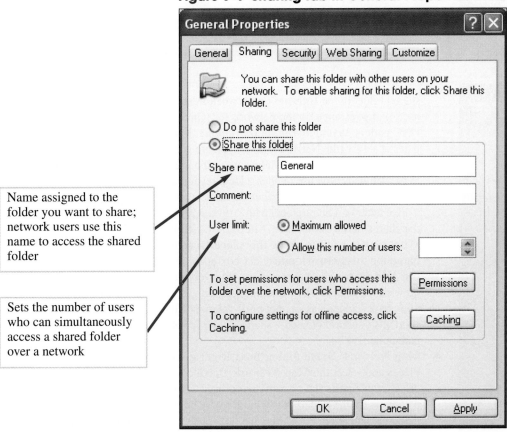

Name assigned to the folder you want to share; network users use this name to access the shared folder

Sets the number of users who can simultaneously access a shared folder over a network

**Figure 9-5  The Add Network Place Wizard**

# skill 2

## *Sharing a Folder (cont'd)*

**exam objective**

Create and remove shared folders. Connect to shared resources on a Microsoft network.

## more

### tip

You can also use a URL path to a Web folder or an FTP (File Transfer Protocol) path to an FTP site.

### tip

You can also map a network drive to a shared network folder (not a local folder) by right-clicking the folder and selecting the **Map Network Drive** command on the shortcut menu.

shared folder in the **Internet or network address** list box. The UNC path is used to connect to any resource on the network for which you have permission. The syntax for the UNC path is: *\\computername\sharename*. The *computername* is the name of the computer or server (the NetBIOS name) you are going to connect to and the *sharename* is the name of the shared folder. Make sure you understand that the UNC path is not the same as the pathname you use to open a local resource. The MS-DOS pathname uses the familiar C:\\*foldername\subfoldername\filename* syntax. The UNC pathname does not include a drive letter or a hierarchical path. You can also enter just *\\computername* to view all of the shares on any computer. After you have entered the UNC, click **Next** to open the **What do you want to name this place?** screen. Name the network place in the **Type a name for this network place** text box and click **Next**. Click **Finish** on the **Completing the Add Network Place** screen. My Network Places serves as a network resource browser for your users, providing them with an easy way to connect to any shared folders you have added as a network place. All that your users will see are the shortcuts you have created—shared folder icons. They will never have to know the UNC pathname.

◆ **Map Network Drive dialog box:** Right-click either My Computer or My Network Places and select the **Map Network Drive** command. In the **Drive** list box, choose any drive letter that is not already being used for the network connection. Enter the UNC pathname for the folder, or use the **Browse** button to locate the folder and it will be automatically entered in the **Folder** list box. Select the **Reconnect at logon** check box if you want the mapped connection to be included in a user's user profile so that they will be able to see it in Windows Explorer each time they log on. You can also use the **Connect using a different user name** link to specify a different user name for making this connection (**Figure 9-6**). After you have mapped a network drive, users will see it as another drive letter in My Computer and Windows Explorer. This is what is called a logical drive, as opposed to an actual physical drive.

◆ **Run command:** You can also specify the UNC path to a shared resource in the Open text box in the Run dialog box (**Figure 9-7**), or you can enter *\\computername* to view a list of the shared folders on that computer (**Figure 9-8**). Then, double-click the share to connect to it over the network.

◆ **NET USE command:** At the command prompt, type: **NET USE (drive letter):** *\\computername\sharename*. In other words, type the drive letter you are going to use for the mapped connection and the UNC for the shared folder.

Mapping a network drive to a shared resource creates a shortcut to the resource. Once this shortcut is created, your users can access the shared resource directly through the shortcut instead of having to use the NET USE or Map Network Drive utilities again.

**Figure 9-6  Map Network Drive dialog box**

Selected by default so the mapped connection will be part of the user profile of users, and they will see it in Windows Explorer each time they log on

Click to specify a different user name for making this connection

**Figure 9-7  Run dialog box**

Enter \\computername only to view all shared folders on that computer

**Figure 9-8  Viewing network resources**

| skill 3 | *Introducing Types of Permissions for Shared Folders* |
|---|---|

**exam objective**

Control access to files and folders by using permissions. Control access to shared folders by using permissions.

**overview**

When you create shares, you can control the level of access network users have to some extent. As you will see in the next lesson, you have much more latitude in setting the level of control users will have when you use NTFS permissions. For shared folders, there are only three levels of access (**Figure 9-9**):

◆ **Read:** The Read permission allows users to display folder names, file names, file data, and the attributes of folders shared on remote systems. Users can also run programs that are in shared application folders.

◆ **Change:** The Change permission allows users to create folders, add files to folders, modify data in files, add data to files, modify file attributes, and delete files and folders, in addition to the actions permitted by the Read permission.

◆ **Full Control:** The Full Control permission allows full access to the shared folder, including all actions permitted by the Read and Change permissions, and users can change permissions on the share.

These three levels of access are controlled by two conditions: Allow and Deny. The default setting is Allow, which gives users the specific permission for the shared folder. Deny, on the other hand, blocks the permission. The Deny setting should not be used very often, because it supersedes the Allow condition; however, it can be useful in cases where you want to deny a specific user in a group the same level of access granted to the group. It is also possible to grant the Change permission, while at the same time denying the Read permission so that a user will be able to delete files based on the file name, but will not be able to read the file before deleting it (**Figure 9-10**). Some important guidelines for assigning shared folder permissions are listed below:

◆ If you assign a specific permission to a user and the user is a member of a group that has a different set of permissions, then the effective permissions for the user are the combination of the user and group permissions. In other words, you add the two permissions together. For example, if a user has been granted the **Read** permission and is a member of a group that has the **Change** permission, the cumulative effect is the **Change** permission, which includes the **Read** permission.

◆ If you deny a permission to a user, it specifically overrides the Allow condition for that permission. Allow gives users the specific permission for the shared folder. Deny *blocks* the permission. For example, if a user has been granted the Read permission by virtue of his or her membership in Group A, but he or she also belongs to Group B, which has been specifically denied the Read permission, the user will not be allowed to access the file.

◆ When you copy or move a shared folder to a new location, the shared folder does not remain shared in the new location.

◆ Organize folders with the same security requirements within a single folder. For example, you can store the folders of various applications within a single folder. Then, you can share the folder containing all of the application folders, instead of sharing each application folder individually.

◆ Assign relevant share names to folders to enable users to locate them easily. Share names should also be short so that they are easier to remember and so that other operating systems can use them. MS-DOS, Windows 3.x, and Windows for Workgroups use 8.3 character names.

**Figure 9-9  Shared Folder permissions**

**Figure 9-10  Share permissions**

# skill 3

## Introducing Types of Permissions for Shared Folders *(cont'd)*

**exam objective**

Control access to files and folders by using permissions. Control access to shared folders by using permissions.

## how to

Assign shared folder permissions.

1. In the **Windows Explorer** window, right-click the General folder in the C: drive, and click the **Properties** command on the shortcut menu to open the **General Properties** dialog box.
2. In the General Properties dialog box, click the **Sharing** tab.
3. Click `Permissions` to open the **Permissions for General** dialog box.
4. By default, **Everyone** is selected in the **Group or user names** list. Click `Remove` to remove this group from the list.
5. Then click `Add...` to open the **Select Users or Groups** dialog box. Here you can select a user, a computer, or a group to which you want to assign shared folder permissions.
6. Confirm that the object type for which you want to assign permissions, in this case Users, appears in the **Select this object type** text box, and that the location is correct in the **From this location** text box. Type the name of the user for whom you want to assign permissions, for example, JSimmons, in the Enter the object names to select text box **(Figure 9-11)**.
7. Click `OK` to select the user and close the **Select Users or Groups** dialog box. The **Group or user names** list displays the user name you added **(Figure 9-12)**.
8. Select the user name and make sure that the **Allow** check box next to the **Read** permission is selected. This will allow JSimmons to read the data in the General folder.
9. Click `OK` to close the **Permissions for General** dialog box, and again to close the General Properties dialog box.
10. Close Windows Explorer.

**Figure 9-11  Selecting a user to assign permissions**

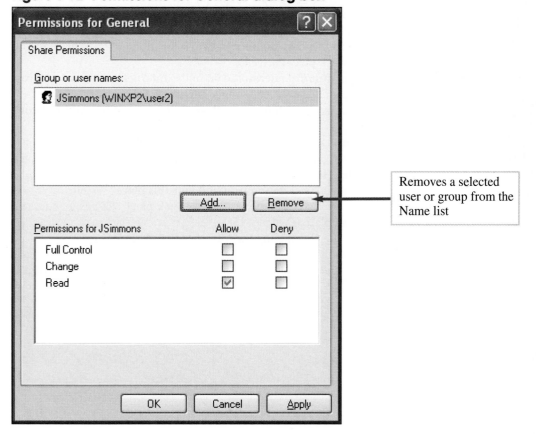

Click for help in finding objects when you are not sure of their exact names

Click for examples of how to phrase object names

**Figure 9-12  Permissions for General dialog box**

Removes a selected user or group from the Name list

# skill 4

## *Accessing Shared Resources on a Windows Network*

**exam objective**

Basic knowledge

**overview**

As you have learned, you can use My Network Places to create shortcuts to shared folders, Web folders, and File Transfer Protocol (FTP) sites on a remote network. FTP is a protocol that is used to make file transfers between local and remote computers possible. Local work-stations upload files to an FTP server, and remote users can then download them. When a URL contains *ftp*, it means that you are accessing an FTP server rather than a Web server. When you view Web pages in your browser, HTTP (Hypertext Transfer Protocol) is used to transmit files so that you can read them, or to transfer or copy them to a local drive. On the other hand, you use FTP to transfer files from a workstation to the file server and vice versa, and on each end they are stored on the hard drive of the receiving computer. Usually you can only access these sites by specifying a user name and password. However, if anonymous access is enabled, you can also gain limited access to the files and folders on an FTP site by logging on anonymously.

**how to**

Use **My Network Places** to access an ftp site. The path address of the site is: **ftp://ftp.microsoft.com**. Log on anonymously to the FTP site and name the new network place **Microsoft FTP**.

1. Click ⚑ **start** and click My Computer to open the My Computer window.
2. Click the **My Network Places** link under Other Places on the left side of the window to open the **My Network Places** window **(Figure 9-13)**.
3. Click the **Add a network place** link under **Network Tasks** on the left side of the window to start the **Add Network Place Wizard**.
4. Click ⬚ **Next >** and select **Choose another network location** on the **Where do you want to create this network place?** screen.
5. Click ⬚ **Next >** and type **ftp://ftp.microsoft.com** in the **Internet or network address** text box to indicate the path to the shared resource **(Figure 9-14)**.
6. Click ⬚ **Next >** to open the **User Name and Password** screen of the **Add Network Place Wizard**.
7. The **Log on anonymously** check box is selected by default. When you log on anony-mously, you do not need to specify a user name and password, and you can use limited resources on the FTP site. However, anonymous logon is not always possible.
8. Click ⬚ **Next >** to open the **What do you want to name this place?** screen.
9. Type **Microsoft FTP** in the **Type a name for this network place** text box to indicate a name for the new network place **(Figure 9-15)**.
10. Click ⬚ **Next >** to open the **Completing the Add Network Place Wizard**.
11. If you would like to open the new network place when you complete the Wizard, leave the **Open this network place when I click Finish** check box selected. If not, clear the check box, and click ⬚ **Finish**.
12. Close the My Network Places window.

**Figure 9-13  The My Network Places window**

Click to open the
Add a Network
Place Wizard

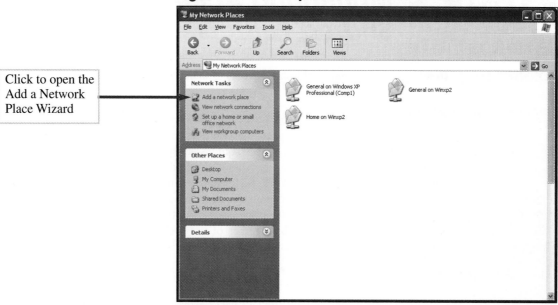

**Figure 9-14  Specifying the location of the ftp folder**

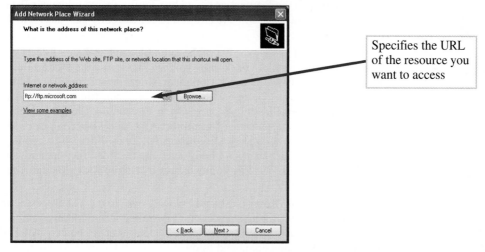

Specifies the URL
of the resource you
want to access

**Figure 9-15  Specifying a name for the new network place**

Name for the
network place

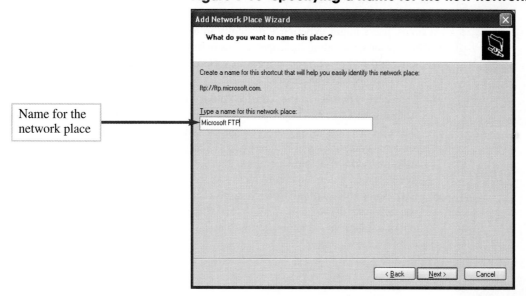

# skill 5

# Monitoring Access to Shared Folders

## exam objective

Manage and troubleshoot access to shared folders. Monitor, manage, and troubleshoot access to files and folders.

## overview

In an organization, there are certain confidential resources that must be safeguarded. Restricted access by only select users must be assigned in order to keep those resources secure. It is also important to monitor such resources at regular intervals. Apart from security reasons, you monitor and manage user access to shared network resources for the following reasons:

◆ **Maintenance:** While performing maintenance tasks on network resources, you may be required to make certain resources unavailable to some or all connected users. You can monitor who is using the resources and notify them before making the resources unavailable.

◆ **Planning:** As the number of users on a network grows, you need to plan for new resources and monitor the usage of existing resources.

You can use the **Shared Folders snap-in** to monitor user access to shared resources in the following ways:

**Determining the number of users accessing a shared folder:** You can view the maximum number of users who can gain access to a folder at one time by selecting the shared folder in the details pane of the Shared Folder snap-in. Then, open the **Action** menu and select the **Properties** command to open the **Properties** dialog box for the shared folder. On the **General** tab, you can see the number of users who are allowed to concurrently gain access to the folder (**Figure 9-16**).

**Monitoring Open Files:** You can view a list of the open files in the shared folders, as well as the users who are accessing the files. To do this, you need to access the **Open Files** folder in the **Shared Folders** snap-in, which is in the Computer Management console. Administrators can also disconnect users from one open file or from all open files when required. You disconnect users from all open files by selecting **Open Files** in the Shared Folders snap-in. Then, open the **Action** menu and select the **Disconnect All Open Files** command, or you can simply right-click Open Files and select Disconnect All Open Files on the context menu (**Figure 9-17**). You close a particular open file by selecting the open file, opening the Action menu, and selecting the **Close Open File** command, or by right-clicking the file you want to close and selecting Close Open File.

Administrators also can use the Shares or Shared Folders nodes to contact users when the user limit has been met and another user must access the open file, or the Administrator must shut down the system for maintenance. To do this, right-click either node, point to **All Tasks**, and click the **Send Console Message** command to open the **Send Console Message** dialog box (**Figure 9-18**). Alternatively, with either node selected, open the **Action** menu, point to **All Tasks**, and click the **Send Console Message** command.

## more

At times, users might experience difficulty in accessing a shared folder. This can be due to various reasons, including improper access permissions. You must identify the cause of these problems and follow corrective measures. Some common problems, their probable causes, and the solutions are listed below:

◆ **User access denied to the Admin$ folder:** This problem arises for non-members of the Administrators or Backup Operators groups. Only members of the Administrators and Backup Operators local groups can access the administrative shares on Windows XP Professional computers and Windows 2000 Server/Server 2003 member servers. Users in the Administrators, Backup Operators, and Server Operators groups can access administrative shares on a domain controller.

◆ **User is not able to modify the contents of a shared folder:** This problem may arise when you only have the Read permission for a shared folder. So that the user can modify the content of a folder, an Administrator must assign the Change or Full Control permission.

**Figure 9-16  Determining the user limit**

Used to set the number of users who can simultaneously access a resource

Makes network files available offline

**Figure 9-17  The Shared Folders node, disconnecting all open files**

Contains commands used to monitor user access

Used to view and monitor shared folders, open files, and open sessions

**Figure 9-18  The Send Console Message dialog box**

Allows Administrator to contact users when the user limit has been met

# skill 6

## *Configuring and Managing Offline Files and Folders*

### exam objective

Manage and troubleshoot access to and synchronization of offline files. Optimize access to files and folders.

### overview

The purpose of offline files and folders is to allow you to work with network documents even when the system is down. If granted permission to do so, Administrators and users can select certain network files and folders to be cached. **Caching** simply means that the data is copied to the local workstation. Network files that are stored locally are called **Offline files**. Offline files are stored in a reserved portion of your system's disk space called the **Cache**. If the network connection malfunctions, users can continue working on the local copy. Then, when the system is restored, Windows XP can synchronize or automatically update the network file.

Caching offline folders is a two-stage procedure. First, you must configure your computer to be able to use offline folders and files. Then, you must configure your computer so that you can make the shared folders stored on your computer available offline to other users on the network.

You give your computer the ability to use offline folders and files on the **Offline Files** tab in the **Folder Options** dialog box. There are two ways to access this dialog box. You can select the **Folder Options** command on the **Tools** menu in the **My Computer** window, or you can double-click **Folder Options** in the **Control Panel**. Then, on the **Offline Files** tab (**Figure 9-19**), you must make sure that the **Enable Offline Files** check box is selected. In Windows XP Professional, this check box, as well as the **Synchronize all offline files before logging off** check box are selected by default, while in Windows 2000 Server you must set them yourself.

Next, you must select the resource that you want to be made available offline. In order to do this, you must use the Map Network Drive Wizard to assign a drive letter to a shared network resource. You must have a link to a network drive in order to make those files available offline. After you have created a link to a network drive, open the **My Computer** window, right-click the drive icon, and select the **Make Available Offline** command (**Figure 9-20**). The first time you create an offline folder, the **Offline Files Wizard** will open (**Figure 9-21**). You will select options related to how the synchronization of the folders should take place, whether you want to receive reminders, and whether you want to have a desktop icon added. Then, the offline files will be copied to your hard drive and a double-arrow icon will be added to the drive icon. Next time you create an offline folder, the Wizard will not be necessary.

To configure shared folders stored on your computer so that network users can cache them, you must open the **Caching Settings** dialog box from the Properties dialog box for the shared folder. To open the Caching Settings dialog box, click the **Caching Settings** button on the **Sharing** tab in the Properties dialog box for the shared folder. The options in the **Setting** list box are listed below:

◆ **Automatic caching of documents:** This option automatically downloads and caches (or copies) all files in a folder as users open them. Old copies of the file that are already stored on the user's hard disk will be automatically replaced with the newer version.

◆ **Automatic caching of programs and documents:** This option makes offline copies of all files from shared folders that have been read, run, or referenced without being modified. Automatic caching for programs enables you to read and execute read-only programs that run from the server without connecting to the network. You cannot change the content of these files.

◆ **Manual caching of documents:** This is the default setting, which lets users manually specify the documents they want to be available offline.

When you reconnect to the network, the changes that you made to the offline files are updated to the network files. This process is called **synchronization**. To configure the synchronization

**Figure 9-19  Synchronizing all offline files**

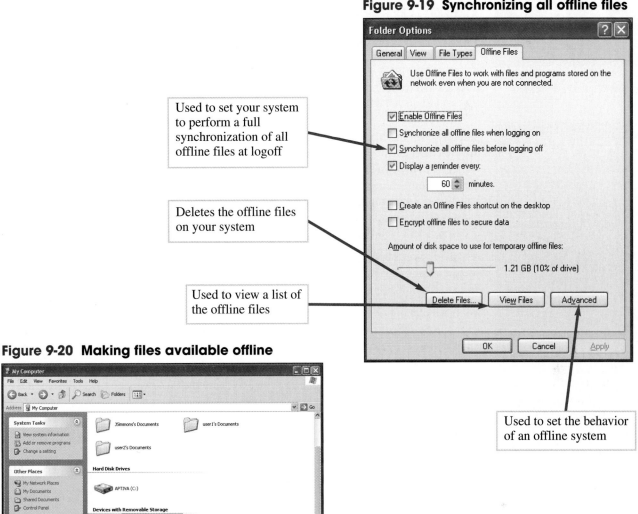

Used to set your system to perform a full synchronization of all offline files at logoff

Deletes the offline files on your system

Used to view a list of the offline files

Used to set the behavior of an offline system

**Figure 9-20  Making files available offline**

Right-click the relevant drive icon to display the shortcut menu

**Figure 9-21  The Offline Files Wizard**

### Welcome to the Offline Files Wizard

Using Offline Files, you can work with network files when you are not connected to the network.

Offline Files are most useful when you are working on a laptop or remotely over a slow network connection.

To continue, click Next.

< Back    Next >    Cancel

# skill 6

## Configuring and Managing Offline Files and Folders (cont'd)

**exam objective**

Manage and troubleshoot access to and synchronization of offline files. Optimize access to files and folders.

## overview

process, open the **My Computer** window and select the mapped network drive. Then, open the **Tools** menu and select the **Synchronize** command to open the **Synchronization Manager Items to Synchronize** dialog box (**Figure 9-22**). Click the **Setup** button to open the **Synchronization Settings** dialog box. On the **Scheduled** tab, click the **Add** button to start the **Scheduled Synchronization Wizard**. You can schedule synchronization tasks to take place daily, only on weekdays, or you can set a schedule for a set number of days between synchronization. The Synchronization Manager is used to update offline files and folders:

◆ Every time you log on or log off your system.
◆ At specific intervals when your system is idle.
◆ At scheduled times.

You have two options for synchronizing files. If you want to perform a full synchronization, leave the **Synchronize all offline files before logging off** check box selected on the Offline Files tab in the Folder Options dialog box. If you only want to perform a quick synchronization, clear the check box.

◆ **Full synchronization:** This ensures that you have the latest version of the offline files on the network.
◆ **Quick synchronization:** This ensures that you have a complete set of offline files on your system, but does not guarantee that they are the latest version.

Computers on a Microsoft network use a file-sharing protocol called Server Message Block (SMB) for network communication. The File and Printer Sharing for Microsoft Networks service (the Server service) used by the computer that hosts the share, and the client computer running the Workstation service (the client redirector) that accesses the share, use this protocol to communicate. This means that non-Microsoft networks, such as Novell NetWare, are not compatible and you cannot set up offline files with them.

## how to

Configure a folder so that network users can cache the files in the share.

1. Log on to your system as an **Administrator**.
2. Open the **Windows Explorer** window.
3. Right-click a folder on your system, for example **Folder1**, and click the **Sharing** command on the shortcut menu to open the **Folder1 Properties** dialog box with the **Sharing** tab active.
4. Click the **Share this folder** option button to make the contents of the folder accessible to users over the network.
5. Click [ Caching ] to open the **Caching Settings** dialog box. Make sure that the **Allow caching of files in this shared folder** check box has not been cleared. (It is selected by default on Windows XP Professional computers.)
6. In the **Setting** list box, select the **Automatic caching of documents** option (**Figure 9-23**).
7. Click [ OK ] to close the **Caching Settings** dialog box.
8. Click [ OK ] to close the **Folder1 Properties** dialog box.
9. Close Windows Explorer.

**Figure 9-22  Synchronizing selected offline files**

Lists the items that you select for synchronization

Synchronizes the items selected in the Name list

Used to specify when synchronization occurs

**Figure 9-23  Caching Settings dialog box**

Provides different caching settings

# Summary

◆ A folder that is shared on a computer, and is accessible to users over a network, is called a Shared Folder or a share.

◆ On FAT, FAT32, and NTFS partitions and volumes, you can use what are called share permissions or shared folder permissions in order to control access to network resources.

◆ This type of access control is only for folders. Individual files within the folders cannot be given their own sets of permissions. To control who can access a particular file, you must grant the appropriate privileges to the folder in which it is stored.

◆ Shared folder permissions are not applicable at the local computer level. They cannot be used to control what users can access locally. By default, all local resources can be accessed by any user, except on NTFS volumes where many system folders and files are protected from access by users. In contrast, shared folders are used for networks, and share permissions must be set up or these folders cannot be accessed by anyone.

◆ After you determine which folders will be shared and which groups or individuals will be able to access them, you set permissions to control what these users will be allowed to do.

◆ You set share permissions in the ACL (Access Control List) for that resource.

◆ The default permission for a shared resource is Full Control for the Everyone group. Generally, you will remove this permission and set your own according to your organizational needs.

◆ Windows XP Professional automatically shares certain folders, whose contents are available to only Administrators and Backup Operators. These administrative shares are appended with a dollar sign (**$**) in order to hide them from other users on the network.

◆ To share a folder over the network, you use the Sharing tab on the Properties dialog box for the folder.

◆ You assign permissions to a user in the Permissions dialog box for that folder.

◆ For shared folders there are three levels of access: Read, Change, and Full Control.

◆ These three levels of access are limited by two conditions: Allow and Deny.

◆ Allow gives users the specific permission for the shared folder. Deny blocks the permission. The Deny setting should not be used very often, because it supersedes the Allow condition.

◆ If you assign a specific permission to a user and the user is a member of a group that has a different set of permissions, then the effective permissions for the user are the combination of the user and group permissions. For example, if a user has been granted the Read permission for a shared folder and is a member of a group that has the Change permission, the cumulative effect is the Change permission, which includes the Read permission.

◆ Shared folders that are copied or moved to another location are not shared at the new location.

◆ You connect to a shared folder using the Map Network Drive Wizard.

◆ Offline files enable you to work on the latest version of network files when you are not connected to the network.

◆ Caching offline folders is a two-stage procedure. First, you must configure your computer to be able to use offline folders and files. Then, you must configure your computer so that you can make the shared folders stored on your computer available offline to other users on the network.

◆ You give your computer the ability to use offline folders and files on the Offline Files tab in the Folder options dialog box. On the Offline Files tab, you must make sure that the Enable Offline Files check box is selected. In Windows XP Professional, this check box and the Synchronize All Offline Files check box are selected by default, while in Windows 2000 Server you must set them yourself.

◆ To configure folders stored on your computer so that network users can cache them, you must open the Caching Settings dialog box from the Properties dialog box for the shared folder.

◆ Users who belong to the Administrator and Server Operators group can share folders on any system in a domain.

◆ You use the Shared Folders snap-in in the Computer Management window to monitor user access to network resources.

# Key Terms

Administrative shared folders
Admin$
C$, D$, E$
Caching
Change permission
Create Shared Folder Wizard
Full Control permission
IPC$ (Interprocess Communications)

My Network Places
Offline files
Offline folders
Open Files folder
Print$
Read permission
Shared Application folder
Shared Data folder

Shared Folder permissions
Shared folder
Shared Folders snap-in
Synchronization
UNC (Universal Naming Convention)
    pathname

# Test Yourself

1. John is a member of two groups: HR Recruitment and HR Strategic Planning at Spearhouse Corp. You assign the Read permission to the HR Recruitment group to access a shared folder named Employee Details. You also assign the Change permission to the HR Strategic Planning group to access the Employee Details folder. The effective permission for John to access Employee Details is:
   a. Read.
   b. Write.
   c. Full Control.
   d. Change.

2. Which of the following types of permissions can you assign to local users for a file system directory on a Windows XP Professional computer if the hard disk is formatted with the FAT32 file system?
   a. Shared folder permissions
   b. File-and-folder permissions
   c. NTFS permissions
   d. None of the above

3. You are the Administrator of a peer-to-peer network at a family-run pharmacy, and you have created a shared folder named Drug Efficacy. The owner asks you to move the folder to a new, more powerful Windows XP computer. After you have moved the folder, the pharmacist complains to you that she can no longer access it. What happened?
   a. You have moved it to an NTFS volume, and the share permissions that you had set are no longer applicable; you must set NTFS permissions for the folder.
   b. The pharmacist must log off and log back on in order to access the folder in its new location.
   c. Folders that are copied or moved to another location are not shared in the new location.
   d. You forgot to allow caching of files in the shared folder after you moved it.

4. Which of the following symbols is used to identify a share created automatically by Windows XP for administrative purposes?
   a. %
   b. &
   c. $
   d. #

5. Suzanne has the Full Control permission for a shared folder on Bill's computer. She also belongs to the Sales group, which has been denied the Full Control permission. What is Suzanne's effective permission?
   a. Full Control
   b. Read
   c. None
   d. Change

6. John is a freelancer working for Pixel Inc. He uses a Windows XP Professional laptop and a dial-up connection to a Windows 2000 server on the network to access the files that he needs. He uses Offline Files so that when he is traveling, he can work on his files without a network connection and can then synchronize his files. He wants to make sure that the cached version on his laptop is always in full synchronization with the network version. What should he do?
   a. In the Settings list box in the Caching Settings dialog box, he should select, Automatic Caching for Documents.
   b. On the General tab in the Synchronization Settings dialog box, he should select the Synchronize all offline files before logging off check box.
   c. On the Offline Files tab in the Folder Options dialog box, he should leave the Synchronize all offline files before logging off check box selected.
   d. On the On Idle tab in the Synchronization Settings dialog box, he should select the Schedule a full synchronization check box.

7. Which of the following is used to view all open files in the shared folders on the network?
   a. Shared folders snap-in
   b. Admin$ folder
   c. Caching Settings dialog box
   d. The Properties dialog box for the shared folder

8. Which of the following do you use to make the content of a folder available to users over a network?
   a. Caching Settings dialog box
   b. Sharing tab
   c. Permissions button
   d. APM tab

9. You can set up offline files with Novell Netware servers running versions 4.0 and higher.
   a. True
   b. False

# Projects: On Your Own

1. Sharing a folder.
   a. Access the **Properties** dialog box of a folder.
   b. Click the **Sharing** tab.
   c. Click the **Share this Folder** option button.
   d. Type the name in the **Share Name** text box.
   e. Share a folder with the specified name.
2. Assign shared folder permissions.
   a. Select a folder and access the **Permissions** dialog box.
   b. Remove the **Everyone** option.
   c. Access the **Select Users or Groups** dialog box.
   d. Select a user or group account and click **Add**.
   e. Access the **Permission** dialog box again and select the user.
   f. Select the **Allow** check box to assign the Full Control permission.
3. Configure Caching to access network files offline.
   a. Log on as **Administrator**.
   b. Access the **Properties** dialog box for a shared folder.
   c. Access the **Caching Settings** dialog box.
   d. Select the **Allow caching of files in this folder** check box.
   e. Select the **Manual caching of documents** option.
   f. Accept the settings.

# Problem Solving Scenarios

1. You work as a project manager at Excelerate, Inc., a fashion industry design house in New York City. You manage a team of 10 assistant designers who share resources on a workgroup network. You are very concerned about security; therefore, you want all team members to keep a local copy of their work on their hard drives, but to back up their files at the end of every day on your machine, as well. Describe in a memo to your instructor how you will create a shared folder named Team Share on your system, and assign permissions to the assistant designers this capability.

2. As a Network Administrator at Excelerate, Inc., you have been asked to assign different share folder permissions to various departments to access a folder named Software on the file server. The departments in the company are divided into groups—for example, the Market Research group, Human Resources group, and Production group. Management wants the following functionality:

   ◆ The Market Research group must be able to edit files in the folder and assign permissions to new users.
   ◆ The Human Resources group should not have access to the Software folder.
   ◆ The Production group must be able to add and delete file folders, but should not be able to change permissions on the share.

   Describe in a memo how you will achieve these objectives.

# 10 Setting Up, Configuring, and Administering Network Printers

Just as you provide accessibility to files and folders and make sure that the correct levels of access are granted, you can also share print resources and assign different levels of access to different sets of users. Although some printing terminology may seem counterintuitive, it can help you to understand how sharing print resources works. In a Windows environment, a printer is considered to be the software that delivers the requests for service from the operating system to the physical print device. A print device, therefore, is the physical hardware that you think of as a printer, which creates the hard copies of your digital files. It is then easy to understand how another resource stored on a disk on the hard drive, (the printer) can be shared with other network users. It is also easy to understand why the ability to configure shared printers is so valuable to a business. Each client does not need its own expensive hardware device.

A print server handles the requests for service for a shared printer. A print server can administer these requests either through a print device that is physically connected to it, or through a print device connected to the network. Network connected print devices are called network-interface print devices and they have their own NIC (network interface card) and network address, or an external network adapter connection. The main point, however, is that a print server receives the requests, queues them, uses a printer driver to translate the digital documents into printer code, and sends the instructions to the print device. Windows XP and 2000 Professional computers, and even Windows 9x computers, can be configured as print servers. However, this ability is limited by the fact that they can, for the most part, only be used on exclusively Microsoft networks. An exception to this is that a Linux system running the SMB (Server Message Block) client can print to a Windows XP, 2000, or 9x print server. However, Microsoft recommends that, if any of the client computers on your network are either Macintosh or Netware, and the print server must support more than ten simultaneous clients, you should use Windows 2000 Server or Windows Server 2003 instead.

As a Network Administrator, you must know how to install and configure new printers, how to manage and share print resources, and how to maintain printer security. You should also know how the printing process works, how to monitor user access to network printers, how to ensure the optimum usage of your print resources, and how to troubleshoot printer problems.

## Goals

In this lesson, you will learn to set up the environment for network printing, add a local printer to your computer, share a printer over a network, connect to a network printer, and configure a network printer. You will also learn to manage printers, troubleshoot printer problems, and control access to network printers by assigning permissions.

## Lesson 10  Setting Up, Configuring, and Administering Network Printers

| Skill | Exam 70-270 Objective |
|---|---|
| 1. Setting up an Environment for Printing | Basic knowledge |
| 2. Adding a Local Printer | Connect to local and network print devices. Connect to a local print device. |
| 3. Connecting to a Network Printer | Connect to local and network print devices. Connect to an Internet printer. |
| 4. Configuring a Network Printer | Monitor, configure, and troubleshoot I/O devices, such as printers, scanners, multimedia devices, mouse, keyboard, and smart card reader. |
| 5. Assigning Access Permissions to Network Printers | Control access to printers by using permissions. |
| 6. Managing Printers | Manage printers and print jobs. Monitor, configure, and troubleshoot I/O devices, such as printers, scanners, multimedia devices, mouse, keyboard, and smart card reader. |
| 7. Troubleshooting Printer Problems | Monitor, configure, and troubleshoot I/O devices, such as printers, scanners, multimedia devices, mouse, keyboard, and smart card reader. |

## Requirements

To complete this lesson, you will need a computer with Windows XP Professional installed on it and a network environment. You will need printers named Printer1 and Printer2, and a printer at a remote location.

# skill 1   *Setting Up an Environment for Printing*

**exam objective**   Basic knowledge

**overview**

Before you can share your print resources, you must set up an environment for network printing and ensure that you have a sufficient number of print devices to meet the needs of all users. The print environment also includes some other utilities and devices besides the printer (the software interface), the physical print device, and the print server (the computer that provides access to the shared printer).

The terminology used in the printing communication environment is described below:

◆ **Printer port:** A **printer port** is the software interface that a computer uses to communicate with a printer. The printer port does not refer to the physical hardware port, but rather to the software that communicates with it. Local connections to a print device can be made using a parallel, serial, infrared, or USB port. Remote connections can be made using either a network cable or a print device that has a NIC called a network-interface print device. The printer port communicates with any of these types of physical connections. In Windows XP, you can use the LPT (line printer), COM, and USB 1.1 interfaces, or IR (Infrared) interfaces, if available.

◆ **Printer driver:** A **printer driver** is the software that contains the information used by the operating system to convert the print commands for a particular model of print device into a printer language such as PostScript. It tells the operating system what attributes the print device has and what print commands it follows so that documents can be properly printed.

◆ **Printer pool:** A **printer pool** is a single printer (that is, the software that delivers the requests for service from the operating system) that can queue print jobs to multiple ports and their associated print devices. Print pooling is used when there are many print devices on a network that can receive instructions from the same type of print driver. Print jobs will be allocated by the printer pool to the first available print device.

When you are setting up your network printing environment, there are several important considerations you must keep in mind (**Figure 10-1**). First, if a print server must handle many requests for service from many printers or for many large documents, it is important that you add enough RAM to the print server to ensure that it can accommodate the load. Insufficient RAM can adversely affect printing performance. Second, you must make sure that you have enough disk space on the print server to store the documents to be printed until they can be sent to the print device. Error messages will be generated if there is insufficient disk space on the print server.

You must also estimate what you expect the printing requirements for your organization to be. Note how many users you have, how often they print and in what quantity, and the length of a typical document. Then, you can determine the type and number of print devices you think you will need in order to accommodate the quantity of requests for service. Next, you must estimate how many print servers your network will need for this number of print devices. Finally, you will need to decide how to place the print devices in the organization so that users can easily collect their printouts. For each computer, you can also define a default printer to be used for requests that are initiated from that workstation.

**Figure 10-1  Requirements for setting up network printing**

Sufficient RAM to process documents

Sufficient disk space on the print server

Determine the company's printing requirement

Determine user's printing requirements

Determine the print server's requirements

Determine the location of printers

# skill 2

# *Adding a Local Printer*

## exam objective

Connect to local and network print devices. Connect to a local print device.

## overview

**Local print devices** are used to print documents from standalone computers that are not on a network, or when a single individual, for example, the CEO, requires exclusive use of a printer. First, you must attach the print device to the computer using a physical port on the computer. A local print device usually uses a parallel (LPT), serial (COM), or USB port. The port enables your computer to communicate with the attached print device. Since most print devices today support Plug and Play, the operating system automatically detects and installs the device when you attach it. If you have a print device that is not Plug and Play, or if you want to add a local printer that is not currently attached to your computer, you must use the **Add Printer Wizard** to create the logical printer; that is, the software interface that delivers the requests for service from the operating system to the physical print device. When you make a request for a print job, the document is spooled (or stored) on the logical printer before it is sent to the actual print device. Only members of the local Administrators or Power Users groups can install a local printer.

## how to

Connect a local printer to your computer.
1. Plug the print device's cable into the appropriate port on your computer.
2. Turn the print device's power on. A **Found New Hardware** information bubble appears from the notification area (**Figure 10-2**). When Windows recognizes the printer, the name is displayed in the information bubble and the necessary printer files are copied.
3. The **Found New Hardware Wizard** dialog box appears to inform you that the software for the print device has been installed. Click [ Finish ] to complete the installation. An information bubble appears from the notification area briefly stating that your printer is installed and ready to use.

Add a non Plug and Play local printer to your computer.
1. Click [ start ] and click **Printers and Faxes** to open the **Printers and Faxes** window.
2. Click the **Add a printer** link under **Printer Tasks** on the left side of the window to start the **Add Printer Wizard**. The **Welcome to the Add Printer Wizard** screen opens.
3. Click [ Next > ] to open the **Local or Network Printer** screen.
4. The **Local printer attached to this computer** option button and the **Automatically detect and install my Plug and Play printer** check box are selected by default (**Figure 10-3**). Clear the Automatically detect check box, and click [ Next > ] to open the **Select a Printer Port** screen.
5. The **Use the following port** option button is selected by default. Accept the default port that is selected in the list box, and click [ Next > ]. The **Install Printer Software** screen opens (**Figure 10-4**).
6. Locate and select the manufacturer of the printer you want to install in the **Manufacturer** scrolling list box. Then, locate and select the name of the printer you want to install in the **Printers** scrolling list box.
7. Click [ Next > ] to open the **Name Your Printer** screen. Accept the printer name provided by the Wizard in the **Printer name** text box. If prompted, select the **Yes** or **No** option button depending on whether you want this printer to be your default printer.
8. Click [ Next > ] to open the **Printer Sharing** screen. Leave the **Do not share this printer** option button selected.
9. Click [ Next > ] to open the **Print Test Page** screen. Select the **No** option button for the **Do you want to print a test page?** setting.
10. Click [ Next > ] to open the **Completing the Add Printer Wizard** screen, which summarizes the settings you have chosen.
11. Click [ Finish ] to copy the drivers for the printer and complete the Wizard. The printer you have installed now appears in the Printers and Faxes window. Close the window.

**Figure 10-2  Automatic detection of a printer**

**Figure 10-3  The Local or Network Printer screen**

Used to add a local printer to a computer or to create a print server

Used to search for printers on network print servers

**Figure 10-4  The Install Printer Software screen**

# skill 3 *Connecting to a Network Printer*

## exam objective

Connect to local and network print devices. Connect to an Internet printer.

## overview

The other way you can access a print device is by using a network connection. When you do this, the Add Printer Wizard creates the logical printer that will connect you to the shared print device. When you choose **Network printer** on the Local or Network Printer screen, the **Specify a Printer** screen will open next. You can either enter the UNC pathname for the shared printer, or browse the network to locate the \\*printservername\sharename* of your choice. You can also use My Network Places to locate and connect to a shared print device just as you would a shared folder, or you can use the Run command on the Start menu and enter the UNC pathname in the Open text box. If your client is running Windows XP, 2000, NT, or 9x, the computer will automatically install the driver needed to deliver the requests for service from the operating system to the physical print device, as long as a copy of the driver is stored on the print server. Windows 3.x and MS-DOS users will have to manually install the print driver and, if your network includes Macintosh, UNIX, and Netware clients, additional services will have to be installed on the print server.

If you are on an Active Directory network, the Specify a Printer screen will include the **Find a printer in the Directory** option button. When you click Next, a dialog box will open in which you can search the Active Directory for a printer based on its name, location, capability, or comment.

You can also connect to remote print devices, such as a print device at a branch office of your company, by connecting to them over the Internet or on your intranet. As long as you have permission for an Internet printer, you can connect to it using its URL. In this case, on the Specify a Printer page, you will select this option and enter the URL.

Many organizations today have network-interface print devices that connect to the Internet using a network interface card (NIC). For these devices, you usually have to configure a TCP/IP port. You can select the **Create a new port** option button on the **Select a Printer Port** screen and select a port type in the **Type of port** list box. Choose **Standard TCP/IP Port**. When you click the Next button, the **Add Standard TCP/IP Printer Port Wizard** opens. On the **Add Port** screen, you will have to enter either the IP address or FQDN (fully qualified domain name) for the print device in the **Printer Name or IP Address** text box. When you enter an IP address, the operating system automatically enters a port name in the **Port Name** text box **(Figure 10-5)**.

Note that if you are connecting to a network-interface print device that does not use the TCP/IP protocol, you will have to install the appropriate network protocol before running the Add Printer Wizard and creating a new port for the protocol.

**Figure 10-5  Specifying the printer for which to add a port**

The operating system will automatically enter a port name based on the information you have entered in the Wizard, but you can change it

# skill 3

## Connecting to a Network Printer
### (cont'd)

**exam objective**

Connect to local and network print devices. Connect to an Internet printer.

## how to

Connect to a network printer.

1. Open the **Printers and Faxes** window from the Start menu.
2. Click the **Add a printer** link to start the **Add Printer Wizard**. The **Welcome to the Add Printer Wizard** screen opens.
3. Click [ Next > ] to open the **Local or Network printer** screen.
4. Click the **A network printer, or a printer attached to another computer** option button.
5. Click [ Next > ] to open the **Specify a Printer** screen. This is where you enter the UNC pathname for a share, or the URL for an Internet or intranet print device.
6. Select the **Connect to this printer** option button. In the **Name** text box, type the path for the network printer, following the syntax, \\*printservername*\*printername* (**Figure 10-6**).
7. Click [ Next > ]. The Wizard copies the necessary printer software, and then opens the **Default Printer** screen. Select the **Yes** or **No** option button, depending on whether you want this printer to be your default printer.
8. Click [ Next > ] to open the **Completing the Add Printer Wizard** screen, which summarizes the printer settings you have specified.
9. Click [ Finish ] to complete the installation of the network printer. An icon for the printer now appears in the Printers and Faxes window (**Figure 10-7**). Close the Printers and Faxes window.

### tip

If IIS (Internet Information Services), Microsoft's Web server software, has been installed on the print server that is servicing the request, you can connect to a printer on the intranet by specifying the path of the printer in the URL text box. You can also locate the printer by browsing the network.

## more

You can also configure a TCP/IP port for a network-interface print device on the **Ports** tab in the **Properties** dialog box for the print device. Simply click the **Add Port** button and select **Standard TCP/IP** port in the next dialog box. This will initiate the **Add Standard TCP/IP Port Wizard**. Once again, you will have to enter either the IP address or the FQDN name for the print device. In the final dialog boxes of the Wizard, you will install and set up the port so that the logical printer will send its instructions to an IP address rather than a local port.

To connect to an Internet printer, select the **Connect to a printer on the Internet or on a home or office network** option button on the Specify a Printer screen of the Add Printer Wizard. Then, enter the URL of the printer in the URL text box, following the syntax, *http://printservername/printername/* (for example, **http://PrintSrv/HPColor2/**).

**Figure 10-6 Specifying a network printer**

**Figure 10-7 Network printer added to the Printers and Faxes window**

# skill 4    *Configuring a Network Printer*

## exam objective

Monitor, configure, and troubleshoot I/O devices, such as printers, scanners, multimedia devices, mouse, keyboard, and smart card reader.

## overview

If you are setting up your computer to be a print server, you will select the Local Printer option button on the Local or Network Printer screen in the Add Printer Wizard. When you select Network printer, all you can do is *locate* a network printer; you cannot create a new printer. You can connect as many print devices as your hardware configuration will allow, and then install their logical printers. If you have not already done so in the Wizard, after you have installed the printer or printers, you can open the Sharing tab in the Properties dialog box for the printer and make it a shared resource, just as you did for a folder (**Figure 10-8**). When you share a print resource, you must set a share name for other users to locate when they browse the available resources on your server. By default, the only driver that is installed when you create a shared printer is the one that is compatible with Windows XP or Windows 2000. If you want to add drivers so that they will automatically download when clients first connect to the share, you can select the **Additional Drivers** button at the bottom of the Sharing tab. This opens the Additional Drivers dialog box where you can choose from a number of other drivers. Then, you can configure the printers to meet the requirements of your organization. If your server will be required to handle a large quantity of printing jobs, several features are useful, including Printer Pooling and Print Priorities.

◆ **Creating a printer pool:** A printer pool is a single logical printer on a print server that is associated with multiple physical print devices. You can use printer pooling when you have a number of the same type, or similar types, of print devices, which all use the same driver so that they can all understand the same sets of commands. Print jobs that are sent to a printer pool will be directed to the least busy print device in the pool. This is a benefit to the Administrator because he or she can manage multiple print devices from a single printer. To create a printer pool, you use the **Ports** tab on the **Properties** dialog box for the printer. At the bottom of the tab, select the **Enable printer pooling** check box and select all of the ports to which you want the logical printer to print. When you enable printer pooling, you cannot control which print device will receive the job; therefore, it is helpful to have the print devices near each other so that your employees can easily find their documents.

◆ **Setting the priority of a printer:** Printer priority is set when multiple configured printers use a common print device. You set printers as high-priority or low-priority to control the order in which their print jobs will be sent to the print device. To set the priority for a printer, you use the **Advanced** tab on the **Properties** dialog box for the printer (**Figure 10-9**). You can rank the priority of the printer from 1 through 99. The number 1 is the lowest rank, and it is selected by default. If you leave the default in place, any printer with a priority from 2-99 will have its jobs sent to the print device first. This can be particularly useful if you have one user or group whose print jobs are critical and must be printed as soon as they are ordered. For example, if you have two logical printers and only one print device, and you want one printer's documents to take priority, you can set this printer's rank to 2 so that its print jobs will be completed first. You can also use the **Available from** option button to make a printer available only at certain times. This can be useful if you have a user or group that has a large volume of low-priority printing jobs.

**Figure 10-8  Sharing a printer**

Makes the printer available to users on a network

Used to add additional printer drivers to a computer

**Figure 10-9  Setting the priority of a printer**

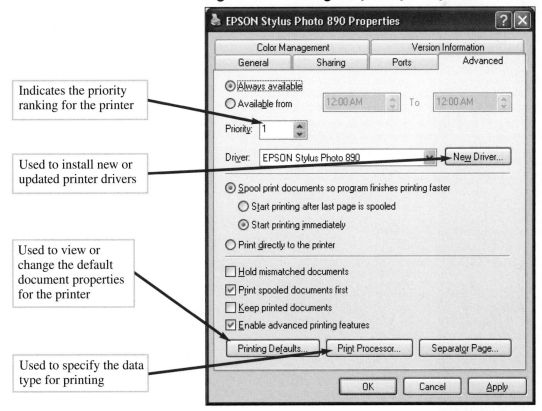

Indicates the priority ranking for the printer

Used to install new or updated printer drivers

Used to view or change the default document properties for the printer

Used to specify the data type for printing

# skill 4

## *Configuring a Network Printer (cont'd)*

**exam objective**

Monitor, configure, and troubleshoot I/O devices, such as printers, scanners, multimedia devices, mouse, keyboard, and smart card reader.

**how to**

Configure a print server to create a printer pool.

1. Log on to the print server as an **Administrator**.
2. Click **start** and click **Printers and Faxes** to open the Printers and Faxes window.
3. Right-click the printer icon for a print device that is attached to the print server. Then, click the **Properties** command to open the **Properties** dialog box for the printer.
4. Click the **Ports** tab and select the **Enable printer pooling** check box.
5. Select the ports for the print devices that you want to include in the printer pool. For example, click **LPT1**, **LPT2**, and **LPT3** in the Port list box (**Figure 10-10**). These multiple print devices connected to the computer will form the printer pool. All will receive their instructions from the one logical printer.
6. Click **OK** to close the Properties dialog box and create the printer pool on the computer.
7. Close the Printers and Faxes window.

**Figure 10-10  Creating a printer pool**

Used to select all of the ports to which you want the logical printer to print

To create a printer pool, you must have a number of the same type, or similar types, of print devices which all use the same driver

# skill 5

## Assigning Access Permissions to Network Printers

**exam objective**

Control access to printers by using permissions.

**overview**

When you install a printer on a network, by default, the Everyone group has the Print permission. Since this is the most restrictive print permission you can assign, you will generally not have to spend much time on printer security. However, you can use printer permissions to limit access to a particular network printer for certain users, and you can allow users who are not Administrators to manage a particular printer. You set print permissions on the **Security** tab in the **Properties** dialog box for the printer. Just like any other permissions, print permissions can be either allowed or denied, and denials override allowed permissions. There are three levels of print permissions:

◆ **Print:** The Print permission enables a user to connect to a printer and send print jobs to it.

◆ **Manage Documents:** The Manage Documents permission enables a user to pause, resume, restart, and cancel all other users' printing jobs. However, a user cannot send documents to the printer or control the status of the printer. Members of the **Creator Owner** group have the Manage Documents permission by default.

◆ **Manage Printers:** The Manage Printers permission grants a user administrative control over a printer. Users with this permission can pause and restart the printer, share a printer, adjust printer permissions, change printer properties, delete a printer, and cancel all other users' documents or all queued documents. Members of the **Administrators** and **Power Users** groups have the Manage Printers permission by default.

**how to**

Assign access permissions for accessing a network printer to a user.

1. Log on to your computer as an **Administrator**.
2. Click ![start] and click **Printers and Faxes** to open the **Printers and Faxes** window.
3. Right-click the printer icon for which you want to set permissions. Then, click the **Properties** command on the shortcut menu to open the **Properties** dialog box for the printer.
4. Click the **Security** tab (**Figure 10-11**).
5. Click [ Add... ] to open the **Select Users or Groups** dialog box. Make sure that **Users** appears in the **Select this object type** text box, and that the computer on which you are working is listed in the **From this location** text box.
6. Type the user name of the user to whom you want to assign printer access permissions, in this case JForester, in the **Enter the object names to select** text box (**Figure 10-12**).
7. Click [ OK ] to close the Select Users or Groups dialog box. The user name you selected now appears in the **Group or user names** list on the Security tab.
8. Select the user name in the Group or user names list.
9. Select the **Allow** check box for the **Manage Printers** permission to assign it to the selected user (**Figure 10-13**).
10. Click [ OK ] to close the printer's **Properties** dialog box, and close the Printers and Faxes window.

**tip**

To remove a user or a group from the permissions list, select the user in the Group or user names list on the Security tab for the printer, and click Remove.

**more**

To view or change the permissions assigned to a printer, click [ Advanced ] on the Security tab. This opens the **Advanced Security Settings** dialog box for the printer, which displays a detailed list of the permissions assigned to users. Any user with the Manage Printers permission can view, remove, or edit a selected permission.

**Figure 10-11  The Security tab**

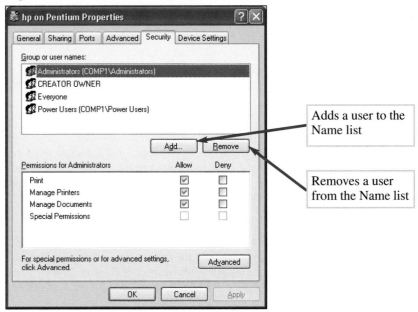

Adds a user to the Name list

Removes a user from the Name list

**Figure 10-12  Selecting a user to be assigned printer permissions**

Enter the user(s) or group to whom you want to assign print permissions

**Figure 10-13  Assigning printer permissions**

# skill 6 *Managing Printers*

## exam objective

Manage printers and print jobs. Monitor, configure, and troubleshoot I/O devices, such as printers, scanners, multimedia devices, mouse, keyboard, and smart card reader.

## overview

Managing printers and print jobs involves pausing and resuming printing; canceling documents; pausing, resuming, or canceling specific documents; restarting print jobs; scheduling documents to print at a later time; and changing the priority of a document so that the printing requirements of your organization can be met. For example, if you urgently need a particular document for a meeting and you have a problem with the default printer on your computer, you can redirect the print job to another printer.

Managing printers involves performing a variety of administrative tasks:

◆ **Specifying paper sizes for paper trays:** A printer has multiple paper trays that hold paper of different sizes; therefore, you must specify the paper size, which you can do on the **Device Settings** tab in the Properties dialog box for the printer **(Figure 10-14)**. When a user selects a paper size and gives a print command, Windows 2000 automatically routes the print job to the correct paper tray. Some common paper sizes are Legal, A4, Envelope #10, and Letter Small.

◆ **Setting a Separator Page:** A Separator page, also called a banner page, is a file that identifies a printed document, usually with the name of the user who requested it, as well as the date and time. It is printed between documents so that you can easily identify the start and end of each print job. You can choose from the four default separator pages by using the **Separator Page** button on the **Advanced** tab in the Properties dialog box **(Figure 10-15)** for a printer to locate your *systemroot*\System32 folder **(Figure 10-16)**, where these pages are stored.

◆ **Performing printing tasks:** A user may need to perform a variety of printing tasks such as pausing, resuming, and canceling the printing of documents. For example, if you send the wrong document to be printed, you can cancel the print job; or if a printer is malfunctioning, you can pause it while you fix the problem and resume printing when it is resolved. To pause all print jobs, open the Printers and Faxes window, right-click the printer icon, and select the **Pause Printing** command. To resume all print jobs, select the **Pause Printing** command again to toggle it off. To pause a particular document, double-click the printer icon, right-click the document, and select Pause Printing. Use the Shift or Ctrl key to select multiple documents. To resume printing specific documents, double-click the printer icon, right-click the documents you want to resume, and select **Resume**. To cancel all documents, right-click the printer icon and select the **Cancel All Documents** command. To cancel one or more specific documents, double-click the printer icon, right-click the documents, and select the **Cancel** command. To restart a print job, right-click the documents and select the **Restart** command.

◆ **Sending documents to a different printer:** If a print device is malfunctioning, you might decide to redirect all queued print jobs. You can do this by adding a port on the **Ports** tab in the Properties dialog box for the printer. First, if there is a working printer of the same type on another local port on the same print server, select the check box for the port, and click OK. Alternatively, if there is a working printer of the same kind on a different print server, click the **Add Port** button. In the **Printer Ports** dialog box, click the **New Port** button. In the **Port Name** dialog box, enter the UNC pathname for the redirect printer in the **Enter a port name** box.

◆ **Changing ownership of a printer:** If the owner of a printer (the person who installed it) leaves the organization and you must pass on the administrative responsibility to a new user, you can change its ownership. Users with the Manage Printers permission and members of the Administrators and Power Users groups can take ownership of a printer on the **Owner** tab on the ACL for the printer. First, open the Properties dialog box for the printer. On the **Security** tab, click the **Advanced** button to open the **Advanced Security Settings for <printername>** dialog box. Then, open the Owner tab and select your user account under **Name** in the **Change owner to** box.

**Figure 10-14  Specifying paper sizes**

Specifies the paper
size to be used by
the front tray of a
printer

**Figure 10-15  Separator Page dialog box**

Enter the file path to
the separator page or
click Browse to
locate the file

**Figure 10-16  Browsing to locate separator page files in the SYSTEM32 folder**

Four default
separator page files

# skill 6

## *Managing Printers (cont'd)*

**exam objective**

Manage printers and print jobs. Monitor, configure, and troubleshoot I/O devices, such as printers, scanners, multimedia devices, mouse, keyboard, and smart card reader.

**how to**

Redirect a document from one printer to another.

1. Click [*start*] and click **Printers and Faxes** to open the **Printers and Faxes** window. Minimize the window.
2. Create a test document in Microsoft Word or WordPad and save it as **Printjob1.doc**. Send Printjob1.doc to the printer.
3. Restore the Printers and Faxes window.
4. Double-click the icon for the printer to which you sent Printjob1.doc. This displays a list of the documents that were sent to the printer for printing.
5. Select the document **Printjob1.doc**, which is the document that you want to redirect to another printer.
6. Open the **Printer** menu and click the **Properties** command to open the **Printer1 Properties** dialog box (**Figure 10-17**).
7. Click the **Ports** tab to display a list of available ports.
8. Click the port to which the alternative printer is assigned (**Figure 10-18**).
9. Click [ OK ]. You have redirected the document **Printjob1.doc** from one printer to another.
10. Close all open windows.

**tip**

To redirect documents to a printer on a different print server, the printer must already exist on the network, and it must be shared on the print server. You can then add a local port for the second print server and provide the print server name, as well as the appropriate share name for the printer.

**more**

There are also tools you can use to manage documents that are in the printing queue. These are found on the General tab in the Properties dialog box for a document. To open the Properties dialog box for a document, double-click the icon for the printer on which the document is printing, and right-click the document in the Printer window. Then, click Properties on the shortcut menu. You can also select more than one document. A notification is used when you want someone other than the person who sent the print job to know that the job is complete. Simply enter the user name in the **Notify** text box. You can also use the **Priority** slider to adjust the priority that was assigned to the document. Finally, you can restrict print times to specific hours by selecting the **Only from** option button and setting a schedule in the **Only from** and **To** spin boxes. You can also manage printers using any computer with a Web browser, even if it is not a Windows XP computer and does not have the correct print driver. When you manage your printers using a Web browser, you can create your own home page containing the location and links to the printers; moreover, you will have access to a page that lists the status of every printer on a print server. Crucial data that does not display in the Printers window, which can be used to correct print device problems, will display instantaneously on this summary page. You can also access all of the printers, or a specific printer, on a print server by entering the path to the print server or to the particular printer in the **Address** text box in the Web browser.

**caution**

To access a printer using a Web browser, the print server on which the printer resides must have Internet Information Server (IIS) installed. IIS is a Web server and responds to user requests from a browser.

**Figure 10-17  Selecting the Properties command**

Indicates the status of documents that are being printed

Used to access the Properties dialog box for a selected document

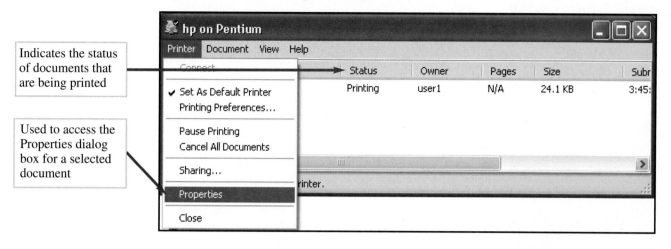

**Figure 10-18  Specifying the port for a printer**

Lists the ports to which printers are connected

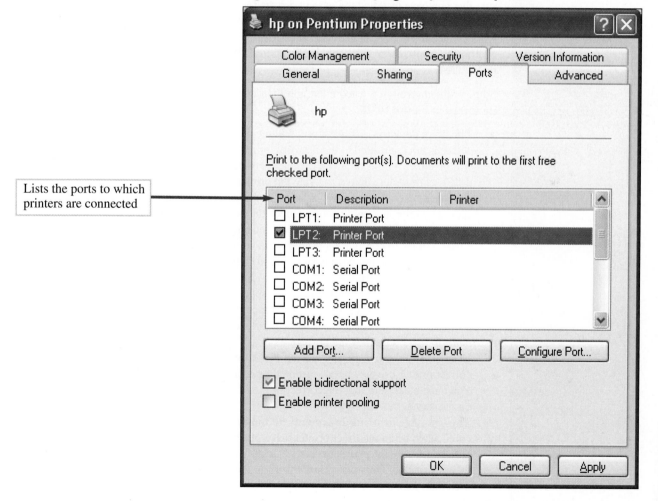

# skill 7 *Troubleshooting Printer Problems*

**exam objective**

Monitor, configure, and troubleshoot I/O devices, such as printers, scanners, multimedia devices, mouse, keyboard, and smart card reader.

**overview**

Troubleshooting printer problems can occupy more time than an Administrator would like. The first thing you should check, as you would when troubleshooting any hardware device, is whether the local devices are plugged in and connected correctly. You should check the cables, make sure the power is on, and check the paper and toner. Then, you can try recreating the logical printer on the client, reinstalling the print driver, and terminating and re-sharing the printer on the print server. Check the print queue for stalled print jobs (click **Start**, click **Printers and Faxes**, double-click the **Printer** icon). If nothing is listed under Status (waiting, paused, or printing), it is likely the print job has stalled. You must also make sure that the print spool service is running (open the **Services** snap-in in the **Administrative Tools** console). Stop and restart the Print Spooler service **(Figure 10-19)**. Make sure that there is enough disk space for spooling on the print server (75 MB is recommended). If the print device is operational and other users can print, the print server is probably not the problem. If other users also cannot print, make sure that the printer on the print server is using the correct driver, and make sure that you have installed the correct drivers for other operating systems on the print server. If you are using a network-interface print device, you should first make sure that there is a network connection between the device and the print server. Make sure that you can see and connect to the print server from the workstation. PING the IP address for a TCP/IP printer to make sure it is operational.

Some problems you may encounter, and their causes and solutions, are described below and illustrated in **Figure 10-20**:

◆ **The print device is offline:** Users will receive this error message when the physical print device is not connected to the network, or is turned off, or has gone offline. Usually there will be either a light or an LCD message to tell you whether the printer is online. Press the Reset or Online button to cycle the printer into online mode.

◆ **The user receives an Access Denied or No Access Available message**: This is usually caused by improper permissions. Check the permissions assigned to both the user and the groups to which he or she is a member, and check for any denied permissions. Sometimes a user will try to configure a printer from an older application and will receive this message when they do not have permission to change printer configurations. You must either change the user's permissions or ask an Administrator to reconfigure the printer.

◆ **A Test page does not print:** This can happen if you select the wrong port when you add a printer. You can solve this problem by configuring the printer again using the correct port. If the printer is using a network-interface print device, check the IP address or DNS name to make sure they are correct.

◆ **User gets an error message stating that a printer driver must be installed:** When the correct printer drivers are not installed on a print server, you will get this error message. You must make sure that the correct printer drivers for each client computer are installed on the server.

◆ **The test page or print documents do not print completely:** The cause of this problem could again be an incorrect printer driver. Install the printer again with the correct driver.

◆ **Documents do not print correctly:** Documents may not print correctly on some printers in a printer pool when the print devices in the pool do not use the same driver. You must use either identical or similar print devices that use the same printer driver.

◆ **Documents do not reach the print server:** This problem may arise as a result of insufficient hard disk space on a computer. To solve this problem, free some space on the hard disk.

**Figure 10-19  The Print Spooler service**

**Figure 10-20  Various printer problems**

A test page does not print

Configuration error

Printer driver installation error

Printer access denied error

A test page does not print completely

Documents do not print correctly

Documents do not reach the print server

# Summary

- In Windows XP, a printer is considered to be the software that delivers the requests for service from the operating system to the physical print device.
- A print device, therefore, is the physical hardware that you think of as a printer that creates the hard copies of your digital files.
- A print server handles the requests for service for a shared printer. A print server can either administer these requests through a print device that is physically connected to it or through a network-connected print device.
- Network-connected print devices are called network-interface print devices and they have their own NIC (network interface card) and network address, or an external network adapter connection.
- Windows XP Professional computers and even Windows 9x computers can be configured as print servers.
- A printer port is the software interface that a computer uses to communicate with a printer. Once again, the printer port does not refer to the physical hardware port, but rather to the software that communicates with it.
- A printer driver is the software that contains the information used by the operating system to convert the print commands for a particular model of print device into a printer language.
- A printer pool is a single printer (that is, the software that delivers the requests for service from the operating system) that can queue print jobs to multiple ports and their associated print devices.
- Print pooling is used when there are many print devices on a network that can receive instructions from the same type of print driver. Print jobs will be allocated by the printer pool to the first available print device.
- Printer priority is set when multiple configured printers use a common print device. You set printers as high-priority or low-priority to control the order in which their print jobs will be sent to the print device.
- Only members of the local Administrators or Power Users groups can install a local printer.
- You can access a print device using a network connection. You use the Add Printer Wizard to create the logical printer that will connect you to the shared print device. On the Locate Your Printer page, you either enter the UNC pathname for the share or browse the network to locate it.
- You can also use My Network Places to locate and connect to a shared print device, just as you would a shared folder, or you can use the Run command on the Start menu and enter the UNC pathname in the Open text box.
- If you are on an Active Directory network, you can use the Find a printer in the Directory option on the Locate Your Printer page to search the Active Directory for a printer based on its name, location, capability, or a comment.
- You can also connect to remote print devices by connecting to the printer over the Internet or on your intranet. As long as you have permission for an Internet printer, you can connect to it using its URL.
- You can configure a TCP/IP port for a network-interface print device on the Ports tab in the Properties dialog box for the print device. Click the Add Port button and select Standard TCP/IP port in the next dialog box to initiate the Add Standard TCP/IP Port Wizard.
- If you are setting up your computer to be a print server, you will select the Local Printer option button on the Local or Network Printer page in the Add Printer Wizard. When you select Network printer, all you can do is *locate* a network printer; you cannot create a new printer.
- There are three levels of printer permissions: Print, Manage Printers, and Manage Documents.
- The Print permission enables a user to connect to a printer and send it print jobs.
- The Manage Printers permission grants a user administrative control over a printer. Users with this permission can pause and restart the printer, share a printer, adjust printer permissions, change printer properties, delete a printer, and cancel all other users' documents or all queued documents.
- Members of the Administrators and Power Users groups have the Manage Printers permission by default.
- The Manage Documents permission enables a user to pause, resume, restart, and cancel all other users' printing jobs. However, a user cannot send documents to the printer or control the status of the printer.
- Members of the Creator Owner group have the Manage Documents permission by default.

# Key Terms

| | | |
|---|---|---|
| Add Printer Wizard | Print permission | Printer port |
| Local print device | Print device | Print server |
| Manage Documents permission | Printer | Separator page |
| Manage Printers permission | Printer driver | |
| Network printer | Printer pool | |

# Test Yourself

1. You are installing a local printer using the Add Printer Wizard. Which of the following options do you need to specify during the installation process?
   a. Share Name
   b. Security settings
   c. Location
   d. Port

2. Which of the following converts print commands into a printer language?
   a. Printer port
   b. Print device
   c. Printer driver
   d. Print server

3. You have multiple identical print devices located in close proximity to the server where the logical printer is configured, and you want print jobs to be sent to the least busy print device so that your print jobs can be serviced as quickly as possible. Which of the following will you use?
   a. Printer pooling
   b. Printer priorities
   c. Redirecting
   d. Printing preferences

4. You want to send your print jobs to a network-interface print device that is connected to your network. Which of the following will you have to enter in the Add Printer Wizard when you are configuring the logical printer? (Choose all that apply.)
   a. Name of the manufacturer
   b. A TCP/IP port
   c. Printer name
   d. IP address
   e. URL of the printer

5. You have multiple printers using a single print device. What rank would you assign to a printer to make it the lowest priority printer in the group?
   a. 99
   b. 999
   c. 89
   d. 1

6. You are the Network Administrator at SpringHead Corp. Mary, the Project Manager at your company, is unable to print her documents using the printer that is configured on her computer. She wants you to redirect her documents to a different printer. Which of the following sequences of steps will you follow in order to do this?
   a. Right-click the printer icon → click Properties → click Advanced tab
   b. Right-click the printer icon → click Printing Preferences
   c. Right-click the printer icon → click Properties → click Ports tab
   d. Right-click the printer icon → click Sharing → click Device Setting tab

7. You work for a large dog food manufacturer. Jane has connected to a printer and sent a print job for a document that she and her partner Samuel need for a meeting after lunch. She has left for lunch and the printer has run out of ink. Samuel rushes over to ask you to pause the printer so that he can refill it. What permission must you have in order to do this?
   a. Printer Pooling
   b. Manage Documents
   c. Print
   d. Manage Printers

8. The Systems Manager of your company, Susan, is allowed to print, pause, resume and restart print jobs sent by other users to a network printer; however, she cannot control the status of the printer. Which of the following permissions does Susan have?
   a. Manage Documents
   b. Print
   c. Manage Printers
   d. Full Control

9. Which of the following can you configure so that documents are sent to the least busy print device in a group of print devices that all use the same driver?
   a. Print server
   b. Network printer
   c. Printer pool
   d. Printer port

# Projects: On Your Own

1. Add a non Plug and Play local printer on a computer.
   a. Access the **Add Printer Wizard**.
   b. Select the local printer option.
   c. Select a port, software, printer name, and share property.
   d. Print a test page and complete the Wizard.
2. Add a network printer on a computer.
   a. Access the **Add Printer Wizard**.
   b. Select the network printer option.
   c. Access the **Specify a Printer** screen.
   d. Connect to the network printer.
   e. Select a default status and complete the Wizard.
3. Assign Access Permissions to a user for accessing a network printer.
   a. Access the **Properties** dialog box of a printer.
   b. Click the **Security** tab.
   c. Access the **Select Users or Groups** dialog box.
   d. Enter the name of a user or group.
   e. Assign the **Print** permission for the user in the **Permissions** section of the Security tab.

# Problem Solving Scenarios

1. You are working as a Systems Administrator at Pitch Inc., a marketing firm in New York City. John Williams, a senior designer, requires color printing of advertising campaign sample pages for several of his projects. Therefore, he wants you to add and configure a color laser printer on his computer. Additionally, he wants this printer to be available to his workgroup members. Outline in a memo the steps you would take to add and configure a color printer on John's computer, and then share it over a network.

2. Your company has recently purchased Hewlett Packard laser printers with enhanced features. These printers have been added and configured on all employee computers. Your company management requires that only managers be allowed to change the print status of the documents sent to printers, and regular employees must be allowed to print documents only. Outline in a memo to company management how you will assign the appropriate print permissions to managers and employees.

On NTFS disks, you can use NTFS permissions, either alone or in combination with share permissions, to control access to network resources. Unlike shared folder permissions, NTFS permissions can also be used to control access to resources that are stored on the computer where the user is physically logged on. Although you will generally choose a file system during the installation of Windows XP Professional, you can convert a drive to NTFS after installation. One reason that NTFS is considered to be superior to the other file systems is that NTFS permissions can be set for both files and folders, and you have many more options for controlling what users can do with a file or folder once they have opened it. This progressive file system also supports large data storage, long file names, compression, encryption, and ownership of files and folders. Each file or folder on an NTFS volume has a set of attributes, including the compression attribute, the encryption attribute, and the owner attribute. NTFS attributes also include the security permissions you set for groups or individual users.

If you are unsure whether you are working with an NTFS volume, you can open Windows Explorer and check the properties for the drive (right-click the drive letter and select the Properties command), or you can open the Properties dialog box for any file or folder to see if the dialog box has a Security tab. When you set NTFS permissions, you do not have to specifically share the file or folder first; you simply open the Security tab to configure the ACL (Access Control List). The Security tab displays the standard NTFS permissions. Setting them involves the same process as configuring the ACL permissions for shared folders; you allow or specifically deny the appropriate level of access. Like share permissions, the Deny condition overrides the Allow condition. By default, the Everyone group is granted the Full Control NTFS permission for the root of a drive, although not for the system subfolders. As with share permissions, you will generally remove this permission and set your own according to your organizational needs.

## Goals

In this lesson, you will learn how to assign NTFS file and folder permissions, and how to assign Special Access permissions to users in order to control user access to objects. Finally, you will learn how to troubleshoot problems related to NTFS permissions.

### Lesson 11  Working with NTFS Permissions

| Skill | Exam 70-270 Objective |
| --- | --- |
| 1. Identifying Types of NTFS Permissions | Basic knowledge |
| 2. Assigning NTFS Permissions | Monitor, manage, and troubleshoot access to files and folders. Control access to files and folders by using permissions. |
| 3. Using Special Permissions | Monitor, manage, and troubleshoot access to files and folders. Control access to files and folders by using permissions. |
| 4. Troubleshooting NTFS Permissions | Monitor, manage, and troubleshoot access to files and folders. Control access to files and folders by using permissions. |

## Requirements

To complete this lesson, you will need a computer with Windows XP Professional installed on it and a volume formatted with NTFS. You will also need a folder named General on the NTFS volume or partition. The exercises will assume it is stored on the C: drive.

Exam 70-270

# skill 1  *Identifying Types of NTFS Permissions*

**exam objective**   Basic knowledge

## overview

One of the most important things to remember about NTFS permissions is that they can be configured for both files and folders. While share permissions are configured at the folder level, and any subfolders or files within the folder inherit the shared folder permissions, you can assign NTFS permissions to a file that are different than the ones assigned to the folder in which the file is stored. File permissions take precedence over folder permissions.

Another important concept is that NTFS permissions, like share permissions, are cumulative, or added together. If a user has the NTFS Read permission granted through membership in one group and the NTFS Modify permission granted through membership in another group, his or her effective permission is Modify.

However, when NTFS permissions are used in combination with share permissions, the most restrictive permission applies. For example, if a user has the Read share permission granted through membership in one group and the NTFS folder Modify permission granted through membership in another group, his or her effective permission when accessing the network share would be Read. Remember, share permissions apply only to users who are connecting over the network, so if users connect to the folder on the computer on which it is being hosted, they will have the NTFS Modify permission locally.

One effective way of handling this contradiction is to create shared folders and leave the default permission, Full Control for the Everyone group, intact. Then, instead of applying any share permissions, use NTFS permissions to secure the resources. Since the most restrictive permission applies, as long as you have fine-tuned your NTFS permissions so that groups have the appropriate level of access, your resources will be secure. Additionally, since NTFS permissions operate locally, you can be confident that security for files and folders on the computers on which they are stored is effective even when more than one user accesses the computer.

**The standard NTFS folder permissions are listed below (Figure 11-1):**
◆ **Read:** Users can open and view the content of files, folders, and subfolders. They can also view the ownership of objects, permissions assigned to objects, and the various folder attributes such as Read-Only, Hidden, Archive, and System.
◆ **Write:** Users can create new files and subfolders in a folder. This permission also allows users to view folder ownership, the assigned permissions, and to use the **Properties** dialog box to change folder attributes.
◆ **List Folder Contents:** Users can only view the names of subfolders and files in a folder.
◆ **Read & Execute:** This permission includes the tasks permitted by the Read and List Folder Contents permissions and gives users the ability to navigate, or traverse, through folders for which they do not have permission, in order to get to files and folders for which they do have permissions. Users may also run program files.
◆ **Modify:** Users can view, create, delete, and modify the content of folders, as well as change attributes. This permission includes all tasks permitted by the Read, Write, and Read and Execute permissions.
◆ **Full Control:** Users can change permissions and take ownership of folders. This permission includes all actions that are permitted by all other NTFS permissions.

**The standard NTFS file permissions are listed below (Figure 11-2):**
◆ **Read:** Users can read the file and view the file attributes, file ownership, and permissions.
◆ **Write:** Users can change the file, change file attributes, and view file ownerships and permissions.
◆ **Read & Execute:** Users can view the contents of files and run program applications.
◆ **Modify:** Users can modify and delete the file, run applications, change attributes, and perform all other actions permitted by the Write and Read & Execute permissions.
◆ **Full Control:** Users can change permissions, take ownership, and perform all actions permitted by the other NTFS permissions.

**tip**
When you assign NTFS permissions to a folder, all files and subfolders in the folder inherit the same permissions by default (This default action can be changed.). On the other hand, NTFS permissions assigned to files cannot be further inherited because files do not contain any objects that can inherit these permissions.

**tip**
You can assign special permissions to both folders and files by clicking the Advanced button on the Security tab of the Properties dialog box for a file or folder.

**Figure 11-1  NTFS folder permissions**

**Figure 11-2  NTFS file permissions**

# skill 2

# *Assigning NTFS Permissions*

Monitor, manage, and troubleshoot access to files and folders. Control access to files and folders by using permissions.

## overview

When you assign NTFS permissions, you must understand not only how they work when combined with other NTFS permissions, as well as how they work when combined with share permissions, but also how they are inherited from the parent folders. By default, whatever permissions you assign to the parent folder are inherited by the subfolders and files stored in that folder. This is true for both share permissions and NTFS permissions. You will know that an NTFS permission has been inherited if it is grayed out and inactive on the Security tab in the Properties dialog box. This indicates that there is no need to assign this permission to the subfolder or file because it has already been inherited. However, for certain files, you may want to prevent the inheritance of some of the permissions granted to the parent folder. This can be accomplished by clicking the **Advanced** button on the Security tab to open the **Advanced Security Settings** dialog box, and then removing the check from the **Inherit from parent the permission entries that apply to child objects** check box at the bottom of the **Permissions** tab. At this point, you can either copy the previously inherited permissions, or you can remove the inherited permissions and keep only those that are explicitly set for the object. The best practice is to copy the existing permissions, because then you can reconfigure the ACL by removing or adding the necessary permissions. If you remove all of the permissions, you will have to reconfigure the entire Security tab.

The important rules for assigning NTFS permissions are recapped and outlined below:

Remember you can assign NTFS permissions to both files and folders, unlike the shared folder permissions, which can be assigned only at the folder level.

You must have the Write permission for the destination folder in order to copy or move an NTFS object to its destination folder. You must have, at least, the Modify permission for the source file or folder in order to move it.

The NTFS permissions for a file or folder copied or moved from an NTFS volume to any other volume, such as FAT or FAT32, are lost because other volumes do not support NTFS permissions.

◆ When you assign multiple permissions to a user, the effective permission for the user is the combination of all of the assigned permissions. For example, if a user has the Read permission for a file, and he/she is a member of another group that has the Write permission for that file, the effective permission for the user is both Read and Write.

◆ When you set the Deny condition, it overrides an allowed permission the user has for accessing the file or folder. For example, if a user named John has the Modify permission for the **Client** folder, which contains two files, Feedback.doc and Requirements.doc, and John is also a member of the Sales group, which has been denied the Modify permission for the Feedback.doc file, John can read and write to only Requirements.doc **(Figure 11-3)**.

◆ When you assign both shared folder permissions and NTFS permissions, the effective permission will be the most restrictive one. For example, if Kelvin is a member of the Team Leaders group and the QA group, and the Team Leaders group has been assigned the Read shared folder permission for the Standards folder, but the QA group has been assigned the Full Control NTFS permission for the Standards folder, the effective permission when Kelvin accesses the folder over the network is Read **(Figure 11-4)**.

◆ NTFS file permissions override NTFS folder permissions. For example, if a user, James, does not have access permissions for a folder named Sales, but James has permission to access a file named data.doc that is stored in the Sales folder, he can access data.doc. However, he must do so by specifying the path for that file in the **Run** dialog box, or use a shortcut to the file. Without permission to read the folder, he cannot view the folder or open it to look for the file.

◆ When you assign NTFS permissions to a folder, the files and subfolders contained in that folder inherit the assigned permissions. However, you can prevent permissions from being inherited by the files and subfolders of a folder.

◆ When you copy or move files or folders, the NTFS permissions often change. When you copy a file from one folder to another, the permissions change because now the file will inherit a new set of NTFS permissions from the new parent folder. When you copy a file, you become the owner of the copy. Once you take ownership of a file, you can change the NTFS permissions.

**Figure 11-3  Denying the Modify permission**

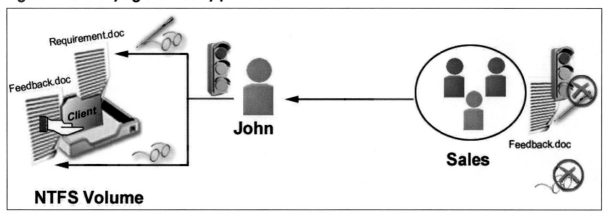

**Figure 11-4  Combining shared folder permissions and NTFS permissions**

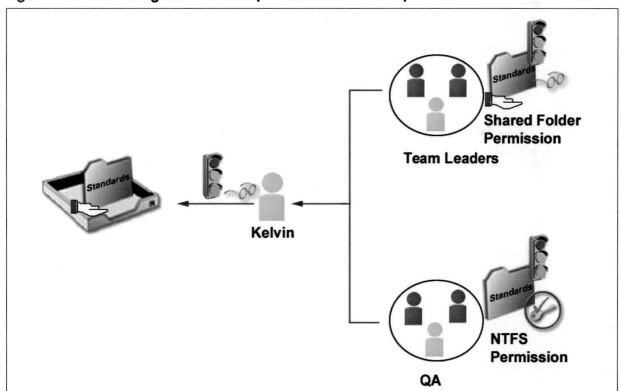

# skill 2

## *Assigning NTFS Permissions (cont'd)*

### exam objective

Monitor, manage, and troubleshoot access to files and folders. Control access to files and folders by using permissions.

### overview

◆ When you move a file, the NTFS permissions may change, subject to the destination directory into which you are moving it. When you move a file or folder within an NTFS volume, the permissions are not changed in the new location because the file is not a new file on the volume, and does not have a new security descriptor. However, when you move a file or folder to a different NTFS volume, the NTFS permission changes because the file is considered new in the destination volume. It is therefore subject to a new security descriptor, inherited from the destination location.

### how to

Assign the Read and Write NTFS permissions to a user for accessing the General folder.

1. Right-click the **General** folder, and click the **Properties** command to open the **General Properties** dialog box.
2. Click the **Security** tab. (Note: If you are working in a workgroup and you do not see a Security tab, simple file sharing is probably enabled on your computer. In Windows Explorer, open the **Tools** menu and click **Folder Options** to open the **Folder Options** dialog box. On the **View** tab, clear the **Use simple file sharing** check box.)
3. Click [ Add... ] to open the **Select Users or Groups** dialog box.
4. Type the user name of the user to whom you want to assign permissions in the **Enter the object names to select** text box (**Figure 11-5**).
5. Click [ OK ] to close the Select Users or Groups dialog box.
6. The user name is added to the **Group or user names** box on the Security tab. The dialog box will show **Joe Foreste**r, the full name you used when you created the account.
7. Select **Joe Forester** in the Group or user names list, and select the **Allow** check box for the Write permission. The Read & Execute, List Folder Contents, and Read permissions should be selected by default (**Figure 11-6**).
8. Click [ OK ] to close the General Properties dialog box.

### tip

If the Allow or Deny check box for a specific permission is grayed out, it indicates that this permission is inherited from the parent object.

### more

In order to effectively assign permissions to multiple users in a large organization, you should follow the guidelines described below:

◆ Assign permissions at the group level rather than at an individual level, according to the level of access that the group requires for each object. This simplifies monitoring access to shared objects over a network. For example, if you have a folder named Sales that contains confidential information and members of the **Managers** group need to modify it regularly, though members of the **Executive** group only need to view and read its contents, assign the **Modify** permission to the Managers group and the **Read** permission to the Executive group. This will prevent you from having to assign permissions to individual members.

◆ Organize folders with the same NTFS permissions within a single folder. For example, you can store the folders of similar applications within a single folder. Then, you can share and assign appropriate access permissions to this single folder, instead of sharing and assigning permissions for each application folder individually.

**Figure 11-5  Selecting a user for assigning permissions**

**Figure 11-6  Assigning permissions to a user**

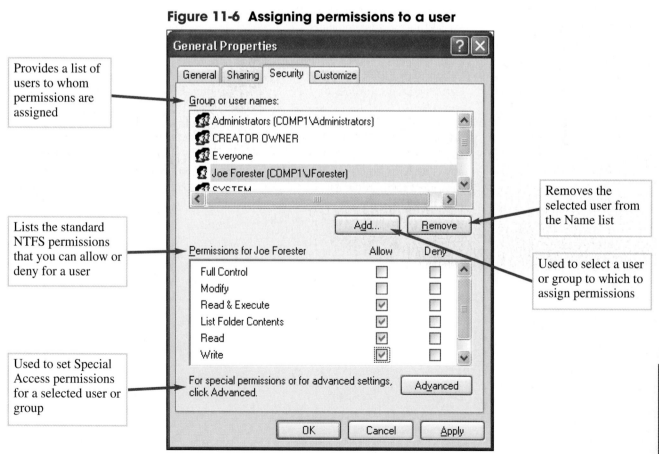

# skill 3

## *Using Special Permissions*

### exam objective

Monitor, manage, and troubleshoot access to files and folders. Control access to files and folders by using permissions.

### overview

As you have learned, on an NTFS volume, you can decide precisely what level of control users will have. This is accomplished using the fourteen **special permissions** to fine-tune your security. These special access permissions are additional security attributes that can be configured on the ACL for a resource. After you assign standard NTFS permissions, you can view the available special permissions by clicking the **Advanced** button on the **Security** tab, and then clicking the **Effective Permissions** tab in the Advanced Security Settings dialog box. The **Change Permissions** and **Take Ownership** permissions are commonly used to further regulate access to files and folders.

The Special Access permissions are described below (**Figure 11-7**):

- **Traverse Folder / Execute Files:** Users can view the directory structure of folders and work on files in those folders.
- **List Folder / Read Data:** Users can view folders and read their content.
- **Read Attributes:** Users can view and read the attributes of folders, for example, Read-only, Archive, and Hidden.
- **Read Extended Attributes:** Users can read the extended attributes of files that are defined by programs.
- **Create Files / Write Data:** Users can create new files on a directory and write data on an existing file on your computer.
- **Create Folders / Append Data:** This permission allows you to create folders and add data to files.
- **Write Attributes:** Users with this permission can change the system-generated attributes associated with a folder or file such as Read-only, Hidden, Archive, compressed, or encrypted.
- **Write Extended Attributes:** Users with this permission can change the program-generated extended attributes associated with a file.
- **Delete Subfolders and Files:** Users can delete subfolders and files in a folder. For example, consider a situation where you need to restrict a user from deleting subfolders in a folder to which he/she has full access. To do this, you deny the Delete Subfolders and Files permission to the user in the Permissions Entry dialog box for the folder.
- **Delete:** Users can delete files and folders.
- **Read Permissions:** Users can view the permissions assigned to a file.
- **Change Permissions:** Users can change permissions for an object.
- **Take Ownership:** Users who are granted this permission can take ownership of a file or folder. They must then explicitly take ownership. Ownership of a resource can be taken, but it cannot be assigned to others. The current owner of a file or folder, an Administrator, or any user with the Full Control permission can assign the Take Ownership permission to another user. That user can then take ownership of the resource on the Owner tab in the Access Control Settings dialog box. For example, an employee named Keith leaves your organization and you want to assign ownership of his files to another employee, Ryan. First, you must assign the Take Ownership attribute to Ryan, and then Ryan must take ownership of each resource.

### tip

The Take Ownership permission can be assigned only by the owner of the object, an Administrator, or a user with the Full Control permission for that object.

Figure 11-7  Various Special Access permissions

# skill 3

## *Using Special Permissions* *(cont'd)*

**exam objective**

Monitor, manage, and troubleshoot access to files and folders. Control access to files and folders by using permissions.

**how to**

Set special access permissions for a user.

1. In Windows Explorer, right-click the **General** folder on the C: drive of your computer, and then click the **Properties** command to open the **General Properties** dialog box.
2. Click the **Security** tab.
3. Select **Joe Forester** in the **Group or user names** list, and then click [ Ad_vanced ] to open the **Advanced Security Settings for General** dialog box.
4. Select **Joe Forester** in the Permission entries list on the Permission tab (**Figure 11-8**).
5. Click [ Edit... ] to open the **Permission Entry for General** dialog box. A list of the special permissions appears.
6. Select the **Allow** check boxes for the **Change Permissions** and **Take Ownership** permissions in the **Permissions** list (**Figure 11-9**). This allows Joe Forester to change the access permissions for the folder and to take ownership of the folder.
7. Click [ OK ] to close the Permissions Entry for General dialog box.
8. Click [ OK ] to close the Advanced Security Settings for General dialog box.
9. Click [ OK ] to close the General Properties dialog box.

### Figure 11-8 Advanced Security Settings for General dialog box

Lists the type of permissions assigned to users

Specifies whether permissions for this object will be inherited from the parent folder

Resets the existing permissions for child objects

Allows you to view and modify the special permissions assigned to a user

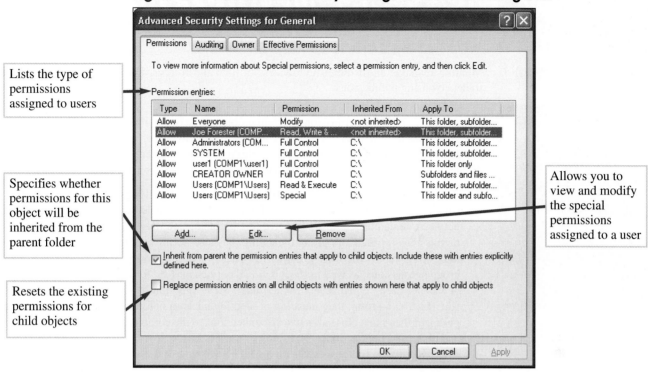

### Figure 11-9 Assigning Special Access Permissions

Lists the special permissions that you allow or deny for a user

Specifies whether you want to apply the permissions to selected folders in the Apply onto text box

Used to change the selected user to which the special permissions are assigned

Clears all of the selected check boxes in the Permissions section

# skill 4

# *Troubleshooting NTFS Permissions*

**exam objective**

Monitor, manage, and troubleshoot access to files and folders. Control access to files and folders by using permissions.

**overview**

After you assign NTFS permissions, certain problems can occur. For example, a user that you thought would be able to access a folder may be unable to do so. You can troubleshoot such problems by identifying their causes and modifying the permissions accordingly. Some of the problems related to NTFS permissions and their solutions are described here:

◆ **A user added to a group is unable to access files or folders:** You add a new user, Charles, to a group named Core. Charles needs to view the content of the Ratings folder, but he is denied access to it. To solve this problem, you may need to update the access permissions for the Core group by adding the Read permission for the Ratings folder to the Core group. If the Core group already has this permission assigned, check the other group permissions, as well as the individual permissions set for Charles to make sure that he has not been denied access to the folder. Most importantly, remember that when you add a user to a group, they must log off and log back on before they become part of that group, or they must close all network connections to the computer where the file is stored and make new connections.

◆ **A user is unable to access a file on an NTFS volume:** If a user is unable to access a file on an NTFS volume, you should first check the location of the file to find out whether it has been copied or moved from one NTFS volume to another. Remember, when you copy or move a file to another NTFS volume, the permissions for the file may change, so you may need to reassign permissions for that user or for an appropriate group to which he or she belongs. If appropriate access permissions were never set, you will also have to reconfigure the ACL for the resource so that the individual, or a group to which he or she belongs, is assigned the correct level of access. Always check to see whether the user, or a group to which the user belongs, has been denied access.

◆ **A user is not allowed to delete the existing content of a file:** If you do not want a user to delete the existing content of a file, you can assign the **Create Folders/Append Data** permission to the user so that he or she can only add data to the file, and cannot delete or modify the existing content. To do this, you use the Permissions Entry dialog box for the file.

◆ **A user with Full Control permission for a folder can delete a file in the folder even though they do not have permission to delete the individual file:** Consider a situation where a user named John has the Full Control permission for the **Report** folder. He deletes a file named Monthly Status that is stored in the Report folder, even though he does not have permission to delete the individual file. To prevent this problem from recurring, you must remove the special permission **Delete Subfolders and Files** so that John will not be able to delete any more files in the folder (**Figure 11-10**).

**Figure 11-10  Troubleshooting problems with NTFS Permissions**

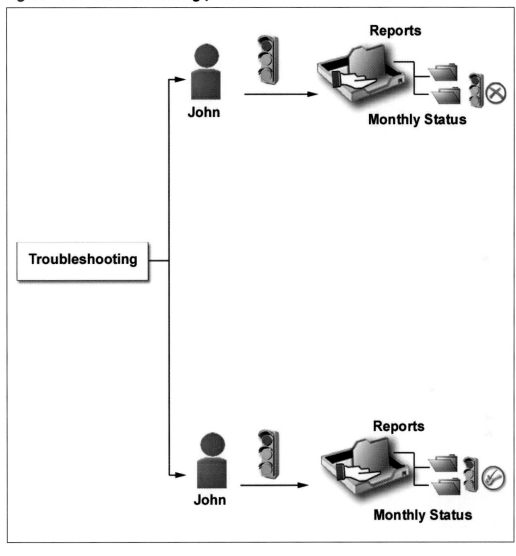

# Summary

- NTFS permissions are used to control access to objects on an NTFS volume, such as files and folders, and to ensure the security of data on an NTFS volume.
- NTFS permissions determine the tasks that users can perform on the content of files and folders.
- NTFS permissions can be configured for both files and folders.
- NTFS folder permissions are assigned to folders and subfolders on an NTFS volume.
- The NTFS folder permissions: Read, Write, List Folder Contents, Read and Execute, Modify, and Full Control.
- NTFS file permissions are assigned to files on an NTFS volume.
- The NTFS file permissions: Read, Write, Read and Execute, Modify, and Full Control.
- NTFS file permissions override NTFS folder permissions.
- The effective NTFS permission for a user with multiple permissions is the sum of all of the assigned NTFS permissions.

- When NTFS permissions are used in combination with share permissions, the most restrictive permission applies when the folder is accessed over the network.
- The Deny condition overrides a specifically allowed permission.
- By default, the files and subfolders in a folder inherit the permissions that are assigned to that folder.
- NTFS permissions often change when files or folders are copied or moved to a new location.
- You assign permissions to groups according to the level of access they require for each resource.
- Permissions should be assigned to a group rather than to individual users.
- Special permissions allow you to fine-tune a specific level of access that users have to objects on the NTFS volume.
- The Access Control List (ACL) for a file or folder is used to assign the Special Access permissions.
- Troubleshooting NTFS permission problems involves identifying the causes of the problems, and then solving them accordingly.

# Key Terms

NTFS file permissions
NTFS folder permissions

NTFS permissions
Special permissions

# Test Yourself

1. You want to disallow some network users from accessing a file on your computer by setting the attribute for the file to Read-Only. Which of the following permissions must you have in order to modify the attributes for the file?
   a. Read
   b. Read & Execute
   c. Write
   d. List Folder Content

2. Harry is a member of two groups at Kemp Corp: Sales and Managers. For a file named Requirements, you assign the Read and Execute Permission to the Sales group, and the Modify permission to the Managers group. The effective permission for Harry for the Requirements file is:

   a. Read.
   b. Modify.
   c. Read and Execute.
   d. Write.

3. Mary has the Read permission for accessing a folder named Reports on an NTFS volume. This folder contains two files, Monthly.doc and Final.doc. Mary is also a member of two groups: Sales and Managers. The Managers group has the Write permission for the Reports folder. The Sales group is denied the Write permission for the Final.doc file. The effective permission for Mary allows her to:
   a. Write to only Monthly.doc.
   b. Read and Write to both of the files.
   c. Only Read the Monthly.doc file.
   d. Write to both of the files.

**4.** Which of the following special permissions allows you to view the directory structure of folders and work on the files in that directory structure?
 a. Read Attributes
 b. Create Folders/Append Data
 c. List Folder Contents
 d. Traverse Folder/Execute Files

**5.** Peter is working as a Marketing Manager at Vector Inc. He has the NTFS Read permission for a folder named Client. As an Administrator, you create a file named Schedule.doc in this folder and assign Peter the Modify permission to change the content of the file. The effective permission for Peter on the file Schedule.doc is:
 a. Write.
 b. Modify.
 c. Read.
 d. Full Control.

**6.** You have the Change shared folder permission for a folder named Analysis, while all other network users only have the Read shared folder permission for this folder. What is your effective permission for the Analysis folder when you log on to the computer where the file is stored?
 a. Full Control
 b. Change
 c. Modify
 d. Read

**7.** Which of the following permissions do you use to fine-tune a specific level of access that users can have for files and folders on an NTFS volume?
 a. Shared folder permissions
 b. Special permissions
 c. NTFS permissions
 d. Read and Execute permission

## Projects: On Your Own

**1.** Assign the Read and Write NTFS permissions to a user named Harry, for accessing the Project folder.
 a. Open the **Project Properties** dialog box.
 b. Open the **Select Users, Computers, or Groups** dialog box.
 c. Select the user name, **Harry**, in the **Name** list.
 d. Select the **Allow** check box for the Read and Write permissions.
 e. Close the **Project Properties** dialog box to assign the Read and Write NTFS permissions to Harry.

**2.** Assign the **Change Permissions** special permission for a folder named **Meeting** to a user, **Jack**.
 a. Open the **Meeting Properties** dialog box.

 b. Open the **Select Users, Computers, or Groups** dialog box.
 c. Enter the user name, **Jack**, in the **Enter the object names to select** list.
 d. Open the **Advanced Security Settings for Meeting** dialog box.
 e. Open the **Permission Entry for Meeting** dialog box.
 f. Select the **Allow** check box of the Special Access permission **Change Permissions**.
 g. Close the **Properties** dialog box to set the special permission, **Change Permissions**, to access the Meeting folder.

## Problem Solving Scenarios

1. You are working as an Administrator at a sporting goods company called Dukes Corporation. Harry Blackmun, the Sales Manager at Dukes, has a folder named Sales on the NTFS drive of his computer. The files in the Sales folder contain information that should be modified by only the Sales Manager. The Sales Representatives who work under Harry will, however, need to have Read access to the files in the Sales folder. He wants you to assign the NTFS Read permission to his team members, and the NTFS Write and Modify permissions to the Sales Manager. Write a memo describing how you would achieve these capabilities. Include how you will handle the combination of shared folder permissions and NTFS permissions, and how you will handle the default permissions.

2. You are working as a regional Sales Manager at Dukes Corporation. The members of your sales team have the Read permission to access a folder named Regional Sales that you create on the NTFS volume of your computer. You want your Administrative Assistant, Susan Olson, to create subfolders and add data to the Regional Sales folder regularly. You also want Susan to be able to set appropriate permissions for the team members to access the Regional Sales folder. Write a report describing the steps you would take to assign appropriate special permissions to Susan in order to enable her to perform these tasks.

Setting group policies is another important part of your overall network security strategy. Group policies are used to manage many different settings for both computers and users, including the desktop appearance, the allocation of software applications, and password limitations. Group policies are most often implemented when you are working with a domain-based network that combines Windows 2000 or 2003 Servers and Windows 2000 and XP Professional clients in an Active Directory environment. You set group policies for sites, domains, and OUs (organizational units) to manage computer configuration, the user environment, and account policies such as minimum password length and length of time a password can be used. Since Windows XP Professional can only be used to set up a peer-to-peer or workgroup network, when you are studying this topic, the emphasis is on setting group policies for individual computers. Group policies for local computers that do not use Active Directory are set using the Local Security Policy console and the Group Policy MMC snap-in. The Local Security Policy console includes account policies, local policies, public key policies, IP security policies, and software restriction policies.

Account policies consist of the password policy and the account lockout policy. Password policies are used to implement specific rules for how all users who log on to a computer must structure their passwords, the frequency with which they must change them, and the length of time they can use their passwords before they must be changed. These policies are not set individually. They apply to all users on a local computer. Account lockout policies are used to set how many invalid logon attempts will be allowed before the account is barred from use. You can also set a specific time period during which the account will remain locked out or configure the policy so that an Administrator must unlock it.

Local security policies are classified as audit policies, user rights assignments, or security options. For example, you can set a security option to prevent the name of the last user that logged on to the computer from displaying in the logon dialog box. User rights assignments prescribe what actions a user can execute. For example, the Increase quotas and Load and unload device drivers user rights are assigned to the built-in Administrators group by default. You can add a user to this group so that they can perform these and other administrative tasks, or you can create your own groups and assign specific rights to them for interacting with the operating system.

Public key policies include the Encrypting File System (EFS) recovery policy. Files and folders are encrypted using a security algorithm and a file encryption key to change the contents into unreadable characters. Either the user who encrypted the file or a user who has been designated as the recovery agent can recover an encrypted file. When other users try to access an encrypted file, they will receive an Access Denied message.

IPSec (Internet Protocol Security) policies are used to protect data as it travels on a TCP/IP network. IPSec policies ensure the security of data packets by encrypting them before sending them to another computer on a public network.

Security templates can simplify the administration of your local security policies in a workgroup setting. Instead of having to set many different policies on each workstation, you can use a security template to apply a group of security settings all at once.

# Goals

In this lesson, you will learn to secure your computer by setting password policies, specifying an account lockout policy, and setting various security options such as preventing the last user name that logged on to the computer from appearing in the logon dialog box. You will also learn how to encrypt and decrypt files using both the Properties dialog box and the Cipher utility, how to add a recovery agent, and how to use IP Security policies to protect data as it travels over a public network. Finally, you will learn how to use the pre-configured security templates in Windows XP, how to perform a security analysis, and how to apply a group of security settings all at once to the local computer.

## Lesson 12   Configuring Local Security Policies

| Skill | Exam 70-270 Objective |
|---|---|
| 1. Introducing Local Security Policies | Configure, manage, and troubleshoot a security configuration and local security policy. |
| 2. Configuring Password Policy | Configure, manage, and troubleshoot account policy. |
| 3. Enhancing Computer Security Using Account Lockout Policy | Configure, manage, and troubleshoot account policy. |
| 4. Configuring Security Options | Configure, manage, and troubleshoot a security configuration and local security policy. |
| 5. Managing Cached Credentials | Troubleshoot cache credentials. |
| 6. Increasing Security Using EFS (Encrypting File System) | Configure, manage, and troubleshoot Encrypting File System (EFS). |
| 7. Encrypting and Decrypting Files and Folders Using the Cipher Utility | Configure, manage, and troubleshoot Encrypting File System (EFS). |
| 8. Recovering Encrypted Files Using Recovery Agents | Configure, manage, and troubleshoot Encrypting File System (EFS). Configure, manage, and troubleshoot a security configuration and local security policy. |
| 9. Securing Data on a Network Using IPSec Policies | Configure, manage, and troubleshoot a security configuration and local security policy. |
| 10. Working with Security Templates | Configure, manage, and troubleshoot a security configuration and local security policy. |

# Requirements

To complete this lesson, you will need administrative rights on a Windows XP Professional computer with an NTFS volume. You will also need a file named Wages.doc stored in the Employees folder and a file named Metadata.doc stored in the Data folder. Both folders must be saved on an NTFS volume. The exercises will assume this is the C: drive. Substitute the correct drive letter in the exercises if necessary. You will also need a file named Accountinfo that was created on the NTFS drive with a Standard or Restricted User account.

# skill 1 *Introducing Local Security Policies*

**exam objective**

Configure, manage, and troubleshoot a security configuration and local security policy.

**overview**

**Group Policies** are used to administer and manage the security of an entire network. They are used at the local level to manage the security of workgroup or standalone computers. Group policies for local computers that do not use the Active Directory are set using **local security policies** in the **Local Security Settings** console and in the Group Policy snap-in. Local security policies are used to set certain conditions, which all users operating the computer will have to abide by. For example, account policies set the rules for the logon process such as the settings for passwords and the procedures that will be followed to lock user accounts after invalid logon attempts. These policies apply to a local computer that is not part of an Active Directory network. If the computer becomes part of a **domain**, higher-level security policies will be set by the Administrator, which may override any local security policies that have been set.

The domain security policies set by the Domain Administrator are applied to sites, domains, and organizational units. Site policies override local policy, domain policies override site policies, and OU policies override domain policies. This default behavior can be controlled using the Block Inheritance and No Override settings.

There are four categories of local security policies: account policies, local policies, public key policies, and IP Security (IPSec) policies **(Figure 12-1)**.

**Account policies** consist of the password policies and the account lockout policies that are used to secure passwords **(Figure 12-2)**. Locking an account will ensure that further logon attempts will not be permitted until a specified time period has passed. In this way you can help to secure your computer from unauthorized access. You can set the number of invalid logon attempts that will be permitted and the time period during which the account will be locked out after this number has been exceeded, or you can lock the account indefinitely until an Administrator unlocks it.

**Local policies** are used to set various security options for your computer such as preventing the last user name that logged on to the computer from appearing in the logon dialog box, or eliminating the requirement that a user must be logged on before they can shut down the computer. You set security options to protect your computer from viruses and unauthorized user access **(Figure 12-3)**. For example, you can configure a local security policy so that the local Guest account will not be able to log on to your computer. Local policies also include audit policies and user rights assignments.

Using **public key policies (Figure 12-4)**, you can set additional recovery agents for a system so that if the owner of an encrypted file forgets his or her password, the recovery agent can copy the encrypted file to that user's computer, and decrypt the file by clearing the **Encrypt contents to secure data** checkbox in the **Advanced Attributes** dialog box for the file. Files are encrypted using a session key called a file encryption key (FEK). After the files are encrypted, the FEK is encrypted using both the user's public key and the recovery agent's public key. The recovery agent has a file recovery certificate, as well as his or her own private key that corresponds to the certificate. EFS requires that a recovery agent be designated before encryption can proceed. On standalone or workgroup computers, you must designate a user account as the recovery agent and a recovery key is placed in this user's personal certificate store on the computer. In a domain, the Domain Administrator account is the default recovery agent for the domain. You can reassign this responsibility or designate additional recovery agents. Recovery agents are required so that encrypted data will never be unrecoverable.

**Figure 12-1  The Local Security Settings console**

Account, local, public key, software restriction, and IPSec

**Figure 12-2  Account Policies**

The two types of Account policies

**Figure 12-3  Local Policies**

Used to protect your computer from viruses and unauthorized user access

**Figure 12-4  Public Key Policies**

Used to set additional recovery agents

# skill 1

## Introducing Local Security Policies
### (cont'd)

**exam objective**

Configure, manage, and troubleshoot a security configuration and local security policy.

**overview**

Finally, you use **IP Security policies** to define security rules for data transmitted across a network so that the data cannot be intercepted or stolen during transit. To configure some of the local security policies, you use the Local Security Settings console. However, in order to see all of the policy settings that are available in Windows XP, you must create a custom Microsoft Management Console (MMC). MMC is the primary administrative tool in Windows XP Professional that provides a method to create, save, and open other administrative tools that are called **snap-ins**. In order to put account policies into operation, you must add the Group Policy snap-in to an MMC.

**how to**

Create a custom Microsoft Management console by adding the Group Policy snap-in to an MMC.

1. Click **start**, and then click the **Run** command to open the **Run** dialog box.
2. Type **mmc** in the **Open** text box **(Figure 12-5)**, and click **OK** to open the **Console Root** window.
3. Open the **File** menu and click the **Add/Remove Snap-in** command to open the **Add/Remove Snap-in** dialog box.
4. Click **Add...** to open the **Add Standalone Snap-in** dialog box. Scroll down the **Available Standalone Snap-ins** list and select **Group Policy (Figure 12-6)**.
5. Click **Add** to initiate the **Select Group Policy Object Wizard**.
6. Click **Finish** to add the Group Policy snap-in as a **Local Computer Policy** in the Console Root window **(Figure 12-7)**. This will be used to configure the Local Group Policy for the computer.
7. Click **Close** to close the Add Standalone Snap-in dialog box.
8. Click **OK** to close the Add/Remove Snap-in dialog box.
9. In the Console Root window, click the plus sign beside the Local Computer Policy node to expand the node.
10. Click the plus sign to expand the **Computer Configuration** node.
11. Click the plus sign beside the **Windows Settings** node, and then the **Security Settings** node to expand the nodes.
12. Expanding the Security Settings node displays the types of local security policies in the details pane of the Console Root window **(Figure 12-8)**.
13. Open the **File** menu and select the **Save** command to open the **Save As** dialog box. Type **Local Group Policy** in the **File name** text box, and click **Save** to save your new custom console. Close the Local Group Policy console.

**more**

Software restriction policies are a new feature in Microsoft Windows XP and Windows Server 2003. They can be used to combat viruses, control what ActiveX controls can be downloaded, and to ensure that only digitally signed scripts can be run. Software restriction policies can also be configured to ensure that only approved software can be installed on network computers and to lockdown a machine. The purpose of software restriction policies is to attempt to maintain system reliability and to simplify network management.

Viruses, worms, and other malicious code can be combated by creating software restriction policies that identify trusted and non-trusted code, and that manage the use of scripts, executable files, and ActiveX controls. A Network Administrator creates a GPO at the site, domain, or organizational level that is then downloaded and applied at the local level. The policy will be activated the next time the user boots up the computer. When the user initiates a program or runs a script, the policy will be consulted and enforced.

**Figure 12-5  The Run dialog box**

**Figure 12-6  The Add Standalone
Snap-in dialog box**

**Figure 12-7  The Console Root window**

Lists the names of vendors associated with a particular snap-in

The Group Policy snap-in has been added to the Console Root window as a Local Computer Policy

**Figure 12-8  The local security policies in the Security
Settings node**

List of local security policies that can be applied on the local computer

# skill 2

# *Configuring Password Policy*

## exam objective

Configure, manage, and troubleshoot account policy.

## overview

Account policies are used to set the user account properties that control the logon process. They include password policies and account lockout policies. **Password policies** are used to supplement the security of your computer by requiring users to change their passwords at specific time intervals, requiring passwords to be a certain length, and by making users keep a password history so that they cannot simply switch back and forth between two passwords. The various password policy options in Windows XP Professional are listed in the **Password Policy** node **(Figure 12-9)**. The Password Policy node is under the **Account Policies** node. Password policies for a local computer are set on the computer itself. However, if the local computer is logged on to a domain, the domain password policies will apply to the local computer.

You can set the following password policy options: Enforce password history, Maximum password age, Minimum password age, Minimum password length, Passwords must meet complexity requirements, and Store password using reversible encryption for all users in the domain.

The **Enforce password history** option is used to set the number of passwords that will be stored in a password history. You can store up to 24 old passwords so that users can refer to their password history and avoid repeating old passwords. This will also help them to create new passwords that are distinctly different from the old ones. You can also leave the value set to the default of 0 if you do not think that maintaining a password history is necessary.

The **Maximum password age** option is used to set the maximum number of days users can keep a particular password. You can set this option as high as 999, although Windows XP Professional allows you to use a password for 42 days by default. Setting a value of 0 indicates that a password will never expire.

The **Minimum password age** option is used to set the minimum number of days during which users must keep the same password. This option can also be set as high as 999 days. Setting a value of 0 indicates that a password can be changed on the same day on which it is set. This setting is particularly useful when a user is compelled to change his or her password by the system so that you can prevent that user from immediately changing it back.

The **Minimum password length** option is used to set the minimum number of characters a password must have. You can set the minimum password length as high as 14 characters.

The **Passwords must meet complexity requirements** option, which is disabled by default, is enabled when you want to require users to follow a minimum password length and a consistent password structure that will require them to construct passwords that contain a combination of capital letters, lower case letters, numbers, or punctuation marks. This policy requires passwords to be at least 6 characters long and to contain characters that include at least three of the following four different types of characters: upper case letters, lower case letters, digits, or non-alphanumeric characters (such as !,$,#,%). The password also cannot include all or part of the user's account name **(Table 12-1)**.

The **Store password using reversible encryption for all users in the domain** option is used to store a reversibly encrypted password for all users. This policy should only be enabled if support is required for applications that use protocols that need to use the user's password for authentication. It is basically the same as storing plaintext versions of passwords. It should not be enabled unless application requirements are more important than password protection. This policy is required when using CHAP authentication through remote access or IAS services. It is also required when using Digest Authentication in Internet Information Services (IIS).

**Figure 12-9  Password Policy node**

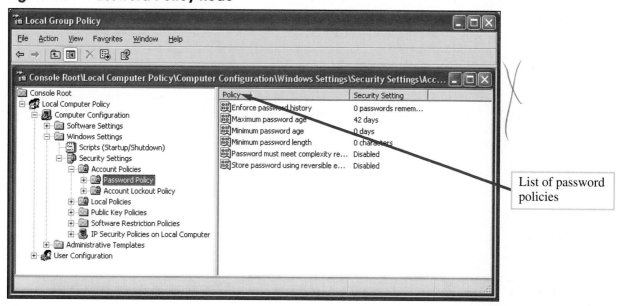

List of password policies

---

### Table 12-1   Passwords must meet complexity requirements

| Requirement | Explanation |
| --- | --- |
| Minimum password length | Password must be at least six characters long. |
| Character complexity | Password must have characters from three of the four categories:<br>(a) Upper case letters (English)<br>(b) Lower case letters (English)<br>(c) Numbers (base 10)<br>(d) Non-alphanumeric characters (`~! @ # $ % ^ & * () _ + -= {} l: " ; ' <> , . /) |
| No duplication of user data | Password cannot contain all or even part of the user's account name. |

# skill 2

# *Configuring Password Policy (cont'd)*

### exam objective

Configure, manage, and troubleshoot account policy.

### how to

Set a password policy that requires users to set passwords with at least 14 characters.

1. Open the **Start** menu, click **All Programs**, point to **Administrative Tools**, and click **Local Group Policy** to reopen the new custom console you created in the previous skill.
2. Expand the **Local Computer Policy** node, and then expand the **Computer Configuration** node.
3. Expand the **Windows Settings** node, and then the **Security Settings** node.
4. Double-click the **Account Policies** node under the Security Settings node, then double-click the **Password Policy** node under the Account Policies node to list the password policies.
5. Double-click the **Minimum password length** option to open the **Minimum password length Properties** dialog box.
6. In the Local Security Policy Setting dialog box, enter **14** in the **Password must be at least** spin box to set a password policy that requires users to set passwords with at least 14 characters **(Figure 12-10)**.
7. Click [ OK ] to save the password policy and close the **Minimum password length Properties** dialog box.
8. Double-click **Enforce password history**. Enter **15** in the **Keep password history for** spin box **(Figure 12-11)**.
9. Click [ OK ] to save the password policy and to close the Enforce password history Properties dialog box.
10. Double-click **Maximum password age**. Enter **60** in the **Passwords will expire in** spin box **(Figure 12-12)**.
11. Click [ OK ] to save the password policy and to close the Maximum password age Properties dialog box. The policies will take effect when you close the console and save the settings.
12. Close the **Local Group Policy** console. Click [ Yes ] to save the console settings.

### more

Local group policies are the first to be applied on a domain-based network in an Active Directory environment. Group policy objects (GPOs) associated with sites, domains and organizational units all take precedence, and the security settings at these levels will override local policy. In a workgroup or on a network on which there are no Windows 2000 or 2003 Server domain controllers, local group policy will be more relevant because there will not be GPOs with policies that override those configured at the local level.

**Figure 12-10  The Minimum password length
Properties dialog box**

**Figure 12-11  The Enforce password history
Properties dialog box**

**Figure 12-12  The Maximum password age
Properties dialog box**

# skill 3 *Enhancing Computer Security Using Account Lockout Policy*

Configure, manage, and troubleshoot account policy.

## overview

Account lockout policy is used to enhance the security of your computer by preventing users from trying to guess passwords. If a user repeatedly attempts to log on to your computer, the computer can automatically lock out the user account according to the specifications you set. You can set the number of invalid logon attempts you will tolerate, the time duration for the account lockout, and the time duration that must pass after an invalid logon attempt before the bad logon attempt counter is reset to 0.

The **Account Lockout Policy** node is contained in the **Account Policies** node. It lists the various account lockout policies. You can set these account lockout options: Account lockout duration, Account lockout threshold, and Reset account lockout counter after (**Figure 12-13**).

The **Account lockout duration** option is used to set the time duration (minutes from 0 to 99999) during which you want the account to be disabled. You can set the value to 0 to lock the account indefinitely until the Administrator unlocks it.

The **Account lockout threshold** option is used to specify the number of invalid logon attempts a user can make, after which the account will be locked and the user will be prevented from making further logon attempts. The default value for this option is 0, meaning that the account will never be locked no matter how many invalid logon attempts are made. You can set the account lockout threshold between 0 and 999.

The **Reset account lockout counter after** option sets the time duration that must elapse after an invalid logon attempt before the account lockout counter is reset to 0. You can reset the bad logon attempt counter between 1 and 99999 minutes.

## how to

Set an account lockout policy so that a user account is locked out after three invalid logon attempts.

1. Open the **Local Group Policy** console.
2. Expand the **Local Computer Policy** node, and then expand the **Computer Configuration** node, if necessary.
3. Expand the **Windows Settings** node, and then the **Security Settings** node, if necessary.
4. Double-click the **Account Policies** node under the Security Settings node, if necessary, then, double-click the **Account Lockout Policy** node under the **Account Policies** node. The account lockout policies are listed in the right pane of the window (**Figure 12-13**).
5. Double-click the **Account lockout threshold** option in the Policy heading in the right pane of the window to open the **Account lockout threshold Properties** dialog box.
6. Type **3** in the **Account will lock out after** spin box to specify that the account should be locked after three invalid logon attempts (**Figure 12-14**).
7. Click [ OK ] to open the **Suggested Value Changes** dialog box (**Figure 12-15**). The Suggested Value Changes window shows the suggested values for the **Account lockout duration** and **Reset account lockout counter after** policies.
8. Click [ OK ] to apply the settings, and close the Suggested Value Changes and Account lockout threshold Properties dialog boxes.
9. Either leave the console open for the next skill, or close it and save the console settings.

## tip

The Suggested Value Changes window appears each time the Account lockout duration is changed to or from zero [0]. It will also appear when the Account lockout duration is set to a number lower than the Reset lockout counter after value, or when the Account duration or Reset lockout duration after value is changed from Not Defined.

**Figure 12-13  Account lockout policies**

**Figure 12-14  The Account lockout threshold Properties dialog box**

**Figure 12-15  The Suggested Value Changes dialog box**

# skill 4

# *Configuring Security Options*

### exam objective

Configure, manage, and troubleshoot a security configuration and local security policy.

### overview

There are many security options you can use to further enhance the security of the data on your computer. For example, you can **Restrict CD-ROM access to the locally logged-on user only** or you can **Prevent users from installing printer drivers**. You can also set the behavior for installing unsigned drivers (**Unsigned driver installation behavior**). You can either set the system to **Silently succeed**, to **Warn but allow installation**, or to disallow the installation of unsigned drivers (**Do not allow installation**). Other security options include allowing automatic administrative logon to the Recovery Console (**Recovery Console: Allow automatic administrative logon**), and shutting down the system immediately if the system is unable to log security audits.

The **Security Options** node, which is found under the **Local Policies** node in the Local Security Settings console, is used to set about 60 types of security options for your computer (**Figure 12-16**). You can set restrictions such as denying unknown connections to your computer, logging off users when the logon time expires, and prompting users to change passwords before the password expires. Some of the commonly used security options include:

### caution

By default, Windows XP Professional does not require users to log on in order to shut down the computer. You must open the Shutdown: Allow system to be shut down without having to log on Properties dialog box for this policy, and select the Disabled option button to prevent unauthorized users from shutting down the system.

◆ Disabling the Allow system to be shut down without having to log on setting.
◆ Additional restrictions for anonymous connections.
◆ Preventing users from installing printer drivers.
◆ Automatically logging off users when the logon time expires.

You can use these options to configure security settings for a computer according to your requirements. For example, if you do not want anybody to be able to shut down your computer unless they have logged on, you need to disable the **Shutdown: Allow computer to be shut down without having to log on** security option.

### how to

Set the **Do not display last user name in logon screen** security option.
1. Open the **Local Group Policy** console, if necessary.
2. Expand the **Local Computer Policy** node, and then expand the **Computer Configuration** node, if necessary.
3. Expand the **Windows Settings** node, and then the **Security Settings** node, if necessary.
4. Double-click the **Local Policies** node under the Security Settings node. Then, double-click the **Security Options** node to display the security options in the right pane of the window (**Figure 12-16**).
5. Double-click the option **Interactive logon: Do not display last user name** in the right pane of the window, to open the **Interactive logon: Do not display last user name Properties** dialog box.
6. Click the **Enabled** option button to program the computer not to display the last user name on the logon screen (**Figure 12-17**).
7. Click [ OK ] to set the security option and close the **Interactive logon: Do not display last user name Properties** dialog box.
8. Close the Local Group Policy console and save the console settings.

### more

The **User Rights Assignment** node under **Local Policies** is used to specify what actions a user can execute within the operating system. Users belong to different groups such as **Administrators**, **Users**, **Guests**, and **Backup Operators**. The User Rights Assignment defines the rights enjoyed by a particular user within a specific group. For example, the Backup Operators have the right to back up and restore any file on the computer. However, they are not given any access to those files, such as to open them or take ownership of them, unless specifically granted *permissions* to do so. The various user rights are listed under the

**Figure 12-16  Security Options**

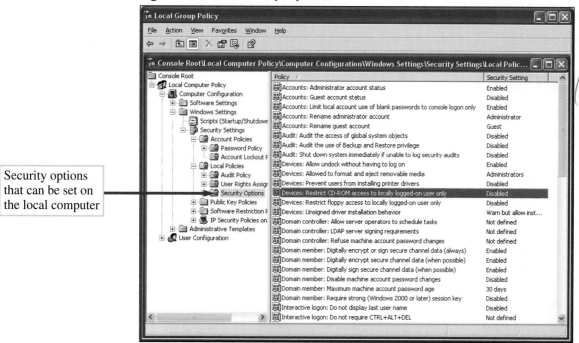

Security options
that can be set on
the local computer

**Figure 12-17  The Interactive logon: Do not display last
user name Properties dialog box**

# skill 4

## Configuring Security Options (cont'd)

exam objective

Configure, manage, and troubleshoot a security configuration and local security policy.

### more

tip

Certain rights are granted to particular groups by default, but no rights are granted explicitly to any particular user account.

User Rights Assignment node under Local Policies security policy (**Figure 12-18**). You can view and configure the groups to which user rights are assigned according to your requirements in the **Properties** dialog box for the user right (**Figure 12-19**). For example, you can grant all groups the right to change the system time. Some of the most commonly used user rights in Windows XP Professional are listed and explained below:

♦ **Access this computer from the network:** This right, which is assigned by default to all built-in groups except the Guests group, enables users to access resources from the computer over the network, provided the user has been given permission to access the resource.

♦ **Backup files and directories:** Only granted by default to the Administrators and Backup Operators groups, this right enables users to backup any file system resource, even if they do not have permission to access that resource.

♦ **Bypass traverse checking:** This right, assigned by default to all built-in groups except the Guests group, allows users to access a resource for which they have been granted permission, that is stored in a parent directory for which they have not been granted access permissions.

♦ **Change the system time:** Granted only to the Administrators and Power Users groups, this right enables users to change the system time.

♦ **Create a pagefile:** This right allows a user to change the default virtual memory settings on the computer. Only Administrators are granted this right by default.

♦ **Deny access to this computer from the network:** This right, which would more accurately be described as a restriction, is not granted to any groups by default. It disallows a user from accessing the computer from the network, no matter what groups he or she belongs to. This right is often assigned to system and service accounts. You can assign it to a user account so that even though a user has been granted the *Access this computer from the network* right by virtue of their membership in the Users group, he or she would no longer be allowed to do so.

♦ **Deny logon locally:** Also one of the restrictive user rights, and also not assigned to any groups by default, this right disallows a user from logging on to a computer locally.

♦ **Force shutdown from a remote system:** Only Administrators are granted this right by default, which enables them to shut down a computer from a remote network location using a remote shutdown utility.

♦ **Increase quotas:** Also only granted to the Administrators group, this right allows users to change the quotas that have been configured on NTFS volumes or partitions.

♦ **Increase scheduling priorities:** This right, granted only to Administrators by default, allows them to reschedule jobs that have been sent to the scheduling service.

♦ **Load and unload drivers:** Only members of the Administrators group can install and uninstall device drivers.

♦ **Log on locally:** Granted to all built-in groups by default, this right must be overridden by the Deny logon locally user right if you do not want to allow local logon.

♦ **Manage auditing and security:** By default, only members of the Administrators group can configure the types of resource access that will be audited on a system.

♦ **Remove computer from docking station:** Granted by default to the Users, Power Users, and Administrators groups, this right enables users to undock a laptop computer from its docking station.

♦ **Restore files and directories:** This user right allows users to restore backup copies of file system resources. It is granted by default to the Backup Operators and Administrators groups.

♦ **Shut down the system:** Members of the Users, Power Users, Backup Operators, and Administrators groups can, by default, shut down the computer locally.

♦ **Take ownership of files of other objects:** Only members of the Administrators group can take ownership of files, directories, printers, and other objects on the computer.

**Figure 12-18  User Rights Assignment**

List of rights you can assign to the user based on the groups to which he or she belongs

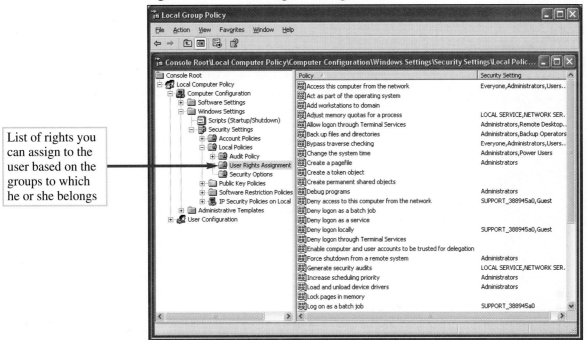

**Figure 12-19  The Change the system time Properties dialog box**

Click to open the Select Users or Groups dialog box where you can add additional users or groups to whom the user right will be assigned

Use to remove a user or a group so that they will no longer be assigned the user right

# skill 5 *Managing Cached Credentials*

**exam objective**

Troubleshoot cache credentials.

**overview**

Credentials in Windows XP refer to the user name and password with which a user identifies him or herself to the local computer, or to the domain, in order to log on and gain access to resources. There are two security options that are used to control how credentials are handled. One of these was discussed and implemented in the previous skill. The **Interactive logon: Do not display last user name in logon screen** policy overrides the default behavior for a system, which is to redisplay the last user name in the logon screen the next time any user attempts to log on.

The other security option handles cached credentials and is called the **Interactive logon: Number of previous logons to cache** policy. This policy is important on domain-based networks in which users may sometimes have to work on a local computer when a domain controller is unavailable, or may at times work away from the network. In Windows XP Professional, such users can log on with a domain user account for a set number of times, which can be configured. By default this policy allows 10 logons using cached credentials. You can set the number of previous logons to cache as high as 50. If you set it to 0, credential caching will be disabled.

Another setting that effects local credential caching is that you can set different passwords for different services and sites in the **Stored User Names and Passwords** dialog box, which you access on the **Advanced** tab in the **User Accounts** utility located in the Control Panel. When you add passwords to your local passwords cache, they are added to your user profile. You can store logon credentials for network locations and Web sites.

**how to**

Set domain cached credential policy and add a password for a user to access a site.
1. Open the **Local Group Policy** console, if necessary.
2. Expand the **Local Computer Policy** node, and then expand the **Computer Configuration** node, if necessary.
3. Expand the **Windows Settings** node, and then the **Security Settings** node, if necessary.
4. Double-click the **Local Policies** node. Then, double-click the **Security Options** node to display the security options in the right pane of the window.
5. Locate and double-click **Interactive logon: Number of previous logons to cache** in the right pane of the window, to open the **Interactive logon: Number of previous logons to cache Properties** dialog box.
6. Change the value in the **Cache** spin box to 15 (**Figure 12-20**).
7. Click [ OK ] to set the security option and close the **Interactive logon: Number of previous logons to cache Properties** dialog box.
8. Close the Local Group Policy console and save the console settings.
9. Open the Control Panel. Double-click the **User Accounts** icon to open the **User Accounts** dialog box. Open the **Advanced** tab (**Figure 12-21**).
10. Click [ Manage Passwords ] to open the **Stored User Names and Passwords** dialog box.
11. Click [ Add ] to open the **Logon Information Properties** dialog box. Enter a server name in the **Server** text box, for example, Server1.com. Enter your user name in the **User name** list box, for example, user1@domain1.com. Enter a password in the Password text box.
12. Click [ OK ] to save the settings and close the Logon Information Properties dialog box.
13. The Stored User Names and Passwords dialog box now reflects that you have stored credentials for accessing a Web site (**Figure 12-22**).
14. Click [ Close ] to close the Stored User Names and Passwords dialog box. Close the User Accounts applet and the Control Panel.

**Figure 12-20  The Interactive logon: Number of previous logons to cache Properties dialog box**

**Figure 12-21  The Advanced tab in the User Accounts dialog box**

Click to open the Stored User Names and Passwords dialog box

**Figure 12-22  The Stored User Names and Passwords dialog box**

You can store logon credentials for network locations and for Web sites

# skill 6

# *Increasing Security Using EFS (Encrypting File System)*

**exam objective**

Configure, manage, and troubleshoot Encrypting File System (EFS).

## overview

As you have learned, the most effective way to protect local resources is to use an NTFS volume and apply NTFS permissions, because share permissions are not effective locally. However, local NTFS permissions can be bypassed by users if they access them by using an operating system other than Windows NT, Windows 2000, or Windows XP, and use another utility such as NTFSDOS. In many organizations, such as defense establishments or in the banking sector where security is of primary concern, the **Encrypting File System (EFS)** can be used to rule out this possibility. You can encode data that is stored on NTFS partitions so that it is non-readable. Other users will not be able to access encrypted files even if they have access to your computer. For example, if Linda and John share the same computer and John does not want Linda to view the files that he uses, he can encrypt them. Linda will receive an Access Denied message if she tries to open one of John's files.

In the EFS encryption technique, important data is secured using a cryptographic key pair: a public key and a private key. Data is encrypted using a session key (file encryption key - FEK). The session key is then encrypted using the user's public key, and later decrypted using the user's private key. If the user who encrypted the file leaves the company and deletes his or her certificate, or has his or her user account deleted, or if a certificate becomes corrupt, another user, who is designated as the recovery agent, can open the file. The recovery agent has a file recovery certificate and his or her own EFS recovery agent private key to decrypt the file so that it can be recovered.

At least one user account in Windows XP Professional must be designated as the recovery agent. On standalone computers or computers in a workgroup, you must designate a recovery agent so that the appropriate recovery key will be placed in the personal certificate store for this user on the local computer. In a domain, the Domain Administrator account is the default recovery agent for the domain.

New files created in an encrypted folder or files copied to an encrypted folder are automatically assigned the encryption attribute. Modifications made to an encrypted file or folder are also automatically encrypted. Backup versions and copies of encrypted files will also be encrypted automatically, as long as they are stored on another NTFS volume.

## how to

### tip

If you are encrypting a folder that contains subfolders or files, the Confirm Attribute Changes dialog box informs you that you are about to encrypt a folder. Click the appropriate option button to encrypt only the selected folder or all subfolders and files in the folder. All new files that are added to an encrypted parent folder are automatically encrypted.

Encrypt a folder.
1. Right-click [ *start* ] and click **Explore** to open Windows Explorer.
2. Locate and then double-click the **Data** folder to open it. The **Metadata** file appears.
3. Right-click the **Metadata** file and click **Properties** to open the **Metadata Properties** dialog box **(Figure 12-23)**.
4. Click [ Advanced... ] to open the **Advanced Attributes** dialog box. In this dialog box, you can set the encryption attribute for the Metadata file.
5. Select the **Encrypt contents to secure data** check box to encrypt the contents of the **metadata** file **(Figure 12-24)**. Note that if you select this check box, you cannot select the **Compress contents to save disk space** check box to compress the data in the file. An encrypted file cannot be compressed, nor can a compressed file be encrypted.
6. Click [ OK ] to close the **Advanced Attributes** dialog box.
7. Click [ Apply ] in the Metadata Properties dialog box to apply the attribute.
8. In the **Encryption Warning** dialog box **(Figure 12-25)**, click the **Encrypt the file only** option button.
9. Click [ OK ] to close the Encryption Warning dialog box.

**Figure 12-23  The Properties dialog box for the Metadata file**

Click to open the Advanced Attributes dialog box

**Figure 12-24  Encrypting a file**

Select to encrypt the file

**Figure 12-25  The Encryption Warning dialog box**

Select this option to encrypt the file and the folder that contains the file

Select this option to encrypt the file without encrypting the rest of the files in the parent folder

# skill 6

## Increasing Security Using EFS (Encrypting File System) *(cont'd)*

**exam objective**

Configure, manage, and troubleshoot Encrypting File System (EFS).

**how to**

10. Click [ OK ] to close the Metadata Properties dialog box.
11. Right-click the **Data** folder and click **Properties** to open the **Data Properties** dialog box.
12. Click [ Advanced... ] to open the **Advanced Attributes** dialog box.
13. Select the **Encrypt contents to secure the data** check box.
14. Click [ OK ] to close the Advanced Attributes dialog box.
15. Click [ Apply ] in the Data Properties dialog box to apply the encryption attribute.
16. The **Confirm Attribute Changes** dialog box opens (**Figure 12-26**).
17. Click the **Apply changes to this folder**, **subfolders**, **and files** option button to encrypt the folder and all of its contents, including all subfolders and files.
18. Click [ OK ] to close the Confirm Attribute Changes dialog box.
19. Click [ OK ] to close the Data Properties dialog box, and then close Windows Explorer.

**more**

An encrypted file or folder remains encrypted if it is copied or moved to:

◆ The same NTFS partition on the same computer.
◆ A different NTFS partition on the same computer.
◆ An NTFS partition on a different computer that runs Windows 2000 or XP.

However, if you move an encrypted file or folder to a File Allocation Table (FAT) partition, or another computer running an NTFS version earlier than NTFS 5, the encrypted file or folder does not retain the attribute. This is because FAT and FAT32 partitions, and NTFS partitions lower than version 5, do not support EFS.

Files also remain encrypted if you rename them, copy them, or back them up, as long as they are stored and restored on an NTFS volume or partition. You cannot encrypt files that have the System attribute, nor would it be a good idea to do so if you were able, and you cannot encrypt any files stored in the %systemroot% directory structure. The %systemroot% folder in Windows XP Professional is by default **\Windows**.

Encrypted files will appear in green by default in Windows XP because the **Show encrypted or compressed NTFS files in color** check box is selected by default on the **View** tab in the **Folder Options** dialog box.

In Windows XP Professional, you can now share access to an encrypted file. To find out who has encrypted a file, or to share access to a file that you have encrypted, click the **Details** button in the **Advanced Attributes** dialog box to open the **Encryption Details** for *filename* dialog box (**Figure 12-27**). Click the **Add** button to open the **Select User** dialog box. Users who have been issued EFS certificates on the system will display. Select the user with whom you want to be able to share access to the encrypted file and click **OK**. On an Active Directory domain, you can use the **Find User** button to locate users who have been issued EFS compatible certificates.

You must grant access to encrypted files individually. You cannot share encrypted folders. Each of the users must have previously encrypted at least one file or folder so that an EFS certificate has been issued to that user from either the local computer or from the Active Directory domain.

**Figure 12-26  The Confirm Attribute Changes dialog box**

Select this option to confirm encryption only for the selected folder and files in the subfolders

Select this option to encrypt the folder and all of its contents

**Figure 12-27  The Encryption Details for C:\Data\Metadata.doc dialog box**

Click to open the Select User dialog box to choose a user with whom you want to share access to the encrypted file

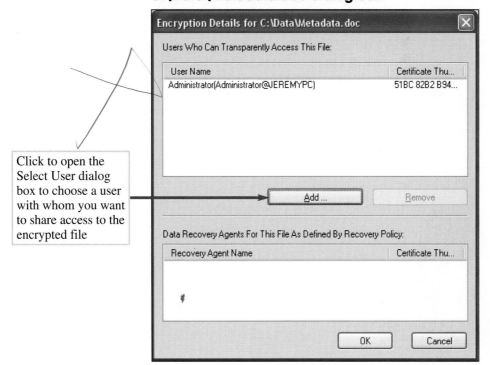

# skill 7

# *Encrypting and Decrypting Files and Folders Using the Cipher Utility*

## exam objective

Configure, manage, and troubleshoot Encrypting File System (EFS).

## overview

Rather than using the Properties dialog box for a file or folder, you can use the Cipher command-line utility to enable encryption. You can also use the **Cipher** utility to view the encryption settings for files and folders, as well as to encrypt and decrypt them.

You execute the Cipher command by typing the following at the command prompt:

**Cipher / [command parameter] [pathname...]**

In the syntax of the Cipher command, **[pathname ...]** denotes the location of the file or folder that you want to encrypt or decrypt. The various parameters that are used with the Cipher command designate various encryption and decryption requirements. **Table 12-2** lists the variables used with the Cipher command.

When using multiple parameters with the command, you must insert a single space between the variables. You can also execute the Cipher command by specifying only the path name.

You can encrypt multiple files at a time using this utility. You can also use wildcards with the **Cipher** utility to specify a group of files with a common attribute such as the same file extension.

### tip

You can also open the command prompt window by typing cmd in the Open: text box in the Run dialog box.

## how to

Encrypt a file using the Cipher command-line utility.

1. Click **start** and click **Command Prompt** to open the command prompt window.
2. Type **cd employees** to access the **Employees** folder.
3. Type **cipher /e /a wages.doc** and press the **[Enter]** key. A message **Encrypting files in C:\employees**\appears. The /e variable is used to denote that the operation used is encryption. The /a variable denotes that the encryption operation is performed on a specific file in a folder.
4. After a few seconds, your file is encrypted and a message appears: **1 file(s) [or directorie(s)] within 1 directorie(s) were encrypted**. You are also warned that converting files from plaintext to ciphertext may leave sections of old plaintext on the disk volume(s). It is recommended to use **CIPHER /W:directory** to clean up the disk after all converting is done. The **/w** switch removes data from available unused disk space on the entire volume. The directory specified can be anywhere on a local volume (**Figure 12-28**).
5. Type **exit** to close the command prompt window. You have successfully encrypted the file **wages.doc** in the **Employees** folder.

## Table 12-2   Variables used with Cipher command

| Variable | Use |
|----------|-----|
| /e | The /e parameter is used to encrypt a folder. Encrypted folders are marked so that any file added to the folder will be automatically encrypted. |
| /d | The /d parameter is used to decrypt an encrypted folder. Files added to a decrypted folder will be automatically decrypted. |
| /s: *dir* | The /s parameter is used to perform the encryption or decryption operation on a folder and all its subfolders. |
| /i | The /i parameter is used to ignore any errors that may occur during the encryption/decryption operation and continue the process. |
| /f | The /f parameter is used to force the encryption or decryption operation on all specified files and folders, even if they have already been encrypted or decrypted. This parameter is used to force the re-encryption of files when, for example, you have set a new recovery agent so that they will be re-encrypted using the new recovery agent key. |
| /q | The /q parameter is used to run the operation in quiet mode so that only the most important information, such as errors that occur during the process, will be displayed. |
| /a | The /a parameter is used to perform the encryption or decryption operation on a specific file. |
| /h | The /h parameter is used so that files with the hidden or system attributes will be listed, which does not occur by default. Hidden and system files are not encrypted by default. |
| /k | The /k parameter is used to create a new file encryption key. When you use this parameter, the cipher utility will ignore all other parameters. |
| /u | The /u parameter is used if the user's file encryption key or the recovery agent's key has changed to update them to the current ones in all of the encrypted files on local drives. It is used in conjunction with the **/n** parameter. |
| /n | The /n parameter is used to locate all of the encrypted files on the local drives, and it prevents the user's file encryption key or recovery agent's key from being updated. It is used in conjunction with the **/u** parameter. |
| /r:*PathNameWithoutExtension* | The /r parameter is used to create a new recovery agent certificate (.cer file) and private key (.pfx file), which are written to files with the file name specified in *PathNameWithoutExtension*. When you use this parameter, the cipher utility will ignore all other parameters. |
| pathname | The pathname parameter is used to specify the path to the file or folder to be encrypted or decrypted. |

### Figure 12-28   Using the cipher utility to encrypt a file

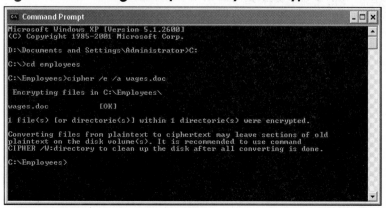

# skill 8

# Recovering Encrypted Files Using Recovery Agents

**exam objective**

Configure, manage, and troubleshoot Encrypting File System (EFS). Configure, manage, and troubleshoot a security configuration and local security policy.

## overview

Files encrypted using EFS can only be opened and used by the user who encrypted them, or by an account that has been designated as the **recovery agent**. The recovery agent has a file recovery certificate, which is needed to decrypt the file or folder. All other users will receive an Access Denied message when they try to open the file, unless they have been granted permission to share access to the encrypted file. Private keys can be lost or damaged during disk crashes or while formatting disks. This is why Windows XP Professional requires that at least one user account be designated as the recovery agent so that encrypted data will never be unrecoverable. By default, if the computer is on a domain, the Domain Administrator account becomes the recovery agent. However, any other user can also be designated as a recovery agent if he or she is provided with a file recovery certificate (.cer file). If your Windows XP Professional is a standalone computer, or is in a workgroup, you must create a recovery agent for the machine. In Windows 2000, the local Administrator account was by default designated as the recovery agent for the local machine, but this has been changed in Windows XP Professional.

To recover encrypted files or folders, the best method is to copy them to the recovery agent's computer where the file recovery certificate and the private key are located. It is not a good idea to have the recovery agent copy his or her private key to the computer where the file is stored, because this can compromise the security of a network. Then, the recovery agent simply clears the **Encrypt contents to secure data** check box in the **Advanced Attributes** dialog box to recover the file.

First, the recovery agent should use Backup or a different backup utility to restore the user's backup version of the encrypted file to the computer where their recovery agent certificate is located. Then, he or she can use the Properties dialog box for the file or folder, or the Cipher utility, to decrypt the file. Finally, the recovery agent should make a backup copy of the decrypted file and send the backup version back to the user/owner.

## how to

Recover a file.
1. Log on to your computer as **user1** (or any other standard or restricted user account you have created on your computer). Create and save a file named **Accountinfo** on the C: drive of the computer (This must be an NTFS disk.). Encrypt the file.
2. Log off and log back on as **user2** (or any other standard or restricted user account you have created on the computer).
3. Open **Windows Explorer**. Double-click **My Computer**. Double-click the **C:** drive in the contents window. Locate the **Accountinfo** file. Right-click **Accountinfo** and click **Properties**.
4. On the **General** tab, click [ Advanced... ] to open the **Advanced Attributes** dialog box. Clear the check from the **Encrypt contents to secure data** check box in the **Compress or Encrypt attributes** section. Click [ OK ].
5. Click [ OK ] to close the Accountinfo Properties dialog box.
6. The **Error Applying Attributes** dialog box opens to inform you that access has been denied (**Figure 12-29**).
7. Click [ Ignore ]. The Advanced Attributes dialog box and the Accountinfo Properties dialog box both automatically close. Close Windows Explorer.
8. Log off and log back on using the local Administrator account.
9. Open the command prompt and type: **cipher /r:filename**.
10. You will be prompted to enter a password to protect the two files that are going to be generated. Enter a password and press **[Enter]**.

## tip

If you are not the owner of an encrypted file, the designated recovery agent, or have not been granted permission to share the encrypted file, you will receive the message shown in **Figure 12-30** when you attempt to open the file.

**Figure 12-29 The Error Applying Attributes dialog box**

Access is denied to an encrypted file for a user who is not the owner or a designated recovery agent

**Figure 12-30 User does not have access privileges message**

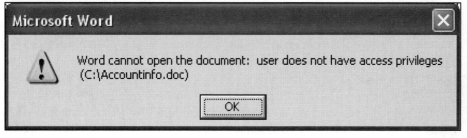

# skill 8

## *Recovering Encrypted Files Using Recovery Agents (cont'd)*

**exam objective**

Configure, manage, and troubleshoot Encrypting File System (EFS). Configure, manage, and troubleshoot a security configuration and local security policy.

**how to**

11. You will be prompted to reenter the password. Reenter the password and press **[Enter]**.
12. A message displays to confirm that two files have been created, a .CER file and a .PFX file (**Figure 12-31**). Close the command prompt.
13. If you do not want the local Administrator account to be the recovery agent, log off and log back on with the user account you want to be the recovery agent.
14. Open the Run dialog box and type **mmc** in the **Open** text box.
15. Open the **File** menu and click the **Add/Remove Snap-in** command to open the **Add/Remove Snap-in** dialog box.
16. Click [ Add... ] to open the **Add Standalone Snap-in** dialog box. In the **Available Standalone Snap-ins** list and select **Certificates**.
17. Click [ Add ] to open the **Certificates snap-in** dialog box. You can create an MMC with the Certificates snap-in to manage certificates for your user account, for the computer, or for a service. Select the **My user account** option button (**Figure 12-32**).
18. Click [ Finish ] to close the Certificates snap-in dialog box.
19. Close the Add Standalone Snap-in and Add/Remove Snap-in dialog boxes. Save the new MMC as **Certificates**.
20. Expand the **Certificates - Current User** node. Right-click **Personal**, point to **All Tasks**, and select **Import** to start the **Certificate Import Wizard**.
21. Click [ Next > ] to open the **File to Import** screen. Enter the path to the **.pfx** file. The two files were saved by default in the Documents and Settings folder for the user account you used when you ran the cipher /r: command.
22. Click [ Next > ] to open the **Password** screen. Enter the password you created to secure the two files and click [ Next > ].
23. On the **Certificate Store** screen, select the **Automatically select the certificate store based on the type of certificate** option button (**Figure 12-33**).
24. Click [ Next > ] to open the Completing the Certificate Import Wizard screen. Click [ Finish ]. The **Certificate Import Wizard** message: The import was successful displays. Click [ OK ].
25. Close the Certificates console and save the settings.
26. Open the **Local Security Settings** console, expand the **Public Key Policies** node, right-click **Encrypting File System** and select **Add Data Recovery Agent** to start the **Add Recovery Agent Wizard**.
27. Click [ Next > ] to open the **Select Recovery Agents** screen. Click [ Browse Folders... ] and navigate to the location of the **.cer** file (in the folder for the user account you used to create it in the Documents and Settings folder) and click [ Open ].

**tip**

If you use the Browse option to locate the .pfx file, you will need to change the setting in the Files of type drop-down list box to Personal Information Exchange (*.pfx, *.p12) in order to find the file.

**Figure 12-31  Using the cipher command to create, a .CER file and a .PFX file**

**Figure 12-32  Creating the Certificates MMC to manage the certificates for the user account**

**Figure 12-33  The Certificate Import Wizard**

# skill 8

# *Recovering Encrypted Files Using Recovery Agents (cont'd)*

## exam objective

Configure, manage, and troubleshoot Encrypting File System (EFS). Configure, manage, and troubleshoot a security configuration and local security policy.

## how to

28. The new recovery agent is displayed as USER_UNKNOWN in the Recovery Agents list box **(Figure 12-34)**. This is how the process works.

29. Click [ Next > ] to open the **Completing the Add Recovery Agent Wizard** screen and click [ Finish ]. The user account you used to log on has now been designated as the recovery agent for all encrypted files on the computer. Close the Local Security Settings console.

30. To recover the **Accountinfo** file, you would open the **Accountinfo Properties** dialog box, click **Advanced** to open the **Advanced Attributes** dialog box and remove the check from the **Encrypt data to secure contents** check box, and click [ OK ]. However, it should be noted that a recovery agent that is added to local security policy only has access to files that are encrypted after the agent is added. If you are the recovery agent and did not have access to the encrypted file before, you are still not going to have access unless you encrypt it again after having added the recovery agent.

## more

The password you entered after using the **cipher /r:** *PathNameWithoutExtension* command is used to secure the two files that are generated: a new recovery agent certificate (.cer file) and private key (.pfx file [Personal Information Exchange]). You can use these two files to make any user a recovery agent. The best practice is to copy the two files to a floppy disk and delete the originals to remove them from the hard drive of the computer. The new recovery agent is listed as USER_UNKNOWN because creating a certificate with the cipher utility does not attach the certificate to a particular user.

If the Windows XP Professional workstation is part of an Active Directory domain, this procedure would not be necessary. The Domain Administrator is the default recovery agent for the domain, as designated by the Default Domain Policy GPO. Additional recovery agents can be added to GPOs at the domain or organizational unit level.

**Figure 12-34  The Select Recovery Agents screen in the Add Recovery Agent Wizard**

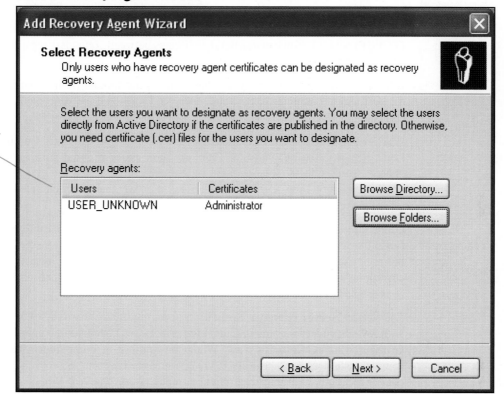

# skill 9

# *Securing Data on a Network Using IPSec Policies*

**exam objective**

Configure, manage, and troubleshoot a security configuration and local security policy.

## overview

**Internet Protocol Security (IPSec)** policy settings are used to protect confidential data on a public network. Data packets are encrypted before they are sent to a destination computer in order to make sure that they are secure and cannot be intercepted, stolen, or modified in transit. IPSec policies are functional on a **Transmission Control Protocol/Internet Protocol (TCP/IP)** network. You can transfer data packets between computers regardless of the type of partitions that are used.

IPSec policies ensure that encrypted files that are transmitted from a source computer reach the destination computer in the same encrypted form and are decrypted at the destination computer.

IPSec policies are configured in the **IP Security Policies on the Local Computer** node in the Local Security Settings console. There are three preconfigured policy templates you can choose from: Client (Respond Only), Secure Server (Require Security), and Server (RequestSecurity). You set IPSec Policies based on whether your computer is performing the role of a client or a server on the network **(Figure 12-35)**.

Of the three policy options, the **Client (Respond Only)** policy is used to provide maximum flexibility when negotiating security with the server computers on the network. By default, this policy sends data packets to server computers without applying security measures such as encryption. However, if specifically requested by a server, the policy ensures that the data will be encrypted before it is sent.

The **Secure Server (Require Security)** option minimizes the number of client computers with which you can communicate over a network, because all communications must be secured using Kerberos trust. When the number of computers with which you can communicate decreases, security is greatly enhanced. When you set this policy, unsecured communications with untrusted client computers are blocked. Whether or not a client is trusted is determined by the authentication mechanism used by the client. Windows XP Professional provides several authentication mechanisms, notably Kerberos V5. When a user attempts to access a network service, authentication mechanisms, such as Kerberos V5, confirm the identification of the user to the network service.

The **Server (Request Security)** option helps provide secure communication by requesting security using Kerberos trust from client computers. This means that, for all IP traffic, clients will be requested to provide security using authentication mechanisms, but communication with unsecured clients will not be denied. Data packets will still be exchanged, even if Kerberos trust is not established. It is important to note that none of the IPSec policy options are assigned to the computer by default. For an existing IPSec policy option, you can either add a new IP security rule or edit an existing IP security rule in the **<policy name> Properties** dialog box.

## tip

Using EFS, you can move or copy data only from one NTFS 5 or above partition to another. Moving or copying data to a different version of NTFS or to a FAT partition is not possible because data does not remain encrypted. EFS encrypted files are not encrypted as they traverse a network.

## how to

Assign the **Client (Respond Only)** IPSec policy and add a new security rule to the policy.

1. Open the **Local Group Policy** console.
2. Expand the **Local Computer Policy** node, and then expand the **Computer Configuration** node, if necessary.
3. Expand the **Windows Settings** node, and then the **Security Settings** node, if necessary.
4. Double-click the **IP Security Policies on Local Computer** node. The IPSec policy options appear in the details pane.
5. Right-click the **Client (Respond Only)** policy option and click **Assign** to assign the policy **(Figure 12-36)**.

**Figure 12-35  The IPSec policies**

Check to view a list of actions

Click to list options to customize the window

Click to organize Favorites folder and view list of Favorites

The various IPSec policy options

**Figure 12-36  Assigning the Client (Respond Only) IPSec policy**

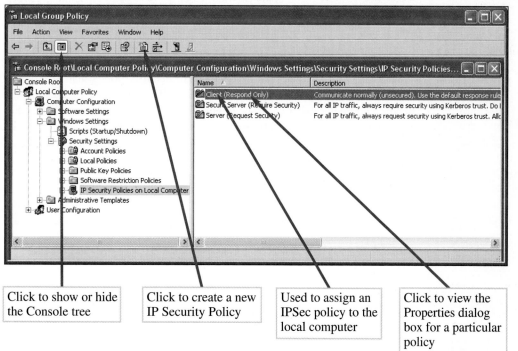

Click to show or hide the Console tree

Click to create a new IP Security Policy

Used to assign an IPSec policy to the local computer

Click to view the Properties dialog box for a particular policy

# skill 9

## Securing Data on a Network Using IPSec Policies *(cont'd)*

### exam objective

Configure, manage, and troubleshoot a security configuration and local security policy.

### how to

6. Right-click the **Client (Respond Only)** policy and click **Properties** to open the **Client (Respond Only) Properties** dialog box. You can also open the **Client (Respond Only) Properties** dialog box by double-clicking the Client (Respond Only) policy option.
7. Click [ Add... ] to initiate the **Security Rule Wizard (Figure 12-37)**. The Security Rule Wizard is used to add a new IP security rule.
8. Click [ Next > ] to open the **Tunnel Endpoint** screen.
9. The **This rule does not specify a tunnel** option button is selected by default. Click [ Next > ] to open the **Network Type** screen.
10. In the **Select the network type:** section, click the **Local area network (LAN)** option button to apply the security rule to computers on the local area network (LAN) only **(Figure 12-38)**.
11. Click [ Next > ] to open the **Authentication Method** screen.
12. The **Active Directory default (Kerberos V5 protocol)** option button is selected by default. Click [ Next > ] to open the **IP Filter List** screen.
13. In the **IP filter lists:** section, click the **All IP Traffic** option button to apply the security rule to all IP traffic. The IP filter list shows the list of IP traffic, such as all ICMP (Internet Control Message Protocol) or all IP traffic. The IP security rule applies to the IP traffic that is selected on the IP filter list.
14. Click [ Next > ] to open the **Filter Action** screen.
15. Click the **Request Security (Optional)** option in the **Filter Actions** section **(Figure 12-39)** to provide secure communication by requesting security from clients.
16. Click [ Next > ] to move to the last screen of the Security Rule Wizard.
17. Click [ Finish ] to save the settings and exit the Security Rule Wizard.
18. Click [ Apply ] to apply the rule. Click [ OK ] to close the Client (Respond Only) Properties dialog box.
19. Close the Local Group Policy console and save the console settings.

### caution

Kerberos is only used for network authentication on a domain-based network. If you are on a workgroup network, a Warning dialog box to this effect will open. Click **Yes** to continue and save the rule properties. You will have to remove the rule after you complete the exercise.

### more

When IPSec policies are configured, the two computers that are attempting to establish a connection will negotiate and agree upon the security policy that is the most stringent that both computers support. Encryption of IP traffic is handled by the IPSec driver on each sending computer using its IPSec policy. Decryption of IP traffic is handled at the receiving computer before the data is transferred to the destination application or process. IP traffic is encrypted at the IP layer (in the Internet layer) in the conceptual model. The result is that all protocols can use the same security packages.

**Figure 12-37  The Client (Respond Only) Properties dialog box**

Lists the rules in the particular IPSec policy; the checkmark indicates that the rule is currently active

Click to add a new rule to the policy

Click to edit an existing rule

**Figure 12-38  The Network Type screen in the Security Rule Wizard**

Select to apply the rule only to the local area network connections on the local computer

**Figure 12-39  The Filter Action screen in the Security Rule Wizard**

The selected policy is the active action for the security rule

# skill 10 *Working with Security Templates*

## exam objective

Configure, manage, and troubleshoot a security configuration and local security policy.

## overview

Security templates are valuable on a workgroup network because rather than configuring your local security policies and local group policies one by one, you can use a security template to apply a whole range of security configuration settings all at once. You can create a custom MMC with the **Security Templates** and **Security Configuration and Analysis** snap-ins to provide a centralized tool, where all of the security attributes are organized in one place, and you can analyze the security configuration of the computer. A security template can include password and account lockout policies, local security policies, user rights assignments, Registry key security, group memberships, and permissions for the local file system. On a domain-based network, you can apply a security template to a Group Policy object so that all of the settings are put into operation on a site, a domain, or an OU (organizational unit). You use the Import Policy command on the shortcut menu for the Security Settings node to import a security template to a Group Policy object so that you can configure the security settings for multiple computers at one time. Security templates are saved as .inf files. You can copy, paste, import, and export some or all of the security settings from these text files to apply them to a Group Policy object. All security attributes, except IPSec and public key policies, can be stored in a security template. The Security and Configuration Analysis snap-in is used to compare the current security configuration of the computer to one of the security templates, to create custom templates, and to apply a template to either the local computer or to a Group Policy object.

## how to

Create a custom Security Templates console and use the Security and Configuration Analysis tool to analyze the current security configuration of the local computer. Customize one of the predefined security templates and apply it to the local computer.

1. Click **start** and click the **Run** command to open the **Run** dialog box.
2. Type **mmc** in the **Open** text box and click **OK** to open the **Console Root** window.
3. Open the **File** menu and click the **Add/Remove Snap-in** command to open the **Add/Remove Snap-in** dialog box.
4. Click **Add...** to open the **Add Standalone Snap-in** dialog box. Scroll down the **Available Standalone Snap-ins** list to locate and select the **Security Templates** snap-in. Click **Add**.
5. Select the **Security Configuration and Analysis** snap-in and click **Add**.
6. Click **Close** to close the Add Standalone Snap-in dialog box.
7. Click **OK** to close the Add/Remove Snap-in dialog box.
8. Open the **File** menu and click the **Save** command to open the **Save As** dialog box.
9. Type **Security Templates** in the **File name** text box and click **Save**. By default, the console will be saved in the Administrative Tools folder.
10. Expand the **Security Templates** node. Expand the **%systemroot%\security\templates** node. The pre-configured security templates appear as shown in **Figure 12-40**. The predefined templates are explained in **Table 12-3**.
11. Right-click the **Security Configuration and Analysis** node and select **Open database** to open the **Open database** dialog box.
12. Type **Local PC** in the **File name** text box and click **Open** to open the **Import Template** dialog box.
13. Select **securews.inf** in the contents window and click **Open** to open the template for a high-security workstation.

**Figure 12-40  The predefined security templates**

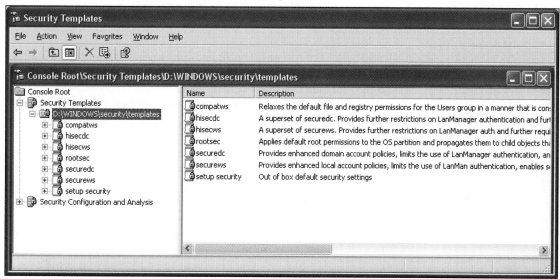

## Table 12-3   The Predefined Security Templates

| | |
|---|---|
| compatws | Compatible workstation: Used on workstations that must be compatible with older applications. Users group access controls are less stringent for certain files, folders, and Registry keys that older applications often need to access so that they can be run with no problem by members of the Users group. This template is used if you need compatibility with non-Windows 2000 and XP applications. |
| hisecws | The template for a maximum security workstation, The Power Users group will have fewer user rights than normally. When you apply this template, security areas are configured to protect network traffic, and the protocols that are used in data exchanges between two Windows XP computers. Communication with down-level clients is likely to be hampered. |
| securedc | The template for a high security domain controller. |
| securews | The template for a high security workstation. Basically the middle ground between the maximum security and the compatible templates, this template will relax security so that older applications can run, but will not inhibit all applications except those specifically written for Windows 2000 or XP. |
| Setup security | The default template that is applied during Setup. It contains all of the security settings that will be needed if you need to restore the system after a disaster. It should never be applied using a Group Policy. |
| rootsec | The root security template includes only the most basic security data, and it defines the default security configuration for the root volume on an NTFS volume. When you apply this template, no permissions will be reset for the folders on the drive. |

# skill10 *Working with Security Templates*
*(cont'd)*

**exam objective**

Configure, manage, and troubleshoot a security configuration and local security policy.

**how to**

14. Right-click the **Security and Configuration Analysis** node and select the **Analyze Computer Now** command. Click [ OK ] in the **Perform Analysis** dialog box to confirm the path to the log file.

15. When the analysis is complete, open the **Security Configuration and Analysis** node.

16. Open the **Account Policies** node and select **Password Policy**. Policies with a green check mark indicate that the local computer policy meets the requirements for a high security workstation. Policies with a red X do not, as shown in **Figure 12-41**.

17. Double-click **Enforce password history** to open the **Enforce password history Properties** dialog box. The current setting is for 15 passwords to be remembered. The database setting for a high-security workstation is 24. Click [ OK ] to close the dialog box and maintain the setting in the database.

18. Double-click **Minimum password length**. In the **Password must be at least** spin box, enter **14** to make the policy setting in the database match the current computer setting (**Figure 12-42**). Click [ OK ]. Note that there are four password policies on the computer that still do not match the database setting.

19. Click the **Account Lockout Policy** node. Double-click **Account lockout threshold**.

20. Note that the current computer setting allows 3 invalid logon attempts, while the database setting for a high-security workstation allows 5 invalid logon attempts.

21. Change the setting in the **Account will lock out after** spin box to match the current computer setting. Click [ OK ] to define the policy in the database.

22. Expand the **Local Policies** node and select **Audit Policy**. Open the **Audit account logon events Properties** dialog box. Remove the check mark from the **Define this policy in the database** check box, and click [ OK ] to remove this policy setting from the database. You will be configuring this audit policy in the next lesson.

23. Select the **Security Options** node. Double-click **Interactive logon: Do not display last user name in logon dialog box**. Click the **Enabled** option button and click [ OK ] to define this policy in the database. Note that there are a number of security options that do not meet the requirements for a high-security workstation.

24. Right-click the **Security Configuration and Analysis** node and select the **Configure Computer Now** command. In the **Configure System** dialog box, click [ OK ] to confirm the path to the log file. The system is configured with the custom template you designed in the exercise.

25. Right-click the **Security and Configuration Analysis** node and select the **Analyze Computer Now** command. Click [ OK ] in the **Perform Analysis** dialog box to confirm the path to the log file. You will now be able to view the information in the database and compare it with the new computer settings.

26. Expand the **Account Policies** node and select **Password Policy**. Notice that now the current computer settings match the database settings for all of the password policies (**Figure 12-44**).

27. Expand the **Local Policies** node and select **Security Options**. Note that all of the computer settings now match the database settings for the custom high-security workstation template you designed in the exercise.

28. Close the Security Templates console and save the console settings.

**Figure 12-41  Performing a security analysis**

**Figure 12-42  The Minimum password length Properties dialog box**

Enter 14 to make the policy setting in the database match the current computer setting

**Figure 12-43  The Account lockout threshold Properties dialog box**

Enter 3 to make the database match the current computer setting

**Figure 12-44  Password policies configured using the custom security template**

# skill10

## *Working with Security Templates*
### *(cont'd)*

Configure, manage, and troubleshoot a security configuration and local security policy.

## more

There is also a command line tool called SECEDIT.EXE that you can use to perform most of the same functions as the Security Template and Security Configuration and Analysis snap-ins. This utility works from a batch file, script, or automatic task scheduler; for example, you can use a SECEDIT command in a logon script that is used for the entire system. SECEDIT can also be run from the command line to create templates, analyze security, and apply a security template. The SECEDIT tool is particularly useful on a domain-based system to perform analyses on a large number of computers at the same time. The results of the analysis can either be viewed in the Security Configuration and Analysis snap-in or from the command line.

Some of the most commonly used command parameters for SECEDIT are explained in **Table 12-4**.

A new command line utility, GPUPDATE, replaces the refreshpolicy command that was formerly used with SECEDIT. GPUPDATE can be used to refresh both local group policy settings, as well as those applied through a GPO on an Active Directory network. The parameters for the GPUPDATE utility are explained in **Table 12-5**.

Security templates can only be applied to Windows 2000 and XP computers, and some of the security settings are not compatible with earlier versions of the operating system, particularly those related to encryption. This means that when you use one of the high-security or maximum security templates, you may not be able to communicate with computers which are not running Windows 2000 or XP. Use either the default or the compatible template on a network that includes Windows 9x or Windows NT computers.

The first time you use the Security configuration and Analysis utility, instructions will display in the details pane of the console window. When you open a database, you are creating a database that you will work with to analyze settings, make changes, and apply the new configuration. You can also simply use all of the database settings to apply the complete configuration outlined in one of the templates. The templates are .inf files. On a domain-based Active Directory network, you will apply a security template to a GPO to put all of the individual security settings into operation at the domain or organizational unit level.

**Table 12-4 SECEDIT Command Parameters**

| Variable | Explanation |
| --- | --- |
| /analyze | Analyzes the current security settings against the /DB and /CFG parameters you enter.(See below.) |
| /configure | Configures the security settings on the computer based on the /DB and /CFG parameters you enter. |
| /export | Exports a template from a security database to an .inf template file using the /DB and /CFG parameters you enter. |
| /DB *filename* | The path to the database that contains the security configuration settings you want SECEDIT to use to perform the analysis or that you want to be applied. |
| /CFG *filename* | The path to the security template that you want SECEDIT to use to analyze or configure the database you specified with the /DB parameter. You can only use this argument in conjunction with the /DB parameter. If you do not specify a security template, the template that is already stored in the database will be applied, or the analysis will be performed against the configuration settings that are already stored in the database. |
| /validate *filename* | Validates the syntax of a security template that you want to import into a database for analysis or apply to the system. |

**Table 12-5 GPUPDATE Command Parameters**

| Variable | Explanation |
| --- | --- |
| /target:{computer|user} | Used to designate that you only want computer settings or current user settings to be updated. User settings will be updated depending on the switch that is specified. |
| /force | Used to designate that you want to ignore all processing optimization settings for GPOs. All security configuration settings are reapplied. |
| /logoff | Used to log off after the update has completed. This is useful because some Group Policy settings do not automatically refresh as a background process, but will only update when a user logs on. In particular, new Folder Redirection and Software Installation policies will only update when a user logs back on. |
| /boot | Used to reboot the computer after the update. This is useful because some Group Policy settings do not automatically refresh as a background process, but will only update when the computer boots. |

# Summary

◆ Group policies are used to manage many different settings for both computers and users, including the desktop appearance, the allocation of software applications, and password limitations.

◆ Group policies are usually implemented when you are working with a domain-based network that combines Windows 2000 and 2003 Servers with Windows 2000 and XP Professional clients in an Active Directory environment.

◆ Group policies for local computers that do not use the Active Directory are set using local security policies.

◆ Local security policies are used to configure the settings for a local computer, which can be a workgroup or a standalone computer, so that the data can be safeguarded.

◆ Categories of local security policies that can be used to safeguard a local computer include account policies, local policies, public key policies, IP security policies, and software restriction policies.

◆ Account Policies consist of the password policy and the account lockout policy.

◆ Password policies are used to implement specific rules for how all users who log on to a computer must structure their passwords, the frequency with which they must change them, and how long they can use them before the passwords must be changed. These policies are not set individually; they apply to all users on a local computer.

◆ Account lockout policies are used to set how many invalid logon attempts will be allowed before the account is barred from use. You can also set a specific time period during which the account will remain locked out, or configure the policy so that an Administrator must unlock it.

◆ Local policies are classified as audit policies, user rights assignments, or security options.

◆ User rights assignments are used to prescribe what actions a user can execute on the operating system.

◆ Public key policies include the Encrypting File System (EFS) recovery policy. Files and folders are encrypted using a security algorithm and a file encryption key to change the contents into unreadable characters. Either the user who encrypted the file or a user who has been designated as the recovery agent can recover an encrypted file. When other users try to access an encrypted file, they will receive an Access Denied message.

◆ IPSec (Internet Protocol Security) policies are used to protect data as it travels on a TCP/IP network. They ensure the security of data packets by encrypting them before sending them to another computer on a public network.

◆ You can specify and customize your password settings by using various password policy options available in the Password Policy node. For example, you can set a minimum length for passwords or assign a password age to ensure that passwords are changed frequently.

◆ There are two security options that are used to control how credentials are handled. One is the Interactive logon:

Do not display last user name in logon screen policy. This policy overrides the default behavior for a system, which is to redisplay the previous user's name in the logon screen the next time any user attempts to log on.

◆ The other security option, which handles cached credentials, is the Interactive logon: Number of previous logons to cache policy. This policy is important on domain-based networks in which users may sometimes have to work on a local computer when a domain controller is unavailable, or may at times work away from the network. In Windows XP Professional, such users can log on with a domain user account for a set number of times which can be configured. By default, this policy allows 10 logons using cached credentials.

◆ You can set different passwords for different services and sites in the Stored User Names and Passwords dialog box, which you access on the Advanced tab in the User Accounts utility. When you add passwords to your local passwords cache they are added to your user profile. You can store logon credentials for network locations and for Web sites.

◆ You can encrypt your files and folders on an NTFS disk using the Encrypting File System (EFS) so that they cannot be read or modified by unauthorized users.

◆ You can encrypt files and folders in Windows Explorer or by using the Cipher command-line utility.

◆ Either the user who encrypted the file or a user who has been designated as the recovery agent can recover an encrypted file.

◆ You can set additional recovery agents for a system so that, if the owner of an encrypted file forgets the password, the recovery agent can copy the encrypted file to his or her computer and decrypt the file by clearing the Encrypt Contents to Secure Data checkbox in the Properties dialog box for the file.

◆ The Domain Administrator account is, by default, designated as the recovery agent for a domain.

◆ You can set security rules related to data communication on a TCP/IP network using IPSec Policies. IPSec Policies are used to ensure the integrity, confidentiality, and authentication of data packets traveling over a TCP/IP network.

◆ When you log on to your Windows XP Professional computer as a member of a domain, the local security policy settings on your computer may be overridden by the security policies of the domain.

◆ Site policies override local policy, domain policies override site policies, and OU policies override domain policies. This default behavior can be controlled using the Block Inheritance and No Override settings.

◆ Security Templates are valuable on a workgroup network because, rather than configuring your local security policies and local group policies one by one, you can use a security template to apply a whole range of security configuration settings all at once.

◆ The Security and Configuration Analysis snap-in is used to compare the current security configuration of the computer with one of the security templates, to create custom templates, and to apply a template to either the local computer or to a Group Policy object.

◆ A security template can include password and account lockout policies, local security policies, user rights assignments, Registry key security, group memberships, and permissions for the local file system.

◆ There is also a command-line tool called SECEDIT.EXE that you can use to perform most of the same functions as the Security Template and Security Configuration and Analysis snap-ins.

◆ A new command line utility, GPUPDATE, replaces the refreshpolicy command that was formerly used with SECEDIT. GPUPDATE can be used to refresh both local group policy settings and those applied through a GPO on an Active Directory network.

## Key Terms

Account lockout duration
Account lockout policy
Account lockout threshold
Account policies
Cipher utility
Client (Respond Only)
Console
Encrypting File System (EFS)
Encryption
Enforce password history
Group policies
IP filter rule

IP security policies
Kerberos V5
Local policies
Maximum password age
Minimum password age
Minimum password length
Password
Password history
Password policy
Passwords must meet complexity
   requirements
Public key policies

Recovery agent
Reset account lockout counter after
Secure Server (Require Security)
Security Configuration and Analysis
   snap-in
Security Template snap-in
Server (Request Security)
Store password using reversible
   encryption for all users in the
   domain
User rights assignment

## Test Yourself

1. You want to set a password policy for your computer so that the password can be changed on the same day on which it is set. Which of the following policies will you use?
   a. Enforce password history
   b. Maximum password age
   c. Minimum password age
   d. Minimum password length

2. You are the Network Administrator at Healthcare Inc., a pharmaceutical company. Details of drugs the company carries are stored on a computer. Which of the following settings will enable you to minimize the chances of an unauthorized person accessing the computer?
   a. Setting values of 8 and 1 for the Account lockout threshold policy and Account lockout duration policy, respectively.
   b. Setting a value of 3 for the Minimum password age policy.

   c. Setting values of 1 and 8 for the Account lockout threshold policy and the Account lockout duration policy.
   d. Setting a value of 1 for the Account lockout threshold policy and a value of 0 for the Account lockout duration policy.
   e. Setting a value of 3 for the Maximum password age policy.

3. You want to implement a policy that enforces complexity requirements for passwords so that they are more secure. Kelly, Joe, George, Sam, and Michael want to set their passwords as kirstenkelly, #59USA, 29974, SamEmaNuaL, and Boeing29, respectively. Passwords can be set for which of the following people?
   a. Kelly
   b. Joe
   c. George
   d. Sam
   e. Michael

4. Which one of the following settings will you use to lock an account indefinitely if invalid logon attempts take place?
   a. Set a value of 0 for the Account lockout duration option.
   b. Set a value of 0 for the Account lockout threshold option.
   c. Set a value of 99,999 for the Account lockout duration option.
   d. Set a value of 999 for the Account lockout threshold option.

5. The Encrypting File System (EFS) is used to secure:
   a. Passwords.
   b. Data files on local computers.
   c. Data packets traveling on a network.
   d. FAT partitions.

6. Which of the following commands would you use with the Cipher utility to decrypt an encrypted folder and its sub folders?
   a. cipher /e /s folder_name
   b. cipher /d /s folder_name
   c. cipher /d folder_name
   d. cipher /e /f folder_name

7. A folder named Misc is saved on the NTFS 5 partition of your computer. You have encrypted the folder using Encrypting File System. Which one of the following statements is true?
   a. If you move the encrypted folder to a FAT partition on a different computer running Windows 2000 Professional, the folder still remains encrypted.
   b. Any file that is added to the folder would have to be encrypted.
   c. If a file from the Misc folder is transmitted across the network to a computer running Windows 2000 Professional on an NTFS volume that was formatted using NTFS 4, the file is decrypted when it reaches the destination computer.
   d. If you move the encrypted folder to an NTFS 5 partition on a different computer that runs Windows 2000 Professional, the folder is decrypted.

8. Which one of the following statements is true about encrypting files and folders using Encrypting File System (EFS)?
   a. You can encrypt a compressed file.
   b. You can choose to encrypt a specific file within a folder.
   c. You can encrypt files and folders stored on FAT partitions.
   d. Files and folders encrypted using EFS cannot be recovered if the user's private key is lost.

9. Which one of the following conditions holds true when you are implementing a security policy in an organization?
   a. You can enable a security policy at the local and domain level and disable it if the computer is not logged on to the domain.
   b. Policies at the domain level can be applied to sites, domains, and Organizational Units.
   c. You set the various audit policies, user rights assignments, and security options using Account Policies.
   d. You set the minimum number of logon attempts using Security Options.

10. You want to encrypt a folder My data on your computer and also force encryption on all the sub folders even if they are encrypted. Which of the following Cipher commands will you use?
    a. cipher /e /s:folder_name /k
    b. cipher /e /s:folder_name /f
    c. cipher /e /s:folder_name /q
    d. cipher /e /s:folder_name /h

11. You have kept the Allow system to be shut down without having to log on local security policy enabled, and gone out on personal work. Your friend Joe thinks that you have left for the day and he wants to shut down the computer. Joe can shut down your computer.
    a. True
    b. False

12. The /i variable used with the Cipher command is used to:
    a. Perform the encryption or decryption operation on a folder and all its sub folders.
    b. Force the encryption operation on all files and folders, even if they have been encrypted.
    c. Display files with the hidden or system attributes during an encryption or decryption operation.
    d. Continue the encryption or decryption operation in spite of errors that may occur during the operation.

13. Which IP Sec policy minimizes the number of computers with which you can communicate on a network?
    a. Client (Respond Only)
    b. Secure Server (Require Security)
    c. Server (Request Security)
    d. Password

14. Which one of the following statements is true about recovery agents?
    a. The recovery agent has a file recovery certificate and his or her own private key so that encrypted files will always be recoverable.
    b. Backup Operators are by default recovery agents.
    c. To recover an encrypted file, the recovery agent should first uncheck the Encrypt contents to secure data check box in the Advanced Attributes dialog box for the encrypted file.

# Projects: On Your Own

**1.** Set up a local security policy so that any user accessing a computer has the right to change the system time.
   a. Open the **Run** dialog box.
   b. Open the **Console Root** window.
   c. Open the **Add/Remove Snap-in** dialog box.
   d. Open the **Add Standalone Snap-in** dialog box.
   e. Initiate the Select Group Policy Object Wizard.
   f. Close the Add Standalone Snap-in dialog box.
   g. Close the Add/Remove Snap-in dialog box.
   h. Access the User Rights Assignment options and open the Change the system time Properties dialog box.
   i. Add the **Everyone** group so that all users will have this user right and close the dialog box.
   j. Close the console without saving the settings.

**2.** Set a security option so that the user is prompted to change the password a day before the expiration date.
   a. Open the **Run** dialog box.
   b. Open the **Console Root** window.
   c. Open the **Add/Remove Snap-in** dialog box
   d. Open the **Add Standalone Snap-in** dialog box.

   e. Initiate the Select Group Policy Object Wizard.
   f. Close the Add Standalone Snap-in dialog box.
   g. Close the Add/Remove Snap-in dialog box.
   h. Access the Security Options and open the **Interactive logon: Prompt user to change password before expiration Properties** dialog box.
   i. Select **1** day in the spin box, and close the dialog box.
   j. Close the console without saving the settings.

**3.** Encrypt a folder named **Personal** and all its contents from the Windows Explorer.
   a. Open the Windows Explorer.
   b. Open the Properties dialog box of the **Personal** folder.
   c. Open the **Advanced Attributes** dialog box.
   d. Set the encryption property for the folder.
   e. Close the Advanced Attributes dialog box.
   f. Accept and confirm the changes.
   g. Select the option to encrypt the folder along with its contents such as sub folders and files.
   h. Close the Confirm Attribute Changes dialog box.
   i. Close the Personal Properties dialog box.

# Problem Solving Scenarios

1. Rodman Auto Supply is an automobile wholesaler operating in Pennsylvania and Ohio. Located in Pittsburgh, Rodman has 75 employees on a Windows network, and three remote locations. As the Network Consultant, you would like to institute a new password policy for the network. You would like to force users to change their passwords every thirty days, not allow them to re-use old passwords, and to use passwords that have at least six characters, including three of the four different types of characters. Outline in a written report how you would achieve these objectives.

2. The Senior Network Administrator at Rodman Auto Supply has expressed concern that files in the Finance department are open to all employees in Finance. The Financial Manager also is concerned and wants to encrypt selected files. He would like you to ensure that these files can be opened by only himself or his Assistant Financial Manager. In a memo to the Senior Network Administrator, explain how you would achieve this objective. Be sure to include your thinking about designating recovery agents.

# 13 Monitoring Events and Resources

**A** Network Administrator's job includes making sure that the computers on the network function optimally, that resources are secure, that the proper people are accessing the correct resources, and that users who should not be accessing resources are not doing so. Auditing is used to observe and record the events that occur on the network, including logons—both successful and unsuccessful—and access to files, folders, the Registry, and printers. These events are recorded in the Security event log, which you can view using the Event Viewer snap-in in the Computer Management console. These tools are used to keep Administrators informed of such occurrences as a user who is attempting to access a computer by repeatedly guessing account names and/or passwords, users who are accessing files at unusual times of the day, and users who are accessing resources that they should not have access to.

Auditing does not take place automatically. You must configure a local security policy to track the events you think are important, given your environment and the specifics of your situation. Then, you must decide whether you want to track the success or failure of the events. The events you choose will be recorded in the Security event log. The entries in the log will identify the events that are occurring, the users who are performing the actions, and the success or failure, or both, of the events, depending on what you have chosen to record. As a general rule of thumb, you will want to monitor unsuccessful events if you are concerned about possible security breaches, and successful events if you are evaluating the capacity or overall functioning of your system.

In addition, Administrators need to monitor the performance of the computers on a network and take corrective actions if the performance is not up to par. The System Monitor in the Performance console is used to display data from current activity on the network or from log files, so that you can evaluate the day-to-day usage of the system. Administrators can monitor the performance of the memory of the system and the processors, find out if the disks are operating optimally, and evaluate overall network performance by monitoring how well the network cards are functioning and what volume of traffic they are able to handle. The Performance console is also used to create logs that record information about the performance of the resources on a computer, and to configure alerts that perform certain actions based on the captured data.

## Goals

In this lesson, you will learn how to audit various events that occur on a computer, such as logging on, accessing files and folders, and shutting down and restarting a computer. You will also learn to monitor resources of a computer such as the processors and memory. Additionally, you will learn to create logs and alerts using the Performance console.

## Lesson 13 Monitoring Events and Resources

| Skill | Exam 70-270 Objective |
|---|---|
| 1. Introducing Auditing | Configuring, managing, and troubleshooting security. Configure, manage and troubleshoot auditing. |
| 2. Auditing Access to Files and Folders | Configuring, managing, and troubleshooting security. Configure, manage and troubleshoot auditing. |
| 3. Managing Auditing | Configuring, managing, and troubleshooting security. Configure, manage and troubleshoot auditing. |
| 4. Monitoring System Performance | Monitor, optimize, and troubleshoot performance of the Windows XP Professional desktop. Optimize and troubleshoot processor utilization. Optimize and troubleshoot memory performance. Optimize and troubleshoot disk performance. |
| 5. Configuring Alerts | Monitor, optimize, and troubleshoot performance of the Windows XP Professional desktop. Optimize and troubleshoot memory performance. |

## Requirements

There are no special requirements for this lesson.

# skill 1

# *Introducing Auditing*

## exam objective

Configuring, managing, and troubleshooting security. Configure, manage and troubleshoot auditing.

## overview

## caution

Auditing increases the overhead on a computer. File system reads take place frequently, which can overload the Security event log and cause both disk space and performance shortfalls. Therefore, you need to decide which events are important to track for your situation.

Each time a user logs on to a computer or to a network, he or she performs a number of activities, including the logon process itself, and accessing files, folders, printers, and the Registry. These activities are called events. As a Network Administrator, you will want to track and monitor some of these events on a regular basis in order to ensure the security and seamless functioning of the computers on the network. **Auditing** is used to track user activities and object access on the computers on a network. You can only audit object access for files and folders that are stored on NTFS volumes and partitions.

First, you will need to determine which events need to be audited on each computer. Auditing must be set up for each computer. Auditing can be used to track exactly who logged on to a computer and when, what files were accessed or folders were created, what printers were used, and what Registry keys were accessed when and by whom, and what actions the users attempted to perform on them. In order to audit who is accessing which objects and what actions they are performing on those objects, you must first activate the audit object access policy, because there is no auditing set up for workstations and servers by default. Then, you configure the audit object access policy in the Properties dialog box and the System ACL editor for the object.

At this point it might be helpful to distinguish between a System ACL (SACL) and a Discretionary ACL (DACL). A System ACL (SACL) is used to allow the System Administrator to log any attempts at gaining access to an object. The list of ACEs (Access control entries) in the SACL will determine which users and groups will be audited. A Discretionary ACL (DACL), which is used to set permissions, determines which users and groups can and cannot access the object. A Discretionary ACL is controlled by the owner of the object, or anyone who has been granted the right to change the permissions for the object.

In an organization, auditing is used to help prevent security breaches by allowing you to track unauthorized attempts to log on or access folders. Auditing is also used to help conduct resource planning for the computers on your network. For example, you may discover that too many users are accessing a particular printer on the network, and that this printer is overtaxed. Based on this finding, you may decide to install another printer. In order to monitor a particular event, you must define an **audit policy** in the Audit Policy folder under the **Local Policies** node in the **Local Security Settings** window. The audit policy tells the operating system what to record in the Security event log on each computer. The events you can audit in Windows XP Professional are listed in **Table 13-1**. When you define an audit policy, you select the events you want to track and decide whether to track the success or failure, or both, for the event. For example, if you want to audit the system events that occur on your computer, such as when a user restarts or shuts down their computer, you will activate the **Audit system events** policy and specify whether to audit successes or failures, or both.

Audited events are stored in the **Security event log**. You can view the Security log using the **Event Viewer** snap-in in the Computer Management console.

## Table 13-1   Events that can be audited

| Event | Description |
|---|---|
| Account Logon Events | The computer has joined a domain and a request to log on to the domain is sent to the domain controller. |
| Account Management | An account or group is created, deleted, or modified, or a user account is renamed, has a new password set, or was activated or disabled. |
| Directory Service Access | The computer has joined a domain and an Active Directory object, such as a computer or domain, is accessed. |
| Logon Events | Users log on or off a computer, or make or cancel a network connection. |
| Object Access | A file, folder, or printer is accessed. |
| Policy Change | User rights, audit policies, or user security options are changed. |
| Privilege Use | A user right or privilege, such as Take Ownership or Print, is exercised by a user. |
| Process Tracking | A program is executed by a user. |
| System Events | A computer is shut down or restarted or some event that concerns the Security log has taken place. |

# skill 1

## Introducing Auditing (cont'd)

### exam objective

Configuring, managing, and troubleshooting security. Configure, manage and troubleshoot auditing.

### how to

Set audit policies for logon and object access events on a computer. Track only failed logon attempts, but track both successful and failed access attempts for objects.

1. Log on as an **Administrator**. If you have not already done so, make the Administrative Tools command appear on the Start menu. Right-click ⊞ start and select **Properties** to open the **Taskbar and Start Menu Properties** dialog box. Click Customize... to open the **Customize Start Menu** dialog box. On the **Advanced** tab, in the **Start menu items** list box, scroll to locate **System Administrative Tools**. Select **Display on the All Programs and the Start menu**, and click OK to close both dialog boxes.
2. Click ⊞ start, point to **Administrative Tools**, and click **Local Security Policy** to open the **Local Security Settings** window.
3. Double-click the **Local Policies** folder to access the **Audit Policy** folder.
4. Click the Audit Policy folder to display the list of audit policies in the details pane **(Figure 13-1)**.
5. Double-click the **Audit logon events** audit policy to open the **Audit logon events Properties** dialog box.
6. Select the **Failure** check box to track failed logon attempts **(Figure 13-2)**.
7. Click OK to save the settings and close the Audit logon events Properties dialog box.
8. Double-click the **Audit object access** audit policy to open the **Audit object access Properties** dialog box.
9. Select the **Success** check box to track successful access attempts to access objects on the computer.
10. Select the **Failure** check box to track failed object access attempts **(Figure 13-3)**.
11. Click OK to save the settings and close the Audit object access Properties dialog box. This simply enables auditing object access on the computer. Next, you will have to choose which files and folders you want the operating system to monitor.
12. The Local Security Setting console displays the status of the Audit logon events and Audit object access audit policies as **Success** or **Failure**, respectively **(Figure 13-4)**.
13. Close the Local Security Settings console.

### tip

Audit account logon events is used to monitor either successful or failed attempts to log on to a domain.

### more

Simple File Sharing is a new feature in Windows XP Professional, which is enabled by default on standalone Windows XP Professional machines, and on computers that are members of a workgroup. It will be disabled on Windows XP Professional computers that are members of a domain. When Simple File Sharing is enabled, a Shared Documents folder is automatically created. It contains two subfolders: Shared Pictures and Shared Music. When Simple File Sharing is enabled, users who access a shared folder on the computer over the network will be authenticated using the Guest user account.

On standalone Windows XP Professional machines, and on machines that are members of a workgroup, before you can enable auditing for specific objects, you must turn off Simple File Sharing or you will not have a Security tab on the Properties dialog box for NTFS resources. To turn off Simple File Sharing, open the **Folder Options** dialog box either by using the icon in the Control Panel or by using the **Folder Options** command on the **Tools** menu in either **My Computer** or **Windows Explorer**. On the **View** tab, remove the check from the **Use simple file sharing** check box.

**Figure 13-1  Audit policies in the Local Security
Settings console**

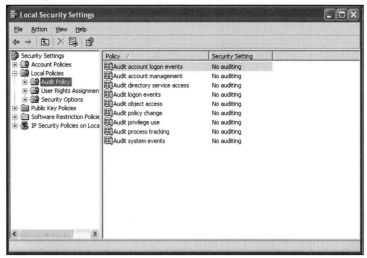

**Figure 13-2  The Audit logon events
Properties dialog box**

**Figure 13-3  The Audit object access
Properties dialog box**

**Figure 13-4  Configured audit policies**

# skill 2

# Auditing Access to Files and Folders

**exam objective**

Configuring, managing, and troubleshooting security. Configure, manage and troubleshoot auditing.

## overview

Now that you have activated object access auditing, you must choose which files and folders you want the operating system to track. Certain files and folders on any computer or network will contain sensitive data that you will want to make sure are only being accessed by authorized users. For example, generally only the Finance Manager and certain other managers will be given access to the files containing the capital expenditures for the company. It is these types of files that you will want to monitor so that you can view unauthorized attempts to access them. You will have to activate the audit object access policy on each computer on which sensitive data that must be tracked is stored. Next, you select the users whose actions you want to audit. You can audit local users or local groups, and if the Windows XP Professional computer joins a domain, domain users, and domain groups. After you select who you are going to audit, you must choose what file system actions you want to monitor in the ACL editor for the file or folder. For example, you can audit who is viewing a folder, creating a file, changing permissions, or viewing permissions.

You can also specify whether or not the subfolders within a folder should inherit the auditing settings. If you are enabling auditing for a subfolder, you can specify whether or not it should inherit the auditing settings of its parent folder. Remember, in order to enable auditing for a file or folder, you must first activate the **Audit object access audit policy** on that computer.

**tip**

You can enable auditing only for a file or a folder that is stored on an **NTFS** drive.

## how to

Enable auditing for a folder named **Reports** located on the **C:** drive of your computer. Log an event every time a user in the Everyone group creates or deletes a file in the **Reports** folder.

1. Open **Windows Explorer** to display the files and folders on your computer.
2. Double-click the **C: drive** icon to display the folders on the drive.
3. Right-click the folder for which you want to enable auditing, for example **Reports**, and click the **Properties** command to open the **Reports Properties** dialog box.
4. Click the **Security** tab, and then click [ Advanced ] to open the **Advanced Security Settings for Reports** dialog box (**Figure 13-5**).
5. Click the **Auditing** tab. The **Inherit from parent the auditing entries that apply to child objects. Include these with entries explicitly defined here** check box is selected by default. This default means that the auditing settings for the parent folder will be inherited by this folder.
6. Select the **Replace auditing entries on all child objects with entries shown here that apply to child objects** check box so that any pre-existing auditing settings on the subfolders in the **Reports** folder will be reset, and will now inherit the settings you are making for the Reports folder (**Figure 13-6**).
7. Click [ Add... ] to open the **Select User or Group** dialog box. In the **Enter the object name to select** box, type the name of the user or group for which you want to enable auditing. For example, type: **Everyone**, to indicate that you want to enable auditing for the **Everyone** group (**Figure 13-7**).
8. Click [ OK ] to close the **Select User or Group** dialog box and open the **Auditing Entry for Reports** dialog box where you can select the actions to be audited.
9. Select the **Successful** check box next to the **Create Files/Write Data** option to indicate that you want to track each time a file is successfully created, or when data is added to a file.
10. Select the **Successful** check box next to the **Delete Subfolders and Files** option to indicate that you want to track each time a file or subfolder is successfully deleted (**Figure 13-8**).
11. Click [ OK ] to save the settings and close the **Auditing Entry for Reports** dialog box.
12. Click [ OK ] to close the **Advanced Security Settings for Reports** dialog box.
13. Click [ OK ] to close the **Reports Properties** dialog box.
14. Close Windows Explorer.

### Figure 13-5  The Permissions tab in the Advanced Security Settings for Reports dialog box

Click to open the Select User or Group dialog box

### Figure 13-6  The Auditing tab

Select to clear any pre-existing auditing settings in the subfolders for this folder so that they will now inherit the settings that you are configuring for the parent folder

### Figure 13-7  Select User or Group dialog box

Enter the name of the object whose actions you want to audit; this can be a local user or local group, or a domain user or domain group, if the computer is a member of a domain

### Figure 13-8  Actions to be audited

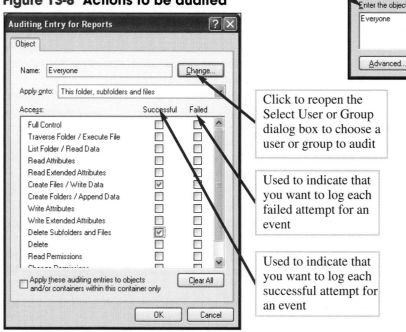

Click to reopen the Select User or Group dialog box to choose a user or group to audit

Used to indicate that you want to log each failed attempt for an event

Used to indicate that you want to log each successful attempt for an event

# skill 3    *Managing Auditing*

**exam objective**

Configuring, managing, and troubleshooting security. Configure, manage and troubleshoot auditing.

## overview

When you implement audit policies, you must understand that auditing increases the overhead on a computer. The CPU will frequently be reading file systems, and the Security event log can become inundated with entries that can cause problems with both disk space and performance. Therefore, you need to decide which events are important to track for your circumstances. Once you have carefully chosen the events you think are important to monitor, for whom you want to monitor them, and what actions you want to track, you must set a schedule for yourself to check the Security log regularly. You can also manage the auditing activities for your organization by managing the operation of the Security event log, which stores the details of the events that are audited.

One important aspect of managing the Security log involves maintaining its size. When events are being regularly recorded, the Security log can become very large. This can quickly use up disk space on your computer. You can control the size of the Security log by specifying a maximum file size in the Event Viewer. When the Security log reaches the maximum file size, you can choose to either overwrite old events as needed, set a specific age for the events you want to be overwritten, or prevent events from being overwritten. If you choose the first option, you could lose data if the log becomes full before you archive it. If you choose the second option, you could lose data that is at least as many days old as you have chosen if you do not archive the log soon enough. If you choose the final option, you must make sure that you monitor the Event Viewer often enough to archive or clear the logs before they become full, because when the log is full the operating system will stop recording events. Archiving is the process you use to save a history of the security events you are auditing so that you can track trends in resource usage. You also use the Event Viewer to archive old log files and store them for future reference.

When you open Event Viewer, the following logs are displayed in addition to the Security log by default:

◆ **Application log:** This log captures the details of events that occur when an application, such as a database application, is run on a computer. Errors, warnings, or information related to these events are recorded automatically.

◆ **System log:** This log records errors, warnings, and information generated by Windows XP Professional, such as a service starts or stops. These events are recorded automatically.

## how to

View events in the Security Log of your computer, set the maximum size of the Security log, and configure the log so that events older than **5** days will be overwritten.

1. Log off of the Administrator account and attempt to log back on as **user1** (or any other user account you have created on the computer). Enter an incorrect user name on your first logon attempt. Enter an incorrect password on your second logon attempt. Log on successfully on your third attempt.
2. Create a file named **Expenses.doc** and save it in the **Reports** folder. Close the file.
3. Log off as user1 and log back on as an **Administrator**.
4. Click ⊞ start , point to **Administrative Tools**, and click **Event Viewer** to open the Event Viewer window.
5. Select **Security Log** in the left pane of the Event Viewer window to open the events in the Security log.
6. Scroll down the list and locate the two Failure Audits (**Figure 13-9**). Double-click the first Failure Audit to open the **Event Properties** dialog box to display the details of the selected event (**Figure 13-10**).

**Figure 13-9  The Security log**

Failed logon attempts are recorded in the Security log

**Figure 13-10  Details of an event recorded in the Security log**

Displays the description of an event

Use to view the Event Properties dialog box for preceding and subsequent events in the Security log

Use to copy the details for the event to the clipboard

# skill 3

## *Managing Auditing (cont'd)*

### exam objective

Configuring, managing, and troubleshooting security. Configure, manage and troubleshoot auditing.

### how to

### tip

The file size can be entered in any multiple, but it will be resized to the closest multiple of 64.

7. Use the up and down arrow buttons to view the next and previous Event Properties dialog boxes for the events in the Security Log. Locate the Event Properties dialog box for the Success Audit in which the Expenses file was saved in the Reports folder (**Figure 13-11**).
8. Close the Event Properties dialog box.
9. Right-click **Security Log** and select **Properties** to open the **Security Properties** dialog box.
10. Indicate the maximum size for the log file in the **Maximum log size** text box. For example, type **384**.
11. The **Overwrite events older than** option button is selected by default. To set the number of days old you want events that are overwritten to be, type **5**, in the **Overwrite events older than** text box (**Figure 13-12**).
12. Click [ OK ] to save the settings and close the Security Properties dialog box.
13. The Event Viewer message box opens to inform you that the Security log has been reduced in size, and to warn you that the new setting will not take effect until you clear the log (**Figure 13-13**). Click [ OK ].
14. Right-click **Security** and select **Clear all Events**. The Event Viewer dialog box opens to prompt you to save the log before clearing it. Click [ No ].
15. Close the Event Viewer.

### more

You must remember to examine the Security event log regularly because the process of auditing will not warn you if security infringements are occurring. Your sensitive files should always be monitored by first setting an audit policy, and then following up to see if unauthorized users are either attempting to access them or succeeding in accessing them. Do not audit events that are not essential either for enhancing the security of your system, or for tracking developments in system usage.

**Figure 13-11  The Event Properties dialog box**

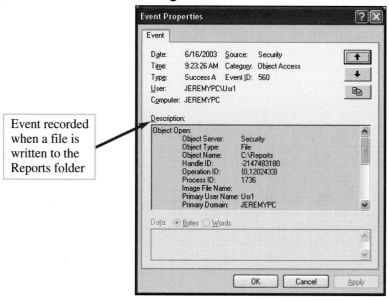

Event recorded when a file is written to the Reports folder

**Figure 13-12  The Security Properties dialog box**

You must check and archive, if necessary, the events in the Security log every 5 days because events older than this will be overwritten if the log file reaches its maximum size

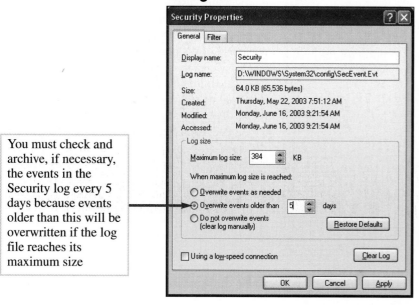

**Figure 13-13  The Event Viewer warning message**

# skill 4

## Monitoring System Performance

**exam objective**

Monitor, optimize, and troubleshoot performance of the Windows XP Professional desktop. Optimize and troubleshoot processor utilization. Optimize and troubleshoot memory performance. Optimize and troubleshoot disk performance.

## overview

At times, the performance of your computer may not be satisfactory. For example, the processing speed may have noticeably decreased so that you are experiencing delays in opening applications. This happens due to bottlenecks, which reduce the speed of the computer system as a whole. A **bottleneck**, in computer parlance, refers to any resource, such as memory or disk space, which causes other resources to delay while it completes its assigned function. For example, if your computer has insufficient memory, memory is the bottleneck that is likely holding up computer functions. The solution to bottlenecks in most situations is to upgrade your system. You may need to add more RAM, get a newer, faster network interface card, buy a more powerful processor, or upgrade your drives. However, you can use the tools in Windows XP Professional to monitor the resources of a computer and determine where and what the bottlenecks are, and how they are adversely affecting the computer's performance. Then, you can attend to the bottlenecks that are causing a noticeable decline in system performance. You can also configure alerts to perform actions based on the performance of the resources on your computer.

First, you must ascertain what the normal operating parameters for the computer are. This is referred to as establishing a baseline or benchmarking the system. The idea is that in order to detect anomalous system behavior, you must first know what level of performance you have during normal usage and under typical workloads. In particular, you should establish baseline behavior when a computer first begins to run on the network and when the hardware or software configuration has been modified so that you can measure the effect made by the update. For example, to determine the baseline behavior for the processors, you can create a counter log using the **Processor—%Processing Time** counter and the **System—Processor Queue Length** counter, which you should run for a few weeks to a month (**Figure 13-14**). This way, at a later date when you make system modifications, you will have a benchmark range of values to evaluate against the new range of values you get after modification (**Figure 13-15**). Sporadic spikes in the values recorded by a counter are generally discarded. The idea is to get a reliable range of values against which future performance can be compared. As a general rule, baselines should be established for all of the important servers on the network.

You monitor the resources on your computer, either to establish a baseline or to diagnose a bottleneck, in the **Performance** console. The **Performance** console consists of the **System Monitor** and the **Performance Logs and Alerts** tools. The System Monitor is used to view a graphical representation of the performance of the resources on your computer. The Performance Logs and Alerts tool is used to record the performance of resources in logs and to configure alerts, which are activated based on threshold values that you set to perform specific actions.

When you open the Performance console, the System Monitor appears by default. It will display the performance of your computer based on objects and counters that you configure. An **object** is a system resource, such as a processor, disk, network interface, or memory, whose performance you can monitor. **Counters** are performance measures for the object that can be calculated and related as numeric figures. For example, if you want to monitor the performance of the processor object, you can monitor counters such as the percentage of time the processor is busy (**%Processor Time**), and the number of times each second that it is interrupted by service requests (**Interrupts/Sec**). Counters can have multiple instances. For example, if a computer has two processors there can be three instances for the %Processor Time counter, one for each processor and one for the total processing time. Processors are not frequently the cause of a bottleneck, but if the %Processor Time counter is consistently above 80%, it will confirm that this is the problem area. You can also use the

**tip**

Some devices that may cause interrupts are adapters, network adapters, the system clock, and the mouse.

**Figure 13-14  The System Monitor**

Using the %Processor Time and Processor Queue Length counters to monitor the Processor and System objects

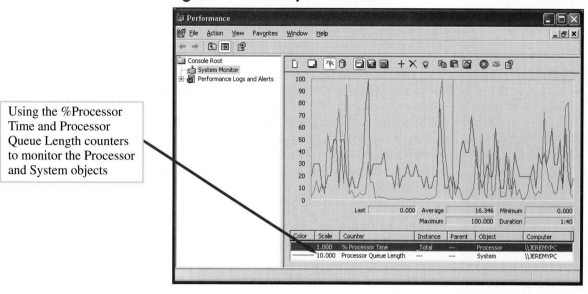

**Figure 13-15  Processor Baseline counter log**

A counter log saved in the Text File-comma delimited (.csv) log file type opens in Excel

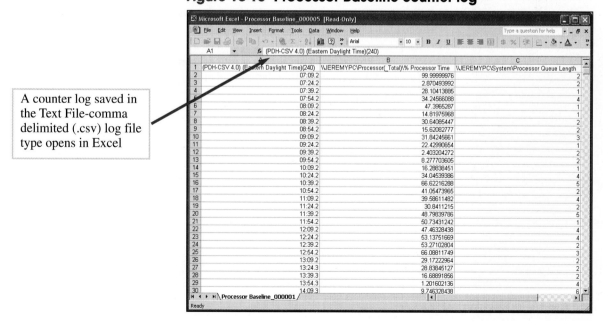

# skill 4

## Monitoring System Performance *(cont'd)*

### exam objective

Monitor, optimize, and troubleshoot performance of the Windows XP Professional desktop. Optimize and troubleshoot processor utilization. Optimize and troubleshoot memory performance.Optimize and troubleshoot disk performance.

### overview

Processor-Interrupts/Sec counter to find out the average number of times the processor is interrupted by hardware device requests for attention. When the system is not in use, the only interrupts are caused by the processor hardware timer which will produce approximately 66 to 100 interrupts per second. First, establish a baseline for normal workloads. This value will depend on the type of processor; 1000 interrupts per second is considered to be a reliable starting point on Windows XP Professional. If system activity has not significantly increased and you note a conspicuous increase in the number of processor interrupts per second, you are likely experiencing a hardware problem. You should consider replacing the network card with one that does more on-board processing itself, as opposed to offloading tasks to the CPU.

In order to monitor performance measures for system objects, you must use the **Add Counters** dialog box to add instances of counters for certain objects to the current graph in the System Monitor. The System Monitor tool captures the data from the counters and displays it as a chart, a histogram, or a report.

### how to

Monitor the average time each of the processors in your computer spends processing service requests and the average number of times per second that they are interrupted by device requests. Display the data as a histogram.

1. Click  start , point to **Administrative Tools**, and click the **Performance** command to open the **Performance** console **(Figure 13-16)**.
2. Click  **+**  to open the **Add Counters** dialog box.
3. Select the **Use local computer counters** option button to indicate that you want to monitor objects on the local computer.
4. **Processor** is selected by default in the **Performance object** list box.
5. Select **%Processor Time** in the **Select counters from list** box.
6. Select the **All instances** option button to monitor all instances of the selected object **(Figure 13-17)**.
7. Click  Add  to add the selected counter.
8. Select **Interrupts/sec** in the **Select counters from list** box.
9. Select the **All instances** option button and click  Add  to add the selected counter to the Performance console.

**Figure 13-16  The System Monitor in the Performance console**

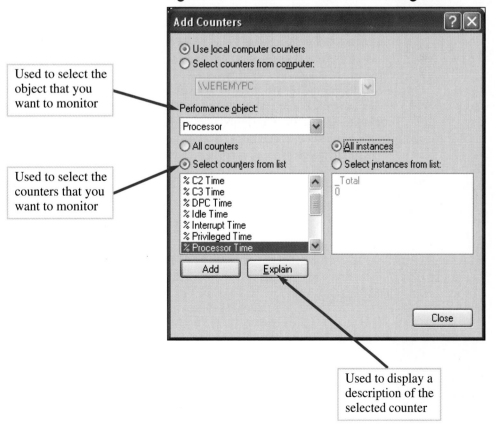

**Figure 13-17  The Add Counters dialog box**

# skill 4
## Monitoring System Performance (cont'd)

### exam objective

Monitor, optimize, and troubleshoot performance of the Windows XP Professional desktop. Optimize and troubleshoot processor utilization. Optimize and troubleshoot memory performance.Optimize and troubleshoot disk performance.

### how to

10. Click [ Close ] to close the Add Counters dialog box and save the data (**Figure 13-18**).
11. Click the **View Histogram** button 📷 to display the captured data as a histogram (**Figure 13-19**). The histogram displays the amount of time all of the processors in your computer have spent processing.
12. Close the Performance console.

### more

There are many other counters you can track with the System Monitor. Since it would be impossible to memorize the purpose of each one, you can select the counter you want to find out about in the Add Counter dialog box and use the **Explain** button to open the **Explain Text** section which provides a description of what the counter measures.

The amount of time it takes for the disk subsystem on a computer to access and display data that is requested by the operating system is referred to as the **disk access time**. In order to monitor disk access time, you can use several counters for the Physical Disk object: **%Disk Time**, **%Disk Read Time**, **%Disk Write Time**, **%Idle Time**, **Disk Reads/Sec**, **Disk Writes/Sec**, and **Disk Transfers/Sec**. You can also use queue length counters, such as **Avg Disk Queue Length**, **Avg Disk Read Queue Length**, **Avg Disk Write Queue Length**, and **Current Disk Queue Length**, to diagnose disk performance bottlenecks.

Most modern high performance disks can handle at least 50 random I/O executions per second. The most up-to-date disks, which have increased rotation speeds, can manage 100 or more I/O operations/second. If you are seeing values that stay in the range of 70% to 85% of the maximum disk capacity, you may have a disk capacity bottleneck. If queue lengths are becoming longer at lower usage rates, the disk may be overtaxed. If the Avg Disk Queue Length is more than twice the number of physical disks on your system, it is very likely that disk performance is causing system delays. Keep in mind however, that disk bottlenecks and memory bottlenecks can cause symptoms that "act" in the same way. If memory is running low, the paging file will have to be accessed more, and the machine will begin reading smaller blocks of code more often. As less and less memory is available, more disk space must be used for the paging file, so the burden on the disks will increase. This is why if you think a disk bottleneck is occurring, you should also monitor memory counters to rule out the possibility that a memory bottleneck is the real cause for concern.

**Figure 13-18  Captured data displayed as a chart**

The View Graph
button: Select to
display data as a
chart

**Figure 13-19  Processor data captured as a histogram**

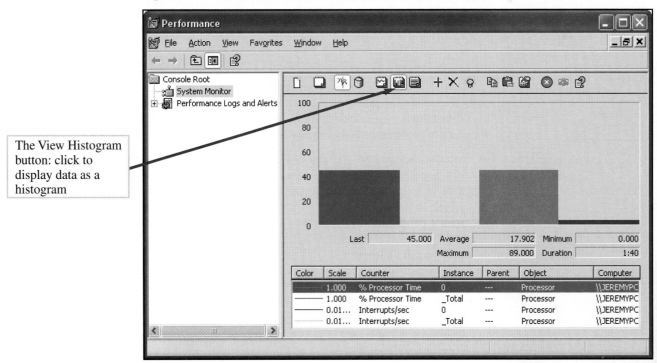

The View Histogram
button: click to
display data as a
histogram

# skill 5

# *Configuring Alerts*

**exam objective**

Monitor, optimize, and troubleshoot performance of the Windows XP Professional desktop. Optimize and troubleshoot memory performance.

**overview**

While the **System Monitor** tool displays graphical representations of the performance measures for various objects, **Performance Logs and Alerts (Figure 13-20)** are used to store the data for future reference. You can create two types of logs: Counter logs and Trace logs. **Counter logs** use the GUI data from the System Monitor to create a log file, which is by default in the *.**BLG** format (Binary LoG). **Trace logs** survey events that take place on the system **(Figure 13-21)**. They do not track performance data, so you do not select counters when you configure them. Instead, you choose the events logged by a system provider or you can add a non-system provider, if available. Both logs store data pertaining to resource usage for a specified time period. You can set begin and end times, or you can start and stop them manually. While Counter logs record the state of object counters at specific intervals of time that you set, Trace logs monitor a particular value continuously.

Based on the performance of resources on your computer, you must take certain actions to enhance the performance of your computer. For example, the most frequent cause of system bottlenecks is memory. There are several counters you can use to evaluate how much memory your system is using. The **Available Mbytes** counter calculates how much memory is left to run a process after all other running processes and the cache are taken care of. The **Pages/sec** counter measures the number of times the processor had to ask for data that was not in RAM (physical memory), but rather had been stored in the page file. The page file is a logical memory location on the root drive where the operating system was installed. If the page file is habitually being called upon, system delays are most likely already perceptible. The Paging file counter **%Usage** will tell you how much of the page file is currently being used. You can use these three counters to monitor the memory on your system and configure an **alert** to send you a message when the value is either under or over certain thresholds. For example, if the available megabytes of memory dips below 4 MB, the paging file usage is consistently more than 99 percent, or if you see frequent peaks over 20 being recorded by the Pages/Sec counter, it is probably time to add more memory to your system. The average number of times per second that the processor has to ask for data that is not in RAM should not exceed 5.

You can also automate actions to be performed when the value of a counter surpasses the threshold value for that particular counter, and you can configure an alert to monitor a particular counter at a scheduled time, or when you manually start the scan. You can configure alerts to perform the following actions:

◆ **Send a message:** Alerts can send messages to computers that are connected to the computer being monitored. For example, you can set up an alert on a computer on your network to send a message to your computer when the available disk space is less than a certain value.

◆ **Run a program:** Alerts can be programmed to run a program. For example, you can configure an alert to run a disk defragmenting program when the available disk space is below a certain limit.

◆ **Start a new log:** Alerts can be configured to create a new log to record events when the counter value is either under or over the threshold you have set. Starting a new log enables you to view events that occur after the alert has been triggered.

◆ **Create an entry in the Application log:** Alerts can create an entry in the Application log. The Application log records events that occur when an application is run. Logging an entry in the Application log enables you to determine the time when an alert was triggered.

You configure alerts by using the **Alert** dialog box in the **Performance** console.

**Figure 13-20  The Performance Logs and Alerts node**

Create a log file to record data from object counters at specific time intervals

Configure actions to be performed when the value of a counter surpasses the threshold value

Survey events that take place on the system and monitor a particular value continuously

**Figure 13-21  Creating a Trace log**

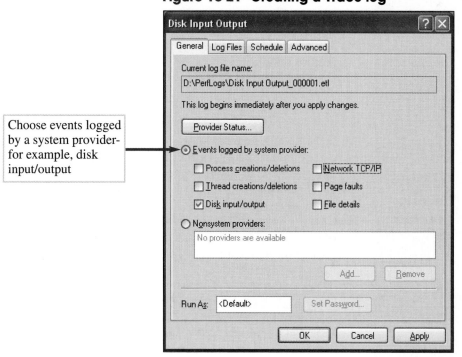

Choose events logged by a system provider—for example, disk input/output

# skill 5

## *Configuring Alerts (cont'd)*

**exam objective**

Monitor, optimize, and troubleshoot performance of the Windows XP Professional desktop. Optimize and troubleshoot memory performance.

**how to**

Create a counter log to evaluate how much memory your system is using at particular points in time, save it in the PerfLogs folder on the **C:** drive of your computer as a text file that has values separated by commas, set the log file size, manually start and stop the counter log so that you can monitor peak usage times, and configure an alert to send a message to another computer when the available memory falls below **4MB**, the **Pages/Sec exceeds 5**, or the **%Usage** of the page file reaches 99%.

1. Click <kbd>start</kbd> , point to **Administrative Tools**, and click the **Performance** command to open the **Performance** console.
2. Click the plus ➕ symbol next to the **Performance Logs and Alerts** node to display the **Counter Logs**, **Trace Logs**, and **Alerts** nodes.
3. Right-click the Counter Logs node and click **New Log Settings** to open the **New Log Settings** dialog box where you designate a name for the new log.
4. Type **Memory Log**, in the **Name** text box to name the new log.
5. Click <kbd>OK</kbd> to open the **Memory Log** dialog box.
6. Click <kbd>Add Counters...</kbd> to open the **Add Counters** dialog box.
7. In the **Performance object** list box, select **Memory**.
8. Make sure that the **Select counters from list** option button is selected. Hold down the **Ctrl** key and select the **Available Mbytes** and **Pages/sec** counters in the scrolling list box (**Figure 13-22**).
9. Click <kbd>Add</kbd> to add the selected counters to the counter log.
10. In the **Performance object** list box, select **Paging File**.
11. In the **Select counters from list** box, select, **%Usage** and click <kbd>Add</kbd> .
12. Click <kbd>Close</kbd> to close the Add Counters dialog box.
13. Enter the time interval at which you want the log to record the data from the selected counters. For example, type **30** in the **Interval** spin box at the bottom of the Memory Log dialog box.
14. Select the unit of the time interval from the **Units** list box. For example, select **minutes** (**Figure 13-23**).
15. Click the **Log Files** tab. Note that the default location for the log file is **%system-drive%\PerfLogs**.
16. In the **Log file type** list box, select **Text File - (Comma delimited)** to indicate that the log file should be a comma-separated text file.
17. In the **End file names with** list box, select **mmddhh** to append the month, day and hour of the day to the name of the log file. You can also append many other different date/time formats or a serial number to the name of the log file, or you can remove the check from the **End file names with** check box to save the counter log with no additional information (**Figure 13-24**).
18. Click <kbd>Configure...</kbd> to open the **Configure Log Files** dialog box. In the **Location** text box, you can change the default location for saving the log file. In the **File name** text box you can change the name for the log file.
19. In the **Log file size** section, you can select the **Limit of** option button and set a size limit in MB for the log file in the spin box (**Figure 13-25**).
20. Click <kbd>OK</kbd> to close the Configure Log Files dialog box.
21. If you accepted the default location and the **PerfLogs** folder has not yet been created, the Memory Log message box will prompt you to create it. Click **Yes**. Click the **Schedule** tab to access the options for scheduling the log file.
22. Select the **Manually (using the shortcut menu)** option button in the **Start log** section to indicate that you will manually start the log.

**Figure 13-22  Adding counters for
the Memory object**

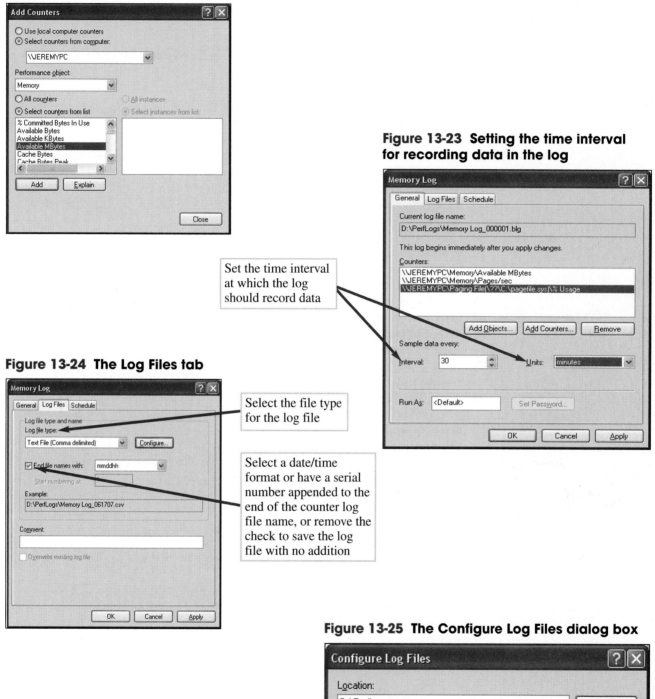

**Figure 13-23  Setting the time interval
for recording data in the log**

Set the time interval
at which the log
should record data

**Figure 13-24  The Log Files tab**

Select the file type
for the log file

Select a date/time
format or have a serial
number appended to the
end of the counter log
file name, or remove the
check to save the log
file with no addition

**Figure 13-25  The Configure Log Files dialog box**

Set a size limit for
the log file

# skill 5

## Configuring Alerts (cont'd)

**exam objective**

Monitor, optimize, and troubleshoot performance of the Windows XP Professional desktop. Optimize and troubleshoot memory performance.

**how to**

23. Click [ OK ] to save the configuration and close the Memory Log dialog box.
24. Right-click the Alerts node and click **New Alert Settings** to open the **New Alert Settings** dialog box.
25. Enter a name for the new alert in the **Name** text box. For example, type **Memory Alert**.
26. Click [ OK ] to open the **Memory Alert** dialog box.
27. In the **Comment** text box on the **General** tab of the Memory Alert dialog box, enter a message for the alert. The comment will be displayed in the Performance Logs and Alerts snap-in. For example, type: **You need to add memory**.
28. Click [ Add... ] to open the **Add Counters** dialog box.
29. In the **Performance object** list box, select **Memory**.
30. Make sure that the **Select counters from list** option button is selected. Hold down the **Ctrl** key and select the **Available Mbytes** and **Pages/sec** counters in the scrolling list box.
31. Click [ Add ] to add the selected counters to the alert.
32. In the **Performance object** list box, select **Paging File**.
33. In the **Select counters from list** box, select **%Usage**, and click [ Add ] to add the selected counter to the alert.
34. Click [ Close ] to close the Add Counters dialog box. The counters are added to the **Counters** list box on the General tab of the Memory Alert dialog box.
35. Select the **Memory\Available Mbytes** counter in the **Counters** list box. In the **Alert when value is** list box, select **Under**, if necessary. In the **Limit** text box, enter the threshold value **4 (Figure 13-26)**.
36. Select the **Memory\Pages/sec counter** in the **Counters** list box. In the **Alert when value is** list box, select **Over**. In the **Limit** text box, enter the threshold value **5**.
37. Select the **Paging File\%Usage** counter in the Counters list box. In the **Alert when value is** list box, select **Over**. In the **Limit** text box, enter the threshold value, **99**.
38. Click the **Action** tab to display the check boxes that you use to specify the action that the alert should perform.
39. Select the **Send a network message to** check box.
40. Enter the name of the computer to which you want the alert message sent. For example, type **\\Computer1 (Figure 13-27)**.
41. Click the **Schedule** tab to display the options for starting the alert scan.
42. Select the **Manually (using the shortcut menu)** option button to indicate that you will manually start monitoring. **Manually** should also be automatically selected in the **Stop scan** section.
43. Click [ OK ] to save the configuration and close the Memory Alert dialog box. To start the alert, right-click its name in the details pane of the Performance console and click **Start**.
44. Close the Performance console.

**Figure 13-26  Setting the threshold value for an alert**

Configure the alert to be triggered when the recorded value is either under or over the threshold value

Set the threshold value for the counter

**Figure 13-27  The Action tab**

Selected by default to automatically create an entry in the Application log when the alert is triggered

Select to send a message to another network computer when the alert is triggered

Select to program the alert to start a new log when the alert is triggered

Select to program the alert to run a program when the alert is triggered

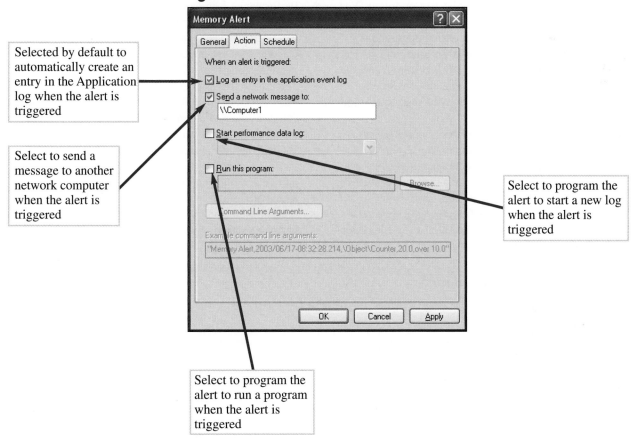

# Summary

- Auditing is used to track user activities and object access on the computers on a network. It must be set up for each computer.
- Auditing is used to help prevent security breaches by allowing you to track unauthorized attempts to log on or access folders.
- It is also used to help conduct resource planning for the computers on your network.
- When you define an audit policy, you select the events you want to track and whether to track the success or failure, or both, for the event.
- Events are activities such as logging on to a computer or a network, and accessing files, folders, printers, and the Registry.
- The success and failure of events that occur on a computer are recorded in the Security log. You use the Event Viewer to view the Security log.
- You can only audit access to files and folders on NTFS disks.
- In order to audit access to files and folders, you must first activate object access auditing on the computer on which the resource is stored. Then, you must choose which files and folders you want the operating system to track.
- Next, you select the users whose actions you want to audit and what file system actions you want to monitor in the System ACL editor for the file or folder. For example, you can audit who is viewing a folder, creating a file, changing permissions, or viewing permissions.
- Auditing increases the overhead on a computer. The CPU will be frequently reading file systems, and the Security event log can become inundated with entries, which can cause problems with both disk space and performance.
- You can control the size of the Security log by specifying a maximum file size in the Event Viewer. When the Security log reaches the maximum file size, you can choose to either overwrite old events as needed, set a specific age for the events you want to be overwritten, or prevent events from being overwritten.
- The Event Viewer is also used to archive old log files and store them for future reference.

- You monitor the resources on your computer, either to establish a baseline or to diagnose a bottleneck, in the Performance console.
- First, you must determine what the normal operating parameters for the computer are. This is referred to as establishing a baseline or benchmarking the system and is used to ascertain the level of performance you have during normal usage and under typical workloads.
- The idea is to get a reliable range of values against which future performance can be compared. As a general rule, baselines should be established for all of the important servers on the network.
- A bottleneck refers to any resource, such as memory or disk space, which causes other resources to delay while it completes its assigned function.
- The Performance console consists of System Monitor and the Performance Logs and Alerts tools.
- The System Monitor displays the performance of your computer based on objects and counters that you configure.
- An object is a system resource, such as a processor, disk, network interface, or memory, whose performance you can monitor.
- Counters are performance measures for an object that can be quantified such as the percentage of time the processor is busy (%Processor Time).
- Performance Logs and Alerts are used to store system performance data for future reference. You can create two types of logs: Counter logs and Trace logs.
- Counter logs use the GUI data from the System Monitor to create a log file.
- Trace logs survey events that take place on the system. They do not track performance data, so you do not select counters when you configure them. Instead, you choose the events logged by a system provider.
- While Counter logs record the state of object counters at specific intervals of time that you set, Trace logs monitor particular value continuously.
- Alerts are used to inform you when a counter has either gone above or below a threshold that you have set, or to perform actions when a threshold value has been crossed.

# Key Terms

| | | |
|---|---|---|
| Alert | Bottleneck | Performance Logs and Alerts |
| Application log | Counter | Security event log |
| Audit object access audit policy | Counter log | System log |
| Audit policy | Event Viewer | System Monitor |
| Auditing | Object | Trace log |

# Test Yourself

**1.** Which one of the following options is a benefit of Auditing?
  a. Runs programs based on the performance of a computer.
  b. Helps prevent security breaches on computers.
  c. Decreases the overhead on a computer.
  d. Records events in the System log.

**2.** Which one of the following actions is audited using the Audit system events audit policy?
  a. Logging on to a computer.
  b. Accessing a printer.
  c. Sending a logon request to a domain controller.
  d. Shutting down a computer.

**3.** You are setting up auditing for a folder on your computer. The audit policy that you select in the Local Security Settings dialog box is:
  a. System events.
  b. Process tracking.
  c. Privilege use.
  d. Object access.

**4.** Which one of the following statements is true about auditing access to files and folders on a computer?
  a. You can select the users to be audited.
  b. The file or folder must be on a FAT drive.
  c. Auditing for privilege use events should be enabled.
  d. You set up auditing for a folder using the Event Viewer.

**5.** The Security event log records events:
  a. Such as the failure of a driver or other system component to load.
  b. For which an audit policy has been configured.
  c. That are generated by Windows XP Professional.
  d. As information, warnings, or errors.

**6.** The Security log of your computer is occupying a large amount of disk space. You want to reduce disk space usage, but you also want to save old events in the log for future reference. Which one of the following actions do you need to perform?
  a. Create a Counter log to record audited events.
  b. Archive the Security log.
  c. Reduce the size of the Security log and archive old events.
  d. Configure the Security log to overwrite events older than 1 day.

**7.** You need to monitor the memory utilization of your computer. To do so, you will use the:
  a. Event Viewer.
  b. Performance console.
  c. Local Security Policy window.
  d. Security log.

**8.** Counters are:
  a. System resources.
  b. Resources that slow down a computer.
  c. Performance measures for an object.
  d. Logs that record data continuously.

**9.** Which one of the following logs records data on the performance of a computer at specific intervals of time?
  a. Security log
  b. Application log
  c. Counter log
  d. Trace log

**10.** You can configure alerts using the:
  a. Event Viewer.
  b. Event Properties dialog box.
  c. Local Security Settings window.
  d. Performance console.

# Projects: On Your Own

**1.** Enable auditing for a folder named **Pictures** on the **D:** drive of your computer. Log an event each time users in the Administrators group create a file in **Pictures**.
  a. Log on as an **Administrator**.
  b. Open the **Local Security Settings** console.
  c. Open the **Audit object access Properties** dialog box.
  d. Select the **Success** check box.
  e. Open **Windows Explorer**.
  f. Open the **Pictures Properties** dialog box.
  g. Click the **Security** tab.
  h. Click **Advanced**.
  i. Click the **Auditing** tab.
  j. Click **Add**.
  k. In the **Enter the object name to select** text box , type the name of the user or group for which you want to enable auditing. For example, type **Administrators**.
  l. Click **OK**.
  m. Select the **Successful** check box next to the **Create Files/ Write Data** option.
  n. Click **OK** to close the Advanced Security Settings for Pictures dialog box.
  o. Close the **Pictures Properties** dialog box.

**2.** Set the maximum size of the Security log on your computer to **320 KB** and program the log to overwrite events that are more than **4** days old.

   a. Open **Event Viewer**.

   b. Right-click **Security** in the left pane of the **Event Viewer** window and select **Properties**.

   c. Type **320** to indicate the maximum size for the log file in the **Maximum log size** text box.

   d. The **Overwrite events older than** option button is selected by default. Indicate the number of days after which the events should be overwritten if the log reaches its maximum size. For example, type **4** in the **Overwrite events older than** text box.

   e. Click **OK** to save the settings and close the **Security Properties** dialog box.

   f. When you are warned that you must clear the log in order for the new settings to take effect, click **OK**.

   g. Clear all events in the log without saving them and close the Event Viewer.

## Problem Solving Scenarios

1. As Network Administrator for Turco's Food Emporium, a regional food distributor in Bedford, New Jersey, you manage a Windows network for 150 employees in a single location. There are many confidential corporate files on the network. You are particularly concerned about files stored in a shared directory on the Financial Manager's machine (the Finance sub-directory). In fact, the Financial Manager has asked you to take steps to secure files in the Finance sub-directory, to audit access to this directory, and to keep track of who is using the files. Outline, in a report, the steps you will take to achieve these objectives.

2. When discussing security issues with the Financial Manager of Turco's Food Emporium, you discover that her computer is not performing well. It seems to be very slow at accessing files and even slower at launching programs. Outline in a brief memo the steps you will take to continuously monitor her computer for one week to try to determine the cause of the problem. What counters will you use?

# 14 Backing Up and Restoring Data

You have carefully planned your network, created user accounts and assigned those users to specific groups, created shared folders, assigned permissions, and set password and account lockout policies. Auditing has been configured to monitor unsuccessful events that could indicate possible security breaches and successful events that will help you to evaluate the capacity and overall functioning of your system. You have encrypted sensitive files and assigned recovery agents so that encrypted data will always be recoverable. IPSec policies have been configured to protect data that is sent over the network and security options have been set to further protect the computers on your network from unauthorized user access and viruses. You are monitoring important system performance measures so that you can anticipate bottlenecks and you have configured alerts to warn you when these resources are either under or over certain thresholds. But what if your system fails? What will you do if a disk drive crashes, or if a virus or power outage wipes out all of the data on the hard drive of one of your computers? How will you recover the operating system and all of that data you have so carefully safeguarded?

There are several tools and utilities that are used to protect your data in the event of such a catastrophe, starting with Windows Backup. The Backup Utility consists of the Backup Wizard, the Restore Wizard, and the Automated System Recovery Wizard. You use the Backup Wizard to create copies of vital enterprise data that are either stored in a backup file on a different hard disk, a Zip or Jaz drive, or other removable storage media such as magnetic tape. If data is lost or damaged, you can use the Restore Wizard to recover it from the backup copies. You must also back up all system files, the startup environment files, the partition boot sector, and the Registry because they can also be accidentally deleted or become corrupt. The Automated System Recovery disk will be used to back up these files so that you can rebuild your system if the system files become corrupt, or the operating system will not start.

Before making backups, you should create a backup plan so that you can retrieve lost data quickly and efficiently. First, you must identify the data that needs to be backed up and the medium you are going to use. Then, you must decide upon a backup schedule and a backup type. Backup types differ depending on how the *archive attribute or backup marker* (also called the archive bit) is treated. The archive attribute is set on a file when it has changed. Some backup types will remove the archive bit when the file has been backed up, while others will ignore it. You must also decide whether to perform network or local backup jobs.

# Goals

In this lesson, you will learn to plan for data backup, decide on the type of backup, and perform the backup operation using the Backup Wizard. You will learn about the different types of backups, as well as how to use them to develop a comprehensive backup and restore strategy. You will also learn to restore data and create an Automated System Recovery disk.

## Lesson 14  Backing Up and Restoring Data

| Skill | Exam 70-270 Objective |
| --- | --- |
| 1. Planning Data Backups | Restore and back up the operating system, System State data, and user data. Recover System State data and user data using Windows Backup. |
| 2. Introducing Backup Types | Restore and back up the operating system, System State data, and user data. Recover System State data and user data using Windows Backup. |
| 3. Backing Up Data | Restore and back up the operating system, System State data, and user data. Recover System State data and user data using Windows Backup. |
| 4. Restoring Data from a Backup | Restore and back up the operating system, System State data, and user data. Recover System State data and user data using Windows Backup. |
| 5. Changing the Default Backup and Restore Options | Restore and back up the operating system, System State data, and user data. |
| 6. Performing an Automated System Recovery Backup | Restore and back up the operating system, System State data, and user data. |

# Requirements

To complete this lesson, you will need a computer running Windows XP Professional that is connected to a network. You will need administrative permissions and a folder named accounts on the C: drive.

# skill 1

## *Planning Data Backups*

**exam objective**

Restore and back up the operating system, System State data, and user data. Recover System State data and user data using Windows Backup.

## overview

Since data can be the most important asset of an organization, you must make sure that it is protected from losses due to viruses, disk drive failures, or user deletion. You can safeguard data by creating copies, or **backups**, of the files and folders on client computers, or on servers on the network. Lost or damaged data can be retrieved if you have conscientiously designed and implemented a comprehensive backup plan.

You can back up files and folders, as well as an entire disk; however, first you must decide what data must be backed up and how frequently it will be backed up. Usually data that is essential to the operation of an organization, such as financial statements and sales reports, should be backed up daily. Employee records should be backed up whenever they are modified. If reports are created on a weekly, monthly, or quarterly basis, and do not change during the interim, they can be backed up accordingly. Data on individual client systems should be backed up regularly or as often as the files are changed.

**tip**

You must make sure that your storage media device is listed in the Windows XP Hardware Compatibility List.

Next, you must decide on the media that you will use. You can back up files to Zip or Jaz drives, to magnetic tape or to the hard drive on a remote file server using the Windows Backup Utility. Magnetic tape has been the most widely used backup medium because it is inexpensive and you can store large amounts of data on it; however, tape can deteriorate over time.

You must also decide whether to implement a network backup or a local backup. When you perform a **network backup**, you can combine essential data from multiple computers on a single disk or tape. This is obviously the most efficient method for Administrators because they will not have to physically visit each client computer and server, possibly dragging the removable storage device with them. **Local backups** can work on small networks where an organizational policy is in effect that requires users to back up their own data on a regular schedule. However, unless you are going to circulate the storage device, each client will need its own Zip, Jaz, or tape drive, and this cost can be prohibitive. You can also adopt a hybrid method that combines both network and local backups. Users can backup data on the local hard drive of their PCs to a network file server, and the Administrator can backup the network drive on the file server locally with a removable storage device.

## more

In order to back up data, you must have the appropriate user rights. Any user can back up files and folders that they have created (files they own), as well as files for which they have the **Read**, **Read and Execute**, **Modify**, or **Full Control** permission. Local **Administrators** and **Backup Operators** can backup any file or folder on the local computer. Domain Administrators and Backup Operators can backup any file or folder in the domain because they are granted the **Back up files and directories** user right by default. They can also perform backups in other trusting domains, as long as they have been granted administrative rights in those domains.

Similarly, to restore a backed up file or folder, you must have the appropriate user rights and permissions. File or folder owners can restore the backup copy. Other users can restore files or folders if they have the **Write**, **Modify**, or **Full Control** permission. Members of the local Administrators and Backup Operators groups can restore any file or folder on the local computer. Administrators and Backup Operators on the domain controller have the **Restore files and directories** user right by default and can restore any backup file or folder on the domain.

**Figure 14-1  The Backup Utility**

**Figure 14-2  Planning backups**

# skill 2

## *Introducing Backup Types*

### exam objective

Restore and back up the operating system, System State data, and user data. Recover System State data and user data using Windows Backup.

### overview

There are five different backup types from which you can choose either in the Backup Wizard or on the Backup Type tab in the Options dialog box. In order to choose one of these types, first you must understand what the **archive attribute** or **archive bit** is and how each backup type handles it. The archive attribute is a property for files and folders that is used to identify them when they have changed. When a file has changed, the **Archive** attribute is automatically selected on the **General** tab in the **Properties** dialog box on a FAT32 partition **(Figure 14-3)**. On an NTFS partition, the Archive attribute can be found in the Advanced Attributes dialog box **(Figure 14-4)**. Some backup types remove the archive attribute to mark files as having been backed up, while others do not. For example, in a **Normal backup** the archive attribute is removed to denote that the file has been backed up; however, in a **Copy backup**, the archive attribute is not removed to mark files as having been backed up. Copy backups are used between Normal and Incremental or Normal and Differential backups (discussed below) so that when they take place, the process will not be affected by the removal of the archive bit.

The archive attribute is used by some types of backups and not by others. Sometimes it is used to identify files that need to be backed up, sometimes it is removed to denote that a file has been backed up, and sometimes it is ignored. For example, in a Normal backup, all selected files and folders are backed up whether they have the archive attribute or not; however, as noted above, the attribute is then removed from any files on which it has been set. Copy backups do not use the archive attribute. All selected files and folders with or without the archive attribute are backed up and, as noted above, the archive bit is not removed. The Copy backup type essentially "ignores" the archive attribute, creating a representation of your data at a particular point in time.

### tip

The archive attribute is also known as a backup marker.

**Figure 14-3  The Archive attribute**

On an NTFS partition, click the Advanced button on the General tab in the Properties dialog box for a file or folder to access the archive attribute

This will be selected when a file has changed

**Figure 14-4  The Advanced Attributes dialog box**

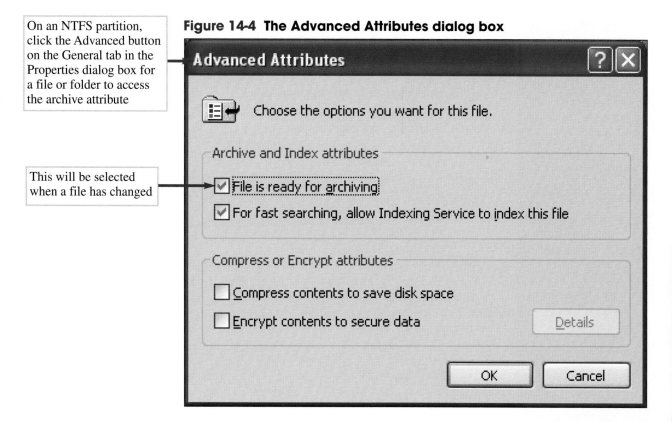

# skill 2

# *Introducing Backup Types (cont'd)*

**exam objective**

Restore and back up the operating system, System State data, and user data. Recover System State data and user data using Windows Backup.

**overview**

An **Incremental backup** backs up only the selected files and folders that have the archive attribute, which is then removed. Thus, if a file has not changed since the previous backup, it will be skipped during the next Incremental backup. A **Differential backup**, on the other hand, backs up only selected files and folders with the archive attribute, which is not removed. Therefore, even if a file has not changed since the previous Differential backup, it will be backed up again because it still has the archive attribute. A **Daily backup** is used to back up all selected files and folders that have changed on that day, but the archive bit is not removed. The different types of backup and their characteristics are explained in **Table 14-1**.

**more**

Organizations use a blend of the different backup types in order to optimize the time spent on both the backup and the restore processes. For example, a Normal backup will take longer than an Incremental backup because all selected files are backed up whether they have the archive attribute or not. However, with a Normal backup you can quickly restore all of your files using the most recent copy of the backup file or tape. On the other hand, if you used only Incremental backups you would not be able to recover all of your data. Since an Incremental backup only backs up files and folders with the archive attribute, you would not be starting with a full set of files. Furthermore, you would have to restore a whole series of backup tapes in order to recapture all of your files because each backup would only include changed files. Therefore, although the backup process would be quick, the restore process would be unwieldy, if not impossible.

For these reasons, you should use a combination of Normal and other backup types to effectively manage your backup and restore times, and ensure that all lost data can be recovered. For example, if you create a backup schedule that uses a combination of the Normal and Differential backup types, you will only have to restore the last Normal backup and the last Differential backup. On the other hand, if you use a combination of Normal and Incremental backups, you will have to restore the last Normal backup and all Incremental backups in the interim. A Normal/Incremental strategy will take less time to back up files because each Incremental backup will only capture changed files, whereas each Differential backup will capture all files that have changed since the last Normal backup. However, a Normal/Incremental strategy will take more time to restore files.

### Table 14-1   Backup Types

| Backup Type | Criteria for Backing Up Files | Archive Attribute |
| --- | --- | --- |
| Normal | All selected files/folders are backed up whether they have the Archive attribute or not. | Archive attribute is removed. |
| Differential | Only the selected files/folders with the Archive attribute are backed up. | Archive attribute is not removed. |
| Incremental | Only the selected files/folders with the Archive attribute are backed up. | Archive attribute is removed. |
| Copy | All selected files/folders are backed up whether they have the Archive attribute or not. | Archive attribute is not removed. |
| Daily | All selected files/folders that have been modified that day are backed up. | Archive attribute is not removed. |

# skill 3

# *Backing Up Data*

## exam objective

Restore and back up the operating system, System State data, and user data. Recover System State data and user data using Windows Backup.

## overview

Once you have planned your backup strategy and decided which backup types to perform at what time intervals, you can use the **Backup Wizard** to configure your backup schedule. You can also manually set backup jobs on the Backup tab. First, you must decide which files to back up. You can either back up all the files and folders on your computer or only specific files and folders. You can also back up the **System State**, which includes such files as the **Registry**, **Ntdlr**, **Ntdetect**, and **boot.ini** files, so that you can restore the operating system to its original state and boot the operating system in the event of a system failure. A System State restore would be performed on a clean installation of the operating system to recover all of the configuration changes.

System State backups should be part of the backup process when any affected system component, such as the Registry, has changed, which can happen quite frequently. When you perform a System State backup, you are backing up the Windows XP Professional boot files, the system files on the boot partition, the Component Service Class Registration (COM+) database, and the Registry. Backing up the System State is a crucial task for the servers on the network. If the server is a certificate server, the Certificate Services database will also be included in a System State backup, and if the server is a domain controller, the SYSVOL directory will be backed up. When you perform a System State backup, you backup all essential boot files, the Registry entries, the COM+ class registrations, and all protected system files (those safeguarded with Windows File Protection (WFP)). A System State restore is performed after you solve a hardware problem on a workstation and restore the user data so that you can rejoin a domain smoothly with all of the computer account settings and system settings in place.

User data, of course, constitutes any files saved by users on the system. It can include database, spreadsheet, word processing, graphics or any other types of files that users do not want to lose. When you perform backups, you must decide whether you are going to backup user data, System State data, or both. Next, you must choose the media you are going to use and the location where you are going to store the data. Finally, you can either start the backup or select advanced backup settings.

## how to

Back up the Accounts folder on the floppy drive of your computer.

1. Log on to your Windows XP Professional computer as an **Administrator**. Insert a floppy disk in the floppy disk drive.
2. Click **start**, click **All Programs**, point to **Accessories**, point to **System Tools**, and click **Backup** to open the **Backup or Restore** Wizard (**Figure 14-5**).
3. Click **Next >** to open the **Backup or Restore** screen. Select the **Backup files and settings** option button, if necessary.
4. Click **Next >** to open the **What to Back Up** screen. The **My documents and settings** option button is selected by default. This selection will backup the My Documents folder, Favorites, desktop, and cookies. You can also back up everyone's documents and settings, or all data on the computer. Select the **Let me choose what to back up** option button (**Figure 14-6**).
5. Click **Next >** to open the **Items to Back Up** screen. Double-click **My Computer** and expand the **C:** drive to select the required folder. Select the check box to the left of the **Accounts** folder (**Figure 14-7**).
6. Click **Next >** to open the **Backup Type**, **Destination**, and **Name** screen. In the **Choose a place to save your backup** list box, select **3 ½ Floppy (A:)**. In the Type a name for this backup list box, type: **Accounts (Figure 14-8)**.
7. Click **Next >** to open the **Completing the Backup or Restore Wizard** screen. The backup settings you have chosen are displayed.

**Figure 14-5 The Backup or Restore Wizard**

**Figure 14-6 The What to Back Up screen**

Select to backup all user data on the computer, as well as to create a system recovery disk

**Figure 14-7 The Items to Back Up screen**

Select the files and folders that you want to back up

**Figure 14-8 The Backup Type, Destination, and Name screen**

Click to save the backup to a hard disk or to a network location

# skill 3

## Backing Up Data (cont'd)

### exam objective

Restore and back up the operating system, System State data, and user data. Recover System State data and user data using Windows Backup.

### how to

8.  Click [ Advanced... ] to open the **Type of Backup** screen. A **Normal** backup is performed by default. Remember that in a Normal backup, all selected files and folders are backed up whether they have the Archive attribute or not and the Archive attribute is removed. Click the list arrow and review the four other backup types (**Figure 14-9**).

9.  Keep Normal as the backup type, and click [ Next > ] to open the **How to Back Up** screen. Select the **Verify data after backup** option button to verify the integrity of the backed up data after the backup process is complete. The default backup in Windows XP creates a volume shadow copy. A **volume shadow** enables you to create shadow backup copies of all files, including those that are open (**Figure 14-10**).

10. Click [ Next > ] to open the **Backup Options** screen. If the backup medium you are using already contains backups, you can choose to either append this backup to the existing backups or to replace the existing backups. If you replace the existing backups, you can also allow only the file owners and the Administrator to access the backup medium, or any backups appended to the medium. Keep the default selection, **Append this backup to the existing backups**.

11. Click [ Next > ] to open the **When to Backup** screen. You can either perform the backup operation immediately or schedule the backup for a later time. Leave the default selection, **Now**.

12. Click [ Next > ] to open the **Completing the Backup or Restore Wizard** screen.

13. Click [ Finish ] to begin the backup process. The **Backup Progress** dialog box opens (**Figure 14-11**).

14. Click [ Report... ] to open the backup log in Notepad (**Figure 14-12**).

15. Close the backup log file, and click [ Close ] to close the Backup Progress dialog box.

### more

The default volume shadow copy backup mode in Windows XP enables you to create exact copies at a particular point in time of all files, including those that are open. In previous versions of Windows this was not the case. Open files would be excluded from the backup process. Because of this new feature, applications can now be writing data to a volume or partition during the backup process, and open files are no longer skipped. This also means that backups can be performed at any time, and users need not be locked out during the process. The way this works is that a duplicate of the volume that is being backed up is immediately created using **Volume Shadow Copy Technology (VSCT)**. The Backup utility then backs up the selected files and folders from the shadow copy rather than from the original. Data that is being written to the volume after the shadow copy is created is not included in the backup. The Backup Utility "sees" these open files as closed because it is viewing the shadow copy, and open files are halted at a fixed point in time when the shadow copy is created.

If you select the **Later** option on the **When to Back Up** screen you can schedule unattended backups to run after working hours. You can also name the backup job, set the start date, and click the Set Schedule button to schedule your backup jobs for different days of the week, or you can schedule them to occur weekly, monthly, or at system startup. On the **How to Back Up** screen, you can select the **Use hardware compression, if available** option button to increase the available data storage space on a tape device. If the tape device supports hardware compression, the option is available; otherwise, it is not. The **Allow only the owner and the Administrator access to the backup data and to any backups appended to this medium** option on the **Backup Options** screen is used to control access to the backup file or tape. You can use this option only when you are replacing an existing backup on a backup medium. It is not available if you are appending data to the existing backup. It is particularly useful when you are backing up the Registry or Active Directory so that other users cannot access the files.

### tip

Volume shadow copy mode is only available on NTFS volumes. There must be enough available free disk space on any of the local NTFS volumes for the shadow copy. If there is not sufficient space on one of the local volumes, the shadow copy will not be created.

**Figure 14-9 The Type of Backup screen**

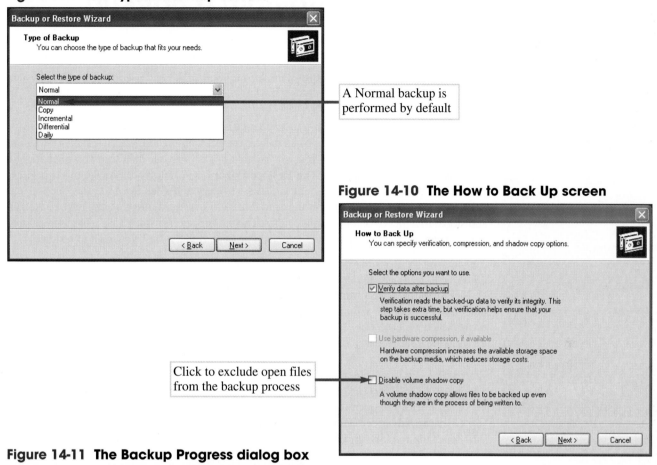

**Figure 14-10 The How to Back Up screen**

**Figure 14-11 The Backup Progress dialog box**

**Figure 14-12 A backup log file**

# skill 4

# *Restoring Data from a Backup*

## exam objective

Restore and back up the operating system, System State data, and user data. Recover System State data and user data using Windows Backup.

## overview

In the event of a hard disk crash, the accidental erasure of data, or damage due to a virus, you will need to restore your backed up data. Experts recommend that you test the restoration process regularly to ensure that you will be able to restore your data to its original state in the event of such a catastrophe. The **Restore Wizard** will help you to make this a painless procedure. You can restore individual drives, folders and files, or an entire backup set. A **backup set** is the compilation of files and folders from one volume that you have backed up and stored in a file, or on one or more tapes. The backup set is displayed as a hierarchical tree that you can use to open drives and folders in order to find the files you want to restore.

You can use the Restore Wizard, or you can manually restore files and folders without using the Wizard. Files and folders that were backed up from an NTFS volume must be restored to an NTFS volume if you want to retain the original NTFS security permissions. If you restore data from an NTFS volume to a FAT or FAT32 volume, any encrypted files will be unencrypted because only NTFS volumes support EFS. Likewise, any disk quota, mounted drive, or Remote Storage configuration settings will be lost.

## how to

Restore the Accounts folder backup.
1. Click **start**, click **All Programs**, point to **Accessories**, point to **System Tools**, and click **Backup** to open the **Backup or Restore Wizard**.
2. Click the **Advanced Mode** link to open the Backup Utility.
3. Select the **Restore and Manage Media** tab. Expand the **File** node in the left pane of the window.
4. Locate and expand the Accounts.bkf backup set. Expand the C: directory and select the Accounts folder (**Figure 14-13**).
5. Use the **Restore files to** list box at the bottom of the window if you are going to restore the folder to a location other than the original location. By default, files and folders will be restored to their original location.
6. Click **Start Restore** to open the **Confirm Restore** message box (**Figure 14-14**). Click **Advanced...** to open the **Advanced Restore Options** dialog box. By default, the **Restore Security**, **Restore junction points, and restore file and folder data under junction points to the original location**, and **Preserve existing volume mount points** option buttons are selected (**Figure 14-15**).
7. Click **OK** to accept the defaults and close the Advanced Restore Options dialog box.
8. Click **OK** to close the Confirm Restore dialog box and start the restore.
9. The Restore Progress dialog box opens (**Figure 14-16**). When the process is complete, click **Report...** to open the backup and restore log in Notepad (**Figure 14-17**).
10. Close the report, the Restore Progress dialog box, and the Backup Utility.

## more

You cannot backup and restore directly to and from a CD-R or CD-RW drive using Windows XP. You must first back up to a file, and then you can copy the .bkf file to a writeable CD. This is due to the mechanics of the process of writing in an uninterrupted flow to a writeable CD.

When you choose to restore a backup set to an alternate location, the directory structure of the backed-up files and folders is preserved in the alternate folder. You use an alternate location when you need some of the files, but you do not want to overwrite or change any of the current files or folders on your disk.

**Figure 14-13  The Restore and Manage Media tab in the Backup Utility**

Used to select an alternate location for the restore, or to restore the backup set to a single folder

**Figure 14-14  The Confirm Restore message box**

Confirm Restore

To set advanced options for restoring your data, click Advanced.

To start restoring your data now, click OK.

OK    Cancel    Advanced...

Click to open the Advanced Restore Options dialog box

**Figure 14-15  The Advanced Restore Options dialog box**

Select to restore the security permissions set on the original files

**Figure 14-16  The Restore Progress window**

Restore Progress

Cancel

Drive:
Label:
Status:  Creating System Restore checkpoint...
Progress:
Elapsed:
Time:
Processing:
Processed:
Files:  0
Bytes:  0

**Figure 14-17  A backup/restore log**

The backup/restore log shows the number of files that have been backed up and restored, the duration of the restore process, the total size of the backed up and restored files, and the start and end time for the operations

# skill 5

## Changing the Default Backup and Restore Options

### exam objective

Restore and back up the operating system, System State data, and user data.

### overview

You can change the default settings for all backup and restore operations in the **Options** dialog box for the Backup Utility. The tabs in the dialog box are listed below:

♦ **General:** On this tab, you can change the default status information for the backup and restore processes, as well as send alert messages, verify data, and list the items being backed up by default. The **Compute selection information before backup and restore operations** option estimates the number of files and bytes being backed up, and displays this information before the backup or restore begins. The **Verify data after the backup completes** option checks the backed-up data and the original data on your hard disk to make sure they are identical. If the data does not match, it indicates a problem with either the media or the file you are using to back up the data. Therefore, you will need to use a different media, or another file, and run the backup again. If you back up data often on a mounted drive, you should select the **Back up the contents of mounted drives** option to make sure that the data, and not just the path information for the mounted drive, are backed up.

♦ The **Show alert message when I start the Backup utility and Removable Storage is not running** option is used when your main backup medium is tape or other media that you use Removable Storage to manage. If you primarily use some kind of removable disk or if you back up data to a file or a hard disk, you do not need to select this option.

♦ **Restore:** On this tab, you can specify the default setting for how to replace existing files with restored files.

♦ **Backup Type:** On this tab, you can change the default backup type that will be chosen in the Backup Wizard.

♦ **Backup Log:** Here you can specify the amount of information that you want to include by default in the backup log.

♦ **Exclude Files:** Here you can specify the files that you want to exclude from the backup process by default. You can exclude a type of file for a specific user, or all users, for security purposes.

### how to

Change default backup options.

1. Click **start**, click **All Programs**, point to **Accessories**, point to **System Tools**, and click **Backup** to open the **Backup or Restore Wizard**.
2. Click the **Advanced Mode** link to open the Backup Utility.
3. Open the **Tools** menu and click the **Options** command to open the **Options** dialog box.
4. On the **General** tab **(Figure 14-18)**, select the **Verify data after backup completes** check box.
5. Click the **Backup Type** tab **(Figure 14-19)**.
6. In the **Default Backup Type** list box, select **Differential** to change the default backup type.
7. Click **OK** to accept the changes and close the Options dialog box.
8. Close the Backup Utility.

### more

The **Tools** menu in the **Backup** window also contains the **Backup Wizard**, **Restore Wizard**, and the **ASR Wizard** commands. These commands will open the **Backup/Restore Wizard** or the **Automated System Recovery Preparation Wizard**. From here, you can proceed to create a backup, restore a backup, or attempt to bring your Windows XP system back to a stable condition, depending on which of the commands you choose.

**Figure 14-18  The General tab in the Options dialog box for the Backup Utility**

Verifies that the backed-up data and the original data on your hard disk are the same

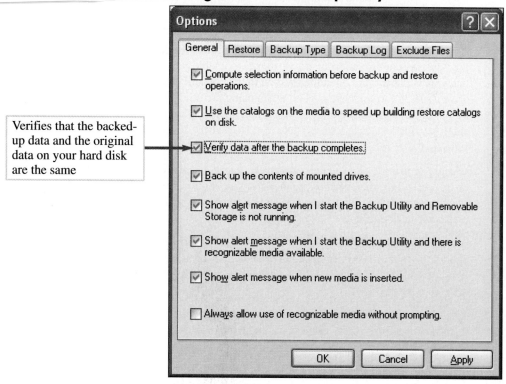

**Figure 14-19  The Backup Type tab**

Used to specify the amount of information to include in the backup/restore log

Used to specify the file types to exclude from the backup process and for which users

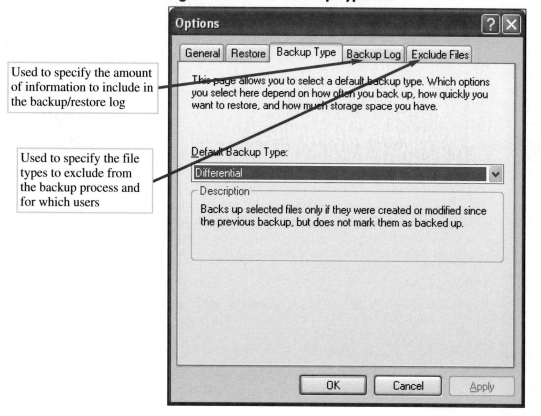

# skill 6

## *Performing an Automated System Recovery Backup*

### exam objective

Restore and back up the operating system, System State data, and user data.

### overview

A new feature in Windows XP is **Automated System Recovery (ASR)**. ASR is a backup of your system configuration that is designed to enable you to repair your system partition so that you can restart the operating system in the event of a complete malfunction due to a hard drive issue or corrupt system files. When using the other system recovery tools, such as Safe Mode, the Last Known Good Configuration, and the Recovery console are not possible, you can use ASR as a last resort. You can also first try to use the System Restore feature in Windows XP Professional, which is discussed in the next lesson.

When you use the Automated System Recovery Wizard, the configuration of your system drive is saved to whatever backup medium you choose. When ASR is applied, it formats the system drive. All user data on the system partition will be lost, and you will have to restore all user data, as well as all system partition data.

An ASR backup should be performed immediately following the successful installation of the operating system. The backup should then be updated whenever you modify the system configuration such as when you add a new device driver or use Windows Update to install a patch or service pack.

To perform an ASR backup, you will need one floppy disk and a backup storage medium that is sufficient in size to store the operating system files, configuration settings, and System State data.

To perform an ASR restore, you will need the bootable Windows XP Professional CD-ROM or the bootable floppy disk set, the most recent copy of the ASR backup, which is generally saved on tape or another removable storage medium, and the most recent ASR backup media set.

The ASR floppy cannot be used to boot a Windows XP system, but if you can boot the computer using the installation CD-ROM or the setup floppies, you can use the ASR floppy and the ASR backup set to repair the system partition. To create the bootable setup floppies, you must download the necessary files from www.microsoft.com/xp. Six disks are needed to create the set.

### how to

Perform an ASR backup.

1. Click **start**, click **All Programs**, point to **Accessories**, point to **System Tools**, and click **Backup** to open the **Backup or Restore Wizard**.
2. Click the **Advanced Mode** link to open the Backup Utility.
3. Click the **Automated System Recovery Wizard** button to start the Automated System Recovery Preparation Wizard **(Figure 14-20)**.
4. Click **Next >** to open the **Backup Destination** screen. Enter the path to the backup media and a name for the backup in the **Backup media or file name** text box **(Figure 14-21)**. Alternatively, you can click **Browse** and navigate to the removable storage drive on which you are going to save the backup of your system files, and name and save the file in the **Save As** dialog box.

**Figure 14-20  The Automated System Recovery Preparation Wizard**

**Figure 14-21  The Backup Destination screen**

# skill 6

## *Performing an Automated System Recovery Backup (cont'd)*

### exam objective

Restore and back up the operating system, System State data, and user data.

### how to

5. Click [ Next > ] to open the **Completing the Automated System Recovery Preparation Wizard** screen.
6. Click [ Finish ] to create a backup of your system files. The **Backup Progress** dialog box will open. Next, the **Selection Information** message box will open and show you the file and byte estimates **(Figure 14-22)**.
7. The entire process can take quite some time. When it is complete, you will be prompted to insert a floppy disk to create the ASR floppy disk.
8. The backup set and the floppy disk together will be used to restore your system in the event of a complete system failure.

### more

ASR replaces the Emergency Repair Diskette (ERD) that was used in Windows 2000 to perform the emergency repair process.

ASR is not available in Windows XP Home edition because that operating system does not support setups from the ASR disks. The option is available in the Backup Utility, but the disk will not be able to be used to recover the system.

**Figure 14-22  The Selection Information message box**

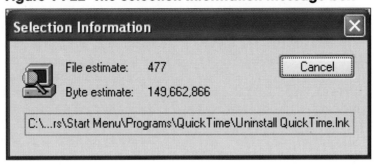

# Summary

- You use the Backup Wizard to create copies of vital enterprise data that are either stored in a backup file on a different hard disk, a Zip or Jaz drive, or magnetic tape.

- Regular data backups ensure that a copy of the data is always present to replace the original damaged or lost data.

- The Backup Wizard in Windows XP Professional can be used to back up data immediately or to schedule unattended data backups at regular intervals.

- There are five backup types from which you can choose: Normal, Copy, Incremental, Differential, and Daily.

- The archive attribute is a property for files and folders that is used to identify when they have changed. When a file has changed, the Archive attribute is automatically selected on the General tab in the Properties dialog box for a file on a FAT32 partition, or in the Advanced Attributes dialog box for a file on an NTFS partition or volume.

- The archive attribute is used by some types of backups and not by others. Sometimes it is used to identify files that need to be backed up, sometimes it is removed to denote that a file has been backed up, and sometimes it is ignored.

- In a Normal backup, all selected files and folders are backed up whether they have the archive attribute or not; however, the archive attribute is removed to denote that the file has been backed up.

- Copy backups do not use the archive attribute. All selected files and folders with or without the archive attribute are backed up and the archive bit is not removed.

- An Incremental backup backs up only the selected files and folders that have the archive attribute, which is then removed. Thus, if a file has not changed since the previous backup, it will be skipped during the next Incremental backup.

- A Differential backup backs up only selected files and folders with the archive attribute, which is not removed. Therefore, even if a file has not changed since the previous Differential backup, it will be backed up again because it still has the archive attribute.

- Organizations use a blend of the different backup types in order to optimize the time spent on both the backup and the restore processes.

- If you create a backup schedule that uses a combination of the Normal and Differential backup types, you will only have to restore the last Normal backup and the last Differential backup.

- If you use a combination of Normal and Incremental backups, you will have to restore the last Normal backup and all Incremental backups in the interim. This will take less time to back up files than a Normal/Differential strategy, but more time to restore files.

- A backup set is the compilation of files and folders from one volume that you have backed up and stored in a file, or on one or more tapes.

- When a backup or restore operation is complete, you can view the backup/restore log in Notepad to view detailed information such as the number of files that have been backed up or restored, the duration of the backup/restore process, the total size of the files backed up or restored, the start and end time for the operation, the backup destination, and the media type and label.

- A new feature in Windows XP is **Automated System Recovery** (ASR). ASR is a backup of your system configuration.

- It is designed to enable you to repair your system partition so that you can restart the operating system in the event of a complete malfunction due to a hard drive issue or corrupt system files.

- When using the other system recovery tools, such as Safe Mode, the Last Known Good Configuration, and the Recovery console are not possible, you can use ASR.

- When you use the Automated System Recovery Wizard, the configuration of your system drive is saved to whatever backup medium you choose.

- When ASR is applied, it formats the system drive. All user data on the system partition will be lost, and you will have to restore all user data, as well as all system partition data.

- An ASR backup should be performed immediately following the successful installation of the operating system. Furthermore, the backup should be updated whenever you modify the system configuration such as when you add a new device driver or use Windows Update to install a patch or service pack.

- To perform an ASR backup, you will need one floppy disk and a backup storage medium that is sufficient in size to store the operating system files, configuration settings, and System State data.

- To perform an ASR restore, you will need the bootable Windows XP Professional CD-ROM, the most recent copy of the ASR backup, which is generally saved on tape or another removable storage medium, and the most recent ASR backup media set.

# Key Terms

Archive attribute
Automated System Recovery (ASR)
Backup
Backup log
Backup set

Backup Wizard
Checksums
Copy backup
Daily backup
Differential backup

Incremental backup
Local backup
Network backup
Normal backup
Restore Wizard

# Test Yourself

1. Which of the following statements is true?
   a. You can only backup data to the hard disk of a computer.
   b. You can back up files and folders, but not an entire disk.
   c. Only Administrators and Backup Operators can back up files.
   d. File or folder owners and users with the Write, Modify, or Full Control permission for a file or folder can restore files and folders.

2. Which of the following statements is true about the Archive attribute? (Choose all that apply)
   a. The Archive attribute is also called the backup marker or the archive bit.
   b. In a Normal backup, all selected files and folders are backed up whether they have the Archive attribute or not. The attribute is removed to denote that a file has been backed up.
   c. The Archive attribute is used to mark files that have been modified since the last backup.
   d. In a Copy backup, all selected files and folders with or without the Archive attribute are backed up, and the Archive attribute is removed.
   e. A Differential backup backs up all selected files and folders, and the attribute is not removed.

3. In a Normal backup:
   a. All selected files/folders are backed up whether they have the Archive attribute or not. The Archive attribute is removed.
   b. Only the selected files/folders with the Archive attribute are backed up. The Archive attribute is removed.
   c. Only the selected files/folders with the Archive attribute are backed up. The Archive attribute is not removed.
   d. All selected files/folders are backed up whether they have the Archive attribute or not. The Archive attribute is not removed.

4. Which one of the following backup types clears the archive attribute?
   a. Daily
   b. Incremental
   c. Differential
   d. Copy

5. Which of the following statements is true?
   a. If you create a backup schedule that uses a combination of the Normal and Differential backup types, you will have to restore the last Normal backup and all Differential backups in the interim.
   b. If you use a combination of Normal and Incremental backups, you will have to restore the last Normal backup and the last Incremental backup.
   c. A Normal/Incremental backup strategy will take less time to back up files than a Normal/Differential strategy, but more time to restore files.
   d. A Normal/Differential backup strategy will take less time to back up files than a Normal/Incremental strategy, but more time to restore files.

6. You are the Network Administrator for a financial services company. Several key files that are updated on a daily, or almost daily, basis are stored on a share. The share and its subfolders total 3 gigabytes in size. You decide that since these files are so crucial, it is necessary to perform a backup every day. You want the backups to take the least amount of time possible, but you also want to be able to restore the files as quickly as possible in the event of a disaster. What backup strategy will you use?
   a. Incremental backups
   b. Differential backups
   c. Normal
   d. Normal and Differential
   e. Normal and Incremental

7. Your company uses a Windows 2000 domain and one of your responsibilities is to backup all of the Windows XP Professional workstations in your department. Your boss has asked you to make sure that the workstations can be restored to the network with all computer account and system settings in place in the event of a hardware malfunction. What must you do to make sure that this requirement is met?
   a. Make sure you back up the Registry on each machine on a daily basis.
   b. Make sure all user profiles on each machine are backed up regularly.
   c. Perform a System State backup on each of the machines regularly.
   d. Perform a differential backup every day.

8. One of the workstations in your department will not start and you suspect that the system files have become corrupt. You cannot use any of the other system recovery tools because you cannot boot the computer. What must you do?
   a. Boot the computer using the Windows XP Professional CD-ROM, and use the ASR disk and backup set to restore your system files.
   b. Boot the computer using the ASR floppy, and use the ASR backup set to restore your system files.
   c. Boot the computer using the bootable setup floppy disk set, and use the ASR backup set to restore your system files.
   d. Boot the computer in Safe Mode, and use the ASR backup set to restore your system files.

## Projects: On Your Own

1. Back up the **My data** folder on the **C:** drive of your computer. Use the **Copy** backup type, verify the backed up folder for data integrity, and specify the backup label as **backup of my data**.
   a. Open the **Backup** window.
   b. Initiate the **Backup Wizard**.
   c. Select the **Back up selected files, drives, or network data** option.
   d. Select the source folder that you want to back up.
   e. Set the default location as the destination of the backup media.
   f. Select the type of backup operation.
   g. Select the option for verifying the data after backup.
   h. Append the backup to the media.
   i. Specify the backup label.
   j. Set the backup time as **Now**.
   k. Complete the backup process.
2. Restore the folder **My data**. Select the alternate location **C:\Restored data** to restore the data.
   a. Initiate the **Restore Wizard** in the **Backup** window.
   b. Select the folder that you want to restore.
   c. Select the backup media from which you want to restore the file.
   d. Restore the desired folder.
   e. Specify the alternate location where you want to restore the data.

   f. Accept the default option of always replacing the file on disk with the restored file.
   g. Clear all of the check box options pertaining to the advanced restore options.
   h. Complete the restoration process.
3. While specifying backup and restore options, in the **Options** dialog box, set the default backup type as **Daily**. Additionally, set options to always verify the data after the backup operation is completed, and show detailed information in the log files.
   a. Open the **Options** dialog box in the **Backup** window.
   b. Select the option for verifying the data after completion of backup.
   c. Set the backup type.
   d. Select the option to view detailed information in the log file.
   e. Confirm the changes.
   f. Close the dialog box.
4. Perform an **Automated System Recovery (ASR)** backup.
   a. Start the Backup or Restore Wizard.
   b. Start the Automated System Recovery Preparation Wizard.
   c. Choose a destination for the backup.
   d. Complete the Wizard and create an ASR floppy disk.

# Problem Solving Scenarios

1. Blackmun's Coffee is an importer of Latin American coffee beans to the United States. Located in Baltimore, Blackmun's has 32 Windows XP Professional workstations on a Windows 2000 network. You have recently been hired as the Information Systems Administrator. You have discovered that the company has no backup policy, and it is left up to individuals to backup and secure their data. The Accounting department seems particularly vulnerable because its computers store all of the financial information for the company. You have decided to implement a firm-wide back up policy. You would also like to backup system data on all the clients. Since the amount of data is quite large, you want an inexpensive external source to store this data, and reduce the load on your hard disk. Explain in a memo how you would implement a regular backup of all of the company's important data.

# 15 Working with the Registry and Boot Process

**T**he Registry is a database that stores information that Windows XP Professional uses to monitor the software and hardware configurations on a computer. Everything from display settings to NIC settings, user profiles, group policies, and hardware profile information is stored in the Registry. The relationships between different portions of the user interface are defined in the Registry. How the operating system starts up, how the desktop is organized and viewed, and how the Start menu and taskbar work, as well as many other interface configuration settings, are all dependent on configuration settings stored in the Registry. The Registry is crucially important to the operation of the operating system, functioning in the areas of security, file location, remembering user preferences, tuning parameters, and device configuration. For example, when you make changes to the display settings on your desktop or add new hardware to your computer, Windows XP Professional stores the display settings or the settings for the new drivers in the Registry. When the operating system or an application you are running malfunctions, if you become knowledgeable enough, you may be able to use the Registry to remedy the problem.

The Registry is organized in a hierarchical structure, which you can view with the Registry Editor. You can access the Registry Editor from the Run dialog box using either of two commands: regedit or regedt32. As with Windows Explorer, you use the plus sign buttons to expand the hierarchical tree to display more branches in the tree. You can also use the Registry Editor to edit information in the Registry such as configuration settings. After you make changes in the Registry Editor, they are automatically saved and applied immediately.

The settings in the Registry file are read during the boot process (the process followed by a computer as it starts). When you are booting your computer and any type of problem occurs that prevents the operating system from starting, you can try to use the Last Known Good Configuration, which is stored in the Registry, to resolve the problem. As its name indicates, the Last Known Good Configuration contains settings saved in the Registry the last time a user successfully logged on to the computer. You can also try to boot the computer in Safe Mode. When you start up in Safe Mode, only the basic drivers and files are loaded and the Registry is activated. You can use Safe Mode to remove corrupt drivers, fix driver conflicts, or uninstall and reinstall applications to resolve possible autostart difficulties. If Safe Mode and the Last Known Good Configuration do not work, you can try the Recovery Console. The Recovery Console enables you to start the operating system when all else has failed. It provides you with a set of administrative command-line tools that can be used to repair your Windows XP Professional installation.

## Goals

In this lesson, you will learn about the Registry and its components, and about how the Registry is edited. You will also learn about the boot process, control sets, and the various advanced boot options that can be used to troubleshoot and correct problems.

### Lesson 15   Working with the Registry and Boot Process

| Skill | Exam 70-270 Objective |
|---|---|
| 1. Introducing the Registry | Configure and manage user profiles and desktop settings. |
| 2. Identifying the Components of the Registry Structure | Basic knowledge |
| 3. Working with the Registry Editor | Basic knowledge |
| 4. Working with Control Sets | Basic knowledge |
| 5. Introducing the Boot Process | Basic knowledge |
| 6. Identifying Advanced Boot Options | Troubleshoot system restoration by starting in safe mode. Restore and back up the operating system, System State data, and user data. |
| 7. Modifying the Boot.ini File | Basic knowledge |
| 8. Using the Recovery Console to Troubleshoot and Recover Tasks | Restore and back up the operating system, System State data, and user data. Recover System State data and user data by using the Recovery console. |

## Requirements

To complete this lesson, you will need a Windows XP Professional computer and administrative rights on the computer.

# skill 1 *Introducing the Registry*

## exam objective

Configure and manage user profiles and desktop settings.

## overview

When you configure or change the settings on your computer, most of the information related to the hardware and software settings is stored in a database on your computer called the Registry. For example, if you change the color settings, screen saver, or wallpaper, these changes are saved in the **Registry**. However, although the Registry looks like a single database when you view it in the Registry editor, settings are stored in several different files, mainly **%systemroot%\system32\Config**, and profile folders on the root drive in the Documents and Settings folder. The term %systemroot% refers to the folder where the operating system files are stored, which will most commonly be C:\Windows for Windows XP Professional. The Registry stores all of the information related to the configuration of the software and hardware devices on a computer. The information stored in the Registry can be divided into the following basic categories:

## caution

Incorrectly modifying the Registry can have serious results, including making the computer completely non-functional. Therefore, you should always back up the Registry before making any changes. You can use the Control Panel for most configuration changes.

◆ **User Profiles:** When you customize your desktop environment, which includes the various display settings, network and printer connections, and other specified settings, the information is first copied to the Registry and then to the user profile. This information is recreated each time you boot your computer.

◆ **Device Drivers:** Device drivers use the data in the Registry to configure the hardware peripherals attached to a computer. They also provide information to the Registry about the system resources, which are currently used by the drivers **(Figure 15-1)**.

◆ **Setup programs:** When you install a program on a computer, the configuration data for the program is added to the Registry, and the setup program can search the Registry to find out if the necessary components have been installed.

◆ **Hardware Profiles:** If a computer has multiple hardware configurations, different hardware profiles are created for each configuration. Hardware profiles contain information about the devices that must be started when the computer is booted up and the settings with which the devices will be started. Hardware profiles are updated in the Registry **(Figure 15-2)**.

◆ **General System Configuration:** Control panel parameter configuration and information about all services that are installed on the computer are also stored in the Registry. This includes what services are installed, the services they are reliant upon, and the order in which the services should be initiated.

◆ **Applications:** Configuration data on all software in use on the computer is stored in the Registry.

◆ **Network Protocols and NIC settings:** NIC settings stored in the Registry include the IRQ (Interrupt Request) number, memory base address, I/O channel ready, I/O port base address, and transceiver type.

You view the information in the Registry using the **Registry Editor**. You can also use the Registry Editor to modify the configuration information. To access the Registry Editor window, you can use either the **regedit** command or **regedt32** in the **Run** dialog box.

In Windows 2000, these commands opened two different programs with different views of the Registry and different capabilities, but that is not the case in Windows XP. The version of the Registry Editor program used in Windows XP is similar to the one that was used in the Windows 9.x family. The interface is similar to Windows Explorer and you can view the entire Registry in one window. The regedt32 version of the program available in Windows 2000 was the Windows NT version of the Registry Editor, and it included security features that were not available in the regedit version in Windows 2000. However, in Windows XP you can now set permissions for Registry keys and subkeys in regedit just as you could in regedt32. You set permissions for Registry keys just as you set shared folder and NTFS permissions, in the ACL for the resource.

**Figure 15-1  The HKEY_LOCAL_MACHINE root key in the Registry Editor**

Contains information about the hardware and software configuration, how hardware is used, how drivers are used, and the startup parameters

**Figure 15-2  The HKEY_CURRENT_CONFIG root key in the Registry Editor**

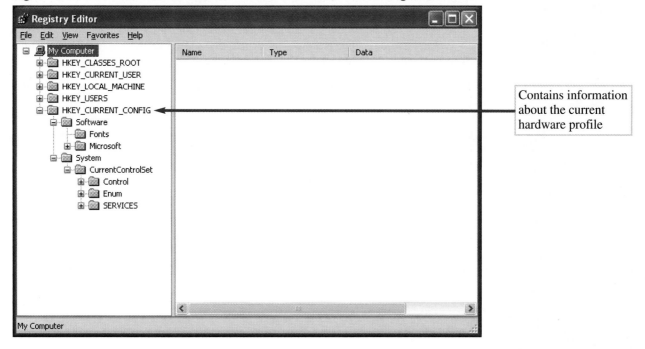

Contains information about the current hardware profile

# skill 2

# *Identifying the Components of the Registry Structure*

## exam objective

Basic knowledge

## overview

When you open the Registry Editor window, the data is organized in a hierarchical tree format. There are five root keys. The root keys, also called **subtrees** or **subtree keys**, are the primary nodes in the Registry structure. Root keys are similar to root folders on a disk. They store other keys and values just as the root folder stores other folders and files. The five root keys in the Registry are outlined below:

◆ **HKEY_LOCAL_MACHINE:** This subtree contains the configuration data for the installed hardware and software and the operating system. It does not change, regardless of what user is logged on to the computer. Data includes the startup parameters, the drivers that will be used, and all hardware and software configuration information. When you manually edit the Registry, you will be working with this root key. The keys in the HKEY_LOCAL_MACHINE subtree are described in **Table 15-1**.

◆ **HKEY_CLASSES_ROOT:** This subtree contains information about the file types that are associated file extensions in Windows Explorer so that the correct application will be used to open a file. For example, a .bmp file is associated with the Paint program, an .mdb file with Access, and an .xls file with Excel. This key is copied from the HKEY_LOCAL_MACHINE/Software/Classes subkey and is not necessary for the operation of Windows XP, but rather is preserved for compatibility with older programs and device drivers.

◆ **HKEY_USERS:** This subtree contains information about the default user profile settings on a computer. It does not pertain to any particular user, but rather is the container for profiles for all users who have ever logged on to the computer, as well as the default user profile. This key is rebuilt each time the computer boots using the default user profile and either Ntuser.dat or Ntuser.man (**Figure 15-3**).

◆ **HKEY_CURRENT_USER:** This subtree contains information about the profile of the user who is currently logged on to a Windows XP Professional computer. The data in this key is copied from the relevant subkey in the HKEY_USERS key when a particular user logs on.

◆ **HKEY_CURRENT_CONFIG:** This subtree contains information about the hardware profile that is currently in use, and it is used when you boot up the computer so that the correct device drivers are loaded and the appropriate system settings are configured. This key is also preserved for compatibility with older programs and device drivers. It is the same data that is now stored in the HKEY_LOCAL_MACHINE\System\ CurrentControlSet\Hardware Profiles\Current subkey.

All Registry data is actually contained in HKEY_LOCAL_MACHINE and HKEY_USERS. HKEY_LOCAL_MACHINE contains the data stored in the SAM, Security, Software and System files. HKEY_USERS contains the data stored in the physical files called NTUSER.DAT, USRCLASS.DAT, and DEFAULT. HKEY_CURRENT_CONFIG, HKEY_CLASSES_ROOT, and HKEY_CURRENT_USER really just point to subkeys in HKEY_LOCAL_MACHINE and HKEY_USERS.

| Table 15-1 | Subkeys in the HKEY_LOCAL_MACHINE root tree |
|---|---|
| **Subkey** | **Configuration information** |
| Hardware | Contains the configuration information about the physical devices to a computer, such as network cards and CD drives. This key is recreated each time you boot the computer. |
| SAM | SAM, or Security Accounts Manager, contains data related to the local security database of the computer. It defines the user account and group membership for a computer. |
| Security | Contains information about the security policies on the computer. It also defines the control parameters, such as password and user rights. |
| Software | Contains information about the software installed on the computer, and the mapped file extensions. |
| System | Contains information that is required to boot a Windows XP computer. This information includes the startup parameters, loading order for device drivers, and behavior of the operating system. |

**Figure 15-3 The HKEY_USERS root key**

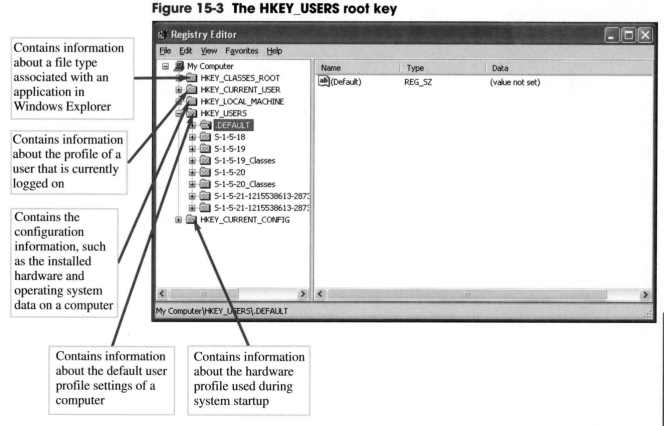

Contains information about a file type associated with an application in Windows Explorer

Contains information about the profile of a user that is currently logged on

Contains the configuration information, such as the installed hardware and operating system data on a computer

Contains information about the default user profile settings of a computer

Contains information about the hardware profile used during system startup

# skill 2

## *Identifying the Components of the Registry Structure (cont'd)*

**exam objective**

Basic knowledge

## overview

In the Registry structure hierarchy, keys are like folders on a hard disk. They are simply containers in which other keys and values are stored, and they are displayed as folders in the left pane of the Registry window. Keys correspond to hardware or software objects, and the information is stored in sections. For example, the HKEY_LOCAL_MACHINE subtree expands to display five **subkeys:** Hardware, SAM, Security, Software, and System. These subkeys are further divided. For example, the System subkey is divided into the subkeys ControlSet001, ControlSet003, CurrentControlSet etc., which are used for setting the computer configuration **(Figure 15-4)**. **Values** or **value entries** are the extremities of the tree. They are the endpoints of a Registry path that serve as parameters to control the configuration settings **(Figure 15-5)**. Value entries are composed of a name, a data type, and a value.

**Value Entries:**

◆ **Name:** The name looks like a capitalized multi-word phrase without spaces, for example, AutoRestartShell or CurrentUser.

◆ **Data type:** The data type determines the format, such as string, binary, or numerical, in which the value will be stored in the Registry. The data types supported by Windows XP Professional are explained in **Table 15-2**.

◆ **Value:** The value is the actual data in the currently selected subkey. The value may be a single binary digit, a string of ASCII characters, or hexadecimal values.

**Hive:** A hive is a distinct group of keys, subkeys, and value entries with its own Registry file and .LOG file. By default, most hive files are stored in the %systemroot%\System32\Config folder.

Because editing the Registry is a risky undertaking that can have potentially damaging results, you should backup the Registry key you are modifying so that you can revert to the former setting. You back up a Registry key using the **Export** command on the **File** menu in the Registry Editor. In the **Export Registry File** dialog box you will save the key in one of several formats. The **Registry Hive Files** format is used to save a binary image of all of the subkeys and values in the selected hive. You cannot view or edit this file, but you can use it to restore the system to its previous state. The **Registration Files** format is used to create a file with the extension .reg, which can be opened in Notepad for editing and then imported back into the Registry. The **Text Files** format (.txt) is also used to create an editable text file, but it cannot be imported back into the Registry. The purpose of saving a Registry key in this format is to create a record of a Registry setting modification that cannot be inadvertently imported back into the Registry. The **Win9x/NT 4 Registration Files** format is used to create a file that can be imported to those down-level operating systems.

In order to revert back to a saved version of a Registry key, simply select the key you are going to restore and use the **Import** command on the **File** menu to open the **Import Registry File** dialog box. After you select the file to import, you will have to confirm that you want to overwrite the selected key and subkeys.

**Figure 15-4 The HKEY_LOCAL_MACHINE root key and subkeys**

**Figure 15-5 Value entries**

| Table 15-2 | Data types supported by Windows XP Professional |
| --- | --- |
| **Data Type** | **Description** |
| REG_DWORD | Displays data in a decimal or hexadecimal format. It is a four-byte binary value displayed with 0x at the beginning and eight hexadecimal digits with no spaces. |
| REG_SZ | Stores data in string format. It is the most common type of value and it can include letters and numbers. |
| REG_EXPAND_SZ | Stores data in string format, which can contain replaceable parameters. |
| REG_BINARY | Stores data in binary format. It is displayed as a series of two-digit, base 16 (one-byte) numbers that are divided with spaces. |
| REG_MULTI_SZ | Stores data as a list of strings that contain values separated by null characters. |
| REG_FULL_RESOURCE_DESCRIPTOR | Stores a resource list for a hardware component or driver in a series of nested arrays. |

# skill 3   *Working with the Registry Editor*

**exam objective**

Basic knowledge

## overview

As a user, you may never need to use or even access the Registry on your computer. However, as an Administrator, it is important that you be familiar with the Registry and that you understand functions such as backing up, viewing, editing, and restoring the Registry. The Registry Editor is automatically installed when you install Windows XP Professional. Regedt32.exe is stored in the **%systemroot%\System32** folder. When you make changes in the Registry Editor, they are automatically saved and applied immediately, and they cannot be undone.

The contents of the HARDWARE subkey can be viewed to determine your system configuration and device settings. All hardware information is stored in the HARDWARE subkey when the operating system starts. You can use this subkey to find out what devices, for example processors and serial ports, were detected at startup and to troubleshoot problems with some devices.

## how to

View the **SystemBiosVersion**, processors on your computer, and the path to the serial controller in the Registry.

1. Click ![start] and then click the **Run** command to open the **Run** dialog box.
2. Type **regedt32** in the **Open** text box, and click [ OK ] to open the **Registry Editor** window.
3. Expand the **HKEY_LOCAL_ MACHINE** subkey. Double-click the **HARDWARE** node and then the **DESCRIPTION** node to expand them.
4. Select the **System** subkey to view the information related to the **SystemBios** (**Figure 15-6**).
5. Expand the **System** subkey. Expand the **Central Processor** key. There will be a key for each processor on the computer. Select one and note the values for the **Identifier** and **VendorIdentifier** value entries (**Figure 15-7**).
6. Expand the **MultifunctionAdapter** subkey. Expand the numbered multifunction adapter subkeys to locate the **SerialController** subkey.
7. Expand the **SerialController** subkey. Each serial controller will have its own key. Select one and note the port it uses, which will be recorded in the **Identifier** value entry (**Figure 15-8**).
8. Close all of the open **HARDWARE** subkeys.
9. Close the Registry Editor window.

### caution

Making even a slight error while using the Registry Editor can lead to serious problems on your computer. You may have to reinstall the operating system.

## more

A utility for directing and managing the XP Registry backup process is a new addition in Windows XP. The **System Restore** utility is used to set system **checkpoints** to ensure that you will be able to return your system to a particular state at a particular date and time. A checkpoint is a snapshot of the system at a particular time interval. This can be particularly important when a significant change has occurred, such as when you have installed a security patch or service pack. The System Restore utility will create a checkpoint before the update is installed. Then, if a crucial file such as a .dll or .exe file is inadvertently deleted, rendering either an application or the operating system unusable, you can use this earlier configuration data to restore the Registry and system settings that were recorded at this time.

**Figure 15-6  Viewing the SystemBios values**

**Figure 15-7  Viewing the Identifier and VendorIdentifier values for a processor**

**Figure 15-8  Identifying the port used by a serial controller**

# skill 4

## *Working with Control Sets*

**exam objective**

Basic knowledge

**overview**

When you are booting a computer, certain configuration information, such as the startup parameters and a list of the installed device drivers and hardware components, must be accessed. This data is stored in **control sets**. The Registry will include more than one control set if you have changed system settings or experienced difficulties with your system settings.

The control sets are stored as subkeys in the **HKEY_LOCAL_MACHINES\SYSTEM** Registry key. The subkeys contain complete information about the boot process and the settings for the storage devices. The subkeys required for booting a Windows XP Professional computer are **ControlSet001**, **ControlSet002**, **CurrentControlSet**, **and Select**. The CurrentControlSet subkey points to one of the ControlSet00x keys.

The **Select** subkey contains value entries with the names: **Current**, **Default**, **Failed**, and **LastKnownGood**. The Current value entry lists the configuration that was used to boot the current session. If you make changes in the Control Panel or modify the Registry, you are changing the CurrentControlSet. The Default value entry contains the control set that will be used when you next boot up your computer, provided you do not choose Last Known Good Configuration on the Hardware Profile/Configuration Recovery or Windows XP Advanced Options menus. It is generally identical to the CurrentControlSet. The Failed value entry contains the control set that was unsuccessful the last time you started the computer, causing you to resort to the Last Known Good Configuration. Finally, the LastKnownGood value entry contains the control set that was saved after the last successful logon (**Figure 15-9**).

After every successful logon, an identical copy of the CurrentControlSet, which contains the data used for configuring the computer, is copied to the LastKnownGood value entry in the Select subkey. When you start your computer, there are two configurations that can be used: the **Default Configuration** or the **Last Known Good Configuration**. The configuration information that is saved when a computer shuts down normally is contained in the default configuration, and the configuration data that was saved after the last successful logon is saved in the Last Known Good Configuration. If your computer is configured for dual booting, you simply select Windows XP on the Please Select the Operating System to Start menu to choose the default configuration. Possible causes of startup failures that might necessitate the use of the Last Known Good Configuration are as follows:

◆  Incorrectly editing the Registry.
◆  Adding a new driver that is either not compatible with your hardware or is defective.
◆  Disabling a critical device driver (such as the SCSIPORT driver).

**more**

**caution**

If you run into difficulties due to a configuration change on your computer and you forget to use the Last Known Good Configuration when you reboot, **do not** log on. The LastKnownGood value entry will be overwritten if you log on.

The Last Known Good Configuration cannot help you to restart the computer if:
◆  There are corrupt or missing files.
◆  A new driver is copied onto an old driver that is still active, the configuration does not change, and reverting to the Last Known Good Configuration will not help.
◆  There are any improper operating system modifications that are not related to the control set (for example, incorrectly configured user profiles or improper file permissions).
◆  A hardware device problem is occurring and you forget to choose Last Known Good Configuration, and then you successfully log on. When you make configuration changes, they are saved in the CurrentControlSet. When you reboot the computer, the kernel copies that information to one of two Registry keys: either ControlSet001 or ControlSet002. On a successful logon, the location of the ControlSet00x key is copied to the LastKnownGood value entry in the Select subkey. Thus, when a user chooses to boot using the Last Known Good Configuration option, the computer looks to the LastKnownGood value entry in the Registry, and then boots using the ControlSet that it specifies.

**Figure 15-9  Value entries in the Select subkey**

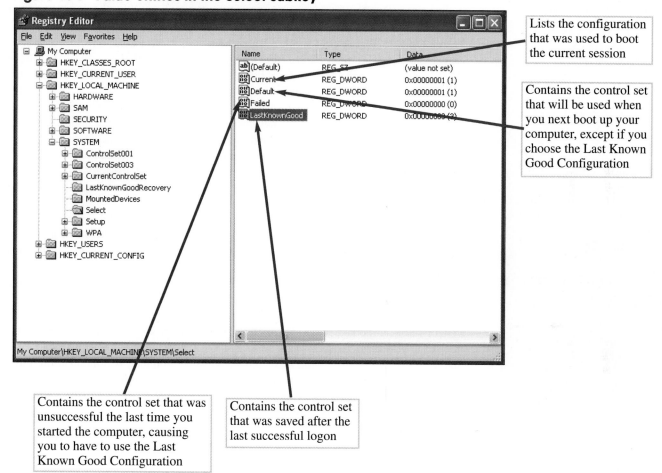

Lists the configuration that was used to boot the current session

Contains the control set that will be used when you next boot up your computer, except if you choose the Last Known Good Configuration

Contains the control set that was unsuccessful the last time you started the computer, causing you to have to use the Last Known Good Configuration

Contains the control set that was saved after the last successful logon

# skill 5

# *Introducing the Boot Process*

**exam objective**    Basic knowledge

## overview

When you start up a computer, the various configuration files and drivers are accessed in sequential order. This series of steps in which files are accessed is known as the **boot** process. Being familiar with the normal boot process will help you to understand the areas where things may be going wrong when startup fails. The files that are initiated during the boot process are summarized in **Table 15-3**. The boot process consists of the following phases:

◆ **Power-On Self Test (POST):** First, the computer runs the POST, which is a built-in diagnostic program that checks the hardware to ensure that the basic hardware components, such as the keyboard and the mouse, are present. The POST also checks the amount of physical memory available on the computer **(Figure 15-10)**.

◆ **Startup:** Next, if the computer has a Plug and Play BIOS (Basic Input Output System), it locates the system board hardware devices. Then, the BIOS finds the boot device and locates and runs the **Master Boot Record (MBR)**, which in locates the boot sector on the active partition, loads the boot sector into memory and loads the hidden system file **Ntldr**.

◆ **Boot Loader:** Next, the **Ntldr** file (the boot loader) puts the CPU into 32-bit memory mode, and loads the FAT and NTFS mini-file drivers so that the operating system can be located and loaded from any type of partition.

◆ **Selecting the Operating System:** Ntldr then reads the **Boot.ini** file. If there are other operating systems on the computer, it is at this point that you will be asked to choose between them on the **Please select the operating system to start** screen. If you choose a DOS-based operating system, Ntldr must run **Bootsect.dos** because this is where the boot sector for the previous OS is stored. If an alternative selection is not made, Ntldr loads the default operating system specified in Boot.ini.

◆ **Detecting the Hardware:** If you select Windows XP or if it is the only operating system on the computer, **Ntdetect.com** takes over **(Figure 15-11)**. This utility performs most of the hardware detection functions, including distinguishing the Bus/adapter type and locating the parallel ports, SCSI adapters, video adapters, communication ports, floppy disks, keyboard, and the mouse/pointing device. The Ntldr utility compiles a list of the installed hardware components and later updates the Registry under the **HKEY_LOCAL_MACHINE\HARDWARE** key.

◆ **Selecting the Configuration:** At this point in the boot process, Ntldr takes over again and you will be asked to choose a hardware profile on the **Hardware Profile/Configuration Recovery** menu if more than one exists on the machine. You will also now be able to press **[L]** to choose the **Last Known Good Configuration**. This will start the computer using the Registry information that Windows saved after the last successful logon. If your computer is configured for dual-booting, you can also access the Last Known Good Configuration by pressing F8 when the **Please select the operating system to start** screen displays to open the **Windows Advanced Options Menu**. Or, if your computer is not configured for dual-booting and it does not have multiple hardware profiles, you can press F8 at boot time to view the Windows Advanced Options Menu. You navigate on any of these menus using the arrow keys. If you do not select a hardware profile during the specified time period, the computer will start with the default hardware profile. If there is only one hardware profile configured on the computer, the Hardware Profile/Configuration Recovery menu does not appear and Windows XP Professional loads using the default hardware configuration.

◆ **Kernel Load Phase:** Next, as the **Starting Windows** screen opens with a progress bar at the bottom of the screen, Ntldr loads the **Ntoskrnl.exe** and **hardware abstraction layer (Hal.dll)** utilities and the **control set**. Hal.dll contains code that interfaces the OS with the hardware devices. The control set, as you will learn, is simply a list of device drivers, services, and settings for the Registry key **HKEY_LOCAL_MACHINE\SYSTEM**, which is loaded into the system from the ***%systemroot%\System32\Config\System*** file.

### Table 15-3  Files initiated during the boot process

| File | Location | Function |
|---|---|---|
| Ntldr | System partition root | The Boot loader for Windows XP Professional computers. |
| Boot.ini | System partition root | Provides the boot menu information. |
| Bootsect.dos | System partition root | Provides the DOS boot information for computers that are configured for dual-booting. |
| Ntdetect.com | System partition root | Detects the hardware attached to the machine. |
| Ntbootdd.sys | System partition root | Allows Windows XP Professional to access the SCSI drive on a computer on which the onboard BIOS is disabled. |
| Ntoskrnl.exe | *%systemroot%*\System32 | The kernel for the Windows XP Professional operating system (%systemroot% refers to the folder on the boot partition where the OS files are stored). |
| Hal.dll | *%systemroot%*\System32 | The code for the hardware abstraction layer. |
| System key | *%systemroot%*\System32\Config | The key that contains the Windows XP Professional Registry data. |
| Device drivers | *%systemroot%*\System32\Drivers | The programs that allow the device drivers to communicate with the operating system. |

### Figure 15-10  The POST screen

### Figure 15-11  The hidden system file NTDETECT.COM on the system partition

NTDETECT.COM performs most of the hardware detection functions

# skill 5

## Introducing the Boot Process *(cont'd)*

**exam objective**

Basic knowledge

## overview

### caution

The Last Known Good Configuration option will not solve problems caused by missing or corrupt drivers or files. Also, any changes made since the last successful startup can be restored only if the user has not logged on again and overwritten the old control set.

### tip

If errors are reported during the boot process, you can check the System log for details after the boot process is complete.

◆ **Kernel Initialization Phase:** Now, as the graphical boot progress screen displays, **Ntoskrnl.exe (Figure 15-12)** creates the **HKEY_LOCAL_MACHINE\HARDWARE** Registry key, which contains information about hardware components on your computer. The kernel also creates an identical copy of the CurrentControlSet, which contains the data used for configuring the computer. The copy of the CurrentControlSet is stored in either the ControlSet001 or ControlSet002 Registry key. After a user successfully logs on, the location of the ControlSet00x key is copied to the LastKnownGood value entry in the Select subkey. The basic device drivers that were loaded during the boot loader phase are now initialized by the kernel, and more device drivers are detected and loaded. If anything goes wrong when the drivers are loading and initializing, an error message is sent to the kernel. These messages are saved in the **System log**, which can be viewed in the **Event Viewer**. After the device drivers are loaded and initialized, the **Session Manager (Smss.exe)** starts the services. The Session Manager is responsible for creating the user-mode environment that provides the visible interface with Windows XP Professional. The set of instructions executed by the Session Manager is listed in **Table 15-4**.

◆ **Logon Process:** Finally, the logon dialog box is displayed as a result of **Winlogon.exe** and **Lsass.exe (Local Security Authority)**, and a final last group of high-level services is started, including the Workstation service and the Server (File and Printer Sharing for Microsoft Networks) service. After logon, Windows 2000 Professional builds the new version of the Last Known Good Configuration.

**Figure 15-12  Ntsokrnl in the System32 folder**

Creates the HKEY_LOCAL_MACHINE\HARDWARE Registry key

---

### Table 15-4  Instructions executed by the Session Manager

| Instructions | Description |
|---|---|
| BootExecute data item | Executes the various commands mentioned in the BootExecute data item and then loads the various services. The BootExecute data item appears under the Registry KEY_LOCAL_MACHINE\SYSTEM\CurrentControlSet\Session Manager \BootExecute. |
| Paging file | Creates the paging file information that holds parts of programs and data files that do not fit in the computer's memory. |
| Symbolic links | Creates the symbolic links that direct some commands to the correct component in the file system. |
| Win32 subsystem | Starts the Win32 subsystem. The Win32 subsystem controls all I/O and access to the video screen. |

# skill 6 — *Identifying Advanced Boot Options*

## exam objective

Troubleshoot system restoration by starting in safe mode. Restore and back up the operating system, System State data, and user data.

## overview

If you are having trouble starting the operating system, you can restart and press F8 at boot time to open the **Windows Advanced Options Menu**. You can use the arrow keys on your keyboard to select from several **Safe Mode** commands (**Figure 15-13**). Safe mode is used to resolve problems that result from faulty device drivers, faulty programs, system service failures, or services that start automatically. Usually, when you start in Safe mode, you will be opening the Control Panel so that you can undo whatever setting you recently configured that may be causing the operating system to malfunction at boot time. You can start or stop a system service, uninstall a recently installed program, change a recently instituted display setting, or uninstall a recently installed device driver. When you boot in Safe Mode, the operating system will only load a basic set of files and drivers for the keyboard, mouse, basic VGA monitor, default system services, and disk. **Safe Mode with Networking** includes networking drivers and services if you must have network access to fix the problem, and **Safe Mode with Command Prompt** opens the command prompt instead of the Graphical User Interface (GUI) environment. The other options on the menu are as follows:

**Enable Boot Logging:** This command will record the loading and initialization of drivers and services in the **Ntbtlog.txt log** file, which is located in the %systemroot% folder. Data pertaining to drivers and services that successfully load, as well as those that do not load or initialize, will be stored here, creating a constructive foundation for your troubleshooting efforts. This option is automatically enabled when you start the computer in any of the safe modes.

**Enable VGA mode:** This command boots the OS with only a basic VGA driver and is useful when your monitor display has been configured at a setting that your monitor does not support.

**Last Known Good Configuration:** This command starts the computer using the Registry information that Windows saved after the last successful logon.

**Directory Services Restore Mode:** On Windows 2000 Server and Windows Server 2003 domain controllers, a server operator can use this option to restore a damaged version of the Active Directory with a backup copy. When he or she boots in Directory Services Restore Mode, they will first be prompted for a password, and the computer will then start in an administrative context. The operator can then correct the problem using a command-line utility.

**Debugging Mode:** This command is used on Windows 2000 Server and Windows Server 2003 machines to send debugging information across a serial cable to another computer that is running a debugger. It is configured to use COM2.

## tip

Safe Mode and Safe Mode with Networking also load the basic VGA driver, **vga.sys**.

## how to

Start your computer in **Safe Mode** and restore the **Display settings**.
1. Shut down and restart your computer.
2. Restart your computer and immediately start pressing the F8 key on your keyboard. If your computer is configured for dual booting, press the F8 key when the **Please select the operating system to start** screen opens.
3. Use the arrow keys to select **Safe Mode** and press the **[Enter]** key to open the **Please select the operating system to start** screen. On a system with only one operating system, press **[Enter]** to open the screen showing a list of drivers used in the safe mode (**Figure 15-14**). If you are configured for dual booting, select Microsoft Windows XP Professional and press **[Enter]**.

**Figure 15-13  The Windows Advanced Options Menu**

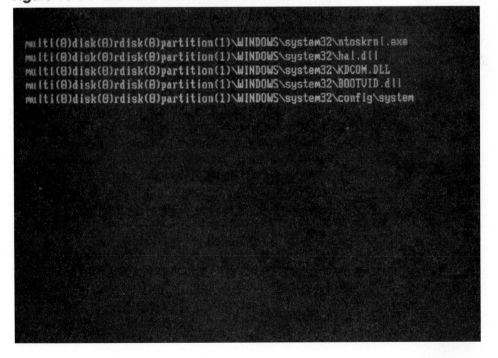

```
Windows Advanced Options Menu
Please select an option:

    Safe Mode
    Safe Mode with Networking
    Safe Mode with Command Prompt

    Enable Boot Logging
    Enable VGA Mode
    Last Known Good Configuration (your most recent settings that worked)
    Directory Services Restore Mode (Windows domain controllers only)
    Debugging Mode

    Start Windows Normally
    Reboot
    Return to OS Choices Menu

Use the up and down arrow keys to move the highlight to your choice.
```

**Figure 15-14  The list of drivers used in Safe Mode**

```
multi(0)disk(0)rdisk(0)partition(1)\WINDOWS\system32\ntoskrnl.exe
multi(0)disk(0)rdisk(0)partition(1)\WINDOWS\system32\hal.dll
multi(0)disk(0)rdisk(0)partition(1)\WINDOWS\system32\KDCOM.DLL
multi(0)disk(0)rdisk(0)partition(1)\WINDOWS\system32\BOOTVID.dll
multi(0)disk(0)rdisk(0)partition(1)\WINDOWS\system32\config\system
```

# skill 6

## *Identifying Advanced Boot Options*
### *(cont'd)*

**exam objective**

Troubleshoot system restoration by starting in safe mode. Restore and back up the operating system, System State data, and user data.

**how to**

4. When the **Welcome to Windows** dialog box opens, press **Ctrl+Alt+Delete** to begin. Log on as an **Administrator** and press the **[Enter]** key.
5. The **Desktop** dialog box informs you that Windows is running in Safe Mode and that some devices may not be available (**Figure 15-15**).
6. Click **Yes** to continue with Startup. When Startup is complete, your desktop will be displayed with no wallpaper and Safe Mode will appear in all four corners of the screen.
7. Click [ *start* ] and click the **Control Panel** command to open the **Control Panel** window.
8. Double-click the **Display** icon to open the **Display Properties** dialog box.
9. Open the **Settings** tab where you can change the screen resolution.
10. Drag the **Screen area** slider to set it at **800 by 600** pixels (**Figure 15-16**).
11. Click [ Apply ]. The screen goes black and the new settings are applied.
12. Click [ OK ] to close the Display Properties dialog box.
13. Close the Control Panel.
14. Restart the computer.

**more**

When you log on in Safe Mode, other tools you can use to attempt to discover the source of your problem are the Device Manager and the Event Viewer. The Device Manager will help you to identify a device with a faulty driver that may need to be disabled or removed. You can also use the Add or Remove Programs utility in the Control Panel to remove a program you suspect may be causing the difficulty.

You can also perform a System Restore after you boot into Safe Mode. In the Desktop warning dialog box, you can click the **No** button to run a System Restore rather than startup in Safe Mode. The System Restore utility, as you have learned, sets system checkpoints so that when a significant system change has occurred and something goes awry, you can return to a previous configuration. To run a System Restore, from the Start menu, point to **All Programs**, **Accessories, System Tools**, and click **System Restore** to start the **System Restore Wizard**. Select the **Restore my computer to an earlier time** option button and click **Next** to open the **Select a Restore Point** screen (**Figure 15-17**). A calendar will display on which highlighted days represent days on which checkpoints were created. When you select a day, the times a system checkpoint was created will display to the right of the calendar. Select the restore point you want and click **Next**. You will have to confirm the selected restore point, close any open programs, and the operating system will then reboot. Recently saved documents will not be lost and you can run a System Restore again to reverse the process. After the computer reboots, a report will open to let you know if the system restore was successful or not. By default, checkpoints are created every 24 hours if the computer is left running. When you shut the machine down, a system checkpoint is created when you reboot if the previous checkpoint was more than 24 hours ago. Performing a System Restore can be useful if you have removed a program that is creating a conflict but uninstalling the program has not fixed the problem. You can also use a System Restore to revert back to a set of drivers you were using with no difficulties before you installed updated drivers.

**Figure 15-15  The Desktop warning dialog box**

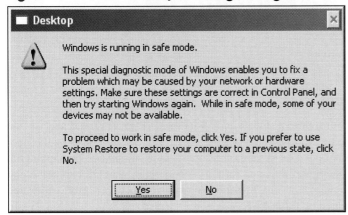

**Figure 15-16  The Display Properties dialog box**

**Figure 15-17  The Select a Restore Point screen in the System Restore Wizard**

# skill 7  *Modifying the Boot.ini File*

## exam objective

Basic knowledge

## overview

The **boot.ini** file is created during the installation of Windows XP Professional and, as you have learned, it is accessed during the selecting the operating system phase of the boot process to find out if any other operating systems are stored on the computer. The boot.ini file is saved in the root of the system partition, and it tells the computer what OS choices to display during startup. It is a hidden, read-only, system file with two sections: **boot loader** and **operating systems**, as explained in **Table 15-5**.

At this point, it is important to make sure that you understand the distinction between the system partition and the boot partition. The system partition is the disk volume that stores the files needed to boot the operating system, Ntldr, boot.ini, Ntdetect, etc. The boot partition is the partition where the actual operating system files (typically \Windows) and the OS support files (typically \Windows\System32) are stored. The boot partition can be the same partition as the system partition. (Refer back to Table 15-3.)

Boot.ini will generally not need to be modified, but you can use a text editor, such as Notepad, to manually change the boot.ini file, if necessary. For example, you can change the "**timeout**" time period, which is the time you will have to choose between alternative operating systems on a dual boot system when the Please select the operating system to start menu appears. You can also change the default operating system on a dual boot system. However, both of these operations can also be performed in the **Startup and Recovery** dialog box, which can be accessed on the **Advanced** tab in the **System Properties** dialog box. Using the Control Panel is the recommended method. However, there are a number of switches you can append to the entries in the operating systems section in the boot.ini file to modify the boot process, which cannot be modified by any other method.

The file attributes for boot.ini can be changed using My Computer or Windows Explorer. In order to edit the boot.ini file, you must use one of these utilities first to remove the hidden, system, and read-only attributes. Then you can either open the file in Notepad directly or use the command prompt to open it in Notepad. To use the command prompt, type **cmd** in the **Open** text box in the **Run** dialog box. Then, at the command prompt, type **boot.ini**. You can also use the command prompt to remove the system, hidden, and read-only attributes by typing: **attrib -s -r -h boot.ini (Figure 15-18)**.

The main reason you will have to edit the boot.ini file is if you want to change the parameters for one of the listed operating systems. In this case, the term parameters refers to the particular features that will be used to start this Windows version. Sometimes when you add a controller or a hard disk, you may have to edit the **ARC path**. The term ARC path (Advanced RISC [reduced instruction set] Computing) refers to the path that points to a valid boot partition containing the Windows operating system files. As you will see when you open the boot.ini file, this path has four parts: **multi**, **disk**, **rdisk**, and **partition**. Multi tells the computer which disk controller to use: 0, 1, 2, and so forth. Multi refers to an IDE disk controller or a SCSI type controller with BIOS enabled. There is also a special case in which the disk controller is SCSI without BIOS enabled and, in this case, you will see **scsi (x)** instead of **multi (x)**. The disk part of the ARC path designates which disk to use on the disk controller indicated in the first section. If a SCSI controller without BIOS enabled is indicated, the disk portion will tell the computer what SCSI address to boot to on the disk. The disk value will always be 0 if the controller is multi. The rdisk component designates which disk to use on the disk controller indicated in the multi section. It will always be 0 if the controller is SCSI. The partition section designates which partition to use on the disk that was pointed to in the first two elements of the path, not including the zeros entered to nullify a possibility. (The disk partitions run from 1 upward. Zero would not be a valid entry here.) When you add switches, they are appended to the end of the ARC path.

**Table 15-5   Sections of boot.ini file**

| | |
|---|---|
| Boot loader | **Ntldr:** Contains entries for the default operating system to be loaded, and the time that the computer should wait for an action from you before loading the default operating system. If the timeout is set to zero, Ntldr loads the default operating system as soon as the computer boots. If you want the computer to wait indefinitely for you to make a selection, set the timeout to –1. The computer will not boot unless you select an operating system and press the **[Enter]** key. |
| Operating systems | Contains entries for all of the operating systems installed on the computer. Each entry for an operating system contains the path to the boot partition for that operating system. The entry also contains the text that will appear on the boot loader screen. Each entry has four parts:<br><br>• **multi**: Indicates which disk controller to use (0,1,2) if it is either an IDE disk controller or a SCSI disk controller with BIOS enabled.<br>• **disk**: Indicates the SCSI address to boot to on the disk if the disk controller is SCSI without BIOS enabled. This value will always be 0 if the controller is multi.<br>• **rdisk**: Indicates which disk to use on the disk controller indicated in the multi section. This value will always be 0 if the controller is scsi.<br>• **partition**: Indicates which partition to use on the disk that was pointed to in the first two elements of the path, either multi and rdisk or scsi and disk. |

**Figure 15-18  Using the command prompt to remove file attributes**

Removes
system attribute

Removes read-only
attribute

Removes
hidden attribute

# skill 7

# Modifying the Boot.ini File *(cont'd)*

**exam objective**

Basic knowledge

**how to**

Edit boot.ini using the Startup and Recovery dialog box or by directly editing the file in Notepad.

1. Open the Control Panel. Double-click the **System** icon to open the **System Properties** dialog box.
2. Open the **Advanced** tab, and click [ Settings ] in the **Startup and Recovery** section to open the **Startup and Recovery** dialog box.
3. In the **Time to display list of operating systems** spin box, change the default timeout period to 5 seconds **(Figure 15-19)**. Notice that you can also change the default operating system in the **System startup** section of the dialog box. This is the recommended method for editing the boot.ini file for these two settings.
4. Change the value back to 30 to complete the rest of the exercise.
5. Close the Startup and Recovery and System Properties dialog boxes.
6. Double-click the **Folder Options icon** to open the **Folder Options** dialog box.
7. Open the **View** tab. Under **Hidden files and folders**, select the **Show hidden files and folders** option button.
8. Remove the check from the **Hide protected operating system files** checkbox **(Figure 15-20)**.
9. A warning dialog box will caution you against displaying protected operating system files. Click [ Yes ]. Click [ OK ] to close the Folder Options dialog box.
10. Open Windows Explorer. Select the drive containing the boot.ini file (the drive where the operating system is installed).
11. Locate boot.ini, right-click it, and select **Properties**. On the **General** tab, in the **Attributes** section at the bottom of the dialog box, remove the check mark from the Read-only check box. Click [ OK ].
12. Double-click boot.ini to open it in Notepad.
13. In the **timeout** section, change the default timeout period of 30 seconds to 5 seconds **(Figure 15-21)**.
14. Open the **File** menu and click the **Save** command to save the setting.
15. Close Notepad and Windows Explorer. Before you close the Control Panel, you should reopen the Folder Options dialog box and replace the hidden and system attributes for protected files.

**caution**

Do not update the boot.ini file if you are unsure of the repercussions of the change. Always back up the **boot.ini** file before making any changes.

**more**

A few of the switches, which are predefined parameters that you can add to the operating systems section to provide additional functionality, are listed below:

◆ **/basevideo:** Boots the computer using the standard VGA video driver. This is useful if you receive a message telling you that your video driver is missing or corrupt, or that an invalid driver was installed for the hardware.
◆ **/fastdetect=[comx | comx,y,z.]:** Disables the detection of the serial mouse.
◆ **maxmem:n:** Specifies the maximum amount of RAM used by Windows XP Professional. This is useful if you are trying to find out if you have a faulty memory chip.
◆ **/noguiboot:** Boots the computer without showing the graphical boot status screen.
◆ **/sos:** Displays the names of the device drivers as they load. This is a useful troubleshooting tool.

**Figure 15-19  The Startup and Recovery dialog box**

Used to change the default timeout period

This is the preferred method for setting the default operating system

**Figure 15-20  The View tab in the Folder Options dialog box**

Clear the check to remove the system attribute from protected system files

**Figure 15-21  Editing boot.ini**

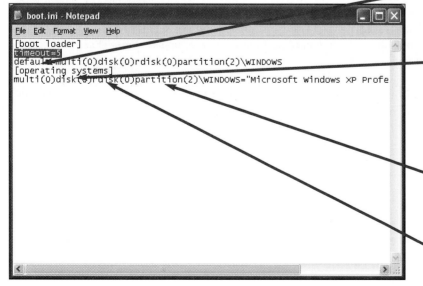

Tells the computer which disk controller to use (0,1,2) if it is either an IDE disk controller or a SCSI disk controller with BIOS enabled

Tells the computer which SCSI address to boot to on the disk if the disk controller is SCSI without BIOS enabled; this value will always be 0 if the controller is multi

Specifies the disk partition that contains the operating system files

Specifies which disk to use on the disk controller indicated in the multi section; this value will always be 0 if the controller is scsi

# skill 8

## *Using the Recovery Console to Troubleshoot and Recover Tasks*

### exam objective

Restore and back up the operating system, System State data, and user data. Recover System State data and user data by using the Recovery console.

### overview

If you are unable to fix boot problems using the Last Known Good Configuration, Safe Mode, or a System Restore, the final tool you can turn to is the **Recovery Console**. It allows you to start the operating system when you cannot get it to start using the other methods. You can use the Recovery Console to stop the specific software or driver causing the problem. The Recovery Console does not start the Registry, so you can use it to copy your Registry backup to %systemroot%\System32\Config to restore the Registry. The %systemroot% will most commonly be C:\Windows. The Recovery Console is a command-line interface used to perform a variety of functions, including the following:

◆ Troubleshoot and recover tasks.
◆ Copy, rename, or replace operating system files and folders.
◆ Format hard disks.
◆ Repair the file system boot sector or the Master Boot Record (MBR).
◆ Read and write data on the local drive of your computer.

The Recovery Console provides you with a limited set of administrative commands that can be used to repair your Windows XP Professional installation. **Table 15-6** lists and describes a number of these commands.

You start the Recovery Console by booting your computer with a Windows XP Professional CD or from the Windows XP Professional Setup disks. Remember, you run the Makeboot.exe tool from the Bootdisk folder on the Windows XP CD-ROM, or Makebt32.exe if accessing the tool from within Windows XP to make the set of Setup floppy disks. Before deciding whether to start from a CD or floppy disks, you should first try booting the computer in Safe Mode. The Recovery Console method is recommended only if you are an advanced user or Administrator who can use basic commands to identify and locate problems relating to drivers and files.

### how to

Install and run the Recovery Console.

1. Insert the Windows XP Professional CD into the CD-ROM drive of your computer.
2. Click ⏽ start and click the Run command to open the Run dialog box. Enter: **X\:i386\winnt32.exe /cmdcons**, where **X** represents the drive letter for your CD-ROM drive, and click [ OK ].
3. A **Windows Setup** warning dialog box will open to let you know that you can install the Windows Recovery Console as a startup option and that it will require 7 MB of hard disk space (**Figure 15-22**). Click [ Yes ] to start Windows Setup.
4. First the computer will attempt to perform a dynamic update. Press **[Esc]** to cancel the search for updates. Click [ Yes ] to cancel the download. This dialog box will appear whether you are connected to the Internet or not.
5. Select the **Skip this step and continue installing Windows** option button, and click [ Next > ] to open the **Copying Installation Files** screen.

## Table 15-6  Recovery Console commands

| Commands | Description |
| --- | --- |
| attrib | Changes attributes of a file or folder |
| Chdir | Displays the name of the current folder or enables you to change to a different directory by specifying the directory name |
| Chkdsk | Checks and displays the status of a disk |
| Cls | Clears the screen |
| Copy | Copies a file to a given location |
| Delete (del) | Deletes specific file or files |
| Dir | Displays all the files and sub folders under a folder |
| Disable | Disables a device driver or a system service |
| Enable | Enables or starts a device driver or a system service |
| Exit | Exits the recovery console and restarts your computer |
| Fdisk | Manages partitions on your hard disk |
| Fixboot | Writes a new partition boot sector on the system partition |
| Fixmbr | Fixes the Master Boot Record of the system partition |
| Format | Formats a disk |
| help | Displays the list of commands that can be used in the Recovery Console |
| logon | Allows you to log on to Windows 2000 installation |
| Map | Displays the drive letter mapping |
| Type | Displays the specified text file |
| Mkdir | Creates a folder |
| Rename (ren) | Renames a file |
| rmdir | Removes a directory |
| systemroot | Sets the current folder to the system root folder |

**Figure 15-22  Installing the Recovery Console**

# skill 8

## Using the Recovery Console to Troubleshoot and Recover Tasks *(cont'd)*

**exam objective**

Restore and Backup the Operating System, System State Data, and User Data. Recover System State data and user data by using the Recovery Console.

**how to**

6. In less than a minute, a **Microsoft Windows XP Professional Setup** dialog box will open to inform you that the Recovery Console has been successfully installed (**Figure 15-23**). Click [ OK ].

7. Restart the computer. When the **Please select the operating system to start** screen opens, select **Microsoft Windows Recovery Console** and press **[Enter]**.

8. You will be asked which Windows installation you would like to log on to; usually there will only be one installation. Type: **1**, and press **[Enter]**.

9. You will be prompted to log on using an Administrator password. Enter the password and press **[Enter]** to open a command prompt.

10. Type **Help**, and press **[Enter]** to view a list of the Recovery Console commands.

11. Press **[Enter]** to scroll down the list of commands.

12. At the command prompt, type **fixmbr** and press **[Enter]** to repair viruses that may have affected the Master Boot Record. Viruses commonly affect the MBR on the hard drive.

13. Type **Exit** and press **[Enter]** to restart the computer.

**Figure 15-23  The Windows Recovery Console has been successfully installed message box**

# Summary

- The Registry is a database that stores information that Windows XP Professional uses to monitor the software and hardware configurations on a computer. Everything from display settings to NIC settings, user profiles, group policies, and hardware profile information is stored in the Registry.

- Although the Registry looks like a single database when you view it in the Registry Editor, settings are stored in several different files, mainly %systemroot%\system32\Config, and profile folders on the root drive in the Documents and Settings folder.

- The term %systemroot refers to the folder where the operating system files are stored, which will most commonly be C:\Windows for Windows XP Professional.

- The Registry stores all of the information related to the configuration of the software and hardware devices on a computer. The information stored in the Registry includes data appertaining to user profiles, device drivers, setup programs, hardware profiles, general system configuration, applications, network protocols, and NIC settings.

- You view the information in the Registry using the Registry Editor. You can also use the Registry Editor to modify the configuration information. To access the Registry Editor window, you can use either the regedit or regedt32 command. Both will open the single Registry Editor included with Windows XP Professional.

- When you open the Registry Editor window, the data is organized in a hierarchical tree format. There are five root keys. The root keys, also called subtrees or subtree keys, are the primary nodes in the Registry structure. They are: HKEY_LOCAL_MACHINE, HKEY_CLASSES_ROOT, HKEY_USERS, HKEY_CURRENT_USER, and HKEY_CURRENT_CONFIG.

- In the Registry structure hierarchy, keys are like folders on a hard disk. They are simply containers in which other keys and values are stored, and they are displayed as folders in the left pane of the Registry window. Keys correspond to hardware or software objects and the information is stored in sections.

- A hive is a distinct group of keys, subkeys, and value entries with its own Registry file and .LOG file. By default, most hive files are stored in the %systemroot%\System32\Config folder.

- Value entries consist of a name, which looks like a capitalized multi-word phrase without spaces, a data type, which determines the format, such as string, binary, or numerical, in which the value will be stored in the Registry, and a value, which is the actual data stored in the subkey. The value can be a single binary digit, a string of ASCII characters, or hexadecimal values.

- The Registry Editor is automatically installed when you install Windows XP Professional.

- When you make changes in the Registry Editor, they are automatically saved and applied immediately, and they cannot be undone.

- The System Restore utility is a new tool for directing and managing the XP Registry backup process. It is used to set system checkpoints so that you can ensure that you will be able to return your system to a given state that was functional.

- A checkpoint is a snapshot of the system at regular time intervals. This can be particularly important when a significant change has occurred, such as when you have installed a security patch or service pack.

- By default, checkpoints are created every 24 hours if the computer is left running. When you shut down the machine, a system checkpoint is created when you reboot if the previous checkpoint was more than 24 hours ago.

- Performing a System Restore can be useful if you have removed a program that is creating a conflict but uninstalling the program has not fixed the problem. You can also use a System Restore to revert back to a set of drivers you were using with no difficulties before you installed updated drivers.

- When you are booting a computer, certain configuration information, such as the startup parameters and a list of the installed device drivers and hardware components, must be accessed. This data is stored in control sets.

- The control sets are stored as subkeys in the HKEY_LOCAL_MACHINES\SYSTEM Registry key. The subkeys contain complete information about the boot process and the settings for the storage devices.

- When you start your computer, there are two configurations that can be used: the Default Configuration or the Last Known Good Configuration.

- The configuration information that is saved when a computer shuts down normally is contained in the default configuration.

- The configuration data that was saved after the last successful logon is saved in the Last Known Good Configuration.

- The Last Known Good Configuration can be used to restart your computer after a problem has occurred to return to the previous configuration that was functional.

- Safe Mode is used to resolve problems that result from faulty device drivers, faulty programs, system service failures, or services that start automatically.

- Usually, when you start in Safe Mode, you will be opening the Control Panel so that you can undo whatever setting you recently configured that may be causing the operating system to malfunction at boot time.

- You can start or stop a system service, uninstall a recently installed program, change a recently instituted display setting, or uninstall a recently installed device driver.
- When you boot in Safe Mode, the operating system will only load a basic set of files and drivers for the keyboard, mouse, basic VGA monitor, default system services, and disk.
- When you enable boot logging, you record the loading and initialization of drivers and services in the Ntbtlog.txt log file, which is located in the %systemroot% folder. Drivers and services that successfully load, as well as those that do not load or initialize, will be recorded in this log file. This option is automatically enabled when you start the computer in any of the Safe Modes.
- The boot.ini file is created during the installation of Windows XP Professional, and it is accessed during the selecting the operating system phase of the boot process to find out if any other operating systems are stored on the computer.
- The boot.ini file is saved in the root of the system partition, and it tells the computer what OS choices to display during startup. It is a hidden, read-only, system file with two sections: boot loader and operating systems.
- The timeout time period is the time you will have to choose between alternative operating systems on a dual boot system before the default operating system loads.
- You can change the default operating system and the default timeout period in the Startup and Recovery dialog box, or by editing the boot.ini file directly. Using the Startup and Recovery dialog box is the recommended method.

- The main reason you will have to edit the boot.ini file is if you want to change the parameters for one of the listed operating systems, such as when you add a controller or a hard disk.
- To do this, you edit the ARC path. The term ARC path (Advanced RISC [reduced instruction set] Computing) refers to the path that points to a valid boot partition containing the Windows operating system files.
- The ARC path has four parts: multi, disk, rdisk, and partition.
- The System Restore utility sets system checkpoints so that when a significant system change has occurred and something goes awry, you can return to a previous configuration.
- By default, checkpoints are created every 24 hours if the computer is left running. When you shut the machine down, a system checkpoint is created when you reboot if the previous checkpoint was more than 24 hours ago.
- Performing a System Restore can be useful if you have removed a program that is creating a conflict but uninstalling the program has not fixed the problem. You can also use a System Restore to revert back to a set of drivers you were using with no difficulties before you installed updated drivers.
- If you are unable to fix boot problems using the Last Known Good Configuration, Safe Mode, or a System Restore, you can use the Recovery Console, which allows you to start the operating system when you cannot get it to start using the other methods.
- The Recovery Console provides you with a limited set of administrative commands that can be used to repair your Windows XP Professional installation.

## Key Terms

| | | |
|---|---|---|
| Advanced RISC Computing (ARC) path | Hive | Registry Editor |
| Boot loader (Ntldr) | Key | Safe Mode |
| Boot process | Last Known Good Configuration | Session Manager (Smss.exe) |
| Boot sector | Master Boot Record (MBR) | Subkey |
| Boot.ini | Power-On Self Test (POST) | Subtree |
| Control set | Recovery Console | Systemroot |
| Enable boot logging | regedit.exe | Timeout |
| Hardware profile | regedt32.exe | Value entries |
| | Registry | |

# Test Yourself

1. When you boot up your computer, what is the first task that is executed?
   a. Ntldr gathers configuration information.
   b. The boot portion of the hard disk is located.
   c. The POST routines are executed.
   d. BIOS runs the MBR.

2. What is a control set?
   a. Configuration information, such as the startup parameters and a list of the installed device drivers, hardware components, and services that is stored in a Registry key.
   b. A record of the master boot.
   c. A file that contains the information about the operating systems installed on the computer.
   d. A file that detects hardware installed on the computer.

3. What happens when a computer is started in Safe Mode?
   a. The computer does not allow you to execute any application other than System Tools.
   b. Drivers and services for networking are added.
   c. The computer loads information saved in the Registry during the last shutdown.
   d. The computer loads only basic files and drivers.

4. When is the boot.ini file created?
   a. During the installation of Windows XP
   b. After kernel initialization
   c. After the operating system is selected
   d. When Ntdetect and Ntoskrnl files detect hardware

5. A hive is a component of the ___.
   a. Boot.ini file
   b. Registry
   c. Subtree
   d. Control Set

6. What kind of information does the subtree HKEY_LOCAL_MACHINE contain?
   a. Hardware and software configuration settings
   b. User settings
   c. File type to application mapping data
   d. Currently active hardware

7. Which of the following files detects the hardware installed on the computer during the boot sequence phase of the booting process?(Choose all that apply.)
   a. Boot.ini
   b. Ntldr
   c. Ntdetect.com
   d. Lsass.exe
   e. Ntoskrnl

8. What does the Master Boot Record (MBR) do?
   a. Locates the boot sector on the active partition, loads the boot sector into memory, and loads the hidden system file **Ntldr** (the boot loader).
   b. Checks the hardware to make sure that the basic hardware components are on the computer.
   c. Reads the boot.ini file to find out what operating systems are on the computer.
   d. Detects the hardware installed on the computer.

9. Under which of the following conditions can you use the Last Known Good Configuration to boot your computer?
   a. You have incorrectly edited the Registry and you are not able to reboot the computer.
   b. Any problem occurring in the computer due to a change in the user profiles.
   c. The drivers for a device are corrupt.
   d. Any change that was made before the last successful logon needs be reversed.

10. The Registry stores information related to the user and hardware profiles only.
    a. True
    b. False

11. If you think that the boot sector on your system partition is damaged, what command can you use in the Recovery Console to create a new boot sector?
    a. fixmbr
    b. fixbootsector
    c. fixboot
    d. mkdir

12. When you boot in any of the Safe Modes, which log file stores information about device drivers that do and do not load successfully?
    a. Ntbtlog.txt log file
    b. Setuperr.log
    c. Mmdet.log
    d. Schedlgu.txt

# Projects: On Your Own

**1.** View the **System Bios Version** in the Registry.
   a. Open the **Registry Editor** window.
   b. Access the **System** subkey in the **HKEY_LOCAL_MACHINE on Local Machine** window.
   c. View the information related to the **System Bios**.
   d. Close the **HKEY_LOCAL_MACHINE on Local Machine** window.

**2.** Start your computer in **Safe Mode** and change the **Display settings**.
   a. Open the **Windows Advanced Options Menu** screen and select the **Safe Mode** option.
   b. Log on as an **Administrator**.
   c. Open the **Control Panel** window.
   d. Open the **System Properties** dialog box.
   e. Modify the screen resolution to be **800 by 600** pixels.
   f. Accept the changes.

# Problem Solving Scenarios

1. You are an Assistant Network Administrator of the IT Department at AccuTime, Inc., a business consulting firm headquartered in Birmingham, Alabama. The Marketing Director just called and said that her Windows XP desktop system no longer starts up. After discussing the situation, you learn that the screen goes blank during the initial boot process after the director selects the operating system on her dual-boot system. An IT department technician recently installed a new NIC and a new VGA Driver. However, the technician failed to restart the director's machine after each installation even though the system had prompted him to do so. Write down the steps you would take to diagnose and solve the problem.

2. A workstation on your network is configured for a dual-boot with Windows 98 and Windows XP. The workstation's user mainly uses Windows XP, which is the default operating system for the machine. The user reports that the computer recently has taken a very long time to boot up. Now, the user cannot boot it at all. When you test the workstation, you cannot boot to the Last Known Good Configuration or into Safe Mode. The POST successfully runs, but then the boot process simply stops. Describe what you think the problem might be. Outline the steps you will take to fix both the critical problem and the original secondary problem reported by the user. Include two methods for fixing the secondary problem and the specific command you will use to fix the critical problem.

# Configuring Remote Access and Dial-up Networking

So far this book has concentrated on creating local area networks (LANs), either workgroup-based or domain-based. When your LAN is created, various networking components such as cables, routers, and NICs are generally used, although increasingly wireless LANs that use radio frequencies, and wireless LAN adapter cards, or USB devices are becoming cost effective, and thus more popular.

However, when you want to make long distance connections, the Public Switched Telephone Network (PSTN), also referred to as Plain Old Telephone Service (POTS) is most commonly accessed. The telephone system is a circuit switched network: it establishes a dedicated link from the caller to the receiver. Your Windows XP Professional computer uses dial-up networking or Remote Access Services (RAS), as well as virtual private networks (VPNs) to connect to the other systems using this established infrastructure. For example, you might need to access resources on your PC or on your organization's LAN when you are traveling to another state or country, or you might want to make a resource on your computer available to a branch office or even to a single user in another city or state. Your employees might also need Internet access on your local LAN if you do not yet have a continuous connection, or they may need to access their e-mail while on the road. Network and Dialup software or Remote Access Services are used to connect to an ISP (Internet Service Provider) or to your company's network. Users dial in to a RAS server, connect to it through a modem, and the RAS server routes the connection to the LAN via a network interface card. Internet Connection Sharing (ICS) is used to share an Internet link with other computers on your LAN so that just one computer on the LAN functions as the gateway to the Web. This is particularly useful for small networks where it may not be feasible to have separate dial-up connections for different computers on a network.

Security is an important consideration when you access resources over a public network. In order to create secure connections, Windows XP Professional supports several protocols that provide security, authentication, and encryption for RAS connections. Virtual private networks (VPNs) are used to create secure connections over an untrusted public network. VPNs use tunneling protocols to create a secure tunnel within the public Internet through which the corporate LAN can be accessed.

Some features new to Windows XP include the ability to set up a basic firewall using an Internet Connection Firewall (ICF), and the ability to establish Remote Desktop sessions with another Windows XP computer. Remote Desktop sessions can be used by telecommuting or traveling employees to access their desktop computers at the workplace. Remote Assistance allows Windows XP users to contact help desk technicians and support personnel, who are also at a Windows XP machine, to obtain help in resolving system difficulties.

# Goals

In this lesson, you will learn how to use RAS to connect a Windows XP Professional PC to a remote computer or a remote network. You will learn to configure both outbound and inbound connections, as well as how to share an Internet link using Internet Connection Sharing (ICS). You will also learn about the protocols that are used to enhance security and how to create a VPN. In addition, you will learn how to configure an Internet Connection Firewall (ICF), use IE to access local, LAN and Web resources, and how to configure and use Remote Desktop and Remote Assistance.

## Lesson 16   Configuring Remote Access and Dial-up Networking

| Skill | Exam 70-270 Objective |
|-------|----------------------|
| 1. Introduction to the Remote Access Protocols | Basic knowledge |
| 2. Configuring Outbound Connections | Connect to computers using dial-up networking. |
| 3. Creating a Dial-Up Connection to a Remote Access Server | Connect to computers using dial-up networking. Create a dial-up connection to a Remote Access server. |
| 4. Connecting to the Internet by Using a Dial-Up Connection | Connect to computers using dial-up networking. Connect to the Internet using dial-up networking. |
| 5. Setting Up a VPN Connection | Connect to computers using dial-up networking. Connect to computers using a virtual private connection (VPN). |
| 6. Configuring Inbound Connections | Connect to computers using dial-up networking. |
| 7. Configuring Internet Connection Sharing | Connect to computers using dial-up networking. Configure and troubleshoot Internet Connection Sharing (ICS). |
| 8. Setting Up a Firewall | Connect to computers using dial-up networking. Configure, manage, and troubleshoot an Internet connection firewall (ICF). |
| 9. Accessing Resources with Internet Explorer | Connect to resources by using Internet Explorer. Configure, manage, and troubleshoot Internet Explorer security settings. |
| 10. Configuring Remote Desktop and Remote Assistance | Connect to computers using dial-up networking. Configure, manage, and troubleshoot remote desktop and remote assistance. |

# Requirements

To complete this lesson, you will need two Windows XP Professional machines with standard 56.6 Kbps modems and the TCP/IP protocol installed.

# skill 1

## *Introduction to the Remote Access Protocols*

**exam objective**    Basic knowledge

## overview

You set up a dial-in remote access server (RAS) so that telecommuters, employees whose jobs involve traveling, and System Administrators who monitor and manage computers at multiple branch offices, can connect to their office networks and access resources. The connection methods used by clients are either dial-up, VPN (connecting to a VPN server over the Internet), or connecting directly to another computer using an infrared, parallel or serial port.

To establish a dial-up connection, Windows XP Professional uses either the **Point-to-Point Protocol (PPP)** or the **Serial Line Internet Protocol (SLIP)** network protocols **(Figure 16-1)**. The PPP protocol allows remote clients to access network resources and provides error-checking to detect possible problems when data is received. SLIP is an older remote communications protocol that is used by UNIX computers. It does not provide security and transfers data without checking for errors. There is no support for encryption so passwords are sent as clear text. A Windows XP Professional computer can only perform the role of SLIP client. It cannot be a SLIP server. PPP provides a more efficient, but slower method of transferring data due to the error-checking. SLIP has for the most part been replaced by PPP, because although error-checking may slow PPP down somewhat, it is still more efficient because if there are problems, they are detected much sooner, and thus solved more quickly. SLIP also does not support dynamically assigned IP addresses (DHCP) and can only be used on TCP/IP networks. It does not support IPX. The updated CSLIP (Compressed SLIP) uses header compression to reduce transmission overhead.

PPP, which can support many networking protocols besides TCP/IP (IPX, NetBEUI, etc.), uses a variety of authentication protocols **(Table 16-1)**:

◆ **Password Authentication Protocol (PAP):** PAP is the least secure authentication protocol. It uses plain text passwords for authentication. However, PAP is used when a more secure authentication method cannot be used and this protocol may be necessary for creating dial-up connections with non-Windows networks that do not encrypt passwords.

◆ **Challenge Handshake Authentication Protocol (CHAP):** CHAP is a protocol that provides authentication on the basis of a value that is calculated using an algorithm. CHAP sends a challenge message to the client as soon as the client dials in. The client applies an algorithm to the message to calculate a hash value (a fixed-length number), and sends the value to the server. The server also calculates a value and compares this value to the value sent by the client. If the value matches, the connection is established and the user can access shared resources on the server.

◆ **Microsoft CHAP (MS-CHAP):** MS-CHAP is Microsoft's version of CHAP. The challenge message is specifically designed for Windows operating systems and one-way encryption is used. MS-CHAP is used with Windows 9.x and NT and only the client is authenticated. In the extended version, **MS-CHAPv2**, both the client and the server are authenticated.

◆ **Shiva Password Authentication Protocol (SPAP):** SPAP is an authentication protocol that is used if you are connecting to a Shiva server. This protocol is more secure than PAP but less secure than CHAP or MS-CHAP. Data is not encrypted.

◆ **Extensible Authentication Protocol (EAP):** EAP is used to extend and customize your method of remote access authentication. It supports authentication using TLS (Transport Layer Security) or MD5-CHAP. TLS supports smart cards and certificates. It is composed of two layers: the TLS Record Protocol, which uses symmetric data encryption to ensure that connections are private, and the TLS Handshake protocol, which negotiates an encryption algorithm and cryptographic key before the application protocol can transmit or receive any data. Algorithms are mathematical formulas with a

**Figure 16-1 SLIP and PPP**

- ◆ SLIP: No error detection, can only be used on TCP/IP networks, no authentication, does not support dynamically assigned IP addresses

- ◆ PPP: Supports multiple networking protocols (IPX, NetBEUI), error-checking, and a variety of authentication protocols

## Table 16-1 Authentication protocols

| Name | Description |
|------|-------------|
| EAP | An extension of the Point-to-Point (PPP) protocol, EAP provides support for authentication mechanisms such as smart cards, token cards, and certificates to validate remote access server connections. Using EAP, a RAS client and a RAS server negotiate and agree upon an authentication method that both of them support. For example, when a RAS client uses a generic token card, the RAS server separately sends queries to the remote access client to obtain information about the user. As each query is asked and answered, the remote access client passes through another level of authentication. After all questions have been answered, the RAS client is authenticated. |
| PAP | The least secure of all authentication protocols because it sends all information in a clear text format. PAP has no provisions for authenticating the client and the server to each other. Therefore, PAP is only used when minimal security is required. |
| SPAP | Provides more security than the PAP protocol. SPAP is an authentication protocol that is used if you are connecting to servers manufactured by Shiva. |
| CHAP | Considered a more secure protocol than PAP or SPAP, CHAP is used by Unix-based and other non-Microsoft clients to communicate with a RRAS server. CHAP provides authentication on the basis of a value that is calculated using an algorithm. CHAP sends a challenge message to the client when the client dials in. The client applies an algorithm to the message to calculate a hash value (a fixed-length number), and sends the value to the server. The server also calculates a value and compares this value to the value sent by the client. If the value matches, the connection is established and the user can access shared resources on the server. |
| MS-CHAP | Microsoft's version of CHAP. There are two versions: MS-CHAP version 1 and MS-CHAP version 2. MS-CHAP version 1, also known commonly as MS-CHAP, supports only a one-way authentication process. MS-CHAP version 2 supports a two-way authentication process known as mutual authentication. |

# skill 1 *Introduction to the Remote Access Protocols (cont'd)*

**exam objective** Basic knowledge

**overview**

clearly defined endpoint that are used to solve a particular problem. They can be written in any language from English to programming languages. Smart cards store user certificates and public/private keys that are used for authentication purposes in conjunction with a PIN number. Certificates are digital signatures that validate users and networks. MD5-CHAP uses a Message Digest 5 (MD5) algorithm to encrypt user names and passwords. MD5 is a hashing algorithm. Hashing algorithms transform data in such a way that the resulting data is unique and cannot easily be converted back to its original form. Hence, a client can be authenticated, without sending the password over the network.

When you use EAP to set up a smart card, PAP, SPAP, CHAP, MS-CHAP, and MS-CHAP v2 are no longer available **(Figure 16-2)**. For a smart card, you only need EAP; the client and the server will negotiate the authentication method, for example, TLS (Transport Level Security).

**Bandwidth Allocation Protocol (BAP)** is another network protocol used with remote networks that use dial-in connections. It works in conjunction with **Bandwidth Allocation Control Protocol (BACP)**. Both protocols are used with PPP to augment the use of multilinked devices. The term **multilinked devices** refers to combining several ISDN (Integrated Services Digital Network) lines or modem links to obtain greater bandwidth. (ISDN simply refers to the international data transfer format for sending voice, video, and data over digital telephone lines or normal telephone wires.) Multilinking means that multiple physical links are combined to create one logical link. All of the links are pooled and the load is balanced among the physical connection components. BAP and BACP are used to dynamically add or drop links on demand so that only as much bandwidth as is required for the current network traffic is used. This dynamically provides optimum bandwidth and helps in reducing connection costs because you can specify that an extra line be dropped if the connection falls below a specific percentage. However, as the price of broadband decreases, multilinking will become increasingly less cost effective because the cost of extra phone lines and modems will exceed the cost of broadband access, which will yield many times the bandwidth.

Virtual private networks (VPNs) create a secure point-to-point connection across private networks or a public network such as the Internet. A VPN creates a logical link called a tunnel between a remote user and a private network. Secure connections in VPNs are created using either **Point-to-Point Tunneling Protocol (PPTP)** or **Layer Two Tunneling Protocol (L2TP)** along with **Internet Protocol Security (IPSec)**, which provides encryption. When IPSec is used, data packets are encrypted in one of two ways: Transport mode or Tunnel mode. Tunnel mode, which is used for VPNs, encrypts both the data and the message header, while Transport mode encrypts only the data. Both PPTP and L2TP work over dialup lines, public TCP/IP networks (the Internet), local network links, and WAN links. If you use L2PT, a tunnel will be created, but data will not be encrypted. L2TP must be used in conjunction with IPSec, which will provide data encryption. When you use L2TP, the message header is compressed, while PPTP does not use header compression. PPTP uses **Microsoft Point-to-Point Encryption (MPPE)** to furnish encryption **(Figure 16-3)**.

You create a direct connection with a remote computer using serial cables, infrared ports, or parallel cables. In a direct connection, one of the computers acts as the host while the other one acts as the guest. A host computer has access to resources on a network such as the Internet and printers. Using a host connection, the guest computer can also access these resources.

**Figure 16-2  The Advanced Security Settings dialog box**

**Figure 16-3  Tunneling protocols**

# skill 2

# *Configuring Outbound Connections*

**exam objective**

Connect to computers using dial-up networking.

## overview

Dial-up networking connections in Windows XP Professional are configured in the **Network Connections** window. You use the **New Connection Wizard** to set up and configure both outbound and inbound connections. In the New Connection Wizard, you choose from the following three types of connections **(Figure 16-4)**:

◆ **Connect to the Internet:** These are connections from a computer to the Internet through a modem or an ISDN line. You can choose an Internet Service Provider from a list, use the Wizard to find an ISP, or manually enter the configuration settings. When you manually set the configuration settings, you must specify the ISP, enter the phone number that will be used to connect, enter your user logon name and password, and configure a personal firewall.

◆ **Connect to the network at my workplace:** These are connections using a regular or ISDN modem to a private network that are established by dialing in to a RAS server. A private network is a Local Area Network (LAN) of any organization. You also use this option to create connections to a Virtual Private Network (VPN). VPNs are connections to private networks, such as a LAN, through an untrusted public network such as the Internet. These connections use tunneling and encryption protocols to create a virtual tunnel, usually over the Internet, so that information can be exchanged securely.

◆ **Set up an Advanced Connection:** You use this option to connect directly to another computer using a serial, parallel, or infrared port. You must specify whether you want your computer to act as the host or the guest. If your computer is acting as the host, you must select the device that will be used to make the connection, select the users who will be allowed to access the connection, and select the networking components that will be used for the connection. If your Windows XP Professional machine will be the guest in a direct connection to another machine, you will only have to enter the name of the computer to which you will be connecting, and select the device that will be used to make the connection. You can also specify whether only you or all users will be allowed to use the connection. Shared resources are stored on host computers, while guest computers access shared resources on a host. You also use this option to allow your computer to accept incoming connections.

## how to

Create a direct connection with another computer in which your Windows XP Professional computer will be the guest.

1. Click  *start* , click **Control Panel**, and double-click **Network Connections** to open the **Network Connections** window.

2. Click the **Create a new connection** link in the left pane of the window under **Network Tasks (Figure 16-5)** to start the **New Connection Wizard**.

3. Click  Next >  to open the **Network Connection Type** screen. Select the **Set up an advanced connection** option button and click  Next > .

**Figure 16-4  The New Connection Wizard**

**Figure 16-5  The Network Connections window**

Click to start the
New Connection
Wizard

# skill 2

## *Configuring Outbound Connections*
### *(cont'd)*

**exam objective**

Connect to computers using dial-up networking.

## how to

4. On the **Advanced Connection Options** screen, select the **Connect directly to another computer** option button (**Figure 16-6**).

5. Click [ Next > ] to open the **Host or Guest?** screen. Select the **Guest** option button.

6. Click [ Next > ] to open the **Connection Name** screen. Enter the name of the computer to which you are connecting in the **Name** text box. This will be the connection name.

7. Click [ Next > ] to open the **Select a Device** screen. Select the device that will be used for the connection. For example, select **Direct Parallel (LPT1)** if you want to use the parallel port on the computer (**Figure 16-7**).

8. Click [ Next > ] to open the **Connection Availability** screen. Select the **My use only** option button.

9. Click [ Next > ] to open the **Completing the New Connection Wizard** screen.

10. Click [ Finish ] to complete the Wizard.

11. The **Connect (Computer_name)** window opens automatically. Close it.

12. Close the Network Connections window.

## tip

You will only be prompted to select the connection availability if your computer is a member of a domain. Connections created on a computer that is a member of a workgroup will always be shared with all users on that computer.

**Figure 16-6  The Advanced Connections Options screen**

**Figure 16-7  The Select a Device screen**

# skill 3

## Creating a Dial-Up Connection to a Remote Access Server

**exam objective**

Connect to computers using dial-up networking. Create a dial-up connection to a Remote Access Server.

**overview**

You can create a RAS connection to a local area network (LAN) from a remote location, for example, if you are traveling to another city as part of your job and you need to access resources on your office computer. You configure a Windows XP Professional computer as a RAS client using a configured access device, most commonly a modem. Modems change outgoing digital signals from a computer into analog signals that can be transmitted over wires, and they transform incoming analog signals into digital signals that the computer can use. The RAS server and the RAS client must use the same connection medium. If the RAS server uses an Integrated Services Digital Network (ISDN) modem, the RAS client must also use one, and if one uses a regular modem the other must do the same. Using RAS, you simply connect to the LAN by dialing the phone number of the RAS server. When you dial in to the RAS server, it receives the data from the modem and sends it to the LAN through the network interface card (NIC). The RAS server acts as the gateway to the rest of the network, and as a boundary between the remote access user and the LAN (**Figure 16-8**). When the RAS connection has been established, the remote user can access network resources for which they have permissions in the same way they would if they were logged on to the LAN.

**how to**

Create a dial-up connection to a RAS.

1. Click **start**, click **Control Panel**, and double-click **Network Connections** to open the **Network Connections** window.
2. Click the **Create a new connection** link to start the **New Connection Wizard**.
3. Click **Next >** to open the **Network Connection Type** screen. Select the **Connect to the network at my workplace** option button.
4. Click **Next >** to open the **Network Connection** screen. Select the **Dial-up connection** option button (**Figure 16-9**).
5. Click **Next >** to open the **Connection Name** screen. Enter a name for the connection in the **Company Name** text box. You can enter the name of your company or the name of the server to which you will be connecting.
6. Click **Next >** to open the **Phone Number to Dial** screen. Enter the telephone number you will use to dial in to the RAS server in the **Phone number** text box.
7. Click **Next >** to open the **Connection Availability** screen. Select the **Anyone's use** option button to make the connection accessible to all users (**Figure 16-10**). (Note: this step is only applicable if the computer is a member of a domain.)
8. Click **Next >** to open the **Completing the New Connection Wizard** screen.
9. Click **Finish** to complete the Wizard.
10. Close the Network Connections window.

**tip**

You will be prompted to select a device if multiple devices are available.

**Figure 16-8  RAS server**

**Figure 16-9  Creating a dial-up RAS connection**

**Figure 16-10  The Connection Availability screen**

# skill 4

## *Connecting to the Internet by Using a Dial-Up Connection*

**exam objective**

Connect to computers using dial-up networking. Connect to the Internet using dial-up networking.

**overview**

You can establish a connection to the Internet using one of several methods. The most common way is through a modem. You connect to the Internet using a modem if you have a standalone computer, or if you are on a small LAN **(Figure 16-11)**. If you connect to the Internet through a modem, it will either be installed on your computer or you can share a connection to the Internet that is configured on one of the computers on the LAN. A connection to an ISP can also use an ISDN adapter and ISDN line, a cable modem, a Digital Subscriber Line (DSL), or an X.25 network.

Another method of establishing a connection with the Internet is through a **proxy server**. Proxy servers have two purposes. First, they provide a connection to the Internet for computers on a LAN. Second, they provide a means for controlling in-coming and out-going requests for service. For instance, a proxy server can be used by an employer to prevent employees from accessing certain Web sites. A proxy server can also be configured to allow or disallow access from unauthorized computers outside the LAN. If there is a caching server on the LAN, proxy servers can also be used to improve network performance. Web pages that have been requested by network users will be saved for a specified time period by the caching server. This means that when a second user requests the same Web page, the request can be fulfilled by the proxy server rather than being forwarded to the Web server. The proxy server is usually on the LAN, so the request for the page can be carried out more quickly. If your computer is on a LAN that is using a proxy server, you will have to specify the IP address for the proxy server in the New Connection Wizard.

When you set up an Internet connection through a modem, you can sign up for a new Internet account, or transfer an existing Internet account to the computer on which you want to establish the dial-up connection. To transfer an existing Internet account from another computer, you can either call your ISP, or visit their Web site to obtain the settings from them and reenter them in the New Connection Wizard. You can also use the **File and Settings Transfer Wizard** to transfer your files from the other computer. To start the Files and Settings Transfer Wizard, click **Start**, point to **All Programs**, point to **Accessories**, point to **System Tools**, and click **Files and Settings Transfer Wizard (Figure 16-12)**. If you select **Choose from a list of Internet service providers (ISPs)** on the **Getting Ready** screen, you will also be able to launch the File and Settings Transfer Wizard from the **Completing the New Connection** screen.

If you are setting up an Internet connection through a modem, Windows XP automatically detects the modems on your computer and displays a list from which you can select the one you want to use. You can also choose from a list of Internet Service providers that Windows supplies by dialing in to the Windows XP Referral Service, or you can use a CD provided by your ISP.

**how to**

Connect to the Internet using a dial-up modem.

1. Click [🏁 start], click **Control Panel**, and double-click **Network Connections** to open the **Network Connections** window.
2. Click the **Create a new connection** link to start the **New Connection Wizard**.
3. Click [ Next > ] to open the **Network Connection Type** screen. Select the **Connect to the Internet** option button.
4. Click [ Next > ] to open the **Getting Ready** screen. Select the **Set up my connection manually** option button. This selection assumes you have chosen your ISP and have the information provided by the ISP that you will need to enter, such as the phone number for the ISP, and your user name and password **(Figure 16-13)**.

## Figure 16-11  Dial-up connections

## Figure 16-12  The File and Settings Transfer Wizard

## Figure 16-13  The Getting Ready screen

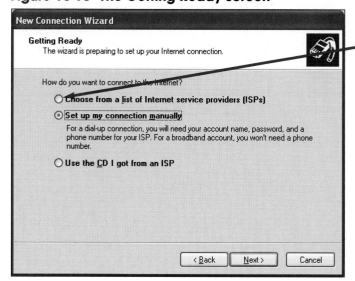

Select to start an MSN Internet account, dial-in to the Windows XP Referral Service, or start the Files and Settings Transfer Wizard

# skill 4

## *Connecting to the Internet by Using a Dial-Up Connection (cont'd)*

**exam objective**

Connect to computers using dial-up networking. Connect to the Internet using dial-up networking.

## how to

### tip

You will be prompted to select a device if multiple devices are available.

### tip

You can also create a desktop shortcut for any connection you create by right-clicking the connection in the Network Connections window and selecting **Create Shortcut**.

5. Click [ Next > ] to open the **Internet Connection** screen. Select the **Connect using a dial-up modem** option button (**Figure 16-14**).

6. Click [ Next > ] to open the **Connection Name** screen. Enter the name of your ISP in the **ISP Name** text box. This name will identify the connection.

7. Click [ Next > ] to open the **Phone Number to Dial** screen. Enter the phone number for the ISP in the **Phone number** text box (**Figure 16-15**).

8. Click [ Next > ] to open the **Connection Availability** screen. Select the **My use only** option button so that only you will be able to access your Internet account. (Note: this step is only applicable if the computer is a member of a domain.)

9. Click [ Next > ] to open the **Internet Account Information** screen. Enter your user name and password in the **User name** and **Password** text boxes. Reenter your password in the **Confirm password** text box (**Figure 16-16**).

10. Click [ Next > ] to open the Completing the New Connection Wizard screen. Select the **Add a shortcut to this connection to my desktop** check box to add an icon for your ISP connection to the desktop (**Figure 16-17**).

11. Click [ Finish ] to complete the Wizard.

12. Close the Network Connections window.

**Figure 16-14  The Internet Connection screen**

If your DSL or cable modem is always connected and your ISP does not require a user name and password, no additional configuration is needed; it is not necessary to run the New Connection Wizard

**Figure 16-15  The Phone Number to Dial screen**

**Figure 16-16  The Internet Account Information screen**

ICF is configured by default for your Internet connection

**Figure 16-17  The Completing the New Connection Wizard screen**

Select to add an icon for the Internet connection to your desktop

# skill 5
## *Setting Up a VPN Connection*

**exam objective**

Connect to computers using dial-up networking. Connect to computers using a virtual private connection (VPN).

**overview**

A **Virtual Private Network (VPN)** is a secure connection across an **untrusted network**. An untrusted network is an open public network that can be accessed by all, i.e. the Internet. This is how a VPN works. First, a remote client creates a connection with the Internet through a dial-up connection, modem, cable, or digital subscriber line (DSL). Then, tunneling and encryption protocols are used to establish a secure channel through the established infrastructure to the LAN. The protocols keep the data flow private even though it is traveling through the public Internet.

Suppose you want to connect two distant offices. Before VPN technologies were introduced, you would have had to create a Wide Area Network (WAN), which is expensive. Using a VPN, the cost is greatly reduced because you can use the existing infrastructure of the Internet. Costs are also reduced because you can use the public Internet rather than making long-distance phone calls to connect to a secure RAS server on your LAN.

A computer must be configured as the VPN server, which will be the terminus of the secure tunnel. Many different types of computers can be configured as a VPN server, including Windows 2000 and 2003 Server computers, Linux computers, and even a Windows 2000 Professional or Windows XP Professional computer for a single connection. Secure connections in VPNs are created using either **Point-to-Point Tunneling Protocol (PPTP)** or **Layer Two Tunneling Protocol (L2TP)**. Both of these protocols work over dial-up lines, public TCP/IP networks (the Internet), local network links, and WAN links. If you use L2PT, a "tunnel" will be created, but data will not be encrypted. L2TP must be used in conjunction with IPSec, which will provide data encryption. When you use L2TP, the message header is compressed, while PPTP does not use header compression. PPTP uses Microsoft Point-to-Point Encryption (MPPE) to furnish encryption.

**how to**

Connect to computers using a Virtual Private Connection.
1. Click ⊞ **start** , click **Control Panel**, and double-click **Network Connections** to open the **Network Connections** window.
2. Click the **Create a new connection** link to start the **New Connection Wizard**.
3. Click [ Next > ] to open the **Network Connection Type** screen. Select the **Connect to network at my workplace** option button.
4. Click [ Next > ] to open the **Network Connection** screen. Select the **Virtual Private Network** connection option button (**Figure 16-18**).
5. Click [ Next > ] to open the **Connection Name** screen. Enter a name for the VPN connection in the **Company Name** text box. You can use the name of your organization or the name of the server you will be dialing in to.
6. Click [ Next > ] to open the Public Network screen. Select the **Automatically dial this initial connection** option button and select the name for your Internet connection on the drop-down list (**Figure 16-19**).
7. Click [ Next > ] to open the **VPN Server Selection** screen. Enter the host name or IP address for the VPN server to which you want to connect in the **Host name or IP address** text box (**Figure 16-20**).
8. Click [ Next > ] to open the **Connection Availability** screen. Select the **My use only** option button. (Note: this step is only applicable if the computer is a domain member.)
9. Click [ Next > ] to open the Completing the New Connection Wizard screen. If desired, select the **Add a shortcut to this connection** to my desktop check box.
10. Click [ Finish ] to complete the Wizard. If you are not currently connected to the Internet the Initial Connection message box opens to ask if you want to create the initial connection. Click **Yes** to connect to your ISP and the VPN, or **No** to cancel. Then close the Network Connections window.

**Figure 16-18  Creating a VPN**

**Figure 16-19  The Public Network screen**

**Figure 16-20  The VPN Server Selection screen**

# skill 6

## Configuring Inbound Connections

**exam objective**

Connect to computers using dial-up networking.

**overview**

Inbound connections are used to allow other computers to connect to yours via either a phone line, the Internet, or through a direct cable. In the New Connection Wizard, you can select the networking components (the protocols, services, and clients) that you will use to establish connections from different kinds of computers. Only the users you select will be able to dial in to the computer. You can accept incoming VPN connections if your computer has a publicly accessible IP address. You can configure an inbound connection to accept dial-up (modem, ISDN, X.25), VPN (PPTP, L2TP), or direct (serial, infrared) connections. On Windows 2000 Professional or Windows XP Professional computers, inbound connections can accept up to three incoming calls, one of each type. The number of inbound connections that can be accepted on a Windows 2000 or 2003 Server machine is restricted only by the hardware configuration of the machine.

Each user that is going to use an inbound connection must have a local user account and must be given the phone number they will dial to connect to your computer. Call back options can be set for each user. If you set a callback number, your computer will authenticate the incoming user, disconnect, and call him or her back at the number you specify. This enhances security because, if an unauthorized user calls in, this number will be called back to establish the connection, not the number of the unauthorized user. You can also use callback options to avoid long distance charges for the connection. The bill will be charged to your phone number, instead of to the client who is calling in. There are three callback options that define how a computer responds when a user dials in. You configure callback options on the **Callback** tab in the Properties dialog box for a user who is allowed to access the connection. To reconfigure callback options after you have created an incoming connection, right-click **Incoming Connections** in the Network Connections window and click **Properties** to open the **Incoming Connections Properties** dialog box. On the **Users** tab, select the user for whom you want to configure callback options and click the Properties button. On the **Callback** tab, set one of the following:

- ◆ **Do not allow callback:** If you select this option, there is no callback. Once the connection is established, the computer stays connected and allows the user to access resources.
- ◆ **Allow the caller to set the callback number:** If you select this option, the computer disconnects as soon as a user dials in and calls them back on the number that they indicate. This setting is useful when users need to dial in from different locations because they can indicate a different number to call back each time they connect.
- ◆ **Always use the following callback number:** If you select this option, the computer calls back only a specified number. Selecting this option enhances the security of your network because users can establish a connection to the computer using only one number.

When you configure inbound connections, you can select the networking components, such as the TCP/IP protocol, to be used for the connection. You must also specify the names of the devices, such as the modem, that will be used for the connection and whether or not the computer should allow incoming VPN connections.

**how to**

Configure a Windows XP Professional computer to accept incoming connections.

1. Open the **Network Connections** window and click the **Create a new connection** link to start the **New Connection Wizard**.
2. Click [ Next > ] to open the **Network Connection Type** screen. Select the **Set up an advanced connection** option button.
3. Click [ Next > ] to open the **Advanced Connection Options** screen. Select the **Accept incoming connections** option button (**Figure 16-21**).
4. Click [ Next > ] to open the **Devices for Incoming Connections** screen. Select the check box for a modem in the **Connection devices** list box (**Figure 16-22**). You can click the [ Properties ] button to open the Properties dialog box for the device.

**Figure 16-21  Configuring an inbound connection**

**Figure 16-22  The Devices for Incoming Connections screen**

You can select a modem, serial, infrared port, or parallel port for the inbound connection

## skill 6

## *Configuring Inbound Connections (cont'd)*

### exam objective

Connect to computers using dial-up networking.

### how to

5. Click [ Next > ] to open the **Incoming Virtual Private Network (VPN) Connection** screen. You can accept incoming VPN connections if your computer has a publicly acces- sible IP address.
6. Select the **Do not allow virtual private connections** option button to disallow inbound VPN connections (**Figure 16-23**).
7. Click [ Next > ] to open the **User Permissions** screen. Select the check boxes for the users who will be allowed to access the inbound connection in the **Users allowed to connect** list box (**Figure 16-24**).
8. Select one of these users in the **Users allowed to connect** list box and click [ Properties ] to open the Properties dialog box for the user.
9. Open the **Callback** tab. Select the **Allow the caller to set the callback number** option button so that they will be able to dial in from different locations (**Figure 16-25**).
10. Click [ OK ] to save the callback setting and close the dialog box.
11. Click [ Next > ] to open the **Networking Software** screen. The **Internet Protocol (TCP/IP)**, **File and Printer Sharing for Microsoft Networks**, and **Client for Microsoft Networks** check boxes are selected by default (**Figure 16-26**).
12. Click [ Next > ] to open the completing the New Connection Wizard screen.
13. Click [ Finish ] to complete the Wizard.
14. Close the Network Connections window.

### more

After you have created an inbound connection, the devices to be used for that connection are converted to answer mode so that, when a user dials in, the computer immediately answers and authenticates the connection. In answer mode, devices can be used by only one inbound connection at a time. You can accept one inbound dial-up connection, one inbound VPN connection, and one inbound direct (serial, infrared) connection at the same time on a Windows XP Professional machine.

You can modify the properties for any connection, such as the name of the connection or the IP address of the destination network in the **<Connection name> Properties** dialog box. Right click the connection in the Network Connections window and select **Properties**. On the **General** tab you can change the device to be used for the connection and either allow or disallow VPN connections. On the **Users** tab, you can select additional users who will be allowed to access the connection and set callback properties for those users. You can also select certain security rules that must be used for the connection. You can require that all users secure their passwords and data, and you can allow directly connected devices such as palmtop computers to connect without providing a password. On the **Networking** tab, you can modify the networking components that are used for the connection.

**Figure 16-23  The Incoming Virtual Private Network (VPN) Connection screen**

**Figure 16-24  The User Permissions screen**

Click to open the Properties dialog box for the user

**Figure 16-25  The Callback tab on the Properties dialog box for a user**

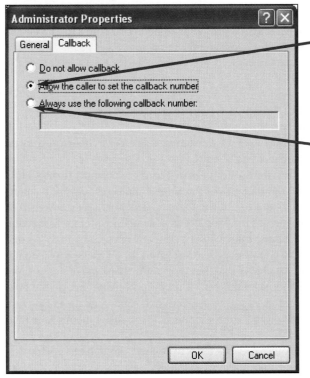

Select to have the computer disconnect after the user dials in and call them back on the number that they indicate

Select to have the computer call back only a specified number; this enhances network security because users can establish a connection to the computer using only one number

**Figure 16-26  The Networking Software screen**

# skill 7

## *Configuring Internet Connection Sharing*

**exam objective**

Connect to computers using dial-up networking. Configure and troubleshoot Internet Connection Sharing (ICS).

**overview**

After you set up an Internet connection on a computer, you can configure **Internet Connection Sharing** so that you can share the link with other computers on your LAN. This computer will then provide the single Internet connection for all computers on the LAN. ICS is most useful for small networks where you want all the computers to use one Internet connection that is shared in the same way as a shared folder.

The other computers on the LAN should be configured to get their IP addresses automatically (in the TCP/IP Properties dialog box). Furthermore, if they have previously established an Internet connection, they will have to open the **Tools** menu in **Internet Explorer** and select the **Internet Options** command to open the Internet Options dialog box. On the **Connections** tab, they will have to select the **Never dial a connection** option button.

If you are on a LAN, the computer on which ICS is configured is assigned a static IP address; thus, any previously established TCP/IP connections will be lost and will have to be reconfigured. The connection to the internal network is configured so that all of the machines sharing the connection are assigned an IP address from a private address range. The ICS machine has both a public IP address and a private IP address. The clients sharing the connection request Internet access from the ICS-enabled machine, which accesses the Internet for them and passes the information to them. ICS automatically assigns unregistered non-publicly-routable private IP addresses to the client computers that are in the Class C subnet range (192.168.0.2 - 192.168.0.254). The ICS enabled machine will be given the IP address 192.168.0.1.

The ICS machine will also assign subnet masks to the other computers on the LAN just like a DHCP server. The default gateway for the other computers on the LAN will be the IP address for the ICS computer. The network adapter in the ICS computer will serve as router for the network (**Figure 16-27**).

**how to**

Configure Internet Connection Sharing (ICS).
1. Open the **Network Connections** window.
2. Right-click a connection icon for an Internet connection and select **Properties** to open the Properties dialog box for the connection.
3. Open the **Advanced** tab. Select the **Allow other network users to connect through this computer's Internet connection** option button. If you have multiple network adapters installed, an additional list box will appear allowing you to select which local area connection you want to enable connection sharing for. If you enabled the Internet connection only for yourself, the **Network Connections** message box will open to remind you that the user name and password for the connection were not saved for all users. If you do not change this setting, ICS will only be able to dial the connection when you are logged on. You must save your user name and password for all users in the **Connect** dialog box. Click [ OK ]. To change this, after you have enabled ICS, right click the connection in the Network Connections windows and select **Connect**. Then, select the **Anyone who uses this computer** option button.
4. After you have selected the Allow other network users to connect through this computer's Internet connection option button, the other ICS options become available and are selected by default (**Figure 16-28**).
5. The **Establish a dial-up connection whenever a computer on my network attempts to access the Internet** option configures the Internet connection to automatically dial and establish a connection to the Internet when another computer on the LAN attempts to access Internet resources through the ICS computer.
6. Remove the check mark from the **Allow other network users to control or disable the shared Internet connection** so that only you will be able to perform these actions.

**tip**

You can also click the **Add** button in the **Advanced Settings** dialog box to add a service that is not listed. You will have to enter the information for the service including a description, the name or IP address for the computer that is hosting the service, the external port number for the service and the internal port number for the service.

**Figure 16-27  Internet Connection Sharing**

Enables workstations on a local
area network to connect to the
Internet through a single IP address

Includes DNS functionality (provides
name resolution services)

Includes DHCP functionality
(assigns IP address)

**ICS-enabled**

**Figure 16-28  The Advanced tab in the Properties
dialog box for an Internet connection**

Select to enable Internet
Connection Sharing

# skill 7

## *Configuring Internet Connection Sharing (cont'd)*

**exam objective**

Connect to computers using dial-up networking. Configure and troubleshoot Internet Connection Sharing (ICS).

## how to

7.  Click [ Settings ] to open the **Advanced Settings** dialog box. On the Services tab, you can select the check boxes for each service running on your network that you want to allow Internet users to access **(Figure 16-29)**.
8.  When you select a service, the **Service Settings** dialog box will open. Here, you can enter the name or IP address for the computer that is hosting this service on your network **(Figure 16-30)**.
9.  Click [ OK ] to close the Advanced Settings dialog box.
10. Click [ OK ] to close the Properties dialog box for the Internet connection.
11. Close the Network Connections window.

## more

After you have set up Internet connection sharing, you can make sure that the computer has been assigned the IP address 192.168.0.1 with a subnet mask of 255.255.255.0 by typing **ipconfig** at the command prompt, or by checking the TCP/IP properties for the LAN connection. You should also check the Internet connection on the ICS enabled computer to make sure that it can successfully connect to the Internet.

Then, you must configure the other Windows XP Professional computers that will be sharing the connection. To do this, open the Local Area Connections Properties dialog box on each of these machines, select **Internet Protocol (TCP/IP)** in the **Connection uses the following items** list box and click **Properties**. Select the **Obtain an IP address automatically** option button. The Windows XP Professional DHCP Allocator will assign IP addresses in the 192.168.0.2- 192.168.0.254 range by default, and the DNS Proxy service will be activated so that the client computers can connect to the shared Internet connection.

To troubleshoot Internet Connection Sharing problems check the following:

♦ **TCP/IP is not enabled on all the computers:** Internet Connection Sharing will not function if the TCP/IP protocol is not installed on the client computers.
♦ **The Internet Connection Firewall (ICF)/ Internet Connection Sharing service has stopped:** If the Internet Connection Firewall (ICF)/ Internet Connection Sharing service has stopped, you must start it again. You can check the status of a service in the **Services** console. You open the **Services** console from the **Administrative Tools folder (Figure 16-31)**.
♦ **Internet Connection Sharing is configured for the wrong connection:** Internet Connection Sharing must be configured for the connection to the Internet. If it has been accidentally configured for a connection with the LAN or for any other connection, users will not be able to connect to the Internet.
♦ **You manually set up the workstations for ICS and incorrectly assign IP addresses or the subnet mask:** Although this is not the recommended procedure (the recommended procedure was followed in the exercise), you can manually configure the ICS clients. If you do, remember that the subnet mask must be 255.255.255.0; the default gateway must be the internally assigned IP address for the ICS enabled machine, 192.168.0.1; and that all IP addresses must be in the Class C subnet range *with no duplicates*.
♦ **ICS clients can only connect if you initiate the connection for them from the ICS enabled machine:** Make sure that the **Establish a dial-up connection whenever a computer on my network attempts to access the Internet** check box is selected on the Advanced tab in the Properties dialog box for the Internet connection.

**Figure 16-29  The Advanced Settings dialog box**

Select the services that are running on your LAN that you want to allow Internet users to access

**Figure 16-30  The Service Settings dialog box**

Enter the name or IP address for the computer on the network that is hosting the service

**Figure 16-31  The Services console**

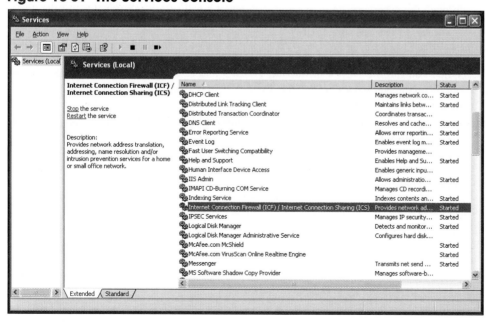

# skill 8        *Setting Up a Firewall*

**exam objective**

Connect to computers using dial-up networking. Configure, manage, and troubleshoot an Internet connection firewall (ICF).

**overview**

As you have seen when you created an Internet connection and when you enabled Internet Connection Sharing, the **Internet Connection Firewall (ICF)** service is now an integral part of the configuration of Internet connections on a Windows network. This feature, new to Windows XP Professional, provides what is referred to as a **stateful firewall** to both Windows XP clients and to machines running Windows Server 2003 Standard and Enterprise editions. ICF is a basic, not overly sophisticated firewall, which monitors all traffic, checking both the source and destination address. A stateful firewall adheres to a security policy that allows for forwarding any data packets that already correspond to an existing connection flow. Packets that are sent from behind the firewall that do not correspond to an existing connection flow will be forwarded only after an entry is recorded in the ICF connection flow table. However, any packets that are received externally that do not correspond to an existing connection flow or port mapping will be dropped **(Figure 16-32)**. Both traffic generating from the computer and incoming traffic to the machine are monitored. If ICS is enabled, this includes all incoming and outgoing data from the ICS clients. Incoming data that is received from the Internet in response to a request by a user, such as entering a URL in the browser, will be permitted. Any other data received from the Internet will, by default, be rejected unless it is connected with one of the services that was selected on the Services tab in the Advanced Settings dialog box for the connection.

You can install ICF in one of four ways:

◆ If you install Windows XP Professional on a standalone computer, during installation of the operating system, you will be asked if you want to connect to the Internet to activate your copy of Windows XP Professional. If the PC has a single network connection and this connection is used to connect to the Internet, at this time you can also create user accounts, and the Welcome to Windows Wizard will enable ICF for the Internet connection.

◆ You can run the **Network Setup Wizard** on a standalone Windows XP Professional computer from the Network Connections window. Instead of the **Network Tasks** category on the menu bar in the left pane of the window, you will see the **Common Tasks** category. Under Common Tasks, select Network Setup Wizard. This Wizard will guide you through the necessary steps to set up a home or small office network. One of the dialog boxes will ask you how you are connected to the Internet. If you select one of the options that specifies that the computer is directly connected to the Internet, ICF will be enabled for the connection.

◆ When you run the **New Connection Wizard** and select the **Connect to the Internet** option on the **Network Connection Type** screen, ICF will be enabled for the connection by default. Refer back to **Figure 16-16**.

◆ Finally, you can select the **Protect my computer and network by limiting or preventing access to this computer from the Internet** check box on the **Advanced** tab in the Properties dialog box for a connection **(Figure 16-33)**. ICF can be enabled on either a standard or wireless LAN, as well as for RAS connections, including PPP over Ethernet (PPPoE) broadband connections, dial-up, and VPN connections.

You can also configure ICF for multiple connections, and each can have its own settings. However, you cannot enable ICF on the ICS private adapter, and you should not enable it for any inbound connections. On an ICS enabled computer that has two network cards, you can enable ICF for the Internet connection but you should not enable ICF for the LAN connection. It is also not possible to enable ICF on a network connection that is part of a network bridge. You must be an Administrator to enable and configure ICF.

**Figure 16-32  Internet Connection Firewall**

**Figure 16-33  Enabling ICF for an Internet connection**

# skill 8

## *Setting Up a Firewall* *(cont'd)*

### exam objective

Connect to computers using dial-up networking. Configure, manage, and troubleshoot an Internet connection firewall (ICF).

### overview

ICF is used to protect the Internet connection on a Windows XP Professional computer that has a direct connection to the Internet through a RAS or LAN. Devices on the Internet can send traffic to this machine, but they cannot gain access to any resources or services on the computer for which access has not been explicitly granted. It is also used to protect a small LAN on which ICS has been enabled.

When you configure ICS, you must decide what types of traffic you are going to block, and what types of traffic you are going to allow. You allow certain types of data packets to pass through the firewall by creating a **port mapping** on the Services tab in the Advanced Settings dialog box. You create a port mapping by setting a particular port number for a particular type of traffic. For example, you can forward inbound HTTP traffic to a Web server on your LAN by mapping port 80 on the computer, which is designated as the port for the HTTP service, to the NetBIOS name or IP address for the Web server **(Figure 16-34)**. Inbound HTTP requests will be forwarded to Internet Information Server (IIS), which hosts the Web site. In this way you can configure a Web server to run behind the firewall.

Furthermore, certain requests must use a different port than the one from which the request was generated, for example, streaming media. You must use a port mapping to handle responses to requests for this type of data. You must also open a port in order to transfer files using Windows Messenger 4.0 or 4.5, because ICF blocks inbound file transfers by default. To do this, click the **Add** button in the **Advanced Settings** dialog box to open a blank **Service Settings** dialog box in which you will use a TCP port number between 6891 and 6900 **(Figure 16-35)**. To handle multiple simultaneous file transfers, you can map several ports within this range. On the Microsoft Network (MSN), inbound computer-to-computer voice calls must be handled by TCP and UDP ports 6901. Computer-to-phone voice calls must be handled by UDP ports 6801, 6901, and 2001-2120.

### more

In order to monitor dropped data packets, either to look for potential security threats or to troubleshoot why data is not being received, you can enable ICF logging. You do this on the **Security Logging** tab in the Advanced Settings dialog box. ICF logging is disabled by default. There are two logging options you can choose: **Log dropped packets** and **Log successful connections**. When you log dropped packets, all rejected packets, whether they are inbound or outbound, will be recorded in the ICF log file. When you log successful connections, all successful connections, both incoming and outgoing, will be recorded. The default location for the ICF log file is **%systemroot%\pfirewall.log**. The default log file size is 4 MB, which can be increased to a maximum of 32MB **(Figure 16-36)**.

In order to allow incoming ICMP echo requests (ping), you must set this option on the **ICMP** tab in the Advanced Settings dialog box. Otherwise, when you are troubleshooting network connections, the ICMP echo request will be blocked and you will not know if there is really a network connectivity issue **(Figure 16-37)**.

**Figure 16-34  Forwarding HTTP traffic to the Web server**

Port 80 is the default port for inbound HTTP requests

**Figure 16-35  Defining a port for Windows Messenger File Transfer traffic**

Use a TCP port between 6891 and 6900 for Windows Messenger File Transfers

**Figure 16-36  The Security  Logging tab in the Advanced Settings dialog box**

Select to log all outbound and inbound dropped packets

**Figure 16-37  The ICMP tab in the Advanced Settings dialog box**

Select to allow ping requests to pass through the firewall

# skill 9

# Accessing Resources with Internet Explorer

**exam objective**

Connect to resources by using Internet Explorer. Configure, manage, and troubleshoot Internet Explorer security settings.

**overview**

As you have learned, you connect to shared network resources using the Universal Naming Convention (UNC) syntax. You use the UNC to map a network location through My Network Places, and to map network drives in the Map Network Drive dialog box, Windows Explorer, or using the NET USE command line utility. To review, the syntax for the UNC path is: **\\\\computername\sharename**

File and Printer Sharing for Microsoft Networks, or the Server service, as you have learned, is the service responsible for making shared folders accessible to other users. The Server service uses the Server Message Block protocol to make shared folders available to all computers that are running Client Services for Microsoft Networks, or the Client service. However, another service is also involved in this process: the Browser service. The function of the Browser service is to maintain a list of all computers that are running the Server service. As computers come online, their Browser service contacts the Master Browser on the subnet. The Master Browser maintains a list of all computers on the subnet that are configured with the Server service. This list is sent to backup browsers on the subnet, which provide redundancy (in case the master browser goes down) and additional capacity for client requests. When a client attempts to locate a network resource, it accesses the Master Browser, which returns a list of backup browsers to the client. Then, the Browser service on the client chooses one of the backup browsers from the list and sends a request for a list of network resources. The Browser service runs automatically in the background and does not need to be configured or managed, but is a necessary component in the process of locating and accessing resources.

Internet Explorer, as you are most likely aware, is the browser utility that is included in and installed with Windows XP Professional, as well as numerous previous Microsoft operating systems. Although IE is primarily used to access HTTP and FTP resources, it can also be used to access both resources that are stored locally and resources on your local area network. Normally, when you access Web resources, you enter the Uniform Resource Locator (URL) in the address bar. However, you can also use the UNC path for a LAN resource or the path to a local resource. The syntax for locating a local resource is: **File://drive:/file_path/filename.ext**

For example to locate a Word document named Reports located on the C: drive of your computer, you would enter: **File://C:/reports.doc** in the Address bar in IE.

When you enter the UNC path to a LAN resource, the same process occurs involving the Server service, the Client service, and the Browser service as when you use My Network Places or the Run dialog box. The new interface in IE 6.0 even has the same look and feel as My Network Places (**Figure 16-38**).

Other methods for connecting to resources using IE include, selecting from the drop-down list on the Address bar, which will include the last 25 entries by default, clicking the History button and using the links on the History bar to locate pages you have previously visited (**Figure 16-39**), and using hyperlinks embedded in Web pages. You can also locate and install printers from Internet Explorer. Simply enter **http://printserver/printers** to view a list of printers on a local printer server.

**tip**

You need to install IIS, and restart the computer after the install, in order to locate and install printers from Internet Explorer.

## Figure 16-38  Accessing LAN resources in IE

## Figure 16-39  Using the History bar in IE

# skill 9 Accessing Resources with Internet Explorer (cont'd)

**exam objective**

Connect to shared resources on a Microsoft network. Connect to resources using Internet Explorer.

**more**

In Internet Explorer, there are four zones by which Web sites and resources are categorized: Internet, Local intranet, Trusted sites, and Restricted sites. Each zone has a particular security level by default, but you can create custom security settings for any zone:

◆ **Restricted sites:** You can place sites that you do not trust in this zone. The security setting for this zone is High by default. All cookies from a site placed in the restricted category will be blocked.

◆ **Trusted sites:** You place sites that you trust into this category. By default, the security setting for this zone is Low. Cookies from trusted sites will be allowed.

◆ **Local intranet:** Sites that do not require a proxy server and all local intranet sites, as well as network paths are placed in this zone. The security setting is Medium-low by default. Cookies from local intranet sites will be allowed.

◆ **Internet:** All other sites that are not placed in any of the other three zones are included in this category. The security setting is Medium by default. You will be prompted before downloading any files, and downloading unsigned Active X files will be blocked. You cannot place sites into this zone.

To add a site to a zone, open the **Tools** menu in IE and select **Internet Options** to open the Internet Options dialog box. On the **Security** tab, select the security zone and click the **Sites** button **(Figure 16-40)**. If you select Trusted sites, the **Trusted sites** dialog box will open, and if you selected **Restricted sites**, the Restricted sites dialog box will open. In either case, enter the URL for the Web site in the **Add this Web site to the zone** text box and click the **Add** button.

If the **Require server verification** check box is selected at the bottom of the Trusted sites dialog box, the URL must begin with https://. IE will make sure that the server for each Web site is secure before making the connection **(Figure 16-41)**. HTTPS (Hypertext Transfer Protocol Secure) provides encrypted data transmission between Web browsers and Web servers. If you select **Local intranet**, and then the **Sites** button, the Local intranet dialog box will open and display a set of three criteria that are applied by default to the zone **(Figure 16-42)**. You can remove the check from any of these settings to customize the security setting for the zone. Click the **Advanced** button to add a site to the zone.

To create custom security settings for any of the zones, select the zone and click the **Custom Level** button to open the **Security Settings** dialog box. Here, you can control behavior such as whether or not signed or unsigned Active X controls will be permitted to be downloaded, if Active X controls will be allowed to run, whether file and font downloads will be permitted, and if desktop item installation will be allowed, among other settings **(Figure 16-43)**.

If the zone is already configured at the default level, you can also use the slider in the **Security level for this zone section** to adjust the security level for the zone without setting specific parameters. Each level, High, Medium, Medium-low, and Low has a particular set of parameters associated with it.

**Figure 16-40  Web content zones**

Click to open the Security Settings dialog box where you can customize the security level for the zone

**Figure 16-41  The Trusted sites dialog box**

The default setting for this zone requires an HTTPS server for the site

**Figure 16-42  The settings that define local intranet sites by default**

Click to add and remove Web sites from the Local intranet zone

**Figure 16-43  The Security Settings dialog box in IE**

# skill10 *Configuring Remote Desktop and Remote Assistance*

**exam objective**

Connect to computers using dial-up networking. Configure, manage, and troubleshoot remote desktop and remote assistance.

**overview**

**Remote Desktop** and **Remote Assistance** provide functionality that is based on Terminal Services so that remote computers can be accessed. Remote Desktop functionality allows you to access a remote computer from a local computer to run applications, open files, and access network resources. Employees can work from their homes while having full access to their workplace computer and the LAN. When you access another computer via Remote Desktop, the screen is locked out so that users physically at the computer cannot use it while you are remotely logged on. The **Computer Locked** message box will display on the desktop of the physical computer hosting the session. Only the remote user's account or an Administrator will be able to unlock it. Remote Desktop client functionality can be used on most previous versions of Windows including Windows 9.x, ME, NT 4.0 and 2000. If the remote computer is not an XP Professional machine, you must install the Remote Desktop Connection client software. You can do this with the Windows XP Professional installation CD. When Setup begins, select **Perform Additional Tasks,** and then **Set Up Remote Desktop Connection** to start the **Remote Desktop Connection InstallShield Wizard (Figure 16-44)**. For very old clients, such as Windows for Workgroups or Windows 3.51, you will have to install the Terminal Services Client.

Remote Assistance is used to request help from an expert, help desk support personnel, a network technician, or simply someone who knows more about a particular problem than you do. The person assisting you must be at another Windows XP computer that has an Internet connection, both parties must be connected to the Internet, and the person requesting help must not be behind a firewall that is blocking port 3389. The person who needs assistance will begin by activating Remote Assistance on the Remote tab in the System Properties dialog box. Next, he or she will send a Remote Assistance invitation through the Help and Support Center, or they can use Windows Messenger or an e-mail to request assistance. The necessary connection information is stored in the invitation, which the recipient opens in order to establish a connection. If both parties have public IP addresses that have been assigned to them by their ISPs, they will establish a direct connection through TCP port 3389. If ICF is enabled, port 3389 will be automatically opened to allow the Remote Assistance session to proceed. Remote Assistance sessions are a bit more problematic, however, if the party requesting help is sharing a DSL or cable Internet connection using a router, for example, those commonly purchased from companies such as Linksys or Belkin, or if there is another mechanism by which networked computers are concealed behind proxy servers or firewalls. In the case of a personal home router, Network Address Translation (NAT) is the mechanism by which machines on a private network access public addresses used on the Internet. These addresses are typically in a class C subnet range that begins with 192.168. What this means is that the IP address that is used to connect to other computers on the Internet is not the one you will find when you use ipconfig to obtain your TCP/IP configuration. Information from the Internet is not sent to this private IP address, but rather to the public IP address for the router.

In order to take advantage of Remote Assistance capabilities when your network is using a private addressing scheme, you must edit the RCTICKET attribute in the Remote Assistance invitation. When the person seeking assistance sends the invitation to the expert or technician, he or she will have to replace the private NAT IP address in the RCTICKET attribute with the public IP address that is being used in communications on the Internet. This address can be found at various Web sites, including **www.whatismyipaddress.com, http://ip.nefsc.noaa.gov/**. The address can also be found at any other sites that determine the public IP address you are using to contact Internet sites, and that they are using to send data back to you. The public IP address will have to be inserted in place of the private NAT address, and port 3389 will have to be opened on the firewall.

**Figure 16-44  Installing the Remote Desktop Connection client on a down-level Windows machine**

# skill 10   *Configuring Remote Desktop and Remote Assistance (cont'd)*

**exam objective**

Connect to computers using dial-up networking. Configure, manage, and troubleshoot remote desktop and remote assistance.

**overview**

Likely the simplest way of requesting Remote Assistance is for both the person requesting assistance and the expert or technician to be using either Windows Messenger or MSN Messenger, or a MAPI-compliant e-mail program such as Outlook or Outlook Express. To make Windows Messenger functional, you must first create a .NET Passport account because use of the Messenger service requires authentication using a Passport account. You can do this by subscribing to the MSN service, signing up for a free Hotmail account, or by signing up for a .NET Passport account with an e-mail address you already have. The .NET Passport information can be saved with either a domain user account or a local user account so that you can use the same logon information with Windows Messenger for Remote Assistance requests and offers.

When you send an assistance invitation, the built-in **HelpAssistant** account is activated (**Figure 16-45**). After the Remote Assistance session is established, the expert or technician can see everything that happens on the other computer, and the two parties can send messages to one and other using chat boxes that are launched on each computer.

**how to**

Configure Remote Desktop and Remote Assistance. You will need two Windows XP Professional computers for this exercise. Both must have Outlook Express configured as their e-mail program and both must be connected to the Internet.

1. On the computer with which you are going to establish a remote connection, open the **System Properties** dialog box from the Control Panel.
2. Open the **Remote** tab. In the **Remote Desktop** section, select the **Allow users to connect remotely to this computer** check box (**Figure 16-46**). Members of the Administrators group, the Remote Desktop Users group, and the HelpServicesGroup will be able to access this computer remotely by default.
3. The **Remote Sessions** message box opens (**Figure 16-47**). Click [ OK ] .
4. Click [ Select Remote Users... ] to open the **Remote Desktop Users** dialog box where you can add additional users who will be allowed to access the computer remotely.
5. Close the Remote Desktop Users dialog box and make sure that the **Allow Remote Assistance invitations to be sent to from this computer** check box is selected in the **Remote Assistance** section.
6. Click [ Advanced... ] to open the **Remote Assistance Settings** dialog box. Make sure that the **Allow this computer to be controlled remotely check box** is selected (**Figure 16-48**).
7. Click [ OK ] to close the Remote Assistance Settings dialog box.
8. Click [ OK ] to close the System Properties dialog box.
9. On the computer you are going to use to establish the remote connection, click [ start ], click **All Programs**, point to **Accessories**, point to **Communications**, and click **Remote Desktop Connection**.
10. In the **Remote Desktop Connection** dialog box, enter the name of the computer to which you want to connect in the **Computer** text box, and click [ Connect ] (**Figure 16-49**).
11. The logon screen for the remote computer will display.
12. Enter your user name and password in the appropriate text boxes to log on.
13. Open the **Administrative Tools** folder. Open the **Services** snap-in and note the services that are running on the computer.
14. Close the open windows. Click [ start ] and select **Log Off** to end the Remote Desktop session.
15. On the computer where help is required, click [ start ], click **All Programs**, and select **Remote Assistance** to open the Remote Assistance page in the Help and Support Center.

**Figure 16-45  The built-in HelpAssistant account**

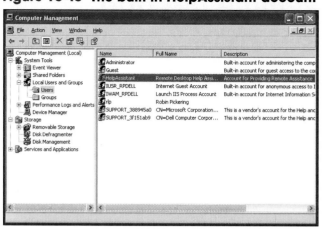

**Figure 16-46  The Remote tab in the System Properties dialog box**

Select to enable Remote Desktop access

**Figure 16-47  The Remote Sessions message box**

**Figure 16-48  The Remote Assistance Settings dialog box**

This must be selected in order for you to take control of the computer

**Figure 16-49  The Remote Desktop Connection dialog box**

Click to display the logon screen for the remote computer

# skill 10

## Configuring Remote Desktop and Remote Assistance (cont'd)

**exam objective**

Connect to computers using dial-up networking. Configure, manage, and troubleshoot remote desktop and remote assistance.

**how to**

16. Click the **Invite someone to help you link** (**Figure 16-50**).
17. Enter the e-mail address for the user at the Windows XP Professional machine that you configured in steps 1-8 in the **Type an e-mail address text** box in the **Outlook Express** section (**Figure 16-51**).
18. Click the **Invite this person** link to open the **Remote Assistance – E-mail and Invitation page**. Enter the name you want to appear in the invitation in the **From** text box.
19. Enter a message regarding the problem you need help with in the **Message** list box.
20. Click [ Continue > ]. Enter a time limit during which the recipient can accept the invitation. For example, change the default 1 hour to 30 minutes (**Figure 16-52**).
21. Type the password the recipient must use to connect to your computer in the **Type password** text box and reenter it in the **Confirm password** text box.
22. Click [ Send Invitation ]. An Outlook Express message box will open to inform you that a program is attempting to send an e-mail message on your behalf. Click [ Send ]. You should receive a message informing you that your invitation has been successfully sent.
23. The person at the remote computer must receive the e-mail and open the attached file, which must be of the MSRC incident type. If they are prompted to save or open the file, they should open it unless the sender is using NAT.
24. Next, they will have to click **Yes** to accept the invitation, and when they are prompted to connect to the sender's computer, they will have to enter the password that you entered (Step #21) and click **Yes** to connect to your computer.
25. On your computer (the sending computer), a **Remote Assistance** message box will open to inform you that your invitation has been accepted (**Figure 16-53**). Click **Yes**.
26. Remote Assistance windows will open on both computers complete with **Message Entry** and **Chat History** sections to allow you and the technician to interact in order to solve the problem.
27. Click the **Disconnect** button to end the remote assistance session and close the Remote Assistance windows on both computers.

**tip**

If you send an assistance invitation and you are using a Network Address Translation device, the receiver must save the invitation file, right-click it and select **Open With Notepad**. Under the RCTICKET attribute, they must replace the private IP address with the public IP address the computer is using. Then, he or she must save the file and double-click it to open the Remote Assistance session.

**more**

A request for assistance can also be issued from the opening page in the Help and Support Center. Under **Additional Resources**, click the **Remote Assistance** link.

The simplest way to access the page where you can *offer* Remote Assistance to someone else is to perform a search on the opening page of the Help and Support Center. The search results for the entry Offer Remote Assistance will return the **Offer remote assistance** link, which you can follow so that you can enter the computer name or IP address for a computer on your LAN for which you have administrative privileges (**Figure 16-54**).

You can add any page in the Help and Support Center to your Favorites list by using the **Add to Favorites** button so that they will be more easily accessed in the future.

**Figure 16-50  Requesting Remote Assistance from the Help and Support Center**

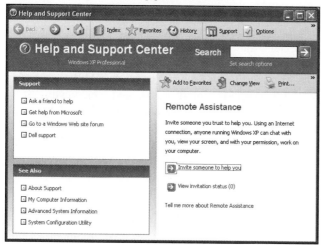

**Figure 16-51  Sending an assistance invitation via e-mail**

**Figure 16-52  The Remote Assistance - E-mail an Invitation page**

You should limit the amount of time during which an invitation is extended to help prevent unauthorized access

**Figure 16-53  The Remote Assistance message box**

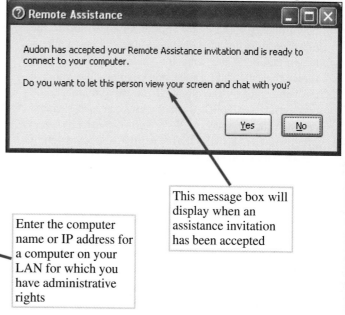

**Figure 16-54  Offering Remote Assistance**

Enter the computer name or IP address for a computer on your LAN for which you have administrative rights

This message box will display when an assistance invitation has been accepted

# Summary

- Your Windows XP computer uses dial-up networking or Remote Access Services (RAS) to connect to other host computers over the established telephony infrastructure.

- To establish a dial-up connection, Windows XP Professional uses either the Point-to-Point Protocol (PPP) or the Serial Line Internet Protocol (SLIP) network protocols.

- The Point-to-Point Protocol (PPP) allows remote clients to access network resources, and provides error-checking to detect possible problems after data is received.

- SLIP is an older remote communications protocol that is used by UNIX computers. It does not provide security, and transfers data without checking for errors. There is no support for encryption so passwords are sent as clear text.

- A Windows XP Professional computer can only perform the role of a SLIP client. It cannot be a SLIP server.

- PPP provides a more efficient, but slower method of transferring data due to the error-checking. SLIP has for the most part been replaced by PPP, because although error-checking may slow PPP down somewhat, it is still more efficient. If there are problems, they are detected much sooner and thus solved more quickly.

- PPP uses a variety of authentication protocols to secure communications.

- Password Authentication Protocol (PAP) is the least secure authentication protocol. It uses plain text passwords for authentication. However, PAP is used when a more secure authentication method cannot be used, and this protocol may be necessary for creating dial-up connections with non-Windows networks that do not encrypt passwords.

- Challenge Handshake Authentication Protocol (CHAP) is a protocol that provides authentication on the basis of a value that is calculated using an algorithm. CHAP sends a challenge message to the client as soon as the client dials in. The client applies an algorithm to the message in order to calculate a hash value (a fixed-length number), and sends the value to the server. The server also calculates a value and compares this value to the value sent by the client. If the value matches, the connection is established and the user can access shared resources on the server.

- Microsoft CHAP (MS-CHAP) is Microsoft's version of CHAP. The challenge message is specifically designed for Windows operating systems and one-way encryption is used. MS-CHAP is used with Windows 9.x and NT, and only the client is authenticated. In the extended version, MS-CHAPv2, both the client and the server are authenticated.

- Shiva Password Authentication Protocol (SPAP) is an authentication protocol that is used if you are connecting to a Shiva server. This protocol is more secure than PAP but less secure than CHAP or MS-CHAP. Data is not encrypted.

- Extensible Authentication Protocol (EAP) is used to extend and customize your method of remote access authentication. It supports authentication using TLS (Transport Layer Security) or MD5-CHAP.

- TLS supports smart cards and certificates. It is composed of two layers: the TLS Record Protocol, which uses symmetric data encryption to ensure that connections are private, and the TLS Handshake protocol, which negotiates an encryption algorithm and cryptographic key before the application protocol can transmit or receive any data.

- Bandwidth Allocation Protocol (BAP) is another network protocol used with remote networks that use dial-in connections. It works in conjunction with Bandwidth Allocation Control Protocol (BACP). Both protocols are used with PPP to augment the use of multilinked devices.

- BAP and BACP are used to dynamically add or drop links on demand so that only as much bandwidth as is required for the current network traffic is used. This dynamically provides optimum bandwidth and helps in reducing connection costs because you can specify that an extra line be dropped if the connection falls below a specific percentage.

- Virtual private networks (VPNs) create a secure point-to-point connection across private networks or a public network such as the Internet. A VPN creates a logical link called a tunnel between a remote user and a private network.

- In a VPN connection, first, a remote client creates a connection with the Internet through a dial-up connection, modem, cable, or digital subscriber line (DSL). Then, tunneling and encryption protocols are used to establish a secure channel through the established infrastructure to the LAN. The protocols keep the data flow private even though it is traveling through the public Internet.

- Secure connections in VPNs are created using either Point-to-Point Tunneling Protocol (PPTP) or Layer Two Tunneling Protocol (L2TP) along with Internet Protocol Security (IPSec), which provides encryption.

- Dial-up networking connections in Windows XP Professional are configured in the Network Connections window. You use the New Connection Wizard to set up and configure both outbound and inbound connections.

- You configure a Windows XP Professional computer as a RAS client using a configured access device, most commonly a modem.

- The RAS server and the RAS client must use the same connection medium. If the RAS server uses an Integrated Services Digital Network (ISDN) modem, the RAS client must also use one, and if one uses a regular modem, the other must do the same.

- Using RAS, you simply connect to the LAN by dialing the phone number of the RAS server. When you dial in to the RAS server, it receives the data from the modem and sends it to the LAN through the network interface card (NIC). The RAS server acts as the gateway to the rest of the network and as a boundary between the remote access user and the LAN.

◆ You can establish a connection to the Internet using one of several methods. The most common way is through a modem. You connect to the Internet using a modem if you have a standalone computer, or if you are on a small LAN. A connection to an ISP can also use an ISDN adapter and ISDN line, a cable modem, a Digital Subscriber Line (DSL), or an X.25 network.

◆ Inbound connections are used to allow other computers to connect to yours via either a phone line, the Internet, or through a direct cable.

◆ Each user that is going to use an inbound connection must have a local user account, and must be given the phone number they will dial to connect to your computer. Call back options can be set for each user.

◆ The call back options are as follows: Do not allow callback, Allow the caller to set the callback number, and Always use the following callback number.

◆ If you select Do not allow callback, the connection will be established and maintained allowing the user to access resources.

◆ If you select Allow the caller to set the callback number, the computer disconnects as soon as a user dials in and calls them back on the number that they indicate. This setting is useful when users need to dial in from different locations because they can indicate a different number to call back each time they connect.

◆ If you select Always use the following callback number, the computer calls back only a specified number. Selecting this option enhances the security of your network because users can establish a connection to the computer using only one number.

◆ Internet Connection Sharing allows you to share an Internet connection link with other computers on your LAN. This computer will then provide the single Internet connection for all computers on the LAN. ICS is most useful for small networks where you want all the computers to use one Internet connection that is shared in the same way as a shared folder.

◆ The other computers on the LAN should be configured to get their IP addresses automatically (in the TCP/IP Properties dialog box) when using ICS.

◆ If you are on a LAN, the computer on which ICS is configured is assigned a static IP address; thus, any previously established TCP/IP connections will be lost, and will have to be reconfigured.

◆ The clients sharing the connection request Internet access from the ICS-enabled machine, which accesses the Internet for them and passes the information to them. ICS automatically assigns unregistered non-publicly-routable private IP addresses to the client computers that are in the Class C subnet range (192.168.0.2 - 192.168.0.254). The ICS enabled machine will be given the IP address 192.168.0.1.

◆ The ICS machine will also assign subnet masks to the other computers on the LAN just like a DHCP server. The default gateway for the other computers on the LAN will be the IP address for the ICS computer.

◆ The Internet Connection Firewall (ICF) service provides what is referred to as a stateful firewall to both Windows XP clients and machines running Windows Server 2003 Standard and Enterprise editions.

◆ ICF is a basic, not overly sophisticated firewall that monitors all traffic, checking both the source and destination address.

◆ A stateful firewall adheres to a security policy that allows for forwarding any data packets that already correspond to an existing connection flow. Packets that are sent from behind the firewall that do not correspond to an existing connection flow will be forwarded only after an entry is recorded in the ICF connection flow table. However, any packets that are received externally and do not correspond to an existing connection flow or port mapping will be dropped.

◆ When you configure ICF, you must decide what types of traffic you are going to block and what types of traffic you are going to allow. You allow certain types of data packets to pass through the firewall by creating a port mapping.

◆ You create a port mapping by setting a particular port number for a particular type of traffic.

◆ You can enable ICF logging on the Security Logging tab in the Advanced Settings dialog box. ICF logging is disabled by default.

◆ There are two logging options you can choose: Log dropped packets and Log successful connections. When you log dropped packets, all rejected packets, whether they are inbound or outbound will be recorded in the ICF log file. When you log successful connections, all successful connections, both incoming and outgoing, will be recorded.

◆ The default location for the ICF log file is %systemroot%\pfirewall.log.

◆ In order to allow incoming ICMP echo requests (ping), you must set the Allow incoming ICMP echo requests option on the ICMP tab in the Advanced Settings dialog box. Otherwise, when you are troubleshooting network connections, the ICMP echo request will be blocked and you will not know if there is really a network connectivity issue.

◆ Remote Desktop and Remote Assistance provide functionality that is based on Terminal Services so that remote computers can be accessed.

◆ Remote Desktop functionality allows you to access a remote computer from a local computer to run applications, open files, and access network resources. Employees can work from their homes while having full access to their workplace computer and the LAN.

◆ Remote Assistance is used to request help from an expert, help desk support personnel, a network technician, or simply someone who knows more about a particular problem than you do.

◆ The person assisting you must be at another Windows XP computer that has an Internet connection, both parties must be connected to the Internet, and the party requesting help cannot be behind a firewall.

◆ If both parties have public IP addresses that have been assigned to them by their ISPs, they will establish a direct connection through TCP port 3389. If ICF is enabled, port 3389 will be automatically opened.

◆ If one or both of the parties are sharing a DSL or cable Internet connection using a router, or if there is another

mechanism by which networked computers are concealed behind proxy servers or firewalls, and NAT addressing is used, you must edit the RCTICKET attribute in the Remote Assistance invitation.

◆ If the person requiring assistance is behind a NAT device, he or she will have to replace the private NAT IP address in the RTICKET attribute with the real IP address that is being used in communications on the Internet.

# Key Terms

Bandwidth Allocation Protocol (BAP)
Callback
Challenge Handshake Authentication Protocol (CHAP)
Extensible Authentication Protocol (EAP)
Generic token card
Inbound connection
Internet Connection Firewall (ICF)
Internet Connection Sharing (ICS)
Internet Explorer
Internet Protocol Security (IPSec)

Internet Service Provider (ISP)
Layer Two Tunneling Protocol
MD5-CHAP
Microsoft CHAP (MS-CHAP)
Multilinked device
Outbound connection
Password Authentication Protocol (PAP)
Point-to-Point Protocol (PPP)
Point-to-Point Tunneling Protocol (PPTP)
Proxy server

RAS client
RAS server
Remote Access Service (RAS)
Remote Assistance
Remote Desktop
Serial Line Internet Protocol (SLIP)
Shiva Password Authentication Protocol (SPAP)
Transport Level Security (TLS)
Tunneling protocol
Untrusted network
Virtual Private Network (VPN)

# Test Yourself

1. You are configuring the callback options for users of an inbound connection on a computer on your network. Which of the following will you achieve by using the Always use the following callback number option button?
   a. Both security and accessibility from all locations
   b. Only Security
   c. Only Accessibility from all locations

2. Which of the following protocols is used to set up a Virtual Private Network?
   a. Bandwidth Allocation Protocol (BAP)
   b. Point-to-Point Tunneling Protocol (PPTP)
   c. Extensible Authentication Protocol (EAP)

3. You are the Network Administrator for a small LAN and you are configuring a Windows XP Professional computer for an employee who telecommutes from her home 70 % of the time. Since this employee sometimes works on a file containing confidential company financial information, you want to make sure she has a secure connection for transmitting that data to the LAN. Which protocols will you use?

   a. NW Link and EAP
   b. IPSec and BAP
   c. PPTP and L2TP
   d. L2TP and IPSec

4. To set up a dial-up RAS connection, you need to make sure that:
   a. An outbound connection is configured on the RAS server.
   b. A POP3 server is present at one end of the connection.
   c. The RAS server and RAS client use the same communication medium.
   d. A proxy server is present on your LAN.

5. You have a small office network with five computers and a single dial-up Internet connection. What will you do to make sure that client computers on the network can access the Internet?
   a. Set up a Virtual Private Network (VPN).
   b. Set up inbound connections on all the computers.
   c. Set up Internet Connection Sharing.
   d. Set up outbound connections on all of the computers.

6. When you configure Internet Connection Sharing on a computer with a dial-up Internet connection, you need to make sure that the computers on the network:
   a. Are configured with an inbound connection.
   b. Obtain IP addresses automatically.
   c. Use tunneling protocols.
   d. Are connected directly to a modem.

7. You need to set up a network to connect the two offices of your company located in New York and New Jersey. The marketing divisions located at the two offices need to exchange confidential data. However, the cost of setting up a WAN connection is prohibitive. Which of the following can you use to exchange data securely without setting up a WAN connection?
   a. Dial-up connection to the Internet
   b. Virtual Private Network
   c. Multilinked devices
   d. Proxy server

8. Transport Level Security (TLS) protocol is associated with:
   a. Smart cards.
   b. A cryptographic system.
   c. Codes that change every time a password is used.

9. You are an Administrator at Spirits Unlimited. You run the New Connection Wizard on your computer and create a dial-up connection to a private network. Your office mate logs on to your computer, but he cannot find the connection. What is wrong?
   a. Only an Administrator will be able to see the connection because you created the connection as an Administrator.
   b. You forgot to create a desktop icon for the connection.
   c. My use only is set.

10. You have received and accepted a Remote Assistance invitation from a coworker, but you find that you can only access the desktop and you cannot perform any actions. What must you tell the person seeking assistance to do?
   a. Tell the user to resend the request for assistance so that you can accept it again.
   b. Open the Help and Support Center and connect to the user's computer from there.
   c. Open the Remote tab in the System Properties dialog box, click the Advanced button, and select the Allow this computer to be controlled remotely check box in the Remote Assistance Settings dialog box.
   d. Open the Remote Desktop Connection dialog box and log on to the computer from there instead.

11. You are working from home and are having difficulty with a particular application that you must use to complete your work. At your workplace, a help desk facility has been established for just such problems. What feature in Windows XP Professional can you use to get help from the technician?

   a. The Application Testing Service
   b. Remote Professional Help
   c. The Web Help and Support Desk
   d. Remote Assistance

12. You are the Network Administrator for a company that has five Windows 2000 Professional workstations, two Windows XP Professional workstations, and one Windows 98 client workstation. One of the servers is configured as the DHCP server for the network. At present, the workstations are using dial-up connections to the Internet. You contact a local DSL company, and they suggest that you use a DSL modem and use their DHCP server for IP address allocation. However, they will only give you two IP addresses, and all of the clients on your network must access the Internet to receive e-mail and do research. You install another network adapter in one of the Windows XP Professional workstations and install the DSL modem on that NIC. What tasks must you perform next? (Choose all that apply)
   a. You must configure all of the clients that will be sharing the Internet connection to obtain their IP addresses automatically.
   b. You must configure all of the clients that will be sharing the Internet connection with static IP addresses.
   c. You must configure the Windows XP Professional computer on which you have installed the DSL modem for Internet Connection Sharing on the Advanced tab in the Properties dialog box for the Internet connection.
   d. You must configure all of the clients with Internet Connection Sharing on the Advanced tab in the Properties dialog box for the Internet connection.

13. You have received an assistance invitation from a friend who is working from a home network that uses a Linksys router. You open the assistance invitation but find that you cannot establish the Remote Assistance session. What must you do?
   a. Save the invitation attachment file, open it in Notepad, and replace the private IP address in the RCTICKET attribute with the public IP address the computer is using.
   b. Disable ICF.
   c. Save the invitation attachment file, open it in Notepad, and replace the private IP address in the Remote Assistance attribute with the public IP address the computer is using.
   d. Tell him or her to install the Remote Desktop Connection client.

# Projects: On Your Own

1. Set up a dial-up connection named **Dial-up1** with a private network that has the phone number **3345222**. Also ensure that all users on the network can use the connection.
   a. Open the **Network Connection Wizard**.
   b. Select the **Dial-up to private network** option button.
   c. Select **Modem—Standard 2400 bps Modem (COM1)** as the device to be used for the connection.
   d. Type **3345222** in the **Phone number** text box.
   e. Click the **For all users** option button, if prompted.
   f. Type **Dial-up1** in the **Type the name you want to use for this connection** text box.
   g. Click **Finish** to save the configuration.

2. Create a VPN connection named **VPN4** to a computer having an IP address **120.9.47.51**. Ensure that the connection can be used only by your profile, if your computer is a member of a domain.
   a. Open the **Network Connection Type** screen of the **Network Connection Wizard**.
   b. Select the **Connect to a private network through the Internet** option button.
   c. Type **120.9.47.51** in the **host name or IP address** text box.

   d. Select the **Only for myself** option button, if applicable.
   e. Type **VPN4** in the **Type the name you want to use for this connection** text box.
   f. Click **Finish** to save the configuration.

3. Set up an inbound connection that uses a **Standard 2400 bps modem**. In addition, the connection should be accessible only by the Administrator user account. Also ensure that callback is disabled.
   a. Open the **Network Connection Type** screen of the **Network Connection Wizard**.
   b. Click the **Accept incoming connections** option button.
   c. Select the **Standard 2400 bps modem** check box from the **Connection devices** list box.
   d. Select the **Administrator** check box from the **Users allowed to connect** list box.
   e. Click the **Callback** tab of the **Administrator Properties** dialog box.
   f. Click the **Do not allow callback** option button.
   g. Click **OK** to save the callback properties.
   h. Click **Finish** to save the configuration.

# Problem Solving Scenarios

1. MidWest Paint and Wallpaper, Inc. is a regional wholesaler and distributor for paint, wallpaper, and other decorating supplies. It sells products to retail stores in the upper-Midwest region from Wisconsin, Minnesota, and the Dakotas, to Montana. Located in St. Paul, Minnesota, MidWest has ten sales reps in the field all the time. They have recently been equipped with laptop computers with Windows XP Professional installed. The laptops have built-in 56k modems. The Sales Director wants to link the sales reps into the company's Windows 2000 network from the field so they can enter orders directly to the order entry system, report sales, and download price files. As Network Administrator, write a document that describes how you will provide remote dial-up access, as well as security for the data.

2. Media Solutions in Ossining, New York, builds multimedia presentations for New York advertising firms. Media Solutions employs twelve artists and programmers in a single office. As a Technical Consultant, you have helped Media Solutions install a Windows XP workgroup network. Now the firm's managers want you to connect the LAN to the Internet so they can share files easily with their customers. In addition, they want you to make it possible for all of the employees to share a single Internet connection. They would like you to write a memo describing how you will connect their firm to the Internet and permit sharing of a single Internet connection.

# 17

# Introducing DNS, Active Directory Services, and Web Server Resources

**A**s you continue to study networking topics, understanding the Domain Name System (DNS) and the services provided by Active Directory will be crucial to your understanding of how Windows networks function. DNS is the main name resolution service for Windows 2000 and 2003 networks. It is used to access computers on a TCP/IP network using the Fully Qualified Domain Name (FQDN) instead of an Internet Protocol (IP) address. IP addresses, as you have learned, are 32-bit numbers consisting of four octets. Each octet represents a binary number in the range 0 to 255 and each octet is separated by a period. Name resolution is the translation of computer names to IP addresses and vice-versa. Name resolution is required so that a user can enter the name of the target computer, and the connection to the other computer can be established using computer language, which is based on binary digits.

As you have learned, user accounts can be stored in one of two places: the local security database on a local machine or the domain database on a domain-based network. In addition to serving as the central security database, Active Directory, which is the domain database for Windows 2000 and 2003, also stores all of the information about how the network is structured and organized. Users access it to identify and locate domain resources. Active Directory (AD) is the directory service for Microsoft Windows 2000 and 2003. A directory service is a database that stores information about users and resources on a network. It also provides ways to access and distribute that information. Active Directory is one of the core features that make Windows 2000 Server and Windows Server 2003 suitable for network administration in large organizations. The Active Directory structure makes it easier for Network Administrators to perform tasks such as designing a network structure, adding, removing, and locating users and resources on a network, as well as managing users and resources. The network administration features of Active Directory are based on the concepts of domains, groups, and user management first introduced with the Microsoft Windows NT operating system. However, Active Directory enhances these concepts to facilitate the management of large domains and networks.

On most networks, computers are connected to the Internet so that users can access information and services from Web sites. Often a separate computer, known as a Web server, is set up by the System Administrator so that users can share resources with other users who are running Web browsers or FTP (File Transfer Protocol) utilities. Web servers are packaged with Internet- and intranet-related programs for sending e-mails, downloading requests for File Transfer Protocol (FTP) files, uploading files, and building and publishing Web pages.

# Goals

In this lesson, you will learn about the DNS service, the name resolution process, and how to configure a Windows XP Professional computer as a DNS client. Additionally, you will learn about the various concepts associated with Active Directory services. This lesson will also introduce the concept of managing Web server resources and teach you how to set up a Web server.

## Lesson 17 Introducing DNS, Active Directory Services, and Web Server Resources

| Skill | Exam 70-270 Objective |
|---|---|
| 1. Examining the DNS Service | Basic knowledge |
| 2. Examining the Name Resolution Process | Basic knowledge |
| 3. Configuring Windows XP as a DNS Client | Basic knowledge |
| 4. Introducing Active Directory Structure | Basic knowledge |
| 5. Introducing Active Directory Concepts and Services | Basic knowledge |
| 6. Managing Web Server Resources | Manage and troubleshoot Web server resources. |

# Requirements

To complete this lesson, you need a Windows XP Professional computer with TCP/IP configured, running on a Windows 2000 Server or 2003 Server network that has the DNS service installed.

# skill 1

## *Examining the DNS Service*

**exam objective**    Basic knowledge

## overview

**tip**

DNS is most commonly associated with the Internet, but is also extensively used by LANs and WANs to resolve and locate computer names on the network.

**caution**

A host name might be different from a computer name if the site developer or the administrator changes the default name given to the computer by the TCP/IP protocol.

Computers on a network must uniquely identify each other in order to communicate with one another. The Internet Protocol (IP) addressing system is responsible for addressing and routing data. It provides the addressing scheme for a network and for the Internet. IP addressing involves assigning each computer a unique identifier, which is a 32-bit number consisting of four octets separated by periods (an octet is an 8-bit value). An IP address contains two identifiers: one for the network and one for the computer or host. The subnet mask is used to divide the network ID from the host ID. It also consists of four octets and is seen by the computer as a string of 32 binary digits (i.e., a series of ones and zeros). The ones identify which of the 32 ones and zeros in the IP address make up the network ID, and the zeros in the subnet mask identify the host ID. This series of ones and zeros representing "off" and "on" is called machine code, and it is the only language that a computer can understand. However, humans prefer names to numbers and find it much easier to access another user's computer by specifying the computer name. Therefore, systems are required for converting computer names to the numbers that make up IP addresses. The core name resolution service for Windows XP is DNS. Windows 2000 and 2003 Server natively use Domain Name System (DNS) servers to perform the task of **name resolution**. Name resolution simply refers to the process by which a name is translated into a corresponding number; in the case of a DNS server, the FQDN (fully qualified domain name) is converted to an IP address. The DNS server maintains a database containing IP addresses mapped to their corresponding names. To access a computer on the network, users need only specify its name.

DNS has a hierarchical structure. The nodes in this hierarchical structure are called domains. Each domain has a name associated with it, for example, domain1. As you add more domains to the DNS hierarchy, the name of the parent domain is added to the child domain or sub-domain. For example, in the domain name **exams.courses.com**, exams represents a sub-domain of the **courses.com** domain, and **courses** is a sub-domain of the **com** domain. The domain at the top of the DNS hierarchy is called a **root domain**. The child domain of the root domain is called a **top-level domain**, and the child domain of a top-level domain is a **second-level domain**. The root domain is represented by a period. The top-level domains are the two- and three-character names you are familiar with in surfing the Web, such as com, net, edu, org, gov, and the various country codes such as uk for Great Britain. Second-level domains have two parts: a top-level name and a second-level name, such as ebay.com, yale.edu, and usmint.gov. A **host name** is at the bottom of the DNS hierarchy and it designates a particular computer either on the Internet or on a private network **(Figure 17-1)**.

By default, TCP/IP uses the name of the computer on which resources are located as the host name. For example, the complete path to the location of a computer named **courses** on the **domain1.com** domain is **courses.domain1.com**.

A **Fully Qualified Domain Name (FQDN)** includes a **domain name** (i.e. a name that follows Internet naming conventions that use dots to separate parts of a name) in addition to the host name. For example, **server1** may be the alias for a computer on a TCP/IP network, whereas **server1.finance.redhen.com**. is the FQDN for the computer. The trailing period indicates the root domain, but even if the period were missing, it is assumed to be there. Com is the top-level domain, designating that this is a commercial organization. Redhen is the second-level domain, indicating the organization name. Finance is a sub-domain of Redhen.com (or third-level domain) indicating the Finance department, and server1 is the name of the computer in the Finance department. The host name is the leftmost part of a FQDN **(Figure 17-2)**. The FQDN represents the exact location of the resource on the network, while the host name can be used by the user at this computer rather than typing the entire FQDN.

**Figure 17-1  DNS hierarchy**

**Figure 17-2  A Fully Qualified Domain Name (FQDN)**

# skill 1

## *Examining the DNS Service (cont'd)*

**exam objective**

Basic knowledge

## overview

On a small network, a DNS server may contain just one database file that stores all of the name-to-IP-address resolution data. However, on larger networks it becomes necessary to divide administrative control and DNS functions into zones. **Zones** are distinct, contiguous segments of the DNS namespace that make a large domain manageable by enabling different administrators to manage different zones. They are areas of authority that consist of one or more contiguous domains. For example, if the resources in **domain1** are related to marketing and finance, the domain can be divided into the zones marketing and finance. The names of the marketing and finance zones will be **marketing.domain1.com** and **finance.domain1.com**, respectively. This partitions or subdivides the DNS namespace to make it easier to manage. Servers in the marketing zone will store all records for the marketing zone and servers in the finance zone will store all records for that zone. There must be at least one **DNS name server** for each zone. However, a single server can host multiple zones.

When multiple DNS servers are created in a zone, there are two kinds of DNS database files: primary and secondary. One DNS name server in the zone will store the primary zone database file and the others will store copies of it called secondary zone database files. Modifications and updates can only be made to the primary zone database file. **Zone transfers** occur to replicate any changes to the primary zone database file to the secondary zone database files. The server where a zone database file is housed is called an **authoritative server** because any query it receives for that zone can be answered with direct knowledge; no other servers must be asked. The purpose of the secondary database file servers is to reduce the traffic and query load on the primary database zone server. Secondary database file servers also provide redundancy; that is, if the primary server is down, the secondary database file servers can service requests instead **(Figure 17-3)**.

Keep in mind that because DNS is fully integrated with Windows 2000, XP, and 2003 Server, a FQDN, such as **www.ebay.com**, can also be the name of a local network. Active Directory is based on DNS, so all Active Directory names are DNS names; for example, redhen.com is a valid DNS name. It can also be used as a Windows 2000 domain name, and **TParks@redhen.com** can function as both an Internet e-mail address and a user name on your LAN. This way, your network users can locate things on the local network in the same way that they locate them on the Internet.

## more

Domain names are not case-sensitive and can be up to 63 characters long; however, a FQDN can have a maximum length of 255 characters. The standard characters supported by the DNS service in Windows 2000 and 2003 are A-Z, a-z, 0-9, and the hyphen. The DNS service also supports the Unicode character set, which contains characters not included in the ASCII (American Standard Code for Information Interchange) character set to support languages other than English. You can use these characters only if all the DNS servers that you are using to administer your site or network support Unicode.

It is advisable to restrict the FQDN to 3 or 4 domain levels. The more domain levels there are, the more administrative effort will be required to maintain them.

**Figure 17-3  DNS Namespace subdivided into zones**

# skill 2
# *Examining the Name Resolution Process*

**exam objective**

Basic knowledge

**overview**

To resolve names to IP addresses and vice-versa, computers send name resolution queries. There are two types of name resolution queries: **forward lookup queries** and **reverse lookup queries**. A computer initiates a forward lookup query when a user attempts to access another computer using a name. These queries resolve names to IP addresses (**Figure 17-4**). Reverse lookup queries resolve IP addresses to names. For example, if a computer named Computer1 has an IP address 142.13.55.2, the forward lookup query will translate computer1 to 142.13.55.2. The reverse lookup query for the same computer will translate 142.13.55.2 to Computer1.

**Forward Lookup query:** When a user enters a name to access a resource, a forward lookup query is initiated. For example, suppose you attempted to access **www.prenhall.com** from your computer, a host inside the **www.school.edu** domain. Your client computer first sends a query to its primary DNS name server. That DNS name server first checks to see if it is authoritative for the zone. If so, it searches its zone database file for an IP address corresponding to the specified name. If it is not authoritative for the zone, the server checks its cache. If the server cannot resolve the name, it sends a query to one of the preset root servers. The root server cannot respond authoritatively for prenhall.com, but it sends a referral to the primary DNS name server for a .com name server. The primary DNS name server then sends a query to the .com name server, which sends a referral for a DNS name server that *is* authoritative for prenhall.com. The primary DNS name server then contacts that name server, which finds the correct host-to-IP address mapping and returns the result to the primary DNS name server, which then relays it to your client computer.

**Reverse Lookup query:** When an IP address must be translated into its corresponding name, a reverse lookup query is initiated. A reverse lookup query is required when a computer needs the name of a computer that has a particular IP address. Since the DNS database is indexed by name and not by IP addresses, the process would be complex, involving an extensive search of all domain names if it were not for **in-addr.arpa**. This second-level domain was expressly created to simplify this task. This domain contains name-to-IP address mappings indexed by IP addresses (**Figure 17-5**).

The in-addr.arpa domain also follows a hierarchical naming scheme, but is based on IP addresses instead of names. The subdomains of the in-addr.arpa domain are named following the numbers in an IP address. The main difference between the in-addr.arpa domain and other DNS domains is that the order of octets in the IP address of the in-addr.arpa domain is reversed. For example, a network ID 135.45.1 on a network would be saved as 1.45.135 in the in-addr.arpa domain. The reversal occurs because IP addresses become more specific from left to right, while domain names get more specific from right to left.

**more**

On a network like the Internet, millions of queries are passed from one name server to another, causing a lot of network traffic. To reduce network traffic, DNS name servers cache query results. A query result can be cached for a specific amount of time called the **Time to Live (TTL)**, after which it is deleted. Updated information will not be sent in response to client requests until the TTL expires. Longer TTL values will increase network efficiency, because requests will be able to be answered more quickly, but shorter TTL values ensure that current data is accessed. The default TTL is 60 minutes.

**Figure 17-3  DNS Namespace subdivided into zones**

# skill 2    *Examining the Name Resolution Process*

**exam objective**     Basic knowledge

## overview

To resolve names to IP addresses and vice-versa, computers send name resolution queries. There are two types of name resolution queries: **forward lookup queries** and **reverse lookup queries**. A computer initiates a forward lookup query when a user attempts to access another computer using a name. These queries resolve names to IP addresses **(Figure 17-4)**. Reverse lookup queries resolve IP addresses to names. For example, if a computer named Computer1 has an IP address 142.13.55.2, the forward lookup query will translate computer1 to 142.13.55.2. The reverse lookup query for the same computer will translate 142.13.55.2 to Computer1.

**Forward Lookup query:** When a user enters a name to access a resource, a forward lookup query is initiated. For example, suppose you attempted to access **www.prenhall.com** from your computer, a host inside the **www.school.edu** domain. Your client computer first sends a query to its primary DNS name server. That DNS name server first checks to see if it is authoritative for the zone. If so, it searches its zone database file for an IP address corresponding to the specified name. If it is not authoritative for the zone, the server checks its cache. If the server cannot resolve the name, it sends a query to one of the preset root servers. The root server cannot respond authoritatively for prenhall.com, but it sends a referral to the primary DNS name server for a .com name server. The primary DNS name server then sends a query to the .com name server, which sends a referral for a DNS name server that *is* authoritative for prenhall.com. The primary DNS name server then contacts that name server, which finds the correct host-to-IP address mapping and returns the result to the primary DNS name server, which then relays it to your client computer.

**Reverse Lookup query:** When an IP address must be translated into its corresponding name, a reverse lookup query is initiated. A reverse lookup query is required when a computer needs the name of a computer that has a particular IP address. Since the DNS database is indexed by name and not by IP addresses, the process would be complex, involving an extensive search of all domain names if it were not for **in-addr.arpa**. This second-level domain was expressly created to simplify this task. This domain contains name-to-IP address mappings indexed by IP addresses **(Figure 17-5)**.

The in-addr.arpa domain also follows a hierarchical naming scheme, but is based on IP addresses instead of names. The subdomains of the in-addr.arpa domain are named following the numbers in an IP address. The main difference between the in-addr.arpa domain and other DNS domains is that the order of octets in the IP address of the in-addr.arpa domain is reversed. For example, a network ID 135.45.1 on a network would be saved as 1.45.135 in the in-addr.arpa domain. The reversal occurs because IP addresses become more specific from left to right, while domain names get more specific from right to left.

## more

On a network like the Internet, millions of queries are passed from one name server to another, causing a lot of network traffic. To reduce network traffic, DNS name servers cache query results. A query result can be cached for a specific amount of time called the **Time to Live (TTL)**, after which it is deleted. Updated information will not be sent in response to client requests until the TTL expires. Longer TTL values will increase network efficiency, because requests will be able to be answered more quickly, but shorter TTL values ensure that current data is accessed. The default TTL is 60 minutes.

**Figure 17-6  The Local Area Connection
Properties dialog box**

**Figure 17-7  The Internet Protocol (TCP/IP)
Properties dialog box**

# skill 4

# Introducing Active Directory Structure

**exam objective**

Basic knowledge

**overview**

On a Windows 2000 or 2003 domain-based network, Active Directory stores information about network objects such as users and groups, printers, and computers **(Figure 17-8)**. Users access Active Directory to locate the resources they need on the network. Active Directory is a searchable database that employs a hierarchical folder structure so that network users can easily find any resource, no matter what server it is located on. Active Directory serves as the central repository for network objects and as a central administrative location so that network administrators do not have to individually manage multiple servers. User and group accounts can all be managed in Active Directory.

Active Directory is based on the domain system. Domains are logical groups of users, computers, and resources. Objects in Active Directory are organized in a logical and a physical structure. Within the logical structure, you can locate any object by name, regardless of its physical location. The physical structure, on the other hand, is used to modify how Active Directory works. If your network is faced with bandwidth limitations that adversely affect the replication and authentication processes, you can create additional **sites**. Sites are defined by creating subnets for each of the physical locations on the network. Additional subnets will be used to establish which server clients will use to log on to the network and locate resources. Additional sites are created when your WAN connections do not have adequate bandwidth to support replication and communication between servers.

The logical Active Directory structure consists of the following organizational elements:

**tip**

Domains use the DNS naming convention and are the building blocks of Active Directory.

◆ **Object:** Any tangible or intangible thing stored in Active Directory. It can be a physical object such as a computer, or a virtual object such as a share. Objects include resources on a network. All objects have attributes or characteristics that are associated with them, which define their properties and behaviors **(Figure 17-9)**. Objects in Active Directory include users, printers, servers, shares, and organizational units (described below).

◆ **Organizational unit (OU):** A subdivision of a domain that is used to group objects in Active Directory. For example, you could have a Finance OU that contains the Cost Accounting OU and the Fiscal Policy OU. Each OU will contain the users, groups, printers, computers, shares, etc., for that OU. The purpose of OUs is to create administrative segments within Active Directory that can be managed by their respective administrators. For example, the head of the Finance department would be the Administrator of the Finance OU and he or she in turn would delegate administrative responsibility for Cost Accounting and Fiscal Policy OUs to their department heads. In this way, administrative control is apportioned without giving any one Administrator access to the entire Active Directory. In Windows 2000 and 2003, OUs are used to reduce the number of domains on a network. On these newer Windows networks, unlike in Windows NT, one domain rather than many can be created with numerous OUs that mimic your organizational structure. Control over the OUs can then be delegated to one or more Administrators.

**Figure 17-8  Active Directory**

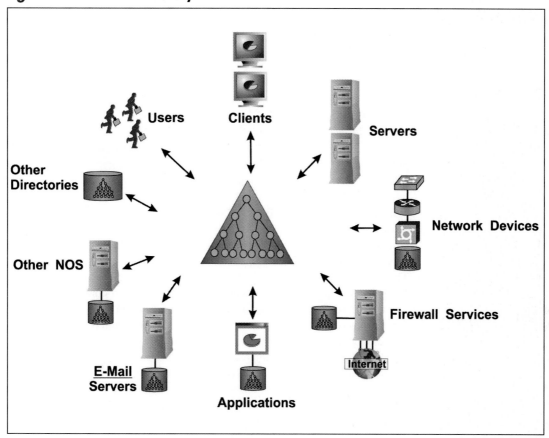

**Figure 17-9  Objects and their attributes**

# skill 4

## *Introducing Active Directory Structure (cont'd)*

**exam objective**

Basic knowledge

## overview

◆ **Domain:** Domains are logical groups of objects that can have their own security policies, can establish trust relationships with other domains, and can hypothetically contain millions of users. Multiple domains in Windows 2000 and 2003 are used mainly when security requirements necessitate multiple domain-wide security policies, such as account policies. Active Directory is stored on a computer that is referred to as a domain controller. You only need to have one domain controller for a domain to exist, but most networks have several domain controllers that store replicas of Active Directory. All domain controllers in a Windows 2000 or 2003 network are equals and directory data is replicated through a process known as **multimaster replication**. This means that all domain controllers replicate Active Directory data rather than having a single master replicator server that is responsible for updating Active Directory on all of the domain controllers. Therefore, when you make changes to Active Directory on any domain controller, the changes are automatically replicated to all other domain controllers in the domain. All domain controllers are responsible for keeping Active Directory up to date.

◆ **Tree:** Domains are grouped in a hierarchical structure called a **tree**. A tree is composed of a contiguous namespace. Trees are used by organizations to create logical domain structures which can be efficiently managed. For example, if you have a domain named *courses.com* and you are going to add a new domain named exams, you can either add the new domain to the existing domain to create a single tree with a parent domain and a child domain, or you can create a new tree, *exams.com*. If you add the new domain to the existing domain, you would create *exams.courses.com*, in which exams is the child domain of courses.com **(Figure 17-10)**.

◆ **Forest:** A **forest** is a group of one or more trees. A forest is the ultimate security boundary on a Windows 2000 and Windows 2003 network. All computers that must share a single Active Directory must be in the same forest, and all domains in a forest share a common schema, configuration, and global catalog. The **schema** is the directory design, which can be extended by adding new object classes or new attributes. A class is the pattern for a set of objects that share a definable set of characteristics. For each class, the schema defines the permanent set of characteristics the class *must* have and the optional attributes that it *may* have. Every object in Active Directory is an instance of one or more classes in the schema. The **global catalog** is a partial read-only copy of all objects in Active Directory that stores commonly used object attributes. Its functions are to respond to logon requests and search queries. All domains in a forest have established transitive trust relationships via the Kerberos V5 authentication protocol. **Transitive trust** means that if a domain has established a trust relationship with another domain, it can also communicate and connect to the domains that that domain trusts and vice versa. The trust relationship is extended to include all other domains that are trusted by that domain. In other words, if domain1 trusts domain2, which trusts domain3, then domain1 and domain3 can communicate because they share a trust relationship with domain2. Domains that do not share a common domain name can be grouped together in a forest and a forest can contain multiple trees. For example, Redhenacct.com and Redhenfinance.com are two different trees because they do not share a contiguous namespace, but they can both be in the same forest in the Active Directory configuration so that users can access resources in the domains in each of the trees **(Figure 17-11)**.

**Figure 17-10  Trees**

**Figure 17-11  Forest**

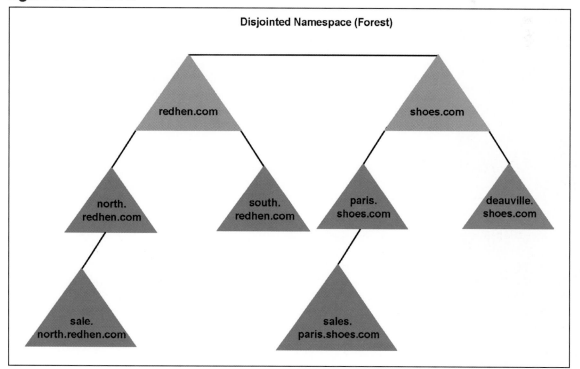

# skill 4

## Introducing Active Directory Structure *(cont'd)*

**exam objective**

Basic knowledge

**overview**

The physical Active Directory structure refers to where objects are located on the network; for instance, where a certain computer or server is located. It outlines, for example, what servers are connected on a LAN and which clients are connected via WANs.

◆ **Sites:** Sites are defined by creating subnets for each of the physical locations on the network. A **site** is a group of TCP/IP subnets with dependable and consistent connections, generally meaning a high-speed link (10Mbps+). **Subnets** are a grouping of devices that share a common network prefix **(Figure-17-12)**. A network prefix (also referred to as a network number) is the part of an IP address that identifies the network on which a host (a computer or other network resource) resides. A subnet, therefore, is a part of a network that has that portion of the address in common. Computers in close physical proximity (i.e., on a LAN) are grouped together to form a subnet. When a user logs on to a domain, his or her client computer is automatically associated with a site according to the subnet on which it exists. On a site, network connectivity is highly reliable, fast, and efficient, as computers on the same site are physically close to each other in a network. On a site, replication is performed among domain controllers in a logical ring format. It spreads from one domain controller to another within this ring until all of the domain controllers are replicated. A domain can span a single site, or it can span multiple sites. Redundant replication paths are set up between domain controllers to ensure that if one of the paths is not available, a second path can be used. Additional sites are typically created when administrators think that the replication latency is too high. Multiple sites are used to control the authentication and replication processes so that network traffic across WAN links can be minimized.

**more**

When you create additional sites, the administrator must create site links. The clients on those sites must be **site aware**, or able to recognize the site-related data that Active Directory is imparting. Windows 2000 and XP Professional and Windows 2000 and 2003 Server machines are, by design, site responsive, but on Windows NT 4.0 and Windows 9.x machines, you must install the Active Directory client extensions to give them site awareness. Installing client extensions will also allow these machines to log on to the domain controller that is nearest to them and to change passwords on any Windows 2000 or 2003 domain controller, as long as the computer is a member of a Windows 2000 or above domain.

**Figure 17-12  Subnets**

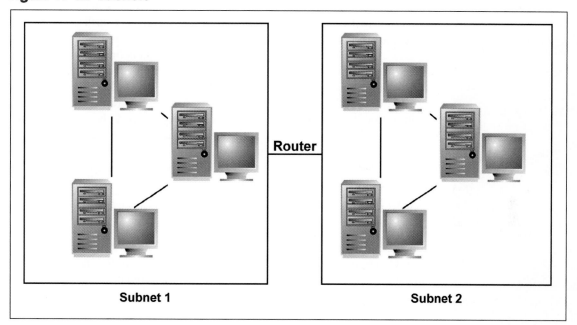

Subnet 1                                              Subnet 2

# skill 5

## *Introducing Active Directory Concepts and Services*

**exam objective**

Basic knowledge

**overview**

To further understand the contents and structure of Active Directory, you must have a broader understanding of the term schema. Schema in general defines the structure of the various objects used in the directory. For all objects in Active Directory, such as computers, users, and groups, the schema defines the attributes of these objects' classes, their parent class, and class properties. For example, for the user object, the schema defines the user attributes such as the first name, last name, and logon name. For each object class, the schema defines the attributes an instance of the class must have such as the object name and object identifier, and additional optional attributes that it may have. Furthermore, the schema defines the parent object class from which the current object class is derived. The schema is created automatically when the Active Directory service is installed. The schema initially contains the definition and attributes of objects that are supported by default such as user accounts, computers, and groups. You can create new classes and assign new attributes to existing objects, thereby extending the schema.

You must also have a broader understanding of the global catalog, as well as be familiar with the concepts of a namespace and a naming convention.

**Global Catalog (Figure 17-13):** The global catalog stores information about objects in a forest. On networks where there is only one domain controller, the global catalog will be stored on the single domain controller and will perform both functions: domain controller and global catalog server. On networks that have several domain controllers, the global catalog will be stored on at least one of them and you can designate additional domain controllers as global catalog servers in order to provide quicker responses to user requests. The global catalog allows users to find directory information no matter which domain it is stored on. The global catalog stores a replica of each object, but not all of its attributes. Only the attributes that are commonly used in searches are stored. This is called a partial replica. Because the global catalog holds a partial replica of every object in Active Directory, all domain data does not have to be replicated to all other domain controllers in order for users to locate data anywhere on the network. When information about objects is updated, a global catalog server exchanges this information with other global catalog servers in a forest **(Figure 17-14)**. This ensures that users have access to the latest information about objects. There must be a global catalog server on the network, or else users—unless they are members of the Domain Administrators group—will not be able to log on to the network; they will only be able to log on to the local computer.

**Namespace:** A naming system is the system by which names are connected with objects, and objects are located based on their names. In other words, the system follows the same set of **naming conventions** (see below). A naming system supplies a naming service to its users for all functions related to naming objects. Directory services, such as Active Directory, extend the naming service so that objects can also be assigned attributes. When objects are also associated with attributes, users can search for objects based on their attributes instead of only being able to perform straight object name searches. DNS is the naming system for Active Directory. The namespace is simply the set of names in the naming system, so a DNS namespace, such as Active Directory, contains the names of the DNS domains. It is the conceptual delimited area in which object names are looked up or resolved. There are two types of namespaces: contiguous and disjointed. In a **contiguous namespace**, the name of the child object always contains the name of the parent domain. Domains that form a single domain tree share a contiguous namespace. In a **disjointed** or **non-contiguous namespace**, there are domains that do not share a common root name, but which are interrelated. Domains in a disjointed namespace, such as an Active Directory forest, are part of the same network, but have different domain names. All domains in a forest share a common schema, configura-

**tip**

You cannot delete a schema object. However, you can deactivate an object.

**caution**

Too many global catalog servers on a network unnecessarily increase replication traffic.

**Figure 17-13  Global Catalog**

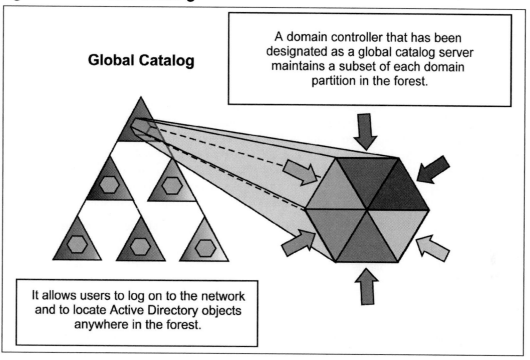

**Global Catalog**

A domain controller that has been designated as a global catalog server maintains a subset of each domain partition in the forest.

It allows users to log on to the network and to locate Active Directory objects anywhere in the forest.

**Figure 17-14  Global Catalog in Active Directory**

Domain1

Complete Information

Global Catalog

Initial Domain Controller

Domain2

Domain Controller 1

Partial Information

Domain Controller 2

# skill 5

## Introducing Active Directory Concepts and Services *(cont'd)*

**exam objective**

Basic knowledge

## overview

tion, and global catalog, and they have all established transitive trust relationships via the Kerberos V5 authentication protocol. However, there can be domains and computers in various locations in the disjointed namespace that have totally unrelated names.

**Naming Conventions:** Active Directory uses four naming conventions: distinguished names, relative distinguished names, globally unique identifiers, and user principal names. The **distinguished name**, or **DN**, is a unique identifier for an object that contains the name of the domain where the object is stored and the full path to the object, including every level of the container objects in which it is stored. A DN also stores information about an object that can be used by clients to retrieve the object from the directory. For example, the user object **Dona Williams**, in the **Users OU**, in the **yourdomain.com** domain can be written as follows:

**CN = Dona Williams, OU = Users, DC = yourdomain, DC = com**

Where CN stands for the common name, OU is the organizational unit, and DC is the domain component.

Another example of this would be:

**CN=Ted Parks, CN=Users, DC=domain1, DC=com.**

If you do not know the exact DN of an object, you can still locate it by searching for one of its attributes. The **relative distinguished name (RDN)** is part of the object name. It is the attribute that identifies it as unique from its peers, usually its "common name," for example, a user account name such as TedParks. RDNs are unique within a specific parent container, meaning that no two objects in the same parent container can have the same RDN or common name. Relative distinguished names consist of one of the attributes for an object that is a part of the DN. The RDN enables you to find an object even if you do not specify the exact DN or if you have changed the DN for an object.

For example, the RDN for the user object Dona Williams is: **CN = Dona Williams**.

A **globally unique identifier** or **GUID** is another unique identifier that is assigned to an object when it is created. A GUID is a 128-bit number that never changes, regardless of changes in the location or the name of the object. When you create an object in Active Directory, the Directory Service Agent (DSA) automatically assigns this number to the object. Even if you move an object from one domain to another, the GUID remains the same. The GUID is used internally by Active Directory, as well as by applications so that they can locate the object again even if it has been moved or renamed. The Windows NT operating system identifies each object in the network by a security identifier (SID). In Windows 2000 and 2003 Server, in addition to a SID, an object is also associated with a GUID. However, unlike a SID, which is unique only within a domain and changes if an object is moved or renamed, a GUID never changes. A GUID is unique across domains, thereby enabling you to track the movement of an object. The GUID is one of the attributes of an object that is stored in the global catalog. **User principal names**, or **UPNs,** contain the user account name, plus the DNS name of the domain where the user account object is stored, separated by an @ sign. For example, **TParks@redhen.com** could be the UPN for the TedParks user account in the redhen.com tree. For the user object Dona Williams in the yourdomain.com domain, the UPN will be: **DonaWilliams@yourdomain.com**.

A user principal name is used to log on to a domain. The UPN of a user object is independent of the DN for the user object. Therefore, you can move or rename a user object without affecting its UPN (**Figure 17-15**).

**Figure 17-15  Active Directory concepts and services**

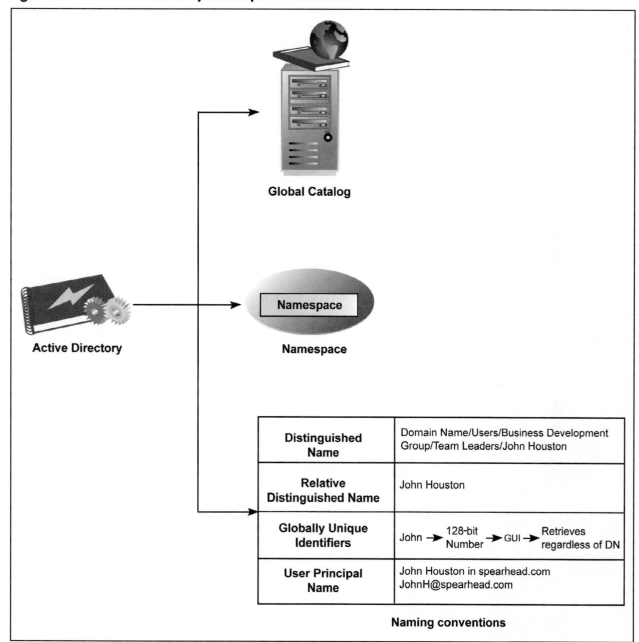

Global Catalog

Namespace

Namespace

Active Directory

| Distinguished Name | Domain Name/Users/Business Development Group/Team Leaders/John Houston |
|---|---|
| Relative Distinguished Name | John Houston |
| Globally Unique Identifiers | John → 128-bit Number → GUI → Retrieves regardless of DN |
| User Principal Name | John Houston in spearhead.com JohnH@spearhead.com |

**Naming conventions**

# skill 6

## Managing Web Server Resources

**exam objective**

Manage and troubleshoot Web server resources.

**overview**

If you want users on your network to be able to share resources with other users who are running Web browsers or FTP (File Transfer Protocol) utilities, you can install **Internet Information Services (IIS)** version 5.1, which comes with Windows XP Professional. This version of IIS does not include as many features as the Windows 2000 and 2003 Server versions. It is intended for use only for small intranets or for a Web site that does not get very much traffic. Sharing Web resources involves publishing your files using HTTP (HyperText Transfer Protocol) rather than the SMB (Server Message Blocks) protocol that is used by the Server service (File and Print Sharing for Microsoft Networks) when you share folders and printers. TCP/IP must be installed before you can install IIS. It is also recommended that you have a DNS server on the network. If it is a very small network, you can use a HOSTS file instead. After you install IIS, an icon for the Internet Information Services Manager will be added to the Administrative Tools folder. This utility is used to manage and configure your Web site. You double-click the Internet Information Services Manager or use the Start menu (Start-All Programs-Administrative Tools-Internet Service Manager) to open the Internet Information Service snap-in where you can configure the properties for the default Web site, as well as the default Simple Mail Transfer Protocol (SMTP) virtual server. By default, an IIS installation includes FrontPage server extensions, the IIS snap-in, the SMTP service, and the WWW service. If you also want a default FTP site, you will have to add File Transfer Protocol (FTP) Service to the default installation.

Like any other resources on your network, shared Web resources must have access controls configured to keep them secure. One simple tip is to disable services that you do not want users to be able to run. This is done in the Internet Information Services snap-in. You can also change the default TCP/IP port for a service so that users will have to know the port number in order to access it. The default port for a Web server is 80, while the default port number for an FTP server is 21. If you change these, users will have to add a colon and the port number to the URL in order to gain access. Furthermore, you can limit the number of incoming connections, restrict which users will be allowed to have Operator privileges, and restrict access to the home directory for either the WWW or the FTP service by setting permissions. In addition, you can either restrict the access allowed by or deny all access to the anonymous user account. You can also only grant access to a specific range of IP addresses, or you can deny access for specific IP or DNS addresses, or a range of addresses. Another method for restricting access is to open the Advanced TCP/IP Property dialog box for the Local Area Connection and set filters so that only certain TCP or UDP (User Datagram Protocol) ports can be used.

**how to**

Install IIS.

1. Click **start** and click **Control Panel** to open the Control Panel.
2. Double-click the **Add or Remove Programs** icon to open the **Add or Remove Programs** window.
3. Click the **Add/Remove Windows Components** icon in the vertical menu bar on the left side on the window to start the **Windows Components Wizard (Figure 17-16)**.
4. Select the **Internet Information Services (IIS)** check box in the **Components** list box **(Figure 17-17)**.
5. Double-click **Internet Information Services (IIS)** to open the Internet Information Services dialog box. The components that are checked are the default installation for IIS. If you want a default FTP site to be created, select the File Transfer Protocol (FTP) Service. Click ☐ OK ☐ to close the Internet Information Services dialog box.

**Figure 17-16  The Add or Remove Programs window**

Click to open the Windows Components Wizard

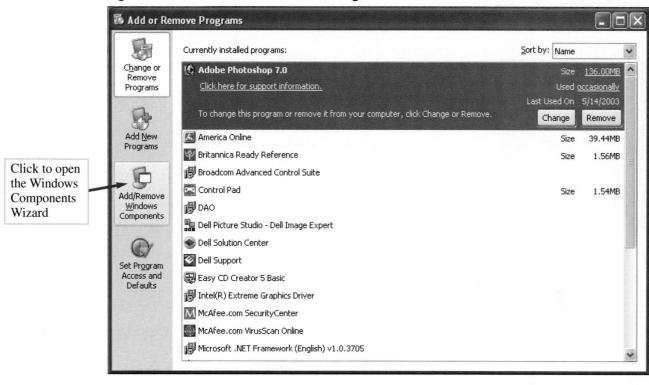

**Figure 17-17  Installing IIS on a computer**

# skill 6

## Managing Web Server Resources (cont'd)

Manage and troubleshoot Web server resources.

6. Click [ Next> ]. The **Configuring Components** screen opens, and then the **Insert Disk** dialog box opens asking you to insert the Windows XP Professional CD in the CD-ROM drive.

7. Insert the Windows XP Professional CD, and click [ OK ] to return to the Configuring Components screen. A progress bar will display the advancement of the installation of the files as they are copied to the system.

8. After all of the files are copied onto the system, the **Completing the Windows Components Wizard** screen opens to inform you that the Wizard has successfully finished (**Figure 17-18**).

9. Click **Finish** to exit the Wizard.

10. Close the Add or Remove Programs window.

11. Open the **Administrative Tools** folder. Double-click **Internet Information Services** to open the Internet Information Services snap-in.

12. Expand the computer name node. Expand the **Web Sites** folder. Expand the **Default Web Site** node (**Figure 17-19**). This console tree represents the logical structure of your default Web site.

13. Close the Internet Information Services snap-in and the Administrative Tools folder.

To modify the settings for the default Web site, right-click **Default Web Site** and select **Properties** to open the **Default Web Site Properties** dialog box. The dialog box includes tabs where you can change the settings for the home directory, directory security, HTTP, ISAPI filters, server extensions, and other settings. To connect to another Web server, right-click the computer name and click **Connect**.

In Windows XP Professional, you can only create one Web site, one FTP site, and one SMTP site, although on Windows 2000 and Server 2003 , you can have many sites of each type. Each site points to content that Web site users will be able to access. The default location of the default Web site is **C:\Inetpub\wwwroot**, if Windows XP Professional is installed on your C: drive. In the console tree, regular folders represent subfolders of Inetpub\wwwroot. Virtual folders are folders that are located either elsewhere on your computer or on other folders on the network.

**Figure 17-18  Completing the Windows Components Wizard**

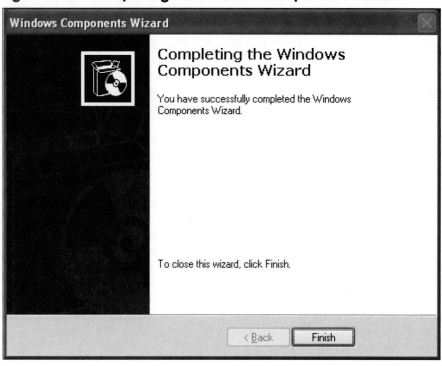

**Figure 17-19  Default Web Site node**

# Summary

- Computers on a network uniquely identify each other using Internet Protocol (IP) addresses.
- An IP address is a 32-bit number consisting of four octets separated by periods (an octet is an 8-bit value).
- Windows 2000 uses the Domain Name System (DNS) service to convert FQDNs to IP addresses (name resolution).
- DNS is a large database containing IP addresses and their corresponding names.
- DNS has a hierarchical structure. The nodes in this hierarchical structure are called domains.
- The domain at the top of the DNS hierarchy is called the root domain (represented by a period). Underneath the root domain are the top-level domains, and underneath the top-level domains are the second-level domains.
- A Fully Qualified Domain Name (FQDN) includes a domain name in addition to a host name.
- Zones are distinct, contiguous segments of the DNS namespace that make a large site manageable by enabling different administrators to manage different zones.
- To resolve IP addresses to names and vice-versa, DNS uses the name resolution process, which consists of forward lookup queries and reverse lookup queries.
- Forward lookup queries are used for resolving names to IP addresses, while reverse lookup queries resolve IP addresses to names.
- in-addr.arpa is a special second-level domain that contains name-to-IP-address mappings indexed by IP addresses.
- In order to use the DNS name resolution service, you must configure your computer as a DNS client.
- To configure your computer as a DNS client, Transmission Control Protocol/Internet Protocol (TCP/IP) must be running on your computer.
- Active Directory organizes objects in a structured hierarchical order. The domain is a logical group of users, computers, and resources.
- Domains are grouped in a hierarchal structure called a tree. A tree is composed of a contiguous DNS namespace.
- A forest is a group of one or more trees that do not share a contiguous namespace. All computers that must share a single Active Directory must be in the same forest, and all domains in a forest share a common schema, configuration and global catalog.
- The schema defines the contents and organizational structure of Active Directory. For all objects in Active Directory, such as computers, users, and groups, the schema defines the attributes of these objects' classes, their parent class, and class properties.
- Computers in close physical proximity are grouped together to form a subnet. On TCP/IP networks, subnets are a grouping of devices that share a common network prefix.

- Sites are defined by creating subnets for each of the physical locations on the network. A site is a group of TCP/IP subnets with dependable and consistent connections, generally meaning a high-speed link (10Mbps+).
- The global catalog is a partial read-only copy of all objects in Active Directory that stores commonly used object attributes. Its functions are to respond to logon requests and search queries.
- The global catalog stores a replica of each object, but not all of its attributes. Only the attributes that will be needed for searches to locate the full copy of the object are stored. This is called a partial replica.
- Because the global catalog holds a partial replica of every object in Active Directory, all domain data does not have to be replicated to all other domain controllers in order for users to locate data anywhere on the network.
- On networks where there is only one domain controller, the global catalog will be stored on the single domain controller and will perform both functions: domain controller and global catalog server.
- On networks that have several domain controllers, the global catalog will be stored on at least one of them, and you can designate additional domain controllers as global catalog servers in order to provide quicker responses to user requests.
- A namespace is a conceptual delimited area in a domain in which an object name is resolved.
- There are two types of namespaces: contiguous and disjointed.
- In a contiguous namespace, the name of the child object always contains the name of the parent domain. Domains that form a single domain tree share a contiguous namespace.
- In a disjointed or non-contiguous namespace, there are domains that do not share a common root name, but which are interrelated. All domains in a forest share a common schema, configuration, and global catalog, and they have all established transitive trust relationships via the Kerberos V5 authentication protocol. However, there can be domains and computers in various locations in the disjointed namespace that have totally unrelated names.
- If you want users on your network to be able to share resources with other users who are running Web browsers or FTP (File Transfer Protocol) utilities, you can install Internet Information Server (IIS) version 5.1, which comes with Windows XP Professional.
- Sharing Web resources involves publishing your files using HTTP (HyperText Transfer Protocol) rather than the SMB (Server Message Blocks) protocol that is used by the Server service (File and Print Sharing for Microsoft Networks) normally when you share folders and printers.

# Key Terms

| | | |
|---|---|---|
| Active Directory | Global catalog server | Schema |
| Authoritative server | Globally unique identifier (GUID) | Second-level domain |
| Contiguous namespace | Host name | Site |
| Directory service | in-addr.arpa | Site aware |
| Disjointed namespace | Internet Information Services (IIS) | Subnet |
| Distinguished name (DN) | Multimaster replication | Top-level domain |
| DNS name server | Name resolution | Transitive trust |
| Domain | Object | Tree |
| Domain controller | Organizational unit (OU) | Time to Live (TTL) |
| Forest | Relative Distinguished Name (RDN) | User Principal Names (UPN) |
| Forward lookup query | Replication | Web server |
| Fully Qualified Domain Name (FQDN) | Reverse lookup query | Zones |
| Global catalog | Root Domain | Zone transfers |

# Test Yourself

**1.** Which of the following are involved in the name resolution process?
   a. Forward lookup queries
   b. Reverse lookup queries
   c. The in-addr.arpa domain
   d. All of the above

**2.** Names are translated into IP addresses using:
   a. Reverse lookup queries.
   b. in-addr.arpa.
   c. Forward lookup queries.
   d. Time to Live (TTL).

**3.** In the domain name reviews.networks.com, which of the following is the root domain?
   a. reviews
   b. com
   c. the final period
   d. networks.com

**4.** You need to configure your computer as a DNS client. To do so, you need to use the:
   a. Add/Remove Programs window.
   b. Internet Protocol (TCP/IP) Properties dialog box.
   c. Internet Information Services Manager.
   d. Windows Components Wizard.

**5.** Which one of the following components must be installed on your computer in order to configure it as a DNS client?
   a. Personal Web Manager
   b. The in-addr.arpa domain
   c. TCP/IP

**6.** A directory service:
   a. Is a database containing IP addresses and their corresponding names.
   b. Is a database of resources and services available on a network.

   c. Is a group of domains.
   d. Contains information regarding all objects contained in a tree.

**7.** Which of the following defines the contents and organizational structure of Active Directory, particularly the attributes, parent classes, and class properties of all object classes?
   a. Schema
   b. Domain
   c. Domain Controller
   d. Site

**8.** Which of the following is both a service and a storage location for a partial replica of every object in Active Directory?
   a. Schema
   b. Global catalog
   c. Namespace
   d. Site

**9.** Which one of the following naming conventions contains the complete path leading to an object, including the name of the domain that holds the object?
   a. Distinguished name
   b. Relative distinguished name
   c. Globally unique identifier (GUID)
   d. User principal name

**10.** When an IIS Web server is installed on a computer running Windows XP: [Choose all that apply.]
   a. The installed Web server is able to manage heavy network traffic.
   b. Two new tools, Server Extensions and Services are added to the Administrative Tools window.
   c. The Web server is packaged with Internet- and intranet-related programs for sending e-mail, downloading requests for FTP files, and building and publishing Web pages.

**Exam 70-270**

## Projects: On Your Own

1. Configure your computer as a DNS client.
   a. Open the **Network Connections** window.
   b. Open the **Local area connection Properties** dialog box.
   c. Open the **Internet Protocol (TCP/IP) Properties** dialog box.
   d. Select the **Use the following DNS server addresses** option button.
   e. Type the IP address of the primary DNS server for the client in the **Preferred DNS Server** text box.
   f. Close the **Internet Protocol (TCP/IP) Properties** dialog box.
   g. Close the **Local area connection Properties** dialog box.

2. Install IIS on a computer running Windows XP Professional.
   a. Log on as **Administrator**.
   b. Open the **Control Panel** window.
   c. Open the **Add or Remove Programs** window.
   d. Start the **Windows Components Wizard**.
   e. Install **Internet Information Services** (IIS) on the computer.
   f. Close the **Windows Components Wizard**.
   g. Close the **Add or Remove Programs** window.
   h. Close the **Control Panel** window.

## Problem Solving Scenarios

1. Grey Polymers Inc. is an industrial supplier of polymer products to small and medium businesses located in Atlanta, Georgia. Grey purchases large quantities of basic polymers from large chemical suppliers. It then re-sells the polymers to smaller firms who use the products in extrusions, moldings, and fabrications. Grey Polymers has expanded rapidly in the last two years, from a small firm with only ten employees to 150 employees at last count. The Network Administrator has asked you to install a DNS server to speed up the name resolution process on the TCP/IP network. There are about 100 clients. Write a memo describing how you will go about configuring each of these clients as a DNS client.

2. Your boss, Sharon Tims, the Systems Administrator at Eagle Sporting Goods Inc., has read about other firms moving various employee human resource applications to corporate intranets. A corporate intranet is a Web site built to run on an internal TCP/IP corporate network. Users access the information on an intranet using their computer's browser. Sharon has asked you to install an Internet Information Server on the company's Windows network. Write a plan in the form of a memo describing how you will install this server.

# Glossary

**Access control entry (ACE)** Entry in an access control list. Contains a set of access rights and a security identifier (SID) that identifies a trustee (ex: user or group) for whom the rights are allowed, denied, or audited.

**Access control list (ACL)** A list of security protections that apply to an object such as files and printers. There are two types: discretionary and system.

**Access token** Contains the security information for a logon session and identifies the user, the user's groups, and the user's privileges.

**Account lockout duration** Used to set the time duration an account will remain locked out once the account lockout threshold has been reached.

**Account lockout policy** Used to set policies relating to locking out user accounts due to invalid logon attempts.

**Account lockout threshold** Number of invalid logon attempts that will be tolerated before a user account is locked out.

**Account policies** Used to set user account properties that control the logon procedure, such as password and account lockout rules.

**ACE** See Access control entry.

**ACL** See Access control list.

**ACPI** See Advanced Configuration Power Interface.

**Action log** Contains information about the events that have transpired during Setup, including the copying of files, the creation of Registry entries, and any errors that may have occurred.

**Active Directory (AD)** Stores information about network objects; used by network users to locate resources.

**Active partition** Partition used to boot the computer.

**AD** See Active Directory.

**Add Hardware Wizard** Used to add, delete, upgrade, and troubleshoot computer peripherals.

**Add Printer Wizard** Used to add and share a local or network printer on your computer.

**Address Resolution Protocol (ARP)** Used to map an IP address to a Media Access Control (MAC) address.

**Admin$** A hidden administrative share that points to the %systemroot% directory.

**Administrative shared folders** Folders available only to Network Administrators and hidden from other users.

**Administrator account** Built-in account used to manage the overall functioning of a computer.

**Advanced Configuration Power Interface (ACPI)** Power management standard that allows the operating system to control and manage power consumption.

**Advanced Power Management (APM)** BIOS controlled method of power management. Uses activity timeouts to determine when to transition devices to low power states.

**Advanced RISC Computing (ARC) path** Points to a valid boot partition containing the Windows XP operating system files.

**Advanced Security Settings dialog box** Provides options to assign special permissions to objects.

**Alert** Generated when a specific counter exceeds or falls below a specified value.

**Answer file** File that contains the inputs required for the Windows Setup program.

**Application layer** Layer of TCP/IP used by applications to gain access to the network.

**Application log** Records events that occur when an application is run.

**Application response setting** Setting that can be accessed in the Performance Options dialog box that enables you to optimize processor performance for foreground applications or background services.

**Archive attribute** Property for files and folders that is used to identify them when they have changed. Also known as an archive bit or backup marker.

**Archive bit** See Archive attribute.

**ARP** See Address Resolution Protocol.

**Assigned application** Application that is automatically installed when the user opens the application from the Start menu or attempts to open a file created using the application. If assigned to a computer, the application will install the next time the computer is started.

**Audit object access audit policy**  Policy that must be activated in order to enable auditing for a file or folder.

**Audit policy**  Sets the types of events you want to monitor in the Security event log of a computer.

**Auditing**  Used to monitor events that occur on a computer, such as who has accessed, or attempted to access, a file.

**Author mode**  Type of console mode that provides users complete access to MMC functionality.

**Authoritative server**  Server where the primary zone database file is located.

**Automated System Recovery (ASR)**  A backup of your system configuration that is designed to enable you to repair your system partition so that you can restart the operating system in the event of a complete malfunction due to a hard drive issue or corrupt system files.

**Automatic Updates**  Windows XP utility that facilitates the downloading and installation of service packs.

**Backup**  Copies of data are created for the purpose of disaster recovery.

**Backup log**  Text file that records backup operations on a computer and is stored on the hard disk of the computer.

**Backup marker**  See Archive attribute.

**Backup set**  Collection of backed up files and folders you have stored in a file or on one or more tapes.

**Backup Utility**  Prevents accidental loss of data due to hardware, software failure or user error. Can be used to schedule automatic backups at regular intervals.

**Backup Wizard**  Used to configure backup jobs by selecting files, drives, or network data, and choosing where to store the data. You can manually back up data or schedule unattended backup jobs.

**Bandwidth Allocation Protocol (BAP)**  Dynamically provides optimum bandwidth by adding and dropping connections and helps in reducing connection costs during remote access.

**BAP**  See Bandwidth Allocation Protocol.

**Basic storage**  Data storage type in which the hard disk is divided into partitions that function as logically separate units of storage.

**Binding order**  Used to establish which protocol should be used first when a network connection is initiated.

**Boot loader**  Known as Ntldr in Windows XP. Responsible for reading information from boot.ini and then loading the appropriate operating system based on user selection or a default timeout.

**Boot process**  Process by which a computer starts.

**Boot sector**  Portion of the hard disk that contains the program that loads the Windows XP Professional operating system and the information about the file system.

**Boot.ini**  Contains information relating to the operating systems(s) installed on the computer.

**Bottlenecks**  System resources that slow down the performance of a computer.

**Built-in local groups**  Used to assign rights to perform system tasks on a single computer.

**Built-in system groups**  Groups whose membership is controlled by the operating system.

**Built-in user accounts**  Default accounts that are created by Windows XP.

**Caching**  Enables you to access the contents of a shared folder offline.

**Callback**  Feature that can be used for inbound connections to increase security for your network and localize long distance charges.

**Change permission**  Allows users to create folders, add files to folders, modify data in files, add data to files, modify file attributes, and delete files and folders, in addition to actions permitted by the Read permission.

**Checksums**  Numerical values that are assigned to files based on their contents. The Emergency Repair process compares the system file checksums on the hard drive with the checksums on the ERD. If there are missing files or files that do not match because they are corrupt, you will be prompted to reinstall them from the installation CD.

**Checkupgradeonly switch**  Used with the Winnt32 command to generate a hardware compatibility report.

**Chkupgrd.exe**  Utility that immediately generates a hardware compatibility report; is much faster compared to checkupgradeonly switch.

**C$ D$ E$**  Drive letter hidden administrative share that points to the root of the corresponding logical drive.

**CDFS**  See Compact Disk File System.

**Challenge Handshake Authentication Protocol (CHAP)** Provides authentication when a user attempts to establish a connection, based on values calculated using an algorithm.

**CHAP** See Challenge Handshake Authentication Protocol.

**Cipher utility** Command-line utility used to encrypt and decrypt files and folders under specified conditions or requirements.

**Client (Respond Only)** IPSec policy used to provide maximum flexibility when negotiating security. Communication will occur with untrusted servers, but encryption will be used when requested by a server.

**Compact Disk File System (CDFS)** File system format used to store data on CD-ROMs.

**Compressed folders** New method of file compression in Windows XP Professional. Compressed folders are standard ZIP files but appear as normal folders.

**Computer name** See NetBIOS name.

**Connectionless communication** Communication in which the host can send a message to the recipient without establishing a channel.

**Console** Administrative tools made up of programs called snap-ins, which are used to perform various management tasks.

**Console tree** Organizes the snap-ins available in a console in hierarchical order.

**Contiguous namespace** Namespace in which the name of the child object contains the name of the parent domain. Domains that form a single domain tree share a contiguous namespace.

**Control set** Contains data about the configuration settings used to control the computer.

**Copy backup** Backs up all selected files and folders with or without the archive attribute and does not remove the archive attribute.

**Counter** Performance measure for an object that can be quantified such as the percentage of time the processor is busy (%Processor Time).

**Counter logs** Uses GUI data from the System Monitor to create a log file.

**Create Shared Folder Wizard** Guides you through the process of selecting the folder you want to share, making it available to network users, and assigning permissions to the users who will be accessing it.

**Custom console** Created by combining preconfigured snap-ins. Used to perform common administrative tasks.

**Daily backup** Backs up the selected files and folders that have been modified during the day and does not remove the archive bit.

**Data Link Control (DLC)** Special-purpose and non-routable protocol designed to access IBM mainframe or minicomputers and certain networked printers. Support for DLC has been greatly reduced in Windows XP.

**Default gateway** Acts as an intermediate device between hosts on different network segments.

**Defragmentation** Process that rearranges files, programs, and unused space to ensure that all related components of files and programs are placed in adjacent sectors of the hard disk, enabling files to open more quickly.

**Details pane** Displays the contents of the snap-in that is selected in the console tree.

**Device driver** Software that enables a specific device, such as a printer, modem, or network card, to communicate with an operating system.

**Device Manager** Utility in Windows XP Professional that you use to view and change device properties, update device drivers, configure device settings, and uninstall devices.

**DHCP** See Dynamic Host Configuration Protocol.

**Differential backup** Backs up selected files and folders on which the archive bit has been set, but the attribute is not removed.

**Digital signature** Code attached to driver files to assure the file is from the correct source—typically the hardware manufacturer or Microsoft.

**Directory database** Central database shared by a group of computers that form a Windows domain.

**Directory service** Provides a directory that stores information about resources and services available on a network.

**Disjointed namespace** Name of a parent object and the name of a child of the same parent are not directly related.

**Disk cleanup** A tool used to free space on the hard drives by removing deleted, orphaned, temporary, or downloaded files.

**Disk defragmenter** A utility that rearranges files, programs, and unused space to ensure that all related components of files and programs are placed in adjacent sectors of the hard disk, enabling files to open more quickly.

**Disk limit** Value for disk quota set on the Quotas tab in the Properties dialog box for an NTFS volume or partition. Designates the amount of space a user is allowed to use.

**Disk Management snap-in** Used to create, delete, and format partitions on a basic disk; lets you create simple, spanned or striped volumes on dynamic disks.

**Disk mirroring** All or part of a hard disk is duplicated onto one or more hard disks. Any change made to the original disk is copied to the other disk.

**Disk properties** Attributes of a hard disk.

**Disk quotas** Used to track and control disk usage on a per-user, per-volume basis.

**Disk striping** A technique that divides data into 64K blocks and spreads it equally in a fixed rate and order among all disks in an array.

**Distinguished Name (DN)** A unique identifier for an object that contains the name of the domain where the object is stored, as well as the full path to the object, including every level of the container objects in which it is stored.

**Distribution server** Network server that stores the installation files for distribution over a network.

**DLC** See Data Link Control.

**DN** See Distinguished Name.

**DNS** See Domain Name System.

**DNS name server** Server containing a zone database file.

**Domain** Logical group of computers on a network that access a common directory database for authentication purposes and that follow common rules and procedures. Domains are the fundamental building block in a Windows 2000 or Windows 2003 network.

**Domain controller** Computer running Windows 2000 Server or Server 2003 on which Active Directory resides.

**Domain local group** Used to assign rights and permissions to users in a particular domain.

**Domain Name System (DNS)** Main name resolution service for Windows. Correlates host names and fully qualified domain names (FQDNs) to IP addresses.

**Domain user account** Used to access the resources of a computer in a domain.

**Dynamic Host Configuration Protocol (DHCP)** Protocol that automatically assigns IP addresses.

**Dynamic disk** Disk that is initialized for dynamic storage.

**Dynamic storage** Storage type supported by Windows 2000 Professional and Server, Windows XP Professional, and Windows Server 2003 that uses volumes instead of partitions.

**Emergency Repair Disk (ERD)** Utility used to create an emergency disk that can be used to repair and restart a Windows 2000 Professional computer if the computer cannot be started on its own. Replaced in Windows XP Professional by Automatic System Recovery (ASR).

**Enable boot logging** Enabled automatically when a computer is started in Safe Mode. Logs all events related to the loading of drivers and services.

**Encrypting File System (EFS)** Feature of Windows XP Professional that enables users to encrypt and decrypt files on a hard disk.

**Encryption** The process of encoding the contents of a file, or all of the files in a folder, so that it is unreadable unless the reader possesses the appropriate key.

**Enforce password history** Used to set the number of passwords that will be stored in the password history.

**ERD** See Emergency Repair Disk.

**Error log** Stores a description of the errors that have occurred and an entry indicating the magnitude of each error.

**Event Viewer** Computer Management console snap-in that allows you to view the Security log.

**Extended partition** A partition in a basic disk created out of any available free space. Only one extended partition can be created on a hard disk.

**Extensible Authentication Protocol (EAP)** Used to extend the logon security process using smart cards or certificates.

**Extension snap-in** Provides additional administrative functionality to other snap-ins.

**FAT** See File Allocation Table.

**FAT16** See File Allocation Table.

**FAT32 file system** The 32-bit version of the FAT file system. Enables the operating system to keep track of the status of various segments of disk space used for file storage.

**Fault tolerance**  The ability of a computer or operating system to respond to a crisis without loss of data.

**File Allocation Table (FAT)**  A table or list maintained by the operating system that keeps track of the status of various segments of disk space used for file storage. Also referred to as FAT16.

**File and Print Services for NetWare (FPNW)**  Enables a NetWare client to use the file and print resources on a computer running Windows 2000 Server or Server 2003.

**File Transfer Protocol (FTP)**  Used to transfer files between a computer running Windows XP Professional and a TCP/IP host running server software and FTP. It also provides directory and file handling services such as listing directory contents and deleting files and selecting file formats.

**Files and Settings Transfer Wizard**  Used to transfer the files and settings of a user's old computer to a Windows XP computer provided that the two computers are connected by a direct cable or a network connection.

**FilterKeys**  Accessibility option that programs the system to ignore repeated keystrokes.

**Finger**  Used to retrieve information about users, including their user name and how long they have been logged on.

**Forest**  Group of trees that share a common schema, global catalog, and configuration.

**Forward lookup query**  Resolves a name to an IP address.

**FPNW**  See File and Print Services for Netware.

**Frame type**  Defines how the network adapter card formats data.

**FTP**  See File Transfer Protocol.

**Full Control permission**  Allows full access to the shared folder, including all actions permitted by the Read and Change permissions; users can also change permissions on the share.

**Fully Qualified Domain Name (FQDN)**  Includes a domain name in addition to the host name.

**Generic token card**  Physical card that provides authentication.

**Global catalog**  A partial read-only copy of all objects in Active Directory that stores commonly used object attributes.

**Global catalog server**  A domain controller that stores a copy of a global catalog.

**Global group**  Used to assign permissions for accessing resources in a domain; are stored in Active Directory.

**Globally Unique IDentifier (GUID)**  A unique identifier that is assigned to an object when the object is created. A GUID is a 128-bit number that never changes, regardless of changes in the location or the name of the object.

**Group**  A collection of user accounts that have similar rights and permissions.

**Group policies**  Used to administer and manage a wide range of network environment settings, including password restrictions, software distribution, and the desktop appearance.

**Guest account**  A built-in account that can be assigned to users who have limited access to a system on a temporary basis.

**GUID**  See Globally Unique IDentifier.

**Hardware Compatibility List (HCL)**  List of devices verified by Microsoft to be compatible with Windows XP Professional.

**Hardware profile**  Contains information about the devices that need to be started when you boot the computer and the settings with which the devices should be started.

**HCL**  See Hardware Compatibility List.

**Hibernate mode**  See Hibernation.

**Hibernation**  Enables Windows XP Professional to save your current system state to your hard disk, and then shuts down the system while you are not working on it. Also referred to as Hibernate mode.

**Hive**  Set of files that contains keys, subkeys, and value entries of the Registry.

**Home folder**  Folder used to store personal files that can be stored on a client computer, but is usually stored on a shared folder on a network server so that it serves as a centralized storage area, which users can access from any workstation.

**Host**  Computer where a resource resides.

**Host ID**  Part of an IP address that represents a specific computer.

**Host name**  Name of a specific computer on a given network.

**Hostname**  Utility used to validate the host name for a local computer

**Hot plugging** See Hot swapping.

**Hot swapping** Ability to add and remove devices without shutting down and restarting the system. Also called hot plugging.

**ICMP** See Internet Control Message Protocol.

**ICS** See Internet Connection Sharing.

**IGMP** See Internet Group Management Protocol.

**in-addr.arpa** Second-level domain expressly created so that a reverse lookup query need not carry out an extensive search of all domain names.

**Inbound connection** Used so that other computers can connect to yours via phone line, the Internet, or direct cable.

**Incremental backup** Backs up only the selected files and folders that have the archive attribute, which is then removed.

**Installation script** Script that enables you to specify the variations in the hardware and software configuration of your computer.

**IntelliMirror** Group of distributed computing technologies that includes roaming user profiles, offline files, and Windows Installer. Allows users to easily move between computers, while still being able to access their own data, applications, and settings.

**Internal network number** Unique number that is used for internal routing purposes to identify a specific computer on the network. Also referred to as a virtual network number.

**Internet Connection Firewall (ICF)** Provides what is referred to as a stateful firewall to both Windows XP clients and to machines running Windows 2003 Server Standard and Enterprise editions. ICF is a basic, not overly sophisticated firewall, which monitors all traffic, checking both the source and destination address.

**Internet Connection Sharing (ICS)** Feature that enables multiple computers on a local area network to share a single Internet connection.

**Internet Control Message Protocol (ICMP)** Enables hosts to exchange status and error information.

**Internet Explorer** Browser utility that is included and installed with Windows XP Professional, as well as numerous previous Microsoft operating systems. Internet Explorer is primarily used to access HTML and FTP resources, but can also be used to access resources that are stored locally and on your local area network.

**Internet Group Management Protocol (IGMP)** Protocol that enables multicast routers on a network to communicate with all member devices in a multicast group.

**Internet Information Services (IIS)** Enables users on a network to share resources with others who are running Web browsers or FTP utilities.

**Internet layer** Layer of TCP/IP that determines the route data will take when data packets are transferred from the source computer to the destination computer.

**Internet Protocol (IP)** Protocol within TCP/IP protocol suite responsible for addressing and routing.

**Internet Protocol Security (IPSec)** Set of security protocols and cryptographic protection services that are used to encrypt data packets in the IP layer and provide secure communications over IP networks.

**Internet Protocol (IP) security policies** Used to configure IPSec security services, which provide a variable level of protection for most types of traffic in existing networks.

**Internet Service Provider (ISP)** Company that provides individuals and organizations access to the Internet.

**IP** See Internet Protocol.

**IP address** A 32-bit number consisting of four octets and containing two identifiers, one for the network and one for the computer or host.

**IP filter rule** Rules defined for an IPSec policy that define the security requirements for the data transmission.

**IP Security policies** Set of policies that are used to define security rules for data transmitted across a network so that the data cannot be intercepted or stolen during transit. IPSec policies are used to configure IPSec services that provide a variable level of protection for most types of network traffic.

**Ipconfig** Used to confirm TCP/IP configuration parameters on a host.

**IPC$ (Interprocess Communications)** Administrative share used to facilitate IPC communication between systems.

**IPSec** See Internet Protocol Security.

**IrDA** Agreed-upon formats for transmitting data over infrared connections, thus allowing other programs and devices to interact with Windows XP.

**ISP** See Internet Service Provider.

**Kerberos V5**  Internet standard security protocol for handling authentication of user or system identity.

**Keys**  Correspond to hardware or software objects on a computer and store the information in sections.

**Last Known Good Configuration (LKGC)**  Enables you to start your computer using the information saved in the Registry after the last successful logon.

**Layer Two Tunneling Protocol (L2TP)**  Tunneling protocol that creates a secure tunnel across an untrusted communication channel.

**Local backup**  Backup method that must be performed at each client and server computer.

**Local group**  A collection of local user accounts stored in the local security database on a single computer.

**Local policies**  Used to set group policies for local computers that do not use the Active Directory.

**Local print device**  Print device that is physically connected to a computer through a physical port.

**Local security database**  Lists user accounts and resource security information for the computer on which the database resides.

**Local user account**  A user account that is stored in a local security database on a particular computer. It can only be used to access resources on the computer on which it was created.

**Local user profile**  Stored locally and accessed from the logon computer.

**Log files**  Information files generated during the Setup process. Include action log and error log, among others.

**Logical drive**  A volume you create within an extended partition on a basic disk.

**Logon script**  A set of command-line operations that are performed when a user logs onto a system.

**Manage Documents permission**  Gives users the ability to pause, resume, restart, and delete documents from all users that have been spooled to be printed.

**Manage Printers permission**  Grants administrative control over a printer. Users can pause and restart the printer and change printer properties.

**Mandatory user profile**  Read-only roaming user profile. In this type of profile, Windows XP does not save the changes a user makes to the desktop environment after the user logs off.

**Master Boot Record (MBR)**  First sector on a hard disk. Contains a partition table with information on the primary and extended partitions including which primary partition is active.

**Master disk image**  Used to copy the installation to other computers.

**Maximum password age**  Used to set the maximum number of days users can keep a particular password.

**MD5-CHAP**  See Message Digest 5 Challenge Handshake Authentication Protocol.

**Media Access Control (MAC) address**  Unique 48-bit or 6-byte number also called the hardware address, physical address, or Ethernet address.

**Member Of tab**  Tab in the User Properties dialog box where a user can be added or removed from a group.

**Member server**  Computer that is not a domain controller of a Windows domain but runs Windows 2000 Server or Windows Server 2003.

**Message Digest 5 Challenge Handshake Authentication Protocol**  Uses the Message Digest 5 (MD5) algorithm to encrypt user names and passwords.

**Microsoft CHAP (MS-CHAP)**  Microsoft version of CHAP.

**Microsoft Management Console (MMC)**  A built-in administrative tool used to manage hardware, software, and network components.

**Minimum password age**  Used to set the minimum number of days during which users must keep the same password.

**Minimum password length**  Used to set the minimum number of characters a password must have.

**Mini-Setup Wizard**  Starts the first time that a computer starts from a disk that has been duplicated by the Sysprep utility. The Wizard gathers any information that is needed to further customize the computer installation.

**Modem**  Device used to communicate between two computers over a telephone line.

**MouseKeys** Enables users to perform mouse functions using the numeric keypad.

**Multicasting** Transmission method for sending identical data to a select group of recipients. The server can transmit a single data stream, regardless of how many clients have requested it. When the data stream crosses a multicast-enabled switch or router, it is copied to the paths where clients that requested the stream are located.

**Multilinked device** Combines several ISDN lines or modem links to create one logical link and obtain greater bandwidth.

**Multimaster replication** Feature of Active Directory that enables changes to Active Directory on any domain controller to be automatically replicated to all other domain controllers in the domain.

**Multiple displays** Enables you to expand the size of your desktop across more than one monitor.

**Multiprocessing** Two or more CPUs carry out one or more processes simultaneously, with each processing unit working on a different set of instructions, or on different parts of the same process.

**My Documents** Folder that provides an area for the users to store their personal files.

**My Network Places** Serves as a network resource browser for users, providing an easy way to connect to shared folders added as a network place.

**Name resolution** Process that resolves names into IP addresses and vice-versa in a domain name system.

**Naming convention** Pattern that is followed for all user logon names on a network to make it easy for users to remember their account names.

**NBT** NetBIOS over TCP/IP.

**Nbtstat** Displays protocol statistics and current TCP/IP connections using NBT (NetBIOS over TCP/IP).

**NetBEUI** Protocol used to share resources in a small LAN.

**NetBIOS** Fifteen-character, or fewer, name given to a computer that must be different from all other computer, workgroup, or domain names. Sometimes referred to as computer name.

**NetBIOS over IPX** Enables a NetWare client running NetBIOS to communicate with a computer running Windows XP Professional and NWLink NetBIOS.

**Netstat** Displays TCP/IP protocol statistics and its network connections.

**Network backup** Backup method in which data from multiple network computers are backed up on a single removable backup medium.

**Network Bridge** Simplifies the process of connecting different segments of networked computers on the same LAN that use different types of network media.

**Network Connection Wizard** Used to select the networking components required to establish connections with different kinds of computers.

**Network ID** Identifies all hosts on the network.

**Network Interface Card (NIC)** Expansion board you insert into a computer so that you can connect to a network.

**Network Interface layer** Layer of TCP/IP conceptual model that consists of physical media.

**Network Monitor Driver 2** Protocol used to collect and displays statistics about the activity detected by the network card on a computer running Windows XP Professional.

**Network number** Unique hexadecimal number that must be specified for each frame type on a network adapter card.

**Network printer** Printer shared with other network users.

**NIC** See Network Interface Card.

**Normal backup** Backs up all selected files and folders, whether an archive bit has been set or not, but removes the archive attribute as necessary to denote that a file has been backed up.

**NTFS compression** Feature that enables the compression of files and folders on an NTFS volume.

**NTFS folder permissions** NTFS permissions configured for folders. Includes Read, Write, List Folder Contents, Read and Execute, Modify, and Full Control.

**NTFS file permissions** NTFS permissions configured for files. Includes Read, Write, Read and Execute, Modify, and Full Control.

**NTFS file system** Advanced file system that may be used with the Windows NT, Windows 2000, Windows XP, and Windows 2003 operating systems.

**NTFS permissions** Permissions used on NTFS disks to control access to network resources.

**Ntldr** See boot loader.

**Ntuser.dat** File that contains the system settings for an individual user account, along with environment settings for the user.

**NWLink** Protocol that enables clients running Microsoft operating systems to access resources on NetWare servers.

**Object** Any tangible or intangible thing stored in Active Directory. Can be a physical object such as a computer, or a virtual object such as a share. In the context of system monitoring, a system resource such as a processor, disk, network interface card (NIC), or memory whose performance can be monitored.

**Octet** An 8-bit value.

**Offline files and folders** Network files that are stored locally so that they are available even if the user is not connected to the network.

**Open Files folder** Used to view a list of open files located in shared folders, and the users who are accessing these files.

**Organizational unit (OU)** Subdivision of a domain used to group objects in Active Directory.

**Outbound connection** Used to dial out and connect to another computer or network.

**PAP** See Password Authentication Protocol.

**Partition** Part of a hard disk drive that has been formatted to act as a logically separate unit of storage.

**Password** Security feature that is used in combination with a logon name to control access to network and local resources.

**Password Authentication Protocol (PAP)** Protocol that uses plain text passwords for authentication.

**Password history** Stores the passwords previously used by a user account.

**Passwords must meet complexity requirements** Used to require users to follow a minimum password length and a consistent password structure to ensure that a combination of capital letters, lower case letters, numbers, or punctuation marks are used.

**PCMCIA card** See Personal Computer Memory Card International Association card.

**Peer-to-peer network** All computers in a network share resources as equals without a dedicated server. Also referred to as a workgroup.

**Performance logs and alerts** Used to record the performance of resources in logs and to configure alerts, which are activated based on threshold values that you set to perform specific actions.

**Permissions** Used to assign the capabilities users have when they gain access to a resource; for example, the Change permission enables users to change and delete data in a file.

**Personal Computer Memory Card International Association (PCMCIA) card** Removable credit-card-sized devices that are plugged into an expansion slot (PCMCIA slot) or a port, generally on a portable computer. Used to add a NIC, modem, or hard disk drive to the portable computer.

**Ping** Utility used to test TCP/IP configurations and identify connection failures.

**PktType** Identifies the packet form (such as Ethernet_II, SNAP, or ArcNet) that must be used.

**Plug and Play** Gives Windows XP Professional the capability to configure newly connected hardware automatically and dynamically, to load appropriate drivers, to register a device notification event, and to use removable and changeable devices.

**Point-to-Point Protocol (PPP)** Used by Windows XP to ensure cross-functionality with other remote access software. PPP settles configuration issues between other networking protocols, including TCP/IP and IPX.

**Point-to-Point Tunneling Protocol (PPTP)** Tunneling protocol that creates secure connections to corporate networks over the Internet.

**POST** See Power-On Self Test.

**Power options** Enable the system to control and manage all of the power requirements of a system in order to manage power consumption.

**Power schemes** Enable Windows XP Professional to automatically switch off a monitor and hard disk when the user is not working on the system.

**Power-On Self-Test (POST)** Built-in diagnostic program that checks the hardware to ensure that basic hardware components are present; also checks the amount of physical memory available on the computer.

**PPP**  See Point-to-Point Protocol.

**PPTP**  See Point-to-Point Tunneling Protocol.

**Preconfigured console**  Console that is a part of the Windows XP Professional operating system by default.

**Primary partition**  Volume created using the unallocated space on a basic disk.

**Print$**  Used by Administrators to monitor shared printers remotely by providing access to the printer driver files.

**Print device**  Hardware that creates the hard copies of your digital files.

**Print permission**  Enables users to connect to a network printer and print documents.

**Print server**  Computer that manages the print requests for a shared printer.

**Printer**  Software that delivers the requests for service from the operating system to the physical print device.

**Printer driver**  Software that contains the information used by the operating system to convert the print commands for a particular model of print device into a printer language such as PostScript.

**Printer pool**  Used to associate a single printer with multiple print devices, which can be either local or network-interface print devices.

**Printer port**  Printer software interface that a computer uses to communicate with a printer.

**Profile tab**  Tab in the Properties dialog box where you set the path for a user profile, logon script, and home folder.

**Protocol binding**  Process of establishing communication between network components on different levels.

**Proxy server**  Provides a connection to the Internet for computers on a LAN, and a means for controlling in-coming and out-going requests for service.

**PSTN**  See Public Switched Telephone Network.

**Public key policies**  Used to configure Encrypting File System (EFS) recovery agents.

**Public Switched Telephone Network (PSTN)**  A collection of the world's interconnected public telephone systems.

**Publishing an application**  Makes application available to any user who wants it; application will appear in the Add/Remove Programs control panel. Applications are published only to specific users, not to computers.

**RADIUS**  See Remote Authentication Dial-In User Service.

**RAS**  See Remote Access Service.

**RAS client**  Computer that establishes a RAS connection with a RAS server.

**RAS server**  Computer with which RAS client establishes a RAS connection.

**RCP**  See Remote Copy Protocol.

**RDN**  See Relative distinguished name.

**Read permission**  Enables users to display folder names, file names, file data, and the attributes of folders shared on remote systems, as well as run programs that are in shared application folders.

**Recovery agent**  Account configured with a recovery agent certificate and a private key that can be used to open and use an encrypted file.

**Recovery Console**  Command-line interface that can be used to perform a variety of troubleshooting and recovery tasks.

**Regedit.exe and Regedt32.exe**  Windows 9x and Windows NT versions of the Registry editor, respectively. Equivalent under Windows XP.

**Registry**  Database in which the Windows XP Professional operating system stores information relating to the hardware and software settings on a computer.

**Registry editor**  Used to view and modify the configuration information in the Registry.

**Relative distinguished name (RDN)**  Part of the object name, and the attribute that identifies an object as unique from its peers, usually its "common name."

**Remote Authentication Dial-In User Service (RADIUS)**  Protocol with a remote user authentication design that is vendor-independent and highly scalable.

**Remote Access Service (RAS)**  Enables you to share and access resources on a computer or a network from remote locations.

**Remote Assistance**  Used to request help from an expert, help desk support personnel, a network technician, or someone who simply knows more about a particular problem than you do. The person providing assistance must be at another Windows XP computer, and the person requesting help must not be behind a firewall.

**Remote Copy Protocol (RCP)**  Copies files between a computer running Windows XP Professional and an RCP host.

**Remote Desktop**  Allows you to access a remote computer from a local computer to run applications, open files, and access network resources. Employees can work from their homes while having full access to their workplace computer and the LAN.

**Remote installation**  Enables an Administrator to install Windows XP Professional on client computers throughout a network from a central location.

**Remote Installation Services (RIS) server**  Windows server that stores an RIS image used for remote installation.

**Remote shell (RSH)**  Runs commands on a Unix host.

**Removable media**  Devices that can be removed from your system while the system is still on.

**Replication**  Process of creating and managing duplicate versions of any database.

**Reset account lockout counter after**  Used to set the time duration that must pass after an invalid logon attempt before the bad logon attempt counter is reset to 0.

**Restore Wizard**  Used to restore lost or damaged data from a backup copy.

**Reverse lookup query**  Resolves an IP address to a name.

**Rights**  Give users the ability to perform an action that interacts with the operating system, for example, changing the system time or shutting the system down.

**RIS server**  See Remote Installation Services (RIS) server.

**Roaming user profile**  Profile that sets up the same desktop environment for a user, no matter which computer the user is using in a domain.

**Root Domain**  The top of the domain hierarchy, represented by a period.

**Root key**  See Subtree key.

**Route**  Displays and modifies the local routing table.

**Router**  Computers that interconnect the multiple computers on a network or the Internet. They use headers and a forwarding table to determine where packets go, and ICMP (Internet Control Message Protocol), an extension of IP, to communicate with each other and configure the best route between any two hosts.

**Routing table**  Used to provide routers with directions they will use to forward data packets to locations on other networks.

**RSH**  See Remote shell.

**Safe Mode**  Starts the computer by loading only a set of basic files and drivers.

**Scheduled Tasks**  Utility used to schedule programs and scripts to run at a specific time.

**Schema**  The database design, which includes the object classes and attributes that are stored in Active Directory.

**Second-level domain**  The names that organizations register for the Internet. They have two parts: a top level name and a unique second-level name, for example, yale.edu.

**Secure Server (Require Security)**  IPSec policy that minimizes the number of clients with which you can communicate over a network, thereby enhancing security. Unsecured communications with untrusted clients will be blocked.

**Security Configuration and Analysis snap-in**  Used to compare the current security configuration of a computer or Group Policy object with one of the predefined security templates, to create custom security templates and to apply a template either to the local computer or to a Group Policy object.

**Security event log**  Records the success and failure of events you have chosen to audit.

**Security Template snap-in**  Used to create a centralized tool where all of the available templates and all of the available security attributes are organized in one place.

**Separator page**  Contains printer commands and is used to identify and separate different documents that are going to be printed.

**Serial Line Internet Protocol (SLIP)** An older remote communications protocol that is used by UNIX computers. It does not provide security and transfers data without checking for errors. There is no support for encryption, so passwords are sent as clear text. A Windows XP Professional computer can only perform the role of a SLIP client.

**Server (Request Security)** IPSec policy that always requests security using Kerberos trust, but does not block communications from unsecured clients.

**Session Manager (Smss.exe)** Responsible for creating the user-mode environment that provides the visible interface with Windows XP Professional.

**Setup** Program that is executed to prepare the hard disk for later stages of installation. Copies the files required to run the Setup program.

**Setup Wizard** Collects setup information such as names, passwords, and regional settings for the computer on which you are installing Windows XP Professional

**Share permissions** See Shared folder permission.

**Shared Application Folder** Contains applications that network users can access from a central location.

**Shared Data Folder** Stores either working or public data. Working data is needed by a select group of users, while public data is more general and used by a large group of users.

**Shared folder** Resources that are made available to other computers on a network.

**Shared Folder permission** Used to control access to network resources. Also known as share permissions.

**Shared Folders snap-in** Enables an Administrator to monitor access to network resources.

**Shiva Password Authentication Protocol (SPAP)** An authentication protocol used when you connect to a Shiva server.

**ShowSounds** Accessibility function that displays captions for the speech and sounds generated by programs.

**Simple volume** Dynamic disk volume that contains disk space from a single disk.

**Site** Group of TCP/IP subnets with dependable and consistent connections.

**Site aware** Ability of clients on a site to recognize site-related data that Active Directory is imparting.

**Slipstreaming** Process of integrating service packs with the Windows XP installation files.

**Smart card** Credit-card-sized devices used to store passwords, public and private keys, and other types of identifying data.

**SMP** See Symmetric Multiprocessing System.

**Smss.exe** See Session Manager.

**Snap-in** Application present in MMC that enables you to perform administrative tasks.

**SoundSentry** Accessibility function that programs Windows XP to generate visual warnings when the system's built-in speaker plays a sound.

**Spanned volume** Dynamic disk volume that can include disk space from up to 32 disks.

**SPAP** See Shiva Password Authentication Protocol.

**Special permissions** Used to assign a specific level of access to users for objects on an NTFS disk.

**Standalone snap-in** Used to perform administrative tasks.

**Standby** Helps conserve the power used by computer by shutting down power to peripheral devices that are not in use.

**StickyKeys** Accessibility function that configures the system so that users do not have to hold down multiple keys simultaneously.

**Striped volume** Dynamic disk volume that combines areas of free space from multiple hard disks—32 is the maximum number of disks—into one logical volume.

**Store password using reversible encryption for all users in the domain** Used by Network Administrators so that a reversibly encrypted password is stored for all users in a domain.

**Subkey** Key within a key.

**Subnet** Grouping of devices that share a common network prefix.

**Subnet mask** A 32-bit, four-part number used to break up an IP address into the network ID and host ID

**Subtree** Primary node within the Registry structure. Similar to the root folder of a disk, and contains the grouped information of the Registry. Also called root key or subtree key.

**Subtree key** See subtree.

**Symmetric Multiprocessing System (SMP)** Description for the process in which multiple processors execute instructions of an application. The same memory space and the same applications are used.

**Synchronization** Process by which changes to offline files are updated to network files.

**Sysdiff** Utility used with Setup Manager to perform automated installations of applications that do not support scripted installation routines. Includes Sysdiff.exe and Sysdiff.inf.

**Sysprep** See System Preparation tool.

**System Preparation tool (Sysprep)** Used to create a disk image of the Windows XP installation and copy that image to various computers.

**System service** Creates a unique SID when the computer to which master image is copied is started for the first time.

**System log** Records errors, warnings, and information generated by Windows XP Professional.

**System Monitor** Used to view a graphical representation of the performance of resources on your computer.

**Systemroot** Path to the Windows XP Professional installation folder.

**Task Scheduler** Administrative tool that can be used to schedule and carry out routine tasks at specified intervals.

**TCP** See Transmission Control Protocol.

**TCP/IP** Standard suite of protocols that enables you to exchange information across networks.

**TCP/IP host** Computer that is connected to a TCP/IP network.

**Telnet** Terminal emulation protocol often used to manage a remote Web server or another type of server. When you run Telnet from a client machine and connect to a server on the network, you can enter commands that will be carried out as if you were performing them directly on the server terminal.

**TFTP** See Trivial File Transfer Protocol.

**Timeout** Time that the computer should wait for an action from you before loading the default operating system.

**ToggleKeys** Accessibility function that causes the computer to generate sounds when certain locking keys are pressed.

**Top-level domain** The two- or three-character names used to designate the type of organization or its geographic location (com, gov, edu, org, net, uk, au, nz, etc.).

**Trace log** Surveys events that take place on the system.

**Tracert** Checks the route a packet follows to reach its destination.

**Transmission Control Protocol (TCP)** Protocol within the TCP/IP protocol suite used to establish a connection between two hosts so they can exchange streams of data. Operates in Transport layer.

**Transport layer** Layer of TCP/IP that sets up communication sessions between computers and makes sure that messages are delivered in the correct sequence without errors.

**Transport Level Security (TLS)** Protocol used to support smart cards and certificates. It is composed of two layers: the TLS Record Protocol, which uses symmetric data encryption to ensure that connections are private, and the TLS Handshake protocol, which negotiates an encryption algorithm and cryptographic key before the application protocol can transmit or receive any data.

**Trivial File Transfer Protocol (TFTP)** Uses UDP to transfer files between a computer running Windows XP Professional and a TCP/IP host running server software and TFTP.

**Transitive trust** Relationship established between domains so that if a domain has established a trust relationship with another domain, it can also communicate and connect to the domains that the other domain trusts and vice versa.

**Tree** Group of domains that share a contiguous namespace.

**TTL** Time to live, after which the name server deletes the query result from its cache.

**Tunneling protocol** Creates a virtual tunnel between two computers or networks through the established Internet infrastructure.

**UDF** See Universal Disk Format.

**Universal Disk Format (UDF)** File systems used to access DVD drives.

**Universal Serial Bus (USB)** External bus device (communication line) used to transfer data among the components in a computer system.

**UNC (Universal Naming Convention) pathname** Used to connect to any resource on the network for which you have permission. The syntax for the UNC path is: *\\computername\sharename*.

**Uninterruptible Power Supply (UPS)** Supplies backup battery power to a system when there is a sudden loss of electrical power.

**Untrusted network** Open public network that can be accessed by anyone.

**UPS** See Uninterruptible Power Supply.

**User account** Contains all of the required information about a user that is needed to identify the user on the network.

**User account properties** Set of properties associated with a user account.

**User Datagram Protocol (UDP)** Used by applications to transfer small amounts of data at one time.

**User mode** Enables you to distribute a console to other Administrators.

**User principal names** User account name plus the DNS name of the domain where the user account object is stored, separated by an @ sign.

**User profile** Collection of folders that stores the current desktop environment for a user, application settings, and the user's personal data.

**User rights assignment** Used to prescribe what actions a user can execute within the operating system.

**Value entries** Data or values that are contained by the subkeys of the Registry.

**Verbose mode** A mode for running a command that causes messages generated to be displayed to the user.

**Video adapter** Expansion board that plugs into a computer to give it display capabilities.

**Virtual memory** Temporary storage used by a computer to run programs that need more memory than is available at any given point in time.

**Virtual Memory Manager (VMM)** Coordinates the use of physical and virtual memory.

**Virtual network number** See Internal network number.

**Virtual Private Network (VPN)** A secure connection established using tunneling and encryption to transfer data securely over the Internet.

**VMM** See Virtual Memory Manager.

**VPN** See Virtual Private Network.

**WDM** See Win32 Driver Model.

**Win32 Driver Model (WDM)** Common model for device drivers that works across Windows 98, Windows 2000, and Windows XP operating systems.

**Windir** Command to display names and paths of Windows directories.

**Windir\comsetup.log** Registers the Optional Component Manager and Com+ setup routines.

**Windir\debug\netSetup.log** Registers information about joining a domain or a workgroup, including the network computer name, workgroup, and domain validation.

**Windir\setupapi.log** Registers an entry when a line from an .INF file is executed, and error information if the execution was unsuccessful.

**Windows Installer** Application installation technology that now augments the Add or Remove Programs Wizard. One of the main features that reduces the TCO (Total Cost of Ownership) of a Windows network, and one of the IntelliMirror technologies that facilitates users moving from computer to computer.

**Windows Internet Naming Service (WINS)** Service used to map IP addresses to NetBIOS or computer names.

**Windows 2000 Advanced Server** Advanced version of Windows 2000 server that can support high-end network applications.

**Windows 2000 Datacenter Server** Microsoft's most powerful server operating system.

**Windows 2000 Readiness Analyzer** Generates a compatibility report about your computer's current hardware and software.

**Windows 2000 Server**  Operating system for client/server networks.

**Windows Server 2003 Datacenter Edition**  Has even greater power and functionality than Windows Server 2003 Enterprise Edition. Ideal for data warehousing on a large scale.

**Windows Server 2003 Enterprise Edition**  A more powerful version of Windows Server 2003 that enables the use of up to eight processors in large sophisticated corporate networks.

**Windows Server 2003 Standard Edition**  Network operating system for client/server networks. Can be used for Web servers, as well as file, print, and application servers.

**Windows Server 2003 Web Edition**  New product that is designed to be deployed specifically for Web serving and Web hosting.

**Windows XP Professional**  Primary Microsoft client desktop operating system.

**WINS**  See Windows Internet Naming Service.

**Winsock**  Provides support to existing NetWare applications that are compatible with the IPX/ SPX socket interface.

**Winnt.exe**  Program used to install Windows XP Professional over a network on a target computer running a Windows 3.x operating system.

**Winnt32.exe**  Program used to install Windows XP Professional over a network on a target computer running Windows 2000, 98, 95, NT 3.5 or 4.0.

**Workgroup**  A logical group of users who work on a common project and share information and resources, on computers that are interconnected, generally over a local area network (LAN). Also known as a peer-to-peer network.

**Zone transfers**  Replicate any changes in the primary zone database file to the secondary zone database files.

**Zones**  Distinct, contiguous segments of the DNS namespace that make a large domain manageable by enabling different Administrators to manage different zones.

# Index